1000 EVIDENCES

for the Church of Jesus Christ of Latter-day Saints

Part Two
Voice from the Dust

500 Evidences in Support of the Book of Mormon

Allen H. Richardson, M. Ed.
David E. Richardson, Ph. D.
Anthony E. Bentley, M. Sc.

ISBN 0-9711921-4-6

Published by Artisan Press
5473 Kent Circle
Salt Lake City, Utah 84117

and

Thousand Evidences
16 Trujillo Way
Tijeras, New Mexico, 87059-7411

www.1000Evidences.com

DEDICATED

to all who seek the truth.

ACKNOWLEDGMENTS

The authors express their appreciation to the many people who contributed directly or indirectly to this work.. Many of the evidences were condensed from research presented in various studies referenced throughout these volumes. Our gratitude is extended to the authors of these scholarly works.

A special thanks to Deanne Flurer for many hours spent typing the original manuscript, and to Eva R. Bentley, Debbie C. Bentley, Steven R. Bentley, Robert C. Bentley and David C. Nuckols for proofreading and providing much support with the tedious process of double checking the myriad of references listed in this volume.

ABOUT THE AUTHORS

Allen H. Richardson was born and raised in Salt Lake City, Utah. He served a mission for the Church of Jesus Christ of Latter-day Saints in New Zealand and has held many other Church callings, including the high council, stake mission president, Sunday School presidency, Young Men's presidency, teacher of various adult and youth classes, and is presently serving in the bishopric. He also served eight years on the curriculum committee of the church, helping to write many manuals and reference books. Allen has used many of the concepts presented in these volumes to assist in the conversion of many people including active critics of the church and an evangelical minister.

Allen holds a Bachelor of Science degree in speech and drama from the University of Utah and a Masters degree in English education from Utah State University. He has taught speech, drama, journalism, art, English, history, and religion in the secondary grade levels for the past 30 years. Three of those years were spent in the Islands of Tonga, where he was instrumental in the conversion of the first thirteen members of the church from the Gilbert Islands, who were attending school in Tonga.

Allen is also an artist; his works include landscapes, portraits, and murals for two chapels. He illustrated four volumes for W. Cleon Skousen, and draws caricatures professionally. He is also an actor, having performed in plays at the Pioneer Memorial Theater, and three movies, including the later version of "Brigham Young." Allen's second book is called *Prelude to the Dawn*—an historical novel about the early struggles of the pilgrims searching for religious freedom.

Allen and his wife Lana are the parents of eight children, and have three grandchildren.

David E. Richardson, Allen's brother, was also born and raised in Salt Lake City, Utah. He served a three-year mission for the Church of Jesus Christ of Latter-day Saints in Brazil. While on his mission David was instrumental in the conversion of three Methodist ministers Saul Oliveira, Walter Queiroz and Helio Camargo. All three have served as LDS bishops, stake and mission presidents, and Regional Representatives. One of the ex-ministers, Helio Camargo, is an emeritus member of the Second Quorum of Seventy of the Church of Jesus Christ of Latter-day Saints is currently president of the Sao Paulo Brazil Temple. (For the conversion stories of these ex-ministers, see Rector, *No More Strangers*, Volume 2, pp. 104-122.) Upon returning from his mission, David completed his studies at the University of Utah, where he received Bachelor and Master of Science degrees in Mechanical Engineering and a Ph.D. in Metallurgy. He is recently retired from the aerospace industry.

Dr. Richardson has served in many Church positions, including a teacher of youth and adults, mission presidency, bishopric, ward and stake clerk, two stake missions, ward mission leader, three high councils, gospel doctrine instructor and service missionary. He presently serves as the High Priest instructor. David's first book, *These were the Valiant*, is a novel with a Church history setting. Other volumes of the series are currently being written.

In his travels Dr. Richardson has been able to personally verify some of the historical and archaeological evidences reported by professional archaeologists to determine which evidences should be included in these volumes.

David and his wife Elva are the parents of ten children (including two sets of identical twins) and are the grandparents of thirty-four.

Anthony E. Bentley, also from Salt Lake City, served his mission in Argentina. In 1987 he married Debbie Christensen of Orem, Utah, and graduated *Magna Cum Laude* in Electrical Engineering from The University of Utah. In 1989 Anthony received his Master of Science degree in Engineering from the University of California, at Davis. For the past fourteen years he has been employed by Sandia National Laboratories, in California and New Mexico, developing feedback control systems for: precision manufacturing processes, synthetic aperture radar systems, lasers and telescopes for both space and airborne applications.

Anthony is currently serving in the bishopric. He has also served as elder's quorum president, and instructor for the elder's quorum, primary, scouting and Sunday school. Anthony and Debbie are the parents of six children and make their home in Tijeras, New Mexico.

CONTENTS

Foreword vi

Preface vii

Introduction viii

Volume 2: A Voice From The Dust

1. Witnesses of the Book of Mormon 1

2. Another Testament of Jesus Christ 13

3. Book of Mormon Prophecy 83

4. Historical Accuracy of the Book of Mormon 99

5. Book of Mormon Geography 151

6. Book of Mormon Culture 169

7. Names used in the Book of Mormon 219

8. Book of Mormon Literacy 249

9. Ancient American Science 289

10. Warfare in the Book of Mormon 303

Partial Bibliography 324

Index 327

FOREWORD

This collection of evidences is designed for all readers. For the active members of the Church of Jesus Christ of Latter-day Saints, it presents documented evidences to enrich their testimonies. It gives substance to those who have taken for granted that the Church is true. For investigators, it provides resource material that will help lead to a testimony. The array of evidence will stimulate the minds of those who have been indifferent. Skeptics, who are open-minded enough to review the material, will find it difficult if not impossible to explain away the great weight of evidence. And it will answer charges of those who have openly criticized the Church.

The evidences presented in these volumes clearly demonstrate that the Church of Jesus Christ of Latter-day Saints is the same Church that Jesus Christ organized in the meridian of time. Each argument by itself will be convincing to some. However, none will be able to deny the truthfulness of the Church when the evidences are considered as a whole.

This compilation does not claim to contain all available evidences. Since new evidences for the Church are being discovered on a daily basis, this work represents only a portion of the thousands of available evidences. Nor does this work profess to be an in-depth study. Entire volumes have probed the depths of single issues that are only lightly touched upon in this work. However, the authors believe the wealth of evidence presents a broad enough perspective to provide an overall understanding of the strength of the LDS position.

Many interpretations, conclusions and opinions associated with this work are those of the authors, and not necessarily those of any organization with which the authors are affiliated, but are based on years of research. In an effort to leave no stone unturned, the authors have spent thousands of hours in research, and have sincerely considered the works of not only those who are sympathetic with the Church, but also those who are critical of it. Scholars, ministers of other religions, and anti-Mormon writers have been consulted in depth.

This work draws upon many discoveries, findings and conclusions of scientists and scholars. The compilers determined the validity and applicability of the evidence presented. Official sanction of the Church of Jesus Christ of Latter-day Saints is not suggested nor implied. The official doctrine of the Church of Jesus Christ of Latter-day Saints is found in four standard works of Holy Scripture. They include:

1. *The Holy Bible*—King James Version, (a collection of books containing revelations received by prophets of the "Old World"—consisting of the Old and New Testaments of Jesus Christ).
2. *The Book of Mormon—Another Testament of Jesus Christ*, (a collection of books of revelation received by inspired prophets of the "New World"—between 2200 BC and 400 AD).
3. *The Doctrine and Covenants of the Church of Jesus Christ of Latter-day Saints* and
4. *The Pearl of Great Price* (are both revelations and instruction received by inspired prophets of the "Latter-days" as well as ancient times).

These standard works are referenced throughout this work by chapter and verse. For the benefit of those who are unfamiliar with the Latter-day scripture, they are listed below along with the individual books that make up the scriptures. Copies of these scriptures may be obtained by writing to: the Church of Jesus Christ of Latter-day Saints, Referral Office, Floor 12, Salt Lake City, Utah 84150.

<u>The Book of Mormon—Another Testament of Jesus Christ</u>: comprised of the following Books:

1 Nephi	Enos	Words of Mormon	Helaman	Mormon
2 Nephi	Jarom	Mosiah	3 Nephi	Ether
Jacob	Omni	Alma	4 Nephi	Moroni

<u>The Doctrine and Covenants</u> (D&C): sections 1 through 138, and Official Declarations 1 and 2.

<u>The Pearl of Great Price</u>: comprised of the following:

Moses	Abraham	J. Smith—Matthew	J. Smith—History	The Articles of Faith.

PREFACE

The search for truth should be one of active pursuit—not passive inquiry. Too often, when questions arise, Latter-day Saints are heard to say, "just pray about it." While constant prayer is an essential ingredient in the quest for knowledge and wisdom, it should not be relegated to the status of a convenient cure-all for defending one's faith. Our Heavenly Father expects us to do more than just to ask each time we lack understanding. Moroni (10:3) reminds us to "ponder" these things in our hearts before asking God for a manifestation. Some have presumed that exercising faith is not an intellectual function. However, the prophet Joseph Smith taught differently: "when a man works by faith, he works by mental exertion..." (See *Lectures on Faith*, Number 7, Section 3.)

Many years ago, Oliver Cowdery desired to receive spiritual communication as the Prophet Joseph Smith had been receiving. However, he "took no thought" except to ask God (D&C 9:7). The Lord's answer was that Oliver should have studied those things out in his mind before simply asking for knowledge (D&C 9:8). Note that the experience of gaining a confirmation or witness from God is not purely spiritual or psychological in nature, but an intense mental activity as well. Indeed, the Lord had told Oliver that "I will tell you in your **mind** *and* in your heart..." (D&C 8:2. Emphasis added.) God has asked us to open our minds—as well as our hearts—to receive the things of God. Indeed, the Lord has said that those who seek to obtain his word and who *study* it will have his spirit (D&C 11:21-22). He has also said that we should "seek learning by *study* and also by faith." (See D&C 88:118; 109:7, 14. Emphasis added.) Hence, the evidences enumerated in this work provide intellectual nourishment for the mind while the spirit seeks for a confirmation from the heart.

It is not improper to seek for additional evidence that a given principle of the gospel is true, the Lord himself gave a "further witness" to Oliver Cowdery that the work of the restoration was under divine direction (D&C 6:22). As Austin Farrer said: "Though argument does not create conviction, the lack of it destroys belief. What seems to be proved may not be embraced, but what no one shows the ability to defend is quickly abandoned. Rational argument does not create belief but it maintains a climate in which belief may flourish." In the Doctrine and Covenants, the Lord further explained the importance of study for obtaining a testimony, and extended the realm of instruction to include external evidences.

And I give unto you *a commandment* that you shall teach one another the doctrine of the kingdom. Teach ye diligently and my grace shall attend you, that you may be instructed more perfectly *in theory, in principle, in doctrine*, in the law of the gospel, in *all* things that pertain unto the kingdom of God, that are *expedient for you to understand*; Of things both in heaven and in the earth, and under the earth, things which have been, things which are, things which must shortly come to pass; things which are at home, things which are abroad; the wars and the perplexities of the nations, and the judgments which are on the land; and a knowledge also of countries and of kingdoms—*That ye may be prepared in all things when I shall send you...* (D&C 88:77-80. Emphasis added.)

Of course the study of external evidence should **never** *supplant* daily study of the scriptures—only *supplement* the constant "feasting upon the word of Christ" (2 Nephi 31:20). Furthermore, until we have obtained our *foundation of faith* in the scriptures, the value of external evidences will not be fully realized. However, after having developed some level of familiarity with God's word, it is expedient to strengthen our testimony with additional evidence. Elder Orson Pratt, one of the apostles in the early days of the Church, also explained the relationship between spiritual faith and the need for searching analysis.

Faith or belief is the result of evidence presented to the mind. Without evidence, the mind cannot have faith in anything. We believe that a stone will fall, when unsupported, on the evidence of past observation in relation to the falling of heavy bodies. We believe that day and night will continue on the evidence of past experience in regard to the uniformity of nature's laws. We believe that space is boundless, and duration endless, on the evidence, presented by the mind itself, which at once perceives the absurdity of either space or duration being limited. We believe in all self-evident truths, on the evidence that all opposite propositions to these truths are absurd. We believe in all the great truths of science, either on the evidences of our own investigations, or on the researches of others. We believe in historical facts on the evidence of the historian. Faith in every fact, statement, truth, or proposition which we have confidence in, is, in all cases whatsoever, derived from evidence. Therefore, without evidence, faith can have no existence. (Quoted in N. B. Lundwall, *Lectures on Faith* [Salt Lake City: Bookcraft, n.d.], p. 70.)

INTRODUCTION

There is a God. His existence is evidenced by conclusions based on scientific study, the testimonies of witnesses, and by the fulfillment of prophecies.

Since God lives and loves His children, there is a purpose to life. That purpose is to "endure to the end" (Matthew 10:22) while being tried and tested in our obedience to God's commandments, in order that we might prove ourselves worthy "to be accepted by the Lord at the judgment" (2 Corinthians 5:9-10) and have life everlasting (John 12:50).

The *means* to prove ourselves has been disputed for centuries. Since the consequences are so serious and long lasting, it is vitally important to make the correct decisions. The Book of Mormon boldly testifies that the only path to eternal life is through "the merits of him who is mighty to save," Jesus Christ (2 Nephi 31:19). And "there is none other way nor name given under heaven whereby man can be saved in the kingdom of God" (2 Nephi 31:21).

Thus the entire purpose of the Book of Mormon is to bring men to Christ: "And we talk of Christ, we rejoice in Christ, we preach of Christ, we prophesy of Christ, and we write according to our prophecies, that our children may know to what source they may look for a remission of their sins" (2 Nephi 25:26).

In ancient times, Joshua gathered the children of Israel together and exhorted them to "choose ye this day whom ye shall serve..." (Joshua 24:15). Obviously, many in his day had become apathetic and indifferent toward the importance of true worship.

So it is in our day; modern prophets continually exhort us to make right choices. Yet, some choose wrongly, relying on personal opinion rather than prayerful study and logical analysis. To them, external evidences do not seem to be available. For this reason, Elijah the prophet saw the need to provide a demonstration of solid evidence to help the people make a proper choice. Before calling down fire from heaven, he asked them, "How long halt ye between two opinions? If the Lord be God, **follow him**..." (1 Kings 18:21 Emphasis added). The evidence was provided and the people "fell on their faces" and cried, "The Lord He is the God, The Lord He is the God" (1 Kings 18:39).

This work presents an impressive array of solid evidences to help the honest in heart conclude that the Book of Mormon is the word of God and contains the true gospel of Jesus Christ, and that it contains the one "strait and narrow" way to Eternal Life (Matthew 7:14).

However, God, in His infinite wisdom, did not choose to provide absolute proof that the Book of Mormon is His word; nor has He provided absolute proof that He exists or that the scriptures are true. He did not provide absolute proof of these facts in order to: 1) provide a climate of greatest individual freedom of choice; and 2) to identify those who are willing to live by faith on the basis of evidence He has provided through scriptures, history, logic, and through individual revelation to those who seek truth.

God prefers us to weigh the evidence He *has* provided and decide for ourselves. In addition to tangible, external evidences, God has provided the greatest evidence of His true Church—individual witness or testimony given by God to *all* that sincerely seek and pray for it. This internal witness or testimony is sufficient for most people without external evidences. If God says something is true, then it is absolutely true for these people, and further proof is not required.

However, a study of the evidences in support of the Book of Mormon can motivate individuals to seek for their own personal witness that it is true. It can also strengthen existing testimony and inspire feelings of joy. All too often, critics of the Book of Mormon exclaim, "There is no archaeological evidence for the Book of Mormon!" This assumption of a lack of evidence usually comes from hearsay, rumor, and the opinion of the uninformed. Though this collection of evidences is not intended as a defense against the claims of critics, such a study can be illuminating. Indeed, the prophet Joseph Smith taught that "By proving contraries, truth is made manifest" (*History of the Church of Jesus Christ of Latter-day Saints,* vol. 6, p. 428).

In 1841 John Lloyd Stephens published a description of his explorations in Guatemala which included detailed drawings of Mayan ruins by Fredrick Catherwood. Of this work Joseph Smith said "It would not be a bad plan to compare Mr. Stephens ruined cities with those in the Book of Mormon. Light cleaves to light and facts are supported by facts. The truth injures no one..." (*Times and Seasons,* vol. 3, no. 23, p. 927).

The responsibility rests with the individual reader to consider the evidence provided in these two volumes and to make his or her own assessment of its strength. This is similar to evidence presented to a jury during a trial. Some of the evidence is strong and totally convincing. Other evidence presented to the court is circumstantial and less convincing. Each juror must decide how much of the evidence will be considered when making the final judgment. However, as in any trial, no judgment should be made until the available evidence has been presented.

During this process of evaluation and sifting, it is hoped that no reader will become impatient with evidences which are less convincing and "throw out the baby with the bath water" (throw away the sound arguments along with the weaker points). Again, each reader is implored to decide how much of the evidence is convincing to him just as he would do if he served on a jury. Jurists do not always need an "expert" to tell them whether a point is good or bad. They often find the truth without coaching by a learned professor. However, jurors are impressed by expert witnesses, and therefore, expert witnesses (professors, scholars and archaeologists) are quoted and referenced throughout this work.

Depending on the juror's particular background and education, what is strong evidence for him or her may not be strong for another. Scientific evidence carries greater weight with some than with others who are more impressed by feelings and emotions. In any event, it is worthwhile to consider external evidences in order to "prove all things" and to "hold fast that which is good" (1 Thessalonians 5:21).

To those who ridicule a person's belief in the Book of Mormon, we echo the words of a juror in a recent trial spoken to a person who took issue with the verdict: "You did not sit on the jury and hear the evidence. I did."

Similarly, those who study the evidence, such as the 1,000 evidences presented in these volumes, will be led to say to skeptics: "You would believe as I do if you considered the evidence I did, pondered it in your heart, and asked God with a sincere heart and real intent if the Book of Mormon is true and if the Church of Jesus Christ of Latter-day Saints is Christ's true Church."

Many evidences will be convincing for some but not necessarily so for others. For example, the evidences that are valid from a Catholic perspective may not be considered valid by a Protestant or vice versa. Other evidences which are valid for a Christian may not be considered valid by a Jew or Moslem. And others still will not be valid to the atheist, but the vast majority of those who read these volumes will agree that the weight of evidence in favor of the Church of Jesus Christ of Latter-day Saints and the Book of Mormon is truly astonishing.

After considering all the evidence, even the skeptic will be able to agree that a belief in the Church of Jesus Christ of Latter-day Saints is logical and reasonable, and some will agree that it is probable that the Church of Jesus Christ of Latter-day Saints is true. All who consider the evidence, ponder these things in their hearts, and "ask God with a sincere heart and real intent" (Moroni 10:4) will receive a personal witness from God that the Book of Mormon is indeed true.

Elder Spencer W. Kimball wrote the following about the Book of Mormon:

May I tell you of a great adventure? As I traveled to a weekend assignment. I took with me an unusual book, which was my constant companion. I could lay it down only to sleep, eat, and change trains. It fascinated me, captivated me, and held me spellbound with its irresistible charm and engaging interest. I have read it many times.

As I finished it, I closed the book and sat back, absorbed as I relived its contents. Its pages held me, bound me, and my eyes were riveted to them. I knew the book was factual, but as has been said, "Truth is stranger than fiction."

I am constrained to speak to you of it today. It is a story of courage, faith, and fortitude, of perseverance, sacrifice, and super-human accomplishments, of intrigue, of revenge, of disaster, of war murder, and rapine, of idolatry, and of cannibalism, of miracles, visions, and manifestations, of prophecies and their fulfillment.

I found in it life at its best and at its worst, in ever-changing patterns. I hardly recovered from one great crisis until another engulfed me.

Across the stage of this drama of life through the ages, marched actors in exotic, colorful costumes from the blood-painted nudity of the warrior to the lavish, ornamented pageantry of royal courts—some actors loathsome and degraded, others so near perfection that they conversed with angels and with God. There are the sowers and reapers, the artisans, the engineers, the traders, and the toilers, the rake in his debauchery, the alcoholic with his liquor, the pervert rotting in his sex, the warrior in his armor, the missionary on his knees.

This dramatic story is one of the greatest ever played by man. The noted tragedians fumble their lines. It is played "on location" with no false fronts for scenery. It is a fast-moving story of total life, of opposing ideologies of monarchies and judgeships and mobocracies. Its scenes carry the reader across oceans and continents. It promises to tell of the "last days of God," but instead records the "last days of populous peoples" and the triumph of God. Class distinction is there with its ugliness, race prejudice with its hatefulness, multiplicity of creeds with their bitter conflicts.

Since this book, a "best seller" left its first press, it is printed in more than two dozen languages, more than a half million copies a year, and millions of copies are in libraries, public and private, and in numerous hotels and motels along with the Gideon Bible. Even the blind may read it in three thick books of Braille. Can anyone be considered to be well-read who has not perused this pretentious volume which makes such bold claims?

Its story has a vital message to all people. The gentiles will find the history of their past and the potential of their destiny; and the Jewish people, the blueprint of their future. The covenants of God to them are unfolded, as are the promises regarding Jerusalem, their ancient city, and their lands. And it is revealed how the Jews, so long persecuted, scattered and tortured since their dispersion, may come into their own. And the gentiles are warned that they must "...no longer hiss, nor spurn nor make game of the Jews, nor any of the remnant of the House of Israel" for the Lord will remember his covenant to them when they respond. It is the life story of the ancestors of the Indians and accounts for their dark skins.

Archaeologists may be excited as they read of ruins of ancient cities, highways, and buildings; and there may yet be hidden buried gold and priceless records. Locations may be approximated, for instance the narrow neck of land which was fortified from the "East sea to the West sea" was but a "day's journey for a Nephite."

Journalists will find in this book crisis after crisis, presenting rich material for limitless climactic stories, articles, plays and operas. A struggling movie industry might here find material, which could increase box office receipts.

This unparalleled book should intrigue navigators: unprecedented land treks near-unbelievable in length scope, and hazard are chronicled and ocean crossings, and the circling of the world centuries before the Vikings—crossings fraught with all the dangers imaginable, including storms, hidden reefs, hurricanes, and even mutiny. This first recorded ocean crossing was about forty centuries ago, of seaworthy, oceangoing vessels without known sails, engines, oars, or rudders—eight barges like and near contemporary with Noah's ark, long as a tree, tight as a dish, peaked at the end like a gravy boat, (Ether 2:17) corked at top and bottom, illuminated by molten stones (Ether 2:20, 3:1), perhaps with radium or some other substance not yet rediscovered by our scientists. Light and like a foul upon the water, this fleet of barges was driven by winds and ocean currents, landing at a common point in North America probably on the west shores.

The reader may follow with wonder another crossing of the ocean which was made by a Jewish group led by a prince, the son of Jerusalem's king, and of a third migration and voyage, perhaps the greatest in all of history, dimming even that of the Saints from Illinois to the Salt Lake Valley, and even of Moses' Israel from Egypt to their promised land. These people abandoned Jerusalem on the eve of its destruction by Nebuchadnezzar and probably landed on the west coast of South America where the ocean currents drove them later to meet and combine with remnants of the earlier migrants; this greatest movement was made in a ship constructed by a young builder who may never have seen an ocean-going vessel. If the party of the prince sailed west and the prophets cast they would have circumnavigated the world from Jerusalem, their people finally meeting in this western world. The vessels were sufficiently large to carry food and seeds.

There was no welcoming committee to meet these adventurers, as there was to meet Columbus and the pilgrims.

This remarkable book tells again of movements of great bodies of people—5,400 in one group, sailing northward on the Pacific side in very large ships, seeking for new worlds to conquer, some of whom likely drawn into the strong westward ocean currents to find the "isles of the sea" and to become the progenitors of the Polynesians.

The people in Jerusalem knew nothing of the whereabouts of these fellow Israelites in the western world, but those here knew of the happenings in Palestine such as the destruction of Jerusalem and the captivity under Nebuchadnezzar and when the Christ was born in Bethlehem, crucified on Calvary, and when he ascended from the Mount of Olives, yet no ships were carrying mail; no telephone wires were humming; no radio sets were operating; no cables yet snaked across ocean floors.

The student of economics will find in this unusual book the disintegration of nations through pride, soft living, and luxuries, terminating finally in hunger and fetters. He will see unified peoples fighting for liberty and then class wars destroying those freedoms. One will see the land waving with ripening grain, the silkworm spinning, flocks and herds grazing, vineyards and orchards bearing, and a richly adored and bejeweled people. He will see stone quarries and lumber mills and mines and craftshops, and then devastated landscapes, burned homes, parched earth, warring antagonists. and deserted lands. He will see towers and temples and kingly courts and palaces of the rich and their luxury, and dissipation, immorality, and debauchery, comparable to that in Babylon. Jerusalem, and Rome.

He will see people thriving in communal living, and taxed from fifty percent, and then to totalness, to slavery, and to bondage. He will see power-greed paternalistic, centralized governments move toward the inevitable revolution which finally impoverishes but frees the people to begin again from ashes.

The astronomer and geologist here may see signs in the heavens and new stars come into focus, three days without sun or any reflected light, and nights without darkness, bright "as the midday sun" (3 Nephi 1:19) and a vapor of darkness so impenetrable that no glimmer, nor candles, nor torches, nor fire could give any light. A great storm came "such an one as never had been known in all the land" (3 Nephi 8:5), certainly since Noah's forty-day pouring, and perhaps drowning more people than since the deluge, and terrible tempests, thunder, and sharp lightnings, and whirlwinds of tornadic and hurricane proportions, swift enough to carry away people never to be heard of again—twistings, foldings, whirlings, slidings, faultings, and tremblings of hours of duration to cause landslides burning great cities perhaps more extensive than the Bali's, Iran's, Assam's, and Chile's, perhaps interring in a few hours more people than ever in the history of the world. Tidal waves swallowed entire communities, and fire consumed many cities and human bodies. The labors of centuries were embalmed in ashes to a greater degree than Pompeii and Herculaneum; and earth convulsions of such intensity and prolongation that "the face of the whole earth was deformed" (3 Nephi 8:17), these earth spasms being a revolt by the created earth against the crucifixion of its Creator.

Engineers will learn from this great book that those centuries ago, men erected buildings, temples, and highways with cement, and paved roads connected city to city and land to land, and when forests had been denuded, a reforestation program was initiated for the future.

The psychologists may find studies in human behavior and the workings of the human mind and the rationalizing processes where men convince themselves that "good is bad, and that bad is good." Here they will watch history unfold for thousands of years and see not only episodes in the lives of individuals but causes and effects in a total history of races.

The educator will find treasures of literature and poetry. He will see how language used to log their day-to-day experiences can be corrupted when not properly written, from an expressive tongue of the educated to numerous corrupted dialects of degenerated peoples, proving that to survive, people must be educated on every front—physical, mental, spiritual, moral—and that anything short of that will bring ultimate disaster.

This comprehensive book should be studied by politicians, government leaders, kings, presidents, and premiers to see the rise and fall of empires, and the difference between statesmanship and demagoguery. They will see nations born in war, live in war, deteriorate in war, and die in war through the centuries. They may find answers to problems of capital and labor, of dishonesty graft and fraud, of dissensions, internal rupture, and civil wars.

In this uncommon book is seen that chief judges, frustrated by growing corruption, resign from judgment seats to proselyte for righteousness; that princes prefer to teach men rather than to rule over them; that kings have tilled the earth providing their own living to serve the people rather than to become burdensome to them and levy upon them confiscatory taxes; that rulers are loved and not feared.

Scientists will read of unusual instruments never patented or remade or duplicated, of elements which, without recharging, illuminate dark spaces indefinitely, that at least fifteen hundred years before Columbus these Westerners knew that the earth is round and revolved about the sun, and of a special instrument, not yet equaled even in our own day with all of our laboratories and knowledge, like a round ball, made of brass curious in workmanship, with two spindles, so sensitive that it was not limited to the cardinal points of the compass but would actually give guidance regardless of direction, recording the feelings, emotions, and inner rebellions of men and would function properly only where there was not human, mental, and moral discord. This instrument would point the way to the prevalence of animals to be hunted for food and was operated by faith rather than by electricity or other natural elements—an instrument on which would be writing changed from time to time, plain to read, increasing the understanding of those who read it.

Military men may learn much in strategy, intrigue, in movements, in morale. They may learn that centuries before the discovery of America, the ancients had cement buildings, temples, and highways connecting cities and lands, and metal tools for tilling ground, and munitions factories for making weapons of war, and forges to beat "plow-shares into swords, and pruning-hooks into spears." (2 Nephi 12:4.) They may learn how cold war can be kept in deep freeze.

Guerrilla warfare, sieges, and the scorched-earth policy were not originated in Civil War days nor in Russia but were programs of survival, initiated long centuries before Columbus, Pizarro, and Cortez.

They may learn that wars of aggression with soldiers, idolatrous and adulterous, who leave God out of their lives, will in the end be futile and disastrous.

They will learn that great cultures stagnate in war shadows and cease to survive when continuous wars make people migrants, when fields are abandoned, livestock appropriated for non-producing soldiers, forests destroyed without replanting, and when farmers and builders become warriors, and businessmen shoulder arms and teachers mobilize. Men cannot plant, cultivate, and harvest when in camps, nor build when on the run. Long and bloody wars mean sacked, burned, ruined cities, confiscatory taxes, degenerated peoples, and decayed cultures.

Victory and defeat alike leave countries devastated and the conqueror and the conquered reduced. Wickedness brings war, and war vomits destruction and suffering, hate and bloodshed upon the guilty and the innocent.

This impressive book should convince all living souls of the futility of war and the hazards of unrighteousness. A few prophets, swimming in a sea of barbarism, find it difficult to prevent the crumbling and final collapse of corrupt peoples.

To you of the Americas, who are terrified by the daily papers, who tremble at "The sound of a shaken leaf," who build shelters in fear of guided missiles, hydrogen bombs, and biological warfare—to you, there is this conditional promise coming from this book of truth:

"...this land shall be a land of liberty unto the Gentiles, and there shall be no kings upon the land...

"And I will fortify this land against all other nations.

"...I, the Lord, the king of heaven will be their king, and I will be a light unto them forever, that hear my words" (2 Nephi 10:11-12, 14).

This single volume records for historians about twenty-six centuries of stirring life, not generally known even to the most highly trained professors of history. It tells of the ancestries of those whose spectacular monuments are now observed in South and Central America and in the Mexican jungles.

In this wondrous book, ministers and priests can find texts for sermons, and men generally can find final and authoritative answers to difficult questions: Is there life after death? Will the body be literally resurrected? Where do the spirits of men go between death and the resurrection? Can one be saved in unchastity? What is the correct organization of Christ's Church? Can one be saved without baptism? Why is it wrong to baptize infants? Is specific authority essential to administer ordinances? Is continuous revelation necessary and a reality? Is Jesus the actual Son of God?

Here is recorded the glorious coming of the Savior to his temple in America. He blessed the little children and wept as angels descended out of heaven and encircled them. He organized his Church with twelve apostles called disciples to whom were given the same priesthood, authority, and keys which their contemporaries, Peter, James, and John held in the other land.

The coming of the Resurrected Redeemer to this land was spectacular—the small piercing voice from heaven heard at Jordan and Transfiguration's Mount awed them as it announced:

"Behold my Beloved Son, in whom I am well pleased, in whom I have glorified my name—hear ye him." (3 Nephi 11:7.)

And then they saw a man descending out of heaven in white robes, and he stood in their midst saying: "Behold, I am Jesus Christ, ...I am the God of Israel and the God of the whole earth and have been slain for the sins of the world." (See 3 Nephi 11:10, 14.) And the multitude thrust their hands into his side and felt the prints of the nails and knew of a surety that this was the very Christ so recently crucified across the sea, and so recently ascended into heaven, and now among them to teach them his saving gospel.

This historical book tells of three men, who, like John the Revelator, are still on earth though it is nearly two thousand years since their mortal birth—men who have not suffered the pains of death, but who have control over the elements and who make themselves known at will and go anywhere on the globe when needed and who cannot be imprisoned, burned in the furnace, nor buried in pits, nor held in prison, nor destroyed by beasts; for, like the three Hebrews, superhuman power and protection have been given them.

This narrative tells of people with such faith that they buried their weapons to die victims of enemies rather than take lives; of boys who had inherited great faith from their mothers who had trained them to trust in God and they would be protected. It tells of the fulfillment when 2,060 of them were saved though they fought in many battles in which men all around them died, but because of the faith of their mothers and the sons, not one of the 2,060 suffered death. In this battle of defense, not one boy lost his life.

But after all, it is not the book's dramatic crises, its history, its narrative that are so important, but its power to transform men into Christ like beings worthy of exaltation.

It is the word of God. It is a powerful second witness of Christ. And certainly, all true believers who love the Redeemer will welcome additional evidence of his divinity.

This inspiring book was never tampered with by unauthorized translators or biased theologians but comes to the world pure and directly from the historians and abridgers. The book is not on trial—its readers are.

Here is a scripture as old as creation and as new and vibrant as tomorrow, bridging time and eternity; it is a book of revelations and is a companion to the Bible brought from Europe by immigrants and agrees in surprising harmony with that Bible in tradition, history, doctrine, and prophecy; and the two were written simultaneously on two hemispheres under diverse conditions. It records the very words people would say when this hidden record should be presented to them.

"...A Bible! A Bible! We have got a Bible, and there cannot be any more Bible.

"But thus saith the Lord God: O fools, they shall have a Bible; and it shall proceed forth from the Jews, ...

"Thou fool, that shall say: A Bible we have got a Bible, and we need no more Bible...

"...I rule in the heavens above and in the earth beneath; and I bring forth my word unto the children of men, yea even upon all the nations of the earth?

"Wherefore murmur ye, because that ye shall receive more of my word? Know ye not that the testimony of two nations is a witness unto you that I am God that I remember one nation like unto another?...

"And I do this that I may prove unto many that I am the same yesterday, today, and forever... And because that I have spoken one word ye need not suppose that I cannot speak another; for my work is not yet finished;... Wherefore, because that ye have a Bible ye need not suppose that it contains all my words; neither need ye suppose that I have not caused more to be written.

"For I command all men, both in the east and the west, and in the north, and in the south, and in the islands of the sea, that they shall write the words which I speak unto them; for out of the books which shall be written I will judge the world, every man according to their works, according to that which is written.

"For behold, I shall speak unto the Jews and they shall write it; and I shall also speak unto the Nephites and they shall write it; and I shall also speak unto the other tribes of the house of Israel, which I have led away, and they shall write it..." (2 Nephi 29:3-12).

Then he says he will gather the three folds into one fold, and he will be their shepherd. And the records of the ten tribes are still to be recovered. "And it shall come to pass that the Jews shall have the words of the Nephites, and the Nephites shall have the words of the Jews; and the Nephites and the Jews shall have the words of the lost tribes of Israel; and the lost tribes of Israel shall have the words of the Nephites and the Jews.

"And it shall come to pass that my people, which are of the house of Israel, shall be gathered home unto the lands of their possessions; and my word also shall be gathered into one." (2 Nephi 29:13-14.)

We seem to hear the Almighty warn: "Fools mock, and they shall mourn," and, "Woe be unto him that rejecteth the word of God." One prophet wrote: "...And if ye shall believe in Christ ye will believe in these words, for they are the words of Christ, ..." (2 Nephi 33:10.)

In the final chapter of the book is the never-failing promise that every person who will read the book with a sincere, prayerful desire to know of its divinity shall have the assurance.

The book of which I speak is the keystone of true religion, the ladder by which one may get near to God by abiding its precepts. It has been named "The most correct of any book on earth."

My beloved friends, I give to you the Book of Mormon. May you read it prayerfully, study it carefully, and receive for yourselves the testimony of its divinity. This, I pray in the name of our Savior Jesus Christ, Amen. (See Spencer W. Kimball, *Conference Report*, April 1963, pp. 62-68.)

1. Witnesses of the Book of Mormon

THE GREATEST EVIDENCE THAT THE BOOK OF MORMON IS TRUE

<u>Claim</u>: The Book of Mormon promises a spiritual witness from God to all who read it with an open mind and humbly ask God if it is true.

> And when ye shall receive these things, I would exhort you that ye would ask God, the Eternal Father, in the name of Christ, if these things are not true; and if ye shall ask with a sincere heart, with real intent, having faith in Christ, he will manifest the truth of it unto you, by the power of the Holy Ghost. And by the power of the Holy Ghost ye may know the truth of all things (Moroni 10:4-5).

<u>Evidence</u>: Millions of Latter-day Saints and even tens of thousands of non-LDS members have received personal manifestations attesting to the truthfulness of the Book of Mormon. They have experienced the warmth of the Holy Ghost, heard his still small voice, or have experienced dreams or witnessed visions. Many have simply felt a powerful and unmistakable conviction flooding their minds that the book could not have been written by a young farm boy, but is the word of God as revealed to ancient prophets. Regardless of the manner in which a spiritual manifestation is experienced, the result is always the same: The Book of Mormon is a true testament of Jesus Christ and his gospel in the ancient Americas. These experiences represent millions of individual evidences on their own—the most powerful testimony that the book is of God.

The following evidences, which represent the bulk of this volume, provide intellectual confirmation for those who have gained the spiritual conviction that the Book of Mormon is of God.

In discussing the relationship between spiritual faith and intellectual evidence, as it applies to the Book of Mormon, Elder Orson Pratt, one of the apostles in the early days of the Church, wrote that:

> Unless the true principles of salvation be revealed and established by sufficient evidence, there could be no true faith and works by which mankind could obtain salvation; for in the system of salvation, works follow faith, and faith follows evidence and evidence accompanies the revealed truth. For instance, God reveals the great and sublime truths contained in the Book of Mormon. Next, He sends evidence sufficient to convince mankind of the divine authenticity of these truths. Thirdly, this evidence produces faith in the minds of those who candidly and carefully examine it. Fourthly, this faith will lead the honest to do the works required of them in that book. And lastly, through the atonement of Christ, these faith and works, combined together, will surely save them in the kingdom of God. (Quoted in L. B. Lundwall, *Lectures on Faith* [Salt Lake City: Bookcraft, n.d.], p. 73.)

EVIDENCE NO. 501: THE THREE WITNESSES SAW AN ANGEL AND HEARD THE VOICE OF GOD

Claim: The three men who announced to the world that they had seen the gold plates from which the Book of Mormon was translated, also testified that they had seen an angel and had heard the voice of God. Their testimony is printed in the preface to the Book of Mormon:

> Be it known unto all nations, kindreds, tongues, and people, unto whom this work shall come: That we, through the grace of God the Father, and our Lord Jesus Christ, have seen the plates which contain this record, which is a record of the people of Nephi, and also of the Lamanites, their brethren, and also of the people of Jared, who came from the tower of which hath been spoken. And we also know that they have been translated by the gift and power of God, for his voice hath declared it unto us; wherefore we know of a surety that the work is true. And we also testify that we have seen the engravings which are upon the plates; and they have been shown unto us by the power of God, and not of man. And we declare with words of soberness, that an angel of God came down from heaven, and he brought and laid before our eyes, that we beheld and saw the plates, and the engravings thereon; and we know that it is by the grace of God the Father, and our Lord Jesus Christ, that we beheld and bear record that these things are true. And it is marvelous in our eyes. Nevertheless, the voice of the Lord commanded us that we should bear record of it; wherefore, to be obedient unto the commandments of God, we bear testimony of these things. And we know that if we are faithful in Christ, we shall rid our garments of the blood of all men, and be found spotless before the judgment-seat of Christ, and shall dwell with him eternally in the heavens. And the honor be to the Father, and to the Son, and to the Holy Ghost, which is one God. Amen.
>
> OLIVER COWDERY
> DAVID WHITMER
> MARTIN HARRIS

Evidence: The three witnesses had varied backgrounds: a wealthy farmer, a teacher/lawyer, and a successful businessman. Although the three witnesses each left the church for a time due to misunderstandings and intense persecution, they all maintained their testimonies that they not only saw the plates, but saw an angel and heard the voice of God. This they did throughout their lives even though there was no apparent reason for doing so. Each developed bitter feelings toward the church and prophet and had cause to expose him as a fraud, yet they stood fast by their testimonies—even at the threat of death, and all but David Whitmer eventually re turned to full fellowship with the church.

Elder B. H. Roberts asked:

> Would it be within the power of an impostor to cause an angel to come from heaven and stand before these witnesses in the broad light of day and exhibit the Nephite plates and the Urim and Thummim? Could he cause the glory of God more brilliant than the light of the sun at noon-day to shine about them? Could he cause the voice of God to be heard from the midst of the glory saying that the work was true, the translation correct, and commanding the witness to bear testimony to the world of its truth? (See B. H. Roberts, *New Witnesses for God,* [1909], vol. 3, pp. 247-249.)

EVIDENCE NO. 502: ADDITIONAL TESTIMONY FROM DAVID WHITMER

Claim: Many skeptics have conceded that Joseph Smith did indeed have gold plates because of the testimony of David Whitmer.

Evidence: Soon after word got out that Joseph Smith had unearthed a sacred record engraved on gold plates, critics and skeptics began to publish their opinion that Smith had no plates, that no ancient peoples had ever recorded anything on metal plates. Anti-Mormons claimed that the witnesses were persuaded to lie by a deceptive "Joe Smith" in order to substantiate his "ridiculous" claims.

Scientific methods of investigation, research and verification, as well as in judicial courts, accept the testimonies of witnesses as evidence. Eleven witnesses signed their names to solemn testimony to the entire world that they had seen the gold plates from which Joseph Smith translated the Book of Mormon. (See prefatory pages of the Book of Mormon.) Due to intense persecution and misunderstandings, some of the witnesses left the Church and severed their ties with the Church. The world waited for them to deny their testimonies, but they never did. All of the witnesses returned to the Church except David Whitmer. Anti-Mormons became so impatient for David to deny his testimony that they began to publish his (fictitious) denial. In response, Whitmer publicly maintained his original testimony in two newspapers insisting that he had "never at any time denied that testimony or any part thereof." (See *Kansas City Journal*, June 5, 1881; and *Richmond, Missouri Conservator*, March 24, 1881; Both are cited in Hunter and Ferguson, *Ancient America and The Book of Mormon* [1950], pp. 114-115.)

In 1887, Whitmer published a pamphlet *An Address to All Believers in Christ*, (Richmond, Missouri, 1887) restating his testimony and denying false reports printed in the *American Encyclopedia* and the *Encyclopedia Britannica* that claimed he had admitted to not actually witnessing the plates. In his pamphlet he reprinted an imposing list of 21 prominent citizens of his hometown of Richmond, Missouri, who signed a document attesting to Whitmer's integrity and undoubted truth and veracity, which had been published in the *Richmond Conservator*, March 24, 1881 (also cited in Hunter and Ferguson, *Ancient America*, [1950], p. 115).

This certificate rightly claimed that the signers knew David Whitmer well—personal relationships can be traced in many cases, including the six that were pallbearers at his funeral seven years later. None on the list publicly accepted the Book of Mormon, but all admired the man who testified of its truth. The list included two doctors, two bankers, two judges, the mayor, the sheriff, a lawyer, a merchant, a general, and various county officials. The *Richmond Democrat*, February 2, 1888, published his last testimony. The same periodical for January 26, 1888, printed the following eulogy after his death: "Skeptics may laugh and scoff if they will, but no man could listen to Mr. Whitmer as he talks of his interview with the angel of the Lord, without being most forcibly convinced that he has heard an honest man tell what he honestly believes to be true."

David Whitmer remained true to his testimony even after being excommunicated from the church. He was excommunicated for "possessing the same spirit with the dissenters," due to his skepticism of further revelations, and opposition to polygamy. He was jealous of the power and suspected influence of Sidney Rigdon. The following are excerpts from Richard Lloyd Anderson, *Investigating the Book of Mormon Witnesses*, (1981), pp. 70-90:

> David Whitmer's separation just preceded [the] Mormon expulsion from Missouri. The estranged witness remained behind to live nearly a half-century in a society hostile to his religious views... The quiet but immovable ways of David Whitmer turned grudging respect to admiration during the fifty years of his residence in Richmond, Missouri. Three decades of surviving newspapers chronicle many ordinary activities, supplemented by public documents. By his recollections his sole capital in 1838 was a wagon and team. The census records value his real estate at $1,000 in 1850, and his personal and real property in 1860 as $5,000, increasing to $7,000 in 1870. His private assets at death in 1888 were probably worth $10,000.

> ... By 1860 he was listed as a "Livery Keeper" and his newspaper notices are fairly continuous for a quarter of a century for the "Livery and Feed Stable" of "D. Whitmer & Son" or "Whitmer & Co." ... After a time both editorials and paid notices refer to the business as "The Old Reliable Livery and Feed Stable." This title symbolized the record of the firm and is really a comment about its owner.

> ... David was public-spirited, serving on fair boards, and he and his wife entered competition and won prizes. Named in the newspapers as participating in many public meetings, he appears as the elected chairman of some. Shortly after the Civil War [in which he had sworn allegiance to the Union and President Lincoln[1]] he signed as one of the "friends of Johnson, Liberty and Union,"[2] and his temperate voice was most influential in the reconstruction period. As early as 1858 he was nominated for city councilman, a position he subsequently held several times.[3] He was elected to fill the unexpired term of mayor in 1867-1868, during which he sponsored several practical programs.[4] But the active businessman of sixty-three apparently retired from further office seeking; declining to

attempt a second term, he recommended the election of a "younger, more energetic man."[5] His prominence, however, never diminished. The Ray county Atlas of 1877 featured his picture as one of twenty individuals.[6]

... A firm friendship existed between David Whitmer and the editor [of the *Richmond Conservator*] Jacob Child. This journalist was an enlightened reformer of his period and had no party connections with the Book of Mormon witness, who was thirty years his senior. Child was a forthright spokesman for ... supporting the integrity of David Whitmer. The opinions of "the famed publisher of the *Richmond Conservator*" should carry a good deal of weight. Dynamic in local and state politics, he was elected mayor of Richmond and state assemblyman. His fellow editors named him president of the Missouri Press Association, and he was United States ambassador to Siam under President Cleveland.

... Whitmer's election as mayor induced some spiteful remarks. Child's editorial reaction reminded his readers that one with "self respect" would not indulge in vicious gossip: "Mr. Whitmer is a gentleman, and as such represented the views of our people when they cast for him their votes for mayor."[7] Some fifteen years later the vitriolic anti-Mormon lecturer, Clark Braden, came to the hometown of the last Book of Mormon witness and publicly branded him as disreputable. The *Conservator's* response was a spirited front-page editorial unsympathetic with Mormonism but insistent on "the forty six years of private citizenship on the part of David Whitmer, in Richmond, without stain or blemish."[8] Although admitting that theological views were open to question, the prominent journalist insisted that the reputation of his friend was not: "If a life of probity, of unobtrusive benevolence and well doing for well nigh a half century, marks a man as a good citizen, then David Whitmer should enjoy the confidence and esteem of his fellow men." The following year the editor penned a tribute on the eightieth birthday of David Whitmer, who "with no regrets for the past" still "reiterates that he saw the glory of the angel."[9]

... Hiram Parker, who lived in David Whitmer's section of town for a decade, ... said "No one could know Uncle Davy and not like and trust him ... Children liked him, men respected him and trusted him, and I never heard a word from anyone during my ten year's acquaintance with him and those who had known him intimately for years that spoke a harsh word or uttered a doubt as to his truthfulness and general kindness of heart... Hiram Parker spent most of his life in selling in several states but had never met "a more honest, guileless man."[10] ...

If neither the man nor his manner of relating his story is questionable, what of his motives? Can the distorting force of self-interest be detected? His plain courage in ignoring self-interest in the manner of his testimony was the source of admiration earned from community leaders in Richmond, Missouri. Neither unpopularity, danger, nor tedious inconvenience altered his expressed convictions. David occasionally alluded to an ultimatum delivered by about five hundred armed men to force him to repudiate the Book of Mormon. We know that this came in 1833 in the public square at Independence, Missouri, when vigilantes menaced Mormon leaders to force all Mormons from Jackson County. The story was told by New York convert John P. Greene, nearly as old in the church as David Whitmer:

> When the mob again assembled, they went to the houses of several of the leading Mormons. And taking Isaac Morley, David Whitmer, and others, they told them to bid their families farewell, for they would never see them again. Then driving them at the point of the bayonet to the public square, they stripped and tarred and feathered them, amidst menaces and insults. The commanding officer then called twelve of his men. And ordering them to cock their guns and present them at the prisoner's breasts, and to be ready to fire when he gave the word, he addressed the prisoners, threatening them with instant death unless they denied the Book of Mormon and confessed it to be a fraud; at the same time adding that if they did so, they might enjoy the privileges of citizens. David Whitmer, hereupon, lifted up his hands and bore witness that the Book of Mormon was the Word of God. The mob then let them go.[12]

David Whitmer was the most interviewed witness. Over one hundred interview accounts exist and it is said thousands occurred. James Hart, a Missouri businessman alluded to "thousands of people" who interviewed him "sometimes 15 or 20 a day."[13]

Interviewers appealed to him to disclose deceit or admit if he was deluded or could have been hypno tized. James H. Moyle, then a law student but who later became Assistant Secretary of the Treasury in two administrations, interviewed David Whitmer and wrote "and so I begged of him not to let me go through life believing in a vital falsehood." His reply in one instance was, "No sir! I was not under any hallucination, nor was I deceived. I saw with these eyes, and I heard with these ears! I know whereof I speak!"[14]...

Richard Lloyd Anderson continues:

> The believers' estimates of the witness are fully substantiated by the reactions of newspaper reporters, a class generally calloused to empty sentimentality. They measured their man during interviews and also came away impressed. A detailed and restrained report in the *Chicago Times* contained the candid opinion of the interviewer: "And no man can look at David Whitmer's face for a half-hour, while he charily and modestly speaks of what he has seen, and then boldly and earnestly confesses the faith that is in him, and say that he is a bigot or an enthusiast."[15] Joe Johnson, of the Missouri *Plattsburg Democrat,* an astute political analyst, was profoundly affected by the inner conviction of the witness. While describing the vision, David's cold symptoms diminished, "his form straightened," and with "Evidently no studied effort" but with "strangely eloquent" tones, he described the vision and "the divine presence." The seasoned Missouri newspaperman classified what he heard as far more than an oddity: "Skeptics may laugh and scoff if they will, but no man can listen to Mr. Whitmer as he talks of his interview with the angel of the Lord, without being most forcibly convinced that he has heard an honest man tell what he honestly believes to be true."[16]

> ... Despite his vigorous differences with most believers in the Book of Mormon, David Whitmer insisted that no one could evade the challenge of this modern revelation: "Kind reader, ... beware how you hastily condemn that book which I know to be the word of God; for his own voice and an angel from heaven declared the truth of it unto me, and to two other witnesses who testified on their death-bed that is was true."[17] Less than a year after voicing this warning, David Whitmer added his deathbed testimony to the historical record. These dramatic details were published in full by the *Richmond Democrat,* but his more specific closing words were given some two weeks earlier to Angus Cannon. Bedridden and "as helpless as a child," the octogenarian was informed by George W. Sweich that his visitor wanted to hear his testimony of the Book of Mormon. After a lifetime of reiteration, the moment was still sacred to the enfeebled witness. Raising his hand, he declared: "My friend, if God ever uttered a truth, the testimony I now bear is true, I did see the angel of God, and I beheld the glory of the Lord, and he declared the record true."[18]

Finally aware of the overwhelming evidence, the anti-Mormons began to concede that Joseph Smith really did have some metallic plates with the appearance of gold: "Every careful reader must be compelled to admit that Smith did have some plates of some kind..." (John Hyde Jr., *Mormonism, Its Leaders and Designs*, pp. 269, 270). For other anti-Mormon concessions, see Professor J. B. Turner, *Mormonism in All Ages*, (1842), p. 178; Daniel P. Kidder, *Mormonism*, (1842), pp. 52-53; William Harris, *Mormonism Portrayed*, (1841), pp. 4-10.

1. Letter of P. Wilhelm Poulson to *Deseret News,* August 13, 1878, Ogden, Utah, cited in *Deseret Evening News,* August 16, 1878.
2. David Whitmer, *An Address to All Believers in Christ*, (Richmond, Missouri, 1887), p. 14.
3. David Whitmer, *A Proclamation,* (Richmond, Mo., 1881).
4. John P. Greene, *Facts Relative to the Expulsion of the Mormons*, (Cincinnati, 1839), p. 17.
5. Letter of Herman C. Smith to *Saints' Herald,* June 28, 1884, (Grand Prairie, Texas) cited in *Saints' Herald,* vol. 31, (1884), p. 442.

6. Letter of James H. Hart to *Deseret News,* August 23, 1883, Seneca Missouri, cited in *Deseret Evening News,* September 4, 1883.

7. *Richmond Conservator,* June 22, 1867.

8. *Richmond Conservator,* August 22, 1884.

9. *Richmond Conservator,* January 9, 1885.

10. "Mormon Reminiscences," published letter of Hiram Parker, Detroit, February 15 (New York), to Clare Mangus of Goodland Kansas, (great-grand daughter holds original clipping).

11. John P. Greene, *Facts Relative to the Expulsion of the Mormons,* (Cincinnati, 1839), p. 17.

12. Letter of James H. Hart to *Deseret News,* August 23, 1883, Seneca Missouri, cited in *Deseret Evening News,* September 4, 1883.

13. Memoirs of Joseph Smith III, cited in Mary Audentia Smith Anderson, *Joseph Smith III, and the Restoration,* (Independence, Missouri, 1952), p. 311-312.

14. *Chicago Times,* August 7, 1875.

15. *Richmond Democrat,* January 26, February 2, 1888, attributed to "an article written by Joe Johnson."

16. David Whitmer, *Address to All Believers in Christ,* (Richmond, Missouri: David Whitmer, 1887), p. 43.

17. *Journal of Angus Cannon,* January 7, 1888, Cp. Cannon's Tabernacle Speech, *Deseret Evening News,* February 12, 1888.

18. *Journal of Angus Cannon,* January 7, 1888.

EVIDENCE NO. 503: ADDITIONAL TESTIMONY FROM OLIVER COWDERY

Claim: The life of Oliver Cowdery supports his testimony that the Book of Mormon is true.

Evidence: Oliver Cowdery was the most closely associated witness. He spent three months of constant companionship with Joseph Smith during the translation of the Book of Mormon.

Of that time he said: "These were days never to be forgotten—to sit under the sound of a voice dictated by the inspiration of heaven, awakened the utmost gratitude of this bosom! Day after day I continued, uninterrupted, to write from his mouth, as he translated, with the Urim and Thummim, or as the Nephites would have said, 'Interpreters,' the history, or record, called 'The Book of Mormon'."

Mormon and non-Mormon alike generally recognized Oliver Cowdery as an astute and highly intelligent individual, and his mature life was spent in the practical vocation and avocation of law and politics. (Richard Lloyd Anderson, *Investigating the Book of Mormon Witnesses,* [1981], p.53.)

By the fall of the first year of Church organization, Oliver Cowdery led out in the expansion of missionary activity beyond upstate New York. In a journey as spectacular as any of the Apostle Paul, he and three companions proceeded mainly on foot 300 miles west to Kirtland, Ohio, where they "baptized one hundred and thirty disciples in less than four weeks." Adding a convert-companion, they traveled and preached another 600 miles to Saint Louis, and walked the last 300 miles to their destination, Independence, Missouri, in the face of cold and deep snow of a bitter winter in an unsettled country. Oliver did not exaggerate when he later referred to the many "fatigues and privations which have fallen to my lot to endure for the gospel's sake."

Thomas B. Marsh asked David Whitmer and Oliver Cowdery for the truth about the Book of Mormon shortly after they left the church:

> I inquired seriously at David [Whitmer] if it was true that he had seen an angel, according to his testimony as one of the witnesses of the Book of Mormon. He replied, as sure as there is a God in heaven, he saw the angel, according to his testimony in that book. I asked him, if so, how he did not stand by Joseph? He answered, in the days when Joseph received the Book of Mormon, and brought it

forth, he was a good man filled with the Holy Ghost, but he considered he had now fallen. I interrogated Oliver Cowdery in the same manner, who answered me similarly." ("History of Thomas Baldwin Marsh, Written by himself in Great Salt Lake City, November, 1857", printed in *The Latter-day Saints' Millennial Star,* vol. 26, [1864], p. 406.)

While Oliver left the church to practice law, he kept his testimony to himself. Thomas Gregg asked Cowdery's colleague, William Lang, whether the former Mormon leader had "denounced Mormonism." The answer was that he kept this subject to himself: "He would never allow any man to drag him into a conversation on the subject." (See Richard Lloyd Anderson, *Investigating the Book of Mormon Witnesses,* [1981], p. 57.)

On one occasion while in court the opposing attorney challenged Oliver's trustworthiness by questioning his testimony as a witnesses. Instead of being confused, Oliver Cowdery rose to his feet and stated that whatever his faults and weaknesses might be, the testimony he had written and given to the world was literally true.

> I cannot now avoid the responsibility, I must admit to you that I am the very Oliver Cowdery whose name is attached to the testimony, with others, as to the appearance of the angel Moroni; and let me tell you that it is not because of my good deeds that I am here, away from the body of the Mormon church, but because I have broken the covenants I once made, and I was cut off from the church; but, gentlemen of the jury, I have never denied my testimony, which is attached to the front page of the Book of Mormon, and I declare to you here that these eyes saw the angel, and these ears of mine heard the voice of the angel, and he told us his name was Moroni; that the book was true, and contained the fulness of the gospel, and we were also told that if we ever denied what we had heard and seen that there would be no forgiveness for us, neither in this world nor in the world to come. (B. H. Roberts, *Comprehensive History of the Church of Jesus Christ of Latter-day Saints,* 6 vols. [Salt Lake City: Deseret News, 1930], vol. 1, pp. 142–143.)

Oliver Cowdery eventually returned to the church at Council Bluffs, and gave the following testimony at a special conference at Kanesville, Iowa, Oct. 21, 1848:

> Friends and Brethren: My name is Cowdery, Oliver Cowdery. In the early history of this Church I stood identified with her, and one in her councils. True it is that the gifts and callings of God are without repentance; not because I was better than the rest of mankind was I called; but, to fulfill the purposes of God, he called me to a high and holy calling.
>
> I wrote, with my own pen, the entire Book of Mormon (save a few pages) as it fell from the lips of the Prophet Joseph Smith, as he translated it by the gift and power of God, by the means of the Urim and Thummim, or, as it is called by that book, "holy interpreters." I beheld with my eyes, and handled with my hands, the gold plates from which it was transcribed. I also saw with my eyes and handled with my hands the "holy interpreters." That book is true. Sidney Rigdon did not write it; Mr. Spaulding did not write it. I wrote it myself as it fell from the lips of the Prophet. It contains the everlasting gospel, and came forth to the children of men in fulfillment of the revelations of John, where he says he saw an angel come, with the everlasting gospel to preach to every nation, kindred, and people. It contains the principles of salvation; and if you, my hearers, will walk by its light and obey its precepts, you will be saved with an everlasting salvation in the kingdom of God on high. (*Deseret News,* April 13, 1859. Quoted in *Millennial Star,* vol. 27, [January 28, 1865], p. 58; and Kirkham, *A New Witness for Christ in America,* vol. 1, p. 71).

Soon afterward Oliver Cowdery was re-baptized, but while making preparations to come to Utah, he died suddenly in Richmond, Missouri, sixteen months after his reconciliation at Kanesville. Those present at his deathbed report his dying testimony. His wife, Elizabeth Whitmer Cowdery wrote, "From the hour when the glorious vision of the Holy Messenger revealed to mortal eyes the hidden prophecies which God had promised his faithful followers should come forth in due time, until the moment when he passed away from earth, he always without one doubt or shadow or turning affirmed the divinity and truth of the Book of Mormon." (Quoted in R. L. Anderson, *Investigating the Book of Mormon Witnesses,* [Salt Lake City: Deseret Book Co., 1981], p. 63.)

EVIDENCE NO. 504: ADDITIONAL TESTIMONY FROM MARTIN HARRIS

Claim: The exemplary life of Martin Harris lends additional credence to his testimony of the Book of Mormon.

Evidence: The following are excerpts from Richard Lloyd Anderson, *Investigating the Book of Mormon Witnesses*, (1981), pp. 96-117:

None of [Martin Harris's] townsmen exceeded his established reputation as a responsible and honest individual... The first anti-Mormon book, based on ... contrived statements from the native locality of Martin Harris, admitted that "he was considered an honest, industrious citizen, by his neighbors." A similar admission characterizes every major assessment of this Book of Mormon witness, even those that allege flaws in his character. The views on the man that are most significant come from about a dozen prominent acquaintances, none of whom displayed sympathy with his religious convictions.

... The most detailed of the recollections of the background and personality of Martin Harris was printed in the *Palmyra Courier* in 1872 as part of a serial history of the town written by James H. Reeves, who was born in 1802 as a member of an early and prominent family. The series included five installments devoted to Martin and his father, Nathan Harris. This is the source of most of the stories of the prowess of "Uncle Nathan" as a hunter and fisher; that pioneer is also portrayed as a vital individual who dearly loved the sociability of the frontier gatherings. The elder Harris was "universally honored by his neighbors for his kindness of heart and willingness to assist those in need."[1] Reeves considered that Martin fell heir to "the energy and activity of his mother."[2] Until his connection with Mormonism, which was deplored, Martin Harris "was an industrious, hard-working farmer, shrewd in his business calculations, frugal in his habits, and what was termed a prosperous man to the world."[3]

... Martin Harris was a farmer of marked ability. For two decades prior to 1829, he had managed over 240 acres of productive land, together with associated interests. ... He won two fair prizes in 1822, eight in 1823, and three in 1824. He was named as one of the two town managers of the society for Palmyra in 1823. His prominence gives some insight into his farming activity. Since he was named in 1824 to judge swine, he had obvious ability in raising animals, but his prizes in the above years are all in the category of cloth manufacturing. He produced linen, cotton, and woolen ticking, blankets, and worsted and flannel fabrics. The degree of this activity points to sheep raising and regular textile manufacturing on his farm. According to the contract of sale of part of his property in 1831, however, a great portion of his land was sown in wheat, then the staple crop of the area.

Included in community service must be his participation in local campaigns of the War of 1812. Although wealthy enough to engage a substitute to accept his draft assignment, he mustered and served on several occasions for defense against British forces when his region was threatened with invasion. His willingness to involve himself in community causes is shown by his election with a number of very prominent Palmyrans in 1824 to raise money to aid the Greek independence movement. The same point is made by his appointment in 1827 on the Palmyra committee of vigilance, by the Wayne County anti-Masonic convention, a cause long since discredited but which then attracted many public-spirited individuals.

But the most consistent community service of Martin Harris tells the most about him. He was elected by his neighbors in the annual township meetings as overseer of highways for his district in the years 1811, 1813, 1814, 1815, 1825, 1827 and 1829. In almost all of the above years these officials were also assigned to be fence viewers. Such positions might be compared with the functions of a non-commissioned officer who deals on a familiar level with small groups and therefore must possess tact and personal respect to succeed. The overseer of highways directed the work of neighbors on the roads in his district. It is obvious that Martin Harris was not a person with talents for leadership as much as a trustworthy local leader.

By 1829 it was well known in Palmyra that Martin Harris believed in Joseph Smith and the golden plates. As just shown, that year his neighbors still elected him to oversee the highway work in his district. Two years before Martin Harris became a witness of the Book of Mormon, he was sworn without disqualification as a grand juror in his county. In the following year his name appears three times as witness before the chief criminal court of his district...

The only extended evaluation of Martin Harris made in the early period is also the most complimentary. His exodus from Palmyra occasioned a touching tribute placed before the public by E. B. Grandin, Editor of the *Wayne Sentinel*: ... "Mr. Harris was among the early settlers of this town, and has ever borne the character of an honorable and upright man, and an obliging and benevolent neighbor. He had secured to himself by honest industry a respectable fortune—and has left a large circle of acquaintances and friends to pity his delusion."[4]

... Numerous recollections from Palmyra emphasize that he read scripture constantly and could quote the Bible from memory in astounding length...

Pomeroy Tucker, had "frequent and familiar interviews" with Martin Harris during the production of the book [of Mormon]... [He] was thoughtful enough to understand the dilemma of rejecting the printed testimony: "How to reconcile the act of Harris in signing his name to such a statement, in view of the character of honesty which had always been conceded to him, could never be easily explained."[5]

Martin Harris was the most skeptical of the three witnesses. He was very cautious in accepting the truthfulness of the Book of Mormon. Richard Anderson continues:

Martin waited until his wife and daughter had made personal inquiries first [then] he "talked with them separately to see if their stories agreed." After satisfying himself that all of the accounts of the Smith's harmonized with Joseph's, he proceeded to lift the box containing the plates, which he concluded must contain metal as heavy as lead or gold, "and I knew that Joseph had not credit enough to buy so much lead."[6]

... He took a copy of the characters transcribed from the plates to prominent linguists, including the famous Charles Anthon of Columbia College. The professor's recollection of the interview emphasized that the Book of Mormon witness had come for his opinion "as a last precautionary step"[7] in order to be sure that "there was no risk whatever in the manner"[8] before pledging his money for the printing... As Joseph Smith's first Secretary, Martin Harris was vigilant... Finding a stone "very much resembling the one used for translating, Martin made a substitution without Joseph's knowledge. The translator became confused and then frustrated, exclaiming "Martin, What is the matter?" ... Martin's answer shows how constantly the secretary was on guard against deception. "To stop the mouth of fools, who had told him that the prophet had learned those sentences and was merely repeating them."[9]

... Harris' prior history shows why Joseph Smith singled him out on the morning of his vision as in special need to "humble yourself." Upon failure of repeated prayers of Joseph Smith and the witnesses, Martin acknowledged that his attitude was probably the cause of their failure to obtain the promised revelation and he withdrew. After the angel appeared and showed the plates to the remaining group, the prophet found Martin Harris, and after joint prayer both were overwhelmed with the same vision. Joseph Smith remembered Martin's cry of conviction "Tis enough, mine eyes have beheld!"[10]

Although Martin Harris was honored by appointment to the first high council of the church, his main contribution was in the missionary service of formal journeys and private conversations. He and his brother Emer baptized a hundred converts in a few weeks, and Martin was imprisoned for his forthrightness in proclaiming the restored gospel. But the trials of Job descended on the Latter-day Saint community of Kirtland, and the witness was affected. The first steps toward plural marriage rankled him and ... he "lost confidence in Joseph Smith" and "his mind became darkened."[11]

... Several former leaders in Kirtland attempted to reorganize a new church and insisted that the Book of Mormon was "nonsense." A contemporary letter from Kirtland reported: "Martin Harris then bore testimony of its truth and said all would be damned that rejected it."[12]

Although the Latter-day Saints moved from Kirtland, Ohio ... Martin remained at Kirtland for the next thirty years ... His constant and vocal testimony to scores of visitors is all the more remarkable in the light of the psychology of the man in this period. Social pressure should have worked against his bearing testimony at all ... Martin Harris was increasingly a solitary figure in non-Mormon society, which only ridiculed him for his persistence in declaring that he had seen the angel and the plates ...

[Martin Harris changed religious affiliation eight times], but if his doctrinal commitments in Kirtland were fickle, the testimony of the angel and the plates remained an immovable certainty." [For example, on a missionary trip with Strangites, George Mantle records:] "When we came out of the meeting Martin Harris was beset with a crowd in the street, expecting that he would furnish them with material to war against Mormonism, but when he was asked if Joseph Smith was a true prophet of God, he answered yes; and when asked if the Book of Mormon was true, this was his answer: 'Do you know that is the sun shining on us? Because as sure as you know that, I know that Joseph Smith was a true prophet of God, and that he translated that book by the power of God.'..."[13]

During his period in Kirtland, scores of people talked with him directly about his testimony, which was given with consistent particulars and uncompromising conviction...

Upon his decision to return to the Latter-day Saints in Utah in 1870, the patriarch expressed his views to attentive listeners. His precise views upon returning were recorded in some detail by a disinterested reporter... "Mr. Harris is now in his 88th year, though still quite vigorous and uprightly, and he is Mormon, soul and body... The old gentleman evidently loves to relate the incidents with which he was personally connected, and he does it with wonderful enthusiasm." [14]

Later in Utah, a highly practical man of thirty, George Godfrey, attended the venerable Harris in his last illness and deliberately waited for a semiconscious moment to suggest that his testimony was possibly based upon deception. The response was vigorous: "I know what I know. I have seen what I have seen, and I have heard what I have heard. I have seen the gold plates ... an angel appeared to me and others."[15]

1. H. W. McIntosh, *History of Wayne County, New York,* (Philadelphia, 1877), p. 134.

2. McIntosh, *History of Wayne County,* p. 134.

3. *Palmyra Courier,* May 24, 1872.

4. *Wayne Sentinel,* May 27, 1831.

5. Pomeroy Tucker, *Origin, Rise and Progress of Mormonism,* (New York, 1867), p. 71.

6. Joel Tiffany, "Mormonism—No. II," *Tiffany's Monthly,* vol. 4, (1859).

7. Cited in E. D. Howe, *Mormonism Unveiled,* (Painesville, Ohio, 1834), p. 271.

8. Cited in John A. Clark, *Gleanings by the Way,* (New York, 1842), p. 235.

9. Edward Stevenson, "One of the Tree Witnesses," *Deseret News,* December 13, 1881.

10. Joseph Smith, "History of Joseph Smith," *Times and Seasons,* vol. 3, (1842), p. 898.

11. Cited in *Saint Louis Luminary,* May 5, 1855.

12. Letter of George A. Smith to Josiah Fleming, (Kirtland, Ohio, March 30, 1838).

13. Cited in *Autumn Leaves,* vol. 2, (1889).

14. *Daily Iowa State Register,* August 28, 1870, also cited in Joseph Grant Stevenson, *The Stevenson Family History,* (Provo, Utah, 1955), vol. 1, pp. 156-157.

15. Affidavit of George Godfrey, October 29, 1921, original still held by attesting notary John J. Shumway, Garland, Utah.

EVIDENCE NO. 505: EIGHT WITNESSES

Claim: Eight witnesses (in addition to the three who saw the angel and heard the voice of God) saw and handled the plates of gold from which the Book of Mormon was translated.

Evidence: The eight witnesses willingly signed a statement that was published to the world testifying that they had seen the plates (from the preface to The Book of Mormon):

BE IT KNOWN unto all nations, kindreds, tongues, and people, unto whom this work shall come: That Joseph Smith, Jr., the translator of this work, has shown unto us the plates of which hath been spoken, which have the appearance of gold; and as many of the leaves as the said Smith has translated we did handle with our hands; and we also saw the engravings thereon, all of which has the appearance of ancient work, and of curious workmanship. And this we bear record with words of soberness, that the said Smith has shown unto us, for we have seen and hefted, and know of a surety that the said Smith has got the plates of which we have spoken. And we give our names unto the world, to witness unto the world that which we have seen. And we lie not, God bearing witness of it.

Christian Whitmer	Hiram Page
Jacob Whitmer	Joseph Smith, Senior
Peter Whitmer, Junior	Hyrum Smith
John Whitmer	Samuel H. Smith

EVIDENCE NO. 506: FAMOUS SCHOLARS & STATESMEN ON THE BOOK OF MORMON

Claim: Famous people who were not Latter-day Saints have expressed positive opinions about the Book of Mormon.

Evidence: Moses Colt Tyler, noted professor of American history, made a positive statement about the Book of Mormon at Cornell University a number of years ago:

We shall never get the correct answer to our problems of American history as long as we so persistently ignore important factors, and amongst those important factors, which we do so ignore, the "Mormon" question stands in the front rank. We have to consider it. Then you have heard something regarding the Book of Mormon. Now, if there had been published in this country or anywhere in the world, a volume that is consistent as is the Book of Mormon ... having as much the appearance of genuineness as that book this university would have been among the first to equip an expedition, put it in the field, and send it off there to investigate the subject ... we have never taken the trouble to look into the matter. (See *Deseret Evening News*, Oct. 26, 1912, Section 2, p. ix.)

In 1899 Perry Benjamin Pierce said the following about the Book of Mormon: "In this publication (the Book of Mormon) we have a work of the greatest anthropological, ethnological, and archaeological interest, struck off in one complete, full, perfect act..." (See *American Anthropologist*, vol. 1, P. 678. Both of the above references are also cited in Harris, *Book of Mormon Message and Evidence*, [1961], pp. 79-81.)

Just a few months after the Book of Mormon was first published, the editor of *The Ohio Painesville Telegraph* wrote: "It may perhaps be useless to condemn the thing (Book of Mormon) by positive and absolute assertions. Time will discover in it something of vast importance to men or a deep laid plan to deceive." (December 7, 1830)

The following are quotes from Weldon, *The Book of Mormon Evidences Joseph Smith a Prophet,* pp. 27-28:

Napoleon Hill said: "It was faith which revealed to Joseph Smith fragmentary evidences of a civilization which preceded the American Indians on this continent at least a hundred years before positive evidence of such a civilization was unearthed on the North and South American continents. Incidentally, the revelations wrought by this faith led to his assassination at the hands of a mob whose leaders resented this modern day revelation of 'miracles' through faith, thus indicating how doggedly mankind has fought all who dared to turn the spotlight of understanding on the principle of faith." (See Napoleon Hill, *The Law of Success,* [1928] vol. 2, p. 145.)

Henry A. Wallace, former vice-president of the United States, said in an address before the New York National Book Fair in New York City: "Of all the American religious books of the nineteenth century, it seems probable that the Book of Mormon was the most powerful. It reached perhaps only 1 per cent of the United States, but affected this 1 per cent so powerfully and lastingly, that all the people of the United States have been affected" (*New York Times,* November 5, 1937).

Sir Richard Burton the famed explorer of the 1800's said: "America, like Africa, is a continent of the future; the Book of Mormon has created for it an historical and miraculous past." (See Richard Burton, *City of the Saints,* [1861] p. 314.)

The noted German historian, Edward Meyer, observed the complete harmony of the Nephite account with the Judeo-Christian writings of the Old World. He said, "A Bible for America, in absolute harmony with the Old and New Testaments, but at the same time an explanation and fulfillment of their teachings which restore the primitive purity of revelation or the Gospel, that is the thought which runs through the entire Book of Mormon, and in which it is rooted." (Quoted in, Hunter and Ferguson, *Ancient America and The Book of Mormon,* [1959], p. 68.)

EVIDENCE NO. 507: THE FAME OF THE BOOK OF MORMON

Claim: With over one hundred million copies of the Book of Mormon circulating throughout the world in ninety-four different languages, it is now one of the most famous and influential books ever published in America. Some fifteen thousand copies of the Book are printed each day. (See *Ensign of the Church of Jesus Christ of Latter-day Saints,* May 2000, p. 112.)

Evidence: Franklin S. Harris noted the following in *The Book of Mormon Message and Evidence,* (1961), p. 7.:

In The spring of 1946, in New York City, the Grolier Club selected and exhibited 100 books, published before 1900, which most influenced the life and culture of the American people (*New York Times Book Review,* April 21, 1946). These were such books as *The Autobiography of Benjamin Franklin*; Noah Webster's *An American Dictionary*; ... Abraham Lincoln's Gettysburg Address; and *The Book of Mormon,* which was given to the world by Joseph Smith in 1830. This recognition of the influence of the Book of Mormon recalls a letter written by the late Charles H. Hull, Professor of American History, Cornell University (*Millennial Star* [1972], vol. 89 p. 682. He wrote:

"I am perfectly willing to say to anyone that I suppose the Book of Mormon to be one of the most famous and widely discussed books ever published in America. I think an arguable case can be made for the assertion that it is the most famous and widely discussed book ever first published in America."

More recently, an Associated Press release from Washington dated November 20, 1991, announced that The Book of Mormon tied with 2 other books for sixth place in a nationwide reader survey on what book made the biggest difference in their lives. The survey had been mailed to a random sample of five thousand book club members—of which 1032 responded. Readers mentioned altogether 935 book titles. This is highly significant considering that only one percent of the United States is Latter-day Saint. At a symposium of the Library of Congress it was announced that survey respondents said their book choices had enhanced their intellectual or spiritual understanding of life. (See *Deseret News,* November 21, 1991, [Salt Lake City, Utah], p. 41.)

2. Another Testament of Jesus Christ

EVIDENCE NO. 508: ANOTHER TESTAMENT OF JESUS CHRIST

Claim: The Book of Mormon professes to be "Another Testament of Jesus Christ." The title page of the Book of Mormon plainly makes this claim and states that its primary purpose is to convince both Jew and Gentile that Jesus is the Christ.

Evidence: The Book of Mormon makes reference to Jesus Christ more often than does the Bible. On average the Book of Mormon prophets mention Jesus Christ by many of His various titles once every 1.7 verses. By comparison, the New Testament writers mention Him at an average rate of once every 2.1 verses. (See Susan Easton Black, *Finding Christ Through the Book of Mormon,* [Salt Lake City, Utah: Deseret Book Co., 1987], p. 15; Lee A. Crandall, *New Testament Study on the Use of the Names of Deity,* [Mesa, Arizona: n.p., 1985].)

EVIDENCE NO. 509: THE BOOK OF MORMON A LATTER-DAY MIRACLE

Claim: Only ancient prophets of God could have written the Book of Mormon as it claims. (See title page of Book of Mormon.) This sacred book could not have been written by Joseph Smith nor any of his contemporaries because there simply was not enough secular information available to Joseph Smith to have produced this work in the short period of time it took him to translate it.

Evidence: The Book of Mormon itself is one of the greatest evidences that Joseph Smith was a prophet of God and that the Church of Jesus Christ of Latter-day Saints is true. The Book of Mormon was translated in a day when there were no modern conveniences, such as electric lights. There were no computers, no word processors, and no copy machines to make the job easier. Libraries of that day had only limited information and were few and far between. There was less time to write in those days when there were many chores that had to be done. Yet the book was completed in a matter of a few months—hardly more than 75 days, and probably less. (See John W. Welch, "Was There a Library in Harmony, Pennsylvania?" *Foundation for Ancient Research and Mormon Studies Update,* No. 92, [January 1994], p. 2; and "How Long Did it Take Joseph Smith to Translate the Book of Mormon?" *Insights, An Ancient Window,* [FARMS: February 1986].)

Little or no scientific exploration and research had been conducted in the Americas prior to the publication of the Book of Mormon. V. W. Von Hagen writes "It was a simple bibliographic fact in 1829 that there was no literature available to the American reader on the ancient American civilizations...Actually, before one could attempt literary research on these pre-Columbian civilizations...one would have to create an entire manuscript library." (Victor Wolfgang Von Hagen, *Maya Explorer: John Lloyd Stephens and the Lost Cities of Central America and Yucatan*, [University of Oklahoma Press, 1947], p. 78. Cited in Harris, *Book of Mormon Message and Evidences*, [1961], p. 60.)

In 1851 the editors of *Harper's* Magazine wrote the following about the Book of Mormon. "We do not hesitate to say it, Joe Smith, or whoever was its author, has made a book superior to that of the Arabian prophet [Mohammed], deeper in its philosophy, purer in its morality, and far more original..." ("The Editor's Table," *Harper's New Monthly Magazine*, [1851], vol. 3, p. 701).

Most critics agree that Joseph Smith could not have written the Book of Mormon himself because he was young and inexperienced, and had very little schooling. Instead they suggest that he drew upon other contemporary sources.

A. Some have suggested that Oliver Cowdery was the author. Yet Cowdery always insisted that Joseph was the translator and the book was of divine origin. Cowdery never recanted his testimony that he had seen an angel with the gold plates, even during the years he was out of harmony with the Church. He also testified that he was scribe for most of the volume. This, in spite of the fact that he had nothing to lose in denying his testimony and he had nothing worldly to gain in reaffirming it.

B. Another popular explanation for the origin of the Book of Mormon was the claim that it had been copied from the Spaulding manuscript. Solomon Spaulding had written a story of a Roman ship washed ashore on the American coast after it had been lost at sea. However, most present-day critics have concluded that the contents of the Spaulding manuscript were much too foreign compared to the contents of the Book of Mormon to have provided any basis for the writing of the latter. For example, the Spaulding manuscript is only about one-sixth the length of the Book of Mormon, hence, it could have provided very little, if any, of the content of the Book of Mormon. Some few argue that it might have provided Joseph Smith with a basis for the idea of Israelites migrating to America, from which Smith could have embellished. However, Spaulding wrote that a group of Romans, not Israelites, made the voyage. Neither the Indians nor Indian ancestors were supposed to have crossed the ocean. Furthermore, none of the names in the Spaulding manuscript bear any resemblance to the names in the Book of Mormon.

C. Others have suggested that Sydney Rigdon must have authored the book—having copied ideas from Mr. Spaulding. Yet Rigdon, like Cowdery, insisted, even while out of the Church, that the book was of divine origin. The Rigdon theory breaks down for several reasons:

> First of all, the style of the Book of Mormon is very different from the embellished rhetoric Sidney Rigdon exhibited in his sermons. Second, there is no proof to show that Sidney Rigdon ever came in contact with the Spaulding manuscript. And third, the attempts to show him secretly communicating with Joseph Smith are simply unfounded. During the writing and printing of the Book of Mormon, from 1827 to 1830, Sidney Rigdon was a popular preacher in northeastern Ohio, and his whereabouts were known to a number of people. Yet none ever indicated that he was involved in such a conspiracy, and neither did any of Joseph's associates. Such a complicity would have been virtually impossible to carry out, especially since it would have involved either Joseph Smith or Sidney Rigdon periodically traveling about three hundred miles to see the other and consequently being gone from their areas of residence for long periods of time, taking into account the primitive modes of travel in those days.

> Sidney Rigdon continued avidly to teach his Reformed Baptist faith until he heard the message of the Restoration from the first Latter-day Saint missionaries in his area, almost eight months after the publication of the Book of Mormon and the organization of the Church. This, of course, would have been extremely unlikely if he had really been the author of the book and thus the originator of much

early Latter-day Saint theology. In fact, if Sidney Rigdon had written the Book of Mormon, it is improbable that a man of his prominence would have let Joseph Smith found the Church and be the leader and then later let Joseph publicly censure him several times when he opposed the Prophet's policies. Even when Rigdon was excommunicated in August 1844 because of his opposition to Brigham Young's leadership of the Church, he made no intimation that he was the author of the Book of Mormon. Late in his life, long after parting with Brigham Young and the body of the Latter-day Saints, Sidney Rigdon forcefully reiterated to his questioning son that he had nothing to do with writing the Book of Mormon. He added that Joseph Smith was a prophet and that the Book of Mormon was true. (John A. Tvedtnes, *A Sure Foundation* [Salt Lake City, Utah: Deseret Book Co., 1988], pp. 57-58.)

D. Still others claim that the Book of Mormon was copied from Ethan Smith's *View of the Hebrews*, first published in Vermont in 1823. *View of the Hebrews* contains very few similarities to the Book of Mormon and does not provide an intelligent alternative. One might as easily suggest that Ethan Smith borrowed from DeFoe's *Robinson Crusoe*. The similarity that a ship in each story sailed to a foreign land where the voyager(s) made their new home does not account for the many overwhelming differences. Besides, *View of the Hebrews* contains a wealth of information on ancient American culture, which is not found in the Book of Mormon. Could an impostor have ignored such tempting information? Also, it appears that there was no available copy of Ethan Smith's book because the *Times and Seasons* (vol. 3, pp. 813-814) quoted it from a secondary source. (See Harris, *Book of Mormon Message and Evidences*, [1961], p. 59.)

After the Book of Mormon was presented to the world, skeptics waited for the scientific world to prove it false. Instead, time has shown the book to be accurate and authentic. It would have been impossible for even the cleverest deceiver to guess with such extreme accuracy, with such continued consistency down to the minutest details throughout the entire volume. In the fields of science "a theory which asserts more, and thus takes greater risks, is better testable than a theory which asserts very little." Even if some source material might have been in existence, Joseph Smith had no time to search for it due to his responsibilities to provide the necessities of life in those rough frontier times. (See Karl R. Popper, "Science: Problems, Aims, Responsibilities," *Federation Reports American Societies for Experimental Biology*, [1963], vol. 22, p. 963.)

The best explanation for the origin of the Book of Mormon is the one given by its translator, Joseph Smith—that it was written by ancient American prophets who were inspired by God, and translated by Joseph Smith through the gift and power of God.

EVIDENCE NO. 510: A TESTAMENT TO THE DIVINE AUTHENTICITY OF THE BIBLE

Claim: While translating the Book of Mormon, Joseph Smith recorded that the Bible is an authentic ancient document containing the word of God. (See 1 Nephi 5:10-13; 14:18-27; 17:26-32, 40-42; 20-21; 2 Nephi 7-8, 12-24; 25:1-8; 26-27; Helaman 8:11-5; 3 Nephi 16:17; 20:11; 22; 23:1-3; 24-25; Mormon 8:23.)

Evidence: Undoubtedly, Joseph Smith was aware of the new philosophies becoming popular in his day regarding religion in general and the Bible in particular. With the new freedoms provided by the Constitution, people everywhere were forming new organizations and societies that had not previously been allowed. The statements in the Book of Mormon testifying to the truthfulness of the Bible appeared in a day when many skeptics, agnostics, and atheists were insisting that the Bible was false. (See Jon Murray & Madalyn Murray O'Hair, *All the Questions You Ever Wanted to Ask American Atheists,* [Austin, Texas: American Atheist Press, 1983]; James Thrower, *A Short History of Western Atheism,* [London: Pemberton Books, 1971]; William McCarty, *Bible, Church and God,* [New York: Truth Seekers Company, 1943]; David M. Brooks, *The Necessity of Atheism,* [New York: Freethought Press Association, 1933].)

Nevertheless, the Bible's authenticity has been verified by the discovery of the *Tel El Amarna* tablets in Egypt, the Moabite stone, the Dead Sea Scrolls, the 2,000 Babylonian tablets, and other archeological discoveries.

EVIDENCE NO. 511:   DELETIONS FROM THE BIBLE

<u>Claim</u>: While the Book of Mormon testifies to the authenticity of the Bible, it does not claim that the Bible is without error. It specifically states that there were many "plain and precious things" that were deleted from its pages through the evil works of men. (See 1 Nephi 13:20-32; 19:10-12; 20:1-3; 2 Nephi 3:5-22; Alma 33:3, 13, 15; 34:7; 46:23-27; Helaman 8:19-20; 15:11; 3 Nephi 10:14-17; 12:13, 17-19, 22, 29-30; 14:1.)

<u>Evidence</u>: Scholars of the Bible have found indisputable evidence that the Bible has indeed suffered many deletions. For example, see Vincent Taylor, *Expository Times*, 71, 1960, p. 72; L. Wallis, *The Bible and Modern Belief*, Duke University Press, 1949, p. 32; Father Herbert, *Expository Times*, 72, 1958, p. 33; The Catholic Bible Quarterly, 5, 1943, pp. 115-59. Above references are cited in Nibley, *Since Cumorah* (1988) p. 32.

Non-Mormon scholarship has concluded that the gospels found in the New Testament have also been manipulated. See W. Schneemelcher, *Neutestamentliche Apokryphen* (Tiibingen: Mohr, 1959), vol. 1, pp. 9, 11-12, 44, 46-47 who refers to Eusebius in *Church History*, vol. 3, p. 24; vol. 5, p. 25. Cited in Nibley, *Since Cumorah* (1988) p. 26-27.

Critics often ask for specific examples of any "plain and precious things" found in the Book of Mormon that are not also found in the Bible. Below is a brief list of a few such examples:

1. The importance of keeping records (1 Nephi 3:1-7; 4:13-16; Omni 1:14, 17; 3 Nephi 23:9-13)
2. The Lord prepares a way for us to keep all of His commandments (1 Nephi 3:7)
3. How mysteries are made known unto man (1 Nephi 10:19; Mosiah 2:9; Alma 12:10; 26:22)
4. The spirit of God led Columbus and the pilgrims to the new world (1 Nephi 13:12-20)
5. America—a promised land for the righteous (1 Nephi 13:12; 14:2; 17:13-14; 18:8, 22)
6. The colonists were delivered from England's tyranny by the power of God (1 Nephi 13:17-19)
7. The process for receiving revelation and inspiration (1 Nephi 17:45; Enos 1:10)
8. The gentiles to assist the house of Israel (1 Nephi 22:8-11; 2 Nephi 10:18)
9. The law of consecration (2 Nephi 2:2)
10. The reason God allows evil and opposition to continue in the world and the importance of moral agency (2 Nephi 2:2, 10-16)
11. The purpose of Adam's fall (2 Nephi 2:22-25)
12. The purpose of man's existence (2 Nephi 2:25)
13. The lost prophecy of the latter-day Joseph (2 Nephi 3:6-16)
14. Jerusalem is not to be the only location for the House of the Lord (2 Nephi 5:16)
15. The true relationship between grace and works (2 Nephi 25:23)
16. The manner in which the doctrine of Christ should be taught (2 Nephi 25:26-27)
17. The definition of priestcraft (2 Nephi 26:29; Alma 1:16)
18. The identity of the "sealed book" spoken of in Isaiah 29:11-12 (2 Nephi 27:6-21)
19. God's word is not limited to the Bible (2 Nephi 29:3-13)
20. The responsibility of stewardship (Jacob 1:19)
21. How to magnify one's office (Jacob 1:19; 2:2)
22. The symbolism of Abraham's sacrifice of Isaac (Jacob 4:5)
23. The lost teachings of Zenos, a prophet who lived in Jerusalem in Biblical times (Jacob 5:1-77)
24. The fate of those who seek for a sign (Jacob 7: 15-20; Alma 30:59)
25. The true meaning of service (Mosiah 2:17)
26. The eternal indebtedness of mankind to the Lord (Mosiah 2:20-25)
27. A description of the natural man, and how to overcome (Mosiah 3:19; Alma 5:6-45)

28. How to retain the remission of sins (Mosiah 4:11-16)
29. The limits of discipleship (Mosiah 4:27)
30. The true process of being *born again* (Mosiah 5:2-9; Alma 5:6-45)
31. The office and calling of a seer (Mosiah 8:13-17)
32. The necessity of organized religion (Mosiah 26:21-28)
33. The law of common consent (Mosiah 29:25-26)
34. Man cannot be saved in his sins (Alma 11:37)
35. The resurrection is literal—not figurative (Alma 11:43-44; 40:23)
36. The key to rending the veil of unbelief (Alma 19:6; 33:21)
37. The manner in which faith is developed and maintained (Alma 32:26-34)
38. A description of the doctrine of desire (Alma 32:27; 41:5)
39. The relationship between justice and mercy—"mercy cannot rob justice" (Alma 34:15-16)
40. The state of the soul between death and the resurrection (Alma 40:11-14)
41. Christians and Christianity flourished before the time of Christ (Alma 46:13-16)
42. The symbolism of the remnant of Joseph's coat (Alma 46:23)
43. The perpetual cycle of the human experience: obedience→blessings→prosperity→pride→sin→ punishment→humility→repentance→obedience…(Helaman 12:1-3)
44. The sacrifice of a broken heart and a contrite spirit (3 Nephi 9:20)
45. The "other sheep" spoken of in John 10:16 are identified (3 Nephi 15:16-24)
46. The true church should bear the name of Christ (3 Nephi 27:8)
47. The powers of translated beings (3 Nephi 28:36-40)
48. Why people are given weaknesses (Ether 12:27)
49. Baptism is only for those who are accountable (Moroni 8:5-23)
50. The manner in which all truth may be verified (Moroni 10:4-5)

EVIDENCE NO. 512: SCRIPTURES MISSING FROM THE BIBLE

<u>Claim</u>: Many "plain and precious things" were deleted from the Bible. Indeed, entire books have vanished altogether that were at one time considered sacred.

<u>Evidence</u>: To substantiate their own records, the prophets of the Bible refer to books that do no longer exist in our current Bible. For example see:

Numbers 21:14	"book of the wars of the Lord"
Joshua 10:13	"book of Jasher" (See also 2 Samuel 10:25.)
1 Kings 11:41	"book of the acts of Solomon"
1 Chronicles 29:29	"book of Nathan the Prophet" (See also 2 Chronicles 9:29.)
1 Chronicles 29:29	"book of Gad the seer"
2 Chronicles 9:29	"book of Ahijah the Shilonite"
2 Chronicles 9:29	"visions of Iddo the seer"
2 Chronicles 12:15	"book of Shemaiah the Prophet"
2 Chronicles 13:22	"the story of the Prophet Iddo"
2 Chronicles 20:34	"book of Jehu"
2 Chronicles 33:19	"written among the sayings of the seers"
Matthew 2:23	the prophets' foreknowledge that Jesus "shall be called a Nazarene"
1 Corinthians 5:9	A previous epistle to the Corinthians
Jude 1:14	"Enoch also...prophesied of these"

EVIDENCE NO. 513: BIBLE SCHOLARS ON MISSING SCRIPTURES

Claim: Several Bible scholars have concluded that there are many passages of scripture that were deleted from the canonical Bible in use today.

Evidence: Adam Clarke quoted Justin Martyr, an early Christian writer who taught that a certain passage had been taken out of the Book of Ezra: "And Ezra said to the people; This Passover is our Savior and our Refuge; and if ye will be persuaded of it, and let it enter into your hearts, that we are to humble ourselves to him in a sign, and afterwards shall believe in him, this place shall not be destroyed forever, saith the Lord of Hosts: But if ye will not believe in him, nor hearken to his preaching, ye shall be a laughing-stock to the gentiles. ...This passage," Justin says, "the Jews, through their enmity to Christ, blotted out of the book of Ezra. He charges them with canceling several other places through the same spirit of enmity and opposition." (Justin Martyr, *Dialogus cum Tryphone [Dialogue with Trypho]*, Section 2 cited in Adam Clarke, *The Holy Bible, With a Commentary and Critical Notes*, vol. 2, p. 752.)

Also in "Dialogue with Trypho," Justin Martyr writes: "And since this passage from the sayings of Jeremiah is still written in some copies (of the Scriptures) in the synagogues of the Jews (for it was only a short time since they were cut out), ...from the sayings of the same Jeremiah these have been cut out: 'The Lord God remembered His dead people of Israel who lay in the graves; and He descended to preach to them His own salvation.'" (See: *The Ante-Nicene Fathers*, vol. 1, p. 234-235. See also John P. Lundy, *Monumental Christianity or the Art and Symbolism of the Primitive Church*, Second Edition, [New York: J. W. Bouton, 1882], p. 73-74.)

The deleted text clearly makes reference to the Savior's visit to *the spirit world*, during the time that His body *slept* in the tomb—as recorded in Peter's first general epistle (1 Peter 3:18-20; 4:5-6).

The following is quoted from an article by Daniel C. Peterson and Stephen D. Ricks, entitled "Comparing LDS Beliefs with First-Century Christianity," (*Ensign*, Salt Lake City, Utah, March 1988, p. 9.):

In the earliest period of the Christian church, it is difficult to see a distinction being made between canonical writings and some books not in the present Protestant canon. For example, the Epistle of Jude draws heavily on non-canonical books such as 1 Enoch and The Assumption of Moses. As E. Isaac says of 1 Enoch, "It influenced Matthew, Luke, John, Acts, Romans, 1 and 2 Corinthians, Ephesians, Colossians, 1 and 2 Thessalonians, 1 Timothy, Hebrews, 1 John, Jude (which quotes it directly) and Revelation (with numerous points of contact) ... In molding New Testament doctrines concerning the nature of the Messiah, the Son of Man, the messianic kingdom, demonology, the future, resurrection, the final judgment, the whole eschatological theater, and symbolism." (E. Isaac, "First [Ethiopic Apocalypse of] Enoch," in *The Old Testament Pseudepigrapha*, edited by J. H. Charlesworth, 2 vols. [Garden City, New York: Doubleday, 1983] vol. 1, p. 10. See also "Apocrypha," in *The Interpreter's Dictionary of the Bible*, edited by G. A. Buttrick [Nashville, Tennessee: Abingdon, 1935] vol. 1, pp. 161-169.)

The so-called Muratorian Fragment, dating from the late second century AD, shows that some Christians of the period accepted the Apocalypse of Peter as scripture. Clement of Alexandria, writing around AD 200, seems to admit a New Testament canon of thirty books, including the Epistle of Barnabas, the Epistle of Clement, and the Preaching of Peter. Origen recognized the Epistle of Barnabas and the letter form the Shepherd of Hermas. (Clyde L. Manschreck, *A History of Christian Tradition* [Chicago: University of Chicago Press, 1974], p. 33.)

Even in more recent times, the question of canon has not been unanimously resolved. Martin Luther characterized the Epistle of James as "an epistle of straw"—largely because it seemed to disagree with his teaching of justification by faith alone—and mistrusted the book of Revelation. Roman Catholics and the Orthodox churches tend to accept the Apocrypha as canonical—books included in their Bibles but left out of most Protestant Bibles, including the current King James Version. In fact, the Eastern Orthodox churches have never settled the question of canon. A number of scholars have pointed out that the church has priority, both logically and historically, over the Bible—that is, a group of believers existed before a certain body of texts, such as the books of the Old and New Testament, were declared canonical. (See R. Bainton, *Here I Stand: A Life of Martin Luther*, [Nashville, Tennessee: Abingdon-Cokesbury Press, 1950], pp. 177, 331-332; Max Lackmann, *Sola Fide: Eine exegetische Studie uber Jakobus 2 zur reformatorischen Rechtfertigungslehre*, [Gutersloh, West Germany: C. Bertelsmann Verlag, 1949]; H. Holzapfel, *Die Sekten in Deutschland*, [Regensburg, West Germany: Verlag Josef Koesel & Friedrich Pustet A. G., 1925], pp. 20, 23-27; P. Johnson, *A History of Christianity* [New York: Atheneum, 1983], p. 22.)

EVIDENCE NO. 514: MISSING PROPHETS

Claim: The Book of Mormon mentions *Old World* prophets such as *Lehi, Zenos* and *Zenok* who are not included in the Bible. (See 1 Nephi 1:5, 19:10, 12.) This has caused considerable criticism by those who claim that the *complete* list of true prophets of God is found in the Bible.

Evidence: The Bible does not mention all the prophets who ever lived. Recently it has been discovered that the words of some true prophets of God were obliterated along with their names. Dr. Hugh Nibley writes: "In 1893 M. R. James published Greek and Latin versions of an ancient text entitled 'The Vision of *Zenez* the Father of Gothoniel.' Since the father of Othniel in the Bible is Kenaz and not Zenez, James translates the title 'The Vision of Kenaz,' though the name which appears in some manuscripts is Zenez, and James confesses himself at a loss to explain how C or K could have been 'corrupted into Z'—but there it is." See Montague R. James, *Apocrypha Anecdota,* second series (Cambridge University Press, 1897), pp. 174-177; Jean Danielou, *The Dead Sea Scrolls and Primitive Christianity* (Baltimore: Hilicon, Mentor Omega Books, 1958), pp. 81-84. See also Erwin R. Goodenough, *Jewish Symbols in the Greco-Roman Period* (New York: Pantheon, 1953), vol. 1, pp. 20-21; and Damascus Covenant (*Zadokite Document*), 5:2; cited in Nibley, *Since Cumorah*, (1988) pp. 277-278, 286.

See related information in the chapter on "Names Used in the Book of Mormon."

EVIDENCE NO. 515: MISSING PRAYERS

Claim: The Book of Mormon states that there are many "plain and precious things" missing from the Bible (1 Nephi 13:26, 28, 40). Some of these plain and precious things are missing prayers.

Evidence: In the Bible, Jesus gave the world His prototype of a simple prayer (Matthew 6:9-13), together with much instruction as to how to pray, where to pray, why we should pray, etc. (Matthew 6:1-15). While our secret or personal prayers are vital, there are other prayers of equal or greater importance that are missing from the Bible. The Bible is missing the prototype, the wording and the instructions on the following prayers:

1. The blessing of little children.
2. The words of the baptism ceremony.
3. The laying on of hands for bestowing the Gift of the Holy Ghost.
4. The blessings on the emblems of the Sacrament of the Lord's Supper.
5. The prototype of the marriage ceremony.
6. The instructions for conferring priesthood authority.
7. The ordaining of men to the various offices in the priesthood.
8. The anointing of the sick with oil.

These ordinances and ceremonies are only briefly mentioned in the Bible. But, even an indirect reference to them in the word of God demonstrates their great importance. Yet, in order to participate in these rituals, non-Mormons must turn to non-Biblical prayer books that were admittedly produced by fallible men. It is ironic that, while they use their non-Biblical works, they criticize the Latter-day Saints for using non-Biblical scriptures provided them through the grace of God.

EVIDENCE NO. 516: MISSING INSTRUCTIONS ON ORDINANCES

Claim: Among the many "plain and precious things" which have been taken from the Bible are the instructions on how to perform certain ordinances and covenants (1 Nephi 13:26).

Evidence: The answers to the following questions are missing from the Bible or are very obscure:

1. Should baptisms be performed by sprinkling, pouring or immersion, or by the touch of a moist finger on the candidate's forehead?
2. Should infants be baptized?
3. Since not all baptisms are acceptable (Acts 19:1-6), what authority is required to baptize?
4. Since some who baptized in Bible times did not have the authority to lay on hands for the gift of the Holy Ghost (Mark 1:6-8; Acts 8:12-20), what authority is needed for this ordinance?
5. Who is authorized to bless the Sacrament of the Lord's Supper?
6. How often should believers partake of the sacrament?
7. What are the differences between elders and bishops? Many Bible scholars say they are synonymous. Why are they listed separately?
8. Should the monetary sacrifices of believers be used to pay ministers to preach?

These questions and others have been serious enough to splinter Christianity into more than 2,000 separate sects throughout the world today.

EVIDENCE NO. 517: MISSING INSTRUCTIONS ON DUTIES OF OFFICERS

Claim: Some of the "plain and precious things" which were taken from the Bible (1 Nephi 13:26, 28, 40), including vital instruction on the duties of officers in the Church, were restored by modern revelation.

Evidence: The Bible mentions certain officers, such as deacons, elders, bishops, apostles, etc., in such verses as 1 Corinthians 12; Ephesians 4:11-14; Titus 1:5; Philippians 1:1, but gives no hint of their duties. Hence, a man who is given the title of elder in one church may have entirely different duties than one who is called an elder in another church. It is the same for all other titles mentioned in the Bible. Merely addressing a man as a deacon does not make him a deacon—unless he is properly ordained and his duties are the same as deacons performed in the ancient Church of Jesus Christ. There has never been any guesswork in the Church of Jesus Christ of Latter-day Saints concerning the duties of the various officers within its organization. Their duties were clearly de fined by revelation and recorded as scripture in passages such as: Doctrine and Covenants Sections 20, 84, 107.

EVIDENCE NO. 518: THE BOOK OF MORMON RESTORES ORIGINAL TEXT FROM THE BIBLE

Claim: Critics claim that Joseph Smith plagiarized some passages from the Bible, inserting them into the Book of Mormon. Yet a careful comparison of those Book of Mormon passages that are shared with the Bible shows that the Book of Mormon actually restores original text from the Bible and makes many clarifications of the Biblical wordings.

Evidence: Joseph Smith did not simply copy verses from the Bible as critics assume. Of the 433 Isaiah verses that are also found in the Book of Mormon, less than half of these passages read the same as the King James Version. The following is quoted from Robert F. Smith, "Textual Criticism of the Book of Mormon" *Foundation for Ancient Research and Mormon Studies Update,* September 1984; Reprinted in *Reexploring the Book of Mormon,* edited by John W. Welch, (1992), pp. 77-79:

> Although he generally followed the King James Version of the Bible both 1) for an acceptable scriptural idiom of translation, and 2) for direct quotations from Isaiah, Joseph Smith sometimes departed precedent. At 2 Nephi 20:39, for example, Joseph dictated *Ramath* instead of the usual *Ramah* of the parallel King James Version Isaiah 10:29. Indeed, there is no -t- in the Hebrew text, the Greek Septuagint, nor even in the Syropalestinian Aramaic version. However, we do find the -t- in the Jewish Aramaic translation known as Targum Pseudo-Jonathan, as well as in the Christian Syriac Peshitta version (*Ramata* and *Rameta,* respectively, as is also evident in the Old Syriac *Rametha* for New Testament Arimathea—compare to Matthew 27:57). Neither source was available to Joseph.

> Another departure from the King James Version came when Joseph Smith was dictating from Isaiah 48:11 in I Nephi 20:11. Among other things, Joseph added an "I" which is not attested in the Greek or Hebrew texts. However, the "I" *is* in one Syriac manuscript, in one Jewish Aramaic Targum manuscript, and in a scribal correction to the large Isaiah Scroll from Qumran Cave One (the latter being the earliest Hebrew text).

> King James Version's "Ariel," a poetic term for *Jerusalem,* is not found in the 2 Nephi 27:3 quotation of Isaiah 29:7. However, it is also absent from the Jewish Aramaic Targum—which replaces it with "the City." The Book of Mormon reads "Zion" instead. This fits well, however, since "Mount Zion" appears at the end of the verse (Isaiah 29:8), and "Zion" and "Mount Zion" parallel each other here.

Another example is found by a careful study of 2 Nephi 23:3 which reveals a much clearer translation of what was said in Isaiah 13:3. The Isaiah passage reads, "I have commanded my sanctified ones, I have also called my mighty ones, for mine anger, *even* them that rejoice in my highness." The Book of Mormon passage reads the same as Isaiah only to the word "anger." It clarifies the nonsense of the King James translation from the Mesoretic text: "for mine anger *is not upon* them that rejoice in my highness."

John A. Tvedtnes has noted that the original error was probably scribal and may have been written erroneously into the Mesoretic text because of the almost identical appearance of the Hebrew versions of Isaiah and 2 Nephi. For more information, see John A. Tvedtnes featured in *A Sure Foundation* (Salt Lake City, Utah: Deseret Book Co., 1988), pp. 24-5; and also in "Isaiah Variants in the Book of Mormon" in *Isaiah and the Prophets,* Edited by Monte S. Nyman, (Provo, Utah: Religious Studies Center, Brigham Young University, 1984).

Still another example can be found by comparing Isaiah 2:16 with 2 Nephi 12:16. The Book of Mormon reads: "And upon all the ships of the sea, and upon all the ships of Tarshish, and upon all pleasant pictures." The Greek Septuagint includes the phrase "and upon all the ships of the sea," which the King James Version leaves out, and the Septuagint omits "and upon all the ships of Tarshish," which the King James includes, and changes the third phrase slightly. On this comparison Franklin S. Harris states the following: "The Book of Mormon contains all three phrases, the Authorized Version and the Greek Septuagint two each, This is an excellent example of what often happens in translation and copying. This indicates that the Hebrew lost the first phrase which the Greek Septuagint preserved, and the reverse was the case on the last phrase." (Franklin S. Harris, *The Book of Mormon Message and Evidences* [Deseret News Press: Salt Lake City, 1961], p. 50.)

In 2 Nephi 24:4, the Book of Mormon adds the phrase "And it shall come to pass in that day," which is not found in the Hebrew (Isaiah 14:4). However, the Codex Alexandrinus, (now in the British Museum, to which Joseph Smith did not have access) includes similar wording: "and thou shalt say in that day." The King James Version of Isaiah 51:15 reads: "But I am the Lord thy God, that divided the sea, whose waves roared: The Lord of Hosts is *his* name." The Book of Mormon corrects the poor grammar by changing *his name* to *my name,* which is also found in both the Septuagint and the Latin.

These and several other examples led Franklin Harris to the following conclusion: "These changes show that the Book of Mormon writers actually had a copy of the early Old Testament records, and is valuable in studying the text of the Bible, since it dates from 600 BC and until recently the oldest Hebrew manuscript of any considerable portion of the Old Testament was the ninth century AD, and the earliest versions and relatively complete codices date from the forth century AD." (Franklin S. Harris, *The Book of Mormon Message and Evidences* [Deseret News Press: Salt Lake City, 1961], pp. 49-52. See also: The master's degree thesis of H. Grant Vest, *The Problem of Isaiah in the Book of Mormon,* [Brigham Young University, 1938]; and Sidney B. Sperry, *Our Book of Mormon,* Chapters 14-16; S. B. Sperry, *Improvement Era,* vol. 42, [1939] p. 594; S. B. Sperry, *The Book of Mormon Testifies,* [1952], chapter 21.)

EVIDENCE NO. 519: INSPIRED CONTENTS

Claim: The Book of Mormon was written by prophets of God who were not only inspired, but who also possessed great wisdom.

Evidence: It is extremely improbable that an uneducated, backwoods farm boy could have produced such profound statements of wisdom and beauty without aid from a higher source. The following statements are only a small sampling of the many inspired passages to be found within the pages of the Book of Mormon:

And it came to pass that I, Nephi, said unto my father: I will go and do the things which the Lord has commanded, for I know that the Lord giveth no commandments unto the children of men, save he shall prepare a way for them that they may accomplish the thing which he commandeth them (1 Nephi 3:7).

For it must needs be that there is an opposition in all things. If not so…righteousness could not be brought to pass, neither wickedness, neither holiness nor misery, neither good nor bad. Wherefore, all things must needs be a compound in one; wherefore, if it should be one body it must needs remain as dead, having no life neither death, nor corruption nor incorruption, happiness nor misery, neither sense nor insensibility (2 Nephi 2:11).

And now, behold, if Adam had not transgressed he would not have fallen, but he would have remained in the garden of Eden. And all things which were created must have remained in the same state in which they were after they were created; and they must have remained forever, and had no end. And they would have had no children; wherefore they would have remained in a state of innocence, having no joy, for they knew no misery; doing no good, for they knew no sin. But behold, all things have been done in the wisdom of him who knoweth all things. Adam fell that men might be; and men are, that they might have joy (2 Nephi 2:22-25).

Wherefore, men are free according to the flesh; and all things are given them which are expedient unto man. And they are free to choose liberty and eternal life, through the great Mediator of all men, or to choose captivity and power of the devil; for he seeketh that all men might be miserable like unto himself (2 Nephi 2:27).

O that cunning plan of the evil one! O the vainness, and the frailties, and the foolishness of men! When they are learned, they think they are wise, and they hearken not unto the counsel of God, for they set it aside, supposing they know of themselves, wherefore, their wisdom is foolishness and it profiteth them not. And they shall perish. But to be learned is good if they hearken unto the counsels of God (2 Nephi 9:28-29).

For we labor diligently to write, to persuade our children, and also our brethren, to believe in Christ, and to be reconciled to God; for we know that it is by grace that we are saved, after all we can do (2 Nephi 25:23).

...and he inviteth them all to come unto him and partake of his goodness; and he denieth none that come unto him, black and white, bond and free, male and female; and he remembereth the heathen; and all are alike unto God, both Jew and Gentile (2 Nephi 26:33).

Therefore, wo be unto him that is at ease in Zion! Wo be unto him that crieth; All is well! Yea, wo be unto him that harkeneth unto the precepts of men, and denieth the power of God, and the gift of the Holy Ghost! Yea, wo be unto him that saith: We have received, and we need no more! And in fine, wo unto all those who tremble, and are angry because of the truth of God! For behold, he that is built upon the rock receiveth it with gladness; and he that is built upon a sandy foundation trembleth lest he shall fall (2 Nephi 28:24-28).

And behold, I tell you these things that ye may learn wisdom; that ye may learn that when ye are in the service of your fellow beings ye are only in the service of your God (Mosiah 2:17).

See that ye are not lifted up unto pride; yea, see that ye do not boast in your own wisdom, nor of your much strength. Use boldness, but not overbearance; and also see that ye bridle all your passions, that ye may be filled with love; see that ye refrain from idleness (Alma 38:11-12).

Do not suppose, because it has been spoken concerning restoration that ye shall be restored from sin to happiness. Behold, I say unto you, wickedness never was happiness (Alma 41:10).

Thus saith the Lord God—Cursed shall be the land, yea, this land, unto every nation, kindred, tongue, and people, unto destruction, which do wickedly, when they are fully ripe; and as I have said so shall it be: for this is the cursing and the blessing of God upon the land, for the Lord cannot look upon sin with the least degree of allowance (Alma 45:16).

And behold, all things are written by the Father; therefore out of the books which shall be written shall the world be judged. ... Therefore, what manner of men ought ye to be? Verily I say unto you, even as I [Jesus Christ] am (3 Nephi 27:26-27).

And if men come unto me I [God] will show unto them their weakness. I give unto men weaknesses that they may be humble; and my grace is sufficient for all men that humble themselves before me; for if they humble themselves before me, and have faith in me, then will I make weak things become strong unto them (Ether 12:27).

Wherefore, my beloved brethren, if ye have not charity, ye are nothing, for charity never faileth. Wherefore, cleave unto charity, which is the greatest of all, for all things must fail—But charity is the pure love of Christ, and it endureth forever; and whoso is found possessed of it at the last day, it shall be well with him. Wherefore, my beloved brethren, pray unto the Father with all the energy of heart, that ye may be filled with this love, which he hath bestowed upon all who are true followers of his Son, Jesus Christ; that ye may become the sons of God (Moroni 7:46-48).

And when ye shall receive these things, I would exhort you that ye would ask God, the Eternal Father, in the name of Christ, if these things are not true; and if ye shall ask with a sincere heart, with real intent, having faith in Christ, he will manifest the truth of it unto you, by the power of the Holy Ghost. And by the power of the Holy Ghost ye may know the truth of all things (Moroni 10:4-5).

EVIDENCE NO. 520: WORSHIPPING THE FATHER

Claim: While the Book of Mormon teaches that *both* the Father *and* the Son (Jesus Christ) are the true objects of godly worship (2 Nephi 25:16, 29; Jacob 4:5; 3 Nephi 11:17; 4 Nephi 1:37), it further clarifies that the true followers of Christ will direct their prayers to the Father—not the Son (2 Nephi 32:9; 3 Nephi 18:19-23; 18:30; 19:6-7; 20:31; 28:30; Moroni 7:48).

However, many non-Mormon Christians do not pray to the Father, but only to "Lord Jesus," and maintain that the real focus of our worship should be on Jesus—not the Father.

Evidence: A number of non-Mormon Bible scholars and theologians have independently arrived at the same conclusion as the Church of Jesus Christ of Latter-day Saints. They feel that the whole thrust of Biblical scripture points to the Father who we worship through the Son.

One Jewish scholar who has embraced Christianity, Dr. Aaron Rogers, writes the following commentary on Matthew 7:23-23:

> There are many who teach a false belief as the following: "All you need is Jesus." There are many variations on this theme, but many ministers, pastors, and evangelists teach this false doctrine. The truth is that *Yeshua* [Jesus] taught as follows:

Rogers then quotes many scriptural references such as Matthew 12:50; 26:39, 42; Luke 2:49; John 8:28; 10:37; 20:21, after which he continues:

> Jesus said that we shall worship the Father in spirit and in truth. Two things are clearly evident here. First, our primary duty is to worship the Father, for this is what Jesus taught. There are many who concentrate so heavily on the worship of the Son, that they forget what God they worship...

> How many times have we heard that *Yeshua* is the one standing on the right hand of God's throne?...Can we focus so much on the Holy Messiah standing beside the throne to the point we don't reverence the Father who sits *on* the throne? (G. Aaron Rogers, *The Messianic Jewish Book of Why,* [Camden Court Publishing 1997], vol. 2, pp. 38-41, 60.)

EVIDENCE NO. 521: SALVATION BY GRACE

Claim: The Book of Mormon teaches the true relationship between grace and works. "For we labor diligently to write, to persuade our children, and also our brethren, to believe in Christ, and to be reconciled to God; *for we know that it is by grace that we are saved after all we can do.*" (2 Nephi 25:23. Emphasis added.)

Evidence: Grace is divine help and is offered through the mercy and love of Jesus Christ. It is through the grace of the Savior, made possible by His atoning sacrifice, that mankind will be resurrected. Additionally, through individual faith in Christ, the grace of God gives to faithful Christians the strength and assistance necessary to do the works which are required for salvation. "And remember, after ye are reconciled unto God, that *it is only in and through the grace of God that ye are saved*" (2 Nephi 10:25).

The Church of Jesus Christ of Latter-day Saints clearly teaches that man cannot merit nor earn his own salvation. In fact, the Book of Mormon teaches that "since man had fallen he could not merit anything of himself" (Alma 22:14). Indeed the word *earn* does not appear anywhere in the cannon of LDS scripture. The word *merit* occurs eight times in the scriptures, however, each time it is mentioned, it refers to "the merits of him who is mighty to save"—Jesus Christ (2 Nephi 2:8; 31:19; Mosiah 2:19; Alma 22:14; 24:10; Helaman 14:13; Moroni 6:4; and D&C 3:20). "There can be nothing which is short of an infinite atonement which will suffice for the sins of the world" (Alma 34:8-16). Salvation and exaltation are an inheritance from our Father in Heaven—the greatest gift of God (D&C 14:7). All our good works cannot compare to the grace provided by our Savior, Jesus Christ. But, insignificant as they are, good works are necessary as a token of our belief in the Savior. (See also Dallin H. Oaks, "What Think Ye of Christ?" *Ensign*, November 1988, p. 67.)

The Book of Mormon further clarifies that "Wherefore, ye must press forward with a steadfastness in Christ, having a perfect brightness of hope, and a love of God and of all men. Wherefore, if ye shall press forward, feasting upon the word of Christ, and endure to the end, behold, thus saith the Father: Ye shall have eternal life. And now, behold, my beloved brethren, this is the way; and *there is none other* way nor *name given under heaven whereby man can be saved in the kingdom of God*" (2 Nephi 31:20-21).

EVIDENCE NO. 522: SALVATION BY WORKS

Claim: The Book of Mormon teaches that we are saved by grace "after all we can do" (2 Nephi 25:23). Because of his idea, that salvation is not totally dependent on God, critics wrongly claim that Mormons are not Christians.

Evidence: It is inconsistent that other churches, which also teach of the necessity of works, are not likewise labeled non-Christian. Some churches agree that water baptism is absolutely essential. Others speak of seven essential *sacraments* and encourage infant baptism to lessen the risk of an unbaptized child being denied access to the "supernatural vision of God." Yet their status as *Christian* remains unquestioned. It is also strange that those who believe in grace alone—without the need for saving works—contradict their own dogma. They insist that man can do nothing to better his own chances for salvation, yet they do not believe that everyone is automatically saved. What, then, must a man do to be saved? They answer that he must do certain things, which they do not label as works (but clearly are), such as exercising faith, confession of sin to God in sincere prayer, and calling upon Jesus to save.

Works alone cannot save man. Man cannot be saved by grace alone. It is truly the grace of Jesus Christ that makes salvation possible, "unto all them that obey him" (Hebrews 5:9).

Some have misinterpreted certain scriptures by assuming that mankind can be saved by grace alone—without obedience to the commandments of God.

If the scriptures are read in proper context, they can be interpreted more correctly according to the original intent. When we read that "whosoever believeth in him should ... have everlasting life" (John 3:16), we should remember that other scriptures define belief as incorporating obedience to Christ (Romans 3:16, John 14:12, Titus 1:16, James 2:14-18). "Thou believest that there is one God; thou doest well; the devils also believe, and tremble. But wilt thou know, O vain man, that faith without works is dead? Was not Abraham our father justified by works, when he had offered Isaac his son upon the altar? Seest thou how faith wrought with his works, and by works was faith made perfect?" (See James 2:19-22 and 2:23-26.) James is saying that works is inseparable from faith, that without works there is no real faith. Where faith is "dead," it does not exist.

Those who insist that works have no part in salvation unintentionally invalidate the Bible. The vast majority of the Bible constantly stresses the need for good works. Yet, critics say good works will automatically be performed out of the natural righteousness of a "saved" individual. Why then, should the Bible promote obedience—if those who would *automatically* perform good works do not require such motivation?

One popular work which advocated salvation by grace without works tells of a very religious man named Mac who is told that "if you died tonight, you'd go straight to hell." His damnation was due to his belief that Jesus expected him to perform certain good works when he should have relied solely on faith. "He should have believed in a Jesus who saves without asking for obedience to commandments."

On another page in the same book, the author claims that "a man who lied, stole, cheated, and lived a wicked life, could say, 'Jesus save me,' and be saved in the last hours of his life" This seems to clearly fit the description of the type of false doctrine against which the apostle Peter had warned in the quote below. He wondered why Christians of his day could believe in a God who:

> ...saves adulterers and murderers if they know him; but good and sober and merciful people who don't happen to know him, simply because they have received no information concerning him, he does not save! A great and good god, forsooth, whom you proclaim, not only saving the wicked but showing no mercy on the good! (See *Recognitiones Clementinae [Clementine Recognitions]*, II, 58, in *Patrologiae Cursus Completus ... Series Graeca*, J. P. Migne editor, [Paris: 1857-1866], vol. 1 p. 1276 quoted in Nibley, *Mormonism and Early Christianity*, [1987], p. 102.)

So why do some Christians believe in salvation without works? Often, the scriptures speak of salvation from death as a free gift to all. Yet these scriptures are referring to *physical salvation* (the reunification of the spirit and the body) not *spiritual salvation* (the reunification of the spirit of man with the spirit of God). Other scriptures seem to speak of the uselessness of "the law" (Acts 13:39; Romans 3:20, 28; Galations 2:21). The Law of Moses was eliminated with Christ (Galatians 3:24-25; Hebrews 7:19). While obedience to the Law of Moses will not save us, we cannot be saved without obedience to the laws of Christ. However, our small works might be compared to *reaching out and receiving the hand of Jesus Christ as He pulls us out of bondage.* He cannot save us if we do not reach out to Him, nor take his hand. Yet, works should be more than simple mechanical actions. They must originate from conviction of the heart.

Tens of thousands of verses admonishing us to do good works fill the pages of the Bible. But, since many of those verses do not specifically mention salvation, some *born-again* Christians apparently ignore such passages. They say that those who are *saved* will automatically obey the commandments—not because they must, not out of fear of losing salvation, but because their new spiritual nature makes them *want* to *do good.* While this state of salvation—where an individual loses all desire to commit sin, whose only passion is for righteousness, can and should be attained by every sincere Christian, it cannot be done while that individual continues in willful disobedience to God. To believe that man can be saved **in** his sins is to negate 99% of the Bible. If the commandments have nothing to do with our salvation, why do they appear in the Bible—which should only contain information pertinent to our salvation? If men will automatically live righteously after being *born again*, why not distill the Bible down to a few verses which, (when taken out of context with the whole) seem to say that man is saved only by the grace of God?

The Savior outlined in detail the *way* in which individuals may claim discipleship and eventual salvation. He said that there are requirements; certain things we <u>should</u> *do* and certain other things we should <u>not</u> *do.* At the great and last judgment, He will say to those on His right hand: "Come, ye blessed of my Father, inherit the kingdom prepared for you from the foundation of the world: For I was an hungered, and ye gave me meat: I was thirsty, and ye gave me drink: I was a stranger, and ye took me in: Naked, and ye clothed me: I was sick, and ye visited me: I was in prison, and ye came unto me" (Matthew 25:34-36). Nowhere else in the scriptures is the necessity of works so simply taught. Yet even so, there are many who continue to insist that good works have nothing to do with salvation. It would seem unjust and unmerciful for God to deny salvation to so many who sincerely serve their fellow man—even when their motivation for service is to secure their own salvation. Surely, God is not displeased with those who are genuinely sincere, even though their efforts are insufficient or misdirected. The heathen, who may have no knowledge of Christ, yet is sincerely trying to do right, can be assured that his prayers are heard and that God will bless him. But those who **have** the light of Christ and knowledge of God's commandments, and ignore them, God will also ignore. In short, God rejects those who reject Him and His commandments.

Jesus commanded us to *do the work* of searching the scriptures in order to gain eternal life (John 5:39). As we search the scriptures we also learn that He also said that whoever does not *do the work* of partaking of the emblems of His flesh and blood has no *life* in them. But whoever *does such work* has eternal life and will be raised up by Him at the last day (John 6:53-57). Continuing our search, we also learn that other ordinances are also required for salvation. Jesus warned Peter that if he refused to allow his feet to be washed, he would have no part with Him (John 13:8). This ordinance, which Peter was told he must experience, should not be confused with the related commandment of Jesus that His disciples should serve one another (John 13:12-17).

In addition to the many thousands of Biblical passages which command the reader to obey God, the following verses specifically warn that good works are essential to one's salvation: **Psalms** 15:1, 2; 24:3; **Matthew** 5:6-12, 19, 22, 28-32, 43-47; 48; 7:21-27; 6:1-6, 14-18; 7:1; 10:22; 13:44-46; 19:16-22; 24:13; 25:31-46; **Mark** 10:17-21; 29-30; 13:13; 16:16; **Luke** 11:41-42; 12:33; 18:22; **John** 5:29; 6:53-54; 12:50; 13:8; 15:2-8; **Acts** 5:32; **Romans** 2:6-15; 6:16-23; 8:17, 24; 10:13-21; 11:22; 13:6-12; **1 Corinthians** 1:21; 6:9-10; 9:24-27; **2 Corinthians** 1:6; 4:17; 7:10; 13:7, 11; **Galatians** 2:17; 5:19-21; 6:7-9; **Ephesians** 3:20-21; 5:5; **Philippians** 1:17, 19; 2:12; **Colossians** 3:24; **1 Thessalonians** 2:12; **2 Thess.** 1:7-8; **1 Timothy** 4:16; 61:12,18,19; **2 Timothy** 4:7-8; **Titus** 2:11-15; **Hebrews** 5:8-9; **James** 1:12; 4:17; **1 John** 1:5-7; 3:2, 3; **1 Peter** 3:21; 4:17-18; **2 Peter** 3:9; **Jude** 3; **Revelation** 2:7, 11, 17, 26; 20:12-15; 21:7; 22:14.

EVIDENCE NO. 523: MERCY CANNOT ROB JUSTICE

<u>Claim</u>: The ancient prophet Alma taught that "the plan of mercy could not be brought about except an atonement should be made; therefore God himself atoneth for the sins of the world, to bring about the plan of mercy, to appease the demands of justice, that God might be a perfect, just God, and a merciful God also. ...For behold, justice exerciseth all his demands, and also mercy claimeth all which is her own; and thus, none but the truly penitent are saved. What, do ye suppose that mercy can rob justice? I say unto you, Nay; not one whit. If so, God would cease to be God" (Alma 42:9-25).

<u>Evidence</u>: Many Christians insist that the supremacy of Christ's *gospel of mercy* over the Mosaic *law of justice* should guarantee *unconditional* forgiveness and salvation to those who have accepted Jesus as their master. However, the parable of the two debtors in Matthew 18:23-35 clearly teaches that God cannot forgive those who do not repent and forgive others—for one who has sincerely repented will surely forgive others also. Speaking of this parable Dr. G. Aaron Rogers, a respected authority on both Judaism and Christianity, writes: "The Lord God wishes to show mercy unto each of us, yet will be forced to perform harsh judgment to us if we do not show His mercy to others" (G. A. Rogers, *The Messianic Jewish Book of Why,* [Camden Court, 1997], vol. 2, p. 24).

EVIDENCE NO. 524: URIM AND THUMMIM

<u>Claim</u>: In the Book of Acts we discover an ancient prophecy (that has apparently been deleted from the Old Testament) which speaks of a "period of restoration of all things" (Acts 3:21—New American Standard Bible). Part of the "restoration of *all* things" is the return of the *Urim and Thummim*—or *interpreters* used anciently by the Hebrew prophets (Exodus 28:30; Leviticus 8:8; Deuteronomy 33:8; Ezra 2:63; Nehemiah 7:65).

When Joseph Smith uncovered the gold plates of the Book of Mormon, he also unearthed several other sacred objects, including the Urim and Thummim—a pair of "seer stones" that would assist him in his work of translation. See Joseph Smith—History 1:35, 52; D&C 10:1. See also Ether 4:5. No other church, known to the authors, has claimed to know of a restoration of these sacred stones.

<u>Evidence</u>: The following is from Bruce R. McConkie, *Mormon Doctrine* (pp. 740-742):

> From time to time, as His purposes require, the Lord personally, or through the ministry of appointed angels, delivers to chosen prophets a *Urim and Thummim* to be used in receiving revelations and in translating ancient records from unknown tongues. With the approval of the Lord these prophets are permitted to pass these instruments on to their mortal successors.

> A Urim and Thummim consists of two special stones called seer stones or interpreters. The Hebrew words urim and thummim, both plural, mean lights and perfections. Presumably one of the stones is called Urim and the other Thummim. Ordinarily they are carried in a breastplate over the heart. (Exodus 28:30; Leviticus 8:8.)

> Because of the sacred nature of these holy instruments, they have not been viewed by most men, and even the times and circumstances under which they have been held by mortals are not clearly set forth. Undoubtedly they were in use before the flood, but the first scriptural reference to them is in connection with the revelations given the Brother of Jared (Ether 3:21-28).

Elder LeGrand Richards wrote the following with regard to the Urim and Thummim in his book *A Marvelous Work and A Wonder*, (1950), pp. 72-73:

> Would it be unfair to ask what the spiritual leaders of Joseph Smith's day knew about the Urim and Thummim? Would Joseph Smith, of himself, have thought of claiming that he translated the Book of Mormon with the assistance of the Urim and Thummim? Yet, the use of the Urim and Thummim was known to the prophets of old:

Urim and Thummim, mentioned as the means by which the High Priest inquired of the Lord, Exodus 28:30; Leviticus 8:8; Numbers 27:21; Deuteronomy 33:8; 1 Samuel 28:6. The Urim and Thummim were clearly material objects of some kind; it has been suggested that they were 1) stones in the High Priest's breastplate, 2) sacred dice, 3) little images of "truth" and "justice" such as are found hung around the neck of an Egyptian priest's mummy. The Urim and Thummim did not exist after the Captivity—Ezra 2:63. (*A Concise Biblical Encyclopedia*, p. 154.)

Ancient Jewish tradition has proclaimed that a great servant of God from the House of Joseph would come in the latter days to prepare the way for the coming of Shilo, the Great Messiah. They began calling him, "Messiah ben Joseph," and called their Shilo, "Messiah ben David." Literally translated, these appellations mean, "The anointed One, son of Joseph," and "The anointed One, son of David." (See Joseph Klausner, *The Messianic Idea in Israel*, [New York: the Macmillan Co., 1955], chapter 9 is devoted exclusively to this subject.)

The chapter on Joseph Smith in volume 1 of this same work shows that this great servant of God was none other than the latter-day prophet Joseph Smith. In Dr. Klausner's doctoral dissertation on the Messiah ben Joseph at the Heidelberg University in 1904, he estimated that the Urim and Thummim, which had been lost since the destruction of the first temple, would be returned during the time of the Messiah ben Joseph. (See Klausner, *Die Messianische Vorstellungen Volkes im Zeitalter der Tannaiten*, [Berlin: Verlag M. Poppelhauer, 1904], pp. 61, 115-119, cited in Vestal and Wallace, *The Firm Foundation of Mormonism,* [1981], p. 208.)

EVIDENCE NO. 525: EARLY CHRISTIAN KNOWLEDGE OF SAINTS BEYOND THE OCEAN

Claim: While many secular historians maintain that the ancient Americans were all pagans, the Book of Mormon claims that many ancient Americans were Christians, having been taught the same gospel that was taught in Palestine (2 Nephi 25:26). However, the early Christians knew that Jesus Christ is the God of the whole earth and that His same gospel principles would be found across the ocean.

Evidence: Clement, who comes close to being the earliest Christian writer after the apostles, has been quoted as saying: "The Ocean is not to be crossed by men, but those worlds which lie on the other side of it are governed by the same ordinances of a guiding and directing God as these." (Origen, "Peri Archon, [On First Things]," in *Patrologiae Cursus Completus ... Series Graeca,* edited by J. P. Migne, [Paris: 1857-1866], vol. 11, p. 194 cited in Nibley, *Lehi in the Desert* [1988], p. 250.)

The Book of Mormon further claims that the ancient inhabitants of America are Israelites (2 Nephi 3:4). Isaiah prophesied that Israel would dwell in the isles and coast lands of the north and the west (Isaiah 49:1, 3, 6, 12).

Jeremiah saw Israel dwelling in the country beyond the sea, but his words do not appear in the King James Version. The Alexandrian Codex supplies us with the missing text: "Judah shall be saved, and Israel shall dwell [in the country beyond the sea] safely" (Jeremiah 23:6).

Religious Beliefs and Practices of the Ancient Americans

The specific resemblances between ancient American religions and the religions of the Near East are too close to be accidental, and thus provide additional evidence that the ancient American Peoples emigrated from the Near East as the Book of Mormon claims (1 Nephi 1:1-4).

When the first Catholic missionaries arrived in the "New World" they found a culture and religion that had many elements of Christianity. However, since these beliefs differed significantly from Catholic doctrine, and because of obvious corruptions (such as human sacrifice), they concluded that the doctrines had been taught by Satan in order to pervert the *true* gospel of Jesus Christ and thereby prevent the Catholic officials from making a full conversion. Consequently, many of the ancient records of these cultures were systematically destroyed. However, a sampling of these ancient doctrines were preserved by insightful priests and natives who were inspired to record these beliefs for posterity.

Since few of these documents predate the Spanish conquest, many critics suggest that the Native Americans picked up these elements of Christianity from the Spanish. However, while that possibility my be somewhat plausible, it is unlikely that those who had seen their people slaughtered and their sacred books destroyed would be so anxious to assimilate the religion of their conquerors—and particularly when these native authors were specifically trying to preserve their own heritage for future generations.

The following is quoted from the abstract of a paper by M. Wells Jakeman entitled "The Mesoamerican Pantheon" (*University Archeological Society Newsletter* 16.02), also cited it Christensen, *Progress in Archaeology,* (1963), pp. 114-115:

> By 'Mesoamerican pantheon' we mean all the gods believed in by the ancient civilized peoples of central and southern Mexico and northern Central America. An understanding of this pantheon is basic to Mesoamerican archaeology because most of the higher culture traits of the area were religious in character, such as the temple architecture, symbolic art, hieroglyphic (i.e. 'sacred') writing, and advanced calendar system featuring a sacred almanac—all doubtless developed by the ruling priest-groups at the religious ceremonial centers or temple-cities.

> A study of the pantheon of ancient Mesoamerica is also important as a test of the Book of Mormon claim that the earliest civilized peoples of this area had a biblical Near Eastern religion. Comparing the deities of the Book of Mormon peoples with those of ancient Mesoamerica evidenced by the early chronicles and archaeology, we discover in fact a number of close correspondences. The most striking are those between 'the Lord' of the Book of Mormon peoples, a life and rain god (identified as 'the Lord'—Yahweh or Jehovah—of the Israelites and the Messiah of the Christians), and Itzamna or Chac (in the language of the Maya people of northern Central America) and Quetzalcoatl or Tlaloc (in the language of the Nahua or Toltec-Aztec people of central Mexico), the life and rain god of these later Mesoamerican peoples according to the evidence of the Chronicles and archaeology. As many as eighteen different aspects of the Book of Mormon deity can be shown to be exactly duplicated in the Mesoamerican beliefs regarding Itzamna-Quetzalcoatl. This leads us to the following conclusions:

> (1) There are almost too many close correspondences for the resemblance to be accidental. This, therefore, establishes at least the possibility that the essentially monotheistic Book of Mormon religion was the earliest in Mesoamerica in the era of its ancient civilizations.

> (2) Evidence from the Chronicles and archaeology indicate paganization in the post-Book of Mormon period (Classic and Militaristic epochs), though the life and rain god—a deity resembling 'the Lord' of the Israelites and Christians—remained supreme:

>> a. 'Idol gods' were added, some of them clearly identifiable with certain 'idol gods' of the Near Eastern and Book of Mormon peoples.

>> b. Aspects of the life and rain god were personified as partially separate deities (for example, Itzamna and Chac, Quetzalcoatl and Tlaloc).

(Many of the eighteen similarities between Jesus Christ and Quetzalcoatl mentioned above, are listed later on in this same chapter as separate evidences.)

It is the position of the authors that, while it is possible that *some* of these parallels were assimilated by the Natives from the missionaries, it is highly unlikely that *all* were learned from their European oppressors when considering all of the evidence as a whole—especially when many of these doctrines held sacred by the Natives are more closely tied to Book of Mormon teachings than to the Catholic doctrine. A number of these similarities are included in the evidences that follow:

EVIDENCE NO. 526: THE ETERNAL GOSPEL BEFORE THE TIME OF CHRIST

Claim: The Book of Mormon teaches that the Gospel of Jesus Christ is universal and eternal, and was taught throughout the entire history of man's sojourn upon this earth (except during periods of apostasy) *before* and after Christ. (See Alma 46:15; 48:10. See also Joseph Smith Jr., *History of Church of Jesus Christ of Latter-day Saints*, vol. 2: pp. 16-17.)

Evidence: As the *"first"* Christians claimed: "that which is called the Christian religion existed among the ancients, and never did not exist from the beginning of the human race." Origen referred to "the Christians that were before Christ." Ambrose said, "We admire the mysteries of the Jews...But I can promise you that the Christian sacraments are both holier and older." (See Augustine, *Epistolae Retrac*, 1.13:3 in Gerald Heard, *Vedanta for Modern Man*, [New York: 1962] p. 17; Ambrose, *De Sacrum*, 1:4. All three above references are cited in Seaich, *Ancient Texts and Mormonism,* [1983], pp. 13, 120.)

The Dead Sea Scrolls also reveal that the gospel of Jesus Christ was known and practiced before his birth. (See R. K. Harrison, *The Dead Sea Scrolls, an Introduction*, Harper Touchbook, 1961, p. 102; F. F. Bruce, *Second Thoughts on the dead Sea Scrolls*, Grand Rapids; W. Eerdmans, 1961, p. 144; K. Stendahl, *The Scrolls and the New Testament*, New York: Harpers, 1957, p. 1; A. Dupont-Sommer, *The Dead Sea Scrolls*, [New York: Macmillan, 1952], p. 96; Frank M. Cross, *Christian Century*, [August 3, 1955], p. 889; Frank M. Cross, *The Biblical Archaeologist*, [February 1954], p. 4; *Time*, September 5, 1955, pp. 33-34; Graystone, G., *The Catholic World*, April 1956, p. 11; J. Telcher, "The Habakkuk Scroll," *Journal of Jewish Studies*, vol. 2, 1954, pp. 47-59.)

Some scholars believe the Gospel of John was actually adapted from certain pre-Christian teachings—a fully developed gospel of which the Mandaean writings are representative. (See Rudolph Bultmann, *Zeitschrift fur die Neutestamentliche Wissenschaft*, Beiheft 24 [1925], p. 139. Cited in Nibley, *Since Cumorah*, [1988], p. 274.)

The church established by the Son of God in the meridian of time was actually a restoration of a more ancient organization with a long history upon the earth. (See Edmund Wilson, *The Scrolls From the Dead Sea* [Oxford: Oxford University Press, 1955], pp. 75-76. Cited in Robinson, *Christ's Eternal Gospel* [1976], p. 106.)

"The authors of most books written about the Dead Sea Scrolls refer to these many apparent parallelisms and conclude that Jesus and His disciples must have borrowed many of the theological concepts from these and other sources." One writer even suggests that Jesus may have actually been a member of one of the earlier sects during his pre-ministry years. (See Edmund Wilson, *The Scrolls From the Dead Sea* [Oxford: Oxford University Press, 1955], p. 94; Robinson, *Christ's Eternal Gospel* [1976], pp. 128-129.)

Dr. Truman G. Madsen wrote:

> The Qumran community—only a part of their records are so far translated—was, as Frank Cross calls it a "church of anticipation." Many things that Christians had heretofore supposed were original, unique, and singular in Jesus are very patently there—as much as two hundred years before. That, to them, is a terrible indictment of Christ. For us, it is exactly what he himself has taught—a dispensation plan and pattern of history. Christ came before; and Christ will come after. He was the Jehovah who manifested himself to the Old Testament prophets. And Adam and Eve, both genuine historical persons, were by him taught the fullness—the all—of the gospel. (*The Ancient Library of Qumran and Modern Biblical Studies,* [Garden City, NY: Doubleday, 1968], pp. 181-184; cited in Madsen in "Are Christians Mormon?" *Brigham Young University Studies,* vol. 15, [Autumn 1974], p. 91.)

Similarly, Christian Jewish Scholar Dr. G. Aaron Rogers concluded from his studies that *"Yeshua* [Jesus] did not start a new religion, but rather defined and brought forward the religion that The Father, He, and The Spirit had been bringing to the nations from the beginning." (G. Aaron Rogers, *The Messianic Jewish Book of Why,* [Camden Court Publishing Co., 1997], vol. 2, p. viii.)

EVIDENCE NO. 527: THE NAME OF CHRIST KNOWN BEFORE THE CHRISTIAN ERA

Claim: The Book of Mormon states that true believers took upon themselves the name of Christ and were called Christians long *before* Jesus Christ was born. For example, see Alma 46:15-16. The idea that there could have been Christians before the time of Christ has been heavily criticized. However, the discovery of the Dead Sea Scrolls provided new evidence (not available at the time of Joseph Smith) to support this belief.

Evidence: *The Gospel of Philip* shows that the word *Christ* existed before the Christian era by explaining that *Christ* is the Greek translation of the more general term *Messiah.* "The name Jesus [Yeshua] does not exist in any other tongue [than Hebrew], but is always called Jesus. But Christ is Messiah in Syriac, while in Greek it is the Christ." See *Gospel of Philip* 56:5-9; 62:6-17 cited in Nibley, *Since Cumorah* [1988], p. 167, note 103.

This is also brought out in John 4:25, which quotes a Samaritan woman as saying "I know that Messias cometh, which is called Christ: when he is come, he will tell us all things." Had there not existed the word *Christ* as a specific use of the term *Messiah* then her statement would have been meaningless.

Dr. Hugh Nibley has written the following in his book *Since Cumorah*, ([1988], p. 168.):

> A number of studies have recently come forth dealing with the origin of the name *Christian*, all of them unsatisfied with the conventional idea that it was a term of derision first applied to the followers of Christ at Antioch. These studies agree that it was the Christians themselves who first took the name—as in the Book of Mormon, and that for them the mere uttering of the name was "a summary confession of faith." This is exactly how it was taken in the Book of Mormon. See J. Moreau, "Le nom des chretiens," *Nouvelle Clio* 1-2 (1949-1950) pp. 190-192; Elias J. Bickerman, "The Name of Christians," *Harvard Theological Review* vol. 42 (1949) pp. 109-124; Harold B. Mattingly, "The Origin of the Name *Christiani,*" *Journal of Theological Studies* vol. 9 (1958) pp. 26-37; W. Lowrie, "The Name Which is Above Every Name," *Theology Today* vol. 8 (1951), p. 19.

EVIDENCE NO. 528: GODHEAD OF THREE DEITIES IN ANCIENT AMERICA

Claim: The Book of Mormon teaches that the Godhead consists of three separate and distinct beings. See, for example, Ether 12:41, which describes their differing missions and functions and, hence, their separate personalities. 1 Nephi 11:27 distinguished between at least two of the Godhead.

Evidence: According to ancient American theology, the earth was created by a Godhead of three distinct personages: "Then they planned the creation, and the growth of the trees and the thickets and the birth of life and the creation of man. Thus it was arranged in the darkness and in the night by the Heart of Heaven who is called *Huracán.* The first is called *Caculhá Huracán.* The second is *Chipi-Caculhá.* The third is *Raxa-Caculhá.* And these three are the Heart of Heaven." *Chipi-Caculhá* is also referred to as, *Gucumatz* and is identified with the Fair God—*Quetzalcoatl.* See *Popol Vuh: The Sacred Book of the Ancient Quiche Maya,* English translation by Goetz and Morley, (Reprinted from Adrián Recinos, 1950, by the University of Oklahoma Press), pp. 77-84, 165–169; cited in Franklin S. Harris, Jr., *The Book of Mormon: Messages and Evidences,* (1961) pp. 76-78 and Hunter and Ferguson, *Ancient America and the Book of Mormon* (1950), p. 93.

Peter DeRoo writes the following in his work, *History of America Before Columbus* (1900), vol. 1, p. 372:

> The mystery of the Blessed Trinity seems not to have been altogether unknown to the Mexicans. On the 20th of March they celebrated the first feast of their year, in honor of an idol which, although one, they worshipped under three different names, and although having three names, they worshipped as one and the same god; almost in a manner in which we believe in the most holy Trinity. The names of the god were "Totec," the frightful and terrible Lord; "Xipe," the disconsolate and *maltreated Man*; "Tlatlauhquitezcatl," the Mirror flaming with splendor. And this idol was not a local one, but its feast was celebrated all over the land as being that of the universal deity.

The natives of Campeche assured the Spanish missionaries that their religious teacher, Quetzalcoatl, had given them images to explain his doctrine, and, in particular, a triangular stone, as an illustration of the Blessed Trinity, with which mystery they were well acquainted, says Sahagun, and in whose name they were baptized.

Peter DeRoo goes on to tell of the Quiché trinity in Guatemala called "Tohil, Awilix, and Gucumatz," and the Chiapan trinity called "Icona, Bacab and Echuac." The above is also cited in Cheesman, *The World of the Book of Mormon* (1978), p. 5; See also Lewis Spence, *Myths and Legends: The North American Indians* (Boston: David P. Nickerson, 1932), p. 3.

EVIDENCE NO. 529: JESUS CHRIST AS ELDER BROTHER

Claim: While most churches teach that Jesus Christ is really God the Father in the flesh, Latter-day Saints believe that He is our elder Brother, being the firstborn of God the Father in the spirit and the only begotten of God in the flesh. (Note: Latter-day Saints also claim Jesus Christ as our adoptive father. Thus, according to Latter-day Saint doctrine, Jesus is both our elder brother through birth, and our father through adoption. See Mosiah 5:7; Bruce R. McConkie, *Mormon Doctrine* [1979], p. 214.)

Since the Book of Mormon claims that the ancient inhabitants of the Americas were taught the fulness of the gospel, it follows that such concepts as the belief in a godly elder Brother, should be found among their legends and histories.

Evidence: Not only is this belief in harmony with the Bible (since Jesus as a God was "in the beginning ...*with* God" [John 1:1] and was "the firstborn of every creature" [Colossians 1:15]), but it was also a sacred belief of the ancient Americans. Since this concept was not taught of the Roman Catholic Church, none can legitimately claim that the Native Americans learned this concept from the Catholic missionaries.

According to the research of John Bierhorst, the Pima tribes of Southern Arizona believed that the "Earthmaker created the sky and the earth, and the two touched, giving birth to a second deity, called Elder Brother." The legend goes on to say that Elder Brother was killed. "After four years, however, Elder Brother revived and followed the setting sun into the underworld." (Compare to 1 Peter 3:18-20.) See John Bierhorst, *The Mythology of North America,* (New York: William Morrow and Co., 1985), pp. 103-104.

EVIDENCE NO. 530: JEHOVAH—YEHOWA

Claim: Since the Book of Mormon claims to be written by people from a Hebraic culture, one would expect to find traces of the Hebrew language in the language and culture of the ancient Americas. For example, one of the most sacred words in the Hebrew language is the name of God: *Jehovah,* pronounced *Yahweh.* A variation of this sacred name was also used by Ancient Americans to describe their god.

The name *Jehovah* was so sacred to the Jews that it could only be spoken in utmost reverence. Eventually it became too sacred to write the name, and was thus removed from the Bible in several passages. A more correct spelling would be *Yehovah* because the Hebrews did not pronounce the "J" sound, but used the "Y" sound instead. (William Smith, *A Dictionary of the Bible,* [MacDonald Publishing Co.: McLean, Virginia], p. 284.)

Evidence: Lewis Spence observed that among the North American Indians, *Yehowa* was the name of a "great and glorious being. His name was never to be mentioned in common talk...*Yehowa* created the world..." (Spence, *Myths and Legends: The North American Indians* [Boston: David P. Nickerson, 1932], p. 3; cited in Cheesman, *The World of the Book of Mormon,* (1978), p. 3.)

EVIDENCE NO. 531: THE MAORI GOD IO AND THE HEBREW IAWEH OR YAHWEH

<u>Claim</u>: The Book of Mormon teaches that some ancient Americans (who were of Hebraic origin) left the continent in ships to settle new lands (Alma 63:5-8). The Church of Jesus Christ of Latter-day Saints teaches that Polynesia, including New Zealand, was settled at least in part by these early Americans, who took with them a knowledge of their God, Jehovah. (See 2 Nephi 22:2; also Cole and Jensen, *Israel in the Pacific* [1961], p. 388.)

As stated in the previous evidence, the Hebrew God Iaweh or Yaweh was a secret deity, whose name was so sacred that only the priest could utter it, doing so only on the most solemn occasions.

<u>Evidence</u>: In New Zealand *Io* was hallowed as a secret God whose name was known only by a few high-ranking tohunga, or priests. *Io* was the one god, the creator, omniscient, omnipotent, and uncreated. Before 1865, the typical Maori probably would not have made any connection between the Maori God *Io* and the Hebrew God *Yaweh*, or *Jehovah*. The name *Yah* or *Iah*, usually spelled <u>Jah</u>—as in Halleluj<u>ah</u>, is the shortened form of *Yaweh*. (See R. Lanier Britsch, *Unto the Islands of the Sea* [1986], pp. 276-277; and James Strong, *A Concise Dictionary of words in the Hebrew Bible*, [New York, Abingdon Press, 1890], entry number 3050, p. 47.)

EVIDENCE NO. 532: THE POLYNESIANS CAME FROM AMERICA

<u>Claim</u>: Although some scholars insist that the Polynesian ancestors came from the Orient and sailed east to settle Polynesia, the Church of Jesus Christ of Latter-day Saints has always taught that they sailed west from America. In 1813, Stuart Meha, a Maori Latter-day Saint from New Zealand, sent a telegram to the Church leaders thanking them for the privilege of allowing a group of Maori saints to travel to Salt Lake to go through the temple. In the telegram, Brother Meha added the words: "Who knows but that some of Hagoth's people have returned—perhaps!" (Hagoth, a shipbuilder of ancient America, mentioned in the Book of Mormon, took a group of people from America and sailed "into the west sea [Pacific] by the narrow neck which led into the land northward. ... And ... they were never heard of more." [Alma 63:5-8].)

> Later, the First Presidency of the Church, and some of the General Authorities, gave a welcome, in Wandermere Park, in honor of this party of Maori Saints from New Zealand. In a speech delivered on that occasion, President [Joseph F.] Smith replied to the telegram: 'I would like to say to you brethren and sisters from New Zealand, you *are* some of Hagoth's people, and there is NO PERHAPS about it!' Continuing, President Smith told how it had been given to him by the spirit, while laboring in Hawaii, that the Polynesians were descendants of Lehi. Brother Meha testifies that these statements touched his heart, and he had no more uncertainties as to whether the Polynesians were truly of the House of Israel. (From "The Personal Testimony of Stuart Meha," Waipawa, H. B., New Zealand. A signed manuscript, recorded May 20, 1937, in the *Missionary Journal, First Mission*, Elder Elwin W. Jensen, Salt Lake City.)

<u>Evidence</u>: Many evidences from tradition, legend and artifacts of ancient Polynesian culture have surfaced that clearly indicate a relationship between the American Indian and the Polynesian. There are many leading scientists and ethnologists who concur in this conclusion. In the past, some scholars seemed to deliberately avoid exploring the possibility of a connection between the Polynesian and the Native American, lest such evidence prove that "Mormonism" and the Book of Mormon were true. Direct scientific fact cannot be denied, however, and many ethnologists now believe there is a direct connection between the Polynesian and the Native American, rather than indirect relationships through common Oriental ancestors as previously believed. (See *University Archeological Society Newsletter*, No. 70, November 25, 1960, published by Brigham Young University, Provo, Utah. The entire issue is devoted to a review of recent publications dealing with speculation on the racial origin of the Polynesian.)

Sir Peter Buck, a Maori and former Director of the Bishop Museum in Honolulu, was persuaded by the evidence, and presents certain facts in one of his publications (Peter Buck, *Vikings of the Sunrise*, [New York: J. B. Lippincott Co., 1938] chaper 21). See also Thor Heyerdahl, *American Indians in the Pacific* (Chicago: Rand McNally and Co., 1952) which shows that there definitely was contact between the peoples of the American continent, and Polynesia.

Another evidence that has caused some American scientists to accept the "American origin" theory of the Polynesian people, is the discovery of the American sweet potato throughout the Pacific. Dr. E. S. Craighill Handy, a well-known and learned ethnologist in Hawaii, points out that America is the original homeland of the "kumara" (the sweet potato, a staple food plant of Polynesia). Dr. Handy writes: "This humble, but valuable vegetable botanically and ethnologically may be the key to an early Polynesian migration westward. ("Forbears and Posterity in the Pacific Isles," by E. S. Craighill Handy and Mary Kawena Pukui, *Improvement Era*, vol. 53, p. 616 [Salt Lake City, Utah: 1950]. Several of the above references are also cited in Jensen and Cole, *Israel in the Pacific* [1961], pp. 384, 388.)

The kumara of America is called "kumala" in some Polynesian islands, such as Tonga. The similarity of these names for the same type of plant is remarkable indeed.

EVIDENCE NO. 533: THE POLYNESIANS ARE DESCENDANTS OF ISRAEL

Claim: The Book of Mormon teaches that descendants of the ancient Israelites were scattered about the islands of the Sea (1 Nephi 22:3-4). President Joseph F. Smith said, "Away off in the Pacific Ocean are various groups of islands form the Sandwich Islands (Hawaii) down to Tahiti, Samoa, Tonga, and New Zealand. On them are thousands of good people, dark-skinned but the blood of Israel. When you carry the gospel to them, they receive it with open hearts." (See *The Utah Genealogical and Historical Magazine*, [Salt Lake City, Utah, 1916] vol. 7, p. 25; cited in Cole and Jensen, *Israel in the Pacific* [1961], p. 388; see also *Journal of Discourses* vol. 14, pp. 325-330, 333.)

Evidence: Long before the first "Mormon" missionaries set foot in New Zealand, the Maori people of the Ngatikahungunu tribe believed they were scattered remnants of the House of Israel. A covenant written in 1881 stated that they believed they were some of "the lost sheep of the House of Israel." An English translation of the covenant is found in R. Lanier Britsch, *Unto the Islands of the Sea* (1986), p. 275. A photocopy of the covenant in the Maori language is found in Cole and Jensen, *Israel in the Pacific* (1961), p. 392.

EVIDENCE NO. 534: THE POLYNESIAN CONCEPT OF EARTH'S CREATION

Claim: In contrast to mainstream Christian theology which generally accepts the concept of creation *ex nihilo*, the Church of Jesus Christ of Latter-day Saints teaches that the earth was *organized* out of pre-existing unorganized materials rather than *created out of nothing*. This concept was shared with the early Christians as well as the ancient Egyptians. (See *Teachings of the Prophet Joseph Smith*, pp. 350-352; *The Ante-Nicene Fathers* [Grand Rapids, Michigan: Erdmans, 1953], vol. 1, p. 165; Duchesne, *Histoire ancienne de l'Eglise*, vol. 1, p. 154; *Patrologiae Graeca*, J. P. Migne editor [Paris: 1857-1866], vi: 40, 416-417; *The Bible and the Greeks*, p. 103; *Theological Dictionary*, vol. 3, p. 1016; *Brigham Young University Studies*, [Spring 1977], vol. 17, pp. 297-300; Veronica Ions, *Egyptian Mythology* [New York: Peter Bedrick Books, 1986], p. 34; and E. A. E. Reymond, *The Mystical Origin of the Egyptian Temple* [Manchester University Press: 1969], p. 187.)

As an important part of the timeless gospel of Jesus Christ, the true concept of the creation was also known among the children of Lehi, some of whom sailed with Hagoth (Alma 63:5-8) and, according to Latter-day Saint belief, helped to populate the Pacific Islands.

Evidence: According to Dr. John Martin, the islanders of the Pacific, specifically the Tongans, believed that the ocean and sky existed with the heavenly bodies, even before the earth was created. They believed that the sky contained solid matter and that the islands of Tonga were not brought into sudden existence out of nothing, but were taken up from the bottom of the sea. (See John Martin, *An Account of the Natives of the Tonga Islands*, [Boston: Charles Ewer, 1820], pp. 327, 333. See also T. Barrow, *Art and Life in Polynesia*, [Wellington, New Zealand: Reed, 1972], p. 11.)

See also the evidences related to the creation in volume 1 of this same work.

EVIDENCE NO. 535: THE CREATION RECORDED IN A HIDDEN BOOK

Claim: The Book of Mormon claims that the ancient inhabitants of America had an in-depth knowledge of the creation of the earth as recorded in the scriptures of Moses (1 Nephi 5:10-11; Mosiah 28:17; Ether 1:1-4). The Book of Mormon further claims that these ancient scriptures were hidden in a hill called *Cumorah* (Mormon 6:6; 8:14). Various aspects of the creation as taught in the scriptures are strikingly similar to Native American beliefs.

Evidence: Some remarkably close similarities to Latter-day Saint scripture are found in Native American histories. For example, the *Popol Vuh*, written by an Indian at Chichicastenango, Guatemala between the years 1554 and 1558 AD, contains many remarkable parallels to the Book of Mormon. For those who would assume that the writers of the *Popol Vuh* were influenced by the Spanish priests, note that many of the creation concepts of the *Popol Vuh* are closer to the Latter-day Saint understanding of the creation than that of the Catholics.

The Quiché-Mayan author claimed that there was a prevalent tradition among his people that his distant ancestors had at one time possessed a *sacred* book, written in hieroglyphics which was *hidden*, so he wrote his manuscript to replace that *lost* book. It was discovered in 1600 AD by Father Francisco Ximenez, a Catholic priest who officiated in the St. Tomas church at Chichicastenango. Ximenez obtained the manuscript from the Quiché-Maya Indians for the purpose of translating it from Quiché into Spanish. After his work was completed, Father Ximenez's translation of the Indian document remained in manuscript form for approximately two hundred fifty years before it was discovered and published in the Spanish language. It was not until 1950, that Delia Goetz and Sylvanus G. Morley translated it in English. Of this work Dr. Morley said: "This manuscript is, without doubt, the most vigorous, literary significant effort achieved by the American Indian in the field of mythology and history." (Goetz and Morley, *Popol Vuh, The Sacred Book of the Ancient Quiche-Maya*, [University of Oklahoma Press: Norman, Oklahoma, 1950], p. 75; cited by Milton R. Hunter, in *Conference Report*, [April 1955], p.105.)

Some of these striking similarities between the *Popol Vuh* and the scriptural accounts (including the Bible, the Book of Mormon, and the Pearl of Great Price) are listed below from Goetz and Morley, *Popol Vuh*, pp. 77-84, and 165–169; cited in Franklin S. Harris, Jr., *The Book of Mormon: Messages and Evidences*, (1961), pp. 76-78; and Hunter and Ferguson, *Ancient America and the Book of Mormon* (1950), pp. 90-93:

Popol Vuh	**Scripture**
"the original book, written long ago, existed, but its sight is hidden to the searcher and to the thinker. Great were the descriptions and the account of how all the sky and earth were formed, how it was formed and divided into four parts; how it was partitioned, and how the sky was divided; and the measuring cord was brought, and it was stretched in the sky and over the earth, on the four angles, on the four corners, as was told by the Creator …"	"And it came to pass…Ammaron, being constrained by the Holy Ghost, did hide up the records which were sacred—yea, even all the sacred records which had been handed down from generation to generation, which were sacred …" (4 Nephi 1:48). "Lehi, took the records which were engraven upon the plates of brass, and he did search them from the beginning. And he beheld that they did contain the five books of Moses, which gave an account of the creation of the world, and also of Adam and Eve, who were our first parents" (1 Nephi 5:10-11).
"This is the account of how all was in suspense, all calm, in silence; all motionless, still, and the expanse of the sky was empty. This is the first account, the first narrative. There was neither man, nor animal, birds, fishes, crabs, trees, stones, caves, ravines, grasses, nor forests; there was only the sky."	"For I, the Lord God, created all things, of which I have spoken, spiritually, before they were naturally upon the face of the earth…and not yet a man to till the ground; for in heaven created I them; and there was not yet flesh upon the earth, neither in the water, neither in the air" (Moses 3:5).

Popol Vuh (Continued)

"The surface of the earth had not appeared. There was *only the calm sea* and the great expanse of sky. There was nothing brought together, nothing which could make a noise, or tremble, or could make noise in the sky. There was nothing standing; only the *calm water*, the placid sea, alone and tranquil. Nothing existed..."

"Then came the word. Tepeu [God] and Gucumatz [the Fair God—Quetzalcoatl] *came together* in the darkness, in the night, and Tepeu and Gucumatz *talked together*. They talked then, *discussing and deliberating*; they agreed they united their words and their thoughts. Then while they meditated, it became clear to them that when dawn would break, man must appear."

"Then *they planned the creation*, and the growth of the trees and the thickets and the birth of life and the creation of man. Thus it was arranged in the darkness and in the night by the Heart of Heaven who is called Huracán. The first is called Caculhá Huracán. The second is Chipi-Caculhá. The third is Raxa-Caculhá. And these three are the Heart of Heaven [Godhead]."

"Then Tepeu and Gucumatz *came together*; then they conferred about life and light, what they would do so that there would be light and dawn, who it would be who would provide food and sustenance. Thus let it be done! Let the emptiness be filled! Let the Water recede and make a void, let the earth appear and become solid; let it be done. Thus they spoke. Let there be light, let there be dawn in the sky and on the earth! There shall be neither glory nor grandeur in our creation and formation until the human being is made, man is formed. So they spoke."

"Then the earth was created by them. So it was, in truth, that they created the earth. Earth! they said, and instantly it was made. Like the mist, like a cloud, and like a cloud of dust was the creation, when the mountains appeared from the water; and instantly the mountains grew...instantly the groves of cypresses and pines put forth shoots together on the surface of the earth. And Gucumatz was filled with joy, and exclaimed; "Your coming has been fruitful, Heart of Heaven; and you Huracán, and you, Chipi-Caculhá, Raxa-Caculhá!"

"Here, then, is the beginning of when it was decided to make man, and what must enter into the flesh of man was sought."

Scripture (Continued)

"And the earth was without form, and void; and darkness was upon the face of the deep. And the Spirit of God moved upon the face of the waters" (Genesis 1:2). See also *Teachings of the Prophet Joseph Smith*, Section Six, p. 350, which states that the earth was created from pre-existing materials.

"In the beginning was the Word, and the Word was with God, and the Word was God. The same was in the beginning with God. All things were made by him; and without him was not any thing made that was made" (John 1:1-4). Compare with the Latter-day Saint concept of the Godhead—three distinct Gods who confer together as one, instead of the Trinity concept believed by the Catholics and others.

"And the Gods said: Let us prepare the earth to bring forth grass; the herb yielding seed; the fruit tree yielding fruit, after his kind, whose seed in itself yieldeth its own likeness upon the earth; and it was so, even as they ordered" (Abraham 4:11).

"...the Father, and of the Son, and of the Holy Ghost, which is one God..." (2 Nephi 31:21).

"And God said, Let there be light: and there was light...And God said, Let the waters under the heaven be gathered together unto one place, and let the dry land appear: and it was so...And God said, Let the earth bring forth grass, the herb yielding seed, and the fruit tree yielding fruit after his kind, whose seed is in itself, upon the earth: and it was so" (Gen. 1:3-11).

"for the LORD God had not caused it to rain upon the earth, and there was not a man to till the ground" (Genesis 2:5).

"And the earth brought forth grass, and herb yielding seed after his kind, and the tree yielding fruit, whose seed was in itself, after his kind: and God saw that it was good" (Genesis 1:12).

"And God saw every thing that he had made, and, behold, it was very good. And the evening and the morning were the sixth day" (Genesis 1:31).

"And the Gods formed man from the dust of the ground, and took his spirit (that is, the man's spirit), and put it into him; and breathed into his nostrils the breath of life, and man became a living soul" (Abraham 5:7). See also Genesis 2:7; Job 33:4.

Popol Vuh (Continued)

"And the Forefathers, the Creators and Makers, who were called Tepeu and Gucumatz said: 'The time of dawn has come, let the work be finished, and let those who are to nourish and sustain us appear, the *noble sons*, the civilized vassals appear; let man appear, humanity, on the face of the earth.' Thus they spoke."

"They assembled, came together and held council in the darkness and in the night; they sought and discussed, and here they reflected and thought. In this way their decisions came clearly to light and they found and discovered *what must enter into the flesh of man*."

"It was just before the sun, the moon, and the stars appeared over the Creators and Makers."

"After that they began to talk about the creation and the making of our first mother and father; of yellow corn and of white corn they made their flesh; of corn-meal dough they made the arms and legs of man. Only dough of corn meal went into the flesh of our first fathers, the four men, who were created...It is said that they only were made and formed, they had no mother, they had no father, they were only called men..."

"They were endowed with intelligence; they saw and instantly they could see far, they succeeded in seeing, they succeeded in knowing all that there is in the world...."

"But the Creator and the Maker did not hear this with pleasure. 'It is not well what our creatures, our works say; they know all, the large and the small,' they said. And so the Forefathers held counsel again. 'What shall we do with them now? Let their sight reach only to that which is near; let them see only a little of the face of the earth! It is not well what they say. Perchance, are they not by nature simple creatures of our making? Must they also be gods? And if they do not reproduce and multiply when it will be dawn, when the sun rises? And what if they do not multiply?' So they spoke." (Note the allusion to the Latter-day Saint [non-Catholic] concept of Godhood.)

"Thus they spoke, and immediately they changed the nature of their creatures. Then the Heart of Heaven blew mist into their eyes, which clouded their sight as when a mirror is breathed upon. Their eyes were covered and they could see only what was close, only that was clear to them...."

Scripture (Continued)

"Now the Lord had shown unto me, Abraham, the intelligences that were organized before the world was; and among all these there were many of the *noble and great ones*. And God saw these souls that they were good, and he stood in the midst of them, and he said: These I will make my rulers..." (Abraham 3:22-23).

"And the Gods took counsel among themselves and said: Let us go down and form man in our image, after our likeness; and we will give them dominion over...every creeping thing that creepeth upon the earth" (Abraham 4:26).

"And the Gods organized the two great lights, the greater light to rule the day, and the lesser light to rule the night; with the lesser light they set the stars also" (Abraham 4:16).

"And I, the Lord God, formed man from the dust of the ground, and breathed into his nostrils the breath of life; and man became a living soul, the first flesh upon the earth, the first man also; nevertheless, all things were before created; but spiritually were they created and made according to my word" (Moses 3:7).

"And Adam called his wife's name Eve; because she was the mother of all living" (Genesis 3:20).

"And the LORD God said, Behold, the man is become as one of us, to know good and evil: and now, lest he put forth his hand, and take also of the Tree of Life, and eat, and live for ever" (Genesis 3:22).

"For God doth know that in the day ye eat thereof, then your eyes shall be opened, and ye shall be as gods, knowing good and evil" (Genesis 3:5).

"And now, behold, if Adam had not transgressed he would not have fallen, but he would have remained in the garden of Eden. And all things which were created must have remained in the same state in which they were after they were created; and they must have remained forever, and had no end. And they would have had no children; wherefore they would have remained in a state of innocence, having no joy, for they knew no misery; doing no good, for they knew no sin" (2 Nephi 2:22-23).

"Therefore, as they had become carnal, sensual, and devilish, by nature, this probationary state became a state for them to prepare; it became a preparatory state" (Alma 42:10). "We define the veil as the border between mortality and eternity; it is also a film of forgetting that covers the memories of earlier experiences" (Neal A. Maxwell, *All These Things Shall Give Thee Experience*, [1980], p.9).

Popol Vuh (Continued)

"Then their wives had being, and their women were made. God himself made them carefully. And so, during sleep, they came, truly beautiful their women, at the side of Balam-Quitzé, Balam-Acab, Mahucutah, and Iqui-Balam."

"There were their women when they awakened, and instantly their hearts were filled with joy because of their wives...."

Scripture (Continued)

"And the LORD God caused a deep sleep to fall upon Adam, and he slept: and he took one of his ribs, and closed up the flesh instead thereof; And the rib, which the LORD God had taken from man, made he a woman, and brought her unto the man" (Genesis 2:21-22).

"And Adam said, This is now bone of my bones, and flesh of my flesh: she shall be called Woman, because she was taken out of Man. Therefore shall a man leave his father and his mother, and shall cleave unto his wife: and they shall be one flesh" (Genesis 2:23-24).

See also the account of the creation found in "Works of Ixtlilxóchitl" in Hunter and Ferguson, *Ancient America and the Book of Mormon* (1950), pp. 21, 89. The *Works of Ixtlilxóchitl* is also found in Lord Kingsborough, *Antiquities of Mexico* (London: Henry G. Bohn 1830-1848), vol. 9.

EVIDENCE NO. 536: THE LIVING EARTH

Claim: In a latter-day restoration of ancient scripture, the prophet Enoch explains that the earth is alive, that it is the "mother of men" (Moses 7:48-49). Whether Enoch was speaking literally or figuratively, these same personifications were handed down from generation to generation with the ancient scriptures, even across the ocean and into the descendants of Lehi.

Evidence: The Indians also believed that the earth "is a living entity, in which living entities have origin and destiny." Similarly, the Navajo Indians referred to our planet as "Mother Earth." (*The World of the American Indian,* edited by Jules B. Billard et. al., [Washington DC: National Geographic Society, 1974], pp. 16, 23.)

EVIDENCE NO. 537: THE EARTH TO BE CLEANSED BY FIRE

Claim: The Book of Mormon prophets taught that the earth would be cleansed by fire before the Millennium. See 2 Nephi 30:8-12.

Evidence: The early Americans also held that same belief. See Lewis Spence, *Myths and Legends: The North American Indians* (Boston: David P. Nickerson, 1932), p. 3; cited in Cheesman, *The World of the Book of Mormon* (1978), p. 3.

EVIDENCE NO. 538: A MOTHER IN HEAVEN

Claim: The Book of Mormon claims that the ancient Americans were taught the gospel (for example, see 2 Nephi 30:5). One of the "mysteries" of the gospel is that we have a Mother in Heaven.* This concept was first taught and publicly announced in *The Mormon* (August 29, 1857, pp. 348-351). It is also mentioned in an early poem by Eliza R. Snow called "O My Father," which was later set to music and has become a favorite LDS hymn (see *Hymns of the Church of Jesus Christ of Latter-day Saints*, [1985], Hymn no. 292, verse 3).

Evidence: An evidence that the Church of Jesus Christ of Latter-day Saints is the true church is the fact that the ancient Americans also believed in a Mother in Heaven. Though this concept is not mentioned in the Book of Mormon, it is an important principle of the eternal gospel that was taught in its fullness in ancient America. According to Laurette Sejourne, the ancient Americans believed in "a place where there are the great God and Goddess." See also Laurette Sejourne, *Burning Water: Thought and Religion in Ancient Mexico* (Berkeley: Shambhala, 1976), pp. 56, 78.

---

* The Latter-day Saint concept of a Mother in Heaven is that of a glorified, perfected, and eternal woman who has lived with The Father as His eternal companion from the beginning—She is not Mary the mother of Jesus as taught by a few other religions. Likewise, Latter-day Saints do not worship, nor do they pray to Her.

Other ancient American documents speak of a heavenly Father and Mother of Life. According to the *Popol Vuh*, (a modern translation of the ancient history of the Quiché Maya of Guatemala): "These are the names of the divinity, arranged in pairs of creators in accord with the dual conception of the Quiché: *Tzacol* and *Bitol*, *Creator* and *Maker*, ... *Mother* and *Father*; they are the Great Father and the Great Mother, so called by the Indians, according to Las Casas; and they were in heaven" (Goetz and Morley, *Popol Vuh*, translated by Recinos, [Norman, Oklahoma: University of Oklahoma Press, 1950], pp. 78-84, footnote 3; Frey Bernardino de Sahagun, *Florentine Codez: General History of the things of New Spain*, translated by Arthur J. O. Anderson & Charles E. Dibble, (Santa Fe, New Mexico: School of American Research, 1963), vol. 10, p. 169; and Paul R. Cheesman, *These Early Americans* [1974], pp. 42, 53).

EVIDENCE NO. 539: PRE-MORTAL EXISTENCE

<u>Claim</u>: The Book of Mormon teaches of the pre-mortal existence of mankind where the inhabitants of this earth lived as spirit children of our Father in Heaven prior to birth (Alma 13:3; 40:11 ; Helaman 14:16-18). Additional Book of Mormon passages, which imply the doctrine of the pre-mortal existence, are found in 1 Nephi 17:36 and Mosiah 7:26-27. Other churches do not believe in this doctrine even though the Bible clearly supports it. (See Job 12:10; 38:4-7; Ecclesiastes 12:7; Isaiah 42:5; 57:16; Jeremiah 1:5; Zechariah 12:1; John 9:1-2; Hebrews 12:9; Ephesians 1:3-6 and Titus 1:1-2.)

<u>Evidence</u>: The belief in a pre-mortal existence was also had among the Native Americans. See Clarke, *Indian Legends of the Pacific Northwest*, p. 133; Laurette Sejourne, *Burning Water: Thought and Religion in Ancient Mexico* (Berkeley: Shambhala, 1976), pp. 56-59; *Anales de Cuauhtitlan* [Imprenta, Universitaria, México, 1945], pp. 10-11; Ernest Thompson Seton, *The Gospel of the Red Man* [Garden City, New York: Doubleday, 1937], pp. 68-69. Cited in Cheesman, *The World of the Book of Mormon*, [1978], p. 5).

Similarly, the ancient Polynesians, specifically the Tongans, believed that all men came from *Bolotoo*, the chief residence of the gods. This belief seems to suggest that God dwells in a specific location. This aspect is also shared with the Latter-day Saints, who believe that God's primary residence is near the planet Kolob. (See John Martin, *An Account of the Natives of the Tonga Islands*, [Boston: Charles Ewer, 1820], p. 328; and explanation of Facsimile No. 2 from the Book of Abraham, Figure 1.)

EVIDENCE NO. 540: THE PRE-MORTAL COUNCIL IN HEAVEN

<u>Claim</u>: Another concept that is unique to the Church of Jesus Christ of Latter-day Saints is that of the pre-mortal council in heaven. In this great council, the eternal plan of salvation was discussed—including the creation, the fall and the atonement of mankind. The need for a savior was presented, who would take upon himself the sins and infirmities of all mankind. Two of the sons of God responded to the call—the first was Jehovah, or Jesus Christ, and the second was Lucifer, who subsequently rebelled and became Satan:

> And the Lord said: *Whom shall I send?* And one answered like unto the Son of Man: Here am I, send me. And another answered and said: Here am I, send me. And the Lord said: I will send the first. And the second was angry, and kept not his first estate; and, at that day, many followed after him (Abraham 3:28).

Since the Nephites had a detailed account of the plan of salvation (Alma 24:14), it is certain that they also knew about this grand council of the Gods, and that remnants of these accounts should be found among the Mesoamerican legends. Indeed a remarkable parallel to this account has been found in ancient Aztec tradition.

<u>Evidence</u>: The Aztecs had a similar belief. Prior to the creation of their world, "It is told that when yet all was in darkness, when yet no sun had shone and no dawn had broken—it is said that the gods gathered themselves together and took counsel among themselves...*Come hither, O gods! Who will carry the burden? Who will take it upon himself to be the sun, to bring the dawn?*" It turns out that two Gods volunteered for the honor of becoming the Sun; Nanauatzin and Tecuziztecatl. The first eagerly ignited himself and became the Sun of the new age while the face of Tecuziztecatl was darkened by the Sun's flame. The second then became the charred moon." (See Brian M Fagan, *The Aztecs*, [W. H. Freeman & Co. 1984], Chapter 1, p. 34.)

(Note that the Bible refers to Jesus Christ as the Sun in Malachi 4:2, and also refers to Lucifer as the fallen "son of the morning" in Isaiah 14:12.)

EVIDENCE NO. 541: THE ANTICIPATED FALL OF MAN

Claim: The Book of Mormon teaches that the fall of Adam was no surprise to the Lord, but was actually expected according to the fore-knowledge of God, and was part of his original plan. See 2 Nephi 2:22-25. See also Moses 5:11. These passages, among many others, speak of the *necessity* of the fall in bringing about mortality, which is a prerequisite for immortality. Elder Bruce R. McConkie, of the Quorum of the Twelve Apostles, has written the following in his book entitled *Mormon Doctrine* (pages 268-269 in the 1990 edition):

> According to the foreordained plan, Adam was to fall; that is, "in the wisdom of him who knoweth all things" (2 Nephi 2:24), Adam was to introduce mortality and all that attends it, so that the opportunity for eternal progression and perfection might be offered to all the spirit children of the Father.
>
> In conformity with the will of the Lord, Adam *fell both spiritually and temporally*. Spiritual death entered the world, meaning that man was cast out of the presence of the Lord and died as pertaining to the things of the Spirit which are the things of righteousness. Temporal death also entered the world, meaning that man and all created things became mortal, and blood became the life preserving element in the natural body. In this mortal condition it became possible for the body and the spirit to separate a separation which by definition is the natural or temporal death (Alma 42:6-12; D&C 29:40-42).
>
> In this state of mortality, subject to both spiritual and temporal death, man thus was in a position to be examined relative to his worthiness to inherit eternal life. He became subject to corruption, disease, and all the ills of the flesh. Spiritually he was required to walk by faith rather than by sight; a knowledge of good and evil could now come to him by actual experience; and being mortal he could now have children, thus providing bodies for the pre-existent hosts. "Adam fell that men might be" (2 Nephi 2:19-25; Moses 5:11; 6:45-48; Smith, *Doctrines of Salvation*, [1955], vol. 1, pp. 107-120).

Evidence: Many churches teach that the fall of Adam was a surprise to God—a terrible blunder that disrupted his plans and sent him searching for a solution of redemption for all mankind. Some of these churches are critical of the Church for its stand. It is ironic that Bible-believing Christians would believe notions which are contrary to the Bible. The Bible teaches that as the fall was anticipated, likewise, the atonement of Christ was planned from the beginning. In Revelation 13:8, the apostle John speaks of the "Lamb slain before the foundation of the world." This means that the atonement was anticipated even before the world was created. Clearly, if the atonement was anticipated, the *reason* for the atonement or the fall was also anticipated.

The early Christians looked upon the fall of Adam as a great blessing. If it was to be considered by some to be iniquity, they preferred to call it *"blessed* iniquity." (See Borsch, *Son of Man*, p. 405, cited in Seaich, *Ancient Texts and Mormonism*, [1983], p. 41.)

EVIDENCE NO. 542: ADAM'S FALL PROVIDED AGENCY AND OPPOSITION

Claim: The Book of Mormon teaches that the *fall of Adam* allowed men to become free (2 Nephi 2:25-27) and provided *opposition in all things,* which was essential for man's eternal progression. The prophet Lehi taught that "it must needs be that there is an opposition in all things. If not so... righteousness could not be brought to pass, neither wickedness, neither holiness nor misery, neither good nor bad" (2 Nephi 2:11). Lehi goes on to say that without this required opposition there can be no existence (2 Nephi 2:12-13).

The Book of Mormon further teaches that the purpose of our life here on earth is to provide a "time for men to prepare to meet God; yea, behold, the day of this life is the day for men to perform their labors" (Alma 34:32). See also Alma 12:24 and Abraham 3:22-28.

Evidence: These concepts were taught to Lehi's descendants who populated the ancient American continent, and have resurfaced among the native inhabitants of the Americas. Laurette Sejourne indicates that to the early Americans, earth is the meeting ground of opposing forces (Laurette Sejourne, *Burning Water: Thought and Religion in Ancient Mexico* [Berkeley: Shambhala, 1976], pp. 67, 114).

Furthermore, these concepts were also taught anciently in the Old World: "All things have their opposites, good and bad. It is the Good which is the foil and proof of the Bad, and vice versa." (See *Sefer Yeshira,* vol. 6, p. 2, cited in *Nibley on the Timely and the Timeless,* [1978], p. 35, note 89. See also Wilson, *The Gospel of Philip* [London: Mowbray, 1962], pp. 29, 101:14-15, 140, 66:10-30.)

The Jewish *Zohar* (1:23) says that, "if God had not given men a double inclination to both good and bad, he would have been incapable either of virtue or of vice; but as it is he is endowed with a capacity for both." Irenaeus taught that men's freedom to choose their own way "makes them envied by the angels." And according to Clementine, this world exists for mankind to make a choice of upper and lower worlds. (See Irenaeus, *Contra Haereses,* IV, 37, 1; *Clementine Recognitions* 1:24; cited in Nibley, *The Timely and the Timeless,* [1978], p. 53.)

EVIDENCE NO. 543: EVE WAS THE FIRST TO PARTAKE OF THE FORBIDDEN FRUIT

Claim: The Book of Mormon teaches that the ancient Americans had a sacred record which contained "an account of the creation of the world, and also of Adam and Eve" (1 Nephi 5:10-13). They also had knowledge of the sequence of events leading to the fall and expulsion from the Garden of Eden as is recorded in the Bible. According to the Bible, it was Eve who first partook of the forbidden fruit (Genesis 3:6). This detail has also been preserved among the legends of the ancient Americans.

Evidence: According to ancient Aztec legend, "The 'woman of discord'... reminds us of the 'feast of discord' during which, as Father Rios tells us, the transgression committed by a woman, 'cause of all the misfortunes' in the original paradise, was commemorated." (See Michel Graulich, *Myths of Ancient Mexico,* [University of Oklahoma Press, 1997], p. 240.)

EVIDENCE NO. 544: THE WHITE FRUIT OF THE TREE OF LIFE

Claim: In the Book of Mormon Lehi describes the Tree of Life which he saw in a vision, the fruit of which was surpassing in whiteness to anything he had ever seen before (1 Nephi 8:10-11).

Evidence: Ancient records, which have come to light since the publication of the Book of Mormon, describe the Tree of Life as resembling a cypress, with fruit that is perfectly white. See "On the Creation of the World," (II, 5, and XIII, 2), 110.13 in *The Nag Hammadi Library in English,* edited by James M. Robinson, (San Francisco: Harper, 1977), p. 169; *Creation Apocryphon,* 158:16-17, cited in Nibley, *Since Cumorah* (1988), p. 161.

EVIDENCE NO. 545: THE GREAT FLOOD, THE TOWER, THE CONFUSION AND SCATTERING

Claim: As recorded in the Book of Mormon, the ancient Americans possessed a knowledge of Biblical history including the flood, the tower of Babel, the confusion of tongues, and the scattering of the people upon all the face of the land (Ether 6:7; Omni 1:20-22; Mosiah 28:17; Ether 1:33-37).

Evidence: The *Popol Vuh* was first translated into English in 1950 by Delia Goetz and Sylvanus G. Morley. In a newspaper interview by Martha Kearney, Goetz says there is no way of accounting for the inclusion of the Biblical themes in the religion of the isolated and otherwise pantheistic tribe. "She is particularly struck by the Quiché version of what can readily be recognized as the Biblical flood." (Goetz and Morley, *Popol Vuh, The Sacred Book of the Ancient Quiche-Maya,* [University of Oklahoma Press: Norman, Oklahoma, 1950], pp. 90-93, 186.) Martha Kearney's interview with Delia Goetz is published in the *Deseret News,* March 26, 1950.

According to the account of the flood by Ixtlilxóchitl, the survivors escaped destruction in an enclosed vessel they called a *toptlipetlocali:*

It is found in the histories of the Toltecs that this age and first world, as they call it, lasted 1,716 years: that men were destroyed by tremendous rains and lightnings from the sky, and even all the land, without the exception of anything, and the highest mountains, were covered up and submerged in water fifteen cubits (caxtolmolatli); and here they added other fables of how men came to multiply from the few who escaped from this destruction in a 'toptlipetlocali'; that this word nearly signifies a closed chest; and how, after men had multiplied, they erected a very high 'zacuali,' which is today a tower of great height, in order to take refuge in it should the second world (age) be destroyed. Presently their languages were confused, and, not being able to understand each other, they went to different parts of the earth. (Lord Kingsborough, *Antiquities of Mexico*, [London: Henry G. Bohn 1830-1848], vol. 9, p. 321; cited in James E. Talmage, *Articles of Faith*, [12th edition 1974], p.506.)

See also Hunter and Ferguson, *Ancient America and the Book of Mormon* (1950), pp. 22, 89-91; Pedro Sarmiento de Gamba, *History of the Incas* (Hakluyt Society, 2nd Series, No. XXII, Cambridge, 1907), pp. 30-32; Peter DeRoo, *The History of America Before Columbus*, [1900], vol. 1, Chapter 16; Jean Francois Alvert du Pouget de Nadaillac, *Prehistoric America*, (London: John Murray, 1885), p. 525, Chapter 10; Paul Herrmann, *Conquest by Man*, (New York, 1954), p. 178; Hasteen Klaw, *Navajo Creation Myth*, Bulletin No. 1, p. 75; Harold Osborne, *South American Mythology*, (Middlesex: Hamlyn Publishers Group Ltd., 1968), p. 61, cited in Cheesman, *The World of the Book of Mormon* (1978), p. 2; Reagans, *Pima Flood Myth*, vol. 3, pp. 97-99; also Nunez de la Vega, *Constituciones Diocesana del Obispado de Chiappa*, (Rome, 1702), preamble paragraph 34, section 30, p. 9; Frey Bernardino de Sahagun, *Florentine Codex: General History of the things of New Spain*, translated by Charles E. Dibble and Arthur J. O. Anderson, (Santa Fe, 1963); *Popol Vuh*, pp. 90-93, cited in Harris, *The Book of Mormon Message and Evidence* (1961), p. 76. See also William Prescott, *Conquest of Mexico* (New York: McKay Co., 1847), vol. 2, p. 43, cited in Weldon, *The Book of Mormon Evidences Joseph Smith a True Prophet*, pp. 22-23.

EVIDENCE NO. 546: HAIR AS A SYMBOL OF STRENGTH

Claim: The Book of Mormon indicates that the ancient Americans once had an in-depth knowledge of Old Testament history which was contained in the brass plates (1 Nephi 5:10-13). It follows, therefore, that these ancient Americans also knew of the Nazarite Samson and his miraculous strength which he retained as long as he did not shave his head (Judges 16:17).

Evidence: The fact that Native Americans held a similar belief strengthens the Book of Mormon claim that the Mesoamericans knew the history of the Old Testament. Hair "had a special meaning to the Indian, and like the Biblical Samson, he felt that he gained strength and life from his hair" (Eugene Rachlis and John C. Ewers, *Indians of the Plains,* [New York: American Heritage Publishing Company, 1960], p. 39).

EVIDENCE NO. 547: AN ISRAELITE FASTING CUSTOM IN ANCIENT AMERICA

Claim: The Book of Mormon records that the ancient Americans practiced the ancient Israelite custom of putting ashes on one's head while fasting (Mosiah 11:25). A Mayan fasting ritual is similar to this ancient Israelite practice and provides additional evidence that the Book of Mormon is true.

Evidence: According to Landa, it was the custom of the Maya to cover themselves with soot or black paint while fasting. (Diego de Landa, *Relación de las Cosas de Yucatán*, translated by Alfred M. Tozzer, *Harvard University, Peabody Museum of American Archaeology and Ethnology Papers*, [Cambridge: Peabody Museum, 1941], vol. 18, pp. 103, 152, 165. See also Recinos, *Popol Vuh*, vol. 2, p. 35, cited in Cheesman, *The World of the Book of Mormon*, p. 17.)

This practice clearly originates with the ancient Israelite custom of covering the head with ashes as a means of cleansing and purification and in times of grief, mourning, and fasting (Daniel 9:3; Isaiah 58:5; Esther 4:3).

EVIDENCE NO. 548: THE PURPOSE OF THE FAST

Claim: The Book of Mormon clearly teaches that fasting is a principle of righteousness (Omni 1:26; Mosiah 27:22-23; Alma 5:45-47; 6:6; 8:26; 10:7; 17:2-3, 9; 28:6; 30:2; 45:1; Helaman 3:34-35; 3 Nephi 27:1; 4 Nephi 1:12). Thus, Latter-day Saints regularly set aside one Sunday of each month as a day of fasting and prayer, in which the members of the church are encouraged to abstain from food or drink for twenty-four hours, and pray for those in need. The money saved by those meals not consumed (and for those who can afford it, much more) is then donated to the church and used to feed, clothe and provide employment for the poor.

Evidence: This principle of fasting in order to give food to the poor was also practiced among the ancient Americans: "Thou know how to deprive thyself of food to give them [the poor and hungry]." (Laurette Sejourne, *Burning Water: Thought and Religion in Ancient Mexico* [Berkeley: Shambhala, 1976], p. 10.)

EVIDENCE NO. 549: THE SACRAMENT OF THE LORD'S SUPPER

Claim: The Book of Mormon teaches that the ancient inhabitants of the Americas practiced the *Sacrament of the Lord's Supper* in remembrance of the sacrifice of Jesus' life to atone for the sins of the world (3 Nephi 18:2-9). The true followers of Christ partook of the bread in remembrance of the body of Christ which was slain for us, and drank the wine in remembrance of his blood which was shed for us. To those who worthily partake of the sacrament the Lord promised to send "his spirit to be with them" (Moroni chapters 4 and 5).

The ancient American prophet Moroni, who recorded the sacramental prayers in the Book of Mormon, ended his record by documenting that his people had become depraved and degenerate, had perverted the principles of the Gospel and had even become cannibals (Moroni 9:7-15). Upon the death of the prophet Moroni, the gospel in its fulness had disappeared from the New World, but remnants remained in corrupted forms. One of the ordinances of the true gospel, which remained in a grossly perverted form, is the Sacrament of the Lord's Supper.

Evidence: Many Christians of today take the symbology of the Lord's supper much farther than do Latter-day Saints, to the extent that they believe that the bread of the sacrament actually *becomes* the flesh and blood of Christ. Latter-day Saints believe that the sacrament merely *represents* his flesh and blood. From the ancient legends of the American Indians, it is apparent that after the death of Moroni, the Mesoamericans also began to take the sacrament more literally.

Among the writings of the Quiche Maya is a strange legend that tells of eating the flesh of a God who had died. "And when he had died, thereupon they broke up his body...distributed and divided [it] up among all...And afterwards it was divided up among them, to *each in his order*, each year when they ate it. [Each] year [those of] two neighborhoods ate it, and also the old men of two tribal temples. And when they divided up among themselves his body [made of] amaranth seed dough, [it was broken up] exceeding small, very fine, as small as seeds. The youths ate it. And [of] this which they ate, it was said: 'The god is eaten,' and of those who ate it, it was said: 'They guard the god.'" (Recinos, *Popol Vuh of the Quiche Maya*, vol. 3, p. 6; cited in Cheesman, *The World of the Book of Mormon*, [1978], p. 17.) Note the similarity to the Latter-day Saint custom of passing the sacrament first to the person highest in authority.

A Spanish writer, Jose de Acosta, was sent as a missionary to America in 1571. After his return to Spain, he published a history. Writing about the ancient American version of the sacrament, he assumed that it was introduced by the Devil as a counterfeit to the true sacrament: "In what manner hath the Devil labored in Mexico to counterfeit the feast of the Holy Sacrament and communion used in the holy church." (Jose de Acosta, *The Natural and Moral History of the Incas*, pp. 345-354, 356-360.) See also Frey Bernardino de Sahagun, *Florentine Codez: General History of the things of New Spain*, translated by Charles E. Dibble and Arthur J. O. Anderson, (Santa Fe, New Mexico, 1963), vol. 3, pp. 5-6, who also writes of the ancient American sacrament. Both Acosta and Sahagun are cited in Cheesman, *The world of the Book of Mormon*, (1978), pp. 17, 74.

The fact that the Spanish assumed that Satan instituted the New World sacrament shows that the Native Americans did not copy the sacrament from the Spanish priests. Herera and Ondegardo, reaffirming the conclusion of Acosta, felt sure that the devil had counterfeited the "sacrament of confession" among the ancient Americans (W. H. Prescott, *History of the Conquest of Peru*, [New York, 1898], vol. 1, pp. 97, 786).

The concept of eating the flesh of Christ may well have also been the *inspiration* for the degenerate Iroquois manner of torture and sacrifice. According to Jules Billard, it "had overtones of religious sacrifice. Victims might be feasted before their ordeal, treated with deference through it. Eating a bit of the body was a way to get some of the fortitude of an especially courageous sufferer." This clearly brings to mind the promise given in the sacramental prayer that the spirit of God would be with those who worthily partake of the sacrament (Moroni chapters 4 and 5). See Jules B. Billard, *The World of the American Indian,* (Washington, DC: National Geographic Society, 1974), p. 129.

EVIDENCE NO. 550: A POLYNESIAN SACRAMENT

Claim: Not only was the sacrament practiced in ancient America, but it was also observed anciently in the Polynesian islands—which were colonized, at least in part, by the children of Lehi who emigrated with Hagoth the great ship builder (Alma 63:5-8).

Evidence: Most of the Polynesians have ceremonies in which a drink is passed around a circle of men. The ritual often includes the chewing of the Kava' root and partaking of a drink made from the Kava' plant and mixed with water. The drink is first passed to the highest-ranking member of the circle who usually recites his genealogy to prove his seniority. (See John Martin, *An Account of the Natives of the Tonga Islands,* [Boston: Charles Ewer, 1820], pp. 369-379. See also T. Barrow, *Art and Life in Polynesia,* [Wellington, New Zealand, 1972], pp. 40, 42.) The John Martin source is particularly significant because it provides evidence that predates the arrival of the first Christian missionaries.

EVIDENCE NO. 551: THE FEAST OF THE PASSOVER

Claim: The Book of Mormon claims to be a record of peoples who descended from Israel, and who "were strict in observing...the Law of Moses" (Alma 30:3). Some critics have branded this sacred record as a forgery because they find no mention of the feast of the Passover, which was an integral part of the Law of Moses.

However, the stated purpose of the Book of Mormon is to testify of Christ—not to testify of its Israelite origin. Even so, the Book of Mormon makes several clear references to indicate that the people of ancient America did indeed observe the feast of the Passover, and were quite familiar with its purpose.

Evidence: The Passover meal commemorates the protection of the Israelites from the destroying angel that slew the firstborn of Egypt. Below are enumerated several Passover themes that are captured in the Book of Mormon:

1. This sacred festival required the fathers to gather their sons and remind them of the things the Lord did for them in Egypt. (Compare Exodus 10:2 with Alma 35:16.)
2. The father then instructed his sons and was required to "spell out the sequence of sin, suffering, repentance, and redemption." Alma discusses these same concepts in his admonitions to sons Helaman, Shiblon, and Corianton (Alma 37-39). (See Abraham P. Block, *The Biblical and Historical Background of the Jewish Holy Days,* [New York: Ktav Publishing, 1978], p. 131.)
3. Traditionally, the sons would be called upon to ask their father certain questions at specific points in the Passover meal. The first question was asked by a wise son: "what is the meaning of the testimonies, and the statutes and the ordinances which the Lord our God hath commanded you?" (Deuteronomy 6:20). The second question, "what does this service mean to you?" was asked by a wicked son, guilty of social crimes, who believed in false doctrines (Exodus 12:26). He is told that he will be punished for his sins, and that had he been in Egypt, he would not have been redeemed. The third question, "what is this?" (Exodus 13:14), was asked by the uninformed son. This son needed to be taught "what the law is" and was given instruction to keep him from breaking the law (Block, *Jewish Holy Days,* pp. 159-164).

Alma answers all three of these same questions in his instruction to his three sons. To the righteous son Helaman he gives the answer to the first question by mentioning wisdom at least eight times as he explains the meaning of the laws and testimonies of God as contained in their sacred books of scripture (Alma 37). The answer to the second question is directed to Alma's rebellious son Corianton who had left the ministry, caused social problems by his immoral behavior, and had followed after false doctrines. Corianton is told of Alma's personal sufferings for sin, and taught about the redemption from sin (Alma 39:3, 11; 41:3-9). Finally, to Shiblon, Alma teaches the importance of his diligence to the gospel and charges him to live to a high code of conduct (Alma 38:11-14).

4. The importance of calling upon God for deliverance from affliction as was done at the Passover is described in Deuteronomy 26:7-9. Alma gives this same injunction to his son Helaman in Alma 36:3, 18, 27.

5. The bondage of the Israelites was symbolized as a "night of darkness" in both (Exodus 12:30 and Alma 41:7).

6. The "bitter herbs" of the Passover, like the "bread of affliction," symbolized the bitter suffering of the Israelites in Egypt. (Compare Exodus 12:8 with Alma 36:18, 21.)

7. The hardness of Pharaoh's heart is compared to the hardness of the hearts of the people. (Compare Exodus 11:10 with Alma 35:15.)

8. The first Passover (or deliverance) was proceeded by three days and nights of darkness that is compared to Alma's deliverance from hell after his three days and nights of pain and darkness. (Compare Exodus 10:22 with Alma 36.)

EVIDENCE NO. 552: REENACTMENT OF THE CRUCIFIXION

Claim: The whole purpose of the Book of Mormon, as stated in its title page, is to teach that Jesus is the Christ and to bring men to His service. Indeed, the Book of Mormon prophesied of the mission of Jesus Christ some 600 years before His coming to earth, and gives added insights into His mission as Savior and Redeemer of the world, and expounds on the necessity of His death and resurrection. It teaches that Jesus died to bring the blessings of immortality and eternal life to mankind (1 Nephi 11:33; 2 Nephi 10:25).

Evidence: In addition to perverting the Sacrament of the Lord's Supper, the ancient Americans also "celebrated" the sacrifice of the Lamb of God, in their own manner through a gruesome ceremony called the Sun Dance. Almost all of the Plains tribes practiced this dance, in one form or another, although some details of the dance varied from tribe to tribe. The following table compares the similarities of the Sun Dance with the crucifixion of our Lord Jesus Christ. All items under the "Sun Dance" column are documented in *Indians of the Plains*, (New York: American Heritage Publishing Co., 1960), pp. 67-70.

Crucifixion	Sun Dance
1. Jesus willingly gave himself up to be tortured and killed (John 10:18; 18:11).	The Indian braves willingly participated in the Sun Dance.
2. Jesus fasted for forty days to prepare for his mission—which culminated in his suffering (Matthew 4:2).	The Indians would fast for extended periods of time until they would faint.
3. Jesus was disrobed and brought to an open shame (Matthew 27:28; Hebrews 12:2).	"Those who were to dance only had for clothing a wrapping about their loins."
4. We are told that we must "suffer with Christ" (Romans 8:17).	The onlookers "had their arms slashed by the medicine man's knife."
5. Jesus was whipped, marred and stabbed (Isaiah 50:6; John 19:34).	The dancers usually performed "acts of self-torture."
6. The nails in Jesus' palms brought healing to the world as the "balm in Gilead" (Jeremiah 8:22).	An attendant "rubbed the palms of [the dancer's] hands with sage and other green herbs."

Crucifixion

7. Jesus' flesh was "pierced" in order to hang him on the cross (Psalms 22:16; Zechariah 12:10; John 19:37; Revelation 1:7).

8. Jesus was "lifted up" and hung upon the cross, "tree" or "pole" (Numbers 21:8; John 3:14; Acts 5:30; 10:39).

9. Jesus Christ is called the "Sun of righteousness" who shall "arise with healing in his wings" (Malachi 4:2).

10. The purpose of Christ's suffering was to bring blessings such as purification from sin, salvation from the enemy of death, and the assurance of eternal life (Numbers 19:17; 1 Corinthians 15:26; John 3:14-16).

Sun Dance

Slits were cut into the dancer's chest or shoulders where "sticks or skewers where thrust. To each of these, a string was fastened."

"Then the victim was lifted up and the strings were fastened to a lariat hanging from a pole."

During the ordeal the dancer gazes as the sun, or a symbol of the sun is tied on top of the pole.

The Sun Dance purified the dancer, and served to "protect the tribe from its enemies," and to assure the arrival of the buffalo for the hunt, which in turn provided life to the Indians.

Evidences Concerning the Book of Mormon Claim that Jesus Christ Personally Ministered in Ancient America After His Resurrection

EVIDENCE NO. 553: CHRISTIANITY IN THE NEW WORLD BEFORE COLUMBUS

Claim: Striking similarities to Christian teachings found in ancient America are further evidence of a righteous Nephite civilization in ancient America and of Christ's visit to the Americas as recorded in the Book of Mormon. The Book of Mormon proclaims to be another testament of Jesus Christ—containing the teachings and ministry of the Savior who personally taught the ancient American people after His death and resurrection.

Evidence: This claim is supported by discoveries that Christianity was practiced in America before Columbus. The usual response of critics is that the Indians learned about Christianity from the first Catholic missionaries who arrived with the Spanish explorers. However, when the Spanish missionaries first attempted to introduce Christianity to the Indians, they recorded their surprise that the American Indians already knew many elements of Biblical Christianity.

Even before the Catholic priests had uttered the first words of their teachings, the Indians had already bowed down to the first explorers, whom the Indians believed to be the returning great white god. The conquistadors wasted no time in launching their brutal attack upon the Indians—slaughtering, torturing and enslaving the people. Needless to say, the Indians developed a hatred for the white people and their religion, which they brought with them. History records many uprisings by the Indians who resisted European domination.

It was the mistaken conclusion of the Catholic priests that the devil had preceded them, and had taught the Indians a "degenerate" form of the Christian philosophy to foil their "true" missionary efforts. Las Casas, Solorzano, Garcilasso de la Vega, Oviedo, Charlevoix and Acosta were among those who believed that the Indian knowledge of Biblical Christianity originated from the devil. (See Peter DeRoo, *History of America Before Columbus*, [1900], vol. 1, pp. 206, 423-424.)

Torquemada, Acosta and Las Casas believed that devil teachers purposely taught Christianity among the Indians in order to cause them to have no interest in being baptized into a church which appeared to be a counterfeit of their own. (See Acosta, *The Natural and Moral History of the Incas*, pp. 356-360, 345-354; W. H. Prescott, *History of the Conquest of Peru*, [Modern Library edition.]; and J. M. Sjodahl, *Introduction to the Study of the Book of Mormon* [1927], pp. 484-485.)

Scholars have shown that Quetzalcoatl was an actual ancient American character, not merely a figure of mythology. Miles Poindexter indicates that Quetzalcoatl was not borrowed from the Spanish missionaries because the Indian religions were more advanced and more involved than Spanish Catholicism. (See Miles Poindexter, *The Ayar-Incas* [New York: 1930], vol. 1, p. 175; Paul Herrmann, *Conquest by Man* [New York: 1954], pp. 171-172.)

According to Peter DeRoo, the Native Americans had Christianity long before Columbus or the Spaniards. He indicates that each missionary who wrote, recorded their wonder that the American Indians were already Christians. (See Peter DeRoo, *History of America Before Columbus* [1900], vol. 1, pp. 229, 111-112, 196-197, 423-424, 449, 558.)

The following is from Harris, *The Book of Mormon Message and Evidences*, [1961] pp. 146 and pp. 151-153:

> F. A. MacNutt has written: "So numerous and striking were the analogies to Christian teachings presented by the Mexican beliefs and rituals that the conviction was obtained amongst many, that this mysterious personage was no other than a Christian priest or bishop. The Mexican traditions concerning his appearance amongst the Toltecs, his teachings, his miracles, and his final disappearance, seem to be hopelessly interwoven with legends of other deities, his personality became merged in that of other mythical characters, with a plumed serpent for his emblem; but there still remained a sufficient number of intelligible and authentic doctrines and practices traceable to him, to argue their Christian origin." (F. A. MacNutt, *Fernando Cortez* [1909], pp. 65-66.)

> What has been the effect of these Christian beliefs and practices? Have they been convincing to observers?

> In 1930, Charles S. Braden in discussing Quetzalcoatl said: "Father Duran supposes that one of the apostles preached in Mexico; Garcia, Becerra Tanco, and particularly the eminent writers Siguenza and Gongora believe that it was the Apostle St. Thomas who left the tradition of his coming and passing which have come to surround the figure of Quetzalcoatl. The last mentioned writer has a work of 517 pages in which he deals with the subject." (Charles S. Branden, *Religious Aspects of the Conquest of Mexico* [Duke University Press], pp. 36-37.)

> "It certainly seems to me that in some way (the Indians) must have received some light from the cross of our Redeemed Christ." Castaneda, chronicler of Coronado's expedition. (Walter J. Sloan, *Ms. on B. of M.*, p. 41 [Church Historian's Office].)

> Waldeck in 1838 (*Voyage Picturesque*, p. 45) thought there were Christian dogmas apparent in the Toltec cult. From 1831-1848, Edward King, Viscount Kingsborough, published his magnificent nine-volume *Antiquities of Mexico* costing him $160,000 in which he gathered all possible evidence that could possibly be construed for Christianity in pre-Columbian America. During this time in 1843, George Jones published his *History of Ancient America* for which part of the subtitle reads "and the Introduction of Christianity into the Western Hemisphere by the Apostle St. Thomas."

> In 1880 the Mexican historians Orozco and Berra (*Historia Antigua y de la Conquista de Mexico*, vol. 1, p. 98) expressed themselves as willing to accept some evidences of Christianity. At the end of the last century Peter DeRoo was working in the Vatican Archives on some historical problems and occasionally came across original and unpublished material pertaining to the religious history of America, either of the time of the Spanish discovery or before it. He met with, on every side, "vestiges of a Christianity which evidently was not introduced by the relatively late Northmen." One of his two-volume work, *History of America Before Columbus*, [1900] is entirely devoted to a detailed discussion of evidences for a pre-Columbian introduction of Christianity into America.

> More recently a German archaeologist, Dr. Carl Maria Kaufmann, published *Amerika und Urchristentum*, setting forth some of the evidence which made him conclude that Christianity had been in the Maya and Inca realms long before the time of Columbus. He says: "In 1922 I referred to previously unknown world routes of primitive Christianity, whose study lies close to the probability of direct relations between the Old World and America in pre-Columbian times. Clues leading in this direction I met frequently...Christianity must have taken foot in Central and South America in an epoch which was closer to the middle of the first millennium than to its end."

Since the research of these authors presents such a compelling evidence for the truthfulness of the Book of Mormon, skeptics have been quick to discredit their conclusions. While these authors have not found wide acceptance, in light of the vast amount of evidence presented, it would be difficult to dismiss entirely the pre-Columbian evidence of Christian philosophy in America.

EVIDENCE NO. 554: JESUS CHRIST VISITED ANCIENT AMERICA

Claim: The Book of Mormon states that Jesus Christ personally ministered in the American continent after His death and resurrection in Palestine (3 Nephi 11:10).

Evidence: Space does not permit listing all of the references from non-Mormon scholars relative to the ancient American tradition of a great white god fitting the description of Jesus Christ who visited this hemisphere. A few of the many references are listed below.

The following is from Harris, *The Book of Mormon Message and Evidences,* [1961], pp. 143-146:

The late Dr. George C. Vaillant tells us: "Quetzalcoatl, 'the Feathered Serpent,' God of Civilization and the planet Venus, seems to have been widely venerated but under different guises... Quetzalcoatl had several forms shared by distinctive divinities. The sculptures of Teotihuacán and Chichén Itzá show that a feathered snake was honored, and the local records mention Quetzalcoatl and Kukulcan, Nahuatl and Maya names having the same meaning." (Vaillant, *Aztecs of Mexico,* [Doubleday, 1940], p. 176.)

In contrast to the other gods, Quetzalcoatl was gentle. (See P. A. Means, *The Maya and Their Neighbors,* p. 433.)   In fact his character was such as to elicit the following remarkable statements from J. T. Short: "The doctrines of the benign and saintly Quetzalcoatl or Kukulcan must be classed among the great faiths of mankind, and their author, alone of all the great teachers of morals except Christ himself, inculcating a positive morality, must be granted a precedence of most of the great teachers of Chinese and Hindu antiquity." (J. T. Short, *North Americans of Antiquity* [1880], p. 515.)

...These accounts refer to events of many centuries before. Henry R. Wagner, says: "All the native writers assure us that this legend, for legend it was, had been generally believed in by the Mexicans for a long time; in fact, it may have originated several hundred years before." (Wagner, *The Rise of Fernando Cortez* [1944], p. 187.)

In the Aztec belief, Quetzalcoatl was the divine ruler of the second era of the creation. (See George C. Vaillant, *Aztecs of Mexico,* [Doubleday: Garden City, New York, 1950], p. 171; and Henry R. Wagner, *The Rise of Fernando Cortez,* [1944] p. 194.)

The historian Bancroft concluded that: Quetzalcoatl's "teachings according to the traditions, had much in common with those of Christ in the Old World." (Hubert Howe Bancroft, *The Native Races of the Pacific States,* [San Francisco: 1883], vol. 5, p. 201. See also, J. Eric S. Thompson, *Rise and Fall of the Maya* [1954], pp. 259-260.)

D. G. Brinton writes: "We thus arrive, still in primitive conditions, to such personal ideals as Quetzalcoatl among the Aztecs of whom it was said in their legends that he was of majestic presence, chaste in life, averse to war, wise and generous in actions, and delighting in the cultivation of the arts of peace; or, as we see among the Peruvians, in their culture hero, Tonapa, of whose teachings a Catholic writer of the sixteenth century says, "So closely did they resemble the precepts of Jesus, that nothing was lacking in them but his name and that of his Father." (D. G. Brinton, *Religions of Primitive Peoples* [1897], p. 251.)

Nadaillac writes of an ancient American tradition that "a white man, wearing a long beard, had taught the inhabitants the art of building houses and sowing seed, after which he disappeared, to live for two thousands years in retreat before reappearing upon the earth. (See Jean Francois Alvert du Pouget de Nadaillac, *Prehistoric America,* [London: John Murray, 1885], p. 527.) See also: H. Beauchat, *Manuel d'Archeologie Americaine* (1912) p. 488; A. L. Kroeber in *Handbook of South American Indians* vol. 2, pp. 908, 909 (1946); Sylvanus G. Morley & G. W. Brainerd, *The Ancient Maya,* (1956), pp. 222-223.

Non-Mormon archaeologist and anthropologist L. Taylor Hansen, the daughter of Professor Taylor, co-originator of the famous Taylor-Wegener Theory of Continental Drift, has spent over thirty years gathering and documenting various Indian legends from throughout North and South America. These legends collectively verify that Jesus Christ did indeed visit the Americas after his death and resurrection in Palestine. Many fascinating accounts of the Savior's teachings in America are documented in her book: *He Walked the Americas* (Amherst Press: Amherst, Wisconsin, 1963).

EVIDENCE NO. 555: BIBLICAL EVIDENCE THAT QUETZALCOATL WAS JESUS CHRIST

<u>Claim</u>: The Book of Mormon teaches that Jesus Christ was represented by a serpent (see Alma 33:19). Many Latter-day Saint scholars believe that the Aztec God Quetzalcoatl is in fact Jesus Christ. "Did [Moses] not bear record that the Son of God should come? And as he lifted up the brazen serpent in the wilderness, even so shall he be lifted up who should come. And as many as should look upon that serpent should live, even so as many as should look upon the Son of God with faith, having a contrite spirit, might live, even unto that life which is eternal" (Helaman 8:14-15).

<u>Evidence</u>: William Prescott remarked: "None of the deities of the country (Mexico) suggested such astonishing analogies with Scripture as Quetzalcoatl." Critics of the Book of Mormon hastily reject the idea that Quetzalcoatl may have been Jesus Christ because they say the Aztec deity was pagan. They claim that the word Quetzalcoatl, which means "feathered serpent," links the ancient American god with Satan—the serpent in Eden (Genesis 3:1-5, 13-14). However, the possibility that a serpent could have represented Christ, has a clear Biblical precedent. In Old Testament times, Moses was commanded by Jehovah to fashion a brazen serpent, attach it to the end of a pole, and raise it up so the sick and afflicted of his camp could look upon it and be healed (see Numbers 21:9). Jesus compared himself with Moses' serpent, by saying that just as the serpent was lifted up to heal sickness, the "son of man" would be lifted up to heal believers of their sins (John 3:14-15). (See Prescott, *Conquest of Mexico* [Modern Library edition], p. 695; see also pp. 694-698.)

Similarly, ancient Jewish Zohar portrays the Lord as a serpent: "As there is a serpent below which is still at work in the world, so there is a sacred serpent above, which watches over mankind in all the roads and pathways and also restrains the power of the impure serpent." (See A. E. Waite, *Secret Doctrine in Israel*, p. 87.)

The following is quoted from Wallace E. Hunt, Jr. in his article "Moses' Brazen Serpent as It Relates to Serpent Worship in Mesoamerica," *Journal of Book of Mormon Studies*, edited by Stephen D. Ricks (1993), pp. 121-131:

> Archaeologists and scholars agree there are countless documented instances of serpent worship in varying forms throughout human history. Yet, despite the innumerable varieties of serpent worship, only in Mesoamerica do we find a preponderance of "feathered" serpent worship. Carrasco emphatically states that "there is no doubt that serpent symbolism and more specifically feathered serpent symbolism is spread throughout the architecture of ceremonial centers in Mesoamerica."[1] The God who was represented by statues and pictorial representations of feathered serpents was known as "Quetzalcoatl."

> Although the ancient peoples of Mesoamerica worshipped many different gods, the beauty of an indigenous bird so captured their interest that they not only borrowed its name, but used its form as well to represent their principal and most revered God, called "Quetzalcoatl" by the Toltecs and Aztecs, and "Kukulcan" and "Gucumatz" by the Maya.[2] Native to the highlands of Chiapas, Mexico, and Guatemala, the quetzal is a strikingly beautiful creature with a three-foot long iridescent green tail, crimson breast, and a myriad of other bright colors on its coat.[3]

> Although Quetzalcoatl's origin is clouded in obscurity, the legends, the few pre-Columbian writings extant today, and the early post-conquest writings contain an abundance of material on this ancient and revered god. These accounts are contradictory and vary widely both on the god's attributes and the details of how he was worshipped,[4] undoubtedly due to a millennium of digressions from the original

concept from the end of the Book of Mormon to the time of the Conquest. However, through all this maze, we find that the Mesoamericans consistently endow Quetzalcoatl with many Christ-like attributes, some of which are listed below:

- Quetzalcoatl was the creator of life.[5]
- Quetzalcoatl taught virtue.[6]
- Quetzalcoatl was the greatest Lord of all.[7]
- Quetzalcoatl had a "long beard and the features of a white man."[8]
- The Mesoamericans believed Quetzalcoatl would return.[9]

Although at first glance the meaning of the name "Quetzalcoatl" might strike one as a far cry from the concept of the Christian deity, it is quite possible that this depiction could have originated from an experience of the Israelite nation on their journey from Egypt as related in both the Old Testament and the brass plates of Laban. After traveling for approximately thirty-eight years in the desert, the Israelites received the last miracle of their exodus, one that carried with it a most important lesson and symbol. As before, the people rebelled and complained. (See Numbers 21:5-9.)

...But why did God use the word fiery in his command, "Make thee a fiery serpent?" Although most Bible scholars concede that the serpents in this area were very colorful, even of a "glowing fiery red color,"[10]...Interestingly, the brazen serpent was kept by the Israelites for some 500 years, during which time the sacred symbol was devalued into "an object of popular worship in Judah,"[11] until Hezekiah, a righteous King, "brake in pieces the brazen serpent that Moses had made: for unto those days the children of Israel did burn incense to it" (2 Kings 18:4). Even though the Israelites were the Lord's chosen people, they, having lost sight of its meaning and spiritual symbolism, had degenerated into worshipping the serpent as an idol.

Actually, the five verses above from the book of Numbers comprise only a very brief summary of this important event, which eventually led to this idolatrous serpent worship. The passages contain surprisingly little detail and absolutely no indication of its true significance. A glimpse of its importance is revealed in the third chapter of John...Because there are so few references in the Bible, to fully understand the Lord's lesson, we must turn to the Book of Mormon and the people of Mesoamerica.

...Although the brazen serpent event is described five separate times in the Book of Mormon (2 Nephi 25:20; Alma 33:19-22; 37:46; Helaman 8:14-15) ,[12] the most significant account is where Nephi refers to the event in admonishing his brothers. Note Nephi's use of the word flying in his description of the serpent:

> And he did straiten them in the wilderness with his rod; for they hardened their hearts, even as ye have; and the Lord straitened them because of their iniquity. He sent fiery flying serpents among them; and after they were bitten he prepared a way that they might be healed; and the labor which they had to perform was to look; and because of the simpleness of the way, or the easiness of it, there were many who perished (1 Nephi 17:41).

...It now becomes imperative to explore why the biblical account refers only to "fiery serpents," whereas the Book of Mormon refers to "fiery flying serpents," for the use of the word flying is important in understanding what took place in Mesoamerica. If Joseph Smith had personally authored the Book of Mormon instead of merely translating it, he would have been foolish to interject the term flying into the description of Moses' serpent, since the term flying is not used in the biblical account of this event. This term does, however, appear later in the Old Testament. In two of his prophecies unrelated to the brazen serpent account, Isaiah uses the phrase "fiery flying serpent" (Isaiah 14:29; 30:6). Since Nephi describes the serpent as not only "fiery," but also "flying," we can theorize the Bible originally depicted a "fiery flying serpent," but somewhere along the way, the term flying was changed or omitted as various scribes and editors translated and retranslated the Bible over the centuries.

...This usage of the term flying in association with Moses' brazen serpent is indirectly supported by numerous works of modern scholars. For example, Karen Joines notes in her exhaustive study of this subject that to the Hebrew word for serpent used in Numbers "may be attributed wings."[13] Joines further states that neither "the Revised Standard Version nor the Septuagint translations of the Hebrew Bible has been at great care to make consistent translations of the Hebrew words for serpents."[14] Henry also suggests that the serpents "flew in their faces and poisoned them."[15]

In addition, there are isolated accounts of winged serpents in this area of the desert. Joines quotes Herodotus as believing "this desert to be a haven for flying serpents."[16] Bush, while he does not give the concept credence, does agree that "the popular idea has for some cause invested these serpents with wings...[and] it is supposed that the epithet flying was given from their power of leaping to a considerable distance in passing from tree to tree."[17]

...In his extensive work on native antiquities, Frey Bernardino de Sahagun, one of the early fathers to come to New Spain, in the context of a description of a serpent named after Quetzalcoatl, stated, "And when it flies or descends, a great wind blows. Wherever it goes, it flies."[18] Thomkins also quotes Sejourne's description that "Teotihaucan was the place where the serpent learned miraculously to fly."[19] Another example of a flying serpent can be found in The Maya, in which Coe displays a gold disc found at the Sacred Cenote at Chichén Itzá. On the disc is a serpent surrounded by clouds, thus implying a flying serpent.[20]

In this connection, it is important to focus upon why the word quetzal was selected as the first element in their God's name, Quetzalcoatl. Since the quetzal bird was revered for its magnificent color, beauty, and elusiveness, it inspired awe and reverence and was capable of evoking the image of a "fiery flying serpent" in the minds of its beholders. This perception applied not only to the quetzal's overall appearance, but also to the bird's individual attributes. For example, since feathers are the source of a bird's ability to fly, and since birds are, in fact, distinguished from other creatures by their flying, the "feathered" (or "quetzal") portion of the name could have easily and naturally emanated originally from the word "flying" as used by Nephi in the phrase "fiery flying serpents." Feathers connote flying!

Also, since the term fiery was illustrated by Moses' usage of a material which imparted vivid color, the Mesoamerican usage of the quetzal bird's name was a natural choice, since the bird was so brightly colored. With the blazing equatorial sun shining on its crimson breast and its iridescent green three-foot long tail rippling in the wind, the quetzal itself could seem to appear as some type of formidable "fiery flying serpent."[21]

Naming their God after the venerable quetzal bird was certainly a natural and instinctive choice for the Mesoamericans. Further, since they also used the word coatl, or serpent, their vision of their deity must have embodied attributes symbolized both by this vividly colored flying bird and by serpents. Could it be that this embodiment was actually rooted in a version of Nephi's "fiery flying serpent" that was corrupted over time?

Some have asked, "*Which* Quetzalcoatl was Jesus Christ supposed to have been?" They say at least seven men bore that title and lived much later than the time of Christ. The fact that there may have been other men who were known as Quetzalcoatl does not mean that Jesus could not have been the first. Just as the name *Caesar* became a name-title for Roman leaders, the Book of Mormon mentions that the Nephites began naming their kings *Nephi* after their first king in the new land (Jacob 1:11). Similarly Quetzalcoatl became a title for others.

[1.] David Carrasco, *Quetzalcoatl and the Irony of Empire* (Chicago: University of Chicago Press, 1992), p. 50; see also J. Eric S. Thompson, *The Rise and Fall of Maya Civilization* (Norman: University of Oklahoma, 1986), p. 121.

[2.] Because these titles refer to the same god, their interpretation—"feathered" or "plumed" serpent—is the same. The *Aztec* word *quetzal* is the name of a bird and also means "tail feather." The word *coatl* means snake.

Similarly the Maya word, *Kukulcan*, is a combination of two words, kukul meaning "feather" and *can* meaning "snake." In the Quiché Maya name *Gucumatz, guc* means "green feathers" and *cumatz* means "serpent." Anne L. Bowes, "The Quetzal," *National Geographic* (January 1969): p. 141; see also Charles Gallenkamp, *The Riddle and Rediscovery of a Lost Civilization: Maya*, 3rd edition (New York: Penguin, 1987), pp. 165, 118; and *Popol Vuh,* Translated by Delia Goetz and Sylvanus G. Morley, (Norman, OK: University of Oklahoma Press, 1975), p. 78.

3. Thompson, *The Rise and Fall of Maya Civilization*, (1986), p. 20. Of interest is the fact that the quetzal bird cannot survive in captivity, for once confined, it ceases to eat and dies. The highly revered quetzal is the national bird of Guatemala. Its currency bears the bird's name.

4. This may be due in part to the confusion and intermingling of stories surrounding the rulers (most notably Topiltzin of Tollan or Tula) who adopted for themselves the name of Quetzalcoatl. Legends made each such leader an "Hombre-Dios" (Man-God); Carrasco, *Quetzalcoatl and the Irony of Empire*, (1992), p. 88. To further add to the entanglement, the Mesoamericans saw their rulers in some manner as avatars of the spirit or gods. Reality blends into the mystic; see Roberta H. Markman and Peter Markman, *The Flayed God: The Mesoamerican Mythological Tradition,* (San Francisco: Harper, 1992), p. 269.

5. Markman, *The Flayed God,* (1992), p. 32; Goetz and Morley, *Popol Vuh,* (1975), p. 83.

6. Gallenkamp, *The Riddle and Rediscovery of a Lost Civilization: Maya*, (1987), p. 166.

7. Carrasco, *Quetzalcoatl and the Irony of Empire*, (1992), p. 43.

8. T. A. Willard, *Kukulcan: The Bearded Conqueror,* (Los Angeles: Murray & Gee, 1941), p. 159.

9. Bernal Diaz, *The Conquest of New Spain*, translated by J. M. Cohen (London: Penguin, 1963); see also Carrasco, *Quetzalcoatl and the Irony of Empire*, (1992), p. 48; and Brian M. Fagan, *Kingdoms of Gold: Kingdoms of Jade,* (New York: Thames and Hudson, 1991), p. 37; and Adrian Recinos and Delia Goetz, *The Annals of the Cakchizuels,* (Norman, OK: University of Oklahoma, 1953), p. 40.

10. George Bush, *Notes, Critical and Practical, on the Book of Numbers* (Oxford: Oxford University, 1868), p. 313. See also J. Jones et al., *The Old Testament: According to the Authorized Version* (New York: Pott & Young, 1878), Numbers 21.

11. George B. Gray, *The International Critical Commentary on the Holy Scriptures of the Old & New Testaments,* (Edinburgh: Clark, 1965), p. 274.

12. To comprehend fully the widespread use of this event by the Nephites, we should keep in mind that Mormon (who wanted to communicate emphatically that the Book of Mormon contains only a very small part of the Nephite activities) tells us five times that, in his abridgment, he wrote less than "a hundredth part" of the written record (Jacob 3:13; Mormon 1:5; Helaman 3:14; 3 Nephi 5:8; 26:6). Therefore, it is reasonable to assume that the Nephite records may have contained many more references to the brazen serpent account.

13. Karen R. Joines, *Serpent Symbolism in the Old Testament,* (Haddonfield, NJ: Haddonfield House, 1974), p. 8. John Sturdy also indicates the word is sometimes translated "flying serpents"; John Sturdy, *Numbers,* (Cambridge, England: Cambridge University, 1976), p. 148.

14. Joines, *Serpent Symbolism in the Old Testament*, (1974), p. 100.

15. Matthew Henry, *An Exposition of the Old and New Testament*, (New York: Carter & Bros., 1853), vol. 1, p. 543.

16. Joines, *Serpent Symbolism in the Old Testament*, (1974), p. 44.

17. Bush, *Notes, Critical and Practical, on the Book of Numbers*, (1868), p. 313.

18. Frey Bernardino de Sahagun, *Florentine Codex: General History of the Things of New Spain*, translated by Charles E. Dibble and Arthur J. O. Anderson, 12 vols. (Santa Fe, New Mexico: School of American Research and University of Utah, 1963), vol. 11, p. 85.

19. Peter, Tompkins, *Mysteries of the Mexican Pyramids,* (New York: Harper & Row, 1987), p. 388.

20. Michael D. Coe, *The Maya* (London: Thames and Hudson, 1987), p. 136.

21. In his *Bird of Life, Bird of Death,* (New York: Dell, 1987), p. 215, Jonathan E. Maslow recounts his quest to find and observe the "resplendent" quetzal, the male bird is described as flying straight down the mountainside, shrieking loudly, and flying in an undulating movement so that the long tail feathers stream and sway behind it "like a flying serpent...if snakes could fly."

EVIDENCE NO. 556: MANY SIGNS AND WONDERS AT CHRIST'S BIRTH

<u>Claim</u>: Traditions of ancient Americans support the Book of Mormon claim that there were many signs and wonders at the time Jesus was born, such as a night without darkness. (See Helaman 14:3-8; 3 Nephi 1:15-21).

<u>Evidence</u>: The Bible speaks only of a new star and choirs of angels heralding the birth of Jesus. Had Joseph Smith been the author of the Book of Mormon, he would have put himself in a very untenable position by claiming that there were additional signs. However, according to recent discoveries, there *were* more signs observed, such as three suns and a meteor. Dr. Immanuel Velikovsky's book entitled *Worlds in Collision*, discusses numerous ancient traditions from both the Old and New worlds which claim that the sun stood still. (See Fulton Oursler's Review of Dr. Velikovsky's Book in, *Reader's Digest,* March 1950, pp. 139-148).

In traditions of the American Indians there is support for the "many signs and wonders in the heavens" that are recorded in the Book of Mormon. Juarros tells of a day when three suns were seen. Ixtlilxóchitl and Veytia refer to a tradition that "the sun stood [still] for a natural day without moving from one spot." (See *Works of Ixtlilxóchitl;* English translation in Hunter and Ferguson, *Ancient America and the Book of Mormon* [1950], pp. 298-301; and Hubert Howe Bancroft, *The Native Races of the Pacific States,* [San Francisco: 1883], vol. 5, pp. 209-210, 566).

Bastian reports that at the disappearance of Quetzalcoatl, both sun and moon were covered and a single star appeared in the heavens (Quoted by Peter DeRoo, *History of America Before Columbus* [1900], vol. 1, p. 431; cited in Franklin S. Harris, *The Book of Mormon Message and Evidences* [1961], p. 147.)

Keeping in mind that much evidence exists that Quetzalcoatl was Jesus Christ, according to ancient American legends, there was no darkness in the Americas on the night of Quetzalcoatl's birth. See Don Mariano Veytia, *Antiquities of Mexico*; Prescott, *Conquest of Mexico,* [New York: McKay Co., 1847], vol. 1, p. 40.

EVIDENCE NO. 557: CALENDAR CHANGED TO COINCIDE WITH THE BIRTH OF CHRIST

<u>Claim</u>: The tradition that Quetzalcoatl taught the people a version of the calendar is consistent with the Book of Mormon peoples reckoning their years from the birth of Christ (3 Nephi 2:4-8).

<u>Evidence</u>: The following is from Harris, *The Book of Mormon Message and Evidence* (1961), p. 146:

> The birth and visit of Christ made such an effect on the Book of Mormon peoples that they reckoned their years from his birth (3 Nephi 2:8; Moroni 10:1). It is interesting to note that there is a tradition that Quetzalcoatl taught the people a version of the calendar, and another that he started the year count. Torquemada says he invented the calendar. Kukulcan [the Mayan term for Quetzalcoatl] was the inventor of the calendar. (Vaillant, *Aztecs of Mexico,* [Doubleday 1940] p. 177; Herbert J. Spinden, *The Maya and Their Neighbors,* p. 165; Hubert H. Bancroft, *Native Races of the Pacific States,* [1882] vol. 3, pp. 259, 274; T. A. Joyce, *British Museum Guide to the Maudslay Collection of Maya Sculptures* [1923], p. 40. See also Christensen, *Progress in Archaeology* [1963] p. 137).

Non-Mormon scholars have discovered that the ancient Americans dated their histories according to the custom initiated at the night of no darkness. (See Helaman 14:1-4; 3 Nephi 1:19. See also Juan de Torquemada, *Monarquia Indiana*, Madrid, Spain, 1723, Vol. 2, pp. 40-50; Stacy Judd, *Ancient Mayas*, p. 54.)

EVIDENCE NO. 558: THE PLACE OF JESUS' BIRTH

<u>Claim</u>: The Book of Mormon states that the ancient Americans knew that Christ would be born "at Jerusalem, the land of our forefathers" (Alma 7:9-10). Critics of the Church have been quick to point to this as evidence that the Book of Mormon is false. However, this is actually another evidence of its truthfulness.

Evidence: The Bible also refers to *Bethlehem, The City of David* as "the Land of Jerusalem" (Luke 2:11 and 2 Kings 14:20). Joseph Smith was most likely unaware of these scriptural parallels, as were thousands of critics who have overlooked them for over 150 years.

On the middle Nile in 1887 the *Amarna letters* were found written on clay tablets. They are "the actual documents of the official correspondence between the Egyptian Government and the rulers of the various principalities of Palestine and Syria about 1400 BC, at the very time the Hebrews were entering Palestine." These letters revealed that it was actually a common practice in early times to refer to all areas and towns surrounding a major city by the name of that city rather than the individual towns themselves. (Nibley, *Approach to the Book of Mormon,* [1988], p. 101, note 16, cites Jörgen A. Knudtzon, *Die El-Amarna-Tafeln* [Leipzig: Hinrich, 1915; reprinted Aalen: Zeller, 1964], vol. 1, pp. 864-867, 872-875; vol. 2, pp. 876-877. This source tells of Bet-Ninib, a city of "the Land of Jerusalem." See also A. Alt, "Die Syrische Staatenwelt vor dem Einbruch der Assyrer," *Zt-Schr. der dt. Morgl. Ges.,* N.F., 13 [88], 1934, pp. 247-249; and Wilhelm Nowack, *Lehrbuch der Hebraeischen Archaeologie* [Freiberg, 1894], p. 194. See also Nibley, *Lehi in the Desert and the World of the Jaredites* [1952], pp. 5-7; and Robert F. Smith, "Land of Jerusalem: The Place of Jesus' Birth," *Re-exploring the Book of Mormon*, edited by John W. Welch, [1992], pp. 170-171.)

Nibley goes on to say on page 469 of *Approach to the Book of Mormon*:

> As a matter of fact, there is "a striking disagreement between the canon and the apocryphal literature" regarding the exact birth place of Jesus, the latter sources, which are often very old, placing it at a point half-way between Jerusalem and Bethlehem.* Foerster thinks that the disagreements are so clear, so persistent and so old that the misunderstanding on the subject goes right back to the beginning, for example, some sources favor a cave, others a stall. The only thing that sources agree on is that the birth took place "in the land of Jerusalem." So serious are the differences on the subject that they have been the subject of at least one entire (and quite shallow) book, which defends the credibility of the Gospel of Luke; William J. Ramsay, *Was Christ Born at Bethlehem?* 3rd edition (London: Hodder & Stoughton, 1905).

---

* Werner Foerster, "Bemerkungen und Fragen zur Stätte der Geburt Jesu," *Zeitschrift der Deutsch-Palästina Vereins*, vol. 57 (1934), pp. 1-7.

EVIDENCE NO. 559: QUETZALCOATL, BORN OF A BEAUTIFUL VIRGIN

Claim: The Book of Mormon verifies the Biblical claim of Jesus' miraculous nativity—being born of a virgin who conceived through the power of the Holy Ghost (1 Nephi 11:13-21; Matthew 1:18; Luke 1:35). Furthermore, the Book of Mormon supplies additional knowledge about "the mother of the Son of God" not found in the Bible, that Mary was "a virgin, most beautiful and fair above all other virgins" (1 Nephi 11:15). This little known fact as well as the knowledge of Jesus' birth are both verified in the ancient legends of the pre-Columbian Americans.

Evidence: Peter DeRoo writes the following in his work, *History of America Before Columbus* (1900), vol. 1, p. 426-427, 430-431:

> We did not in our researches find any of the more savage American tribes to have any idea of the Son of God made man, if we except some parts of Brazil, where we also met with traces of the apostle Saint Thomas's preaching. One of the Manaicas' traditions states, indeed, that *a woman of accomplished beauty*, who had never been wedded to man, gave birth to a most lovely child. This child, after growing up to man's estate, worked many wonders, raised the dead to life again, made the lame walk and the blind see. Finally, having one day called together a great number of people, he ascended into the air and was transformed into the sun who enlightens this earth. (Paul Gaffarel, *Histoire de la Decourverte de l'Amerique* [Paris: 1892], vol. 1, p. 428.)

Note how the ancient legend reveals in passing that Mary, the mother of Jesus, was "a woman of accomplished beauty." While the Book of Mormon expounds upon this fact, the Bible makes no mention of Mary's great charm. Thus, it is significant that the descendants of those prophet writers in the Book of Mormon preserved this detail of Christ's mother as an additional witness of the Book of Mormon.

Peter DeRoo continues:

...We have mentioned already, the belief of the Chiapans, according to which the god Bacab was born of a *virgin*, Chibirias, who is now in heaven with him. Sahagun relates that the Tlascaltecs designated one of their principle gods by the name "Camaxtle," which means the Naked Lord. He was to them what Christ represented on the cross is to us, for they asserted that he was endowed with both the divine and the human natures, and was born from a devout and holy *virgin* named "Coatlicue," who brought him forth without lesion of her *virginity*, on the mount Coatepec de Tulla. All this information, says Sahagun, was first given to the Toltecs by Quetzalcoatl.

This Quetzalcoatl is often confounded with his divine master, whose doctrine and precepts he published and observed...Quetzalcoatl is he who was born of the *virgin*, called Chalchihuitzli, which means the precious stone of penance, says the author of the "Explanation of the Codex Talleriano-Remensis." Tonacatecotl, the Mexican supreme deity, begot Quetzalcoatl, not by connection with woman, but by his breath alone, when he sent his *ambassador* [the Holy Ghost—Matthew 1:18; Luke 1:35] to the virgin of Tulla. They say it was Quetzalcoatl who effected the reformation of the world by penance. His father had created the world, but men had given themselves up to vice, on which account it had been frequently destroyed, but now had Tonacatecotl sent his son into the world to reform it. (See Lord Kingsborough, *Antiquities of Mexico,* [London: Henry G. Bohn 1830-1848], vol. 5, pp. 135-136, 184.)

Quetzalcoatl undertook the reformation of the sinful world through preaching, by word and example, the virtues of self-denial and fasting, of chastity and piety, of charity towards men, and of a pure religion towards the one true God. For a time he succeeded in Tulla, where according to some reports, his *virgin-mother*, Chimalma, lived; but in spite of all the wondrous good he did in that province, like Christ, he was persecuted, and finally driven out by the majority of the people. Carrying a cross, he came to the valley of the Zapotecs. We have noticed before that the Chiapan son-god, Bacab, who had been scourged by Eopuco and crowned with thorns, had also been the divine son of the Mexican virgin goddess. The same son of Chibirias or Chimalma had been put to death by crucifixion; and this sacrilegious crime had been perpetrated on a Friday. So had the Chiapans been informed by bearded men who in ancient times had taught them to confess their sins and to fast every Friday in honor of the death of Bacab. (See Lord Kingsborough, *Antiquities of Mexico,* [London: Henry G. Bohn 1830-1848], vol. 6, pp. 507-508; Hubert Howe Bancroft, *The Native Races of the Pacific States,* [San Francisco: 1883], vol. 5, p. 2; and San Bartolome de las Casas, *Colección de Documentos Inéditos para la História de España*, [Collection of Unpublished Documents for the History of Spain], vol. LXVI, chapter cxxii, p. 453.)

Another circumstance of our Savior's death seems to be remembered in Mexico, for it is related in its traditions that at the disappearance of Topiltzin or Quetzalcoatl, both the sun and moon were covered in darkness, while a single star appeared in the heavens.

Our Lord's resurrection is plainly brought to mind by the statement of the venerable Chiapan chief, who asserted that the crucified Bacab remained dead three days and on the third day came to life again.

EVIDENCE NO. 560: THE ISLANDERS OF THE PACIFIC BELIEVED IN A GREAT WHITE GOD

Claim: Many of the first Polynesians came from ancient America and believed in Jesus Christ. The Book of Mormon mentions two ships that sailed from America in 55 BC out into the west (Pacific) sea to migrate northward (Alma 63:5-8). They were never heard of again. The Latter-day Saints believe that the Polynesians are the descendants of those ancient Americans who sailed away.

Evidence: Evidence that the Polynesians originated from ancient America, and took with them their belief in Jesus Christ comes from such sources as the journals of the British sea voyager, Captain James Cook. During the middle to late 1700's Cook sailed among the Polynesians in the islands of the Pacific. Everywhere he went native peoples fell on their faces and worshipped him as a god. He later discovered that they believed his arrival to be the long-anticipated return of the white god Lono. (See Oliver E. Allen, *The Pacific Navigators*, [Alexandria, Virginia: Time-Life Books, 1980], pp. 164, 167-168).

EVIDENCE NO. 561: THE ISLANDERS OF THE PACIFIC COMMEMORATED CHRIST'S SACRIFICE

Claim: The first Polynesians, having come from Book of Mormon lands, knew of the sacrifice of Jesus Christ and his charge to symbolically eat his flesh in remembrance of his sacrifice.

Evidence: During Old Testament times, the prophets knew of the coming sacrifice of Jesus Christ and offered sacrifices of their own in anticipation of His ultimate sacrifice. The Book of Mormon prophets, like their Hebrew counterparts in the Near East, also offered sacrifice. (See, for example, Mosiah 2:3).

In the South Pacific islands, descendants of the Book of Mormon people offered a type of sacrifice which also resembled a form of the Sacrament of the Lord's Supper. However, since the islanders became isolated from the prophets and ancient church of America, their beliefs evolved significantly from the truth, until only a few fragments survived along with much perversion of the truth.

In Tahiti, the British voyager Captain Cook observed a ceremony in which a man was bound to a long pole and killed. Certain dignitaries were then given small portions of the body, which they pretended to eat. Captain Cook made no comparison to the crucifixion of Jesus Christ nor to the Sacrament of the Lord's Supper, but the close similarity, albeit grossly perverted, is remarkable. (See Dorthy and Thomas Hobbler, *The Voyages of Captain Cook*, [New York: G. P. Putnam's Sons; 1983], p. 158. A Sketch of the incident made by one of Cook's men is shown in John R. Hale, *Age of Exploration*, [New York: Time, Inc., 1966], p. 156.)

EVIDENCE NO. 562: THE ANCIENT AMERICAN SAVIOR WAS HUNG ON A POLE OR CROSS

Claim: The ancient Americans knew of the crucifixion. Introduced in 1 Nephi 11:13-34, over 600 years before it actually took place, prophecies of the crucifixion were taught throughout the entire Book of Mormon period.

Evidence: According to the findings and conclusions of scholars, the ancient Americans believed that Quetzalcoatl died for the sins of man. They believed their great white god had been whipped and hung from a pole. This is especially convincing (since it does not mention the cross) for those who may argue that the Catholic religion, which came with the first explorers, influenced ancient American legend and folklore. The crucifix was an indispensable token of Catholic regalia and architecture. The ancient Americans said that he had been lashed and placed on a timber with his arms stretched out. Las Casas called him Baca, the son. (See Juan de Torquemada, *Monarquia Indiana*, [Madrid, Spain, 1613; 1723 edition], p. 15; Las Casas cited by Peter DeRoo, in *History of America Before Columbus* [1900], pp. 373, 431; *Apologetica Historia de las Indias*, [written 1550, pub. 1875 in Madrid, Spain], see chapter CXXIII; and Sahagun, *Anales de Cuauhtitlan*, [Codice Chimajpopoca, Imprenta Universitaria Mexico, 1945].)

Quetzalcoatl gave the ancient Americans the cross—telling them that he was lifted up on it at his death. It was also said to be a symbolic representation of the Tree of Life. See *Works of Ixtlilxóchitl,* English translation in Hunter and Ferguson, *Ancient America and the Book of Mormon,* (1950), pp. 210-212. See also Alan W. Watts, *Myth and Ritual in Christianity* (London and New York, 1954, p. 159); and Warren and Ferguson, *The Messiah in Ancient America,* (1987), pp. 77-84.

Figure 1 below shows a collection of crosses from the Mesoamerica. See Désiré Charney, *The Ancient Cities of the New World,* translated by J. Gonino and Helen S. Conant, (New York: Harper and Brothers, 1887), p. 86. See also the evidence regarding TREE SYMBOLISM in the chapter on "Book of Mormon Culture" in this same volume, which shows several Mesoamerican renderings of the *Tree of Life,* fashioned in the shape of a cross.

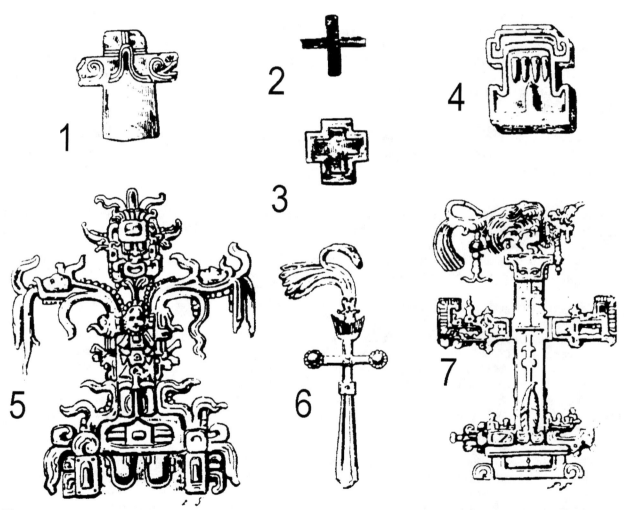

Figure 1. Mesoamerican crosses: No. 1 is a serpent cross; No. 2, cross shown on Quetzalcoatl's tunic; No. 3, cross from Mayapan, Yucatan; No. 4, cross of Teotihuacán (near Mexico City) with Symbol of Life at the top; No. 5, cross from the tablet of the Foliated Cross Temple at Palenque, Chiapas; No. 6, cross and Tree of Life from Yaxchilan, Guatemala, with serpent-like tail feathers extending from the tail of the bird at the top of the cross; No. 7, tree and cross from the Tablet of the Cross at Palenque, Chiapas.

EVIDENCE NO. 563: GREAT DESTRUCTION AT THE TIME OF THE CRUCIFIXION

Claim: At the time of Christ's crucifixion in the Middle East, there was great destruction as recorded in the Book of Mormon (3 Nephi 8:5-23).

Evidence: Concrete evidence of the great destruction unleashed in Mesoamerica at the time of the crucifixion can be found in Southwestern Mexico City where a thirty-foot thick layer of volcanic lava covers the archeological site of Copilco. Radiocarbon dating suggests that the lava was deposited in 30 AD—almost exactly the time of the Savior's death in Jerusalem. (See Bruce W. Warren and Thomas S. Ferguson, *The Messiah in Ancient America,* [1987], p. vi.)

Ancient American history also attests to great destruction at a time that coincides with the date of the crucifixion. This cataclysm became a turning point in the history of the ancient Americans. *The Works of Ixtlilxóchitl* (English translation by Hunter and Ferguson, *Ancient America and the Book of Mormon* [1950], pp. 189-190) gives two checks on the date of the destruction. It occurred 166 years after the great council (which convened 132 years before the night of no darkness) and 270 years after the ancient ones had been destroyed (236 years before the night of no darkness). The night of no darkness in ancient America occurred on the night of Christ's birth in Bethlehem.

Ixtlilxóchitl further wrote that "The earth trembled, and the rocks broke, and many other things and signs took place...This happened in the *ce Calli,* which adjusting this count with ours comes to be at the same time when Christ our Lord suffered." (*Works of Ixtlilxóchitl,* English translation by Hunter and Ferguson, *Ancient America.*, pp. 189-194).

The Book of Mormon records earthquakes, hurricane winds, valleys becoming mountains, mountains becoming valleys, cities sinking in the sea, and a thick darkness (3 Nephi 8). Dr. Adolph Bandelier sums up traditions of Viracocha the equivalent of Quetzalcoatl, in Peru, who descends out of the sky. He even made high places level; plains were broken up and made into great heights; springs burst forth and rocks were rent. In fact, the whole topography of the land was changed. (See *American Anthropologist* [1904], Vol. VI, No. 1, p. 203.)

The following are quotations from Harris, *The Book of Mormon Message and Evidences* (pp. 148-149):

> At the death of Christ, as recorded in the Book of Mormon (3 Nephi 8), there was a great destruction by earthquakes, winds, fire and darkness which lasted for three days. Isaac B. Ball (*Improvement Era,* vol. 34, pp. 387,457 [1931]) has shown that the Book of Mormon account is a good description of the action and effects of hurricanes and earthquakes. There may also have been volcanic action. Wagner has suggested that the tradition of the great wind that was raised when Quetzalcoatl was deposed as god seems to have some bearing on his worship as god of the air or wind (Henry R. Wagner, *The Rise of Fernando Cortez,* [1994] Ref. 10, p. 189).

> There are many traditions of darkness, earthquakes and great destruction in the far past. Ixtlilxóchitl, for example, gives a Toltec tradition that some time after the invention of the Toltec calendar, "the sun and moon were eclipsed, the earth shook, and the rocks were rent asunder, and many other things and signs happened, though there was no loss of life" (Hubert Howe Bancroft, *The Native Races of the Pacific States,* [San Francisco: 1883], vol. 5, p. 210; see also B. H. Roberts, *Improvement Era* [1917] vol. 20, pp. 574; and George C. Vaillant, *Aztecs of Mexico,* [Doubleday 1940], pp. 53, 171).

> The Pedregal lava sheet which flowed centuries ago from the volcano Xitli in Central Mexico covered at least two ruins near Copilco and Cuicuilco just south of Mexico City. These cultures flourished for perhaps a thousand years around the time of Christ (Vaillant, *Aztecs of Mexico,* [1940], pp. 43-47; see also Sylvanus G. Morley & G. W. Brainerd, *The Ancient Maya,* [1956], p. 386).

About the time of Christ there were cataclysmic volcanic eruptions in the Central part of El Salvador which rendered it uninhabitable and greatly influenced the rest of the people of that region to move elsewhere (Samuel K. Lothrop, "Pottery Types and Their Sequences, in El Salvador," *Indian Notes and Monographs. Museum of the American Indian Heye Foundation*, vol. 1, no. 4, [1927], p. 214; see also Kingsborough, *Antiquities of Mexico,* [London: Henry G. Bohn 1830-1848], vol. 8, p. 193.)

Elder LeGrand Richards quoted an Indian legend that recorded the type of destruction of which the Book of Mormon spoke:

Long time, heap long time. Maybe one hundred years, injun no sabe, white man sabe. My grandfather's father, he heap old man. Maybe two, three hundred years, me dunno, Carson Valley, Waso Valley, Truskee Valley, Long Valley, Pilamid Lake, Lublock, eblywhere all water, plenty pish, plenty duck. Big pish too, now no see him no more, all go away, no come back.

Wasu Injun, he lib big mountains [pointing to the Comstock and Pyramid range]. Sometime Wasu Indian take em boat go see Piutee, maybe Piutee he take em boat go see Wasu Indian, Yash he good friend, all time.

Pointing to the Sierra to the west of Washoe Valley, the old Indian continued:

Big mountain all time pire, plenty boom, boom, heap smoke, injun heap flaid! Byme bye, one day, mountain heap smoke, heap noise, glound too much shake, Injun heap flaid, pall down, plenty cly. He sun ebly day come up [pointing to the northeast] he go down, [pointing to the southwest]. One day no come up, Injun no sabe, mountain heap smoke, glound plenty shake, wind blow, water heap mad. *Maybe two, tlee day sun he no come,* injun no eat, no sleep, all time, cly, cly. Yash, heap flaid. Byme bye water make plenty noise, go plenty fast like Tlukee Liver; water go down, down, mountain come up, come up, plenty mud, plenty pish die, byme bye sun come back over this mountain [pointing to the southeast] he go down ober there [pointing to the northwest]. Yash, white man sabe, injun no sabe,

Maybe two, tlee week, mud he dly up, Piutee. Wasu Injun wal, no more boat. All water he go; maybe little water Pilamid Lake, Honey Lake, Wasu Lake, too much mountain, he come purty quick. Yash, injun no sabe, water, big pish no come back. No see him no more. (Mrs. M. M. Garwood, *Progressive West Magazine*, reprinted in *Deseret Semi-Weekly News*, February 5, 1906.)

The narrative is lacking in detail, but it is sufficiently clear to indicate that the aborigines of this country have preserved, in legendary form, some account of the terrible cataclysms that have convulsed the American continents. (Richards, *A Marvelous Work and a Wonder* [1950], p. 76)

EVIDENCE NO. 564: DESTRUCTION IN THE FIRST DAYS OF THE YEAR

Claim: The Book of Mormon specifies that the great destruction in the Americas at the time of Christ's crucifixion in Jerusalem took place in the first days of the year (3 Nephi 8:5).

Evidence: It is a well-known fact that the crucifixion took place during the Passover—which was held during the first month of the Jewish lunar-solar year *Abib* (Matthew 26:2, 17; Mark 14:1, 12; Luke 22:1, 7; John 18:39; 19:14). This month (later called *Nissan*) coincides with late March or early April on the Gregorian calendar.

This is also verified in the *Works of Ixtlilxóchitl*, which speaks of the great destruction that occurred in ancient America, precisely during the time that Christ was crucified in the Old World. It not only specifies the exact year, but also states that the destructions "happened during the first days of the year." See *Works of Ixtlilxóchitl*, English translation by Hunter and Ferguson, *Ancient America and the Book of Mormon*, (Kolob Book Company, Oakland, California: 1950), pp. 189-194.

EVIDENCE NO. 565: APPEARANCE OF NEW MOUNTAINS

Claim: According to the Book of Mormon, new mountains appeared during the great cataclysm at the time of the crucifixion of Jesus Christ. See 3 Nephi 8:10; 9:8.

Evidence: Marquis Nadaillac wrote the following regarding Ancient American traditions which verifies this claim from the Book of Mormon: "Other traditions allude to convulsions of nature, to inundations, and profound disturbances, to terrible deluges, in the midst of which mountains and volcanoes suddenly rose up." (See Jean Francois Alvert du Pouget de Nadaillac, *Prehistoric America,* [London: John Murray, 1885], pp. 16, 17, 527; who cites D'Eichtal, "Etudes sur les Origines Bouddhiques," part 1, p. 65.)

EVIDENCE NO. 566: SUBMERGENCE OF CITIES

Claim: The Book of Mormon records that during the cataclysm at the time of the crucifixion some cities sank into the ocean (3 Nephi 8:9; 9:4).

Evidence: Many have dismissed the idea that there could have been a cataclysm of sufficient magnitude to submerge whole cities. However, recent discoveries have been made which provide conclusive evidence that this phenomenon occurred in the very areas spoken of in the Book of Mormon. See Cortez, *Five Letters*, p. 65; see also *Salt Lake Tribune*, Monday, December 15, 1980, p. 8A by Fernando Irusta, Reuter News Agency, La Paz, Bolivia.

A false prophet would not have dared to declare greater cataclysms on the Western Hemisphere, than mentioned in the Bible at the time of the crucifixion. The fact that these cataclysms did occur, supports our claim that Joseph Smith was a true prophet of God, and that the Book of Mormon is a true and accurate history.

EVIDENCE NO. 567: LIGHTNING DURING THE EARTHQUAKE

Claim: The Book of Mormon records that "exceeding sharp lightnings..." occurred during the earthquakes in the Americas at the time of Christ's crucifixion in Jerusalem (3 Nephi 8:6-7).

Evidence: It is interesting that the Book of Mormon would mention "sharp lightnings" during the terrible earthquake—especially since it makes no mention of rain. Russell H. Ball writes about a certain "type of volcanic eruption in which intense lightning can be generated within the ash cloud above the volcano:"

> A full-color photograph of such an eruption of the Sakura-jima Volcano in southern Japan on November 17, 1987 was published in the April 1988 issue of *Discover*. This volcano erupted more than one hundred times in 1987 and spewed molten rock and hot gases into the sky. During these eruptions a small amount of magma was released constantly, rather than all at once, as at Mount St. Helens. The surprising feature of the photo is the presence of a large number of lightning bolts in the ash cloud above the volcano. The lightning is triggered by the buildup of static electricity in the cloud of erupting ash. Friction among the swirling particles causes them to become electrically charged. (Russell H. Ball, "An Hypothesis Concerning the Three Days of Darkness Among the Nephites," *Journal of Book of Mormon Studies,* vol. 2, no. 1, [Spring 1993], pp. 107-123.)

While the Book of Mormon does not specifically mention volcanic eruptions during the earthquake, it does state that many new mountains rose up (3 Nephi 8:10; 9:8). Intense volcanic activity would be a logical explanation for both the appearance of new mountains and the "sharp lightnings" as recorded in the Book of Mormon. See also Juarras, cited by H. J. Spinden, "Shattered Capitals of Central America," in *The National Geographic Magazine*, vol. 35, no. 3 (Sept. 1919), p. 202; P. Byerly, *Seismology* (New York: Prentice Hall, 1942), p. 76. Both above sources are cited in Nibley, *Since Cumorah* (1988), p. 233.

EVIDENCE NO. 568: A THICK VAPOR OF DARKNESS

Claim: The Book of Mormon states that at the time of Christ's crucifixion, *thick vapor of darkness* prevented the lighting of any fires (3 Nephi 8:20-22; 10:13). According to the record, the people could even *feel* the vapor. Because this description sounds improbable, critics have mocked this passage in the Book of Mormon. However, it is actually another evidence that the book is true.

Evidence: *The Works of Ixtlilxóchitl* (English translation in Hunter and Ferguson, *Ancient America and the Book of Mormon* [1950], pp. 190, 218) record that the sun and moon were eclipsed at the time of the crucifixion. See also Benaduci, Boturini, *Idea de Una Nueva História General de la America Septentrional*, (1746); Francisco Javier Clavigero, *Historia Antiqua de Mexico*, 1780 (1945 edition) vol. 1, chapter 2, p. 179; Ordonez and Augiar, *Historia de la Creación*, etc., 1907 edition, p. 2. All three sources are cited in Hunter and Ferguson, *Ancient America*, [1950], p. 198.) See also T. A. Willard, *Kukulcan, The Bearded Conqueror*, p. 103; and Cieza de Leon cited in Thor Heyerdahl, *American Indians in the Pacific*, (Stockholm, 1952), p. 715.

The following statement is quoted from a *Readers' Digest* review of Dr. Velikovsky's book *Worlds in Collision*: "Nations and tribes in many other places have traditions about a cosmic catastrophe during which the sun did not shine; the long darkness is remembered in Finland, Babylonia and Peru, by the American Indians, by peoples all over the world. Hundreds of thousands of men and animals were killed during an upheaval that shook the earth" (Fulton Oursler's Preview of Dr. Immanuel Velikovsky's, *Worlds in Collision, Readers' Digest*, March 1950, pp. 139-148; cited in Hunter and Ferguson, *Ancient America and the Book of Mormon* (1950), pp. 298-301).

In addition to ancient writings which record that thick darkness occurred at the time of the crucifixion, the following sources state that such a phenomenon preventing the lighting of fires is possible and has occurred on other occasions. See Werner Knop, "The Day The Earth Exploded," *Saturday Evening Post*, March 20, 1954, 25, 114; John Lear, "The Volcano that Shaped the Western World," *Saturday Review*, November 5, 1960, pp. 57-66; August H. Sieberg, "Auffallender Nebel und Wundersame Dicke Luften," *Handbuch der Erdbebenkunde*, (Braunschweig: Vieweg, 1904), p. 123; Herbert J. Spinden, "Shattered Capitals of Central America," in *National Geographic Magazine*, vol. 36, no. 3, September 1919, p. 211. The last four sources are also cited in Nibley, *Since Cumorah*, (1988), p. 236.

EVIDENCE NO. 569: ANCIENT AMERICAN KNOWLEDGE OF THE RESURRECTION

Claim: The Book of Mormon account that the ancient Americans knew about the resurrection of Jesus Christ (for example, see Mosiah 3:8-12) and of the resurrection of all mankind (first introduced in 2 Nephi 9:6-11) is supported by evidence.

Evidence: It has been established that the ancient Americans did, indeed, believe in a universal resurrection, as well as the resurrection of their great white god, whom Latter-day Saints know to be Jesus Christ. (See Peter DeRoo, *History of America Before Columbus* [1900], Vol. 1, pp. 373, 425, 430, who cites a letter from Francis Hernandez to Las Casas. See also *Anales Cuauhtitlan* [Codice Chimalpopoca, Imprenta Universitaria Mexico, 1945], p. 9.)

This evidence is especially significant in light of the fact that many Christian churches teach that there is not really a literal resurrection of the physical body. They defend this notion with such Biblical passages as 1 Corinthians 15:50 which states that "flesh and blood cannot inherit the Kingdom of God." Therefore, it is unlikely that the Indians of the Americas could have learned of this doctrine from Spanish missionaries.

EVIDENCE NO. 570: APPEARANCE IN THE LAND OF BOUNTIFUL

Claim: The Book of Mormon indicates that Christ appeared in the land called *Bountiful* (3 Nephi 11).

Evidence: The great white god of ancient America appeared in Huehuetlapallan, which means *"ancient Bounti-ful land."* See *Works of Ixtlilxóchitl,* English translation by Hunter and Ferguson, *Ancient America and the Book of Mormon*, (1950), p. 149.

EVIDENCE NO. 571: FEEDING A GREAT MULTITUDE

Claim: The Book of Mormon account that sufficient bread was miraculously provided while giving sacramental bread to the great multitude (3 Nephi 20:6) is supported by the traditions of ancient Americans.

Evidence: Non-Mormon sources from ancient American histories indicate that Quetzalcoatl miraculously fed a great multitude. (See Paul Herrmann, *Conquest by Man* [New York: 1954], p. 178.)

EVIDENCE NO. 572: THE RESURRECTED CHRIST HEALED THE SICK

Claim: The Book of Mormon claim that the resurrected Christ worked mighty *miracles* and *healed* many people (3 Nephi 17:7, 9; 26:15; Mosiah 3:5-8) in ancient America is supported by non-LDS sources.

Evidence: The great white god of the ancient Americas was often called "The Healer" by many native American tribes scattered from South America up into Canada. (See Laurette Sejourne, *Thought and Religion in Ancient Mexico*, pp. 136-137; T. A. Willard, *Kukulcan-The Bearded Conqueror* [Hollywood, California: 1941], pp. 127, 131-133, 148-149; Bernardo de Lizana, *History of Yucatan and Spiritual Conquest*, 1633; Constance Irwin, *Fair Gods and Stone Faces*, [New York: St. Martin's Press, 1963], pp. 33, 100.)

EVIDENCE NO. 573: QUETZALCOATL ORDAINED PRIESTS AND CHOSE TWELVE APOSTLES

Claim: Historical findings support the Book of Mormon claim that Christ personally organized his priesthood upon the Nephites, and that his priesthood continued among the Nephites with new priests being ordained in the name of Jesus (3 Nephi 18:5; Moroni 3:1-4). The name of this priesthood was "the Holy Priesthood after the Order of the Son of God" (Alma 5:44, 49; 13:1-16; D&C 107:1-4). The members of this priesthood were required to "take upon [themselves] the name of Christ" (Mosiah 5:7-10; 3 Nephi 27:5).

The Book of Mormon further states that Jesus Christ chose twelve from among the priesthood of the Nephites to serve as His apostles on the American continents (3 Nephi 12:1-2; 13:25-26; 15:11-12).

Evidence: Ancient Aztec traditions relate that Quetzalcoatl founded a priesthood and that priests were named after him. Torquemada says: "He (Quetzalcoatl) had priests whom were called quequetzalcohus, that is to say 'priests of the order of Quetzalcoatl.'" Other sources indicate that these priests "took upon themselves his name" and performed rituals in his name. (Adolph E. Bandelier, *Archeological Reconnaissance Into Mexico* [1884], p. 172; George C. Vaillant, *Aztecs of Mexico* [Doubleday & Co., Inc., 1940], pp. 52, 177, 186; Laurette Sejourne, *Thought and Religion in Ancient Mexico*, pp. 25, 27, 30. See also Harris, *Book of Mormon Message and Evidences* [1961], p. 146.)

Among the natives Americans that once thrived in Oklahoma is a legend of prophet healer who "was born across the ocean, in a land where all men were bearded. In this land he was born of a virgin on a night when a bright star came out of the havens and stood over His city." The supernatural being known as the "Dawn God," came among them and, "chose from the priesthood His twelve disciples, and lectured to all the people." (See Louise Taylor Hansen, *He Walked the Americas,* [Amherst Press: Amherst, Wisconsin, 1963], p. 48.)

EVIDENCE NO. 574: THE ASCENSION OF CHRIST

<u>Claim</u>: The account in the Book of Mormon of the ascension of Jesus Christ into Heaven after his brief ministry among the Nephites (see 3 Nephi 18:37-39) is supported by traditions of ancient Americans.

<u>Evidence</u>: This is validated by several sources including "no less an authority than the first bishop of Chiapas, San Bartolome de las Casas himself," who found that the Indians:

> … believed in a God who dwells in the heavens, and that God is Father, Son, and Holy Ghost. The Father's name was Icona, and he had created man and all things; the Son had for name Bacab, and he was born from a maiden always virgin, called Chibirias, that lives in the heavens with God. The Holy Ghost they called Echuac. They say that Icona means the Great Father; of Bacab, who is the Son, they tell that Eopuco put him to death, had him scourged, and placed a crown of thorns on his head, and hung him with extended arms from a pole; not meaning that he was nailed, but bound to it; and to better explain the chief extended his own arms. There he finally died, and remained dead three days, and the third day he came to life again and *ascended to Heaven*, where he is now with his Father. Immediately after came Echuac, who is the Holy Ghost and who supplied the earth with all that was needed. (San Bartolome de las Casas, *Colección de Documentos Inéditos para la História de España*, [Collection of Unpublished Documents for the History of Spain], vol. LXVI, chapter cxxii, p. 453.)

The above is also cited in Peter DeRoo, *History of America Before Columbus*, (1900), vol. 1, p. 373. More evidence comes from the Manaicas Indians of Brazil, and the natives of Upper California. Peter DeRoo continues on pp. 426-427, 432-433:

> One of the Manaicas' traditions states, indeed, that a woman of accomplished beauty, who had never been wedded to man, gave birth to a most lovely child. This child, after growing up to man's state, worked many wonders, raised the dead to life again, made the lame walk and the blind see. Finally, having one day called together a great number of people, *he ascended into the air* and was transformed into the sun who enlightens this earth. (Paul Gaffarel, *Histoire de la Decourverte de l'Amerique* [Paris: 1892], vol. 1, p. 428. Emphasis added.)

> …Resuming the ancient American history of our Savior where we left it, we should next inquire as to the reminiscences of his *ascension to heaven*. Such souvenirs are actually found in several parts. The supreme god of Upper California, Chinighchinigh, was believed to be an immortal sprit, and yet underwent the penalty of death. When asked where he desired to be buried, his answer was that he would go up into heaven, where he would take an account of the actions of all men, and reward or punish them accordingly. "When I die I shall ascend above the stars," he said, "where I shall always behold you; and to those who have kept my commandments I shall give all they ask of me; but those who obey not my teachings nor believe them I shall punish severely."

While some critics assume the natives learned Christianity from the Catholic clergy, it is significant that the first Catholic officials testify they first heard these teachings from the natives themselves. See also William Montgomery McGovern, *Jungle Paths and Inca Ruins*, pp. 276-280. The above sources are also cited in Peter DeRoo, *The History of America Before Columbus* [1900], vol. 1, pp. 373, 427, 430, 433.

EVIDENCE NO. 575: JESUS CHRIST PROMISED TO RETURN

<u>Claim</u>: Before his ascension into Heaven, Jesus Christ promised the ancient Americans that he would return (see, for example, 3 Nephi 21:25 and 3 Nephi 28:7).

<u>Evidence</u>: See A. Hyatt Verrill, *America's Ancient Civilizations* [New York: 1953], p. 104.) It is a fact of history that the natives of the Americas who saw the first explorers, such as Columbus and Cortez, believed them to be the great white god who had promised them that he would return.

EVIDENCE NO. 576: QUETZALCOATL AND CHRIST AS THE SOURCE OF LIFE

Claim: To the ancient Americans, the Lord was a giver of rain and hence, life, as recorded in the Book of Mormon (Helaman 11:17).

Evidence: Some scholars have noted that the name Quetzalcoatl, which means feathered serpent, represents the green quetzal bird and the green stone because of its "precious color." To the ancient Americans, green symbolized "life-giving water or rain." See John L. Sorenson in *Man Across the Sea: Problems of Pre-Columbian Contacts*, edited by Carroll J. Riley et al. (Austin: University of Texas Press, 1971), pp. 234-235, cited in Sorenson, *An Ancient American Setting for the Book of Mormon* (1985), p. 328.

The ancient Americans taught that Quetzalcoatl rose from the dead. Marine shells, which are another symbol of Quetzalcoatl, also represent resurrection from the dead. Jesus rose from the dead—the relationship is clear. See Stephan F. de Borhegyi, "Shell Offerings and the Use of Shell Motifs at Lake Amatitlan, Guatemala, and Teotihuacan, Mexico," *Actas y Memórias, 36a Congreso Internaciónal de Americanistas*, (España, 1965, vol. 1 (Seville, 1968), pp. 356,359; Laurette Sejourne, *Burning Water: Thought and Religion in Ancient Mexico* [Berkeley: Shambhala, 1976], pp. 25, 83-85; Idem, "El Simbolismo de los Rituales Funerarios en Monte Alban," *Revista Mexicana de Estudios Antropologicos*, (1960) vol. 16, pp. 85-90; Rene Millon, *The Teotihuacan Map*, vol. 1, (Austin: University of Texas Press, 1973), pp. 55-56; cited in Sorenson, *An Ancient American Setting*, (1985), p. 328.

EVIDENCE NO. 577: THE BLOOD OF QUETZALCOATL RESTORES LIFE

Claim: The Book of Mormon teaches that mankind will be restored to life by the blood or atonement of Jesus Christ (2 Nephi 31:20; Ether 3:14). Similarly the Bible teaches:

Then Jesus said unto them, Verily, verily, I say unto you, Except ye eat the flesh of the Son of man, and drink his blood, ye have no life in you. Whoso eateth my flesh, and drinketh my blood, hath eternal life; and I will raise him up at the last day (John 6:53-54).

Further evidence that Quetzalcoatl is Jesus Christ is found in the ancient Aztec legend of how life is restored by the blood of Quetzalcoatl.

Evidence: Professor Brian M. Fagan writes the following:

The most common legend has Quetzalcoatl descending into the underworld to obtain the bones and ashes of previous human beings in order to recreate humanity. Quetzalcoatl delivers the bones to the assembled gods in Tomoanchan, where the bones are ground into a powder and placed in a vessel. [Led by Quetzalcoatl], the gods then undergo mass auto-sacrifice, their blood drips into the sacred vessel, and this fertilizes the pulverized bone...*those who deserve and [were] brought back to life because of penance*" (Brian Fagan, *The Aztecs*, [W. H. Freeman & Co. 1984], Chapter 9, p. 226).

Compare the above reference to Quetzalcoatl's trip into the underworld to the Biblical account of Christ's visit to the spirits that were imprisoned (1 Peter 3:18-20; 4:6). Aztec poets philosophized the significance of Quetzalcoatl's supreme act of sacrifice as cited in Miguel Leon-Portilla, *Pre-Columbian Literatures of Mexico*, translated by Jack Davis, (University of Oklahoma Press, 1963), p. 111:

Perchance, it is true?
Did our Lord, our prince Quetzalcoatl, bring man back to life;
He who invents man, he who creates man?
Perchance, was it determined by the Lord and Lady of Duality?
Was not the Word handed down?

EVIDENCE NO. 578: SUDDEN DECLINE OF QUETZALCOATL WORSHIP AROUND 200 AD

Claim: The Book of Mormon records that 200 years after Jesus Christ personally established His church on this hemisphere, new religions came about that rejected Christ and his teachings, and eventually dominated the religious scene in Mesoamerica (4 Nephi 1:26-41). This transition in the history of pre-Columbian America is echoed in the archeological ruins of the great city of Teotihuacán near Mexico City.

Evidence: The following is quoted from John L. Sorenson, "The Decline of the God Quetzalcoatl at Teotihuacán," *Foundation for Ancient Research and Mormon Studies Insights,* No. 84, (September 1992), p. 2:

Some Latter-day Saints have long been struck with the similarity between certain characteristics of the god Quetzalcoatl, as known from native traditions in Mexico, and Guatemala, and Jesus Christ, whose visit to Lehi's descendants is described in Third Nephi. In the book, *An Ancient American Setting for the Book of Mormon* (1985), the dramatic decline of the god Quetzalcoatl in the period around AD 200 at the giant city of Teotihuacán near Mexico City was discussed in comparison with Fourth Nephi. The book relied on a study by Mexican scholar Enrique Fiorescano ("Quetzalcoatl: Espiritualismo del México Antiguo," *Cuadernos Americanos,* 105/4 [1959], pp. 127-139.) A new study now presents even clearer parallels. (See Rubén Cabrera C., "La Secuencia Arquitectónica del Edificio de los Animales Mitológicos en Teotihuacán," in *Homenaje a Román Piña Chan,* [México: UNAM, 1987], pp. 349-372.)

The face of what Mexican archaeologists term "the old Temple of Quetzalcoatl" at Teotihuacán has been photographed by innumerable tourists. Dramatic symbolic representations of Quetzalcoatl as a serpent dot the facade of this impressive structure. Additional mapping, ceramic study, and excavation have definitely established that this building was constructed at the same time as the huge Pyramid of the Sun—between AD 150 and 200 (Cabrera, P. 364, reports a new carbon-14 date of AD 148). As visitors clearly see, the original building was later covered over with another structure bearing very different symbols.

In Book of Mormon history, this half century was the golden age following the appearance of the resurrected Jesus to the Nephites in Bountiful; however, Fourth Nephi gives only two brief verses about this period (see 4 Nephi 1:19-20). (Of course we do not positively know that Teotihuacán was one of the cities of the Nephites or Lamanites, but the change in deities that Cabrera reports is so striking that we may at least speculate that worship of Jesus Christ, under the name translated by the later Aztecs as Quetzalcoatl, prevailed there.)

Cabrera's picture of the transition between the two sacred buildings is interesting: "the Plumed Serpent [representing Quetzalcoatl]...acquired for this period of time a preponderance of force in the political and religious aspect of Teotihuacán. This is shown by the ostentatious, sculpture-decorated structure, which to construct required enormous labor...making it one of the great glories of Teotihuacán." But what was the reason, the author goes on, for them to mutilate many of the enormous plumed serpent heads and then construct a new edifice of lesser quality covering the first one? The change was not simply one of architectural style. More likely it had to do with changing political and religious power.

Cabrera continues, "the band or group of priests representing Quetzalcoatl held power at Teotihuacán from at least the time when the first structure was erected, before AD 200. But then other religious groups arose who were represented by the symbolism of jaguars, coyotes, birds and fishes along with other mythological beings." Priests or followers of this new religious persuasion eventually gained control of the city; the date for this change is not known precisely but is usually considered after approximately AD 300. Paintings and sculptures of jaguars and other symbolic animals are found widely throughout the sacred portion of the metropolis thereafter.

Fourth Nephi 1:26-41 reports the rise of new "churches" rivaling "the church of Christ," and which eventually came to dominate the society. This took place about AD 210 to 260, a reasonable approximation to the scholars' estimate of AD 300.

Cabrera concludes with questions about this "period of social crisis whose causes are unknown": "Do the phenomena mentioned represent other Teotihuacán groups, or groups coming from elsewhere, intent on establishing at Teotihuacán their own religion?" Or, "what was going on in Teotihuacán society in the area of religious and political organizations in the interval between AD 200 and 350?"

Those who read the Book of Mormon as authentic ancient history will feel that they already have a useful explanation. But we too would like, in the author's final works, "better information, to establish more exact dates of these social events and determine their causes."

Evidences From the Cuna Indians

The Cuna Indians live on the San Blas Islands, just off the northeast coast of Panama. Much of Cuna oral history contains striking parallels to the stories and principles taught in the Book of Mormon and the Bible. After the Church of Jesus Christ of Latter-day Saints gained legal recognition from Panama in September 1965, many Cuna Indians were baptized and church units were organized on the islands. The following five evidences are from the history of the Cuna Indians.

EVIDENCE NO. 579: WICKEDNESS FOLLOWED BY DAYS OF DARKNESS IN ANCIENT AMERICA

Claim: The Book of Mormon testifies that the people "turned from the Lord their God, and they did stone the prophets and did cast them out from among them" (3 Nephi 7:14). It further states that because of their wickedness, three days of such thick darkness covered the land that no fires could be lit (3 Nephi 8:20-5).

Evidence: According to Cuna oral history and tradition, the Cuna god caused eight days of darkness to cover the land because of the great wickedness of the people. There was no light at all, and even fires would not burn. (See Tomas Herrera Porras and Anita McAndrews, *Cuna Cosmology: Legends From Panama* [Washington, DC: Three Continents Press, 1978], pp. 57-59, cited in *Cuna Indians and the Latter-day Saints* [a pamphlet accompanying an exhibition of Cuna Art at the Museum of Church History and Art at 45 North West Temple, Salt Lake City, Utah: The Church of Jesus Christ of Latter-day Saints, 1989].)

EVIDENCE NO. 580: A VOICE FROM THE HEAVENS

Claim: According to the Book of Mormon, after the days of darkness, the people heard a voice which pierced them to their very souls, causing their frames to quake and their hearts to burn (see 3 Nephi 11:3-7).

Evidence: According to Cuna history, after the days of darkness, a golden dawn flooded the sky and a sparkling mist rolled in. The deep voice of a man came like the wind over the mountains (see Porras and McAndrews, *Cuna Cosmology*, pp. 57-59).

EVIDENCE NO. 581: THE APPEARANCE OF A MAN OF LIGHT

Claim: The Book of Mormon testifies that after the voice was heard, which came after the light dispelled the darkness, they saw "a Man descending out of heaven" who introduced himself as the light of the world (3 Nephi 11:8-11).

Evidence: The Cuna legends claim that after the voice was heard, which came after the light dispelled the darkness, they saw a man descend out of heaven who introduced himself as Iberocuna, which means "Man of Light" (see Porras and McAndrews, *Cuna Cosmology*, pp. 57-59).

EVIDENCE NO. 582: THE MAN OF LIGHT TOOK EACH PERSON BY THE HAND

<u>Claim:</u> The Book of Mormon testifies that all the people went forth one by one to feel the prints in the hands of Jesus Christ (3 Nephi 11:15).

<u>Evidence:</u> The Cuna Indian legends describe the "Man of Light" moving without haste from one Cuna to another until he had shook each person's hand and told each one his name (Porras, *Cuna Cosmology*, pp. 57-59).

EVIDENCE NO. 583: THE MAN OF LIGHT EMBRACED THE CHILDREN

<u>Claim:</u> The Book of Mormon testifies that Jesus Christ "took their little children, one by one, and blessed them" (3 Nephi 17:21).

<u>Evidence:</u> According to Cuna history, the children clung to the "Man of Light" and he embraced each child (see Porras and McAndrews, *Cuna Cosmology*, pp. 57-59).

EVIDENCE NO. 584: NEW TESTAMENT REFERENCES IN THE BOOK OF MORMON

<u>Claim:</u> The existence of New Testament teachings in the Book of Mormon is another evidence that the same God inspired the writings of both books.

<u>Evidence:</u> Critics point to references such as Moroni 10:20-22, which they claim was borrowed from the words of Paul's eloquent discourse in 1 Corinthians 13:13 on faith, hope, and charity. The Book of Mormon introduces itself as another testament of Jesus Christ. As such, readers should expect to find the same gospel within its pages as is found in the New Testament.

Biblical scholars have recently discovered that New Testament writers, such as the apostle Paul, often used the writings of classical writers, orators, and used drama, law courts, ancient religious rites, etc. In fact, in some passages, he candidly admits to making allusions to other writers. For example, in Acts 17:28, he makes reference to certain "of your own poets." The *faith, hope and charity* passages, specifically, have been found to originate, not with Paul, but with a much earlier Babylonian culture. See R. Reitzenstein, *Nachrichter v.d. kgl. Gesd. Wiss zu Gottingen*, 1916, pp. 362,416 and 1917 Heft 1, pp. 130-151, and Historische Jeitschrift, 116, pp. 189-202. Also, A. von Harnack, in *t*, 50 (1931), pp. 266ff.; cf. Alf. Resch, "Der Paulinismus u. die Logia Jesu" in *Texte u. Untersuch-ungen. N.F.* XII (1904). All sources cited by Nibley, *Since Cumorah*, (1988), p. 112.

The Babylonians in turn received such passages and other teachings from prophets of God who taught the same gospel in various dispensations of time, from Adam's dispensation on down throughout the annals of history.

EVIDENCE NO. 585: OTHER SHEEP

<u>Claim:</u> The Book of Mormon fulfills the passage in John 10;14-16 in which Jesus says: "And other sheep I have, which are not of this fold: them also I must bring, and they shall hear my voice; and there shall be one fold, and one shepherd."

<u>Evidence:</u> Non-Mormons have difficulty trying to explain this passage. In 3 Nephi 15:16-24, Jesus testified that his appearance to the Nephite people was the fulfillment of the passage in John. Jesus, knowing that his listeners in Palestine assumed the "other sheep" were the gentiles, said:

> And they understood me not, for they supposed it had been the Gentiles; for they understood not that the Gentiles should be converted through their preaching. And they understood me not that I said they shall hear my voice; and they understood me not that the Gentiles should not at any time hear my voice—that I should not manifest myself unto them save it were by the Holy Ghost (3 Nephi 15:20-3).

Those who insist that the gentiles were the "other sheep" of the fold of Christ do not understand that Jesus was sent to preach only "unto the lost sheep of the *house of Israel*" (Matthew 15:24). This is verified by the simple fact that there is no record of Jesus ever preaching to gentiles. Furthermore, sheep are *accustomed* to the voice of their shepherd and none other (John 10:27-28). The gentiles, unconverted as they were at that time, were not yet sheep, and did not *know* His voice. The sheep were followers of the good Shepherd—on both sides of the world—each in their own "fold."

EVIDENCE NO. 586: NEW INSIGHTS ON THE TEACHINGS OF JESUS CHRIST

Claim: As Another Testament of Jesus Christ, the Book of Mormon adds profound insights into the meaning of the life and mission of Jesus Christ.

Evidence: The following is a summarized list complied by Dr. Gilbert W. Scharffs in his article "Unique Insights on Christ from the Book of Mormon," *Ensign*, December 1988, pp. 8-13.

1. Our Redeemer's atonement reaches those who die without law, including little children who die without baptism (2 Nephi 9:25; Mosiah 3:11-12; Moroni 8:11-12).

2. Christ's death brought about a *universal* resurrection for *all* mankind, regardless of a person's belief or performance (2 Nephi 9:22; Mormon 9:13).

3. The Lord's atonement brought about a physical resurrection, not just a spiritual one (2 Nephi 9:4; Alma 11:42-43).

4. So great was Christ's suffering that blood literally came from every pore (Mosiah 3:7).

5. One reason for Christ's atonement was to appease justice (Mosiah 15:9; Alma 42:25).

6. Christ's atonement was part of an eternal plan that included the fall of man (2 Nephi 2:22-27; 9:13; 11:5; Alma 12:25; 42:8; Ether 3:14).

7. Without the Savior's atonement, all the earth's inhabitants would come under Satan's control (2 Nephi 9:8; Mosiah 16:3-12).

8. The Lord's love extends to all races and people (2 Nephi 26:33).

9. The Savior's influence is so great that it enlightens each person's conscience (Moroni 7:16).

10. To become committed followers of Christ, we must have the option to reject him (2 Nephi 2:11-16).

11. The strength and freedom of America depend on its people serving Jesus Christ (Ether 2:12).

12. The source of real freedom for any person or nation is Jesus Christ (Mosiah 5:7-8).

13. Both the *grace of Jesus Christ* and *good works* (of which Christ is the primary model) are necessary to the Plan of Salvation (2 Nephi 2:8; 25:23; 3 Nephi 27:21-22).

14. The Book of Mormon affirms the basic accuracy of the Bible concerning Christ (3 Nephi).

15. The God of the Old Testament is Jesus Christ (1 Nephi 19:10; Jacob 4:5; 3 Nephi 15:5).

16. Jesus Christ's premortal spirit looked like his mortal body (Ether 3:16).

17. The areas of the Savior's earthly ministry included more than Palestine. (3 Nephi 15:21; 16:1. See also John 10:16.)

18. The Book of Mormon teaches us more about baptism (2 Nephi 31:5-9; Mosiah 18:14).

19. Jesus Christ's Sermon on the Mount receives some clarifications in the Book of Mormon. (3 Nephi 12:3, 6. See also Matthew 5:3, 6.)

20. Jesus Christ has an eternal priesthood that can be shared with man (Alma 13:1-12, 18).

21. Christ is the source of continual revelation yesterday, today, and tomorrow (3 Nephi 29:6 ; Mormon 9:7-8).

22. The Book of Mormon prophesies that the Savior would restore his church in our day (2 Nephi 3:5; 27:1-35; Ether 5:1-6).

23. Jesus declared that his church must bear his name (3 Nephi 27:8).

24. The Messiah has not forgotten the Jews (3 Nephi 29:1-9).

25. The Book of Mormon is a modern witness that Jesus is the Christ (1 Nephi 19:10; 3 Nephi 11:10-11).

EVIDENCE NO. 587: ANCIENT AMERICAN TEMPLE RITES

Claim: The Book of Mormon claims that the early peoples of the Americas constructed temples as an important part of their religious activities (2 Nephi 5:16; Jacob 1:17; Mosiah 1:18; Helaman 10:8; 3 Nephi 11:1).

Evidence: In ancient American Kivas, sweat lodges, and pyramids of Mexico, certain rites and ceremonies were performed that were particularly sacred and esoteric. Though having evolved with differing details, the modern remants of ancient ceremonies provide links with the original ceremonies. Brinton wrote the following:

> The priests formed secret societies of different grades and illumination, only to be entered by those willing to undergo trying ordeals, whose secrets were not to be revealed under the severest penalties. The Algonquins had three such grades—the Waubino, the Meda and the Jossakeed, the last being the highest...All tribes appear to have been controlled by the secret societies (Daniel G. Brinton, *The Myths of the New World*, [Philadelphia: 1905], p. 285).

The following is a description of the Kiva construction and celebration from the Anasazi ruins in Aztec, New Mexico (Dr. Gregory A. Kajete, and Theresa Nichols, *A Trail Guide to Aztec Ruins*, [Southwest Parks and Monuments Association, 1994], p. 28):

> The people gathered to build a Great Kiva. In so doing they enacted the joining of the primal pairing of nature that bonded them as one people, male and female: Sky and Earth, sun and moon, winter and summer. The Great Kiva represented the First House created by The People upon their emergence from the Earth's Navel. The Great Kiva was a place where all the clans met to celebrate that First Story. The Great Kiva was the center of the Cosmos, where the six sacred directions symbolically came together, where The People reconnected with their spiritual and mythic origins and were nourished by the spiritual Center, the Earth's Navel.

The concept of building sacred temples was carried to the Pacific Islands as they were populated (at least in part) by the ancient Americans who sailed with Hagoth (Alma 63:5-8). One of the most well-known customs of the Polynesian peoples was to consecrate certain houses and parcels of lands as being too sacred for unworthy persons to touch. (See John Martin, *An Account of the Natives of the Tonga Islands*, [Boston: Charles Ewer, 1820], p. 393. See also T. Barrow, *Art and Life in Polynesia*, [Wellington, New Zealand: Reed, 1972], p. 47.)

It is easy to see a correlation between this custom and the belief in the sacredness of the temple. Just as with the ancient taboos (spelled tapu in some island groups), only those who have met certain requirements of worthiness are admitted into the temples.

EVIDENCE NO. 588: PURIFICATION CEREMONY OF THE ARAPHAHO

Claim: The Book of Mormon prophets instructed their people to cleanse themselves from evil and sin through repentance before attempting to work miracles (3 Nephi 8:1). In addition, since the Nephites were a temple-building people—whose temple was patterned after that of Solomon (2 Nephi 5:16)—it is implied that they also practiced the same purification ceremonies that were performed anciently in the temple (Acts 24:18; Ephesians 5:26; Hebrews 9:10). Latter-day Saints believe that the temple ordinances of *washing and anointing* as revealed in D&C 124:39, are the modern equivalent of the ancient Hebrew ceremonies.

Evidence: There is evidence to suggest that the Nephite temple ceremonies were handed down from one generation to the next, on down to the surviving descendants of Lehi. Hence the temples, towers and pyramids of the ancient Americans all hold clues to the nature of the original Nephite temple ceremonies. A remnant of the initiatory *washing and anointing* ceremony of the ancient temple may be found in the purification rites of the Arapaho Indians of the Great Plains (*Indians of the Plains*, [New York: American Publishing Co., 1960], p. 66):

> Before beginning ceremonies in which sacred objects were used...the Plains Indians often took part in a purification ritual...The steaming-sweating process was carried out a number of times. After the last sweating, the Indian would plunge into a nearby stream in summer, or into a snow bank in winter. Thus purified, he was ready to make an offering or seek a vision.

EVIDENCE NO. 589: AZTEC TEMPLE AND HOLY CITY

Claim: The Book of Mormon testifies that the Nephites were a temple-building people (2 Nephi 5:16; Jacob 2:11; Mosiah 11:112; 3 Nephi 11:1). It further speaks of *Zion* a holy city in which the pure in heart would dwell (1 Nephi 13:37; 22:14; 2 Nephi 8:3, 11; Mosiah 12:22). Inasmuch as the Book of Mormon professes to be a sacred history of the former inhabitants of the Americas, one would expect to find evidences of some of the important concepts such as the temple, and the holy city, among such indigenous peoples as the Aztecs.

Evidence: "The ceremonial centers, such as the holy city built at the heart of Mexico, Tenochtitlan, consisted mainly of temples (*teocalli*), pyramids, whose terminal platform supported the sanctuary proper" (*Encyclopedia Britannica*, [Chicago: William Benton, 1974], Macropedia, vol. 2, p. 551).

There can be little doubt that the pyramids symbolized a mountain. This man-made mountain reinforced the Old Testament concept that the temple was the "mountain of the Lord's house" (Isaiah 2:2-3).

Some critics have questioned the tendency of Latter-day Saints to link the Aztecs and their pagan ceremonies, which included human sacrifice, with the religious history of the Book of Mormon. But as seen in the following evidences, these apostate ceremonies clearly had their origin in pure and undefiled temple ordinances and gospel principles.

Evidences from Aztec Hieroglyphs of the Codex Borgia

To the Aztec people every aspect of life was dominated by their religion. Their works of art were acts of devotion that reflected the more sacred elements of their theology. (See James West Davidson and Michael B. Stoff, *The American Nation*, [Englewood Cliffs, New Jersey: Prentice Hall, 1995], p. 51.)

One of the few surviving codices of the Aztec peoples, *The Codex Borgia* (from Cholula, Puebla, Mexico), is just such a work of devotion. Written between 1350 and 1500 it predates the arrival of the Spanish conquistadors. A pictorial expression of Aztec beliefs, rites and ceremonies, this codex also seems to relate a story that progresses from one drawing to the next. The "reader" is lead from one story to the next by means of passageways drawn in the form of stylized vines, footprints, or entwined, undulating serpent motifs.

This codex is named after the Borgian Museum in Rome where it is housed. Copies of the facsimiles shown in this volume were taken from Lord Kingsborough's *Antiquities of Mexico*, (London: Robert Havell and Colnaghi Son and Co., 1831), vol. 3. Since each facsimile is very complex and detailed, the authors have simplified them by isolating certain portions for ease of reference and discussion.

Claim: The Church of Jesus Christ of Latter-day Saints teaches that part of the temple ceremony known as the *endowment* includes a review of the creation, the fall and the atonement. Elder James E. Talmage wrote the following in his work *The House of the Lord*, (1976), pp. 83-84:

> This course of instruction includes a recital of the most prominent events of the creative period, the condition of our first parents in the Garden of Eden, their disobedience and consequent expulsion from that blissful abode, their condition in the lone and dreary world when doomed to live by labor and sweat, the plan of redemption by which the great transgression may be atoned, the period of the great apostasy, the restoration of the Gospel with all its ancient powers and privileges, the absolute and indispensable condition of personal purity and devotion to the right in present life, and a strict compliance with Gospel requirements.

The Book of Mormon claims that the ancient Americans had detailed knowledge of the creation, the fall and the atonement of mankind (2 Nephi 9:5-10; Mosiah 3:19; 4:6-8; Alma 18:36; 22:13-14; 30:44; Mormon 9:12-13). It follows, therefore, that the ancient Americans also included a review of these central themes in their own temple ceremonies. Indeed, the following four evidences provided justification for this claim.

EVIDENCE NO. 590: A REVIEW OF THE CREATION

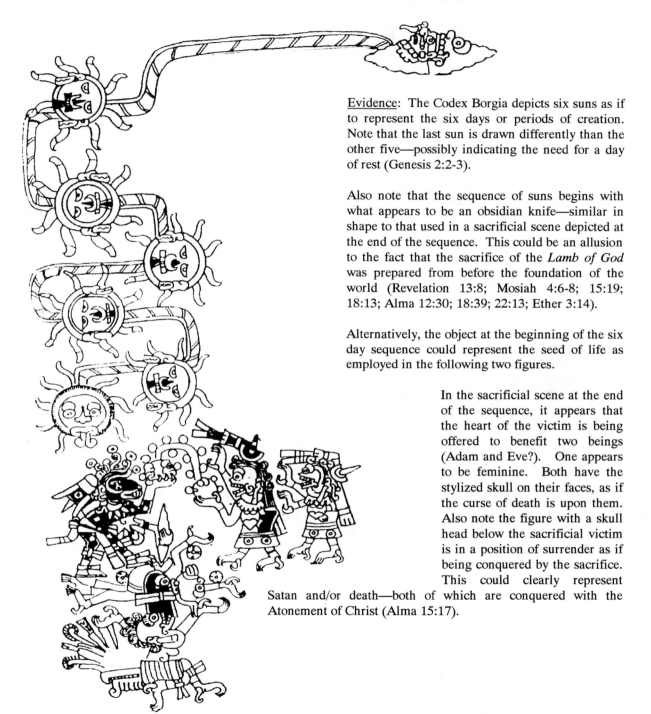

Evidence: The Codex Borgia depicts six suns as if to represent the six days or periods of creation. Note that the last sun is drawn differently than the other five—possibly indicating the need for a day of rest (Genesis 2:2-3).

Also note that the sequence of suns begins with what appears to be an obsidian knife—similar in shape to that used in a sacrificial scene depicted at the end of the sequence. This could be an allusion to the fact that the sacrifice of the *Lamb of God* was prepared from before the foundation of the world (Revelation 13:8; Mosiah 4:6-8; 15:19; 18:13; Alma 12:30; 18:39; 22:13; Ether 3:14).

Alternatively, the object at the beginning of the six day sequence could represent the seed of life as employed in the following two figures.

In the sacrificial scene at the end of the sequence, it appears that the heart of the victim is being offered to benefit two beings (Adam and Eve?). One appears to be feminine. Both have the stylized skull on their faces, as if the curse of death is upon them. Also note the figure with a skull head below the sacrificial victim is in a position of surrender as if being conquered by the sacrifice. This could clearly represent Satan and/or death—both of which are conquered with the Atonement of Christ (Alma 15:17).

Figure 2. Aztec hieroglyphs possibly representing the six days of creation

Note that the scene at left is "framed" with what appears to be seeds (or perhaps eggs)—symbols of new life. The frame could represent the confines of the garden of life where mankind symbolically emerged out of the seeds.

The central figure is two-headed (seeds) possibly representing dual parentage.

Figure 3. Aztec hieroglyphs possibly representing the creation of man and expulsion of Satan

In the same facsimile one being appears to be cast out below what appears to be the underworld—symbolized with skull head and inverted (lifeless) seeds. (All of the seeds that yield fruit [life] have eyes and a mouth—which gives a clear orientation for the seeds.)

EVIDENCE NO. 591: EXPULSION FROM THE GARDEN

Evidence: In another of the facsimiles of the Codex Borgia, (Figure 4) a serpent is perched in or on what appears to be a fruit tree. Standing before the tree is a couple—which very possibly represent Adam and Eve. Note that the person closest to the tree (Eve?) seems to be taking counsel from the serpent, while the other (Adam?) is seemingly resisting that same council.

The pathway that leads *away* from the tree is marked with footprints suggesting that these two individuals depart from the scene. Note that the facsimile does not show six individuals, rather it shows three stages of progress with the *same* couple (note the same facial designs and the same regalia on each of the three couples) as they progress down the path away from the tree. At the top of the path is a feathered being which possibly represents the angel of the Lord stationed to block the way to the Tree of Life (Genesis 3:24).

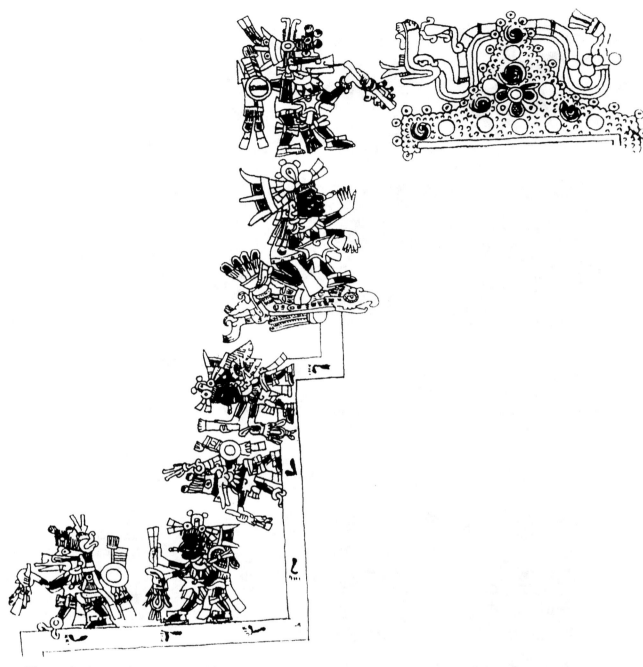

Figure 4. Aztec hieroglyph possibly representing the expulsion of Adam and Eve from the garden

EVIDENCE NO. 592: THE CRUCIFIXION

Evidence: Continuing the temple ceremony themes of the creation, the fall and the atonement, the *Codex Borgia* appears to illustrate the crucifixion of the Savior (Figure 5). Note that the instrument of death is an "X" rather than the traditional cross—prevalent among those of the Christian persuasion. This fact further substantiates that the *Codex Borgia* is properly dated as pre-Columbian, and was not influenced by the Spanish—who revered the cross as central to their Catholic faith.

Figure 5. Aztec hieroglyph of the crucifixion

Because of the high level of detail in this facsimile, it is difficult to discern the central figure stretched over the X-shaped (Saint Andrew's style) cross. However, close observation shows that each of the victims hands are attached to the upper arms of the "X" while the two feet are attached to the lower arms of the "X." Also note that the victim appears to be giving birth—symbolic of the life-giving nature of the Savior's sacrifice. Also apparent are the four deformed beings on each arm of the cross with drooping eyes and limp wrists—symbolic of the Savior's taking upon himself the infirmities of all mankind (Matthew 8:17; 2 Nephi 9:21; Alma 7:12-13).

Note the animals placed around the cross. The animals may represent the fact that the Savior's sacrifice was for the benefit of the whole earth—not just mankind (Genesis 9:9-12; Isaiah 14:5-8; Mark 16:15; Luke 19:40; Colossians 1:23; Revelation 5:12-13; 2 Nephi 24:5-8; Mosiah 27:30).

EVIDENCE NO. 593: THE SAVIOR'S WOUNDS PROVIDE LIFE

Figure 6. Hieroglyph of the Savior and His healing wounds

Evidence: The Bible states that the savior was "wounded for our transgressions" and that through his suffering "we are healed" (Isaiah 53:5). This truth was also taught to the ancient Americans (3 Nephi 11:14-15).

The Codex Borgia demonstrates that the Aztecs had a version of this concept in their beliefs. The central figure shown here is a highly stylized Savior with a circular body resembling the sun. This is consistent with the Old Testament imagery of Malachi: "…shall the Sun of righteousness arise with healing in his wings..." (Malachi 4:2), which concept was also known to the Nephites (3 Nephi 25:2). Noting that its arms and legs have been darkened for emphasis more easily identifies the personage.

Fresh wounds are being made in this Savior figure at both feet, the wrists, and in the side. Additional wounds are being made at the knees shoulder and head. At each wound is a sun, and several beings seem to be extracting sustenance from each. The aliment seems to take two forms—one solid (bread?), being held in one hand, while the other hand seems to be extracting a fluid (blood). This makes a clear allusion to the Sacrament in which the benefactors of the Lord's suffering are provided with the means of life and salvation.

Figure 7. Aztec hieroglyph of the Savior and His healing wounds

In a similar facsimile, the savior figure is again stylized with the sun as his torso. Again, he is providing life-giving sustenance as worshippers partake of what appears to be some form of liquid coming out of a basket of perhaps corn. In this case the wounds are stylized as small holes in the hands and feet. While in this figure the ailment does not come directly out of the wounds, the fact that the food surrounds the savior figure implies that he has supplied it. Also note that in both figures those who are partaking are in the attitude of worship or great respect (bent-knee). Below the sun-bodied savior appears to be a symbol of death—with a head in the form of a stylized skull. He is in the position of defeat, as if to symbolize the Savior's victory over death by means of His suffering (Isaiah 25:8; 1 Corinthians 15:53-57; Mosiah 15:7-9; 16:6-8; Alma 22:14).

EVIDENCE NO. 594: AZTEC INITIATORY ORDINANCES OF WASHINGS AND ANOINTINGS

Claim: Given the fact that the Book of Mormon claims that the Nephites built temples "after the manner of the temple of Solomon" (2 Nephi 5:16), some have questioned whether the ordinances performed in such temples were Mosaic or not. The Church of Jesus Christ of Latter-day Saints testifies that the higher ordinances of Latter-day temples are of ancient origin and that they were made available to the righteous peoples of the Book of Mormon lands and times. (See Joseph Fielding Smith Jr., *Doctrines of Salvation*, [Bookcraft, 1956], vol. 3, p. 93; see also, article on "Altar," in *Encyclopedia of Mormonism*, [1992], vol. 1.)

While Mosaic rituals were indeed performed in parts of Solomon's temple, the Bible makes mention of higher chambers where other ordinances were performed (1 Chronicles 28:11; 2 Chronicles 3:9; Jeremiah 36:10; Ezra 42:5).

In *The Doctrine and Covenants of the Church of Jesus Christ of Latter-day Saints* the Lord revealed that one of the reasons for His covenant people to build temples was to perform "washings" and "anointings" (D&C 124:39). Associated with these temple ordinances are sacred garments worn by faithful members of the Church. Latter-day Saints believe that Isaiah makes reference to this sacred clothing when he speaks of the Lord clothing him "with the garments of salvation" (Isaiah 61:10). See James R. Clark, *Messages of the First Presidency*, (Bookcraft, 1965), vol. 1, p.260.

Evidence: Similarly, one of the main purposes of the Aztec temple was to provide a place for "ritual baths" (*temazcalli*). See *Encyclopedia Britannica*, (Chicago: William Benton, 1974), *Macropedia*, vol. 2, p. 551.

The *Codex Borgia* demonstrates such a ritualistic bath in one of its facsimiles. Though highly stylized, this Aztec temple ceremony appears to be a *washing* and an *anointing* followed by a re-clothing in some kind of sacred garb.

Figure 8. Aztec hieroglyphs possibly representing the ordinances of washing, anointing and clothing

In the above figures note the difference in the fluids being poured over the emphasized figure. In the first stage the fluid appears to be *washing* away particles of dirt—symbolic of sin, evil and death. The stylized skulls may be symbolic of death. In the last figure, note the cloth being draped over the emphasized figures.

EVIDENCE NO. 595: AZTEC PRAYER CIRCLE AND VEIL

<u>Claim</u>: In connection with the claim that the ancient Americans built temples, is the corollary that in their temples they performed the same eternal ordinances that are performed in latter-day temples. Among these would be included the prayer circle and passage through the veil. (See James R. Clark, *Messages of the First Presidency*, [1975], vol. 6, p. 256; James E. Talmage, *The House of the Lord*, [1976], pp. 159-160.)

<u>Evidence</u>: One of the facsimiles in the *Codex Borgia* shows a circle of people with heads bowed and uplifted hands as if in the attitude of prayer or worship. In the center of the circle are two persons, both kneeling with upstretched arms—also in the attitude of worship or reverence to some superior being.

The footprints lead from the circle to some sort of a barrier that could quite possibly represent the veil of the temple. The footprints indicate a clear attempt to pass through the veil and make contact with the supernatural being just beyond the veil. The being obscured by the veil seems to be anticipating (with outstretched arms) the arrival of passengers from the other side.

Figure 9. Aztec prayer circle and veil

EVIDENCE NO. 596: PROTECTIVE SACRED GARMENTS

Claim: The Book of Mormon indicates that the ancient Americans built temples, for the purpose of worshipping the Lord God (2 Nephi 5:16). The Church of Jesus Christ of Latter-day Saints claims that one of the most important ceremonies practiced in temples involves the receipt of sacred garments that are to be worn throughout one's life. These garments represent the "coats of skins" that the Lord God made to clothe Adam and Eve after they partook of the forbidden fruit (Genesis 3:21). Faithful temple patrons are taught that by honoring the covenants associated with the garment they received in the temple, they will be protected against evil. (See Boyd K. Packer, *The Holy Temple*, [Bookcraft, 1980], pp. 76-78; Joseph Fielding Smith, "The Pearl of Great Price," *Utah Genealogical and Historical Magazine*, [July 1930], p. 103.)

While the Book of Mormon does not specifically mention these sacred garments, it is assumed that since it claims that the ancient Americans participated in temple worship, they also believed in the concept of the protective garments.

Evidence: The Arapaho Indians wore a shirt of *buckskin*, which they believed would protect them in battle. "The Sioux believed the designs [on the shirt] protected the wearer from the bullets of the white man" (*Indians of the Plains*, [New York: American Heritage Publishing Co., 1960], p. 137).

EVIDENCE NO. 597: THE SABBATH IN ANCIENT AMERICA

Claim: The Book of Mormon indicates that ancient Americans believed that all people should rest from their labors every seventh day, and consecrate that day unto the Lord. See Jarom 1:5, Mosiah 13:16; 18:23. This claim has now been verified by American Indian mythology.

Evidence: For documentary evidence that the ancient Americans kept one day in seven as a holy day, see Lewis Spence, *Myths and Legends: The North American Indians* (Boston: David P. Nickerson, 1932), p. 3, cited in Cheesman, *The World of the Book of Mormon*, (1978), p. 3.

EVIDENCE NO. 598: BAPTISM IN ANCIENT AMERICA

Claim: The Book of Mormon indicates that the ancient Americans practiced the religious ordinance of baptism (1 Nephi 10:9; 3 Nephi 11:23-26).

Evidence: When the Europeans first arrived in America they were surprised to discover the natives practicing the ordinance of ceremonial washings as a purification rite (baptism). These rites that were practiced by the Maya, Mexican and other ancient Americans, predate the conquest and were strikingly similar in form and meaning to that which was practiced by the Europeans. (See Hubert Howe Bancroft, *The Native Races of the Pacific States*, [San Francisco: 1883], vol. 3, p. 119; E. Seler, *Codexborgia II*, [Berlin, 1906], Codex, p. 31; Sahagun, *Anales de Cuauhtitlan*, [Codice Chimajpopoca, Imprenta Universitaria México, 1945], vol. 6, Chapters 32-37; Diego de Landa, *Relación de las Cosas de Yucatán*, translated by Alfred M. Tozzer, *Harvard University, Peabody Museum of American Archaeology and Ethnology Papers*, [Cambridge: Peabody Museum, 1941], vol. 18; Frans Blom, *Conquest of Yucatan*, 1936, p. 79; A. M. Tozzer's translation of Tomas Lopez Mendel's writings in 1612. Peter DeRoo, *History of America Before Columbus*, [1900], p. 467; Acosta, *Natural & Moral History of the Incas*, p. 369; Frey Bernardino de Sahagun, *Florentine Codex: General History of the things of New Spain*, translated by Charles E. Dibble and Arthur J. O. Anderson, [Santa Fe: The School of American Research, 1963], vol. 1, p. 8.)

Landa gives an account of the ancient American baptism rites as follows:

> Baptism is not found in any part of the Indies except in Yucatan*...a name which means "to be born anew or again," which is the same as *renascor* in the Latin language, for in the language of Yucatan *sihil* means "to be born anew or again," and it is only used in compound words, and so *caput sihil* means "to be born anew." ...We have not been able to find its origin, more than that **it is a custom that has always existed**, and for which they had so much devotion that no one failed to receive it; and so much reverence for the rite that those who had sins, if they were capable of knowing they had committed them, were obliged to make a special confession of them to the priest, in order to receive baptism, and they had such great faith in it that they never repeated it in any way. That which they thought they received by it was a preliminary disposition towards being good in their way of living and not to be injured in their temporal affairs by the evil spirits, and by this means and by a well-ordered life to attain glory. (Diego de Landa, *Relación de las Cosas de Yucatán*, translated by Alfred M. Tozzer, *Harvard University, Peabody Museum of American Archaeology and Ethnology Papers*, [Cambridge: Peabody Museum, 1941], vol. 18.)

The above is cited in Harris, (*The Book of Mormon Message and Evidences*, [1961], pp. 146-148), who also cites M. Wells Jakeman, *The Origins and History of the Mayas* [1945], p. 103.

Not only is this documentation proof that baptism was practiced in ancient America, but it also links the ancient Americans with the Pre-Christian Middle East. See A. Gardiner, "The Baptism of Pharaoh," *Journal of Egyptian Archaeology*, 1950, pp. 3-12, 36.

---

* This statement by Landa is in error as Landa does not appear to have known of the customs in Mexico where baptism was practiced as a purification by the invocation to the goddess Chalchiuhlicue. See Sahagun, *Anales de Cuauhtitlan*, (Codice Chimajpopoca, Imprenta Universitaria Mexico, 1945), vol. 6, p. xxxvii.

EVIDENCE NO. 599: INFANT BAPTISM CONDEMNED

<u>Claim</u>: The Book of Mormon teaches that baptism is for the remission of sins and since infants have no sin, neither are they capable of repentance—a prerequisite of baptism. The practice of baptizing children is contrary to the Gospel of Jesus Christ:

> The whole need no physician, but they that are sick; wherefore, little children are whole, for they are not capable of committing sin; wherefore the curse of Adam is taken from them in [Christ]...it is solemn mockery before God, that ye should baptize little children.

> Behold I say unto you that this thing shall ye teach—repentance and baptism unto those who are accountable and capable of committing sin; yea, teach *parents* that they must repent and be baptized, and humble themselves as their little children, and they shall be saved with their little children. And their little children need no repentance, neither baptism. Behold, baptism is unto repentance to the fulfilling the commandments unto the remission of sins.

> But little children are alive in Christ, even from the foundation of the world; if not so, God is a partial God, and also a changeable God, and a respecter to persons; for how many little children have died without baptism... Behold I say unto you, he that supposeth that little children need baptism is in the gall of bitterness and in the bonds of iniquity; for he hath neither faith, hope, nor charity; wherefore, should he be cut off while in the thought, he must go down to hell. For awful is the wickedness to suppose that God saveth one child because of baptism, and the other must perish because he hath no baptism. Wo be unto them that shall pervert the ways of the Lord after this manner, for they shall perish except they repent. ... He that saith that little children need baptism denieth the mercies of Christ, and setteth at naught the atonement of him and the power of his redemption. Wo unto such, for they are in danger of death, hell, and an endless torment" (Moroni 8:8-26).

Evidence: The notion that infants need baptism was one of the false beliefs of Christianity that alienated the nineteenth century philosopher Robert G. Ingersoll. He expressed his contempt for the doctrine in these words: "The churches teach that the little dimpled child in the cradle is simply a chunk of depravity." (Quoted from *The Works of Robert G. Ingersoll* [New York: The Ingersoll League, 1929], vol. 2, p. 371.)

The following Biblical scriptures clearly demonstrate that those who are accepted for baptism are capable of understanding, believing and repenting (emphasis added):

> But when he saw many of the Pharisees and Sadducees come to his baptism, he said unto them, O generation of vipers, who hath warned you to flee from the wrath to come? *Bring forth therefore fruits meet for repentance* (Matthew 3:7-8).

> John did baptize in the wilderness, and preach the *baptism of repentance* for the remission of sins. And there went out unto him...and were all baptized of him in the river Jordan, *confessing their sins* (Mark 1:4-5).

> He *that believeth* and is baptized shall be saved; but he that believeth not shall be damned (Mark 16:16).

> But when they believed Philip preaching the things concerning the kingdom of God, and the name of Jesus Christ, they were baptized, both men and women...And Philip said, *If thou believest with all thine heart*, thou mayest...And he answered and said, I believe that Jesus Christ is the Son of God (Acts 8:12, 37).

When the Bible speaks of little children, it shows them being blessed—never baptized:

> And they brought young children to him, that he should touch them: and his disciples rebuked those that brought them. But when Jesus saw it, he was much displeased, and said unto them, "Suffer the little children to come unto me, and forbid them not: for of such is the kingdom of God. Verily I say unto you, Whosoever shall not receive the kingdom of God as a little child, he shall not enter therein." And he took them up in his arms, put his hands upon them, and blessed them (Mark 10:13-16; also Matthew 19:13-15; Luke 18:15-17).

> Whosoever therefore shall humble himself as this little child, the same is greatest in the kingdom of heaven...Take heed that ye despise not one of these little ones; for I say unto you, that in heaven their angels do always behold the face of my Father which is in heaven (Matthew 18:4, 10). See also Matthew 28:19-20; Acts 10:34-35, 43, 48; 16:32-34; Luke 3:7; and Acts 2:38-40.

EVIDENCE NO. 600: BIBLE SCHOLARS OPPOSING INFANT BAPTISM

Claim: Bible scholars agree that the practice of infant baptism was not approved in the early church.

Evidence: "Tertullian appears as a zealous opponent of infant baptism, a proof that the practice had not yet come to be regarded as an apostolic institution, for otherwise he would hardly have ventured to express himself so strongly against it." Says Tertullian: "What haste, to procure the forgiveness of sins from the age of innocence? ...Let them first learn to feel their need of salvation; so it may appear that we have given to those that wanted." (Augustus Neander, *General History of the Christian Religion and Church*, vol. 1, p. 312.)

Giesler says: "The baptism of children was not universal, and was even occasionally disapproved." Lange says: "All attempts to make out infant baptism from the New Testament fail. It is totally opposed to the spirit of the apostolic age, and to the fundamental principles of the New Testament." (See Giesler, *Church History*, volume 2, chapter 3, p. 53; and Lange, *Infant Baptism*, p. 101.)

Lindner says: "For whom is baptism appointed? For adults; not for children: for adults at all times—not only of those times. There can be no question about any infant baptism if the Christian Church will remain true to the Gospel. Neither the baptism of John nor Christian baptism can be fulfilled in respect of newborn children." (See Lindner, *Lord's Supper*, p. 275.)

EVIDENCE NO. 601: UNINTENTIONAL SIN

Claim: In King Benjamin's farewell address, he taught that the blood of Christ atones not only for the fall of Adam, but for the sins of those "who have died not knowing the will of God concerning them, or who have ignorantly sinned" (Mosiah 3:11). Modern, Western thought does not consider the possibility of an unintentional breach of the law. Indeed, Western law makes no concession for *ignorance of the law*. Yet, the Book of Mormon professes to be a true and authentic record of peoples who migrated from Palestine. New research has shown that the Book of Mormon peoples shared this concept (of partial innocence due to ignorance) with their ancient ancestors of the Middle East.

Evidence: Those who have made light of the Book of Mormon for teaching this concept of unintentional sin, are themselves guilty of the very sin they criticize. They are unintentionally criticizing the Bible, since the Bible teaches this same concept (Numbers 15:27-29; 19:14; 2 Samuel 6:6-7). Jacob Milgrom has shown that the Old Testament Culture included the concept that inadvertence is a "key criterion in all expiatory sacrifice" (Jacob Milgrom, *Leviticus 1-16*, [New York: Doubleday, 1991], p. 228).

Furthermore, the *Dead Sea Scrolls* state that a small fine should punish "a single inadvertent sin," while a repeated error was apparently not tolerated. (See 1Qs 9:1-2; cited in Gary A. Anderson, "Intentional and Unintentional Sin in The Dead Sea Scrolls," *Pomegranates and Golden Bells*, edited by D. Wright, D. Freedman and A. Hurvitz [Winona Lake: Eisenbrauns, 1995], p. 55.)

Both of the above sources are cited in "Unintentional Sin In Benjamin's Discourse," *Foundation for Ancient Research and Mormon Studies Update*, April 1996, p. 2.

EVIDENCE NO. 602: CHILDREN OF GOD

Claim: The Book of Mormon repeatedly refers to the righteous inhabitants of ancient America as "the children of God" (2 Nephi 6:12; Mosiah 5:7-8; 18:18-26; Alma 6:6; 13:1; 30:42; 3 Nephi 12:9; 4 Nephi 1:17, 39). The Bible goes even farther by referring to man as the *offspring* of God (Acts 17:28-29). Evidence has recently been uncovered that some of the ancient inhabitants of the Americas did indeed consider themselves "Children of God." This provides further support for the truthfulness of the Book of Mormon.

Evidence: In ancient Central America there is a region known as *Tamoanchan*, which some Mormon scholars believe to be the site of the land of Bountiful. *Tamoanchan* is translated by Sahagun to mean "land-of-the-lineage-of-heaven." See Edward Seler cited in an article entitled "Tamoanchan," by Paul Henning, Francisco Plancarte, Cecilio A. Robelo, and Paul Gonzalez in the *Anales del Museo Nacional de Arqueologia*, (Mexico), vol. 4, pp. 433-462 cited in Hunter and Ferguson, *Ancient America and the Book of Mormon* (1950), p. 155.

EVIDENCE NO. 603: MOSES ASCENDS TO HEAVEN

Claim: Critics have noted a contradiction between Deuteronomy 34:5-7 and Alma 45:19 concerning the end of Moses' mortal existence. The Bible records that he died and was buried. The Book of Mormon account that records his ascension into heaven is supported by historical legend.

Evidence: Moses' ascension into heaven was universally known in ancient times. See Mowinckel, *He That Cometh* (Abingdon, 1954), p. 300; Josephus, *Antiquities of the Jews,* English translation by William Whiston, (Kregel Publishing: Grand Rapids, Michigan, 1981), book 4, ch. 8, p. 103; and Spencer J. Palmer, *Deity and Death* (Provo, Utah: Religious Studies Center, Brigham Young University, 1978), p. 84.

Also the ascension of Moses is consistent with his appearing to Christ on the Mount of Transfiguration with Elijah, another prophet who ascended to heaven without tasting of death (2 Kings 2; Matthew 17:2-3).

EVIDENCE NO. 604: SATAN IN ANCIENT AMERICAN BELIEFS

Claim: Another evidence for the authenticity of the Book of Mormon is the fact that the equivalent of the Biblical Satan is found therein (1 Nephi 12:17-19; 22:15; 2 Nephi 2:17-19) as well as in Mesoamerican belief.

Evidence: The following is quoted from a response by Dee F. Green entitled "A Counterpart of Satan in the Mesoamerican Pantheon" (*University Archeological Society Newsletter* 60:50), also cited in Christensen, *Progress in Archaeology* (1963), pp. 115-116:

A Question for the Editor. Sir: Recently we have heard a great deal about comparisons of Quetzalcoatl with the Savior. Does Satan have any counterpart in the mythology of ancient Mesoamerica and if so, what is his relationship to Quetzalcoatl? — B.G.

Answer. Quetzalcoatl, the bearded Fair God of the Toltecs, has for several years been investigated with the possibility that he might be identified with the Savior and the Book of Mormon account of his visit to this continent. Many interesting and curious facts seem to support this conclusion, and scholars and others in the LDS Church agree that the characteristics of the two are so similar that there must be some connection.

Your inquiry as to Satan is extremely interesting, especially since there appears to be such a character in ancient Toltec-Aztec mythology.

Among the pantheon of gods credited to the Toltecs is found one called Tezcatlipoca. He was the god of war, pestilence, darkness, and the underworld. Numerous references by early native and Spanish authors such as Ixtlilxóchitl, Sahagun, and Torquemada describe him as ferocious, wicked, and the author of wars and destruction among the people. One of his titles was " Sower of Discord."

Originally, he was the twin brother of Quetzalcoatl, but opposes him in all things. They are eternal enemies, and several interesting legends are told about the history of their feud.

An early account says that "...one day Quetzalcoatl hit him on the head with a club and Tezcatlipoca was knocked down from his throne up in the sky. As he fell down to the earth, he was transformed into a vicious jaguar that haunted the world, devouring people, nearly wiping out an entire generation..." Later, Quetzalcoatl was defeated and killed in battle by Tezcatlipoca. Quetzalcoatl, however, regained his life and then taught the Toltecs their religion, art, and culture.

Sometime thereafter, a great religious war occurred in which Tezcatlipoca defeated the Toltec followers of the god Quetzalcoatl. It is said that Tezcatlipoca used magic and tricks to defeat and kill them and that he will reign on the earth until the return of Quetzalcoatl.

The resemblances of both these gods to Christian concepts of Christ and Satan are curious indeed.

3. Book of Mormon Prophecies

Many things that have transpired in the history of the world since the Book of Mormon was first published were prophesied within the pages of that sacred volume. Other prophecies of the Book of Mormon itself were recorded in the Bible. These prophecies stand as solid evidence that the Book of Mormon is true, that ancient prophets transcribed its pages under the direction of God.

EVIDENCE NO. 605: THE BOOK OF MORMON DESCRIBED BY ISAIAH

Claim: The Book of Mormon stands as the only possible fulfillment of the prophecy of a sealed sacred book that will open the eyes of the blind.

Evidence: Isaiah prophesied that "In that day shall the deaf hear the words of the book and the eyes of the blind shall see out of obscurity, and out of darkness" (Isaiah 29:18). Most non-LDS Bible students have been at a loss to identify the book spoken of in this Isaiah passage. Obviously, it is not the Bible, which would have been described as "this" book. Also, the Bible has not been "sealed" as was the book described in verses 11-12 of the same chapter. The phrase "In that day" refers to a specific time period, when the Lord promised to "do a marvelous work among this people" (Isaiah 29:14).

Isaiah also described the reaction of closed-minded scholars towards the coming forth of the Book of Mormon: "And the vision of all is become unto you as the words of a book that is sealed, which men deliver to one that is learned, saying, Read this, I pray thee: and he saith, I cannot; for it is sealed" (Isaiah 29:11).

Martin Harris, who sought scientific verification of the truthfulness of the Book of Mormon before mortgaging his farm, wrote the following after his interview with Professor Anthon.

> I went to the city of New York, and presented the characters which had been translated, with the translation thereof, to Professor Charles Anthon, a gentleman celebrated for his literary attainments. Professor Anthon stated that the translation was correct, more so than any he had before seen

translated from the Egyptian. I then showed him those, which were not yet translated, and he said that they were Egyptian, Chaldaic, Assyriac, and Arabic; and he said they were true characters. He gave me a certificate, certifying to the people of Palmyra that they were true characters, and that the translation of such of them as had been translated were also correct. I took the certificate and put it into my pocket, and was just leaving the house, when Mr. Anthon called me back, and asked me how the young man found out that there were gold plates in the place where he found them. I answered that an angel of God had revealed it unto him.

He then said to me, "Let me see that certificate." I accordingly took it out of my pocket and gave it to him, when he took it and tore it to pieces, saying that there was no such thing now as ministering of angels, and that if I would bring the plates to him he would translate them. I informed him that part of the plates were sealed, and that I was forbidden to bring them. He replied, "I cannot read a sealed book." I left him and went to Dr. Mitchell, who sanctioned what Professor Anthon had said respecting both the characters and the translation (Joseph Smith—History 1:64-65).

Following this interview, Harris confidently mortgaged his farm, knowing that Anthon had testified to the truthfulness of the characters from which the Book of Mormon was translated.

Some have expressed doubt as to whether Professor Anthon ever really affirmed that the characters were authentic. They suggest that Harris, in his enthusiasm to prove Mormonism true, might have fabricated some extra dialogue to gain the approval of the more intellectual community. However, Professor Anthon, in his letter to E. D. Howe, admitted that Harris's sole purpose for the visit was to secure verification of the characters before selling his farm to pay for the printing of the Book of Mormon. (See Roger S. Gunn, *Mormonism: Challenge and Defense* [1973], pp. 280-284.)

In spite of the fact that Anthon destroyed the paper on which he had certified the authenticity of the characters, Harris walked away with absolute assurance that the characters were authentic and promptly mortgaged his farm for the printing of the Book of Mormon. Obviously, Harris could understand Anthon's fear of damaging his reputation by supporting such a controversial movement—once he discovered Harris was associated with the young prophet Joseph Smith and that angels were involved in obtaining the plates. The important thing was that he knew that Professor Anthon believed the characters to be authentic.

Truly, the Book of Mormon is the only scripture that fits Isaiah's description of a future sacred book.

EVIDENCE NO. 606: JACOB PROPHESIED OF JOSEPH'S DESCENDANTS IN AMERICA

Claim: The Bible prophecies that descendants of Joseph would come to the Americas. The record of fulfillment of this prophecy is the Book of Mormon.

Evidence: The Bible contains an interesting prophecy about Joseph who was sold into Egypt:

And of Joseph he said, *Blessed of the Lord be his land*, for the precious things of heaven, for the dew, and for the deep that coucheth beneath, And for the precious fruits brought forth by the sun, and for the precious things put forth by the moon, And for the chief things of the ancient mountains, and for the precious things of the lasting hills, And for the precious things of the earth and fulness thereof, and for the good will of him that dwelt in the bush: let the blessing come upon the head of Joseph, and upon the top of the head of him that was separated from his brethren.

His glory is like the firstling of his bullock, and his horns are like the horns of unicorns: with them he shall push the people together to the ends of the earth: *and they are the ten thousands of Ephraim, and they are the thousands of Manasseh*. (Deuteronomy 33:13-17. Emphasis added.)

Concerning this scripture, Elder LeGrand Richards wrote the following:

> When this blessing was given by Moses, the patriarch, it is clear that he first had in mind the new land that would be given to Joseph which would be abundantly blessed of the Lord to produce precious fruits of the land and the precious things of the lasting hills and of the ancient mountains.
>
> When the descendants of Joseph were led to this land of America about 600 BC, they were told that it would be a land choice above all other lands. The reading of Moses' blessing to Joseph indicates that Moses was impressed with this fact and attempted to so describe it. He further indicated that it would be in the "ancient mountains" and the "everlasting hills." The land to which they were led was in the western part of South, Central, and North America, in the Rocky Mountains, which accurately answers Moses' description.
>
> Then Moses further indicated that the good will of him who dwelt in the bush (referring to the God of Israel who dwelt in the burning bush—see Exodus 3:2) would be upon Joseph who was separated from his brethren. Then he refers to his glory as like "the firstling of his Bullock," or the firstborn or heir of his father, and we have already pointed out how Joseph became heir to the birthright. Moses looked beyond to the power and authority that should be given to Joseph's seed and added: "he shall push the people together to the ends of the earth: and they are the ten thousands of Ephraim, and they are the thousands of Manasseh." (See Deuteronomy 33:17.) This seems to look forward to the establishment of the kingdom of God in the earth in the latter-days, which we have previously outlined, and the gathering of Israel. (Richards, *A Marvelous Work and a Wonder* [1950], pp. 64-66.)

Isaac's son Jacob called his children to him and blessed them just prior to his death: "And Jacob called unto his sons, and said, Gather yourselves together, that I may tell you that which shall befall you *in the last days.* Gather yourselves together, and hear, ye sons of Jacob: and hearken unto Israel your father" (Genesis 49:1-2).

Of these verses, Elder Richards commented:

> It is suggested the reader study the entire chapter noting the great difference in the respective blessings. Now let us give careful consideration to the special blessing Joseph received from his father:
>
>> Joseph is a fruitful bough, even a fruitful bough by a well; whose branches run over the wall: The archers have sorely grieved him, and shot at him, and hated him: But his bow abode in strength, and the arms of his hands were made strong by the hands of the mighty God of Jacob; (from thence is the shepherd, the stone of Israel:) Even by the God of thy father, who shall help thee; and by the Almighty, who shall bless thee with blessings of heaven above, blessings of the deep that lieth under, blessings of the breasts, and of the womb; The blessings of thy father have prevailed above the blessings of my progenitors unto the utmost bound of the everlasting hills: they shall be on the head of Joseph, and on the crown of the head of him that was separate from his brethren (Genesis 49:22-26).
>
> This blessing is very similar to that given by Moses, and begins with reference to the land to which Joseph's seed would go: "A fruitful bough by a well; whose branches run over the wall." It seems consistent to assume that the ocean was regarded as the wall over which Joseph's branches were to run "unto the utmost bound of the everlasting hills." Then Jacob indicated that Joseph would be blessed "with the blessings of heaven above … blessings of the breasts, and of the womb," indicating that his posterity would be great, and that his blessings would prevail above the blessings of his progenitors. (Richards, *A Marvelous Work*, pp. 64-66.)

EVIDENCE NO. 607: JERUSALEM TO BE DESTROYED

Evidence: Lehi prophesied a total destruction of Jerusalem. He said that the destruction and scattering would be so extensive, that the refugees would cover "all the face of the earth" (1 Nephi 1:13,18; 22:3-4). Some Bible scholars have assumed that the destruction was only a superficial one and that only the more important citizens were taken to Babylon.

Evidence: Only recently have modern archaeologists begun to find evidence of the full extent of the devastation: "all, or virtually all, of the fortified towns in Judah [were] razed to the ground." (See W. F. Albright, "A Brief History of Judah from the Days of Josiah to Alexander the Great," *The Biblical Archaeologist*, vol. 9 [1946], p. 6. Cited in Nibley, *An Approach to the Book of Mormon* [1988], p. 105.)

EVIDENCE NO. 608: CIVILIZATIONS TO BE SWEPT OFF THE LAND

Claim: Evidence has been found which proves the fulfillment of Book of Mormon prophecies that the Jaredite and Nephite peoples would be swept off the land if they did not serve the true and only God. For example: "whoso should possess this land ... should serve him, the true and only God, or they should be swept off... And it is not until the fulness of iniquity among the children of the land that they are swept off" (Ether 2:8-10).

Evidence: The following is quoted Hugh W. Nibley, *Teachings of the Book of Mormon*—Semester 1: Transcripts of 29 Lectures Presented to an Honors Book of Mormon Class at Brigham Young University, 1988-1990. "Introduction and 1 Nephi 1–Mosiah 5." (Provo, Utah: FARMS, 1993) also found in "The Book of Mormon and the Ruins; the Main Issues," (N-BMA, Nibley Archive, *Foundation for Ancient Research and Mormon Studies*, University Station, Provo, Utah, July 13, 1980), p. 6:

> People often ask, "Where are the great heaps of evidence that would confirm the Book of Mormon?" As William A. Bullard says here in Culbert's book, "The old Classic culture with its social controls was completely sundered and swept away [that's a favorite expression in the Book of Mormon: they shall be swept away as soon as they're ripe in iniquity—they shall be swept from the face of the land]. The Post-Classic is a new chapter, if not indeed a new book....The fabulous cities of the Puuc were totally and finally abandoned.... . Not only the Maya country but the Atlantic Coast, Oaxaca, and the Central Highlands of Mexico were all deserted at once." (See Laurette Sejourne, *Burning Water— Thought and Religion in Ancient Mexico*, p. 179; and T. B. Culbert, *The Classic Maya Collapse*, [University of New Mexico, 1973], p. 240.)

EVIDENCE NO. 609: COLUMBUS TO BE LED BY THE SPIRIT

Claim: The Book of Mormon prophet Nephi stated that Columbus "a man among the gentiles," would be led by the Spirit of God which would come "down and wrought upon the man; and he [would go] forth upon the many waters, even unto the seed of my brethren, who were in the promised land [America]" (1 Nephi 13:12).

Evidence: Dr. W. Cleon Skousen wrote the following regarding what is being discovered about Columbus: "It is only recently that the broad spectrum of this man's biography has begun to be more fully appreciated. A number of things taught concerning Columbus have turned out to be pure myths, whereas the true history of the man is turning out to be a literal and rather amazing fulfillment of everything the scriptures said concerning him." (Skousen, *Treasures from the Book of Mormon*, vol. 1, p. 1103).

For example when Columbus wrote to king Ferdinand of Spain concerning his great discovery, he wrote, "I came to your Majesty as the Emissary of the Holy Ghost." On another occasion Columbus wrote: "The Lord was well disposed to my desire, and he bestowed upon me courage and understanding ... Our Lord with provident hand unlocked my mind, sent me upon the sea, and gave me fire for the deed. Those who heard of my enterprise called it foolish, mocked me, and laughed. But who can doubt but that the Holy Ghost inspired me?" (Jacob Wasserman, *Don Quixote of the Seas*, [Boston: Little, Brown, and Co., 1930], pp. 18, 46).

One of the foremost authorities on Columbus, Samuel Eliot Morison of Harvard University wrote the following:

> For he was not, like a Washington, a Cromwell or a Bolivar, an instrument chosen by multitudes to express their wills and lead a cause; Columbus was a Man with a Mission... He was a man alone with God against human stupidity and depravity, against greedy conquistadors, cowardly seamen, even against nature and the sea, always with God though, in that his biographers were right; for God is with men who for a good cause put their trust in him.

> Men may doubt this, but there can be no doubt that the faith of Columbus was genuine and sincere, and that his frequent communion with forces unseen was a vital element in his achievement. It gave him confidence in his destiny, assurance that his performance would be equal to the promise of his name. This conviction that God destined him to be an instrument for spreading the faith was far more potent than the desire to win glory, wealth, and worldly honors, to which he was certainly far from indifferent. (Samuel Eliot Morison, *Admiral of the Ocean Sea*, [Boston, 1942], pp. 46-47.)

"When Columbus wrote his report concerning the settlement of the New World he expressed the hope that none but devout Christians would be used as settlers, 'since this was the end and the beginning of the enterprise, that it should be for the enhancement and glory of the Christian religion, nor should anyone who is not a good Christian come to these parts.'" (Dr. Samuel E. Morison, *Admiral of the Ocean Sea*, [Little, Brown & Co: Boston, 1942], p. 279; cited in Skousen, *Treasures from the Book of Mormon*, vol. 1, pp. 1103-1104; 1115-1116. See also Bjorn Landstrom, *Columbus*, p. 38; and Arnold K. Garr, *Christopher Columbus: A Latter-day Saint Perspective*, Religious Studies Center Specialized Monograph Series, vol. 8. [Provo, UT: Religious Studies Center, Brigham Young University, 1992]; Salvador de Madariaga, *Christopher Columbus* [London: Hollis and Carter, 1949], p. 16. Pauline Moffitt Watts, "Prophecy and Discovery: On the Spiritual Origins of Christopher Columbus's 'Enterprise of the Indies,'" *American Historical Review* [February 1985], pp. 73-102; Bartolome de las Casas, *História de las Indias* [Mexico City: Fondo de Cultura Economica, 1951], pp. 27-34; George E. Nunn, *The Geographical Conceptions of Columbus*, [New York: American Geographical Society, 1924]; Nibley, "Columbus and Revelation," *The Prophetic Book of Mormon*, [1989], pp. 49-53.)

EVIDENCE NO. 610: LAND TAKEN FROM THE NATIVE AMERICANS

Claim: The Book of Mormon prophesied that "other nations ... will take away from them [the Native Americans] the lands of their possessions" (2 Nephi 1:11). See also 1 Nephi 12:21.

Evidence: Anyone with even a superficial knowledge of American history can see that the Native Americans were cheated out of their lands by broken promises and unkept treaties. The greater part of this land-grabbing occurred after the publication of the Book of Mormon when the West was being settled at a feverish pace. Since that time the natives have been driven from their homelands to be resettled on reservations. Even today contentions arise over questions of Indian lands.

EVIDENCE NO. 611: THE LAMANITES NOT TO BE UTTERLY DESTROYED

Claim: The Book of Mormon states that, though the Lamanites (Native Americans) will suffer great persecution, the Lord would preserve them, and not allow them to be utterly destroyed (2 Nephi 13:30-31).

Evidence: At the time the Book of Mormon was first printed, the universal notion was that the Indians were a perishing race and would soon become extinct. Indeed, whole tribes quickly died off due to exposure to diseases carried by the white people who immigrated into their lands. Liquor had been introduced to the natives, and they seemed to have a weakness for its addictive power—losing the incentive to do the necessary work for survival. Other tribes had been scattered, driven and killed off in the name of government expansion. Many people had been publicly calling for the extermination of the "animal-like savages." For example James M. Cavanaugh, (delegate to Congress from the territory of Montana), declared before the House of Representatives,

"I have never in my life seen a good Indian (and I have seen thousands) except when I have seen a dead Indian." Others, such as General William T. Sherman, were saying, "The more [Natives] we can kill this year, the less will have to be killed [in] the next war! They all have to be killed or maintained as a species of paupers." Colonel John M. Chivington: "I am fully satisfied, that to kill the red rebels is the only way to have peace and quiet." And finally, George Armstrong Custer: "We see him [the Native American] as he is, a `savage' in every sense of the word … one whose cruel and ferocious nature far exceeds that of any wild beast of the desert." (See *The Indians*, edited by Benjamin Capps, [New York: Time-Life Books, 1973], pp. 192, 217.)

Nevertheless, the Lamanites have survived inspite of the schemes of the gentiles who wanted to annihilate them.

EVIDENCE NO. 612: THE GENTILES TO ASSIST THE LAMANITES

Claim: Speaking of the Lamanites, the Book of Mormon states that: "after our seed is scattered the Lord God will proceed to do a marvelous work among the Gentiles, which shall be of great worth unto our seed; wherefore, it is likened unto their being nourished by the Gentiles and being carried in their arms and upon their shoulders" (1 Nephi 22:8).

Evidence: Even more remarkable than the Lamanites surviving the oppression of the gentiles, is the ironic "twist of fate" that would find the gentiles giving them aid and assistance. For example, the *Snyder Act* of 1921 defined the duties of the *Bureau of Indian Affairs* that included Native American opportunities for education, employment and medical benefits. This was followed by the *Johnson-O'Malley Act* of 1934 which dictated improvements in the federal and state education, health care, welfare and agricultural programs for the Indians.

Beginning in 1952, the *Relocation Services* program committed itself to assisting thousands of Indians move from reservations to urban centers. Renamed *The Employment Assistance Program* in 1962, this agency has aided many Indians in finding housing, employment and vocational training.

In the 1960's, the *Bureau of Indian Affairs* began to work with the *Department of Housing and Urban Development* to bring low-rent housing to the reservations. *The Department of Health, Education, and Welfare* has continually worked to improve the living conditions of the Native Americans. (See *World Book Encyclopedia*, [Chicago, 1992], vol. 10, p. 182.)

EVIDENCE NO. 613: EZEKIEL AND JOHN ON THE REMNANTS OF ISRAEL

Claim: The Church of Jesus Christ of Latter-day Saints teaches that Ezekiel's prophecy on *the stick of Joseph* (Ezekiel 37:15-22), and Jesus' prophecy of the *other sheep* (John 10:16) both apply to the people of the Book of Mormon.

Evidence: According to non-Mormon scholar Aileen Guilding, Ezekiel's prophecy of the stick of Joseph was the *background* of Jesus' prophecy concerning his "other sheep." This evidence strengthens the claim of the Church of Jesus Christ of Latter-day Saints that the *other sheep* were not gentiles, but remnants of the House of Israel living in the New World. (See Aileen Guilding, *Jewish Worship and the Fourth Gospel: A study of the Relation of Saint John's Gospel to the Ancient Jewish Lectionary System,* [Oxford: Clarendon, 1960], p. 6, cited in John Fowles, "The Jewish Lectionary and the Book of Mormon Prophecy," *Journal of Book of Mormon Studies,* vol. 3, no. 2, [Fall, 1994], p. 119.)

Guilding reached her conclusions by finding that John recorded the *time* of year of Jesus' prophecy. According to John, it was during the *Feast of Dedication* and that it was winter (John 10:22). This annual Jewish festival, sometimes called Hanukkah, was commenced in the month of *Kislev*, which correlates with December. Another name for this feast is the *Dedication of the Altar*, which is closely related to Solomon's consecration of the temple and the *Feast of the Tabernacles* mentioned in the apocryphal book 2 Maccabees 1:9, 18.

The significance of the time of year for the feast, is that the Jews of the New Testament followed an ancient schedule of reading specific passages of the law on the specified Sabbaths throughout the year. (See Acts 15:21.)

According to Guilding's reconstruction of the reading schedule, the section of the Pentateuch that was read during the *Feast of Dedication* was Genesis 46:28 through 47:31, which prophesied of the reuniting of Judah and Joseph. Along with this was read Ezekiel 37:15-28, which symbolically deals with the reunification of the divided house of Israel by bringing forth the *records* of each kingdom and uniting them together.

EVIDENCE NO. 614: THE AMERICAN INDIANS TO KNOW THEY ARE OF ISRAEL

Claim: The Book of Mormon boldly prophesied that the Indians shall: "know that they are of the house of Israel, and that they are the covenant people of the Lord; and then shall they know and come to the knowledge of their forefathers, and also to the knowledge of the gospel of their Redeemer … and the very points of his doctrine, that they may know how to come unto him and be saved" (1 Nephi 15:14; Alma 9:17).

Evidence: One might say that such a prophecy could be easily fulfilled simply by sending out missionaries to the Indians and teaching them whatever was predicted that they should learn. However, a false prophet, exposed to the popular notions about the "stubborn, wild savages," would have cautiously predicted that the gospel would only be *offered*, but not necessarily accepted. But, to say they would *accept* the message, that they would actually *listen*, and especially that they would *understand*, is too remarkable to have been a prediction of man—only God could foresee such a tremendous acceptance of the gospel among the Indians.

From the early days of the church, the Indians have embraced the gospel in large numbers. For example in 1869, one single missionary (William Lee) sent to the Indians in the western part of Tooele County, Utah, was instrumental in bringing one thousand Lamanite converts into the church. See Milton R. Hunter, *Brigham Young the Colonizer* (Independence: Zion's Printing & Pub. Co., 1945), pp. 292-297.

President Spencer W. Kimball summarized the Indian enthusiasm for the gospel during the mid-1870's:

> There was a period back in 1875-1876 when there were great numbers of Indians who came into the Church. There was Chief Poko-Tel-Lo from the Snake River, who with his entire band, was baptized into the Church…There were fifty from the north who came down. Chief Alma with twenty-two of his people from the Salmon River country came down and were baptized into the Church…Orson Pratt baptized fifty-two and blessed nine papooses down at Mount Pleasant in June of that year. In July there were eighty-five of Kanosh's band who were baptized in the Church, and the following year there were forty-one men and thirty-nine women, Indians, baptized down in Kanab. It seems that there were a great many baptisms also up in the Malad country (*Conference Report*, Oct. 1947, p. 17).

This and the Hunter source are also cited in Ross Warner, *Book of Mormon Prophecies* (1975), pp. 128-129.

Today, natives of North and South America are joining the Church in record numbers. (See Figure 2, Chapter 1, vol. 1 of this same work to see the dramatic increase in church membership among Latin Americans.)

EVIDENCE NO. 615: TRUTH TO COME OUT OF THE EARTH

Claim: The Prophet Joseph Smith testified that he had taken the plates, from which he translated the Book of Mormon, from a burial place on the Hill Cumorah (Joseph Smith History 1:51-54, 59-60). This claim is consistent with Bible prophecy.

Evidence: The Bible speaks of truth coming forth out of the earth (see Psalms 85:11; Isaiah 29:4). Other churches have made no attempt to interpret these passages—except to insist that the Latter-day Saint interpretation is incorrect. Some scholars have stated that "speech out of the dust" (Isaiah 29:4) is an image of a defeated nation which has been "brought down." This, of course, is in accord with the Latter-day Saint interpretation. The defeated Nephite nation, which had originally left Jerusalem, was indeed "brought down, *as* Ariel" was (Isaiah 29:2) when Jerusalem was destroyed. And, of course, the record of the defeated civilization symbolically spoke "out of the ground" (Isaiah 29:4), when Joseph unearthed the plates from the Hill Cumorah.

EVIDENCE NO. 616: HAWAIIAN PROPHECY OF THE "SQUARE BOX"

Claim: According to the legendary Hawaiiloa, the "true religion" would someday come to Hawaii in the form of a "square box." In 1819, the great King Kamehameha outlawed idolatry and virtually made the Hawaiian natives a people without a religion in preparation for events of which not even the king was aware. With the coming of the first Christian missionaries in 1820 followed by the publication of the Holy Bible in Hawaiian in 1839, some Hawaiians were convinced that the Bible was the "square box" to which the ancient seer referred. In actuality, the "square box" relates to the Book of Mormon.

Evidence: With the arrival of ten Latter-day Saint missionaries in Honolulu, December 12, 1850, the fulfillment of the "square box" prophecy took on deeper significance as the natives learned of gold plates delivered from a stone box to Joseph Smith at the hands of an angel. In 1906, Elder Abraham Fernandez baptized Queen Liliuokalani of Hawaii a member of the Church of Jesus Christ of Latter-day Saints. (See Jay Todd, "Hawaii," *The Improvement Era*, [May 1966], p. 383; and R. Lanier Britsch, *Unto the Islands of the Sea* [1986], p. 138)

EVIDENCE NO. 617: THE BOOK OF MORMON TO GO TO ALL NATIONS

Claim: Nephi, the first prophet mentioned in the Book of Mormon recorded the prophetic words of an angel who declared that the Book of Mormon would be made "known to all kindreds, tongues, and people" (1 Nephi 13:40).

Evidence: There are now over one hundred million copies of the Book of Mormon circulating throughout the world. The Book of Mormon has been taken to so many nations for so long, that some editions have gone out of print with dying languages. As of the year 2000 the Book of Mormon, including abridged editions, has been printed in 94 languages. Fifteen thousand copies of the Book are printed each day (*Ensign,* May 2000, p. 112).

EVIDENCE NO. 618: THE BOOK OF MORMON TO BE REJECTED BY MANY

Claim: The Book of Mormon accurately prophesied the negative reaction of the world to its first appearance. One of the criticisms leveled at the volume is that it presents itself as containing words of God in addition to the Bible. Knowing the criticism that was to come, Nephi wrote these words from God:

> Wherefore murmur ye, because that ye shall receive more of my word? Know ye not that the testimony of two nations is a witness unto you that I am God, that I remember one nation like unto another? Wherefore, I speak the same words unto one nation like unto another. And when the two nations shall run together the testimony of the two nations shall run together also.

> And I do this that I may prove unto many that I am the same yesterday, today, and forever; and that I speak forth my words according to mine own pleasure. And because that I have spoken one word ye need not suppose that I cannot speak another; for my work is not yet finished; neither shall it be until the end of man, neither from that time henceforth and forever. Wherefore, because that ye have a Bible ye need not suppose that it contain all my words; neither need ye suppose that I have not caused more to be written (2 Nephi 29:8-10).

Evidence: Dr. Hugh Nibley has noted that the discovery of other ancient and holy texts has lead such devout scholars as F. M. Cross to exclaim: "It is as though God had added to his 'once for all' revelation." (Frank M. Cross, "The Scrolls From the Judean Wilderness," *Christian Century*, vol. 72 [1955], p. 890)

Dr. Nibley writes:

> But where does the Bible itself ever claim "once for all" revelation? Nowhere. As Professor C. M. Torrey points out, our Bible as we have it is the result of picking and choosing by men who claimed no inspiration for themselves, yet on their own authority decided what should be considered "revelation" and what should be labeled apocryphal or "outside" books.

"Outside books?" writes Torrey, "By what authority? The authority was duly declared, but it continued to be disputed … down even to the 19th century … A new terminology is needed … the current classification … as Apocrypha and Pseudepigrapha is outworn and misleading, supported neither by history nor by present fact." (Charles Torrey, *The Apocryphal Literature* [New Haven: Yale University Press, 1945], pp. 4, 10-11, cited in Nibley, *The Prophetic Book of Mormon* [1989], p. 213).

EVIDENCE NO. 619: MANY WILL DECLARE THE BIBLE TO BE SUFFICIENT

Claim: A passage in the Book of Mormon accurately prophesied the reaction of many Christians to its publication.

Evidence: When the Book of Mormon was first published in 1830, it contained the following prophecy: "and because my words [the Book of Mormon] shall hiss forth—many of the gentiles shall say A Bible! A Bible! we have got a Bible, and there cannot be any more Bible" (2 Nephi 29:3).

Just as the Book of Mormon prophesied, many critics of the Church use this line of reasoning in vocalizing their main objection to the Church of Jesus Christ of Latter-day Saints. Often, they use the very same expression—insisting that the Bible is sufficient, containing all necessary revelation from God, when there is no Biblical evidence for such a position.

For evidence to their unfounded objection, critics often cite Revelations 22:18-19, which forbids *mankind* from adding to or taking "away from the words of the book of *this* prophecy," and accuse Joseph Smith of doing just that. They are apparently unaware that this same mandate was given over a thousand years earlier in Deuteronomy 4:2. This reasoning would eliminate the vast majority of the Holy Bible from Deuteronomy chapter 5 on to Revelations chapter 22—over a thousand pages of the *word of God*. Clearly the warnings in Revelations and Deuteronomy apply only to mankind, and not to God. If the great Jehovah wishes to add to His words, who is man to forbid Him?

EVIDENCE NO. 620: PRIESTCRAFTS IN THE LATTER-DAYS

Claim: The Book of Mormon prophesies that the inhabitants of [America] in latter-days will be a nation "filled with all manner of … priestcrafts" (3 Nephi 16:10). It defines priestcraft as the practice in which "men preach and set themselves up for a light unto the world, that they may get gain and praise of the world" (2 Nephi 26:29).

Evidence: This prophecy is especially remarkable since, in 1830 there were no multi-millionaire evangelists living in luxurious mansions supported by mesmerized masses who "praised" them with monetary gifts. Since then, those who proclaim to preach the gospel can, in a very literal sense, be seen as "a light unto the *world*" and can gain the "praise of the *world*." The humble preachers of 1830 could have been a light to a small congregation in a small part of the country, but had no means at their disposal to preach to the world. They may have been able to reach thousands in print, but not the billions of the world. Today, satellite-broadcasting systems have enabled charismatic preachers to be "simultaneously" heard all over the world.

EVIDENCE NO. 621: LYINGS, DECEITS, AND HYPOCRISY OF THE GENTILES

Claim: The Book of Mormon prophesied that the gentiles, who would take this land from the Lamanites, would "be filled with all manner of lyings, and of deceits, and of mischiefs, and all manner of hypocrisy…" (1 Nephi 13:14; 3 Nephi 16:10).

Evidence: An example of the lying and deceitfulness of the gentiles is the fact that the United States (the melting pot of the gentile Nations) broke scores of treaties and promises with the Native Americans during the great Western expansion of the 1800's—robbing them of their homelands.

An illustration of the hypocrisy of the gentiles (in a collective sense) is the manner in which US Government treated the Saints. The US Government denied the Later-day Saints constitutional protection against the mob violence that was being unmercifully poured out upon them by their fellow citizens. A few years later, after the Mormon Battalion had honorably served their country in the longest US military march in history, the federal government sent a large army of US troops to Utah to threaten the saints with war. This was done in response to false reports of a Mormon rebellion against the United States government.

EVIDENCE NO. 622: WHOREDOMS OF THE GENTILES

Claim: The Book of Mormon contains a prophecy from the Lord that the gentiles in this land will be filled with all manner of "whoredoms, and of secret abominations" (3 Nephi 16:10).

Evidence: In 1830 when the Book of Mormon was published, no mortal could have known to what great depths of immorality the people of the gentile nations would eventually fall. In Joseph Smith's day, only the Lord, and the prophets with whom He communicated, knew that adultery and fornication, which were looked upon with abhorrence and disgust by the majority, would actually become popular and generally accepted among the future public. No one knew then that the little-known perversion of homosexuality would, in the future, become tolerated and openly defended as an acceptable "alternative" lifestyle. No one knew in 1830 what pornography was. Even after photography was invented, no one would have believed that peddlers of smut could have become millionaires in a Christian nation such as America. Before the telephone was invented, no one thought of obscene phone calls nor "dial-a-porn." No one in 1830 could have foreseen that the future availability of contraceptives and the legalization of abortion would generate such an upsurge in extra-marital sex.

Truly, the gentile nations have been filled with "whoredoms, and all manner of abominations" (Mormon 8:31).

EVIDENCE NO. 623: MURDERS OF THE GENTILES

Claim: The Book of Mormon also prophesied that the gentiles would be filled with "all manner of ... murders" (3 Nephi 16:10).

Evidence: The United States of America, the gathering place for gentiles from all other nations, inflicted terrible slaughters and massacres upon the American Indians all across the continent with the great westward migration, a tragedy which President Brigham Young rightly called *murder*. (See, for example, his rebuke against an apostate Mormon who had killed an Indian in *Journal of Discourses* vol. 11, p. 263.)

Many saints were also *murdered* in compliance with a corrupt governor's order. In 1838 Governor Boggs of Missouri issued an official "extermination order" against the Mormon people—resulting in such unmerciful slaughters as the *Haun's Mill Massacre*, and the brutal murder of the Prophet Joseph Smith and his brother Hyrum Smith (*History of the Church*, vol. 3, p. 175; D&C 135).

Many other *murders* were also committed in the name of government-instituted wars. For example, hundreds of thousands of civilians were unmercifully killed at the dropping of atomic bombs on Hiroshima and Nagasaki, Japan. President J. Reuben Clark Jr. described this as "the crowning savagery of the war." He added that "the worst of this atomic bomb tragedy is that not only did the people of the United States not rise up in protest against this savagery, not only did it not shock us to read of this wholesale destruction of men, women, and children, and cripples, but that it actually drew from the nation at large a general approval of this fiendish butchery." (See *Conference Report*, October 1946, pp. 86-88. See also President Brigham Young's condemnation of war in which the guilty will be damned, in *Journal of Discourses* vol. 7, p. 137.)

Yet another subtler "manner of murder" is the unholy slaughter of countless millions of innocent children through abortion—which, is not only considered legal and moral by the gentiles, but is actually subsidized through public taxes. Of course on the other end of the spectrum is the equally horrifying murders of abortion clinic workers committed by so called "pro-life" extremists.

EVIDENCE NO. 624: SECRET COMBINATIONS

Claim: The Book of Mormon prophesies the formation of "secret combinations."

Evidence: The Book of Mormon, published in 1830, prophesied that in the last days evil men would swear oaths in secret pacts that would be the cause of death to many people in seeking "to overthrow the freedom of all lands, nations, and countries," in their attempt to "get power and gain" (Ether 8:22-25).

Down through history, there have always been countries that have attempted to conquer other lands, but they have not operated within secret combinations in the same manner as was prophesied in the Book of Mormon. Many passages of the Book of Mormon make reference to these same types of secret combinations which do not always overthrow other cities by frontal attacks in formal warfare, but would secretly infiltrate into the government and among the people with "all manner of wickedness" (Ether 8:16). Such are the tactics of Communism, the Mafia, and the drug cartels.

Who can deny that since the Book of Mormon was first published, a number of secret combinations similar to those described in the Book of Mormon have emerged in various parts of the world. These have caused death, destruction and "all manner of wickedness" in their unrighteous quest for money and power.

EVIDENCE NO. 625: GREAT POLLUTIONS

Claim: The Prophet Mormon wrote that the Book of Mormon would come forth in a day when there shall be great pollutions upon the face of the earth (Mormon 8:31).

Evidence: This prophecy has literal, as well as figurative fulfillments. In our modern day, when the Book of Mormon is being carried forth to the world, we can scarcely watch the evening news, or read the newspaper without learning of pollution. Conservationists lament the chemical pollution from toxic wastes in the rivers and oceans of the world, and almost every large city is turning to extreme measures in order to cut down on automobile emissions and other sources of pollution. The Environmental Protection Agency is enforcing more restrictive regulations on American enterprises than ever before, in an effort to reduce industrial pollution—often at the cost of many thousands of jobs. Radioactive pollutions from nuclear accidents such as Chernobyl, and toxic wastes from forty years of nuclear weapon development, certainly represent a type of pollution that would fulfill the prophecy of Mormon.

Even more devastating is the contamination that fills the airwaves and computer networks with pornography and violence, which pollutes the human mind in the name of "home entertainment." Not only have these evils defiled the air, but with the advent of satellite broadcasting, they have also polluted the heavens.

EVIDENCE NO. 626: PROPHECIES OF NATURALISM, MATERIALISM AND RELATIVISM

Claim: The prophetic Book of Mormon tells of destructive teachers such as *Korihor* whose corrupt philosophies foreshadowed the popular ideologies that spawned the great moral decline of the twentieth century.

Evidence: Dr. Hugh Nibley observed the following in his work *Since Cumorah,* (1988), pp. 380-381:

Korihor insisted on a strictly rational and scientific approach to all problems, anything else being but "the effect of a frenzied mind" (Alma 30:13-16); he crusaded against the tyranny of ancient traditions and primitive superstitions, which led people to believe things which just "are not so" (Alma 30:16), calling for an emancipation from "the silly traditions of their fathers" (Alma 30:31). He called for a new morality with the shedding of old inhibitions (Alma 30:17-18, 25). He called for economic liberation from priestly exploitation (Alma 30:27), demanding that all be free to "make use of that which is their own" (Alma 30:28). He preached a strict no-nonsense naturalism: "when a man was dead, that was the end thereof" (Alma 30:18), and its corollary, which was a strict materialism: "therefore every man fared in this life according to the management of the creature" (Alma 30:17). From this followed a clear-cut philosophy of laissez-faire: "Therefore every man prospered according to his genius, and ... every man conquered according to his strength," with right and wrong measured only by nature's iron rule of success and failure: "And whatsoever a man did was no crime" (Alma 30:17). It was survival of the fittest applied to human behavior, and the removal of old moral and sentimental restraints was good news to many people, "causing them to lift up their heads in their wickedness, yea, leading away many ... to commit whoredoms" (Alma 30:18). Along with his attitude of emancipation Korihor cultivated a crusading zeal and intolerance of any opposition, which has been thoroughly characteristic of his school of thought in modern times, calling all opposition "foolish" (Alma 30:13-14), "silly" (Alma 30:31), and the evidence of frenzied and deranged minds (Alma 30:16). And while for Alma a free society was one in which anybody could think and say whatever he chose (Alma 30:7-12), for Korihor the only free society was one in which everyone thought exactly as he thought (Alma 30:24)— which was also the liberal gospel of Huxley, Dewey, Marx, et al.

The philosophy of Korihor, with its naturalism, materialism, and moral relativism, is the prevailing philosophy of our own day, as was foreseen in the Book of Mormon. "Yea ... there shall be great pollutions upon the face of the earth ... when there shall be many who will say, Do this, or do that, and it mattereth not, for the Lord will uphold such at the last day. But wo unto such, for they are in the gall of bitterness and in the bonds of iniquity" (Mormon 8:31). Enormously proud of their accomplishments, "the Gentiles are lifted up in the pride of their eyes, and have stumbled, because of the greatness of their stumbling block" (2 Nephi 26:20). Their own expertise is the highest court of appeal, as they "preach up unto themselves their own wisdom and their own learning, that they may get gain and grind upon the faces of the poor" (2 Nephi 26:20). The theologians "set themselves up for a light unto the world, that they may get gain and praise of the world" (2 Nephi 20:29), as they "contend one with another, ... teach with their learning, and deny the Holy Ghost"(2 Nephi 28:4).

EVIDENCE NO. 627: THREE NEPHITES NOT TO TASTE OF DEATH

Claim: The Book of Mormon records that three of the twelve Nephite disciples were given a promised that they would remain on earth until the Second Coming of Christ in the same fashion that the apostle John's life was extended until Christ should return (John 21:22-23). These three Nephites were given power to perform miracles (3 Nephi 28:2-40).

Evidence: An ancient Incan legend describes three men who visited their forefathers, with power to perform great miracles, such as walking on water, etc. (See Sarmiento de Camboa Pedro, *História de Los Incas, Segunda Parte de la História Indica*, [Buenos Aires, Argentina: Emece Editores, 1943], pp. 108-109.)

Similarly, the history of Chichén Itza mentions three brothers who lived with them for a time that were called "Lords of Fire." (See Linda Schele and David Freidel, *A Forest of Kings: The Untold Story of the Ancient Maya*, [New York: William Morrow, 1990], p. 360, cited in Jerry L. Ainsworth, *The Lives and Travels of Mormon and Moroni*, [Peacemakers Publishing, 2000], p. 138.)

There are hundreds of accounts in recent LDS history (after 1830 AD) of the three Nephites who performed great services in miraculous ways. Although this is regarded as folklore by skeptics and anti-Mormons, many accounts are considered to be authentic by LDS historians, especially by the descendants of those who personally encountered the three Nephites and particularly those encounters that were witnessed by many people.

Elder Orson Pratt spoke of the work of the three Nephites among Native American people in which there were literally hundreds of witnesses:

It seems that the Lord is working among that people [the Native Americans], and that He is determined this prophecy shall be fulfilled whether we take it in hand or not. What do my ears hear? What do we all hear? Messengers are visiting these wild tribes in the basin, and in the region round about hundreds of miles apart. These messengers come to them, and they speak in their own language in great plainness, and tell them what to do. They tell them to repent of their sins and to be baptized for the remission thereof; tell them also to cease roaming over the country and to cultivate the land; tell them to go to the leaders of this Church and receive the ordinances under their hands.

Who are these messengers? Read the Book of Mormon and you will find what God promised to do for the remnants of Joseph fourteen hundred years ago, about the time that most of them were becoming wicked and corrupt. The Lord said when their record [the Book of Mormon] should come forth in the latter-days that He would send his messengers to them, and among these messengers He mentioned three persons who lived some eighteen hundred years ago, three of the Twelve who were chosen on this land. The Lord made a promise to these three that they should administer, as holy messengers in the latter days for and in behalf of the remnants [Indians] of the house of Israel, ... that they should be instruments in His hands in bringing these remnants to the knowledge of the truth. We hear that these messengers have come, not in one instance alone, but in many instances. Already we have heard of some fourteen hundred Indians, and I do not know but more, who have been baptized. Ask them why they have come so many hundreds of miles to find the Elders of the Church, and they will reply: "Such a person came to us, he spoke in our language, instructed us and told us what to do, and we have come in order to comply with his requirements" (*Journal of Discourses,* vol. 17, p. 299-300).

Other accounts and testimonies of encounters with the Three Nephites may be found in books such as N. B. Lundwall's *Assorted Gems of Priceless Value* (Salt Lake City: Bookcraft, 1947).

EVIDENCE NO. 628: THE LATTER-DAY SAINTS TO SUFFER DEATH

<u>Claim</u>: In 1830, Joseph Smith published the Book of Mormon which contained his translation of Nephi's prophecy that in the last days "the blood of saints shall cry from the ground" (2 Nephi 28:10). The Book of Mormon predicts that this will occur when the Gospel, which had been engraven upon the plates, would come out of the earth (Mormon 8:26-27).

<u>Evidence</u>: The cruel history of the American frontier attests to the hundreds of Latter-day Saint lives lost in the brutal mobbings, lynchings, and massacres poured out upon the church in its early days.

These prophecies must have been ill tidings for the early members of the Church who called themselves *Latter-day Saints*. Clearly, a false prophet would not have prophesied such gloom on his own church. Were the Church not true, none would have taken interest in helping this prophecy to be fulfilled by joining the saints and subsequently giving up their lives. Furthermore, this terrible prophecy would seem highly unlikely to unfold in the one nation where religious tolerance and freedom were guaranteed by a constitution inspired by God—a *civilized* age of modernization, enlightenment, industry and invention. A false prophet, who would obviously be interested in attracting followers, would certainly avoid frightening his prospective disciples with ominous predictions of an unhappy future of violence, suffering and death. Yet because the Book of Mormon is true, it attracted thousands of converts rather than causing fear in prospective members.

EVIDENCE NO. 629: JOSEPH SMITH TO BE MADE STRONG

<u>Claim</u>: In the Book of Mormon, the Lord declared that "out of weakness," Joseph Smith "shall be made strong" (2 Nephi 3:13).

<u>Evidence</u>: Joseph Smith did, indeed, become very influential and inspired tens of thousands of his acquaintances to obtain their own testimonies of the gospel of Jesus Christ. Even many who did not see him as a prophet, admired and commented on his strength of character. One such non-Mormon was Josiah Quincy, mayor of Boston, who said of Joseph: "Born in the lowest ranks of poverty, without book learning and with the homeliest of all human names, he had made himself at the age of thirty-nine a power upon earth." Josiah Quincy, *Figures of the Past,* 5th edition, (Boston: Roberts Brothers, 1883), p. 376.

Dr. Harold Bloom, a Jewish religious scholar, and distinguished professor at both New York and Yale Universities, extols Joseph Smith as "an authentic religious genius, unique in our ... history," and praises "the sureness of his instincts, his uncanny *knowing* precisely what [was] needful for the inauguration of a new faith." Joseph Smith and Mormonism, he further expounds, have contributed to the world "a more human God and a more divine man... I also do not ... doubt that Joseph Smith was an authentic prophet. Where in all of American history can we find his match? ... Nothing else in all of American history strikes me as ... equal to the early Mormons, to Joseph Smith, Brigham Young, Parley and Orson Pratt, and the men and women who were their followers and friends." (Harold Bloom, *The American Religion*, [New York: Simon & Schuster, 1992] pp. 79, 82-83, 95, 100.)

EVIDENCE NO. 630: JOSEPH SMITH TO BE GREAT LIKE UNTO MOSES

<u>Claim</u>: In the Book of Mormon, the Lord announced that the latter-day Joseph "shall be great like unto Moses" (2 Nephi 3:8-9).

<u>Evidence</u>: This bold prophecy has been fulfilled in many ways. Note the remarkable similarities below:

Similarities	**Moses**	**Joseph Smith**
1. Both narrowly escaped death in their youth	Exodus 1-2	*Young Women's Journal*, vol. 17, pp. 537-538.
2. Both spoke with God face to face	Exodus 33:11 Numbers 12:6-8	Joseph Smith—History 1:1-25
3. Both became transfigured	Exodus 34:34-35	*Conference Report*, April 1898, p. 89
4. Both received commandments from God	Exodus 20	D&C 67:1-6
5. Both stood before great governmental leaders	Exodus 7-11	*History of the Church* vol. 4, pp. 40, 80
6. Both led multitudes from oppression to Zion	Exodus	D&C 101:63-80; 103:22-24
7. Yet neither were able to witness the arrival of their people in the promised Zion	Numbers 20:10-12	D&C 135
8. Both depended on a brother for help	Exodus 7:1-2	D&C 135:3
9. Both were in possession of sacred objects, such as the *Urim & Thummim*	Deuteronomy 33:8	Joseph Smith—History 1:35
10. Both were leaders when their people went to battle	Exodus 17:8-13	*History of the Church*, vol. 3, Chapter 12, p. 169
11. Both constructed holy sanctuaries unto the Lord by His commandment	Exodus 25:8-22; 33:7-11	D&C 109:1-20; 115:8
12. Both recorded scripture	Genesis, Exodus, Leviticus, Numbers & Deuteronomy	The Doctrine and Covenants, & The Pearl of Great Price
13. Both were reprimanded by the Lord	Numbers 20:10-12	D&C 3:6-9; 5:2; 20:5; 93:47
14. Both performed great miracles	Exodus	See Chapter 8 of vol. 1 of this same work

EVIDENCE NO. 631: AMERICA RESERVED FOR THOSE WHO WORSHIP GOD

<u>Claim</u>: The Book of Mormon prophesied that America is reserved for those who worship God (2 Nephi 1:6-7).

<u>Evidence</u>: While modern-day detractors constantly strive to rewrite history and discredit our founding fathers, the fact remains that the founders of this great nation were deeply devoted to the God of Israel. See for example, *One Nation Under God, America's Christian Heritage,* (Christian Defense Fund: Springfield, Virginia 1997); Verna M. Hall, *The Christian History of the Constitution of the Unites States of America,* (California: Foundation for American Christian Education, 1978); W. Cleon Skousen, *The Making of America,* (Washington DC, 1985); Jay A. Parry, Andrew M. Allison and Skousen, *The Real George Washington,* (National Center for Constitutional Studies [NCCS]: Washington DC, 1991); Allison, Skousen & M. R. Maxfield, *The Real Benjamin Franklin,* (NCCS, 1987), Allison, Maxfield, K. D. Cook & Skousen, *The Real Thomas Jefferson,* (NCCS, 1983).

Not only did our founding fathers reverence God, but the percentage of US citizens affiliated with a church has steadily risen since this nation was established. Recent surveys show that more than 90 percent of Americans profess a belief in God; 63 percent of the population claim church memberships, more than half say they pray at least once a day, and 44 percent of the adult population attend weekly worship services. Each of these figures are more than any other highly-developed country. A recent Gallup survey found that: "while most survey respondents hold staunchly to the view that one can be a good and ethical person without believing in God, a solid majority (61 percent) say that a democracy cannot survive without a widespread belief in God or a Supreme Being." It further reports that "A substantial majority believe that they will be called before God at Judgment Day to answer for their sins. Americans overwhelmingly attest to a belief in the divinity of Jesus Christ, although what is meant by 'divinity' varies ... Only three out of every 100 Americans say their lives have not been touched at all by Jesus Christ."

Not only is the faith of Americans strong, but this survey also found that those who belong to a church are significantly more charitable with their time and money than those who do not. Moreover, the study found that "as we look at other countries, we generally see an inverse correlation between levels of religious commitment and levels of education. The more highly educated a country's populace is, the less religiously committed and participating it is. The United States is unique in that we have at the same time a high level of religious belief and a high level of formal education." (See George Gallup, Jr., "Religion in America: Will the Vitality of Churches be the Surprise of the Next Century?," *The Public Perspective*, [1995, The Roper Center for Public Opinion Research]. Reprinted by *United States Information Service—Israel*, March 23, 1997, [usis-israel.org.il/publish/journals/society/march97/ gallup.htm]; See also *Christian Daily News*, Dec. 12, 1997, [www.christiannews.org/archives/1997/121297/news/ full.html]; "Church and State," American Civil Liberties Union Briefing Paper Number 3, [aclu.org/library/pbp3.html]; Roger Finke and Rodney Stark, *The Churching of America*, [New Brunswick, NJ: Rutgers University Press, 1992], paper 1993; George Gallup, and Tim Jones, *The Saints Among Us*, [Richfield, CT: Morehouse Publishing, 1992].)

EVIDENCE NO. 632: AMERICA TO BE A LAND OF LIBERTY

Claim: While translating the Book of Mormon, Joseph Smith recorded that the land, which is called America, would be "a land of liberty unto the Gentiles," that no kings would rule over the people that would live within its borders, and should any man *attempt* to rule as king in America—he "shall perish" (2 Nephi 10:11-14).

Evidence: History has witnessed the literal fulfillment of this prophecy. The United States has continually led in the struggle for freedom. Since the Book of Mormon was published in 1830, America has clearly demonstrated that it is a land of liberty, continually rising up in defense of other nations that have been threatened by Nazism, Fascism, Communism, and other world-threatening dictatorships.

In Brazil, the attempt to create a monarchy failed on November 15, 1889, with the deportation of Don Pedro and the establishment of a republic. In Mexico, Maximillian was executed in 1866—two years after his coronation. (For more information, see B. H. Roberts, *New Witnesses for God* [1909] vol. 3, p. 280.)

EVIDENCE NO. 633: A LAND CHOICE ABOVE ALL OTHER LANDS

Claim: The Book of Mormon prophesied that the land of America would become a land "choice above all other lands" (1 Nephi 2:20; 13:30; Ether 2:7). It also foretells that the American Gentiles would become the most powerful people on the face of the earth: "unto the pouring out of the Holy Ghost through me upon the Gentiles, *which blessing upon the Gentiles shall make them mighty above all*" (3 Nephi 20:27).

Evidence: In 1830 when this prediction was first published, it must have sounded quite ludicrous, for this nation had scarcely begun its great experiment with democracy—and could hardly be considered a world power. Today, however, few can dispute the literal fulfillment of this bold prophecy. Not only does America dominate the world economy, and have the largest and best equipped military in the world, but it is also "choice above all other lands" in that it yields the more farm product exports than any other country in the world. It accomplishes this with a work force of only three-percent of the US population. America's farmers are the most productive on earth—with the average farmer producing enough food for 78 people, and creating an annual value of 136 billion dollars (in 1980). The United States also leads all nations in mineral production and in manufacturing which produced about $140 billion and $1.85 trillion per year respectively in 1980. (See "United States of America," *Funk and Wagnalls New Encyclopedia,* [1983], vol. 26, pp. 271-277; and "Industry," *Compton's Interactive Encyclopedia* [Compton's New Media, Inc., 1994].)

The United States became a choice land in a political sense in that it leads the world in the protection of human rights as enumerated in the *Declaration of Independence* and the *Constitution of the United States.* People from all over the world are trying desperately to immigrate to the United States, and participate in this grand experiment in democracy and personal freedom.

EVIDENCE NO. 634: THE UNITED STATES TO BE FORTIFIED AGAINST ALL OTHER NATIONS

Claim: The Book of Mormon prophesies that America will be fortified against all other nations and that those who fight against this land will perish (2 Nephi 10:12-13).

Evidence: No one except a true prophet could have foreseen that Spain, France, or England would not have eventually won back lost territories from a new struggling republic in future conflicts. None except a true prophet of God could have known that the infant nation would never lose a future war that would subordinate the United States under a conquering nation.

EVIDENCE NO. 635: JEWS TO GATHER AFTER THE BOOK OF MORMON COMES FORTH

Claim: The Book of Mormon prophesied that once the Book of Mormon was published to the world, the House of Israel would begin to be restored to their land of inheritance—Palestine (3 Nephi 29:1). The Book of Mormon further prophesied that those who fight against the restored Nation of Israel "shall be turned one against another," to fight among themselves and ultimately destroy each other (1 Nephi 22:14).

Evidence: A remarkable series of events led to the fulfillment of these prophecies. England issued the Balfour Declaration on November 2, 1917. On December 11, 1917, General Sir Edmund Allenby led British troops into Jerusalem to take it peaceably from the Turks. On May 14, 1948 the British gave up control of Palestine to allow Israel to become an independent nation.

Since the Nation of Israel was established, none of her enemies have prevailed against her. Those nations who have helped Israel (such as the United States) have been blessed above all other nations, and those who have not, have been "utterly wasted" (for example in the Gulf War with Iraq).

Perhaps the most miraculous triumph was the six-day war of 1967: "A country no larger that the state of Massachusetts with a population of only 2¾ million was completely encircled by the League of Arab States" representing a population of 110 million. "A military massacre appeared inevitable ... This gave Egypt and her Arab League more than twice as many ground forces as Israel, three times as many tanks and over twice as many fighter and bomber planes ... Every two hours news bulletins from Cairo called for a Jehad—a massive holy war against Israel. On May 28, Egypt's President Gamal Abdel Nasser told the Arab world, 'We intend to open a general assault against Israel. This will be total war. Our basic aim is the destruction of Israel!' It was obvious that unless something almost miraculous happened, Egypt and her Arab League were perfectly capable of fulfilling their own prophecy." Yet, despite their seemingly hopeless predicament the tiny Jewish nation, with the help of Jehovah, celebrated a fantastic victory in less than one week. (See W. Cleon Skousen, *Fantastic Victory* [1967], pp. 3-4; who cites: *U. S. News and World Report,* June 12, 1967, pp. 32-33; *Israel's Swift Victory,* a special edition of *Life,* June 3, 1967, p. 4; and *Israel's Finest Day,* a day-by-day report, [West Pittston, Pennsylvania: Marx Publishing Co.], p. 7.)

4. Historical Accuracy of the Book of Mormon

Claim: As Joseph Smith dictated his translation of the Book of Mormon to each of his various scribes, he did so with remarkable invariance. Upon returning from a break, or when starting a new day of translation, it is said that he did not even have to ask his scribe to read the previous sentence in order to know where they had left off. He would simply resume the translation at the precise location, without losing the continuity of that which was being conveyed. This is especially remarkable when considering that neither the Book of Mormon, nor the golden plates, from which it was translated, contained punctuation marks. Yet the message of the Book of Mormon is amazingly consistent. (See "Statement from Emma Smith to her Son Joseph Smith III," *The Saints Herald*, October 1, 1879, pp. 289-290.)

The authors claim that had Joseph Smith been a fraud, it would not have been possible for him to produce a literary work of such great significance, with such a degree of consistency. Thus, we submit that the only possible explanation for the origin of this scripture is that which Joseph Smith claimed—that it was translated from ancient historical records by the gift and power of God.

Evidence: The following is quoted from John W. Backwoodsman, "Textual Consistency," *Foundation for Ancient Research and Mormon Studies Update* for October 1987; reprinted in *Re-exploring the Book of Mormon*, edited by John W. Welch, (1992), pp. 21-23:

> It is extremely difficult the first time through to dictate a final of a letter, let alone a book. Yet the original manuscript of the Book of Mormon is remarkably clean. There are few strikeovers, and only minor changes were made as the book went to publication. The vast majority of those, involved only spelling, punctuation and grammar.

> Even more remarkable are the extensive, intricate consistencies within the Book of Mormon. Passages tie together precisely and accurately even though separated from each other by hundreds of pages of text and dictated weeks apart. Here are a few striking examples.

> In Alma 36, Alma recounts the story of his conversion. In describing the joy he experienced and the desire his soul then felt to be with God, Alma compared himself to Lehi: "Yea, methought *I saw, even as our father Lehi saw, God sitting upon his throne, surrounded with numberless concourses of angels,*

that for about 500 years before the birth of Christ our Redeemer, this land was populated. (Bernardino de Sahagun, *Introduction al Primer Libro de la Historia,* vol. 1, p. 12; Cited in Hunter and Ferguson, *Ancient America and the Book of Mormon,* [1950], pp. 60-61).

See also Sahagun, *Historia General de las Casas de Nueva España* (Editoria S. A. Mexico, 1946, Vol. 1, p. 12); Karl Jaspers, *The Origin and Goal of History,* (Yale University Press, 1953) p. 8; Helen Augur, *Zapotec,* (Garden City, NY, 1954), pp. 120, 161; Michael Mok, "New Clues to the Mayan Riddle," *Popular Science Monthly,* January 1929, pp. 44, 157, also January 1930, pp. 23, 127; cited in Skousen, *Treasures from the Book of Mormon,* (1974), vol. 1, p. 108.

EVIDENCE NO. 640: SAMUEL THE LAMANITE

Claim: The Book of Mormon tells of a Lamanite prophet who prophesied of the imminent birth of the savior. The record states that his audience tried to kill him, but God protected him such that the angry crowd could not hit him with their stones nor with their arrows (Helaman 13-16).

Evidence: The legends of the *Wintun* Indians speak of a certain man who was protected. "He was no more like himself before, for now no arrow could wound him. Though a thousand Indians should shoot at him, not one flint-pointed arrow would pierce his skin. He was like the Great Man in Heaven for no man could slay him forevermore." (See Ellen Russell Emerson, *Indian Myths, or Legends, Traditions, and Symbols of the Aborigines of America,* [Minneapolis: Ross & Haines, Inc., 1965], p. 595, cited in Tom Cryer, *Visual Testamament and the Israelite Indian,* [1999], p. 370.)

EVIDENCE NO. 641: THE CORRUPT RULE OF THE ELDERS AT JERUSALEM IN 600 BC

Claim: The Book of Mormon paints a dismal picture of Jerusalem in 600 BC. The record also speaks of many prophets who predicted of the impending destruction of Jerusalem because of the iniquities of her inhabitants and leaders. It further states that these prophets, including Lehi, were not well received, were cast out, and forced to flee for their lives (1 Nephi 1:4, 13, 18-20). As it turns out, this description of Jerusalem is fully substantiated in modern research of the era.

Evidence: The following is quoted from Dr. Hugh Nibley in his work *Approach to the Book of Mormon,* (1988), pp. 96-97.

Nephi tells us casually but emphatically that things at Jerusalem were controlled by "the elders of the Jews," who were holding nocturnal meetings with the powerful and influential Laban (1 Nephi 4:22-27). Poor Zedekiah plays no part at all—his name occurs half a dozen times in the Book of Mormon, but only to fix a date. These elders were no friends of Lehi; for if they had been, his life would never have been in danger. As it was, he "was driven out of Jerusalem" (Helaman 8:22; 1 Nephi 7:14) by the only people who could have driven him out, the important people, those responsible for the "priestcrafts and iniquities" that were to be the ruin of them at Jerusalem (2 Nephi 10:5).

Bible students recognize today that affairs at Jerusalem were completely under the control of the "elders." The word "elders" has been understood to mean the heads of the most influential families of a city. In 1935 in the ruins of the city of Lachish, 30 miles southward of Jerusalem, a remarkable body of documents was found. They were military reports written at the very time of the fall of Jerusalem and saved from the flames of burning Lachish by being covered with rubble when the watchtower in which they were stored collapsed. Lachish was the last Jewish town to fall before Jerusalem itself went down, so here, in the fragments of some eighteen letters, we have a strictly first-hand, if limited, account of what was going on. (See Wilhelm Nowack, *Lehrbuch der Hebräischen Archaeologie* [Freiburgh i/B-Leipzig: Mohr, 1894], p. 300; and Harry Torczyner, *The Lachish Letters* [London: Oxford University Press, 1938].)

EVIDENCE NO. 638: RECURRENCE OF HISTORY

<u>Claim</u>: Book of Mormon critics have often charged that Joseph Smith was an amateur fraud and that he plagiarized many Biblical stories and placed them in the Book of Mormon. For example, they point to similarities between the ships and barges that carried the Nephites, and the Jaredites to America and the ark of Noah (Genesis 6-8; 1 Nephi 17-18; Ether 2-6). Lehi's journey through the wilderness to the "promised land" of the Americas is reminiscent of Moses's journey through the wilderness to the "promised land" of Palestine (Exodus 12-40; 1 Nephi 1-18). Nephi's calling to rule over his older brothers had precedent in Isaac's birthright over Ishmael, Jacob over Esau, and Joseph over his older brothers (Genesis 21:12; 27:1-36; 37:3-4; 48:22; 1 Nephi 2:22). Nephi in the mountain calls to mind Moses on Sinai. (Exodus 3:1-3; 1 Nephi 11).

Rather than being a sign of weakness, the recurrence of Book of Mormon events that were foreshadowed in Biblical history, is yet another witness that the Book of Mormon is a true and accurate history.

<u>Evidence</u>: This practice of drawing parallels between *current* and ancient history is well documented in Alan Goff's, article "Boats, Beginnings, and Repetitions," *Journal of Book of Mormon Studies,* (Fall 1992), vol. 1, no. 1, pp. 66-84. In his treatise, Goff refers to many non-Mormon scholars such as Søren Kierkegaard, "Fear and Trembling and Repetition," in *Keirkegaard's Writings,* (Princeton University Press, 1983), Mircea Eliade, *Cosmos and History: The Myth of Eternal Return,* (New York: Harper and Row, 1959), Bernhard W. Anderson, *Creation versus Chaos: The Reinterpretation of Mythical Symbolism in the Bible,* (Philadelphia: Fortress, 1987).

Those who thus criticize the Book of Mormon are unknowingly criticizing the New Testament—which has sustained the very same charges of plagiarism from the Old Testament. For example, there are many parallels between Christ and Elijah. Both spent 40 days in the wilderness, both climbed a mountain for spiritual renewal, both performed healings, raised the dead, caused food to be multiplied, the lives of both were threatened. Both were said to have power to call down fire from heaven, both performed miracles in crossing barriers of water, both ascended into heaven and it was prophesied that both were to make a glorious return. See also Morton Smith, *Jesus the Magician,* (New York: Harper and Row, 1978).

Furthermore, the Old Testament has been accused of plagiarizing other ancient myths and legends that preceded the Bible. For example, the Epic of Gilgamesh resembles Noah and his ark. The infant Sargon's life was saved in the same way as was that of Moses. The Code of Hammurabi contains much that is found in the Mosaic Law. And the brazen serpent that was lifted up by Moses on a pole is reminiscent of Aesculapius, the pagan serpent god of healing.

However, the Bible and the Book of Mormon stand firm as true records of sacred history. And the vast bodies of evidence concerning the veracity of both works speaks louder than the fruitless cries of critics who wish to mock their sacred messages. The evidences that follow in this chapter establish the truthfulness of the Book of Mormon, while the Book of Mormon testifies to the truthfulness of the Bible (2 Nephi 29:4-14).

EVIDENCE NO. 639: NEPHITE HISTORY BEGAN IN 600 BC

<u>Claim</u>: The Book of Mormon opens in the days of King Zedekiah in the year 600 BC (1 Nephi 2:2-6). Subsequently, the Nephites based their historical calendar on this year in which they left Jerusalem (1 Nephi 10:4; 19:8; 2 Nephi 25:19; 3 Nephi 1:1).

<u>Evidence</u>: The Spanish Padre Sahagun wrote the following concerning the first colonizations of the American Indians:

> Touching the antiquity of this people, I learn from investigation that they have inhabited this land which now [16th Century] is called New Spain more than 2000 years because by their ancient writings, it is learned that the famous city, which is called Tula, had already existed about 1000 years when it was destroyed...It is sound and true that more than a thousand years had passed, by which it follows

that for about 500 years before the birth of Christ our Redeemer, this land was populated. (Bernardino de Sahagun, *Introduction al Primer Libro de la Historia*, vol. 1, p. 12; Cited in Hunter and Ferguson, *Ancient America and the Book of Mormon*, [1950], pp. 60-61).

See also Sahagun, *Historia General de las Casas de Nueva España* (Editoria S. A. Mexico, 1946, Vol. 1, p. 12); Karl Jaspers, *The Origin and Goal of History*, (Yale University Press, 1953) p. 8; Helen Augur, *Zapotec*, (Garden City, NY, 1954), pp. 120, 161; Michael Mok, "New Clues to the Mayan Riddle," *Popular Science Monthly*, January 1929, pp. 44, 157, also January 1930, pp. 23, 127; cited in Skousen, *Treasures from the Book of Mormon*, (1974), vol. 1, p. 108.

EVIDENCE NO. 640: MESOAMERICANS—DESCENDANTS OF ISRAEL (JACOB)

Claim: The Book of Mormon indicates that Lehi and his family were descendants of Israel (3 Nephi 10:17; 20:22) who was first known as Jacob (Genesis 32:28).

Evidence: The *Popol Vuh*, the sacred book of the ancient Quiché-Maya in the highlands of Guatemala, mentions that the people of *Llocab* came to this land from the "other side of the sea" in the East. The double "L" in Llocab is pronounced "Y." Thus, Llocab would be pronounced exactly like the Hebrews pronounced the name Jacob—Yah·ak·obe'. (See Delia Goetz and Sylvannus G. Morley, *Popol Vuh*, English translation by Adrian Recinos, [University of Oklahoma Press: 1950], pp. 69-80, 171; James Strong, *Dictionary of the Hebrew Bible*, [1890], word 3290; both cited in Hunter and Ferguson, *Ancient America and the Book of Mormon*, [1950], p. 64).

EVIDENCE NO. 641: THE CORRUPT RULE OF THE ELDERS AT JERUSALEM IN 600 BC

Claim: The Book of Mormon paints a dismal picture of Jerusalem in 600 BC. The record also speaks of many prophets who predicted of the impending destruction of Jerusalem because of the iniquities of her inhabitants and leaders. It further states that these prophets, including Lehi, were not well received, were cast out, and forced to flee for their lives (1 Nephi 1:4, 13, 18-20). As it turns out, this description of Jerusalem is fully substantiated in modern research of the era.

Evidence: The following is quoted from Dr. Hugh Nibley in his work *Approach to the Book of Mormon*, (1988), pp. 96-97.

Nephi tells us casually but emphatically that things at Jerusalem were controlled by "the elders of the Jews," who were holding nocturnal meetings with the powerful and influential Laban (1 Nephi 4:22-27). Poor Zedekiah plays no part at all—his name occurs half a dozen times in the Book of Mormon, but only to fix a date. These elders were no friends of Lehi; for if they had been, his life would never have been in danger. As it was, he "was driven out of Jerusalem" (Helaman 8:22; 1 Nephi 7:14) by the only people who could have driven him out, the important people, those responsible for the "priestcrafts and iniquities" that were to be the ruin of them at Jerusalem (2 Nephi 10:5).

Bible students recognize today that affairs at Jerusalem were completely under the control of the "elders." The word "elders" has been understood to mean the heads of the most influential families of a city. In 1935 in the ruins of the city of Lachish, 30 miles southward of Jerusalem, a remarkable body of documents was found. They were military reports written at the very time of the fall of Jerusalem and saved from the flames of burning Lachish by being covered with rubble when the watchtower in which they were stored collapsed. Lachish was the last Jewish town to fall before Jerusalem itself went down, so here, in the fragments of some eighteen letters, we have a strictly first-hand, if limited, account of what was going on. (See Wilhelm Nowack, *Lehrbuch der Hebräischen Archaeologie* [Freiburgh i/B-Leipzig: Mohr, 1894], p. 300; and Harry Torczyner, *The Lachish Letters* [London: Oxford University Press, 1938].)

Now in the Lachish letters we learn that the men who are running—and ruining—everything are the *sarim*, who actually are the elders, the term *sarim* designating, according to J. W. Jack, "members of the official class, i.e. `officers' acting under the king as his counselors and rulers." In these priceless letters "we find the *sarim* denouncing Jeremiah to the king and demanding that he be executed because of his bad influence on the morale of the people." In accusing the prophet of defeatism, the leading men of Jerusalem were supported by the majority of the people and by a host of popular "prophets" suborned by the court, by whose false oracles "Judahite chauvinism" was "whipped to a frenzy." To oppose this front, as Lehi did, was to incur the charges of subversion and defeatism. (See James W. Jack, "The Lachish Letters—Their Date and Import," *Palestine Exploration Fund Quarterly,* [1938], p. 176. Compare to William F. Albright, "A Brief History of Judah from the Days of Josiah to Alexander the Great," *Biblical Archaeologist,* vol. 9, [February 1946], p. 4.)

EVIDENCE NO. 642: FOUR BROTHERS

Claim: The Book of Mormon tells us that the Hebrew colony from Jerusalem was led by four brothers: Laman, Lemuel, Sam and Nephi (1 Nephi 2:5). Ancient American traditions about four brothers correlate with the record of four brothers in the Book of Mormon, which tells that the youngest (Nephi) ruled over the older brothers.

Evidence: The following are quotations found in Weldon, *The Book of Mormon Evidences Joseph Smith a Prophet,* pp. 8-9:

From the findings of anthropologists and explorers, none of which were available to Joseph Smith, we present a few excerpts:

Lewis Spence says that the great Kiche and his three brothers, according to the Mayas, led the first people to Southern Mexico (Spence, *Myths of Mexico and Peru*, pp. 157-158).

Daniel G. Brinton, University of Pennsylvania archaeologist who spent some forty years collecting and studying American Indian traditions wrote, "The Tupis of Brazil claim a descent from the four brothers. The fourfold division of the Muyscas of Bogota was traced back to four chieftains created by their hero God Negumsteba. Hardly a nation on the continent but seems to have had some vague tradition of an origin from four brothers, to have at some time been led by four leaders or princes, or in some manner to have connected the appearance and action of four important personages with its earliest traditional history" (Brinton, *Myths of the New World*, pp. 94-101).

The *Popol Vuh* a native book written by a Maya Quiche Indian priest and discovered in Catholic Archives in Guatemala by Doctor Scheizer in June 1854 gives us the Maya Quiche version of the four brothers. "Now it came to pass that the time of the death of Balam-Quitze, Balam-Agab, Mahucutah, and Iqi-Balam drew near.... Then they called their sons and their descendants round them to receive their last counsels.... Thus died and disappeared on Mount Hacavitz Balam-Quitze, Balam-Agab, Mahucutah and Iqui-Balam, these first men who came from the east *from the other side of the sea.* Long time had they been here when they died; and they were very old, and surnamed the Venerated and Sacrificers" (*Popol Vuh,* p. 169).

Rivero and Tschudi said concerning Peru, "Its first inhabitants flowed in abundantly toward the Valley of Cuzco, conducted by four brothers, Ayar-Manco-Topa, Ayar-Cache-Topa, Ayar-Auca-Topa and Ayar-Rica-Topa, who were accompanied by their sisters and wives. The youngest of the brothers according to the tradition was at the same time the most skillful and hardy."—*Peruvian Antiquities,* p. 52 (Rivero, a former Director of the National Museum in Peru; Tschudi a scientist).

J. D. Baldwin asserted, "The youngest of these brothers assumed supreme authority, and became the first of a long line of sovereigns" (Baldwin, *Ancient America,* p. 264).

EVIDENCE NO. 643: THE TWO OLDER BROTHERS REBELLED AGAINST THE YOUNGEST

Claim: The Book of Mormon tells of the first two sons of Lehi continually fighting against their younger brother, Nephi, because they believed that Nephi wanted power over them. See, for example, 1 Nephi 16:37-38. This enmity was carried on in the posterity of Laman and Lemuel (called Lamanites) against the posterity of Nephi (called Nephites). For example, see 2 Nephi 4:13; 5:2-4, 14; Mosiah 10:12-17. Eventually the Nephites were largely destroyed by the Lamanite nation (Moroni 9:7-21).

Evidence: The *Popol Vuh* describes the first and greatest enemy against whom the two hero sons fought. They accused him of being "proud, vain, arrogant," whose "only ambition was to exalt himself and to dominate" all of which seemed "very evil" and greatly angered them, so they set out to bring him and his children down to defeat because of his "assumed greatness." See *Popol Vuh*, pp. 103-106, cited in M. Wells Jakeman, *Stela 5*, Izapa, Chiapas, Mexico (Provo: The University Archaeological Society Special Publication No. 2, 1958), p. 24.

Note that except for the Book of Mormon (which was written by the Nephites), the only histories of these Meso-american nations have been passed down from the Lamanites. Naturally the Lamanite perspective of these events would differ from that of the Nephites, and would likely place the guilt on the younger brother against whom they rebelled. Nonetheless, the similarities are remarkable.

EVIDENCE NO. 644: TWO FUNDAMENTALLY DIFFERENT SOCIETIES IN ANCIENT AMERICA

Claim: The Book of Mormon records that the descendants of Laman and Lemuel became degenerate, violent, and full of hatred towards their relatives the Nephites (Alma 43:8-9, 43-47; Mormon 5:15). Indeed, with the exception of a brief period of peace following the appearance of the resurrected savior to the Americas, the record is dominated by the struggle between the generally peace-loving Nephites, and the warmongering Lamanites. Of course there were exceptions among the Lamanites who were at times more righteous than the Nephites (Jacob 3:5; Helaman 6:1), but in general the struggle between good and evil was between the Nephites and the Lamanites.

Evidence: The Mesoamerican historian Ixtlilxóchitl verified that there were two fundamentally different societies in ancient America. He furthermore mentions that these two contrasting groups were descendants from the early settlers. He writes:

> ... All of them take pride in the fact that they are of the lineage of the *Chichimecas*, because all of them descend from them, although it is true that there is a difference from some *Chichimecas* to others, in that some took more culture than others, like the Tultecas; and others took more to being great barbarians (savages), like the *Otomites* and others of their kind. Those ... have been warlike men, warriors, and fond of power and having the rest in subjection; and because some lead a courteous (cultured, polite) life, and others are very harsh and of evil thoughts, or haughty and arrogant, fond of killing, it has come about that there are virtuous and evil rulers ... (*Ixtlilxóchitl*; English translation by Hunter and Ferguson, *Ancient America and the Book of Mormon*, [1950], p. 39).

EVIDENCE NO. 645: ANCIENT AMERICANS WITH FAIR SKIN AND BEARDS

Claim: The Book of Mormon mentions two races of people who inhabited the ancient Americas—one with fair skin and the other with dark skin. The fair-skinned Nephites were for the most part destroyed by the dark-skinned Lamanites. However, the Book of Mormon records that a few of the Nephites did escape the slaughter. (See 2 Nephi 5:1-24; 25:21; 3 Nephi 2:14-16; Mormon 6:15-20.)

Evidence: One of the lesser-known discoveries of Columbus was a whole tribe of about five hundred white-skinned natives living in present day Haiti. The Spanish settlers subsequently killed off the entire native population of this island (then called Hispañola). Of these white natives Columbus said they "went naked as their mothers bore them, and so the women without any shame; and they are the most handsome men and women we had found hitherto; so white that if they went clothed and protected themselves from the sun and air they would be as white as in Spain." Quoted by Samuel Elliot Morison, *Admiral of the Ocean Sea*, (Little, Brown & Co: Boston, 1942), p. 288. Also cited in Skousen, *Treasures of the Book of Mormon,* vol. 1, pp. 1116-1117.

According to the *Popol Vuh, the Sacred Book of the Ancient Quiche Maya,* the first settlers were a race of white men. (See Delia Goetz and Sylvanus G. Morley, *Popol Vuh,* [Norman, University of Oklahoma Press, 1950], pp. 172, 195; Fray Bernardino de Sahagun, *História General de los Cosas de Nueva España: Florentine Codex* [General History of the things of New Spain], translated and edited by Charles E. Dibble and Arthur J. O. Anderson, [Santa Fe: The School of American Research, 1950], chapter 29, vol. 12, p. 118; Ruth Murray Underhill, *Red Man's America, A History of Indians in the United States* [University of Chicago Press, 1953] pp. 1-2; Andrea De Tapia in Francis C. Kelly, *Blood Drenched Altars,* [Milwaukee: Bruce Publishing Co., 1935] p. 38; all cited in Cheesman, *The World of the Book of Mormon,* [1978] pp. 3, 14.)

Similarly, the Shawnees claimed that the ancient inhabitants of Florida were white. See Du Pratz: *History of Louisiana,* vol. 2, (London 1703) p. 175; cited in Jean Francois Alvert du Pouget de Nadaillac, *Prehistoric America,* (London: John Murray, 1885) p. 526. The following are quoted from Weldon, *The Book of Mormon Evidences Joseph Smith a True Prophet* (page 9):

Archaeologist Edward Herbert Thompson said: "The legends of the primitive races of Yucatan and portions of Mexico tell of a fair-skinned race of men who become the rulers and the leaders of the dark-skinned aborigines." (See *People of the Serpent* [University of Oklahoma Press 1953], p. 75.)

University of Pennsylvania archaeologist, Daniel G. Brinton said: "Just as in Mexico, the natives attributed the erection of buildings, the history of which had been lost, to the white Toltecs, the subjects of Quetzalcoatl, so in Peru various ancient ruins, whose builders had been lost to memory, were pointed out to the Spaniards as the work of a white and bearded race who held the country in possession long before the Incas had founded their dynasty." (See Brinton, *American Hero Myths* [New York: Haskell House Publishing] p. 88.)

Concerning murals at Chichen-Itza, Yucatan, a Carnegie Institute bulletin says, "The fair-haired white folk are certainly suffering reverses in battle. One is grabbed by the hair and his face is fittingly distorted ... it cannot help but bring to mind legends rife throughout the American continent concerning the fair-skin and golden hair of a mythical race." (*Carnegie Institute Pub.,* no. 46, [1931] p. 402.)

A dramatic chapter in the story of American archaeology was broadcast to the world by the announcement in 1947 of the discovery of murals depicting dark and light-colored Indians painted on the interior walls of a temple in the southern jungles of Mexico. The Maya name Bonampak meaning painted walls was given to this archaeological site by a famous archaeologist, the late Dr. Sylvanus G. Morley.

The light and dark-skinned Indians of Bonampak are also documented in an article by Otto Done entitled "A Tour and Brief Description of Some of the Ancient Ruined Cities of Northern Central America" (*University Archaeological Society Newsletter* 26.0); cited in Christensen, *Progress in Archaeology,* (1963), pp. 164-165.

Dr. David E. Richardson (one of the authors of this work) has personally visited several museums in South America, which display pottery and tapestry showing both light and dark-skinned people in contact with each other. With particular interest he noted at the museum in Lima, Peru a room full of mummies from the local area. Most possessed dark skin and hair like the Indians of today. However, one mummy possessed light skin and light hair. Another possessed light skin and brown hair. These had been dated to times before the arrival of the Spaniards. When Dr. Richardson asked the Museum director for an explanation, he stated: "You must be a Mormon." "Yes," came the reply. "The Mormon explanation is as good as any," said the director.

See also, Donnely, *Atlantis*, p. 349; Alfredo Chavez, *Obras Históricas de Ixtlilxóchitl*, (1891), vol. l, footnote 2, pp. 49-50; Harold I. Velt, *America's Lost Civilizations*, (1949), p. 84; Miles Poindexter, *The Ayar Incas*, (New York, 1930), vol. 1, pp. 232, 236-239; Thor Heyerdahl, *American Indians in the Pacific*, (Stockholm, Sweden, 1952), who cites Cioza de Leon, Von Humboldt, and W. Bollaert to prove that ancient America had bearded white men as well as a bearded white god: pp. 229-345; Paul Herman, *Conquest by Man*, (New York, 1954), p. 83; A. L. Kroeber, "Cultural Relations Between North and South America," *Proceedings of the 23rd International Congress of Americanists*, (New York, 1930); Andres de Avendano y Loyola, *Relación de las dos Entradas que hize a Pe Ytza*, (1697), English translation by Philip A. Means, *History of the Conquest of Yucatan and of the Itzas*, (1917), p. 22.

EVIDENCE NO. 646: A POPULOUS DARK-SKINNED RACE

Claim: Critics have questioned the logic of the Book of Mormon claim that the Lord "did cause a skin of blackness to come upon" the Lamanites (2 Nephi 5:21). Others have questioned the possibility that the Lamanite population could have grown so much faster than that of the Nephites in such a short period of time—even though some of the wives of the rebellious sons of Ishmael left their husbands and rejoined the Nephites (2 Nephi 5:6; Jarom 1:6; Mosiah 25:3; Alma 2:27; 43:51; Helaman 4:25). However, both questions are answered with evidence, which suggests that Laman and Lemuel, and at least two of the sons of Ishmael, took additional wives while traveling in the Arabian Peninsula. (See Hilton, *Discovering Lehi*, (1996), chapter 11, pp. 139-147.)

Evidence: The evidence for this claim is presented below under eight categories:

1) <u>Dark Skin</u>: In spite of the fact that it was Laman and Lemuel who hated Nephi and had taught their children to hate Nephi's children (2 Nephi 3:14; 4 Nephi 39), the dark skin was given only to the *descendants* of the rebellious brothers rather than to the brothers themselves (1 Nephi 12:23). Most likely it was for this reason that Lehi expressed to the children of Laman his hope that the curse would "be taken from [them] and be answered upon the heads of [their] parents" (2 Nephi 4:6) who were obviously the guilty party that instituted the bitter hatred. It was further stated that anyone who intermarried with the Lamanites did not bring the dark skin upon himself, but upon his seed instead (2 Nephi 5:23; Alma 3:9). Conversely, the curse was removed from Lamanites who became righteous, but their skin color remained the same until they intermarried with the Nephites: "their curse was taken from them and their skin became white *like unto the Nephites*" (3 Nephi 2:14-16).

In relation to this, it would be well to remember that God often operates according to natural laws rather than simply creating all things instantaneously out-of-nothing by the mere power of his words. For example, the Bible states that God "*planted* a garden eastward in Eden" rather than just causing the garden to appear "out-of-nothing" (Genesis 2:8). The dark-skinned Arab women that the rebellious brothers may have married would have provided the most natural means for their children to inherit a dark skin.

2) <u>Polygamy</u>: The Nephites had been strictly forbidden to take more than one wife, which thing would have been an abomination for them at that time (Jacob 2:26-30). Furthermore, they were taught that "David and Solomon truly had many wives and concubines, which thing was abominable before me, saith the Lord" (Jacob 2:24). Laman and Lemuel, on the other hand, were rebellious to God's commandments and believed that the Jews at Jerusalem of that day were "righteous" (1 Nephi 1:19; 17:22), while the prophets had declared that they were guilty of "whoredoms" such as "desiring many wives and concubines" (Jacob 1:15; 2:33), and that they "followed the abominations of the heathen" (2 Chronicles 36:14). Laman, Lemuel and the sons of Ishmael who were also full of "all manner of abominations" (1 Nephi 12:23), most likely also practiced polygamy. In later years, however, it was the apostate Nephites who had begun to desire more than one wife, while the Lamanites had become monogamous (Jacob 3:5).

3) Ishmaelitish Women: There seems to be a distinction drawn in the Book of Mormon between the "daughters of Ishmael" and the "Ishmaelitish women" (Alma 3:7). Clearly the "daughters of Ishmael" were the actual children of father Ishmael whose family had joined Lehi's party (1 Nephi 7:1-2). The "Ishmaelitish women," on the other hand, were most likely descendants of Abraham and Hagar's son Ishmael, living in Arabia, who could have joined Lehi's party while traveling through the peninsula. The dark skin was upon the "Ishmaelite women" (Alma 3:7), but not upon the "daughters of Ishmael," who married Sam, Nephi, and Zoram, nor was it upon Nephi's sisters who married the sons of Ishmael (2 Nephi 5:6; also Erastus Snow, in *Journal of Discourses,* vol. 23, pp. 184-185).

4) Raiding: The Arabic tribes traditionally raided each other, as well as travelers from afar. Likewise, the Lamanites were continually raiding not only their enemies the Nephites, but they also raided each other. (See Mosiah 10:1-7; Alma 17:26-37; Hilton, *Discovering Lehi,* p. 146.)

5) Raw Meat: Arabs have traditionally eaten their meet raw, calling it *baster.* So also the Lamanites lived mainly on "raw meat" (Enos 1:20; Hilton, *Discovering Lehi,* p. 146).

6) Midian: While Midian is clearly an Arabic name, it was also employed by the Lamanites as a name for one of their cities (Alma 24:5; Hilton, p. 146).

7) Dancing: Hebrew men and women traditionally did not dance together, while Arab women were not similarly inhibited. Thus Laman and Lemuel as well as the sons of Ishmael danced with their wives on the ship during the voyage (1 Nephi 18:9).

8) Eagle & Snake Motif: The symbol of Mexico that is featured on their coins and flag depicts an eagle clutching a snake. This symbol is derived from an ancient American legend in which an eagle was seen clutching a snake as a sign that *Mexican* outcasts had finally found their "promised homeland." (See Michel Graulich, *Myths of Ancient Mexico,* [University of Oklahoma Press, 1997], pp. 241-243; and Michael E. Smith, *The Aztecs,* [Blackwell Publishers, 1996], p. 45.)

Coincidentally, this very same symbol was also used anciently in Arabia. Displayed in the museum of Saana, Yemen, is an agate ring, dated between the second and third century BC, in which is carved a rendering of the eagle clutching a snake. (Hilton, *Discovering Lehi,* [1996], p. 146, Figure 11-3.)

EVIDENCE NO. 647: LAMANITES IN POLYNESIA

Claim: The Book of Mormon explains that God caused the children of Laman and Lemuel to have dark skin because they hated Nephi, (their younger brother and spiritual leader), and tried to kill him (2 Nephi 5:21).

Evidence: The same basic ideas are found in the South Pacific, where, according to Latter-day Saint belief, many descendants of the Nephites and Lamanites lived. Alma wrote that Hagoth and a shipload of travelers were lost at sea (Alma 63:5-8). Some of the travelers could very well have been Lamanites. This would partially explain the dark skin among the Polynesian peoples.

Dr. John Martin found that the legends, particularly among the Tongan peoples, included stories of two brothers, one of which was industrious and creative, while the other was lazy and jealous. Eventually the older brother killed the younger, and as punishment, the god Tangaloa cursed the older brother and his children: "You shall be black because your minds are bad, and shall be destitute." Martin insists that this legend was much older than any of the teachings of early Christian missionaries, and was not a corruption of the Cain and Abel story. (See John Martin, *An Account of the Natives of the Tonga Islands,* [Boston: Charles Ewer, 1820], p. 337.)

EVIDENCE NO. 648: PEACEFUL LAMANITES

Claim: While the Book of Mormon usually portrays the Lamanites as a people who did not hesitate to fight, it also tells of a group of Lamanites who converted to Christianity and renounced their violent past by making a vow to never again take up arms (Alma 23:7-12). This group, who referred to themselves as *Anti-Nephi-Lehi*, even refused to defend themselves when they were being attacked by their fellow tribesmen (Alma 24). When the Nephites learned of the slaughter of these Lamanite Christians, they offered the surviving converts refuge in the land of Jershon and set it aside for an inheritance (Alma 27). According to Book of Mormon chronology, this new community was established sometime between 90 and 77 BC.

Evidence: According to recent research, the ancient city of Teotihuacan was established in south central Mexico around 64 BC. The unique feature of this city was that it not only lacked "defensive preparations, but also [lacked] any kind of military organization to come to the city's aid in time of attack." (See Vincent H. Malstrom, *Cycles of the Sun, Mysteries of the Moon,* [Austin: University of Texas Press, 1997], p. 129; cited in Jerry L. Ainsworth, *The Lives and Travels of Mormon and Moroni,* [Peacemakers Publishers, 200], p. 129.)

Undoubtedly, the pacifism of the people of Anti-Nephi-Lehi was carried on among many of their descendants for several generations. Indeed, when the Spaniards arrived in the New World, then encountered a group of Native Americans on the West Coast of Mexico that refused to fight. These natives claimed a tradition of never having fought and stated they would not break that tradition even at the peril of their own lives. In fact, the Pacific Ocean was actually named after these peace-loving natives. Around 1600 AD the Spaniards named the vast body of water "*El Oceano de los Pacificos*"—which literally means "the Ocean of the Peaceful People." (See *México a Traves de los Siglos,* [Mexico City: Editorial Cumbre, 1979], vol. 2, p. 459; also cited in Ainsworth, *Mormon and Moroni,* p. 133).

EVIDENCE NO. 649: THE HIDDEN RECORD OF THE ANCIENT AMERICANS

Claim: The Book of Mormon is the translation of sacred records about ancestors of some of the American Indians, which was handed down from one prophet to the next (usually from father to son), and eventually buried in the earth to come forth many hundreds of years later. (See preface to the Book of Mormon.) The teachings of Jesus Christ (that were personally delivered to the Mesoamericans after his crucifixion and resurrection in Palestine) are the central message of the Book of Mormon. (See 3 Nephi 11-30.)

Joseph Smith testified that he unearthed the gold plates from which he translated the Book of Mormon, hundreds of years after it had been hidden by an ancient prophet of God (Joseph Smith—History 1:51-52, 59-62, 67-68).

Evidence: According to Peter DeRoo, the Otomis tribe tells of a "Divine Book" which had been handed down from father to son and guarded by persons of importance. The natives claim that it told of the crucifixion of Jesus Christ. It is said that out of reverence, the Indians did not touch it with their hands but turned its pages with a small stick. They say that the book perished in the ground where its guardians had buried it. (See Peter DeRoo, *America Before Columbus,* [New York: J. P. Lippincott Co., 1900], p. 425, cited in Cheesman, *The World of the Book of Mormon,* p. 6.)

In the *Popol Vuh,* the sacred record of the Quiché Maya of Guatemala it is written that "we shall write now under the Law of God ... we shall bring it to light because [the original record] ... cannot be seen any more, in which was clearly seen the coming from the other side of the sea. The original book, written long ago, existed, but its sight is hidden to the searcher and to the thinker" (Delia Goetz and Sylvannus G. Morley, *Popol Vuh,* English translation by Adrian Recinos, [University of Oklahoma Press: Norman, 1950], pp. 79-80).

This hidden record contained a history of the creation of the world, much of which was preserved in the *Popol Vuh.* See the evidence regarding THE CREATION RECORDED IN A HIDDEN BOOK in the chapter "Another Testament of Jesus Christ" included in this same volume.

EVIDENCE NO. 650: THE SIGNIFICANCE OF THE DAY THE PLATES WERE UNEARTHED

Claim: On September 22, 1827, Joseph Smith received permission from the angel Moroni to remove the gold plates of the Book of Mormon from Hill Cumorah (Joseph Smith—History 1:59). He had no idea of the significance of that date.

Evidence: September 22, 1827, was the autumnal equinox, which focuses on several important events at the New Year concerning covenant renewal and the re-enthronement of the king. It was also the Jewish New Year's Day. In ancient Israel and Judah, the New Year could come with either the beginning or ending of the harvest season—near either the vernal or autumnal equinox, that is, Passover-Unleavened Bread for Israel, and Trumpets-Atonement-Tabernacles for Judah, respectively. (See Edwin R. Thiele, *A Chronology of the Hebrew Kings* [Zondervan, 1977], pp. 14; cited in "New Year's Celebrations," January 1985 in the *Foundation for Ancient Research and Mormon Studies Monthly Update* for 1985 by FARMS Staff [STF-85u].)

The symbolic significance of this date contains several close parallels to the stated purpose of the Book of Mormon. The following is quoted from an article by Lenet Hadley Read, entitled "Joseph Smith's Receipt of the Plates and the Israelite Feast of Trumpets," in *Journal of Book of Mormon Studies,* (Fall 1993), vol. 2, no. 2, p. 110, (italics added):

> Joseph Smith received the golden plates on the Israelite Day of *Remembrance* (or Rosh ha-Shanah). Biblical references and interpretation by Jewish sages through the centuries set this day as the day God would *remember* his covenants with *Israel* to bring them back from *exile*. Also called the Feast of Trumpets, on this day ritual trumpet blasts signify the issuance of *revelation* and a call for Israel to gather for God's word of redemption. Set at the time of Israel's final agricultural harvest, the day also symbolizes the Lord's final harvest of souls. Furthermore, it initiates the completion of the Lord's time periods, the *Days of Awe*, and signifies the last time to prepare for *final judgment* and the *Messianic Age*. The coming forth of the Book of Mormon is literally fulfilling such prophecies of the day.

Compare the above symbology with the stated purpose of the Book of Mormon, taken from it's title page (italics added): "Which is to show unto the *remnant of the House of Israel* what *great things the Lord hath done* for their fathers; and that they may *know the covenants* of the Lord, that they are *not cast off forever*—And also to the convincing of the Jew and Gentile that JESUS is the CHRIST, the ETERNAL GOD, *manifesting himself unto all nations*—And now, if there are faults they are the mistakes of men; wherefore, condemn not the things of God, that ye may be found spotless at the *judgment-seat of Christ*."

EVIDENCE NO. 651: METAL PLATES IN ANCIENT AMERICA

Claim: The inscribed metal plates Joseph Smith translated into the Book of Mormon were not the only ancient American records engraven on metal plates. (See 1 Nephi 1:1-3; 3:3; 9:1-6; 19:1-6; 2 Nephi 5:14-17, 28-33; Jacob 1:1-4; Mosiah 8:9; 21:27; 28:10-12; Alma 8:21-31; Ether 1:1-5; 15:33-34.)

Joseph Smith claimed that he had been directed by an angel to unearth a set of gold plates that contained engravings of ancient prophets. When he was told to translate an ancient history from the plates, neither he nor anyone else had ever heard of any ancient peoples having recorded anything on metal plates, particularly gold plates. The thought of gold plates was strange and unusual, even to Joseph Smith himself. He knelt in prayer and cried, "O God, what will the world say?" (Elder LeGrand Richards related having heard this account from Elder Charles A. Callis, *Conference Report*, October 1946, p. 125. Cited in Paul R. Cheesman, *The World of the Book of Mormon*, p. Vii.)

Evidence: In answer to Joseph's concern about what the world might say about ancient histories having been engraven on metal plates, the answer from God was, "Fear not, I will cause the earth to testify the truth of these things" (*Conference Report*, 1946, p. 125). This is exactly what has happened. Since this prophetic revelation, hundreds of archaeological finds have been unearthed to prove that the ancient Americans did, indeed, record their histories on metal plates, including plates of gold—as if the very earth is testifying of the truth of the Book of Mormon.

For examples of metal plates discovered in the Amaricas, see Emerson, *Indian Myths*, p. 225; Padre Gay, *Historia de Oxaca*, vol. 1, chapter 4, p. 62; *Geografía y Compendio Historia del Estado Antigua en Columbia*, (Paris, 1885), p. 517; *The Newport, Vermont, Express and Standard*, August 15, 1882; Saville, *The Goldsmith's Art In Ancient Mexico*, 1920, pp. 10, 16, 175, 180; Juan de Torquemada, *Los Viente i un Libros Rituales Monarquia Indiana*, 3 vols., (Madrid, Spain, 1613 and 1723); Sahagun, *Libro Noveno*, chapter 15; J. J. Tschudi, *Peruvian Antiquities*, 1853, p. 105; Turner, *Pioneer History of Western New York*, p. 668; See Ariel Crowley, *Metal Record Plates in Ancient Times* (1947), pp. 6-7; Louis Houch, *A History of Missouri*, vol. 1, pp. 395-403, cited in Cheesman, *Ancient Writing on Metal Plates* (1985), p. 50; Curtis Wright, *Metallic Documents of Antiquity*, p. 457; U. Schmoll in *Zeitschrift der Deutschen Morgenländischen Gesellschaft*, vol. 113 (1964), pp. 512-514; H. Herbert's Paper in *Journal of the American Oriental Society*, vol. 72 (1953), pp. 169. Both cited in Nibley, *Since Cumorah* (1988), p. 221.

EVIDENCE NO. 652: METAL PLATES IN THE MIDDLE EAST

Claim: Joseph Smith claimed that he translated the Book of Mormon from ancient metal plates "with the appearance of gold" that he unearthed near Manchester, New York. (See introduction to the Book of Mormon.) The Book of Mormon claims that the ancient Americans patterned their plates after similar plates in and around Jerusalem (1 Nephi 3:3, 19:1-6). To skeptics and critics this idea was as ridiculous as Joseph Smith's claim to have ancient American golden plates. The skeptical world countered with assertions that no metallic plates were ever used in the ancient Mideastern cultures. Everyone assumed that the ancient scribes of the Middle East wrote only on parchment scrolls—not metallic plates. However, what was originally considered as evidence against the Book of Mormon, has become another evidence that it is true. Historical records of the ancient Near East have recently been discovered that were kept on metal plates, including those made of gold.

Evidence: Many years after Joseph Smith made this claim, the scientific world has found hundreds of examples of ancient people having written on metal plates, including gold, containing ancient history. For example, Hebrew inscriptions on a gold plate were found in Sicily. Three gold plaques were found in Italy with Phoenician engravings. The gold plates of Darius were found in a stone box, similar to the stone box from which Joseph Smith took his plates. The following is quoted from a *Foundation for Ancient Research and Mormon Studies Update,* (July 1994), no. 95, p. 2:

> In the past, critics of the Book of Mormon have attacked the alleged absurdity of the Book of Mormon having been written on golden plates and its claim of the existence of an early sixth century BC version of the Hebrew Bible written on brass plates.[1] Today, however, critics almost universally admit that there are numerous examples of ancient writing on metal plates. Ironically, some critics now claim instead that knowledge of such plates were readily available in Joseph Smith's day. Hugh Nibley's 1952 observation seems quite prescient: "it will not be long before men forget that in Joseph Smith's day the prophet was mocked and derided for his description of the plates more than anything else."[2]

> Recent re-evaluation of the evidence now points to the fact that the Book of Mormon's description of sacred records written on bronze plates fits quite nicely in the cultural milieu of the ancient eastern Mediterranean.

> One of the earliest known surviving examples of writing on "copper plates" are the Byblos Syllabic inscriptions (eighteenth century BC), from the city of Byblos on the Phoenician coast. The script is described as a "syllabary [which] is clearly inspired by the Egyptian hieroglyphic system, and in fact is the most important link known between the hieroglyphs and the Canaanite alphabet,"[3] It would not be unreasonable to describe the Byblos Syllabic texts as eighteenth century BC Semitic "bronze plates" written in "reformed Egyptian characters."[4]

> Walter Burkert, in his recent study of the cultural dependence of Greek civilization on the ancient Near East, refers to the transmission of the practice of writing on bronze plates ... from the Phoenicians to the Greeks. "The reference to 'bronze [plates]' as a term [among the Greeks] for ancient sacral laws would point back to the seventh or sixth century [BC]" as the period in which the terminology and the practice of writing on bronze plates was transmitted from the Phoenicians to the

Greeks.[5] Students of the Book of Mormon will note that this is precisely the time and place in which the Book of Mormon claims that there existed similar bronze plates which contained the "ancient sacred laws" of the Hebrews, the close cultural cousins of the Phoenicians.

---

[1] For example, John Hyde Jr., *Mormonism: Its Leaders and Designs,* (New York: Fetridge, 1857), pp. 217-218; M. T. Lamb, *The Golden Bible,* (New York: Ward and Drummond, 1887) p. 11; and Stuart Martin, *The Mystery of Mormonism,* (London: Odhams Press, 1920), p. 27; See William J. Hamblin, "Sacred Writing on Bronze Plates in the Ancient Mediterranean," available from *Foundation for Ancient Research and Mormon Studies,* for full references and analysis of the issues raised in this Update.

[2] Hugh Nibley, *Lehi in the Desert,* (1988), p. 107.

[3] See David Noel Freedman, editor, *The Anchor Bible Dictionary,* vol. 4, pp. 178-180. Byblos is only about 170 miles north of Jerusalem.

[4] Nibley, *Lehi in the Desert,* (1988), pp. 105-106, mentions these plates, which were not deciphered until 1985.

[5] Walter Burkert, *The Orientalizing Revolution: Near Eastern Influence on Greek Culture in the Early Archaic Age,* p. 30.

See also Wright, *Metallic Documents of Antiquity,* p. 457; Gabriel Barkay, "The Divine Name Found in Jerusalem," *Biblical Archaeology Review,* (1983), vol. 9, no. 2, pp. 14-19; Gabriel Barkay, "Priestly Blessings on Silver Plates" (in Hebrew), *Cathedra,* (1989), vol. 52, pp. 46-59; Michael D. Coogan, "10 Great Finds," *Biblical Archaeology Review,* (May-June 1995), vol. 21, no. 3, pp. 36-47; U. Schmoll in *Zeitschrift der Deutschen Morgenländischen Gesellschaft,* vol. 113, (1964), pp. 512-514; C. Colonna in *Archaeology,* vol. 19, (1966), p. 21. (H. H. Paper, in *Journal of the American Oriental Society,* vol. 72, (1953), p. 169; William F. Albright, *From the Stone Age to Christianity,* (1940), p. 13; George A. Barton, *Archaeology of the Bible* (6th edition 1933), p. 74, fig. 26, p. 87; Anstock-Darga, M. "Semitische Inscariften auf Silbertafelchen aus dem 'Bertiz'-Tal," *Jahrbt. Kleinasiat Forschung,* vol. 1, (1950), p. 199; A. Dupont-Sommer, "Deux Lamelles d'argent a inscription hebreo-arameenne," *Jahrh f. Kleinasiat-Forschung,* vol. 1, (1950), pp. 201-217; H. Bossert, *Orientalia,* vol. 20, (1951), pp. 70-77; W. Andrae, *Hittitische Inschriften auf Bleistreifen aus Assur,* (Leipzig: Hinrichs, 1924); J. Bothero, "Deux Tablettes de fondation, enior et argent, d'Assurnasirpal II," *Semetica* vol. 1, (1948), pp. 25-32; Breasted, *Ancient Records,* p. 202; *Bulletin of the American Schools of Oriental Research* No. 60, p. 3; *Chamber's Encyclopedia,* (1927), vol. 10, pp. 755-756; *Cyclopedia of Biblical Literature,* "Art Lead." John Kitto; Samuel Fallows, *Bible Encyclopedia,* p. 74; A. Von Gall, *Basileia tou Theou,* p. 77; Ali Jawad, *Tarikhal-Arab Qubl al-Islam,* (Baghdad, 1951), vol. 1, p. 14; Sten Konow, "Kalawan Copper-plate Inscription of the Year 134," *Journal of the Royal Asiat Society,* (1932), pp. 950, 965; J. Obermann, "An Early Phoenician Political Document" *Journal of Biblical Literature,* vol. 58, (1939), pp. 229-231; A. Olivieri, *Lamellae Aureau Orphicae in Kleine Texte,* No. 133, (1915); *Bulletin of the American School of Oriental Research,* vol. 73, p. 9; H. Ranke, "Eine Bleitzfel mit hierogl. Inschrift," *Zeitschrift für Ägyptische Sprache und Altertumskunde,* vol. 74, 1938, pp. 49-50; A. H. Sayce, *The Hittites,* (1925), pp. 41, 125, 170; Seck, *From the Pyramids to Paul,* p. 224; F. Thureau-Dangin, "Une tablette en Or provanant d'Umma," *Revue D'Assyriologie,* vol. 34, (1937), pp. 177-183; Richard Watson, *Bible and Theological Dictionary*; William F. Albright, *Bulletin of the American Schools of Oriental Research,* vol. 73, p. 9; E. S. Drower, *The Mandeans of Iraq and Iran* (Oxford: 1937), pp. 23, 132; Henry Guppy, "Human Records, A Survey of Their History From the Beginning," *Bulletin of the John Rylands Library,* vol. 27 (1942-1943), p. 197. All cited in Cheesman, *Ancient Writing on Metal Plates* (Bountiful: Horizon Publishing, 1985), pp. 87-89, Nibley, *Since Cumorah,* (1988) pp. 273-274, William J. Anderson, "Lehi's Jerusalem and Writing on Metal Plates," *Journal of Book of Book of Mormon Studies,* (1994), vol. 3, no. 1, pp. 204-206.

Evidences Relative to the Cave of Lehi

The Book of Mormon records that Lehi's sons fled Jerusalem (most likely to the south—since they were camped in the wilderness south of Jerusalem) after a second failed attempt at obtaining the *brass plates* from Laban. The servants of Laban who were under orders to slay Nephi and his brothers followed them in hot pursuit. Nephi records that after fleeing from the city they hid themselves in a cave (1 Nephi 3:24-27). A cave called *The Cave of Lehi* was recently discovered in the region where Nephi and his brothers most likely hid themselves. It contains several remarkable parallels to Nephi's story. Each provides evidence that the Book of Mormon is true.

EVIDENCE NO. 653: FLEEING TO THE CAVE OF LEHI

Claim: The logical assumption is that Lehi's sons fled southward for it was in a southern direction that Lehi's caravan had traveled in order to be located "by the borders near the shore of the Red Sea" (1 Nephi 2:5). Lehi's sons most likely fled south in the direction of the most logical region—Hebron, the city of refuge—where those who felt unjustly accused could find safety (Joshua 20). See Vestal and Wallace, *The Firm Foundation of Mormonism* (1981), pp. 106-107.

Evidence: Just ten miles east of Hebron is a cave, uncovered during the construction of a highway in 1961. It is very significant that the local populace, knowing of a cave in the region, called it *Khirbet Beit Lei*, "The ruins of the house of Lehi (or "The ruins of Lehi's family," since *beit* may mean either "house" or "family"). This cavern was originally used as a tomb, but was later occupied by refugees fleeing Jerusalem. This and following information is from Joseph Ginat, an anthropologist who served as deputy advisor on Arab affairs to Golda Meier, former Prime Minister of Israel, who presented his findings at the 21st Symposium on the Archaeology of the Scriptures at Brigham Young University on October 16, 1971.

Part of the inscription on the wall of the cave portends danger: "Deliver us O Lord!"

See Joseph Ginat, "The Cave at Khirbet Beit Lei," *Newsletter and Proceedings of The Society for Early Historic Archaeology*, no. 129, April 1972; see also, LaMar C. Berrett, *Discovering the World of the Bible* (Provo, Utah: Brigham Young University Press, 1973), pp. 395-396; also Ross T. and Ruth R. Christensen, "Archaeology Reveals Old Testament History: Digging for the Truth," *Ensign*, February 1974, p. 66. Cited in Vestal and Wallace, *The Firm Foundation of Mormonism* (1981), p. 107.

EVIDENCE NO. 654: THE CAVE WAS OCCUPIED AROUND 600 BC

Claim: The Book of Mormon is very specific about the time Lehi left Jerusalem: It was shortly after "the commencement of the first year of the reign of Zedekiah, king of Judah," six hundred years before the birth of Jesus Christ (1 Nephi 1:4; 10:4; 19:8). Bible scholars estimate that Zedekiah ascended to the throne in approximately 600 BC.

Evidence: By observing that the inscriptions in the walls of the cave are of the pre-captivity style of Hebrew spoken up to 600 BC, scholars have dated the cave occupation to be around 600 BC. Commenting on inscriptions on the wall of the cave, Joseph Naveh of the Hebrew University in Jerusalem said that there is no reason to date them later than the 6th Century BC. (Joseph Naveh, "Old Hebrew Inscriptions in a Burial Cave," *Israel Exploration Journal* [Jerusalem, Israel: 1963], vol. 13, no. 2, p. 89.)

Dr. Frank Moore Cross, Jr. of Harvard agrees that the Beit Lei inscriptions are safely dated to the 6th Century BC. (Frank Moore Cross, Jr., "The Cave Inscriptions from Khirbet Beit Lei," *Near Eastern Archaeology in the Twentieth Century*, edited by James A. Sanders [Garden City, New York: Doubleday and Company, Inc., 1970], p. 304. Both sources cited in Vestal and Wallace, *The Firm Foundation of Mormonism* [1981], p. 107.)

EVIDENCE NO. 655: THE REFUGEES FLED TO AVOID BABYLONIAN INVADERS

Claim: The Book of Mormon states that the family of Lehi left Jerusalem to escape the impending destruction of approaching Babylonian armies (1 Nephi 1:13).

Evidence: Dr. Joseph Ginat commented that "the inscriptions may have been written there (in the cave) by someone fleeing before the Babylonian invaders who destroyed Judah and its capital city in 587 BC" (Ginat, "The Cave at Khirbet Beit Lei," *Newsletter & Proceedings of the SEHA,* April 1972, p. 3).

The Israel Museum states that the text of the inscriptions "appears to be poetic or prophetic, jotted down by refugees hiding from the conquering Babylonian army." (*Inscriptions Reveal Documents from the Time of the Bible, the Mishna and the Talmud* [Jerusalem, Israel: Israel Museum], p. 44. Both cited in Vestal and Wallace, *The Firm Foundation of Mormonism* [1981], p. 107.)

EVIDENCE NO. 656: THE REFUGEES LOOKED FORWARD TO THE REDEMPTION OF JERUSALEM

Claim: Lehi prophesied that after Jerusalem and the House of Israel is scattered, that they would be gathered again (1 Nephi 10:14). Nephi quotes the Lord as saying that he will bring the House of Israel again out of captivity, "and they shall be gathered together to the lands of their inheritance ... and they shall know that the Lord is their Savior and their Redeemer" (1 Nephi 22:12). This was stated after the cave incident, but there is no reason to suppose they were not aware of the redemption of Israel as early as the first warnings of Jerusalem's destruction. Lehi was aware of the "redemption of the world" (1 Nephi 1:19), which would, of course, include the redemption of Jerusalem. Furthermore, most prophecies of the scattering of Israel are followed by a promise of its redemption and gathering.

Evidence: One of the inscriptions on the wall of the cave speaks of the Lord accepting the cities of Judah and promising to redeem Jerusalem. Frank Moore Cross, Jr. suggests that the inscriptions in the cave are a "citation of a lost prophecy" (Cross, "The Cave Inscriptions from Khirbet Beit Lei," p. 304).

Dr. Joseph Ginat says, "only a prophet would dare make such a statement-prophecy accepting the cities of Judah and promising the redemption of Jerusalem" (Ginat, "The Cave at Khirbet Beit Lei," *Newsletter & Proceedings,* April 1972, p. 3). Both are cited in Vestal and Wallace, *The Firm Foundation of Mormonism* (1981), p. 107.

EVIDENCE NO. 657: THE REFUGEES LIVED IN TENTS

Claim: Nephi makes several references to the fact that his family lived in tents after leaving Jerusalem and during their mission to Jerusalem (1 Nephi 2:4; 4:9).

Evidence: Two unusual circles on the north wall of the cave chamber were identified as a camp layout and a tent. "The circular incision on the left ... recalls the schematic plans of the Assyrian camps, the incision on the right is perhaps a tent ... I have to thank Prof. Y. Yadin for this observation." (See Naveh, Joseph Naveh, "Old Hebrew Inscriptions in a Burial Cave," *Israel Exploration Journal* [Jerusalem, Israel: 1963], vol. 13, no. 2, p. 76, footnote 5; Y. Yadin, *Warfare in Biblical Lands in the Light of Archaeology*, Ramat-Gan, 1963, Figs. on pp. 293-294, 393 [Hebrew]. See also Hugh Nibley, "Lehi in the Deseret," *The Improvement Era*, April 1950, p. 276. All sources cited in Vestal and Wallace, *The Firm Foundation of Mormonism* [1981], p. 108, footnote 47.)

EVIDENCE NO. 658: THE REFUGEES LATER SAILED BY SHIP

Claim: The Book of Mormon states that the families of Lehi and Ishmael built and boarded a ship to sail to a new land (1 Nephi 17:7; 18:1-8). As early as 1 Nephi 2:20, they knew they were to be led to a new land.

Evidence: A remarkable find in the cave was the discovery of the drawings of ships on the south wall of the main chamber. (Joseph Naveh, "Old Hebrew Inscriptions in a Burial Cave," *Israel Exploration Journal* [Jerusalem: 1963], vol. 13, no. 2, p. 78, cited in Vestal and Wallace, *The Firm Foundation* [1981], p. 108.)

Evidences Relative to Stela 5, at Izapa, Mexico

Stela 5 is a bas-relief sculpture discovered at Izapa, Chiapas, Mexico near the Guatemalan border. Izapa was occupied between approximately 300 BC and AD 300, between the Olmec and Mayan civilizations. The Stela 5, one of twenty-two found in the region, is the most complex, obviously bearing the most important message. Latter-day Saint scholars have concluded that the Stela was not created during the Book of Mormon time period, but was a later effort by descendants to record a sacred narrative of great importance to their ancestors.

Some scholars have expressed doubts about Stela 5 having any connection with the Book of Mormon account of the Tree of Life vision. Nevertheless, according to several scholars there are many images on the stone that easily correlate to the Book of Mormon interpretation. Dr. M. Wells Jakeman has studied the Stela for many years and has published much information concerning it. Dr. Jakeman has counted at least forty striking parallels between the Stela 5 and the Book of Mormon account of the Tree of Life vision. Below is a sampling of some of the similarities. (See for example, Joseph L. Allen, *Exploring the Lands of the Book of Mormon,* [Orem, Utah: S. A. Publishers, Inc., 1989], p. 119).

Figure 10. The Stela 5 sculpture at Izapa, Mexico

EVIDENCE NO. 659: THE GREAT AND SPACIOUS BUILDING

<u>Claim</u>: In Lehi's dream he sees a large and spacious building which represents the pride of the world. This building was floating "in the air, high above the earth" (1 Nephi 8:26; 11:35-36).

<u>Evidence</u>: In the very top of the image on Stela 5, is what appears to be the decorative lintel or facade of a large structure. The location of the structure above the tree could be an attempt to show that it was "high above the earth," as was the building in the dream.

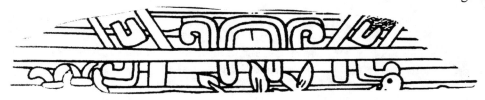

EVIDENCE NO. 660: THE TREE OF LIFE

<u>Claim</u>: The Book of Mormon tells of the vision of the Tree of Life witnessed by Lehi and his son, Nephi (1 Nephi 8, 11). The fruit of the tree was said to be sweet above all that is sweet and was able to fill those who partake until they hunger not. There was also an iron rod that "extended along the bank of the river, and led to the tree" (1 Nephi 8:11-19; Alma 32:42).

Assuming that this important vision was taught to the descendants of these men, representations of this vision could be expected to appear in ancient American art.

<u>Evidence</u>: Non-Mormon scholars, such as Clyde E. Keller, have concluded that the stone gives a representation of the Tree of Life. This conclusion should not have been unexpected because the tree, bearing life-giving fruit to all around it, occupies the central focal point of the entire Stela. (See Clyde E. Keller, "The Cuna Indian Tree of Life," *Bulletin of the Georgia Academy of Science*, vol. 15, no.1 [1957], p. 32, cited in Alan K. Parish, "Stela 5, Izapa: A Layman's Consideration of the Tree of Life Stone," *The Book of Mormon: First Nephi, The Doctrinal Foundation* [Provo: Brigham Young University], 1988], p. 127).

To the left of the tree are two humming birds. These birds provide a unique and unmistakable way to symbolize the sweetness of the fruit. Humming birds are known for their constant search for the sweet nectar from plants such as the honeysuckle. Above the birds is a pair of fish, tied and hanging, as if being saved for a meal. Below them, half way down the tree are the same two fish eating the fruit. This would seem to indicate that these fish are first filled with the fruit and then provided by the tree to fill the needs of the hungry.

At the roots of the tree is a broad thick line, held up by three triangular supports, that runs near the river straight to the tree. This is possibly the rod of iron mentioned in the dream. (See Jakeman, *Stela 5, Izapa, Chiapas, Mexico* [Provo: The University Archaeology Society Special Publication Number 2, 1958], p. 14.)

EVIDENCE NO. 661: THE FOUNTAIN OF LIVING WATER

<u>Claim</u>: The Book of Mormon makes mention of the fountain of living water in Lehi's dream which represents the love of God (1 Nephi 11:25).

<u>Evidence</u>: On the right side of the bas-relief of Stela 5 is the image of water flowing vertically as if from a spring or a fountain. Note that this water is not speckled, as is the water that runs horizontally just under the tree. This would seem to indicate that it is clean and pure.

EVIDENCE NO. 662: A RIVER OF FILTHY WATER

<u>Claim</u>: Lehi claimed that he saw a river of water which was filthy and represented hell (1 Nephi 8:13; 15:27-29).

<u>Evidence</u>: There is a river of water shown flowing by the Tree of Life represented by wavy lines. Note the chiseled marks in the figure below—signifying the filthiness of the water. See M. Wells Jakeman, *Stela 5, Izapa, Chiapas, Mexico* (Provo: The University Archaeology Society Special Publication Number 2, 1958), p. 14.

EVIDENCE NO. 663: LEHI'S NAME GLYPH

<u>Claim</u>: Lehi is the great ancestor of many of the ancient American peoples, who taught his family about his vision or dream of the Tree of Life. See, for example, 1 Nephi 2:1-4; 8; 11; Alma 9:9; 10:3; Helaman 8:22.

<u>Evidence</u>: The principal person depicted on the left side of the tree on the Stela 5 appears to be a religious leader who, with arm raised in gesture, seems to be teaching a family member about the tree. Above this old bearded man is a jaw of a crocodile. It is interesting to note that the meaning of the name *Lehi* in Hebrew is *jaw, jawbone* or *cheek*. See M. Wells Jakeman, *Stela 5, Izapa, Chiapas, Mexico: A Major Archaeological Discovery of the New World* (Provo: Brigham Young University, 1958), pp. 32-33, n. 49; and *Interpreter's Dictionary of the Bible*, 5 vols. (Nashville, Tennessee: Parthenon Press, 1962), vol. 3, pp. 110-111, cited in Alan K. Parrish, "Stela 5 Izapa: A Layman's Consideration of the Tree of Life Stone" in *The Book of Mormon First Nephi, The Doctrinal Foundation*, edited by Monte S. Nyman and Charles D. Tate Jr. (Provo, Utah, 1988), p. 134.

The glyph that shows an upper jaw or cheek is known as the crocodile glyph. In Aztec terminology this glyph is called *cipactli*—which means crocodile. It is interesting to note that the *name* of the ancestor of the ancient

Americans, according to their legends, was known as *Mox* or *Cipactonal*. *Mox, Imox* or *Imix* is Mayan for the Nahuatl or Aztec Cipactli, all of which are names for the sign of the first day of the ancient calendar. This is highly significant because it could have been designed to symbolize the first ancestor of their people by showing his glyph as the first of each year. See Francisco Nunez de la Vega, *Constituciones Dioecesanas del Obispado de Chiappa* (Rome, 1702), pp. 9, 10 cited in Jakeman, *Stela 5*, p. 34.

Incidentally, the name *Mox* (pronounced 'mosh,' the letter X in Mayan orthography, has the sound of "sh") very closely imitates the Egyptian word *Msh* which means "crocodile"—just as the Aztec word *cipactili* means crocodile. This further supports the Book of Mormon claim that the New World culture was influenced by the Egyptian language and culture (1 Nephi 1:2; Mosiah 1:4; Mormon 9:32). See Jakeman, *Stela 5*, p. 35.

Similarly, the ancient Maya of Chichén Itza refer to their original ancestor as "Lord Jawbone." (See Linda Schele and David Freidel, *A Forest of Kings: The Untold Story of the Ancient Maya*, [New York: William Morrow, 1990], p. 362, cited in Jerry L. Ainsworth, *The Lives and Travels of Mormon and Moroni*, [Peacemakers Publishing, an Imprint of Lamar-Lee, Inc., 2000], p. 138.)

EVIDENCE NO. 664: SARIAH'S NAME GLYPH ON STELA 5

Claim: The Book of Mormon introduces Sariah as wife of the prophet Lehi who supported her husband in teaching eternal truths to their children. See 1 Nephi 1:1.

Evidence: The headdress of the person behind Lehi resembles Egyptian representations of a queen or princess, and may be a name glyph representing Sariah, which means "princess of Yahweh." She is situated behind the key figure to lend support and encouragement. (See Jakeman, *Stela 5*, p. 37, cited in Parrish, "Stela 5 Izapa: A Layman's Consideration of the Tree of Life Stone" in *The Book of Mormon First Nephi, The Doctrinal Foundation*, edited by Monte S. Nyman and Charles D. Tate Jr. (Provo, Utah, 1988), p. 135).

EVIDENCE NO. 665: NEPHI'S NAME GLYPH ON STELA 5

Claim: Nephi, known for his large stature, wrote the story of his family's flight from Jerusalem and of his vision of the Tree of Life. See 1 Nephi 1:1 and Chapter 11.

Evidence: The key figure on the right of three on Stela 5 shows a young man of large stature with a serpent projecting out from his forehead and a plant rising above the leaves flowing down his back. A glyph design resembling an ear of corn is above his head. This may very well be a representation of maize (that is, Indian corn or grain) which symbolizes the ancient Egyptian grain god, *Nepri* or *Nepi* (the "p" was aspirated), corresponding even more closely with Nephi of the Book of Mormon. See E. A. Wallace Budge, *The Gods of the Egyptians, or Studies in Egyptian Mythology* (London, 1904), p. 332; G. Maspero, *History of Egypt...* (London n. d.), vol. 1, pp. 51, 54; Alan H. Gardiner, *Egyptian Grammar: Being an Introduction to the Study of Hieroglyphs* (Oxford, 1927), pp. 472,546; Jaroslav Cerny, *Ancient Egyptian Religion* (London, 1952), p. 58. All cited in Jakeman, *Stela 5, Chiapas, Mexico*, (1958), pp. 40, 43-44, cited in Parrish, "Stela 5," pp. 135-136.

It is noteworthy that this figure is shown holding a stick or stylus as if he were writing. This calls to mind the great amount of writing Nephi contributed to the Book of Mormon—especially the account he made of this very incident. Over the Nepri or Nepi glyph is an object with the appearance of an umbrella—the symbol of rulership in Mesoamerica as well as in Egypt (Jakeman, *Stela*, pp. 26-28). This is significant since the Book of Mormon indicates that the Lord called Nephi to be a ruler and teacher over his brethren (1 Nephi 2:22).

EVIDENCE NO. 666: LAMAN AND LEMUEL REPRESENTED ON STELA 5

Claim: The Book of Mormon explains that Lehi lamented Laman and Lemuel's refusal to partake of the fruit of the Tree of Life (1 Nephi 8:17-18, 35-38). Both Laman and Lemuel may have been given their Arabic names during Lehi's travels among Arabic traders.

Evidence: At the base of the tree are seated two persons (one on each side) with their backs to the tree. These are identified with Laman and Lemuel for the following reasons: (1) their backs are turned against the tree—symbolizing their refusal to partake of the fruit; (2) they wear turbans with a neck cloth at the back, after the style of the Arabs—possibly representing their Arabic names; (3) they are much smaller than "Nephi," who was larger in stature both physically *and* spiritually. The first figure (seated before the bearded old man) is most likely Laman since he is seated closer to the old man and woman, as if he were their firstborn son, and the smoke in front of his face could symbolize the cloud of darkness in Laman's mind and his inability to see with the eyes of understanding.

The second of two figures seated with their backs to the tree is most likely Lemuel since he is seated second from the old man and woman as if he were their second child. For more information, see Jakeman, *Stela 5*, pp. 27-29.

EVIDENCE NO. 667: NEPHI'S BROTHER SAM REPRESENTED

Claim: The Book of Mormon portrays Sam as a supportive brother to Nephi in contrast to Laman and Lemuel who objected to Nephi's rule and turned their backs to the tree (see 1 Nephi 2:17-18; 7:6; 8:17-18; 2 Nephi 5:6; Alma 3:6).

Evidence: The figure seated just behind the engraver on the right side of the Stela appears to be in a supportive position, holding an object over Nephi. This clearly fits the personality of Sam, as described in the Book of Mormon. The object appears to be an umbrella or parasol—the Egyptian symbol of rulership—possibly indicating Sam's willingness to accept Nephi's rule (see Jakeman, *Stela 5* [1958], pp. 26-28).

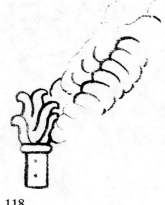

EVIDENCE NO. 668: THE CURTAIN OF FIRE

Claim: The Book of Mormon mentions a curtain of fire that divided the wicked from the righteous, and represented the justice of God (1 Nephi 15:30).

Evidence: The flames rising out of the censer-like object shown between Lehi and Laman, mentioned above, separates the prophet from his rebellious son and could easily represent the curtain of fire referred to in the Book of Mormon.

EVIDENCE NO. 669: THE MISTS OF DARKNESS

Claim: In the vision of *the Tree of Life*, Nephi describes the attempts of the devil to blind the eyes of the children of men who were searching for the tree. "And the mists of darkness are the temptations of the devil, which *blindeth the eyes* and hardeneth the hearts of the children of men, and leadeth them away into broad roads, that they perish and are lost" (1 Nephi 12:17).

Evidence: As mentioned above, a column of smoke between the figure of Lehi and Laman is shown billowing up toward the face of Laman—as if to symbolize his spiritual blindness, and the cloud of error that darkened his mind. Also since the smoke is between the prophet father and his rebellious son, it would seem to indicate the communication barrier between the two which blocked Lehi's teachings from entering the heart of Laman. Also note that Lehi is pointing his finger towards Laman as if he were lecturing him.

Additionally, just to the left of the tree is the figure of a man who appears to have a hood over his head. At least he has no eyes. This might well represent those spoken of in the Book of Mormon who are blinded by the devil and thus cannot find the fruit to partake of it and to enjoy its life-giving nourishment.

EVIDENCE NO. 670: PARTAKERS OF THE FRUIT TURN AWAY FROM THE TREE

Claim: Lehi stated that in his dream he saw people who partook of the fruit but became ashamed and turned away because of the scoffers in the large building. Others turned away before reaching the tree and were also lost (1 Nephi 8:23-28, 32).

Evidence: On Stela 5 is shown a man to the left of the tree holding its fruit, but with his back turned away from the tree as if he were ashamed.

On the right side of the tree between the two figures believed to represent Lemuel and Nephi is a small figure that could also represent those who turned away from the path. Just below the small figure are two lines that seem to represent the pathway or the rod of iron or both. Notice that the body is turned in one direction, while the head is turned back as if they are confused, ashamed or lost. It is significant that he or she is standing between Lemuel and Nephi as if trying to decide whether to follow Lemuel and the wicked or Nephi and the righteous.

EVIDENCE NO. 671: MAN IN WHITE ROBE AND THE SPIRIT OF THE LORD

Claim: During his vision, Lehi followed a man in a white robe who led him to the tree of life (1 Nephi 8:5). Likewise, during Nephi's vision, the Spirit of the Lord introduced Nephi to the tree (1 Nephi 11:1-8).

Evidence: On each side of the tree are strange, human-like figures each wearing the mask of a creature. These two figures correspond to the man in the white robe and the Spirit of the Lord. This interpretation is based on the fact that: (1) they are standing above the others as if in the air, as angels often do; (2) their faces are hidden by masks, leaving the white-robed man unidentified, just as the being in Lehi's dream was unidentified, and also possibly representing the veil between the mortal and spiritual dimensions;* (3) the fearsome faces of the creatures were employed by ancient Americans in their artistic

representations to symbolize the power of a being whom all men must fear; (4) both figures are facing the tree with outstretched arms, as if introducing Lehi and Nephi to the tree; (5) the swirling mist in front of the figure on the left seem to suggest the glory and mystery of a spiritual being; and (6) the headdress on the figure on the right suggests a crown as a symbol of power and authority. For more information see Jakeman, *Stela 5*, p. 46.

* See for example, Exodus 34:29-34, where Moses covered his face with a veil after speaking with God.

EVIDENCE NO. 672: THE BEHEADING OF LABAN

Claim: A Mesoamerican beheading scene from Izapa Stela 21 is similar to the story of Nephi beheading Laban in the Book of Mormon.

Evidence: This Mesoamerican beheading scene, of the Protoclassical era (circa 100-200 AD), is from Izapa Stela 21 is and is found in Greene, *Maya Sculpture*, p. 425, pl. 202. (Many details have been left out.)

"Although the motifs in this Stela are not uncommon, the overall theme of the images bears an interesting general resemblance to the story of Nephi and Laban—a priestly or royal figure decapitates another while additional figures prepare for a journey in the background." (William Hamblin, "Hand held Weapons in the Book of Mormon," *Foundation for Ancient Research and Mormon Studies* [HAM-85]. See also V. Garth Norman, *Izapa Sculpture*, New World Archaeological Foundation, Paper 30 [Provo, Utah: Brigham Young University, 1976].)

Figure 11. Mesoamerican beheading scene, from Izapa Stela 21.

EVIDENCE NO. 673: THE PRACTICE OF SWEARING OATHS

<u>Claim</u>: Nephi and Zoram had just met after Laban was killed. Zoram greatly feared that Nephi would kill him as well. However, Zoram immediately trusted Nephi after Nephi swore an oath (1 Nephi 4:32-37).

About five hundred years later, the Book of Mormon records another incident involving the swearing of oaths. In the record of Alma we find a strange account of a battle between the bloodthirsty Lamanites led by Zerahemnah and the peace-loving Nephites lead by Moroni. After having defeated the Lamanites in battle, Moroni offers to spare the army of Zerahemnah if they would swear an oath of peace. However Zerahemnah, the murderous and unscrupulous leader of the Lamanites, refused saying, "we will not suffer ourselves to take an oath unto you, which we know that we shall break" (Alma 44:8). It is interesting to note the binding power of an oath applied to those who did not value human life. Even the most notorious of criminals were bound to honor their oaths.

<u>Evidence</u>: The Bible relates many instances of righteous men who swore oaths, but did so only when it was necessary. For example Genesis 24:2-4, 37; 26:28-29. Even after the Savior cautioned people against swearing oaths, the practice was continued for sacred and solemn occasions. See, for example, Hebrews 6:16-17 and Revelation 10:6. The Lord himself swore a sacred oath to Abraham as recorded in Hebrews 6:13. In the New Testament, as well as the Book of Mormon, Jesus cautioned the people against swearing oaths unnecessarily (Matthew 5:33-37; 3 Nephi 12:33-37). Both Sahagun and Ixtlilxóchitl speak of the purity of speech among the Tultec Indians whose conversations were limited to little more than "yes" and "no" (see Hunter and Ferguson, *Ancient America and the Book of Mormon* [1950], pp. 323-324).

Swearing by oaths was very common in the Middle East. It was a means of trust in one another. Oaths were never broken, even at the cost of one's life. The most solemn oath included the words "as the Lord liveth." See W. Ewing, *Palestine Exploration Fund Quarterly*, (1895), p. 172; A. Jaussen, "Judgments," *Rev. Biblique*, XII, p. 259; *Survey of Western Palestine*, p. 327; *Survey of Western Palestine Special Papers*, 326; P. Baldensperger, *Palestine Exploration Fund Quarterly*, (1910), p. 261; *Arabia Deserta*, vol. 2, p. 27. See also Nibley, *Lehi in the Desert and The World of the Jaredites*, (1980) p. 118.

EVIDENCE NO. 674: THE COMPASS OR DIRECTOR

<u>Claim</u>: The Book of Mormon records that Lehi's party was miraculously provided a compass or director which they called the *Liahona* (1 Nephi 16:10-16, 28; 2 Nephi 5:12-16; Alma 37:38-40).

<u>Evidence</u>: One of the few ancient American documents to have escaped the destruction of the Spanish conquest was produced in 1554 and is known as *The Title of the Lords of Totonicapán*. In 1834 at the request of the Quiché Indians, Dionisio Jose Chonay, a Catholic priest, translated the document from the Quiché-Maya Indian language of Guatemala into Spanish. The document was "... signed by the kings and dignitaries of the Quiché court" (*Title of the Lords of Totonicapán*, p. 164). It was first translated into English by Delia Goetz and published in 1953. However, Dr. M. Wells Jakeman published English extracts from the Spanish version in 1945, this being the first time that any of this work had appeared in English.

According to this ancient work, the ancestors of the Maya were given a gift from God, called *"giron-gagal,"* in their travels on the other side of the sea before they sailed to this new land. (See *Título de los Señores de Totonicapán*, translated and edited by Adrian Recinos, [Mexico: Fondo de Cultura Economica, 1963]; *El Título de Totonicapán*, translated by Robert M. Carmack and James L. Mondloch [México: Universidad Nacional Autónoma de México, 1983]; *Title of the Lords of Totonicapán*, p. 170; cited in Milton R. Hunter, *Great Civilizations and the Book of Mormon* [Salt Lake City: Bookcraft, 1970], pp. 79-80).

In a similar tradition recorded in the *Popol Vuh*, it was called *"Pizom-Gagal"* and was symbolic of the power of God (Recinos, *Popol Vuh of the Quiche Maya*, p. 205). According to both accounts, this instrument assisted them in their travels. Another tradition speaks of a Gold Wedge with mystic powers which directed early travelers to where they should reside (William H. Prescott, *History of the Conquest of Peru*, [New York, 1898], vol. 1, p. 31).

The Native American art of "arrow divination" also calls to mind the *Liahona*. Like the Liahona, they used "pointers" (not always arrows) as a form of casting lots. The arrowheads (or pointers) are used in ceremonies and rituals with unknown, ancient origin. The "sacred arrows" of the Cheyenne are their most prized possession. A gold rod was said to have directed early Incas. (See Fowkes, *U.S. Bureau of Ethnology*, [1891-1892], vol. 8, p. 116; and E. George Squire, *Peru, Travel & Exploration in the Lands of the Incas*, [M. A. F. S. A.], pp. 301, 331. See also T. Fahd, *Une Pratique Cleromantique a la Ka' ba preislamique, Semitica*, (1958), vol. 8, p. 61; S. Culin, *Games of the North American Indians* (Washington: Smithsonian Institution, 1907), pp. 33, 45, 383;

A "magic arrow" also showed ancient travelers of the Old World where to go. See Roscher's, *Lexicon*, vol. 1, pp. 2815, 2817, 2822; B. Meissner, *Babylonian u. Assyrian* (Heidelberg, 1926), vol. 2, pp. 65, 275. Pauly-Wissowa, *Realenzyklop. der Altertumswiss*, vol. 1, p. 16; J. Wellhausen, *Reste Arabischen Heidentums* (Berlin, 1897), p. 133; G. Jacob, *Altarabisches Bedouinenleben* [Berlin, 1897], p. 110, n. 2). Several of the above sources are also cited in Nibley, *Since Cumorah*, (1988), pp. 251-263.

Some have proposed that the Liahona utilized the principle of magnetism to cause its "spindles" to point the way. Indeed, according to the Book of Mormon, the word *Liahona* specifically meant, "compass" (Alma 37:38). The following is quoted from an Update of the *Foundation for Ancient Research and Mormon Studies*, "Lodestone and the Liahona," (March 1984), p. 1:

> It is worth noting that the function of magnetic hematite was well understood in both the Old and New Worlds before Lehi left Jerusalem. Magnetite or *lodestone* is, of course, naturally magnetic iron (Fe_3O_4), and the word *magnetite* comes from a place in which it was mined in Asia Minor by at least the seventh century BC, namely *Magnesia*. (Thales of Miletus is the first known to have mentioned its strange properties, circa 600 BC). Professor Michael Coe of Yale University, a top authority on ancient Mesoamerica, has suggested that the *Olmecs* of Veracruz, Mexico were using magnetite compasses already in the second millennium BC. This is based on Coe's discovery during excavations at *San Lorenzo-Tenochtitlán* of a magnetite "pointer" (M-160) which appeared to have been "machined," and which Coe placed on a cork mat in a bowl of water in a successful test of its function as a true floater-compass. (J. B. Carlson, *Science*, vol. 189, pp. 753-760; R. H. Fuson, *Annals of the Association of American Geographers*, vol. 59, pp. 508-510; E. Baity, *Current Anthropology*, vol. 14, p. 443.)

EVIDENCE NO. 675: EXTENDED TIME IN THE WILDERNESS

Claim: According to the Book of Mormon, Lehi's party spent eight years traveling through the wilderness (1 Nephi 17:4). Some have wondered why it took so much time, however, current research has verified that this was the custom of the ancient Bedouins.

Evidence: It was customary for travelers to find a good camp and to stay there for as long as six months (W. E. Jennings-Bramley, "The Bedouin of the Sinaitic Peninsula," *Palestinian Exploration Fund Quarterly*, p. 284, cited in Nibley, *An Approach to the Book of Mormon* [1988], pp. 228-229).

EVIDENCE NO. 676: NO FIRES, RAW MEAT

Claim: Lehi's group, which traveled across the Arabian Desert, did not light fires and ate raw meat (1 Nephi 17:12). With recent evidence which has substantiated this claim, the accuracy and truthfulness of the Book of Mormon is confirmed.

Evidence: Joseph Smith, who was not acquainted with the Near Eastern world, would not likely have thought that a party would fear raids in the middle of the desert. However, no fires, and raw meat were the rule while crossing the deserts. See Wiliam C. Palgrave, *Narrative of a Year's Journey Through Central Arabia*, 1862-1863 (London, 1866) I; Zeller, *Palestine Exploration Fund Quarterly*, 1909, p. 256; B. Thomas, *Arabia Felix*, p. 137; Cheesman, *Unknown Arabia*, p. 228, 234, 240, 280; Raswan, *Drinkers of the Wind*, p. 200. (The last three sources are also cited in Nibley, *Lehi in The Desert and The World of the Jaredites*, [1988], pp. 63-64.)

A related evidence discussed elsewhere in this work, "Eastern Route Across the Arabian Desert," presents evidence that Lehi's group may have traveled along a well-known trade route called the *Frankincense Trail*. This being the case, it is even more likely that the travelers would fear attacks from desert bandits.

EVIDENCE NO. 677: THE AZTEC TREE OF LIFE

Claim: Another representation of Lehi's vision of the Tree of Life (1 Nephi 8:2-35) can be found in one of the few surviving codices of the Aztec peoples, the *Codex Borgia* from Cholula, Puebla, Mexico.

Evidence: Written between 1350 and 1500, the Codex Borgia predates the arrival of the Spanish conquistadors. A pictorial expression of Aztec beliefs, rites and ceremonies, this codex also seems to relate a story that progresses from one drawing to the next. This codex is named after the Borgian Museum in Rome where it is housed. The facsimile shown in this evidence was taken from Lord Kingsborough's *Antiquities of Mexico*, (London: Robert Havell and Colnaghi Son and Co., 1831), vol. 3.

Figure 12. Aztec hieroglyphs possibly representing the Tree of Life

One of the facsimiles of the *Codex Borgia* appears to represent the Tree of Life. In the accompanying facsimile, note the foliage in the shape of a tree—which appears to be brimming with fruit. The serpents undulating out from the tree may be enigmatic of Quetzalcoatl—the feathered serpent god of the Aztecs (whom Latter-day Saints believe actually represents Jesus Christ). If so, it would appear that some serpents are breathing new life on creatures who otherwise were destined for death.

Note also the strait (not straight) and narrow path leading to the tree (Matthew 7:14; 1 Nephi 8:20). Next to the path is a set of parallel lines which could easily represent the rod of iron that led along the path to the tree in Lehi's dream (1 Nephi 8:19). Note that there are five people walking along the path with their hand on the "rod" (1 Nephi 8:30). A sixth person who has already arrived at the tree has his hand over the rod, as if reaching up to grasp the fruit.

EVIDENCE NO. 678: HUD AS LEHI

Claim: The Book of Mormon tells of a prophet named Lehi (introduced in 1 Nephi 1) living in Jerusalem who was so outspoken that his enemies plotted to take his life. Ancient accounts of another man called *Hud* match the Book of Mormon description of Lehi on several aspects, and provide further evidence for the authenticity of the Book of Mormon.

Evidence: Interesting parallels exist between the teachings of Lehi in the Book of Mormon and the story of Hud, a messenger sent to pre-Islamic Arabia. Some scholars believe Hud was Jewish. Some Latter-day Saint scholars believe Hud was Lehi. On this subject William J. Hamblin noted the following:

> … it is interesting to examine some possible parallels between the traditions of Hud and the Book of Mormon, a work which Latter-day Saints accept as an ancient scripture and which begins with the story of Lehi, a Jewish prophet in self-imposed exile from Jerusalem with his family. They wandered through the "wilderness" to the Red Sea, built a ship, and voyaged to the New World.

> Although the Book of Mormon provides no specific information on the route, Latter-day Saints generally accept that Lehi and his party traveled through Arabia, ending their journey in Hadramawt, the same region where Hud is supposed to have preached. In a religious sense, Lehi was a Jew, which corresponds with the theory that the name Hud could refer to a Jewish prophet.

> A theoretical reconstruction of Lehi's stay in southern Arabia could run something like this. Lehi and his family eventually arrive in Hadramawt, at that time a highly populated region serving as one of the main trade routes of southern Arabia. There they would have necessarily made contact with the local inhabitants, if only because every well in the region would have been owned by some tribe or city, and strangers would not have been allowed to drink from the wells without permission. The Book of Mormon makes no mention of any contacts with local inhabitants, but Ishmael was buried "in the place which was called Nahom" (1 Nephi 16:34), implying that it was so called by local inhabitants, in contrast to Lehi's usual practice of giving a new name to each place where they stay. (See 1 Nephi 2:14; 16:13; 17:6.) According to this theory, Lehi discusses religion with the local inhabitants of Arabia, possibly converting a few, but at least leaving the impression that a man of God had dwelt among them. The oral tradition eventually becomes the pre-Islamic and Qur'anic traditions of Hud.

> In view of this theory it is possible to examine some parallels between the literary images of Lehi's vision of the Tree of Life and some similar images in the story of Hud, with the assumption, still speculative, that Lehi told the Arabians of his vision in Jerusalem, and its images became, in oral tradition, the activities of the prophet Hud. Take the following examples:

> 1. According to the Islamic Hud traditions, one of the chief sins of the tribe of Ad was pride symbolized by magnificent buildings, as an attempt to create an earthly replica of paradise. For this impious pride, God sent the prophet Hud to call them to repentance. For the most part, the

Adites failed to heed his call. This religious image of the building symbolizing man's pride correlates with the image of the "great and spacious building" of Lehi's vision, filled with mocking men and women representing "the pride of the world" (1 Nephi 8:26, 11:35-36).

2. The city of the Adites was built at a place "beneath which rivers flowed." Likewise a prominent part of Lehi's vision is the "river of water" flowing between the "great and spacious building" and the "Tree of Life." (1 Nephi 8:13; 12:16)

3. When the Adites reject Hud's message, God sends a drought to chasten them. A delegation of Adites prays for rain at Mecca. In response to their prayer, God sends a black cloud and a great windstorm, which destroys them and their city. An important image in Lehi's vision is the "mist of darkness," which causes that men "perish and are lost" (1 Nephi 8:23-24). The black cloud of the Hud story and the "mist of darkness" of Lehi's vision are both religious images relating to the destruction of the wicked.

4. The final vindication of Hud's prophetic calling comes when the magnificent buildings of the Adites, in which they thought they could live forever, are destroyed by the storm. Likewise, in Lehi's vision, the triumph of God over the wickedness of the world is by the destruction of the great and spacious building: "and it fell, and the fall thereof was exceedingly great" (1 Nephi 11:36).

5. Salvation comes to Lehi and his party by partaking of the fruit of the Tree of Life (1 Nephi 8:11-12; 11:24-25). Hud, on the other hand, and those few who believed in his message, are saved in a hazira, "an enclosure for camels made of trees to protect them from the cold and wind." To an Arab transmitter of oral traditions, it would have seemed strange for Hud to be saved from the destroying winds because of a single tree; a barricade of trees would be more reasonable. Although this process of transmutation is hypothetical, it could account for the Tree of Life becoming a hazira; certainly both images have the similar function of providing salvation from the wrath of God.

Although a number of remarkable parallels exist between the stories of Lehi and those of Hud, we cannot conclude that Lehi is the basis of the Hud traditions. The causal link is missing. We can, however, conclude that the record of Lehi, a pre-Islamic prophet of Arabia by Mormon belief, coincides with what Islamic traditions tell us about such prophets. In other words, Lehi fits the pattern of what we know concerning pre-Islamic Arabian prophets.

For more information, see William J. Hamblin, "Pre-Islamic Arabian Prophets," *Mormons and Muslims*, p. 96.

EVIDENCE NO. 679: REMARKABLE PARALLEL TO FIRST NEPHI

Claim: The Book of Mormon account of Nephi is remarkably similar to the ancient narrative of Zosimus.

Evidence: John W. Welch said the following regarding *The Narrative of Zosimus:*

Before the recognition of similarities such as those between the Book of Mormon and the Narrative of Zosimus, it was possible to reserve interest in the Book of Mormon by wondering why no other Ancient Near Eastern books existed which closely resembled it. On that score, one need wonder no longer."

...This article demonstrates certain similarities existing between texts in 1 Nephi in the Book of Mormon and a little-known document entitled "The Narrative of Zosimus." The Narrative's core material was written originally in Hebrew and appears to be at least as old as the time of Christ, and perhaps much older. There is no evidence that any knowledge about the Narrative of Zosimus existed in any English-speaking land prior to the publication of the Book of Mormon.

While no one knows who, if anyone, Zosimus was, or even what the name Zosimus means or where it may have come from, the ancient narrative which bears this name records traditions about a righteous people who left Jerusalem at the time of the Prophet Jeremiah. They were led by God to an ideal land across the ocean. The text is of obvious interest to students of the Book of Mormon, which relates a similar history.

The many parallels between the early chapters of the Book of Mormon and this Narrative require little elaboration: dwelling in the desert (1 Nephi 2:4), being led by prayer and faith (1:5; 11:3; 16:29), wandering through a dark and dreary waste (8:7), being caught away to the bank of a river (8:13), crossing to the other side of a river or abyss and passing through a great mist (8:23), coming to a tree whose fruit is most sweet above all (8:11), eating and drinking from the tree which was also a fountain of living waters (11:25), being greeted by an escort (11:2-3), being interrogated as to desires (11:2), beholding a vision of the Son of God (1:6; 11:27), keeping records on soft metal plates (3:24), recording the history of a group of people who escaped the destruction of Jerusalem at the time of Jeremiah (1:4; 7:14), being led to a land of promise and of great abundance due to righteousness (18:25), practicing constant prayer (Alma 34:21-27), living in chastity (Jacob 2:25-28), receiving revelations concerning the wickedness of the people of Jerusalem (1 Nephi 10:11), and yet obtaining assurances of the mercy to be extended to the inhabitants of Jerusalem (1 Nephi 1:14; 10:3). (John W. Welch, *BYU Studies,* vol. 22 [Summer 1982], pp. 311-332.)

A more detailed comparison of the two texts is included in the above referenced article by John W. Welch.

EVIDENCE NO. 680: LARGE POPULATION IN MESOAMERICA

Claim: The Book of Mormon tells of large numbers of people who lived in ancient Mesoamerica. For example, Mormon 6:10-15 mentions that 230,000 warriors were killed at Cumorah.

Evidence: Some have doubted the truthfulness of the Book of Mormon on the assumption that reports of such great numbers of people living in Ancient America could not be substantiated. Dr. John L. Sorenson, professor of Anthropology at Brigham Young University, noted that the figures on Mesoamerican population offered by demographers decades ago could not be reconciled with statements in the Book of Mormon about the numbers of people who were destroyed in Nephite and Jaredite wars. However, current data does substantiate the Book of Mormon Claims. Dr. Sorenson writes, "Now, analysis of the data on lands occupied, ecology, settlement, sizes, war casualties, and other population-related factors in the Book of Mormon text shows striking consistency and realism in the reported demographic changes." (See John L. Sorenson, "Digging into the Book of Mormon," *Ensign,* September 1984, p. 34.)

EVIDENCE NO. 681: THE NEPHITES BUILT GREAT CITIES WITH LARGE BUILDINGS

Claim: In a day when the American Indians were regarded as uncivilized pagans, the Book of Mormon announced that the ancient inhabitants of the American continents built huge cities with massive temples (2 Nephi 5:15-17; Jarom 1:8; Helaman 6).

Evidence: At the time of Joseph Smith the great architectural accomplishments of the ancient Americans were virtually unknown to the English-speaking world. For example, in 1848 the following was published by the Smithsonian Institution regarding the origin of the ancient mounds found in the Eastern United States. "They, [Native Americans] were hunters, adverse to labor and not known to have constructed any works approaching in skillfulness of design or in magnitude [to these mounds] under notice." (Ephraim George Squier of the American Ethnological Society, quoted in Lionel Casson, et. al. *Mysteries of the Past,* edited by Joseph J. Thorndike, Jr., [American Heritage Publishing Co., New York: 1977], p. 122).

Until recently, critics have insisted that all of the great Mesoamerican temples and cities are of a post-Nephite period, dating only as early as 800 AD. The advent of radio-carbon dating has since silenced these claims and has established that the great cities date back to long before pre-classic era of Aztec culture—back to 250 BC. See J. R. Arnold and W. F. Libby, "A Determination by Radio-Carbon Content Checks With Sample of Known Age," *Science Magazine* 1949; "How Old Is It?" *National Geographic*, August 1958; Morley, *The Ancient Maya*, 1946, pp. 42, 344-345; P. DeRoo, *History of America Before Columbus*, (Philadelphia, 1900), p. 111;

The following is quoted from Daniel C. Peterson, *Review of Books on the Book of Mormon*, pp. 45-46:

It is so widely recognized in the academic community that true cities existed in pre-Columbian Meso-america that such ideas can be found even in introductory textbooks.[1] Teotihuacán, the only pre-Hispanic site which even Bartley will grant to have been an actual city, represents no minor exception to his dismissal of Mesoamerican urban life: It was evidently larger in area than imperial Rome.[2] In a section entitled "Teotihuacán: An American Metropolis," one major archaeological atlas notes that, in AD 500, "Teotihuacán was the sixth largest city in the world."[3] Now, it is true that Teotihuacán, near Mexico City, was once thought by many Americanists to be not merely the pre-eminent Mesoamerican urban center, but the first one. Recent discoveries, however, have clearly shown such beliefs to be incorrect. El Mirador, for instance, flourished from about 150 BC to AD 150—long before the few immediately pre-Columbian quasi-urban concentrations that Bartley grudgingly acknowledges. Ongoing excavations conducted by the University of California, Los Angeles, at Nakbe, in El Petén, Guatemala, have revealed "a highly developed city" dating back to approximately 500 BC and sitting "in the heart of the lush forests of Central America."[4] And, within only the past few years, excavators have unearthed what is now termed the oldest city in North America, an Olmec center in Mexico called Teopantecuanitlan ("The Place of the Jaguars' Temple"). This site, which appears to have been inhabited from at least 1500 BC to 600 BC, and which may indeed date back to 2000 BC, covers an area of 241.5 acres and probably served as the residence for approximately 15,000 people. (This was a sizable population for the period, almost anywhere.) The homes of the city's people line the local riverbanks. Two stone irrigation canals, each half a mile long and five feet deep, tell of a rather highly developed agricultural life at Teopantecuanitlan.[5] "Large architectural complexes forming the centers of Maya cities were fundamental to their civilization. The plan of such ceremonial centers was established in the earliest days of the Maya, dating back to 2000 BC."[6]

---

[1] See, for instance, Ruth Whitehouse and John Wilkins, *The Making of Civilization* (New York: Knopf, 1986), pp. 61-62 ("Chapter 3, Cities"), where the general problem is discussed, and pp. 78-79, where fifth century AD Teotihuacán is discussed as a prime example of pre-Columbian cities in Mesoamerica. See also, the comparative perspective offered in Paul Wheatley, *The Pivot of the Four Quarters: A Preliminary Enquiry into the Origins and Character of the Ancient Chinese City* (Chicago: Aldine, 1971), which also discusses Mesoamerican cities. Michael Coe expresses some reservations about the word "city," applied to Mesoamerica, but frequently uses it nonetheless. See Michael D. Coe, *The Maya*, 3d edition (New York: Thames and Hudson, 1984), pp. 53-55, and passim. The F.A.R.M.S. Update for April 1985, "Nephi's Garden and Chief Market," contains yet other useful references.

[2] See René Millon, "Teotihuacán," *Scientific American*, vol. 216 (June 1967): pp. 38-48.

[3] *Past Worlds: The Times Atlas of Archaeology,* edited by Chris Scarre, (London: Times, 1988), p. 216.

[4] See Harlan Lebo, "Mayan Mysteries," *UCLA Magaine,* vol. 2 (Spring 1990), pp. 29-33. The dig at Nakbe is directed by Richard Hansen, a graduate of Brigham Young University, and includes scientists from both UCLA and BYU, as well as from the University of San Carlos in Guatemala.

[5] See the account given in the *Chicago Tribune*, 13 July 1986, sec. 6, p. 1, col. 4.

[6] Scarre, *Past Worlds*, p. 218.

Miguel Covarrubia writes, "Most archaeologists now agree that many of these artistic masterpieces date back to the beginning of the Christian era." The 4th Century BC already had great buildings, the cultures which followed 400 AD evolved from a greater civilization or a "mother culture" with a higher degree of civilization. See Miguel Covarrubias, *Mexico South-The Isthmus Tehuantepec*, (Mexico, 1946), p. 80; Laurette Sejourne, *Burning Water: Thought and Religion in Ancient Mexico* [Berkeley: Shambhala, 1976], pp. 31-83; and Helen Augur, *Zapotec*, (Garden City, New York, 1954), pp. 143-144, 146.

Ross T. Christensen writes the following about two of the great cities built by the Mesoamericans in an article entitled "A Tour and Brief Description of Some of the Ancient Ruined Cities of Central and Southern Mexico or 'land northward' of the Book of Mormon." (The authors have added emphasis to bring out key points):

Cholula. Near Puebla is located Cholula, an ancient city containing the largest pyramid in the world, a much eroded structure of adobe bricks which covers *twice the area of the great Pyramid of Cheops at Gizeh in Egypt.*

Cholula was the ancient city where Quetzalcoatl-worship was kept alive until the coming of the Spaniards. Aside from the main pyramid-temple, some 400 smaller temples were counted by Cortez at his arrival in 1519.

A maze of tunnels has been cut in all directions through the ancient structure by archaeologists in an effort to understand its history and composition. The guide, Sr. Davila, reported the 1953 discovery of a smaller circular pyramid buried beneath the masonry in one corner of the large pyramid. This structure may date to the "Late Preclassic" period, [600 BC to 1 AD] when circular pyramids first appear in Mesoamerica (compare the Cuicuilco pyramid in the Valley of Mexico). Figurines found on the surface in the vicinity of the Pyramid indicate a still earlier occupation of the site in the "Middle Preclassic" (late Jaredite) period [1100-600 BC]. ...

Monte Alban. Undoubtedly the most spectacular ruins visited by the Tour were those of Monte Alban, an ancient Zapotec religious center crowning a mountain ridge above the modern state capital of Oaxaca. Excavated by Alfonso Caso in the 1930's, the discovered occupation of the site dates back to the eighth century BC ("Middle Preclassic" period), according to radiocarbon evidence, and continued through several periods all the way up to the fifteenth century AD, or *just before the coming of the Spaniards.* The excavators have preserved the layered evidence of the successive occupation periods.

A vast array of large stone temple-pyramids surrounds a group of connected plazas. The fourteen main structures are believed to have been temples erected for the worship of the fourteen principal gods of the Zapotecs. Outstanding discoveries in one plaza are low-relief sculptures of human figures in a variety of dancing (?) or other poses (the "Danzante" carvings, probably dating to the second or "Late Preclassic" occupation). *One heavily bearded individual is portrayed.* [See related evidence on ANCIENT AMERICANS WITH FAIR SKIN AND BEARDS in this same chapter.]

Over 150 tombs have been excavated in the vicinity of the temples, some of which were visited by Tour members. Tomb No. 7, dating to the final period (when Monte Alban was ruled by the Mixtec kings), contained one of the greatest finds of treasure in the history of archaeology. The rings and other jewelry and ornaments of gold, silver, jade, pearls, and rock crystal, and thin sheets or plates of gold and silver, from this fabulous tomb treasure were viewed in the state museum at Oaxaca City. (See Christensen, *Progress in Archaeology*, [1963], pp. 150-156.)

EVIDENCE NO. 682: LINEN AND SILK IN ANCIENT AMERICA

Claim: Linen and silk are described in the Book of Mormon (Alma 4:6).

Evidence: Some have questioned the authenticity of the Book of Mormon, claiming that the ancient Americas had neither linen nor silk. However, Bernal Diaz, who served with Cortez, described seeing natives wearing garments made of *henequen*, a type of linen made from the maguey plant. Some conquistadors described seeing a type of silk, which apparently had been made of fine thread, spun from fine hair on rabbits' bellies and from the pod of the ceiba tree. (I. W. Johnson, "Basketry—Textiles," *Handbook of Middle American Indians,* edited by Robert Wauchope, vol. 10, part 1, [Austin: University of Texas Press, 1971], p. 312; Matthew Wallrath, *Excavations in the Tehuantepec Region, Mexico, American Philosophical Society Transactions,* no. 57, part 2 [1967], p. 12; A. M. Tozzer, *Landa's Relación de las Cosas de Yucatan, Harvard University, Peabody Museum of American Archaeology and Ethnology, Papers* vol. 18, [Cambridge, 1941], pp. 201, 205; J. E. S. Thompson, *Thomas Gage's Travels in the New World* [Norman: University of Oklahoma Press, 1958], p. 149. Cited in Sorenson, *An Ancient American Setting* [1985], p. 232; See also John L. Sorenson, "Possible Silk and Linen in the Book of Mormon," *Re-exploring the Book of Mormon*, edited by John W. Welch, [1992], pp. 162-164.)

EVIDENCE NO. 683: A PROMISED LAND

<u>Claim</u>: A recurring theme of the Book of Mormon is that the land of the "New World" was a Promised Land. (See 1 Nephi 2:20, where this concept is first introduced.) Until the Book of Mormon was published in 1830, the only known *land of promise* was Palestine—promised by God as an inheritance unto the seed of Abraham (Genesis 24:7). Yet the Book of Mormon boldly tells of a group of Israel's children leaving Abraham's Promised Land for yet another land of promise in the "New World" across the sea.

<u>Evidence</u>: For evidence that the ancient Americans believed that their land was, indeed, *a land of promise,* see Charles R. Enock, *Mexico* (New York: Scribner, 1910), p. 21.

EVIDENCE NO. 684: CITIES DESIGNED WITH SPACES FOR GARDENS

<u>Claim</u>: The Book of Mormon indicates that Nephi had a garden at his residence within the city of Zarahemla (Helaman 7:10).

<u>Evidence</u>: Readers who have assumed that cities in ancient America with high-density populations had no room for gardens near dwelling places have wondered about the accuracy of this verse. However, according to studies that have been conducted since the publication of the Book of Mormon, it has been discovered that some large cities did, indeed, contain gardens immediately adjacent to habitations. (See P. G. Krotser, "The Life Style of El Tojin," *American Antiquity*, Vol. 38, 1973, pp. 109, 204; and R. Diehl, "Tula," *HMAJS*, both cited in John L. Sorensen, "Nephi's Garden and Chief Market," *FARMS Update*, April 1985; reprinted in *Re-exploring the Book of Mormon*, Edited by John W. Welch [1992], p. 236.)

EVIDENCE NO. 685: PRIESTS WHO WERE NOT OF THE TRIBE OF LEVI

<u>Claim</u>: The Book of Mormon states that Lehi and his family were descendants of Joseph who had been sold into Egypt (2 Nephi 3:4). Yet, the children of Lehi were ordained priests (2 Nephi 5:26).

<u>Evidence</u>: When the faultfinders discovered these verses, they immediately referred to Bible passages that designate the Levites as those who were to perform priestly duties. (For example see Deuteronomy 21:5. In fact the Mosaic Law specified that death was the penalty for any "stranger" who would attempt to perform priestly duties [Numbers 3:10].) More specifically, only Aaron and his sons, who were descendants of Levi, could hold the office of priest. Their duties included offering sacrifices, burning incense, teaching the law, transporting the Ark of the Covenant, etc.

However, the Bible tells of other men, not of the tribe of Levi, who offered sacrifices in place of a priest. Gideon, who was not a Levite but an Abi-ezrite, lived in the territory of Manasseh. He was not a priest but a warrior—"a mighty man of valour" (Judges 6:11-15). Yet, he was commanded by the Lord to offer a sacrifice upon an altar

(Judges 6:26) just as a Levitical priest would do. An angel of God instructed Manoah, who was of the tribe of Dan to sacrifice burnt offerings to the Lord (Judges 13:2, 15-21). David, another non-Levite (of the tribe of Judah) offered sacrifices and blessed the people (2 Samuel 6:18; 1 Chronicles 16:2-3) as if he were a Levitical priest. (See also Mark 2:25-28, where Jesus recognized and accepted David's priestly acts.) The Bible also mentions that King David's sons, were Priests (2 Samuel 8:17). In fact, the Bible specifically differentiates between priests and Levites (1 Kings 8:4; Ezra 2:70; John 1:19). Isaiah records the word of the Lord saying that He would *make gentiles priests and Levites* (Isaiah 66:19-21).

Therefore, those who criticize the Book of Mormon for allowing non-Levites to perform priestly functions are indirectly criticizing their own Bible for doing the same.

EVIDENCE NO. 686: TEMPLES OUTSIDE JERUSALEM

<u>Claim</u>: The Book of Mormon tells of a temple that was built "after the manner of the temple of Solomon" in the Western Hemisphere, by the authority of the prophet of God (2 Nephi 5:16). Likewise, the Church of Jesus Christ of Latter-day Saints, which claims to be modern-day Israel, has built many temples throughout the world. Critics ask why Israelites would build a temple that was not located on Mount Zion in Jerusalem, which they assume, is the only proper location for an Israelite temple.

<u>Evidence</u>: Six years after the publication of the Book of Mormon, scholars discovered the writings of a Jewish colony at Elephantine in Egypt. This colony erected a temple far away from Jerusalem. After a hostile local governor destroyed it, the Jews applied to the directors of the temple at Jerusalem to rebuild it. Permission was granted. See E. G. Kraeling, *The Brooklyn Aramaic Papyrus*, pp. 41, 44-46, 95; cited in B. Porten, in *Journal of the American Oriental Society*, vol. 81 (1961), pp. 38-42. See also A. E. Cowley, *Aram Papyri from the Fifth Century B. C.*, (Oxford, 1923). All cited in Nibley, *Since Cumorah*, (1988), p. 242. Also M. L. Margolis, *Jewish Quarterly Review*, vol. 2, (1911-1912), pp. 430-435.

EVIDENCE NO. 687: SYNAGOGUES BEFORE THE DESTRUCTION OF THE TEMPLE

<u>Claim</u>: The Book of Mormon, professing to be an authentic history as well as sacred scripture, refers to synagogues between BC 559 and 545. (See 2 Nephi 26:26; also Alma 16:13; 21:4; 31:12.)

<u>Evidence</u>: Skeptics have insisted that there were no synagogues before the destruction of the temple, because they assume synagogues were built as a type of substitute for the temple. While no one knows exactly when or how the first synagogues were built, many historians have approximated the development of the synagogue in the era *before* Jerusalem was destroyed and Israel exiled. These include Leopold Loew, Julian Morgenstern, Louis Finkelstein, and Azriel Eisenberg. See Joseph Gutmann, *The Synagogue: Studies in Origins, Archaeology, and Architecture,* (New York: KTAV, 1975). See also S. Zeitlin in *American Academy of Jewish Research*, 1930-1931, pp. 78-79. Cited in Nibley, *Since Cumorah* (1988), pp. 164-165. See also, George Buttrick, "Synagogue," *The Interpreter's Dictionary of the Bible,* (New York: Abingdon Press, 1962), pp. 479-480; Joseph Gutmann, *The Synagogue: Studies in Origins, Archaeology, and Architecture,* (New York: KTAV, 1975); both cited in John W. Welch, "Synagogues in the Book of Mormon," *Re-exploring the Book of Mormon,* (1992), pp. 193-195.

Furthermore, the word *synagogue* is of Greek origin, meaning "to gather" or "to bring together." Regardless of what the original Hebrew word was that Joseph Smith translated as *synagogue,* its usage fits well into the context of the Book of Mormon, for they "built synagogues, and that they did *gather* themselves *together*" (Alma 31:21).

EVIDENCE NO. 688: COMMON AGRICULTURE BETWEEN OLD AND NEW WORLDS

Claim: The Book of Mormon states that the ancient Americans cultivated barley (Mosiah 9:9; Alma 11:7) and other Grains (Mosiah 9:9; Enos 1:21; Alma 11:7). For many years, critics have questioned the possibility of these grains in Mesoamerica, saying that there has been no evidence to substantiate such a claim. However, findings relating to these and other plants found in ancient America as well as the Old World help substantiate the Book of Mormon claim that ancestors of the early Americans came from the Middle East.

Evidence: The December 1983 issue of Science 83, reports on the discovery of pre-Columbian, domesticated barley among the ruins of the Hohokam civilization in Arizona. The Hohokam (who were described in the May 1967 issue of National Geographic, pp. 670-695) are believed to be immigrants from Mesoamerica into Southern Arizona around 300 BC. See Foundation for Ancient Research and Mormon Studies Update, December 1884.

This evidence validates the claim for barley in pre-Columbian America, and thus the authenticity of the Book of Mormon. The following is quoted from John L. Sorenson, "What Archaeology Can and Cannot Do for the Book of Mormon" (manuscript at Brigham Young University Library), pp. 6-7:

> The sequence of cultural development within the Book of Mormon record itself generally accords with what the expert in culture history expects as well as agreeing with the archaeological record. For example while the first Nephites are said to have planted Old World cereals, such as wheat and barley—"And it came to pass that they did grow exceedingly; wherefore, we were blessed in abundance" (1 Nephi 18:24)—later references to foodstuffs show a changing picture. By the time of Mosiah 7:22 and 9:9 (about 200-120 BC) "corn" (a plant of New World origin) is listed first in a series of crops. In the same period (9:14) corn is mentioned as the only grain taken from the Zeniffites by robbing Lamanites. Barley is mentioned once thereafter, but all other references are simply to "grains." Of course the dominance of corn in the Middle American diet was overwhelming by the time the Europeans arrived. The fate of the other grains is suggested by a comparison with Colonial Mexican history. Bishop Landa of Yucatan wrote in the 16th century: "We have set them to raising millet and it grows marvelously well and is a good kind of sustenance," words recalling distinctly Nephi's description of their first crop. Yet Lundell reported after a lengthy botanical survey of Yucatan for the Carnegie Institution a few years ago that no species of millet whatever could be found.

The following (Quoted in Ross T. Christensen, Progress in Archaeology [1963], pp. 72-73) is based on an article by Bruce W. Warren entitled "Findings with Respect to Some of the Agricultural Plants of Ancient America Seem to Indicate a Transoceanic Influence in the Origin of the American Civilizations" (University Archaeological Society Newsletter, vol. 14, p. 10):

> One of the first studies giving rise to the new interest in the possibility of transoceanic influence in the origin of the ancient American civilizations is a paper published in 1950, entitled "The Grain Amaranths: A Survey of their History and Classification," by Jonathan Deininger Sauer (Annals of the Missouri Botanical Garden, vol. 37, pp. 561-632), which investigates the origin of some of the plants cultivated in the agriculture of the American civilizations. Dr. Volney H. Jones of the University of Michigan, in a review of Sauer's work dated July, 1953 (American Antiquity, Vol. 19, No. 1, pp. 90-92), gives the following opinion:

> > Until recent years it was axiomatic in American anthropology that the cultural developments of the Old World and New World were independent and that any influences between the hemispheres were only by deculturizing northern routes. Almost the heart of the argument for this view was the essentially distinct inventory of crop plants and field methods in agriculture. It was recognized that the gourd and cotton did not quite conform, but there was a feeling that if we did not notice these problems they might go away. They are still with us, and recruits have been added in such crops as the sweet potato, corn, coconut, and we can now add the grain amaranths (a widespread genus, certain species of which produce abundant edible seeds about 1 mm. in diameter). These recalcitrant domesticates and perhaps others, refuse to remain neatly compartmentalized in one hemisphere or the other.

EVIDENCE NO. 689: OLIVE HORTICULTURE

Claim: The Book of Mormon contains a description of olive horticulture that is accurate in every detail. The description is used as symbolism in an allegory from the writings of an ancient prophet named Zenos who lived in Palestine long before Lehi fled from the country. (See Jacob 5-6.) An uneducated farm boy could not have known of the precise aspects of olive horticulture.

Evidence: Modern agricultural science has enumerated the many complexities of olive horticulture. Although Joseph Smith did not have access to this information at that early period and in his isolated environment, the detailed description of olive horticulture that he translated from the Book of Mormon coincides remarkably well with what modern botanists know. Both the Book of Mormon (Jacob Chapters 5-6) and modern science concur on the following (See Nibley in *Since Cumorah*, [1988] pp. 269-270):

1. Olive trees have to be diligently pruned and cultivated.
2. The top branches are the first to wither.
3. The new shoots come right out of the trunk.
4. The Olive is the most resilient of trees, surpassing even the willow in its power to survive the most drastic flailing and burning.
5. Superior fruit is very rare and difficult to obtain and perpetuate.
6. The ancient way of strengthening the old trees (especially in Greece) was to graft in shoots of the oleaster or wild olive.
7. Shoots from valuable old trees were transplanted to keep the stock alive after the parent tree should perish.
8. Surprisingly, the olive prefers rocky ground, whereas rich soil produces inferior fruit.
9. Too much grafting produces a nondescript and cluttered yield of fruit.
10. The top branches, if allowed to grow as is done in Spain and France, will sap the strength of the tree, producing a poor crop.
11. Fertilizing with dung is very important.

EVIDENCE NO. 690: VINEYARDS OF OLIVE TREES

Claim: The references in the Book of Mormon to olive trees in "vineyards" (such as in Jacob 5:3) provide additional evidence that the Book of Mormon is true.

Evidence: In the past, critics of the Book of Mormon have been quick to point out that "olive trees do not grow in vineyards, grapes do." However, what was originally viewed as an error, is now evidence that the Book of Mormon is true.

According to *Webster's Unabridged Dictionary*, the word vineyard has multiple meanings. One is a field of labor especially in the religious or missionary sense. A vineyard can also refer to a collection of fruit trees. (See Vestal and Wallace, *The Firm Foundation of Mormonism*, p. 40.)

Furthermore, Dr. Hugh Nibley has pointed out that olive trees were commonly planted in vineyards and that the word "carmel" can mean either an olive orchard or a vineyard. Tourists who visit the Holy Land are told that the proper word for a group of olive trees is not an *orchard*, but is a *vineyard*. See Hugh Nibley, *Since Cumorah*, (1988), p.191, 468, note 32.

EVIDENCE NO. 691: THE MIGRATORY EXPEDITIONS OF HAGOTH

Claim: Hagoth, the ship builder, maritime explorer and settler, who led a large migratory expedition "into the land northward" is mentioned in Alma 63:5-8. The description of Hagoth, and his followers as found in the Book of Mormon clearly resembles that of the *Hohgates* (Indian settlers of Northern California).

Evidence: In the tradition of the Book of Mormon, groups of people were always named after their leader. For example, *Nephites* followed Nephi, *Lamanites* were the followers of Laman, *Zoramites*, the descendants of Zoram, *Jaredites*, the followers of Jared, *Mulekites* the followers of Mulek and even the *Anti-Nephi-Lehites* (*Lamanite* descendants of *Lehi*, who were dissimilated from their brethren and wanted to be associated with the *Nephites*). See 2 Nephi 5:14; Jacob 1:13; Alma 23:17; Moroni 1:23.

Similarly, according to Native American tradition, early settlers of Northern California were called *Hohgates*: "...the Hohgates, the name [the Natives gave] to seven mythical strangers who arrived in the country from the sea, and who were the first to build and live in houses. The Hohgates killed deer, sea-lions, and seals..." (Jean Francois Alvert du Pouget de Nadaillac, *Prehistoric America*, [London: John Murray, 1885], pp. 64-66; cited in B. H. Roberts, *New Witness for God*, vol. 3, [1951], pp. 79-82.)

See also the evidence THE POLYNESIANS CAME FROM AMERICA in the chapter on "Another Testament of Jesus Christ" of this same volume, which relates that during Hagoth's last voyage he was driven off course and landed in the Pacific Islands.

EVIDENCE NO. 692: ORACLE STONES IN ANCIENT AMERICA

Claim: Stones were used by Book of Mormon prophets to assist in receiving revelations and in translating records. (See Omni 20-22; Mosiah 8:13; 28:11-16; Alma 37:21-26; Ether 3:23-28.)

Evidence: The fact that seer stones were used in Mesoamerica is documented in "Landa's Relación de las Cosas de Yucatán," Translated by A. M. Tozzer, *Harvard University, Peabody Museum of American Archaeology and Ethnology, Papers*, vol. 18, (Cambridge: Peabody Museum, 1941), p. 130. Tozzer is cited in a paper by John L. Sorensen entitled "Incense Burning and 'Seer Stones' in Ancient Mesoamerica; New Evidence of Migration of Biblical Peoples to the New World" (*University Archaeological Society Newsletter* 21:00) who writes:

"Additional evidence of such a connection is seen in the use of oracle or 'seer' stones by peoples of ancient and even modern Mesoamerica, especially Yucatan and Guatemala. The *Urim and Thummim* of the Israelites [Exodus 28:30; Leviticus 8:8; Numbers 27:21; Deuteronomy 33:8; 1 Samuel 28:6] was only one example of widespread use of such stones in the Old World for predicting the future. A certain traditional account from ancient Mexico strongly suggests that one colonizing group arrived there by sea in the distant past, divinely guided by means of a sacred stone." (Quoted in Christensen, *Progress in Archaeology*, [1963], p. 119.)

EVIDENCE NO. 693: SEVEN TRIBES

Claim: The Book of Mormon record of seven different tribes is consistent with the tradition of ancient Mesoamerican that they descended from seven famous caves or lineages. The main Book of Mormon colony divided itself into seven family tribal groups (Jacob 1:9-14). These groups retained their identity throughout Book of Mormon history (4 Nephi 1:35-38).

Evidence: According to the *Popol Vuh*, the first settlers were divided into six groups but named their first settlement "Seven." (Delia Goetz and Sylvanus G. Morley, *Popol Vuh*, [1950], pp. 62-67; cited in Hunter and Ferguson, *Ancient America and the Book of Mormon*, p. 231; See also John L. Sorenson, John A. Tvedtnes, and John W. Welch, "Seven Tribes: An Aspect of Lehi's Legacy," *Re-exploring the Book of Mormon*, edited by John W. Welch, [1992], pp. 93-95.)

Other similar legends claim that the inhabitants of Mesoamerica all sprang from "seven caves" or lineages. See George C. Vaillant, *The Aztecs of Mexico*, (Harmondsworth: Penguin, 1950), pp. 97-98.

The following is quoted from *Foundation for Ancient Research and Mormon Studies Update*, November 1987, entitled "Seven Tribes: An Aspect of Lehi's Legacy":

Several years ago it was observed that the descendants of Lehi's party consistently divided themselves into seven tribes. Three times in the Book of Mormon these seven are mentioned, each time in the rigid order of 'Nephites, Jacobites, Josephites, Zoramites, Lamanites, Lemuelites, and Ishmaelites' (Jacob 1:13; 4 Nephi 38; Mormon 1:8). Significantly, these references come from the earliest as well as the latest periods of Nephite history, indicating the importance and persistence of kinship as a basic element in this society. See, for example, John L. Sorenson, *An Ancient American Setting for the Book of Mormon*, pp. 310-313. Now it has been discovered that the origin of this societal structure can be traced back to the words of Lehi himself.

One of the many enduring legacies of Lehi's last will and testament appears to be the organization of his descendants into seven tribes. After speaking to several of his sons collectively (2 Nephi 1:1-29), Lehi spoke first to Zoram (2 Nephi 1:30-32), second to Jacob (2 Nephi 2), third to Joseph (2 Nephi 3), fourth to the children of Laman (2 Nephi 4:3-7), fifth to the children of Lemuel (2 Nephi 4:8-9), sixth to the sons of Ishmael (2 Nephi 4:10), and seventh to Nephi and Sam together (2 Nephi 4:11). This seems to be the precedent that established the social and legal order that lasted among these people for almost one thousand years. The seven groups recognizable here are exactly the same as those listed in Jacob 1:13, 4 Nephi 38 and Mormon 1:8.

... Thus, the division of the people into seven groups was an important feature of Nephite civilization. It may even have been considered prototypical. After all, Alma established "seven churches in the land of Zarahemla" (Mosiah 25:23), and traditions, mentioned by Sorenson, (*An Ancient American Setting*, p. 313), and Ross T. Christensen, ("The Seven Lineages of Lehi," *New Era*, vol. 5, no. 5, [1975] pp. 50-51), claim that the ancient Mesoamericans sprang from seven famous caves or lineages.

EVIDENCE NO. 694: THE NEPHITES UNITE WITH THE MULEKITES

Claim: The Book of Mormon indicates that the Nephites which migrated from the Middle East encountered and joined the *Mulekites* which had independently crossed the ocean from the Middle East (Omni 1:12-13, 17-19). According to the Book of Mormon, the place where the two groups of settlers united was *Zarahemla*, in the region just south of a narrow neck of land (Helaman 6:10; 8:21; Alma 22:29-31; Ether 7:6, 16-17).

Evidence: Torquemada wrote that the group of settlers, "departing from Panuco, made their way with fine diligence ... and it was by chance that they arrived at Tullan where, on arriving, they were hospitably received by the natives of that province." See *Torquemada*, (1723 edition), vol. 1, pp. 254-255, cited in Hunter and Ferguson, *Ancient America and the Book of Mormon* (1950), pp. 126-129 and chapter 13.

Hunter and Ferguson note that both the time (200 BC) as well as the location of this merger correspond to the episode mentioned in the Book of Mormon.

Evidences Regarding King Benjamin's Address

A key event in the Book of Mormon is recorded in Mosiah chapters 2 though 6, and is referred to as "King Benjamin's address." Benjamin was a humble and righteous king who reigned over the Nephite civilization, and refused payment for his services as king. Rather, he "labored with [his] own hands " to provide for his family so that his people would "not be laden with taxes" (Mosiah 2:12-15). Upon appointing his successor, he gathered the people together to give them his famous farewell address. Several profound principles of doctrine, unique to the Book of Mormon, are introduced in this sermon.

The following three evidences are related to King Benjamin's address. They provide evidence that the events depicted in the Book of Mormon actually occurred as recorded therein, that the Book of Mormon is a true history of the ancient inhabitants of the Americas, and that it was truly translated by Joseph Smith through the gift and power of God.

EVIDENCE NO. 695: A GREAT GATHERING HELD APPROXIMATELY 130 BC

Claim: During the reign of King Benjamin, peace was established in the land, which continued after his death. During this period of peace, a large gathering of the people came together to hear an address from their king, according to Book of Mormon chronology, about 124-130 BC (Mosiah 2:1-2, 5, 8). This may be the same gathering reported by Ixtlilxóchitl.

Evidence: According to the Aztec historian Ixtlilxóchitl, after a great period of peace was established in the land … a great council was held … in 132 BC (according to their methods of dating). See *Works of Ixtlilxóchitl*, English translation by Hunter and Ferguson, *Ancient America and the Book of Mormon* (1950), p. 147.

EVIDENCE NO. 696: THE GREAT ASSEMBLY OR YEAR RITE

Claim: The Book of Mormon account of the great gathering to hear King Benjamin's address fits all of the characteristics of the ancient *Great Assembly* or the *Year-Rite*.

Evidence: These characteristics are listed below with documentation that each was part of the ancient rite:

	Characteristic	Mosiah	Ancient "Great Assembly"
1.	A proclamation was sent out to announce the event.	2:1	*Western Political Quarterly,* vol. 2 (1949), pp. 331-34
2.	Many tents and booths were erected.	2:5-6	Raymond W. Muncey, *Our Old English Fairs* (London: Sheldon, 1935), p. 33; Athenaeus, *Deipnosophistae.* vol. 6, p. 150; *Contemporaries of Marco Polo* edited by M. Komroff, (NY: Liveright, 1928), p. 98
3.	A tower was erected from which King Benjamin delivered his speech.	2:7	Herodian, *History* vol. 6, p. 9; Dio, *Roman History,* LIX, p. 25.
4.	The firstlings of their flocks were offered as a sacrifice and burnt offering to the Lord.	2:3	The firstlings of the flocks acted as the New Year offering just as the great Hag was celebrated to give thanks after the Exodus of Israel from Egypt (Nibley, *An Approach to the Book of Mormon,* (1988), p. 299).
5.	King Benjamin begins address by asking his people to open their ears, hearts and minds.	2:9	At the ceremony, the king's address always started with a "silentium." (*The Assembly of Animals and Men in the Presence of the King and the Genies,* edited by F. Dieterici, [Leipsig, 1881], p. 52).
6.	King Benjamin prophesied about the things he had seen in vision.	3:1-2	Divination of the future was a standard part of the *Great Assembly* (G. Widengren, *Ascensio Isaiae,* p. 16).
7.	King Benjamin confers the kingdom upon his son Mosiah.	2:30; 6:3	The central act of the Great Year Rite was for the king to confer the kingdom on one of his sons. (P. E. Dumont, *l'Asvemedha,* Paris, 1927, pp. vii, 50
8.	King Benjamin gives Mosiah charge of the ancient records, the sword of Laban, and the Liahona.	1:16-17	It was also a traditional part of the coronation rite to consign the national treasures for safekeeping. (R. Grousset, *l'Asie Orientale,* [Paris, Presses University, 1941], p. 448).
9.	The people were so numerous that they could not be counted—implying that an attempt was made to take a census.	2:2	A census was always taken during these rites. (*Western Political Quarterly,* vol. 2, 1949, pp. 334-337.
10.	King Benjamin reminds his people that they had been begotten through a divine parent.	5:7-8	This ancient belief was nearly always revived at the *Great Assemblies.* (S. Hooke, *The Labyrinth, Passim and Myth and Ritual,* p. 8).

Characteristic	Mosiah	Ancient "Great Assembly"
11. King Benjamin asks the people to enter into a covenant that would be sealed. The names of those who entered the covenant to be registered in the Book of Life, the Lord would seal them as His own.	2:16-19; 5:15; 6:1	During these ceremonies, the people entered into covenants and their names were recorded. (H. Frankfort, *Kingship and the Gods: A Study of Ancient Near Eastern Religions as the Integration of Society and Nature* (Univ. of Chicago Press, 1948); A. Wensinck, "The Semitic New Year and the Origin of Eschatology," *Acta Orientalia I*, (1925), p. 172.
12. The people fell to the earth at the end of the king's address.	4:1	During the ceremonies, the "proskynesis" was a demonstration of submission to higher authority. (B. Meissner, *Babylon u. Assyria*, vol. I, pp. 63, 138; vol. 2, p. 166; Caiger, *Bible and Spade*, p. 181).
13. The people respond to the king in one voice with an acclamation on the theme of eternity during the great gathering.	4:2	A traditional part of the Great Assembly was to repeat phrases in unison, usually under the direction of a presenter: (Nathan Ha-Babli, "The Installation of an Exilarch," chap. 10 of B. Halper, *Post-biblical Hebrew Literature* [Philadelphia: Jewish Pub. Society of America, 1943], pp. 64-68; J. G. Graevius, *Thesaurus Antiquitatum Remanarum*, vol. 6, p. 1697).
14. King Benjamin's address was recorded so that all would know his words.	2:8	This was the normal procedure. (*Classical Journal*, vol. 40, 1945, 527, pp. 19-20).

The above references, along with several others are cited in Nibley, *An Approach to the Book of Mormon,* (1988), pp. 301-306.

EVIDENCE NO. 697: THE KING AS GUARDIAN OF THE COVENANT

Claim: The kings in the Book of Mormon followed the practice of guarding the covenant between God and his people, as was the practice among the kings of Israel.

Evidence: The Foundation for Ancient Research and Mormon Studies reported the following:

The King and the Covenant of the Lord. Unlike kings of other peoples of the ancient Near East, the king in Israel had the responsibility of acting as the guardian of the covenant between the Lord and his people. The king in ancient Israel was one "from among the people of Yahweh who, because of the singular privilege of being anointed to kingship, bore a special responsibility of guardianship for the faith of the nation." Helen A. Kenik, "Code of Conduct for a King: Psalm 101," *Journal of Biblical Literature* vol. 95, (1976), p. 391. In a similar manner, kingship and covenant are inextricably connected in Benjamin's speech (Mosiah 2:29-30). Benjamin commanded his son to gather the people together in order that he might proclaim his son king and "give this people a name" (Mosiah 1:10-11). This "name" is "the name of Christ," to be accepted by all "that have entered into the covenant with God that ye should be obedient unto the end of your lives" (Mosiah 5:8). Much of Benjamin's address is concerned with admonishing the people to keep the covenant. Kingship, covenant, and the observance of commandments are again conjoined in Mosiah 6:3 where Benjamin appointed priests "to teach the people, that thereby they might hear and know the commandments of God, and to stir them up in remembrance of the oath which they had made." (*FARMS Update*, "The Ideology of Kingship in Mosiah 1-6," August 1987.)

EVIDENCE NO. 698: THE CORONATION CEREMONY

Claim: The coronation of King Mosiah in the Book of Mormon follows very closely the coronation ceremony of ancient Israel.

Evidence: No coronation ceremony of a king is described in significant detail in the Bible. Yet, some critics believe Joseph Smith, a 23-year old backwoods farm boy, fabricated in his own mind what an actual ancient coronation was like. Yet the detailed description of the coronation of Mosiah conforms almost perfectly to discoveries of the scholars. Intensive research has produced a profile of what a coronation was like in the days of ancient Israel that is precisely followed in the coronation of King Mosiah:

	Characteristic	Mosiah
1.	The coronation always occurs at the temple	1:18
2.	The elders officiate if the old king is dead. Since King Benjamin is still alive, he officiates.	1:9
3.	All the people are summoned.	1:10
4.	The people are told to bring gifts. King Benjamin's people bring animals to make sacrifices.	2:3
5.	In return, the king provides a great feast.	
6.	The day before the coronation a great wooden tower is built	2:7
7.	Its sides are covered to conceal a trained choir, which under the direction of a precentor, leads the congregation in hymns and recitations. King Benjamin's people cry with "**one**" voice" a lengthy exclamation of over 230 words as if they had been rehearsed or led by the choir.	5:2-5
8.	The king appears at the top of the tower.	2:8
9.	The people stand until the king sits down on one of three thrones.	
10.	The other two thrones are for governmental officials, counselors, or scribes.	2:8
11.	Over the king's head is a *baldachin* or royal tent.	
12.	The precentor, or the king imparts royal blessings on the new king. King Benjamin proclaims that Mosiah will be the new king.	1:10
13.	The chorus in the tower shouts "Amen!"	
14.	The king gives a royal speech, all three on the tower showing deference to one another to demonstrate unity. In this case, King Benjamin gives the speech.	2:9-4:30
15.	The speech is given as if the words were revealed from heaven. The angel of the Lord delivers King Benjamin's words, "that the mysteries of God may be unfolded."	4:1 / 2:9
16.	All listen in total silence. King Benjamin's people fall to the earth.	4:1
17.	After the speech the king asks questions.	5:1, 13-14
18.	The people answer in the person of an old man of wisdom and experience. King Benjamin's people answer "with **one** voice."	5:2
19.	The precentor, or old king, pronounces a blessing on the people which is to last for life. King Benjamin says they will retain a remission, be guiltless, made free, and be found at the right hand of God.	4:26 / 5:8-9
20.	The precentor, or old king, blesses the new king and his two counselors.	6:3
21.	The precentor makes a formal roll call of the people.	6:1
22.	The precentor presents the book of the law to the new king.	1:16
23.	The king reads the covenant into which the people are entering.	5:5-6; 6:3
24.	The king delivers a discourse on the law.	4:6-29
25.	The precentor again blesses the new king by the book of the law. After King Benjamin consecrates Mosiah to be king, he charges him to teach the people the commandments.	6:3
26.	Officers of the kingdom are re-ordained to establish the political order under the new king.	6:3
27.	There is an investiture with royal insignia, such as a scepter or a sword.	1:16
28.	All say "Amen!" No doubt, the people echoed King Benjamin's Amen.	6:15

See Nathan Ha-Babli, "The Installation of an Exilarch," Chapter 10 of B. Halper's, *Post-biblical Hebrew Literature*, (Philadelphia: Jewish Publication Society of America, 1921, reprinted 1946), vol. 1, pp. 37-40; vol. 2, pp. 64-68. Cited in Nibley, *Since Cumorah*, (1988), pp. 247-248. See also "More Perspectives on Benjamin's Speech," *Foundation for Ancient Research and Mormon Studies Update*, (February 1986).

Another study of the coronation tower points out that: "the tower built by Benjamin was evidently more than just a way to communicate to the people. It was a rich symbolic part of ancient Israelite tradition in which the king stood on a platform at the temple to officiate between God and his people" ("Benjamin's Tower and Old Testament Pillars," *Foundation for Ancient Research and Mormon Studies Update,* [October 1995], no. 102, p. 2). The *FARMS* article cites T. R. Hobbs, *2 Kings*, vol. 13, of *Word Biblical Commentary,* (1985), p. 142; Roland deVaux, *Ancient Israel,* (1965), vol. 1, pp. 102-103; Gerhard von Rad, "The Royal Ritual in Judah," in *The Problem of the Hexateuch and other Essays,* translated by E. W. Trueman Dicken (1966), p. 222; H. J. Kraus, *Worship in Israel,* translated by Geoffrey Buswell (Richmond: John Knox Press, 1966), p. 224; George Widengren, "King and Covenant," *Journal of Semitic Studies,* (1957), vol. 2, p. 10; and H. Frankfort, *Kingship and the Gods,* (1948), pp. 245-246.

This article points out that the tower could also be symbolic of the pillar of fire or cloud "that stood before the Tabernacle, signaling God's presence at that holy sanctuary." It further notes that the raised platform in the center of the modern Jewish synagogue (called a *bimah*), from which the Torah is to be read, can also be connected to this tower at the temple.

To assume that a young, uneducated, Joseph Smith could have created such an accurate and complex ceremony that so closely matches the ancient prototype, is to go way beyond the realm of possibility.

EVIDENCE NO. 699: KING BENJAMIN'S FAREWELL ADDRESS

<u>Claim</u>: The Book of Mormon presents remarkable resemblances between King Benjamin's speech (recorded in Mosiah chapters 1 through 5) and the classical farewell address of ancient times.

<u>Evidence</u>: Scholars have noted a number of consistent similarities in the farewell speeches of many ancient religious and political leaders. They have found that each speaker appeared to be following a customary pattern. William S. Kurz has published a detailed study, comparing twenty-two addresses from the classical and Biblical traditions. He has identified twenty elements common to the farewell addresses in general. John W. Welch finds King Benjamin's speech to be "the fullest and the most complete example of this ancient speech typology anywhere in world literature." The logical inference from this discovery is that King Benjamin understood this tradition and followed its pattern consciously. These parallels indicate yet another ancient Near Eastern influence on the Nephite record. See William S. Kurz, "Luke 22:14-38 and Greco-Roman and Biblical Farewell Addresses," *Journal of Biblical Literature*, vol. 104 (1985) pp. 251-268; John W. Welch and Daryl R. Hague, "Benjamin's Speech: A Classic Ancient Farewell Address," *FARMS Update* June 1987; reprinted in *Re-exploring the Book of Mormon*, edited by John W. Welch, (1992), pp. 120-123.

The chart below compares the characteristics of the traditional farewell sermon with King Benjamin's speech.

Kurz' Criteria	Reference in Mosiah
1. The speaker summons successors	1:9-10; 2:1, 9
2. Cites his own mission as an example	2:12-14, 18
3. His innocence; fulfilled his duty	2:15, 27-31
4. Impending death	2:26, 28; 1:9
5. He exhorts his audience	4:9-10; 2:9, 40-41; 5:12
6. Warnings/final injunctions	4:14-30; 2:31-32, 36-39; 3:12, 25; 5:10-11
7. He blesses his audience	Not Clearly found, but we see "blessed" in 2:41
8. Farewell gestures	Possibly implied in 2:28; see also 2 Nephi 9:44
9. Tasks for successors	1:15,16; 2:31; 6:3
10. Theological review of history	2:34-35; 3:13-15
11. Speaker reveals future	3:1, 5-10

12.	Promises are given	4:12; 2:22, 31; 5:9
13.	Appoints/refers to successor	1:15-16; 2:31; 6:3
14.	Audience bewails the loss of the leader	Not found
15.	Future degeneration is addressed	3:23-27; 4:14-15
16.	Sacrifices and covenant renewal	2:3; 5:1-7
17.	Care of those left	4:14-26; 6:3
18.	Consolation to inner circle	5:15
19.	Didactic speech	3:16-21
20.	Ars moriendi	Possibly in 2:28

EVIDENCE NO. 700: KING'S RENUNCIATION OF ABSOLUTE POWER

Claim: The idea of a powerful monarch publicly and willingly abridging his own powers is extremely unlikely. Yet this is precisely what two kings are recorded as doing in the Book of Mormon. King Benjamin renounced his absolute power in Mosiah 2:10-14, and King Mosiah in Mosiah 5:7.

Evidence: Anciently, this practice was not as uncommon as people in the 1800's may have thought. See K. H. Bernhardt, *Das Problem der Altorientalischen Konigsidealogie im Alten Testament* (Leiden: E. J. Brill, 1961) Chapter 6; G. Fohrer in *Zeitschrift für die Alttestamentliche Wissenschaft,* vol. 71 (1959), pp. 1-22; and George Widengren in *Journal of Semitic Studies,* vol. 2, (1957), pp. 1-32. All cited in Nibley, *Since Cumorah,* [1988], pp. 250-251.

EVIDENCE NO. 701: THE LAW OF CONSECRATION IN ANCIENT AMERICA

Claim: The Book of Mormon teaches that after the Savior personally ministered to the ancient Americans, and instituted his gospel among them, the people became so righteous that they shared their wealth with all. Having "all things common among them; therefore, there were not rich and poor, bond and free, but they were all made free..." (4 Nephi 1:2-3; see also 3 Nephi 26:17-21). This superior way of life which, when fully implemented eliminates poverty, is called the *Law of Consecration* (D&C 42:29-34).

Evidence: There is evidence that the Ancient Americans anticipated a time when the *law of consecration* would be realized in the Americas. The Hopi Indians believed that "as the Day of Purification approaches the *True White Brother will come*...The earth will become new as it was in the beginning. The people saved *will share everything in common*, speak one tongue, and adopt the religion of the Great Spirit" (Frank Waters, *Mexico Mystique,* [Chicago: Sage Books, 1975], p. 272, emphasis added.)

The above reference to "one tongue" is additional evidence of the Book of Mormon claim that the corruption of language accompanies the corruption of morals in society (Omni 1:17). Naturally the reverse should also hold true: living in peace and unity would be expected to yield an uncorrupted universal language. Hence, the Hopi prophesy that the righteous survivors will "all speak one tongue." Another writer quoted from the laws of an ancient Indian tribe: "he that hath more than he needs" shall give surplus "to those that have need." See Thompson, *The Gospel of the Red Man,* (Seton Village, 1966), pp. 13, 27-29.

The peaceful Indian tribes were often surprised that in the flood of white men covering their lands, so few of them were willing to share the land and its resources. Indeed, by and large, the Indians had no concept of private land ownership until after the white man claimed the land for himself. Often the Indian tribes followed the principle that "he who has, divides with him who has not" (*The World of the American Indian,* edited by Jules B. Billard et. al., [Washington DC: National Geographic Society, 1974], p. 323).

EVIDENCE NO. 702: THE LAW OF CONSECRATION IN POLYNESIA

Claim: Evidence that the Polynesians practiced the law of consecration substantiates the claim that the Polynesians came from American, through the voyages of Hagoth (Alma 63:5-8), and that they are descendants of the children of Lehi who also practiced the law of consecration (4 Nephi 1:2).

Evidence: According to several eyewitness accounts, the aboriginal Polynesians were completely unselfish with their possessions. They were known for their charity and kindness especially to strangers. One of the authors, Allen Richardson, who spent five years in the South Pacific, noted this tendency first hand among the Maori of New Zealand, the Tongans, Hawaiians, Tahitians and the Fijian natives with whom he associated.

Dr. John Martin wrote in 1820 that the Tongans, typical of other Polynesians, share "whatever they have, whether much or little" with "all present. Those who get more than they want never fail to supply others who have not enough. Selfishness is a very rare quality among them: If a man has a piece of yam, though it be not enough for a meal, he will readily give half away to anyone who may want it; and if anybody else comes afterward in like need, with the greatest good nature he will give half the remainder; scarcely giving himself any, though he may be very hungry."

Among the native Tongans, it was not considered a crime for a hungry person to take food from a another without permission. Stealing another's valuable possessions, on the other hand, was a crime that carried severe penalties. Dr. Martin writes that when the Tongan chieftain Tooi Tooi [now spelled Tuitui] learned that the customs of the European culture would not allow a hungry, destitute person to take food from a neighbor without invitation, he laughed and expressed his disdain for the stupidity of such a custom. (John Martin, *An Account of the Natives of the Tonga Islands,* [Boston: Charles Ewer, 1820], pp. 68, 195, 352-353, 357, 390, 393, 460.)

EVIDENCE NO. 703: CRIME IN THE BOOK OF MORMON

Claim: The Book of Mormon prophetically describes the manner in which crime infested the Nephite society, (Helaman chapters 2 & 6; 2 Nephi chapters 3 and 4) and contributed to the ultimate downfall of their civilization (Helaman 6:22-32; Moroni 9:19).

Evidence: The type of crime described in the Book of Mormon was not typical of any crime that may have been practiced in the backwoods of New York in the 1820's. It was, however, much like the type of crime that would sweep across America and other countries over a hundred years later.

The following is also quoted from Dr. Hugh W. Nibley in an article entitled "The Book of Mormon and the Ruins; the Main Issues," (N-BMA, Nibley Archive, *Foundation for Ancient Research and Mormon Studies*, University Station, Provo, Utah, July 13, 1980), pp. 6-7:

> What was "the fullness of iniquity" in question? This takes us to the *dark side* of early American civilization. A 16th Century description *of Rites and Ceremonies ... employed by the Indians of This New Spain* discovered in 1856, [tells] about sacred gatherings for a sacrament that recalls in detail the events of the Savior's visit in 3 Nephi. And then proceeds to tell how those same practices became corrupted to a nightmare of cruelty and bloodshed. The Quetzalcoatl religion has two opposite sides according to Eduard Seler. The one was the religion of Quetzalcoatl, the great prophet and savior who departed with the promise to return; the other was the cult traced to the time of King Uemac, "at which time the people turned to war and human sacrifice." The Book of Mormon tells us a good deal about both religions. The wickedness of the Nephites was the perversion of what had been good: Moroni 9:19: "And they have become strong in their perversion and they are alike brutal, sparing none." What Mormon describes in his letter to his son in the 9th Chapter of Moroni is clearly the bloody warrior cult of later times. (Eduard G. Seler, *Gesammelte Abhandlungen zur Amerikanischen Sprach und Alterthumskunde,* [Berlin: Behrend, 1908], vol. 3, p. 330.)

The evil has two aspects in the Book of Mormon. (A) General corruption and licentiousness, with frequent mention of their "delight in the shedding of blood" which is "the favorite theme of the Warrior Age after the 10th Century." (See Sejourne below) and (B) The domination of secret societies with their oaths, signs, insignia, etc. These lasts are very much in evidence in all the Post-classical Art. Eduard Seler maintains that the word *Nauatl* from *naual* means disguised, masked, secret; also that the purpose of the vast display of overwhelming symbolism, especially of the lion or jaguar, eagle and snake motifs was to make the society members objects of terror to all the world. In the Book of Mormon, the ubiquitous eagle, lion and snake motifs are only hinted at, but in the correct context. When Nephi tells us how "upon the wings of his Spirit hath my body been carried away upon exceeding high mountains. And mine eyes have beheld great things, yea, even too great for man; therefore I was bidden that I should not write them" (2 Nephi 4:25), he came as near as possible to describing the experience of an initiate in the Quetzalcoatl mysteries and some of our own Plains Indians (L. Sejourne, *El Universo de Quetzalcoatl*, [Mexico: Fondo de Cultura Economica, 1962], pp. 13, 16, 164; Eduard G. Seler, *Gesammelte Abh...*, [Berlin: Asher, 1904], vol. 2, pp. 75, 616).

EVIDENCE NO. 704: SECRET CRIMINAL SOCIETIES IN ANCIENT AMERICA

Claim: The Book of Mormon describes "secret combinations;" or secret societies, that thrived on murder and robbery in order to "get gain." See, for example, Helaman 7:12; 3 Nephi 7:12; 4 Nephi 1:46; Ether 8:9. These bloodthirsty outlaws bound themselves together with secret oaths and signs (Helaman 1:11; 2:7; 6:21-22; 3 Nephi 3:8). The Book of Mormon description of these secret societies and the subsequent discovery that such secret societies did indeed exist in Ancient America is further evidence that the Book of Mormon is filled with authentic details. Details, which testify that Joseph Smith was an inspired prophet and seer and that it was through the gift and power of God that he translated it.

Evidence: Sahagun compared the secret and violent *Nahualistas* of Mesoamerica to the assassins of the Near East. See Miguel Covarrubias, *Mexico South: The Isthmus of Tehuantepec* (New York: Knopf, 1947), pp. 77-78, cited in Sorenson, *Ancient American Setting...* (1985), p. 80.

Josephus describes similar bands of organized mayhem in *Wars of the Jews,* 4, 408; See also H. Lutz, "Alleged Robbers' Guild in Ancient Egypt," *University of California Publications in Semitic Philology,* (1937), vol. 10, pp. 240, 242, both cited in John W. Welch, "Theft and Robbery in the Book of Mormon and Ancient Near Eastern Law," (*Foundation for Ancient Research and Mormon Studies*, 1985), pp. 6-7.

Dr. Hugh Nibley observed that:

> In Joseph Smith's day (1805-1844) whole nations were not controlled as they are now by secret combinations to get power and gain (as described in Helaman 2). In his day such a thing as a general strike was unknown (such as described in 3 Nephi 4). Big bosses did not write smooth and flattering letters to competitors making deals and offering protection (as described in 3 Nephi 3). The selling of protection by huge gangs operating in high places was unknown (as described in Helaman 6). The art of manipulating public opinion as practiced by the Gadianton society (as in Helaman 6) had not been discovered until our own day. This is no picture of the rustic America of the 1820's but of the world of the Nephites and of Twentieth-Century America. See Nibley, *An Approach to the Book of Mormon*, (1957), pp. 315-334.

EVIDENCE NO. 705: THIEVES AND ROBBERS

Claim: The Book of Mormon correctly distinguishes between the words *thieves* and *robbers* and correctly preserves the Hebrew usage of each. For example, Helaman 2:4 describes a ruthless criminal, Gadianton, as being expert in the secret work of murder and *robbery*, while Alma 11:2 indicates that those who did not pay what they owed were cast out as *thieves*. Note that the term robbery as used in the Book of Mormon is directly associated with murder*, and thus it was considered just to execute capital punishment on robbers, who were by definition also murderers, (1 Nephi 3:13), while thieves were merely cast out as mentioned in Alma 11:2.

Evidence: The Hebrew word *gánab* (to steal) and *gannáb* (thief) denote stealing in secret. In contrast, *gazal* (to rob) and *gazlán* (robber) normally meant taking property openly, most often by force. (See Bernard S. Jackson, *Theft in Early Jewish Law*, [Oxford: Clarendon Press, 1972], pp. 2-5, and H. Botterweck and H. Ringren, *Theological Dictionary of the Old Testament*, vol. 2, pp. 456-460; both cited in John W. Welch, "Theft and Robbery in the Book of Mormon and Ancient Near Eastern Law," (*Foundation for Ancient Research and Mormon Studies*, 1985), p. 2.

John W. Welch, Professor of Law at BYU, has also written that:

> In the ancient world there was a significant distinction between a *thief*, who stole property from one of his neighbors, and a *robber*, who was a highwayman living in bands outside of settled communities. The Book of Mormon is consistent in the use of the terms thieves and robbers. Thus, the Gadianton robbers are never called thieves—always robbers.* The King James translators, however, rendered the Greek and Hebrew words for thief and robber indiscriminately since in English common law, the same distinction did not exist. (See Bernard S. Jackson, *Theft in Early Jewish Law*, [Oxford: Oxford University Press, 1972]; Welch's contribution to "New Developments in Book of Mormon Research," *Ensign*, [February 1988], p. 12. See also John W. Welch, "Thieves and Robbers," *Re-exploring the Book of Mormon*, [1992], pp. 248-249.)

In ancient times, the thief, a common criminal from the local area, was tried and punished by the local government, and was required to make restitution to his victims. Robbers, on the other hand, were not usually considered part of the community, and hence were dealt with by military force and martial law. This often resulted in execution. See Laban's threat to Laman (who had left the community of Jerusalem and was hiding in the wilderness with his family) in 1 Nephi 3:13. See also Helaman 2:10; 6:37; 11:28, 3 Nephi 4:14, 27-28, and compare to Bernard S. Jackson, "Some Comparative Legal History: Robbery and Brigandage," *Georgia Journal of International and Comparative Law*, (1970), vol. 1, pp. 63, 79, 86; Jackson, *Theft*, (1972), pp. 16, 38, 180, 251-252; *Code of Hammurabi*, Section 22; H. Lutz, "Alleged Robbers' Guild in Ancient Egypt," *University of California Publications in Semitic Philology*, (1937), vol. 10, p. 232; Josephus, *Wars of the Jews*, 1, 204, and *Antiquities of the Jews*, 14, 159; all cited by Welch.

---

* See for example, Helaman 2:10; 6:18-21; 11:26-32; 3 Nephi 2:11-18; 4:1-26; 5:4; 4 Nephi 1:17; Mormon 2:8-10; Ether 10:3; 13:26.

EVIDENCE NO. 706: ROBBERS AS INSTRUMENTS OF DIVINE JUSTICE

Claim: The Book of Mormon authentically portrays the robbers corrupting the government by the use of extortion, infiltration and ransom (Helaman 6:38; 7:4; 3 Nephi 2:11; 3:6-10; 4:4). While these lawless gangsters were diabolic in nature, nevertheless, they were symbolized as instruments of divine retribution upon the unrighteous *chosen* people (Helaman 11:34; 12:3).

Evidence: The historical significance of the robber's effect on God's covenant peoples is documented in Hosea 7:1; Jackson, *Theft*, pp. 15, 35, 251-260; Lutz, "Alleged Robbers' Guild," pp. 232, 234; Josephus, *Wars of the Jews*, 2, 278; all cited in John W. Welch, "Theft and Robbery," pp. 9, 13.

EVIDENCE NO. 707: CANNIBALISM AND SELF-MUTILATION

Claim: The Book of Mormon mentions that cannibalism and mutilation were practiced by the more wicked inhabitants of Ancient America (Moroni 9:8, 10). When Joseph Smith translated the Book of Mormon he would not have known that modern research would substantiate this claim.

Evidence: That Cannibalism and self-mutilation was indeed performed in Mesoamerica is documented in W. T. Sanders, *The Cultural Ecology of the Teotihuacan Valley* (State College, Pennsylvania: Penn. State University, 1965), p. 179; "Landa's Relación de las Cosas de Yucatán, a Translation," edited by A. M. Tozzer, *Harvard*

University, Peabody Museum of American Archaeology and Ethnology Papers, vol. 18 (Cambridge: Peabody Museum, 1941), vol. 18, pp. 118-20; *Man Across the Sea—Problems of Pre-Columbian Contacts*, edited by Carroll L. Riley, J. Charles Kelley, Campbell W. Pennington, and Robert L. Rands, (Austin: University of Texas Press, 1971), p. 233, all cited in Sorenson, "The Book of Mormon as a Mesoamerican Codex," *Foundation for Ancient Research and Mormon Studies,* (1976), p. 5.

The Book of Mormon further mentions that the lawless gangs of robbers that terrorized the ancient inhabitants of America committed gruesome acts of ritual sacrifices (3 Nephi 4:7; Mormon 2:10; 4:14-21; 9:10). This strange behavior has been documented as a typical rite of ancient robber clans. See H. Lutz, "Alleged Robbers' Guild in Ancient Egypt," *University of California Publications in Semitic Philology,* (1937), vol. 10, pp. 240-242; Achilles *Tatius*, III, 12, 1. Both cited in John W. Welch, "Theft and Robbery in the Book of Mormon and Ancient Near Eastern Law," (*Foundation for Ancient Research and Mormon Studies*, 1985), p. 7.

EVIDENCE NO. 708: LEPROSY IN ANCIENT AMERICA

Claim: The Book of Mormon records that when Jesus visited the inhabitants of Ancient America, He commanded that they bring forth their lepers so that he could heal them (3 Nephi 17:7). Book of Mormon critics have pointed out that there is no medical evidence for the existence of leprosy in Ancient America. However, one record of the early Spanish Padres records that leprosy did exist anciently in the Americas.

Evidence: Of course one possible explanation for the lack of medical evidence of leprosy in America, is that the disease was completely eradicated by the Savior when he healed their lepers. However, there has also been some question as to what the word *leprosy* really meant in Biblical times and whether or not the Biblical use of the world is translated correctly.

Regardless of the conflicting opinions as to the specific type of skin disease that has been labeled as *leprosy* in the Bible, Father Sahagun reported that one of the diseases attributed to the god Tloac was what he labeled "leprosy." (See *Codex Florentino*, vol. 1, p. 287, and J. E. Thompson, *Mexico Before Cortez*, [New York: Scribner's, 1933], p. 50, both cited in *Foundation for Ancient Research and Mormon Studies Update,* [September 1994], no. 96, p. 2.)

EVIDENCE NO. 709: EVIDENCES LINKING MORMON WITH HEUMAN

Claim: Mormon, the man after whom the Book of Mormon is named, is first introduced in The Words of Mormon, located between the books of Omni and Mosiah.

Evidence: Ixtlilxóchitl describes a man named Heuman who fits the Book of Mormon profile of Mormon in a surprising number of details. Sources from the *Works of Ixtlilxóchitl* are found in Hunter and Ferguson, *Ancient America and the Book of Mormon* (1950), pp. 337-343.

1. Their names are similar—each having two syllables and ending with the suffix "mon" or "man."
2. Both lived during the same period of time.
3. Both were prophets (Mormon 1:15).
4. Both were historians (Mormon 2:17-18).
5. Both were generals (Mormon 2:1).
6. Both led a great army into battle in 326 AD (Mormon 2:1-7).
7. Both led their people in a great exodus from the land called Bountiful (Mormon 6:5-6). (The word Bountiful is not given in the Works of Ixtlilxóchitl, but the English equivalent of the ancient name means the same thing.)
8. Both negotiated an important treaty in 350 AD (Mormon 2:28-29).
9. Both were forced to lead their people into the northern countries (Mormon 2:29).
10. Both had temporary hope and optimism for their people (see Mormon 2:10-12).

11. Each were notified by the enemy of plans to attack, according to the law of the land (Mormon 3:4).

12. Mormon was given 10 years of peace (Mormon 3:4); Heuman was given 3 years.

13. Each led his army into a final battle of extermination in which all but a few were killed (Moroni 1:2).

14. The Book of Mormon Lamanites were ancestral relatives of the Nephites—Ixtlilxóchitl describes the enemy as "their own fierce kindred (Moroni 1:4)."

15. Each wrote a sacred book shortly before death (Mormon 1:1-5; 6:5-6; Words of Mormon 1:11). Ixtlilxóchitl's book was called Teoamoxtli, which means Various Things of God and Divine Book.

16. Each abridged the ancient records that contained history from the creation to their day (Introduction to the Book of Mormon). Ixtlilxóchitl called his a resume.

EVIDENCE NO. 710: THE PERIOD OF MIGRATION INTO MEXICO AND NORTH AMERICA

Claim: The Book of Mormon records that the people of Mesoamerica entered into the "north countries" around 327 AD as the Nephite nation fled from destruction by the Lamanite nation (Mormon 2:3). This correlates with both Mayan and North American History.

Evidence: M. Wells Jakeman noted the following in his article "The Ancient Middle American Calendar System: Its Origin and Development" (*University Archaeological Society Newsletter*, 31.0, Cited in Ross T. Christensen, *Progress in Archaeology* [1963], p. 135):

> Another noteworthy result of this study is that of calendrical and hieroglyphic evidence fixing the time of the final migration from Central America into Mexico of the "Ulmeca-and-Xicalanca," "Huehuetl-apallaneca," or original "Tulteca" of the Chronicles (i.e. the ancient urbantheocratic people of Mesoamerica in the latter part of the "Preclassic" period, the followers of the life-god "Quetzalcoatl," who correspond in time and character to the Nephites of the Book of Mormon). This migration occurred sometime between about the dates 8.13.0.0.0. and 8.16.0.0.0. of the Maya chronological era ("Long Count"), or 297 and 357 of the Christian era (in the 11-16 correlation of these eras). This agrees closely with the Book of Mormon date of the final migration of the Nephites from the "land southward" or—very probably—northern Central America into the "land northward" or southern and central Mexico, viz. circa AD 327 (Mormon 2:3 *et seq.*; it will be noted, in fact, that the mean date from the calendrical evidence is also circa AD 327).

Bruce W. Warren has come to a similar conclusion about North America: "... direct Mesoamerican cultural influence ... occurs, however, in the Ohio-Mississippi and adjacent regions of southeastern United States, appearing about AD 400 (!) and becoming strong only as late as AD 1000 in this region. All this evidence has an important bearing on the interpretation of the Book of Mormon, as to the indicated movements of its peoples into eastern United States." ("Their Mouths Are Stopped With Dust," by William A. Ritchie *University Archaeological Society Newsletter* 15.0; also cited in Christensen, *Progress in Archaeology,* [1963], p. 209.)

EVIDENCE NO. 711: THREE SEPARATE MIGRATIONS TO AMERICA

Claim: While the Book of Mormon does not claim to be the record of *all* peoples who migrated to America, it specifically mentions three separate migrations from the Old World: the Jaredites (Ether 6:11-12), the people of Mulek (Mosiah 25:2) and the people of Lehi (1 Nephi 18:8-23).

Evidence: A sixteenth century document known as *Titulo de los Señores de Totonicapan,* translated into Spanish from the ancient histories of the Quiché Mayas of Guatemala, reveals that "three nations passed [to the New World] ... arrived here from the other side of the sea." Similarly, Ixtlilxóchitl writes of three major groups who migrated to this land: 1) The ancient ones, or giants, 2) The *Tulteca,* and 3) the *Ulmec.* (Note the similarity between *Ulmec* and *Mulek.*) Both sources are cited in Hunter and Ferguson, *Ancient America and the Book of Mormon,* (1959), pp. 12-13.

EVIDENCE NO. 712: JAREDITE LANGUAGE NOT CONFOUNDED

Claim: The Jaredites did not experience a confusion of tongues as the rest of the world did at the time of the *Tower of Babel* (Ether 1:35, 37). Critics argue that the Biblical account seems to make the confusion all-inclusive (Genesis 11:7).

Evidence: According to ancient American legends, a group of families were spared the curse of the confusion of languages. From them descended the Toltecs, Aztecs, Acolhuas. See Humbolt, *Vues des Cordilleres*, vol. 1, p. 114-115; vol. 2, pp. 175-178; vol. 3, pp. 65-67, 148; and Eoturini, *Idea de una Historia*, pp. 113-114.

Hunter and Ferguson quote yet another early American source, which verifies that the language of the first migrants who came from the tower was not confounded:

> [The Tulteca history tells] how afterwards men, multiplying made a very tall and strong Zacualli, which means the very high tower, in order to shelter themselves in it when the second world should be destroyed. When things were at their best, their languages were changed and not understanding each other they went to different parts of the world; and the Tultecas, *who understood their language among themselves*, came to these parts, having first crossed large lands and seas... (*The Works of Ixtlilxóchitl*, English translation by Milton R. Hunter and Thomas Stuart Ferguson, *Ancient America and the Book of Mormon*, [1959] pp. 24-25.)

Since the concept of not confounding the languages of *all* the people is unique to the Book of Mormon—and not Biblical, it is unlikely that Ixtlilxóchitl could have assimilated this incident from the Spaniards. Some readers may question the possibility that the Bible would allow for exceptions to its statements of absolute, categorical totals. However, the Bible indicates that just before the exodus *all* the cattle of the Egyptians were killed (Exodus 9:6) yet a few verses later the Bible implies that some Egyptian cattle survived (Exodus 9:20). Likewise, all the horses were said to have been destroyed (Exodus 9:3), yet some survived (Exodus 14:9).

EVIDENCE NO. 713: LUMINOUS STONES

Claim: The Book of Mormon explains that, during the voyage of the Jaredites, their barges were lighted by luminous stones (Ether 3:4).

Evidence: Critics scoffed at this "wild idea" that was considered "patently ridiculous" until the following sources were found which claimed that Noah also had a luminous stone that lighted his ark. The Rabbis, according to the Midrash Rabbah, could not explain the *Zohar*. All they knew was that it was the light source for the ark. Rabbi Levi said it was a precious stone. Rabbi Levi quoted R. Phineas as saying that Noah had a polished gem that he hung up to light the interior of the ark. See H. Freedman's translation of the *Midrash Rabbah* (London: Soncino Press, 1939), vol. 1, p. 244; vol. 31, p. 11.

The Jerushalmi or Palestinian Talmud reports that Noah possessed precious stones that shone forth in the darkness of night. See *Talmud Jerushalmi Pesahim*, Schwab Translation, (Paris, 1882), vol. 1, p. 1; cited by E. Mangenot, in F. Vigouroux, *Dictionnaire de la Bible* (Paris, 1894), vol. 1, p. 923. All sources for luminous stones are cited in Nibley, *An Approach to the Book of Mormon*, (1988), pp. 337-339.

Currently, scientists at Sandia National Laboratories, (in New Mexico) have developed radio-luminescent lights (using "aerogel," phosphates, and tritium gas) that provide an interesting parallel to the Jaredite lights, and give a possible scientific explanation for these strange lights. These new lights, which require no external power source, nor batteries, were developed specifically to "serve the needs for lighting where no electricity is readily available." While these lights are powered by the radioactive decay of the tritium, the beta radiation is contained inside the aerogel while the majority of the light escapes to the outside—thus providing a very efficient and safe source of bright light. With a life expectancy of 20 years these intense lights, or some variation thereof, would clearly meet the specifications mentioned in the Book of Mormon. (See *Sandia National Laboratories News Release*, [September 27, 1990], pp. 1-3.)

If mankind, with his limited tools and knowledge can devise such an ingenious source of light, it is entirely conceivable that God, with his infinite resources and wisdom, altered the clear stones of the Jaredite prophet to produce a similar radioactive isotope resulting in the phosphorescent effect. It is interesting to note that almost thirty years before Sandia scientists developed these fantastic lights, a Latter-day prophet, Elder Spencer W. Kimball proposed that the Jaredite stones might have been illuminated "with radium or some other substance not yet rediscovered by our scientists" (*Ensign*, April 1963, pp. 63-64). Both of the above sources are also cited in *Foundation for Ancient Research and Mormon Studies Update*, (July 1992), p. 2.

EVIDENCE NO. 714: ELEPHANTS IN ANCIENT AMERICA

Claim: The Book of Mormon mentions that elephants lived in ancient America (Ether 9:19). However, when the Spanish conquistadors arrived in America there were no elephants on either of the American continents. Recently discovered proof of elephants, mastodons and mammoths in ancient America, during the time span of the Book of Mormon, is another evidence that the book is true.

Evidence: For many years critics have assumed that there is no evidence to support the Book of Mormon claim that elephants lived in ancient America. However, overwhelming evidence has been recently documented which conclusively proves that there were elephants in ancient America. The critics are now silent on this issue. Scholars have produced evidence that early American man had contact with elephants. Arrowheads and spear points have been found with skeletal remains of elephants. (See *Narrative and critical history of America*, edited by Justin Winsor, [New York: AMS Press, 1967] p. 438; John Boyd Thatcher, *Christopher Columbus: his life, his work, his remains*, [New York and London, G. P. Putnam's sons, 1903], vol. 2; and Francesco Saverio Clavigero, *History of Mexico*, [Philadelphia: Thomas Dobson, 1817], p. 19.)

Although some of the evidences of ancient man with the elephant in America predates Book of Mormon times, much evidence is dated concurrently with the time of the Book of Mormon (2200 BC to 400 AD). For example, *Scientific Monthly* reports that a pictograph near Moab, Utah "appears to be an authentic link between aboriginal man and the elephant or mastodon, for it is highly improbable that any primitive artist could have achieved so good a likeness without having seen such a creature or having at least seen a picture of one done by some fellow artist." (See *Scientific Monthly*, [1935], vol. 41, pp. 378-379.) See also J. Eric Thompson, *Mexico Before Cortez*, (Charles Scribner's Sons: 1933), p. 5; Douglas Leechman, *American Antiquity*, (1950) vol. 16, p. 157; J. L. B. Taylor, "Did the Indians Know the Mastodon?" *Natural History*, (1921) vol. 21, p. 591; Loren C. Eiseley, "Men, Mastodons and Myth," *Scientific Monthly*, (1946) vol. 62, p. 517; W. Balfour Gourley, *Man*, (June 1940); and W. D. Strong, *American Anthropologist*, (1934), vol. 36, p. 81. These were also cited in Harris, *Book of Mormon Message and Evidences*, (1961), pp. 87-92.

M. F. Ashley Montagu in *American Anthropologist*, (1944), vol. 46, p. 568, says: "There is even a possibility that in certain parts of the country the mammoth may have lingered on up to as recently as five hundred years ago. In several conversations with the writer, Professor William Berryman Scott, the dean of American paleontologists, has given it as his opinion that, had the first of the Spanish discoverers of America penetrated into the interior, it is quite possible that they might have met with the living mammoth." (See also *Science*, [1942], vol. 95, p. 380; M. F. Ashley Montagu and C. Bernard Peterson, "The Earliest Account of the Association of Human Artifacts With Fossil Mammals in North America," *American Philosophical Society Proceedings*, [1943], vol. 86, p. 236; L. H. Johnson III, "Men and Elephants in America," *Scientific Monthly*, [1952], vol. 75, pp. 216, 220; M. F. Ashley Montagu, *Introduction to Physical Anthropology*, 2nd Edition [1951], p. 221; Helmut de Terra, *American Antiquity*, [1947] vol. 13, p. 40; de Terra, *Man and Mammoth in Mexico*, [1957] p. 102.)

The following quotes are from Ludwell H. Johnson III, "Men and Elephants in America," *Scientific Monthly* vol. 75, October 1952, pp. 215-21.

> Strong, in his valuable article, reproduced a Naskapi account concerning a creature called Katchee-tohuskw. The story is too long to be set down in full here, especially as the body of it is not particularly significant; the really important point is the Indians' description of the monster. "When asked to describe Katcheetohuskw, the informants said he was very large, had a big head, large ears and teeth, and *a long nose with which he hit people*" (italics supplied). "His tracks in the snow were described in their stories as large and round." (See W. D. Strong, *American Anthropology*, [1934], vol. 36, pp. 81-86.)

In another narrative the beast is described as having teeth "long enough to pierce seven hunters, a lip as long as seven paces, and an unconquerable strength...." Only one animal could fit this description. (See F. G. Speck, *American Anthropology*, [1935], vol. 37, pp. 159, 163, 161.)

Strong gives a number of other, less graphic, legends that may be briefly itemized. (1) *Ojibwa and Iroquois*: a vague belief concerning a large animal which could crush trees in its path; (2) *Algonkian*: the "Great Moose," which used a fifth leg rooted between its shoulders to prepare its bed; (3) *Alabama and Koasati*: insist on translating "man-eater" (*Atipa teoba*) as "elephant;" (4) *Chitimacha*: "A long time ago a being with a long nose came out of the ocean.... It would root up trees with its nose to get at persons who sought refuge in the branches, and people lived on scaffolds to get away from it.... When the elephant was seen it was thought to be the same creature...." (5) *Atakapa of Louisiana*: one of the earliest records of this tribe "tells of their tradition that a beast of enormous size perished in one of several nearby watercourses. Duralde, the chronicler, adds that the subsequent discovery of an elephant skeleton in Carancro bayou seemed to realize this tradition."

... In short, although it is not difficult to disbelieve one tradition, or two, or even three, the cumulative effect of all the available stories is irresistibly persuasive. That there have been misinterpretations, distortions, leading questions, and outright inventions cannot be denied. But when all due allowance has been made for these, there remains a solid foundation of genuine folk memories of the elephant that refuses to be explained away.

A. L. Kroeber said "In an earlier stage, while man's numbers were few and his arts and weapons undeveloped, these species may have continued to live alongside him without serious molestation. Once better equipped and organized, Indian tribes may well have put an end to piedmont bison, horses, camels, mastodons, and mammoths; possibly in a few centuries in a given terrain." (See A. L. Kroeber, *The Maya and Their Neighbors* [Appleton-Century Crofts, Inc.: 1940], p. 475. See also, Ivan T. Sanderson, *Living Treasure* [1941], pp. 39, 53, 126, 127. Above sources also cited in Harris, *The Book of Mormon Message and Evidence*, [1961] pp. 89-92.)

EVIDENCE NO. 715: HORSES IN ANCIENT AMERICA

Claim: The Book of Mormon also mentions that horses were used by the ancient inhabitants of America (1 Nephi 18:25; Ether 9:19).

Evidence: Critics also made light of the Book of Mormon because it mentions the use of horses in America, whereas when the Spanish conquistadors arrived they found none. However, once again, what was once considered a flaw, has now become another evidence that Joseph Smith was indeed a prophet of God and that the book he translated is true.

For example, a wheeled toy vehicle from Oaxaca in the possession of the American Museum of Natural History, shows a man <u>mounted</u> on an animal, possibly a horse. Also, twelve petroglyphs of men on horseback are depicted on a section of rock in Indian Creek Canyon near Monticello, Utah. Bows and arrows are depicted, but no guns. (See Christensen, *Progress in Archaeology*, [1963], pp. 97-98; Weldon, *The Book of Mormon Evidences Joseph Smith a True Prophet*, p. 16.)

M. F. Ashley Montagu says the following concerning the existence of the horse in America: "Another distinguished American paleontologist, whose special interest is the horse, is, I understand, of the opinion that the horse never became extinct in America." (See M. F. Ashley Montagu in *American Anthropologist*, [1944], vol. 46, p. 568-569.)

The following references contain proof that horses existed in the Americas before Columbus: Chester Stock, *Rancho Labrea, A Record of Pleistocene Life in California*, pp. 42-43; Alvin M. Josephy, *The Indian Heritage of America* (New York: Alfred Knopf, 1968), p. 44; *National Geographic*, October 1969, p. 437; Graham E. Clark, *World Pre-History*, 2nd Edition (New York: Cambridge University Press, 1969), p. 272; Alma M. Reed, *The Ancient Past of Mexico* (New York: Crown Pub., 1966), p. 3; Matthew and Chubb, *Evolution of the Horse*, p. 13; *University of Nebraska News Museum Notes*, January 1963; and Leo Deuel, *Conquistadors Without Swords* (New York: St. Martin's Press, 1967), p. 538. The above nine sources also cited in Cheesman, *The World of the Book of Mormon* (1978), pp. 91-92.

See also Professor W. D. Matthews, *American Museum Journal*, supplemental edition 2 (1905); *Touring Topics*, November 1932, p. 22; W. H. Proctor, *Life*, October 24, 1938, p. 9; George C. Marshall, "Giant Effigies of the Southwest," *National Geographic*, September 1952, p. 389; Setzler, Frank M. and Richard H. Stewart, "Seeking the Secret of the Giant," *National Geographic*, September 1952, p. 390-404; all five above sources also cited by Harris, *The Book of Mormon Message and Evidence* (1961), pp. 89-90.

The following sources document both the horse and elephant living coincidentally with ancient American man. Hannah Marie Wormington, *Ancient Man in North America*, 2nd Edition (Denver: Colorado Museum of Natural History, 1944), pp. 5, 13, 15, 35, 38, 57, 58; *Early Man as Depicted by Leading Authorities at the Academy of Natural Sciences*, edited by G. G. Mac-Curdy, (Philadelphia: March 1937), p. 192, contains papers of 36 experts; E. N. Fallaise, *Science Progress*, vol. 32, p. 132 (1937-1938);

Frank Roberts says: "The first migrants were unquestionably hunters, and many of the animals that served them as game were essentially the same as those existing today. In addition there were a number that now are extinct. Among those represented by the bones associated with the remains of camps and tools left by these hunters are … mammoth … and the horse." (Frank H. H. Roberts, *Essays in Historical Anthropology of North America Published in Honor of John R. Swanton, Smithsonian Miscellaneous Collections*, [1940], vol. 100, p. 104.) All above sources were also cited by Harris, *The Book of Mormon Message and Evidence* (1961), pp. 88-89. See also John L. Sorenson, "Horses," *Re-exploring the Book of Mormon*, edited by John W. Welch, (1992), pp. 98-100.

Below is a drawing of an interesting ceramic toy animal located in the American Museum of Natural History that once functioned as a wheeled toy (cat. no. 30.0-3274). On the back of this animal is a man, although the top half is missing. According to Dr. Ignacio Bernal, and Dr. Gordon Ekholm, this toy appears to be pre-Columbian. Writing about this toy Dr. Ekholm says:

> The really extraordinary feature is the rider, unfortunately incomplete, seated on the animal's back with legs clasping the sides of the animal in a manner exactly like that of a horseback rider. There are also clay fillets behind and in front of the rider, which obviously represent some form of saddle. (Gordon F. Ekholm, "Wheeled Toys in Mexico," *American Antiquity*, [Society for American Archaeology, 1946], vol. 11, pp. 224-226.)

While this animal does not much resemble a modern horse, it clearly shows that the Mesoamericans did indeed ride some sort of fairly large animal. It may well be that the *horses* mentioned in the Book of Mormon, did not at all resemble the well-bred horses of today, rather when translating the Book of Mormon Joseph Smith chose to call these now extinct animals *horses* for lack of a better word. Furthermore, it may be that this toy was not fashioned after any living animal, but was perhaps the product of conjecture based on the descriptions from legends of when the Horse was still found in America. (See Diane Wirth, *A Challenge to the Critics*, [Horizon Publishers, 1986], p. 54. See also the evidence regarding THE WHEEL IN ANCIENT AMERICA in the chapter on Ancient American Science.)

Figure 13. Pre-Columbian ceramic wheeled toy with rider and saddle.

EVIDENCE NO. 716: CURELOMS AND CUMMOMS

<u>Claim</u>: Along with elephants and horses, the Book of Mormon also mentions two unidentified animals called *cureloms* and *cummoms* (Ether 9:19). Apparently these were domesticated animals and were highly useful to the ancient inhabitants of America. Because Joseph Smith did not translate the names of these animals into familiar English designations, it is generally assumed that these animals no longer exist. While we have no idea what these animals were like, scientists have now unearthed evidence that the ancient Americans had contact with many animals now extinct.

<u>Evidence</u>: Alfred Louis Kidder, in referring to various discoveries says these "prove beyond possible doubt that man was present in the New World contemporaneously with many mammals now extinct." (See *Essays in Anthropology in Honor of Alfred Louis Kidder*, [1936] p. 144.)

M. R. Harrington, "Gypsum Cave Nevada," *Southwest Museum Papers*, No. 8, April (1933), page 172, shows a map of 23 locations where extinct animals have been associated with man in America. Pages 184-185 present ancient associations of man with the mammoth, mastodon, camel, and horse.

Another possibility is that the Book of Mormon was making reference to animals of which an uneducated farm boy, such as Joseph Smith would have no knowledge—such as the tapir or the llama.

EVIDENCE NO. 717: "GIANTS" IN ANCIENT AMERICA

<u>Claim</u>: The Book of Mormon states that the Jaredites who came to the Americas from the Tower of Babel were "large," "mighty" and of "great stature" (Ether 6:16, 44, 73, 99) and larger than the Nephites (Mosiah 8:10). Ancient American traditions support this claim.

<u>Evidence</u>: The following is quoted from B. H. Roberts, *New Witnesses for God*, vol. 2, p.479:

> On the way between Vera Cruz and the capital not far from the modern city of Puebla, stands the venerable relic, with which the reader has become familiar in the course of this narrative—called the temple of Cholulua. It is, as he will remember, a pyramidal mound, built, or rather cased, with unburnt brick, rising to the height of nearly one hundred and eighty feet. The popular tradition of the natives is that it was erected by a family of giants, who had escaped the great inundation, and designed to raise the building to the clouds; but the gods, offended with their presumption, sent fires from heaven on the pyramid, and compelled them to abandon the attempt. The partial coincidence of this legend with the Hebrew account of the Tower of Babel, re-received also by other nations of the east, cannot be denied (William H. Prescott, *Conquest of Mexico*, [New York: McKay Co., 1847], vol. 2, pp. 43, 386, 387).

The following are quotations from Weldon, *The Book of Mormon Evidences Joseph Smith a Prophet* (pp. 22-23):

> Hubert H. Bancroft says, "The Quinames or giants are mentioned as the first inhabitants of Mexico." (*Native Races of the Pacific States*, [New York: McGraw-Hill, 1883], vol. 1, p. 670. Se also vol. 3, pp. 67, 68.)

> William Gates in his *Yucatan, Before and After the Conquest* (John Hopkins University, 1910), p. 85 comments: "Landa says in demolishing one building they found a very large jar containing the ashes and bones of a man. These were greater people—their bones very large and thick showing them to be very strong and great of strength. Also those figures found in cement on the walls denote men of great height as well as the height and width of the steps."

> H. H. Bancroft reports three different claims of discovery of giants' bones in Mexico. (See *Native Races of the Pacific States*, vol. 4, pp. 547, 576, 600, 609.)

> Nadaillac said: "One fact is now incontestably secured to science: The first Americans were a large and powerful race, and were contemporary with gigantic animals.... They had to contend with the

mastodon, the megatherm, the mylodon, the elephant and a jaguar larger than that of the present day." (*Prehistoric America* [New York: Random House, Inc., 1885], p. 15.)

Dr. Alfred M. Tozzer, Harvard archaeologist, in his *Landas' Relación de Los Cosa's de Yucatan* (Boston: Peabody, 1941), note 633, said: "The Tultecs according to ancient histories were the second settlers of these lands after the giants."

According to H. H. Bancroft the early Spanish writer Veytia doubted that a race of giants actually existed, although admitting that there were doubtless individuals of great size among them. (*Native Races of the Pacific States*, vol. 3, p. 67; vol. 5, p. 198)

Hunter and Ferguson in their *Ancient America and the Book of Mormon*, p. 136 quote Ixtlilxóchitl, the native Tezcuyan historian, as follows: "On the banks of the Atoyac river, which is the one that passes between Puebla and Cholula, they (the Olmecas) found some of the giants that had escaped the calamity and extermination of the second age. It is a tale of men arriving at Panuco by sea ... with them came sages and soothsayers, men able to write ... four old men undertook to regulate the calendar ... the tradition connects these ancient new comers with the building of the pyramids 'by giants'."

Later peoples referred to the first group as "the giants." See *Works of Ixtlilxóchitl*, W. Jiminez Moreno, "El Enigma de los Olmecas;" *Cuadernos Americanos*, vol. 2, p. 5, 1942; Miguel Covarrubias, *Mexico South, the Isthmus of Tehuantepec*, (1946), p. 116. All cited in Hunter and Ferguson, *Ancient America and the Book of Mormon* (1950), p. 46.

See also Boturini, *Idea de una Historia*, pp. 113, 114; Clavigero, *Storia Antes del Messico*, vol. 1, pp. 129, 130; vol. 2, p. 16; *Spiegazione delle Tavole del Codice Mexicano* (Vaticano) tav. 7, in Lord Kingsborough, *Mexican Antiquities*, vol. 5, pp. 164, 165; Gemelli Carreri, in *Churchill's Colossians Voy.*, vol. 6, p. 481; Humboldt, *Vues des Cordilleres*, vol. 1, pp. 114, 115; vol. 2, pp. 175-178; Tylor, *Anahuac* pp. 276, 277; Gondra, in Prescott, *Conquesta de Mexico*, vol. 3, pp. 1-10. All cited in H. H. Bancroft, *Native Races of the Pacific States*, (New York: McGraw-Hill, 1883), vol. 3, pp. 67, 68.

EVIDENCE NO. 718: THE CALAMITY OF SERPENTS

Claim: The Book of Mormon tells of a great curse of serpents that spread over a part of the land after a severe drought, which hindered animals and people from passing through the area (Ether 9:30-31).

Evidence: Critics have mocked the idea of serpents preventing passage in articles with such preposterous titles as "Cowboy Snakes." However, history records several other similar situations that occurred in ancient times. Pompey the Great for example, could not get his army into Hyrcania because snakes along the Araxes stream barred the way. (See James Darmesteter, *The Zend-Avesta*, [Oxford University Press, 1895], Part 1, p. 5, n. 3.)

The Absurtitani were driven from their country by snakes, and Esarhaddon of Assyria records a dangerous march by his army through a land "of serpents and scorpions, with which the plain was covered as with ants." (James A. Montgomery, *Arabia and the Bible* [Philadelphia: University of Pennsylvania Press, 1934], p. 50).

Dr. Hugh Nibley writes: "In the thirteenth century A. D. Shah Sadrudin set his heart on the building of a capital which should surpass all other cities in splendor; yet the project had to be abandoned after enormous expense when during a period of drought, the place so swarmed with serpents that no one could live in it. It is interesting in this connection that the plague of serpents in Ether is described as following upon a period of extreme drought" (Ether 9:30). See Fikret Isiltan, *Die Seltschuken-Geschichte des Akserayi, Sammlung Orientalistischer Arbeiten*, (Leipzig: Harrassowitz, 1943), vol. 12, p. 97. See also Herodotus, *Histories*, vol. 1, p. 140. All above sources on serpents are cited in Nibley, *Lehi in the Desert*, (1988), pp. 221-222.

Another similarity can be found in Josephus' account of "How Moses Made War With the Ethiopians," (Flavius Josephus, *Antiquities of the Jews*, Book 2, Chapter 10).

5. Book of Mormon Geography

Introduction

Throughout the Book of Mormon, detailed descriptions are given of geographical locations such as cities, rivers, seas, mountains, wildernesses, isthmuses, coastal regions, and even the length of time needed to travel from one place to another. With this wealth of information, students of the Book of Mormon have been able to piece together maps of the various civilizations that existed anciently. Geographical descriptions in the Book of Mormon match modern maps (unavailable at the time of Joseph Smith) of both the Middle East, where the story of the Book of Mormon begins, and of Central America, where most of the history unfolds. Volumes have been written which discuss the many parallels. (See, for example, John L. Sorenson, *An Ancient American Setting for the Book of Mormon* [Salt Lake City: Deseret Book Co., 1985], and Joseph L. Allen, *Exploring the Lands of the Book of Mormon* [Orem, Utah: S. A. Publishers, Inc., 1989]).

Skeptics say that Joseph Smith might have been able to consult maps of Central America. But it is highly unlikely that such maps were available to him in the small, remote town of his day. However, not only does the geography correlate, but the precise locations and names of various ruined cities also correlate. The vast majority of these ruins were discovered many years after the Book of Mormon was first printed. Some of the first of such explorations were those of John Lloyd Stephens which did not occur until the 1840's and were not published until years later. So even if Joseph Smith had access to maps of South and Central America, they would not have contained the detailed information that he would have needed to fabricate the intricate details unfolded in the Book of Mormon.

The following evidences demonstrate the remarkable correlation between cities and lands of the Book of Mormon with those that have since been discovered. They demonstrate that neither Joseph Smith, nor any of his contemporaries could have authored the Book of Mormon, rather it was translated from ancient records as testified by Joseph Smith and his scribes.

EVIDENCE NO. 719: THE BOOK OF MORMON CONVERTS A SCHOLAR OF ANCIENT CULTURES

Claim: The remarkable correlations between the Book of Mormon and Ancient American history, culture, and geography have prompted serious investigators and scholars to join the Church.

Evidence: Scholars are typically skeptical about things of a spiritual nature, and tend to dismiss the Book of Mormon without seriously giving it a chance to sand on its own merits. For example, in 1982 the Smithsonian Institution published a statement stating that it finds "no connection between the archaeology of the New World and the subject matter of the Book [of Mormon]." This statement was made without first examining the volumes of work by *Brigham Young University*, which clearly show many such connections. (See John L. Sorenson, "An Evaluation of the Smithsonian Institution's 'Statement' Regarding the Book of Mormon," *Foundation Ancient Research Mormon Studies Papers*, [Provo, Utah, 1982].)

However, honest scholars who examine the Book of Mormon with an open-mind find a host of evidence supporting the veracity of the Book of Mormon. One example is Alpheus Hyatt Verrill, author of several works on Ancient American culture and history, who joined the Church in his later years (correspondence from Dr. John L. Sorensen to Allen Richardson). Brother Verrill was tutored by his father Dr. Addison Verrill professor of Zoology at Yale University. He published over one hundred books on ancient American natural history and allied subjects, including: *The American Indian* (New York: New Home Library, 1943); *America's Ancient Civilizations* (New York: G. P. Putnam's Sons, 1953), *The Deep Sea Hunters; Foods America Gave the World; The Golden City; Great Conquerors of South and Central America; My Jungle Trails; The Incas' Treasure House; The Islands and Their Mysteries; Minerals, Metals and Gems* (New York: Grosset and Dunlap, 1939); *The Ocean and Its Mysteries; Old Civilizations of the New World; Perfumes and Spices; Under Peruvian Skies* (Plymouth: Mayflower Press); *Rivers and their Mysteries; Shell Collectors Handbook* (New York: G P. Putnam's Sons, 1950); *Smugglers and Smuggling* (New York: Duffield and Co., 1924); *Strange Sea Shells and Their Stories* (Boston: L. C. Page and Co., 1936); *Strange Insects and Their Stories* (Page, 1937); *Strange Reptiles and Their Stories; Strange Birds and Their Stories* (Page, 1938); *Strange Fish and Their Stories; Strange Animals and Their Stories; Strange Customs Manners and Beliefs* (Page, 1946); *Strange Prehistoric Animals and Their Stories* (Page, 1948); *The Strange Story of our Earth; Strange Creatures of the Sea* (Page, 1955).

Lehi's Travels in Arabia

The Book of Mormon tells of a prophet named Lehi who was commanded by God to leave his home in Jerusalem and take his family into the wilderness (1 Nephi 2:1-2). It says that they traveled southward to the Red Sea, and on through what is now known as Arabia in a south-southeastern direction (1 Nephi 16:13). It mentions that Lehi's party spent eight years traveling through the Arabian Peninsula—making several encampments along the way (1 Nephi 17:4). Clearly, they spent a considerable amount of time "tarrying" at each camp. They spent some time hunting (1 Nephi 16:18, 31), and it appears that they also stopped to plant and harvest gardens, and store the food before leaving on each leg of their voyage (1 Nephi 8:1). In addition to the eight years it took for Lehi's party to travel from Jerusalem to the coast of Arabia, it must have taken at least two or three more years for Nephi to build their ship (1 Nephi 17:7-18).

The references in the Book of Mormon to the "wilderness" may bring to mind desolate wastelands. However, the text alludes to the fact that others were traveling the region at the same time. It says that the Lord did not allow them to have fires and made their meat sweet so that they could eat it raw (1 Nephi 17:12). The only logical reason for this was that the smoke of their fires would have been seen by others with evil intentions. Indeed, according to the histories of the time and locale, there were nomadic tribes and well-traveled trade routes in that region along the borders of the Red Sea.

There is significant evidence that Lehi and Nephi left their mark and their names on the local cultures as they traveled throughout the Arabian Peninsula. The next several evidences deal with Lehi's journey through Arabia and the evidence he left behind along the way.

EVIDENCE NO. 720: LEHI'S CONVERTS IN THE ARABIAN PENINSULA

<u>Claim</u>: The Book of Mormon records that, Lehi and Nephi both spent much of their time in the wilderness studying and pondering the contents of the brass plates, and sharing what they read with their family. There must have also been many opportunities to share the gospel message with other travelers and nomads. And since Lehi was unafraid to preach the gospel before unfriendly crowds in Jerusalem (1 Nephi 1:18-20), it is entirely conceivable that he and his family made a lasting impression on some of the local inhabitants as they journeyed through Arabia.

<u>Evidence</u>: Six hundred years after Lehi left Jerusalem, after Lehi's message had time to spread about the land, the scribe who penned the Book of Acts recorded that "there were dwelling at Jerusalem Jews, devout men, *out of every nation under heaven*" (Acts 2:5), among which were Arabians (Acts 2:11). Indeed, historians have recently found evidence that support the theory that Lehi made converts in the Arabian Peninsula.

On October 22, 1983, a paper was presented by Hope and Lynn Hilton at the 32nd annual Symposium on Archaeology of the Scriptures at Brigham Young University, entitled "The Lihyanites." It made a strong case for the possibility that Lehi converted some Arabs during his travels through the wilderness. The Hiltons refer to a *Smithsonian* article which dates the origin of the Lihyanite culture at 600 BC—precisely the year that Lehi took his family out of Jerusalem to travel across the wilderness of Arabia to the sea (1 Nephi 2:2-5; 10:2-4). See Dora Jane Hamblin, "Treasures of the Sands," *Smithsonian Magazine*, September 1983, p. 43.

The Hiltons also note that "the Saudi Arabian archaeological department describes the Lihyanites as a tribal group who probably followed the common practice of taking their name from some respected leader." The name *Lihyan* is "so similar to *Lehi*, one would think the Mormons had made it up themselves."

The Lihyan culture replaced the Dedan culture of the northwestern portion of present day Arabia in 550 BC—just 50 years after Lehi passed through the area. See Dr. Abdulrahman, al-Ansari's (professor of archaeology at King Saud University, Riyad, Saudi Arabia) article, "The Chronology of Lihyan," *Journal of the Eighteenth Recontre Assyriologique Internationale*, (paper read at a conference held, June 29-July 3, 1970, at Munich, Germany), pp. 53-59. Cited in Lynn M. and Hope A. Hilton, *Discovering Lehi*, (Springville, Utah, 1996), p. 81. See also Hilton, pp. 75, 78, 80-81, 95.

The Lihyanite culture is also referred to in an article on "Arabia," in *Encyclopedia Americana*, (Danbury, Connecticut: Grolier, Inc., 1983), vol. 2, p. 162. Dr. Abdulrahman, refers to the Lihyans in Muslim tradition in the *Encyclopedia of Islam*, (Leiden University Press, 1986), edition 2, vol. 5, p. 763. See also vol. 3, p. 540 for an article with related information by Professor G. Rentz.

The name of Lehi is also associated with several cities in Yemen in the southwestern corner of the Arabian Peninsula. At approximately 14° north and 48° east is the town of *Lahij*. Located on the coast of Arabia at approximately 16° north and 43° east, is the town of *Luhaiya* (also known as *Laheia*). See *Hammond World Atlas*, (Maplewood, New Jersey, MCMLXXXVI), p. 58. See also Figure 14 below which marks the locations of the above-mentioned site, along with the proposed route for Lehi's travels through Arabia.

According to the Qur'an (Sura 7), a prophet named *Salih* preached to the people of *Midian Salih-al Ula*. His message was identical to that of Lehi: "... repent or be destroyed." (Compare to 1 Nephi 1:13.) Tradition also connects him to the Lihyan temple of al-Ula, (see following evidence), but no one seems to know exactly who he was nor where he came from.

That this mysterious prophet *Salih* could actually have been Lehi is suggested by: 1) the similarity of their message, 2) the similarity of their names—If the prefix *Sa* is removed, the remaining *Lih* forms the phonetic lettering for the first half of Lehi's name, 3) that both were connected to temple worship, 4) that both lived at the same time and locale, and 5) that both men were prophets who traveled through Arabia. (See Hilton, *Discovering Lehi*, [1996], p. 83.)

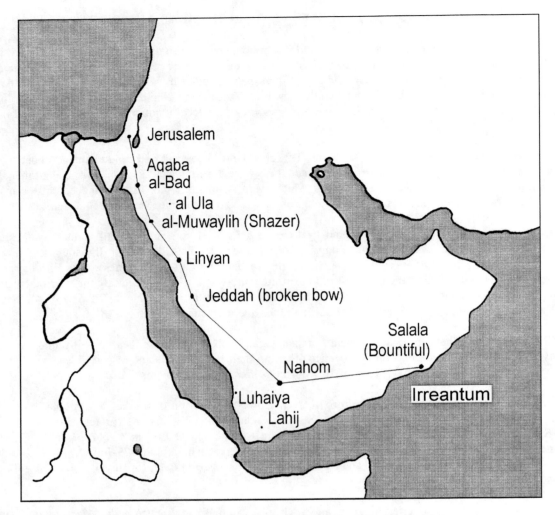

Figure 14. Lehi's travels through the Arabian Peninsula

EVIDENCE NO. 721: THE LIHYANITE TEMPLE

<u>Claim</u>: Another factor that strengthens the case for Lehi having converted Arabs to the Israelite religion is the discovery of a Lihyanite temple.

<u>Evidence</u>: Dr. F. Winnett a respected archaeologist said that the ruins of an ancient Lihyanite temple at al-Ula, Saudi Arabia, is the most unusual of archaeological remains yet discovered in the entire Arabian peninsula. (Winnett, and Reed, *Ancient Records from North Arabia,* [University of Toronto Press, 1970], p. 40.)

In the center of an open court at the Lihyanite temple site is a sandstone vessel, 12 feet in diameter and 7 feet deep—very close to the dimensions of the "brazen sea," from Solomon's temple (1 Kings 7:23-26). Inside the vessel are steps for people to enter and leave. However, there is no evidence that it had rested on the backs of 12 oxen, as did Solomon's. Mohammed Naif, al-Juhaineh, director of the al-Sodia School at al-Eis said that some of the Lihyanite structures were built by Jews, such as the fort at al-Eis. Professor G. Levi Della Vida also acknowledged "the presence of Judean elements" in the Lihyanite civilization. Also, A. J. Drews reports that Hebrew inscriptions have been found in the area of al-Ula, the same vicinity of the Lihyanite temple and font. (See *Encyclopedia of Islam,* [Leiden, University Press, 1963], edition 1, vol. 3, p. 27; edition 2, vol. 5, p. 172. All cited in Lynn M. and Hope A. Hilton, *Discovering Lehi,* [Springville, Utah, 1996], pp. 85, 97-99.)

EVIDENCE NO. 722: THE NAME OF NEPHI IN SOUTHERN ARABIA

Claim: During the eight years that Lehi's party traveled in the wilderness, and also during the time their ship was under construction, they surely had opportunities to share the gospel message with local residents. Most of their time in the wilderness was spent tarrying "for the space of a time" (1 Nephi 16:17, 33)—which must have been several months at each location, in order for them to take eight years to arrive at the coast (1 Nephi 17:4).

Knowing that Nephi was exceptionally diligent and obedient to the Lord, we should expect to find that, like Lehi, he too left his mark along the way as he followed his father's example of missionary labor. Indeed, in a revelation given to the prophet Joseph Smith, the latter-day missionaries were told: "Open your mouths and they shall be filled, and you shall become even as Nephi of old, who journeyed from Jerusalem in the wilderness" (D&C 33:8). This makes a clear reference to Nephi's missionary efforts while in the wilderness. Thus it would not be surprising to find the name of Nephi preserved as a legendary hero in the secular history of Arabia.

Evidence: In al-Ula, not far from the proposed route of Lehi's travel, (see map above), is found a Lihyanite inscription carved in stone next to a tomb bearing the word *NFY* for the personal name of Nephi. With these consonants, Arabs usually insert the vowels "A" and "I" to read *Nafi*. (See F. V. Winnett and W. L. Reed, *Ancient Records from North Arabia*, [University of Toronto Press, 1970] inscription 6:42; reprinted in Hilton, *Discovering Lehi*, [1996], p. 87.)

Furthermore, the name of Nephi can be found in the local geography. Within an eight-hour drive from Yanbu, lies the rural town of *Nafee*. In the Jeddah phone book, there are 27 families listed with the name of *al-Nafi*. (See Hilton, *Discovering Lehi*, [1996], pp. 78, 87, 89.)

EVIDENCE NO. 723: THE VALLEY OF LEMUEL AND THE RIVER LAMAN

Claim: The Book of Mormon tells of a river that flowed into the Red Sea (1 Nephi 2:5-8). Critics have maintained that there never was a river in such a locale. The Book of Mormon goes on to mention that this river ran through (or perhaps near) a valley which was "firm and steadfast, and immovable" (1 Nephi 2:9-10).

Evidence: Explorers have affirmed that rivers once flowed into the northeastern arm of the Red Sea. (See Edward H. Palmer, "The Desert of The Tíh and the Country of Moab," in *Survey of Western Palestine Special Papers*, [London: Palestine Exploration Fund, 1881] vol. 4, p. 67; "Lieutenant Claud R. Conder's Reports," in *Palestine Exploration Fund Quarterly*, 1875, p. 130; Gray Hill, "A Journey to Petra—1896," *Palestine Exploration Fund Quarterly*, 1897, p. 144; W. Ewing, "A Journey in the Hauran," *Palestine Exploration Fund Quarterly*, 1895, p. 175; all cited in Nibley, *Lehi in the Desert and The World of the Jaredites*, (1980), pp. 86, 145.

A valley that matches the description given in the Book of Mormon has also been identified in the area specified by the Book of Mormon. It is located three-days journey from Aquaba in a south-southeastern direction. The Wadi Afal at the oasis of al-Bad, which "has a precipitous, breath-taking canyon." It is the only significant oasis for 150 miles and there are nearby mountains where Nephi could have seen his visions (1 Nephi 2:16-24). There is a *river* that flows south, (though it is ephemeral) in the Wadi *Afal*. Frequent thunderstorms during the winter season result in literal torrents of water that last for two or three days. The spring at Al Beda forms a stream that flows south for 21 miles and empties into the Red Sea. See Lynn M. and Hope A. Hilton, *Discovering Lehi*, (Springville, Utah, 1996), pp. 30, 45, 54; and Lynn M. Hilton, *In Search of Lehi's Trail* (Salt Lake City: Deseret Book Co. 1976) p. 64.

The Hiltons also note that the Hebrew word *nachalah* which is only a "winter torrent," is often translated as *river*, such as was the case with the Arnon River. Ever-flowing rivers such as the Nile or the Euphrates are both translated from the Hebrew word *nahar* (Hilton, *Discovering Lehi*, [1996], pp. 52-53).

EVIDENCE NO. 724: THE TRAVEL ROUTE ALONG THE RED SEA

Claim: The Book of Mormon tells that Lehi and his family traveled in a south-southeastern direction along the "borders near the shore of the Red Sea."   It further mentions that they traveled along the "borders which are *nearer* the Red Sea;" then after Ishmael's burial at Nahom, they turned eastward until they arrived at the coast (1 Nephi 2:5; 17:1).

Evidence: Non-Mormon scholars have found that there was just such a route that existed in that time period. Called the Frankincense Trail, it follows a south-southeastern direction along the Red Sea and turns eastward across the peninsula. See Gus W. Van Beek, "The Rise and Fall of Arabia Felix," *Scientific America*, December 1969, pp. 36-44, cited in Hilton, *In Search of Lehi's Trail*, (1976), p. 32.

Furthermore, a study of modern-day maps of the area shows that the western Arabian coastal plain is an area lying between the Red Sea and the mountains of the Arabian Peninsula. Its greatest width is 48 miles in the area close to Jeddah, near present-day Mecca, which is located approximately midway along the length of the Red Sea. At its narrowest width there is no beach at all—the mountains drop directly into the sea. The wadi called *al-Afal* could clearly represent the "borders near the Red Sea," while the beach of *Tihama* could easily have been referred to as the "borders nearer the Red Sea." (See Hilton, *In Search of Lehi's Trail*, [1976], p. 49).

EVIDENCE NO. 725: NAHOM REDISCOVERED

Claim: Nephi states that Lehi's caravan traveled south along the coast of the Red Sea until they arrived at a place "which was called Nahom" (1 Nephi 16:14, 16, 33, 34). The record does not state that Lehi or any of his company named the place—it therefore may have been an already-existing town.

Evidence: There is a site in the Arabian Desert that is known as *Nehum*. Located on the fifteenth parallel north latitude near the borders of the Red Sea, this site was found in a chart by Carsten Niebuhr who explored the Arabian Peninsula under the direction of King Frederick V of Denmark. Alternate spellings of this town include: *NHM, Nah'm, Neh'm*. See Thorkild Hansen, *Arabia Felix: The Danish Expedition of 1761-1767* (1964), pp. 232-233, cited in Ross T. Christensen, "The Place Called Nahom," *Ensign*, August 1978, p. 73 and in Vestal and Wallace, *The Firm Foundation of Mormonism* (1981), p. 110; See also Warren P. and Michaela J. Aston, Stephen D. Ricks and John W. Welch, "Lehi's Trail and Nahom Revisited," *Re-exploring the Book of Mormon*, edited by John W. Welch, (1992), pp. 47-49; and Hilton, *Discovering Lehi,* (1996), pp. 5, 21, 124-127.

More recently, an ancient altar which dates to at least 700 BC has been discovered at a site in Yemen on the south-west corner of the Arabian peninsula. This altar "contains an inscription confirming *Nahom* as an actual place that existed in the peninsula before the time of Lehi" (*Ensign*, February 2001, p. 79).

EVIDENCE NO. 726: THE BROKEN BOW INCIDENT

Claim: The Book of Mormon tells of a strange incident in which Nephi's steel bow breaks, and the bows of his brothers loose their springs. This event occurred in the area between Shazer and Nahom (1 Nephi 16:15, 17).

Evidence: Assuming that Lehi's party traveled approximately twenty miles per day, a four-day journey from the previous camp at the Valley of Lemuel would put *Shazer* at an oasis called *al-Muwaylih*—a natural stopping place for weary travelers.

The area where Nephi broke his bow roughly matches the vicinity of Jeddah, Saudi Arabia, where the weather is a merciless combination of heat, humidity, sand and salt forces strong enough to destroy steel. In the same locale, the Hilton explorers witnessed holes rusted through car fenders in only a few months' time. See Hilton, *In Search of Lehi's Trail,* (1976), p. 81; and Hilton, *Discovering Lehi*, (1996), pp. 30-34, 109.

EVIDENCE NO. 727: ARABIA'S INTERIOR CLIMATE

Claim: The Book of Mormon implies that Arabia's interior was a hot, dry desert, which was very difficult to cross (1 Nephi 16:35; 17:1-6). This was possibly the first accurate description of that part of the world.

Evidence: It is well known that the interior of the Arabian Peninsula is very hot and dry. However, had Joseph Smith been the author rather than the translator of the Book of Mormon he would have most likely described Arabia's interior as green, fertile and abounding in game. That was the prevailing notion at the time, described in the popular but erroneous guidebook by Josiah Conder, *A Popular Description of Arabia,* Modern Traveler Series, (London: Duncan, 1825) pp. 9, 14-15, 348-349, cited in Nibley, *Lehi in the Desert* (1980), p. 127.

EVIDENCE NO. 728: IRREANTUM

Claim: After leaving Nahom, the families of Lehi and Ishmael traveled eastward over land to reach the sea which they "called *Irreantum,* which, being interpreted, is *many waters*" (1 Nephi 17:5). This strange word has been the subject of ridicule by critics of the Book of Mormon. However, not only has it been shown to be an authentic name for that area, but the meaning of the name is the same as given in the Book of Mormon.

Evidence: The Greeks of the first century called the sea in this area *Erythreum.* The similarity of Irreantum and Erythreum becomes clearer when both words are spelled phonetically: *Ir-re-thre-um* vs. *Ir-re-ant-um.* See Hilton, *Discovering Lehi,* (1996), p. 21. On page 88 of Hilton, is shown a map printed in Latin and dated at 1661 which shows the word *Erythreum* just off the southern coast of the Arabian Peninsula.

Furthermore, it is interesting to note that the Egyptians called the sea to the east, "Many Waters." See W. Spiegelberg, *Koptisches Handwoerterbuch,* pp. 204, 258; also cited in Nibley, *Lehi in the Desert,* (1952), pp. 89-91.

The word, *Irreantum,* can be traced back to some derivation containing *wr* (great) and *nt* (Coptic *noret* "standing water"), and to identify the final-*um* with the common (eg., Coptic Hebrew) *yem, yam, yum,* "sea" and the rest of the word with Coptic *irnahte* "great or many." Also, *Iaru* is an Egyptian name for Red Sea, and *Iny-t* is Egyptian for describing large bodies of water. See J. R. Towers, *Journal of Near Eastern Studies,* vol. 18, (1959), pp. 150-153. Also cited in Nibley, *Since Cumorah* (1976), pp. 195-196.

EVIDENCE NO. 729: ARABIA'S BOUNTIFUL

Claim: After Lehi's party had traveled eastward across the desert (1 Nephi 17:1), they arrived at a place of many waters which they called Bountiful (1 Nephi 17:5), a land of fruit and honey, near mountains (1 Nephi 17:7), with enough trees to build a ship (1 Nephi 17:8). Arabia's coastal region in the area of the nineteenth parallel, near the Qara Mountains, were correctly described, perhaps for the first time, in the Book of Mormon as being green, fertile and with bounteous vegetation—in stark contrast to the hot desert of its interior.

Evidence: The Frankincense Trail's natural end near the Qara Mountains is the one place along the 1,400 mile southern coast of Arabia near the 19th parallel that perfectly fits the description given in the Book of Mormon. It is now called *Khor Kharfot,* which means "Fort Inlet" in English. Surrounded on three sides by the Qara mountains it is a fertile, well-watered valley, abounding in gardens, palm trees, fruits, flowers, honeybees, and animal life. (See Lynn M. and Hope A. Hilton, *Discovering Lehi,* [Springville, Utah, 1996], pp. 4-6, 152-154.)

According to *Foundation for Ancient Research and Mormon Studies Insights,* no. 5, (September 1993): "Khor Kharfot and its environs have all the features mentioned in the Book of Mormon in connection with the Old World Bountiful. It has no features that would conflict with the Book of Mormon account. A survey of alternative sites in the Arabian Peninsula has turned up no others that come close to fitting the criteria for Bountiful so well." For a description of this place, see Wilfred Thesiger, *Arabian Sands* (Middlesex, England: Penguin Books Ltd., 1964), p. 47. Cited in Lynn M. Hilton, *In Search of Lehi's Trail,* (1976), p. 40.

Again, Josiah Conder's *Popular Description of Arabia* (cited above)—which was quite popular in Joseph Smith's day, depicts the geography exactly opposite from reality. While Conder imagined forests and lakes in the interior of that desert country, he states that the whole coastline was" a rocky wall ... as dismal and barren as can be not a blade of grass or a green thing" to be found anywhere. (Josiah Conder, *A Popular Description of Arabia,* Modern Traveler Series, [London: Duncan, 1825], pp. 9, 14-15, 348-349, cited in Nibley, *Lehi in the Desert* (1980), p. 127.

Neither Joseph Smith, nor any of his contemporaries could have authored the Book of Mormon as critics claim, because there were no accurate references available at the time to provide such a curiously accurate description of that strangely diverse and largely unexplored land. In fact the first recorded crossing of the Great Desert or Empty Quarter of Arabia was not until 1928—a whole century after Joseph Smith translated Nephi's accurate account as recorded in the Book of Mormon (Nibley, *Lehi in the Desert,* [1988], p. 112). See also Robert E. Cheesman, *In Unknown Arabia,* (London: Macmillan, 1926), pp. 67-71.

EVIDENCE NO. 730: MINERAL DEPOSITS IN THE OLD WORLD BOUNTIFUL

Claim: The Book of Mormon indicates that Nephi obtained ores in the area of Bountiful, in order to make the tools necessary to build a ship (1 Nephi 17:9-10).

Evidence: Eugene Clark, former geologist for ESSO in Oman, has prepared a report of mineral deposits in the *Dhofar* region where *Wadi Sayq* is located—the presumed site of the Old World Bountiful. The report identifies a number of geological possibilities for copper or iron ore accessible to Wadi Sayq, based on published geological studies and surveys.

Most promising among the published studies are reports of specular hematite found in small, random deposits on the Mirbat plain east of Salalah. Specular hematite is the most readily available form of high-quality iron and would have been most attractive as a low-tech smelting source for Nephi's tools. The report also notes that Dhofar irons would usually occur in mixtures with manganese and carbon, yielding higher-quality steel that would be superior for tools ("Preliminary Study Identifies Possible Sources for Nephi's Ore," *Foundation Ancient Research Mormon Studies Insights,* June 1995, p. 5).

EVIDENCE NO. 731: THE ENVIRONMENT OF BOOK OF MORMON LANDS

Claim: The study of Mesoamerican lands has elucidated and substantiated certain cultural and geographical aspects of the Book of Mormon.

Evidence: The following is quoted from the abstract of a paper by John L. Sorenson entitled "Further on Authentication and Elucidation of the Book of Mormon" (*University Archaeological Society Newsletter,* [BYU: Provo, Utah], vol. 6, p. 3):

Climatic change shown by geological and archaeological data now appears to have caused a dry period in Mexico (at least the central part) about the same time that the Nephites colonized the Land Northward (i.e. southern and central Mexico), much of which is stated to have been barren of forest at that time. The "wilderness" of tropical forest around the ruins of Central America fits ideally the Book of Mormon wilderness around the cities of the Land Southward, which were full of wild beasts and impeded travel, causing parties to get lost continually. The division of Guatemala and adjoining regions into two distinct archaeological zones corresponding to the highlands and the lowlands may indicate some basic physical and economic reasons for the enmity of the highland Lamanites toward the lowland Nephites.

EVIDENCE NO. 732: THE SYMBOLIC TEMPLES AT TEOTIHUACAN

Claim: Striking parallels exist between the ruins of Teotihuacan, Mexico and the teachings of the Book of Mormon.

Evidence: Near Mexico City lie the ruins of the great city of Teotihuacán which was the sixth largest city in the world in 500 AD and is thought to be the first pre-eminent Mesoamerican urban center. The dominant feature at Teotihuacán is the Pyramid of the Sun that was dedicated to the worship of Quetzalcoatl (Jesus Christ). On the southern end of the site are twelve evenly-spaced, smaller pyramid-temples—described by Ross T. Christensen:

> Pyramid of the Sun at the Place of God: Near the village of San Juan Teotihuacán in the northeastern part of the Valley of Mexico, [we] visited the magnificent ruins of the ancient ceremonial-center or temple-city of Teotihuacan. This is an Aztec name meaning Place of God (or the Gods), and the center was anciently dedicated to the worship of Quetzalcoatl, the Fair God. The dominant feature is the great Pyramid of the Sun, an enormous rectangular structure some 180 feet (15 stories) high, rising in four sloping terraces.

> Twelve Small Pyramid Temples: At the southern end of the site is a large complex known as the Citadel. A bulwark or very thick wall surrounds a large rectangular court. Upon the bulwark, on each of three sides, four platform-altars or small pyramid-temples are spaced evenly, making a total of twelve. (Ross T. Christensen, "A Tour and Brief Description of Some of the Ancient Ruined Cities of Central and Southern Mexico or 'Land Northward' of the Book of Mormon," *Progress in Archaeology* [1963], pp. 149-150.)

The above makes a striking parallel with Lehi's vision of Jesus Christ and his twelve apostles (1 Nephi 1:8-11). On the eastern side of this complex are three larger structures similar to the twelve pyramid-temples which could clearly make reference to the Godhead (2 Nephi 31:13, 21; Mormon 7:7; Ether 5:4) or perhaps the three Nephite Apostles who were allowed to remain on the earth until the Lord should return in His glory (3 Nephi 28:1-12).

Incidentally, the name *Teotihuacan* literally means "the place where men become Gods." This further substantiates that the Ancient Americans had the true gospel of Jesus Christ that clearly teaches this sacred principle. (See Matthew 5:48; John 10:34; Acts 17:29; Romans 8:17; Galatians 4:7; Revelations 3:21; D&C 76: 50-70; Joseph L. Allen, *Exploring the Lands of the Book of Mormon,* [Orem, Utah: S. A. Publishers, Inc., 1989], p. 97.)

EVIDENCE NO. 733: POSSIBLE LOCATION OF THE WILDERNESS OF HERMOUNTS

Claim: The Book of Mormon identifies a wilderness called *Hermounts* located in the land northward which was infested by wild and ravenous beasts (Alma 2:37).

Evidence: Comparative geographies between ancient America and the Book of Mormon would place Hermounts in the area known today as Tehuantepec—located north of an isthmus (the isthmus of Tehuantepec) just as Hermounts was located north of the "narrow neck of land." Linguist Calvin Tolman said that the word *Tehuantepec* means land or mountains of wild beasts. *Tepec* in the Nahuatl (Aztec) language means hill, or mount. *Tecuani* in Nahuatl, or Tehuan (Spanish pronunciation) means "wild beasts"—hence the meaning of Tehuantepec is "wilderness of wild beasts." (See Antonio Penafiel, *Nombres Geográficos de México* [Mexico City: Litoimpresores, 1977], p. 54; cited in Joseph L. Allen, *Exploring the Lands of the Book of Mormon,* [1989], p. 40.)

For additional information on Hermounts, see the related entry in the chapter on Names in the Book of Mormon.

EVIDENCE NO. 734: POSSIBLE LOCATION OF THE LAND OF KING LAMONI

Claim: The land called Ishmael in the Book of Mormon was governed by King Lamoni (see Alma 17:21). The Book of Mormon claims that it was located in the east wilderness.

Evidence: Joseph L. Allen has noted that, "In the small country of Belize, which borders the Peten of Guatemala, are the remains of an archaeological site that carries the name of *Lamanai*. This Maya site dates to 100 BC which is the Book of Mormon time period when a man by the name of Lamoni was the Lamanite king."

Allen explains further that the Belize/Peten area is an excellent candidate for the east wilderness referred to in the Book of Mormon as the land in which the city of Ishmael was located. (Joseph L. Allen, *Exploring the Lands of the Book of Mormon*, [1989], p. 39.)

Evidences Correlating the River Sidon with the Rio Grijalva

Claim: The Book of Mormon makes frequent mention of an ancient American river of substantial size called *Sidon* (Alma 2:15-35; 43:22-53; Mormon 1:10). Several specific details regarding its headwaters and direction of flow are included. For many years critics have hastily claimed that there is no river in all of South or Central America that meets the specifications given for the Sidon River. However, a river in Central America has now been identified that perfectly matches the description of Sidon—which strengthens the claim of the geographical accuracy of the Book of Mormon. The following several evidences are presented to support this claim.

EVIDENCE NO. 735: THE HEADWATERS FLOW WESTWARD

Evidence: According to a recent report, the *Rio Grijalva* (formerly *Rio San Miguel*), which flows over the border between Guatemala and Mexico, appears to be the best candidate for the Sidon river of Book of Mormon times. (See John L. and Janet F. Hilton, "A Correlation of the Sidon River and the Lands of Manti and Zarahemla with the Southern end of the Rio Grijalva," *Journal of Book of Mormon Studies* vol. 1, no. 1, [1992]: pp. 142-162.)

Scientific studies have concluded that "There has been no appreciable change that would affect the size or cause major relocation of the rivers [in that area] over the last 2000 years ... The exact shape of the river's meanderings through the alluvial deposits that exists at the bottoms of the geologically 'old' canyons are expected to vary a few meters from year to year as the high water floods cause considerable local re-channeling" (Hilton, p. 154). But in general the river should run the same course, as has the Jordan River in Palestine since ancient times.

The head of the Sidon river flowed from east to west (Alma 22:27). The source of the Rio Grijalva (called by another name—*Rio Cuilco*), also flows westward, but becomes the Rio Grijalva as it turns northward on the border of Southwestern Guatemala and Mexico.

EVIDENCE NO. 736: THE RIVER TURNS NORTHWARD NEAR A HILL TO REACH THE SEA

Evidence: The Book of Mormon implies that the Sidon River flowed northward as it made its way to the sea. Several passages refer to the East and West banks of the river Sidon—thus establishing that the river either flowed north or south (Alma 2:15-17, 34; 6:7; 8:3; 16:6-7; 43:27-32, 53; 49:16; and 50:11). This, together with the knowledge that the "head of the river Sidon" was in the South near Manti, (Alma 16:6-7; 17:1; 22:27), implies that the river flowed in a northern direction.

The Book of Mormon tells of a great battle that occurred on the banks of the river Sidon which gives further details on the geography of the river. It species that at the "hill Riplah," near the "head of the river Sidon," the river had turned to flow northward. It further implies that the bend in the river occurred near the hill Riplah, since it mentions that the Lamanites (who were pursued by the Nephites from both the *north* and the *east*), were forced to cross to the *western* shore of the Sidon rather than fleeing to the *south* (Alma 43:22, 31-35, 40-41).

Similarly, the *Rio Cuilco* makes a sudden turn northward to become the *Rio Grijalva*. And at the corner is a substantial hill-like mountain at the end of the *Cuilco* range behind which Lehi's men could have easily been obscured and over which they could have traversed as recorded in Alma chapter 43.

After flowing Northward, both the river Sidon and Rio Grijalva empty into the sea. (See Alma 3:3; 44:22; Hilton, "A Correlation of the Sidon River" [1992], pp. 147, 151-158, 192.)

EVIDENCE NO. 737: THE SIDON RIVER WAS CROSSED ON FOOT AND CARRIED BODIES TO SEA

Evidence: The Sidon was not so swift and deep as to prevent an army from wading across it (Alma 2:12), and yet it was strong enough to carry thousands of bodies out to sea (Alma 2:34; 3:3; 43:39-40; 44:22). It also must have had a hard flat bottom to allow for crossing.

At the Rio Grijalva, John L. and Janet F. Hilton, "...calculated field measurements verified a minimum and maximum estimate of the needed water flow rate. To carry thousands of bodies out to sea, the needed water flow rate would measure about 10 cubic meters per second or greater; for a river to accommodate pedestrian fording, we estimate the water flow to measure less than about 72 cubic meters per second (for a river of perhaps 25 to 60 meters wide with a hard flat bottom)" (Hilton, "A Correlation of the Sidon River" [1992], p. 144).

EVIDENCE NO. 738: SIDON FLOWED ON THE EAST SIDE OF MANTI

Evidence: The city of Manti was located west of the Hill Riplah, west of the Sidon River, upstream and south from Zarahemla (Alma 17:1; 43:35, 39-42).

A short distance north and downstream from where the Rio Cuilco turns and becomes the Rio Grijalva, and on the west side of the Rio Grijalva, in the *Chicomuselo* valley, is the Modern-day village of *Cercadillo*. The location of this village fits the description of the location of the city of Manti.

Incidentally, the village of Cercadillo is located in the valley of the stream *Lincum*. The name *"Lincum"* would fit very well into Book of Mormon culture. The affix *"cum"* is used in many Book of Mormon names such as *Teancum, Cumeni, Kishkumen, Cumorah, Cumenihah, Moriancumer, cumoms,* and *Ripliancum* (Alma 50:35; 56:14, Helaman 1:9; Mormon 6:2, 14; Ether 2:13; 9:19; 15:8).

EVIDENCE NO. 739: AMNIHU AND GIDEON EAST OF THE SIDON

Claim: According to the Book of Mormon the Hill *Amnihu* lay adjacent to the valley of *Gideon* on the east side of the Sidon River (Alma 2:15; 6:7).

Evidence: Approximately 40 kilometers downstream from where the Rio Cuilco turns north and becomes the Rio Grijalva, is an "unusual hill sufficiently separated from the other hills. This spectacular landmark with its unusual double column of limestone rock rising 20 or 30 meters above the hill base is located just on the east side of the river ... Immediately downstream from the hill is a valley which could correspond to the valley of Gideon, suggesting that this landmark hill might fit as the ancient Nephite hill *Amnihu*..." (Hilton, "A Correlation of the Sidon River" [1992], p. 157).

EVIDENCE NO. 740: BOUNTIFUL—THE ANCIENT AMERICAN CITY

<u>Claim</u>: The original city of *Tulan* or *Plain of Abundance* in the Gulf Coast region of Central America fits descriptions of *Bountiful* as described in the Book of Mormon (for example, see Alma 22:29). The land around that city fits the description of *The Land of Bountiful* described in the Book of Mormon.

<u>Evidence</u>: See *Works of Ixtlilxóchitl*, (cited in Hunter and Ferguson, *Ancient America and the Book of Mormon*, p. 149), for verification of Ixtlilxóchitl's interpretation of the meaning of the ancient city Tulan meaning *Bountiful*. See Professor Mark E. Bercerra, *Nombres Geográficos Indigenas de Estado de Chiapas*, 1930, p. 140; Le Comte H. de Charencey, *Les Cites Votanides, Valeur Symbolique des Nombres dans La Nouvelle Espagne*, (1885), pp. 52-56; Bernardino de Sahagun, *Historia de Las Cosas de Nueva España*, translated by Anderson and Dibble (Santa Fe, 1950), vol. 3, Chapter 3, Prologue; Libro Octavo, *Xahila and Chronicle of Mani*, written in 1500, published in 1882; Juan de Torquemada, *Los Viente y un Libros Rituales y Monarquia Indiana*, 3 vols., (Madrid, Spain, 1723), cited in Hunter and Ferguson, *Ancient America and the Book of Mormon* (1950), p. 149.

The following is quoted from the abstract of a paper by M. Wells Jakeman, "The evidence to date tends to locate the City of Bountiful on the Gulf-Coast Region of Southern-Western Campeche" (*University Archaeological Society Newsletter* 22.02, 59.23, 75.0), also cited in Christensen, *Progress in Archaeology* [1963], pp. 178-179):

Now the early historical writings of Mesoamerica, in the native Indian and Spanish languages, make it clear that one of the most important lands of that area in ancient times was a certain region called *Tulapan*—a Maya name apparently meaning 'Abundant' or 'Bountiful land'—described as a "very opulent land," a "land of rain" and "nine rivers," a "land of verdure" and "abundance," a "terrestrial paradise," and explicitly located in or comprising the Gulf Coast region of Central America—in other words a region or land identical, in both name and location, to the region called the land Bountiful in the Book of Mormon, according to the "Tehuantepec" interpretation of the Book of Mormon geography. In this Gulf Coast land of rain and abundance, moreover, there was an ancient city called *Tullan*, an Aztec name of Maya derivation meaning 'Place of Abundance' (or *Tullan*, a purely Maya name meaning 'Bountiful').

(There were other cities of this name located in this region as well as elsewhere in Mesoamerica, for example, the famous city Tullan, Tollan, or Tula in central Mexico, capital of the Toltecs—but of much later date and probably named after this original Tullan.) *This original "city of Abundance," according to indications given by Sahagun and other early chroniclers, was founded by a group of "wise men" or civilized people who had come from the northeast coast of Mexico, after first landing there from ships (at Panutla or Panuco, "place where they arrived who came by sea") more than four hundred years before Christ.*[emphasis added]). The correspondence of this migration and founding, on the Gulf coast of Central America, of a city called Place of Abundance or Bountiful, to the migration of the Book of Mormon colony of Mulek (a group of highly civilized people who came across the sea to a first landing on the east coast of the Land Northward—that is, very probably Mexico—in about 585 BC, and then journeyed to a second landing on the coast of the Land Southward, i.e. very probably the Gulf coast of Central America) and their founding, on or near the latter coast, of a city called Bountiful, is so complete and arbitrary that it seems inconceivable that these are not one and the same series of events, and that consequently the original city Tullan or Place of Abundance of the Chronicles in the Gulf Coast region of Central America was not in fact the city Bountiful of the Book of Mormon.

Santa Rosa Linked With the Nephite City of Zarahemla

<u>Claim</u>: Zarahemla, an important city often mentioned in the Book of Mormon, was the capital of the Nephite civilization for several hundred years (Helaman 1:27). The following several evidences establish the connection between the Mayan city now called Santa Rosa, and the Nephite city of Zarahemla. The following evidences are cited in Vestal and Wallace, *The Firm Foundation of Mormonism*, (1981), pp. 78, 130-131.

EVIDENCE NO. 741: SUDDEN GROWTH OF ZARAHEMLA AND SANTA ROSA

Evidence: Zarahemla, originally settled by the Mulekites, was a relatively small settlement prior to 300 BC. It experienced significant expansion and improvement when the Nephites, who arrived shortly thereafter, discovered it (Omni 1:12-19). According to the findings of Dr. Brockington, of San Diego State, Santa Rosa suddenly began its major growth around 275 BC. (See Donald L. Brockington, "The Ceramic History of Santa Rosa, Chiapas, Mexico," *Papers of the New World Archeological Foundation*, #23 [Provo, Utah: BYU, 1967] pp. 4, 68.)

EVIDENCE NO. 742: A TEMPLE AS THE CITY'S CENTRAL STRUCTURE

Evidence: According to the Book of Mormon, the first major task of the Nephites upon arriving in the land of Nephi was to erect a temple (2 Nephi 5:16). Likewise, after the Nephites arrived in Zarahemla, the temple appears to be of central importance (for example, see Mosiah 1:18; 2:1, 5-7). Similarly, the central structure at the site of Santa Rosa is a temple mound (Brockington, "The Ceramic History of Santa Rosa," pp. 60-61).

EVIDENCE NO. 743: THE CITY CONSISTED OF TWO GROUPS

Evidence: The original settlers of Zarahemla were Jews who brought King Zedekiah's son, Mulek, from Jerusalem to the ancient Americas. They were later joined by the Nephite colony, which was of the tribe of Joseph. The two were then "gathered together in two bodies" (Mosiah 25:4).

The city of Santa Rosa was divided into two separate residential areas, determined by pottery fragment distribution. Brockington reports that even the temple base was divided into two sides, as evidenced by two different construction materials (Brockington, "The Ceramic History of Santa Rosa," pp. 60-61).

EVIDENCE NO. 744: THE CITY REACHED IT'S PEAK AROUND 50 BC

Evidence: The Book of Mormon describes Zarahemla as reaching the peak of its prosperity in about 40 BC (Helaman 3:36-37). Following this crest the land became engulfed in war, and many inhabitants were slain (Helaman 4:1-5). Contentions continued (with only short episodes of peace) until the city was finally devastated by fire in 34 AD (3 Nephi 8:1-25).

Similarly, Dr. Brockington reports that Santa Rosa reached its apex around 50 BC. Although some structures at Santa Rosa were constructed of stone, many were built with wood. Radiocarbon dates taken at the site indicate that these structures burned sometime between 40 BC and 30 AD (Brockington, "The Ceramic History of Santa Rosa...," pp. 89; also Agustin Delgado, "Excavations at Santa Rosa, Chiapas, Mexico," *Papers of the New World Archeological Foundation*, #17 [Provo, Utah: BYU, 1965] #17, pp. 77-78).

EVIDENCE NO. 745: THE REBUILT CITY ENJOYED A SECOND APEX

Evidence: After the cataclysm, Zarahemla was rebuilt and enjoyed a great period of peace and prosperity from 100 to 200 AD (4 Nephi 7-8, 22, 23, 14-18). Santa Rosa also reached a second apex at a later time. (See Gareth Lowe, "The Chiapas Project," *Papers of the New World Archaeological Foundation*, [Orinda, California, 1959], p. 5; cited in Vestal and Wallace, *The Firm Foundation of Mormonism* [1981], pp. 78, 131.)

EVIDENCE NO. 746: A TURNING POINT AFTER 200 AD

Evidence: The Book of Mormon explains that the period of peace ended around 200 AD and was followed by pride and worldliness, false religions, class-structured society, crime, and war (4 Nephi 24-29, 31-43).

Dr. Brockington reported that after about 200 AD a "break with earlier traditions" occurred in Santa Rosa. During this period, Santa Rosa experienced a marked escalation of militarism that swept the entire Mayan regions, and may have contributed to the establishment of priestly classes, which became typical of the classic Mayan period. (Brockington, "The Ceramic History of Santa Rosa," pp. 4, 61; See also David L. Webster, "Warfare and the Evolution of Maya Civilization," *The Origins of Maya Civilization*, edited by Richard E. W. Adams [Albuquerque: University of New Mexico Press, 1977].)

EVIDENCE NO. 747: THE PLACE WHERE LACHONEUS GATHERED HIS PEOPLE

Claim: The Book of Mormon states that Lachoneus, governor of the land of Zarahemla, gathered his people together at a certain place to defend themselves from their enemies (3 Nephi 3:22-24). The people who moved to the defensive location intended to stay there for at least seven years and most likely named their new land after their governor (3 Nephi 4:4).

Evidence: Joseph L. Allen suggests that the battle took place in the valley and the area called *Lacanha*. Today the *Lacandone* Indians occupy the area. Allen has concluded that this site together with the nearby *Lacantun* River and the *Lacanha* archaeological site were all named after Lachoneus. See Joseph L. Allen, *Exploring the Lands of the Book of Mormon*, [1989], p. 38.

Evidences Linking San Lorenzo with the Jaredite City Built by Lib

Claim: The Book of Mormon mentions a great Jaredite city built under the reign of King Lib (Ether 10:20). The following several evidences establish the connection between the Olmec city now called San Lorenzo, and the Jaredite city mentioned in the Book of Mormon. This connection was first postulated by V. Garth Norman, who submitted his findings and conclusions to the *Society for Early Historic Archaeology*, (SEHA) which were later reprinted by the *Foundation for Ancient Research and Mormon Studies* (FARMS).

EVIDENCE NO. 748: THE TIME OF SETTLEMENT

Evidence: Jaredites arrived in Central America between 2400 and 2500 BC. This is determined by the fact that Ether 1:3 dates the beginning of the Jaredite civilization as being contemporary with the Tower of Babel and the confusion of tongues.

The earliest possible antecedents of Olmec ceramics were found in the highlands of Mexico between 2400 and 2500 BC. (See V. Garth Norman, "San Lorenzo as the Jaredite City of Lib," *FARMS Reprint* [Provo, Utah: Foundation for Ancient Research and Mormon Studies], NOR-83, p. 6; also Fred W. Nelson, "Recent Developments in Olmec Archaeology," in *SEHA Newsletter and Proceedings* No. 133, Aug. 1973, pp. 1-9.)

EVIDENCE NO. 749: THE CITY WAS BUILT ON AN ISTHMUS

Evidence: The city of Lib was built on a "narrow neck of land ... where the sea divides the land" (Ether 10:20). San Lorenzo was built in approximately 1450 BC on the Isthmus of Tehuantepec on the large navigable Rio Coatzacoalcos, which divides the land, forming an island (see Norman, "San Lorenzo as the Jaredite City of Lib," pp. 5-6; and Nelson, "Recent Developments in Olmec Archaeology," pp. 1-9).

EVIDENCE NO. 750:   THE CITY WAS A CENTER OF GOVERNMENT AND TRADE

Evidence: The city of Lib is described as a "great city" of the Jaredite King Lib (Ether 10:20). San Lorenzo was the principal governing Olmec center. The city of Lib was also a center of trade for the surrounding regions which were covered with a large number of cities (Ether 10:19,22). It has been well documented that San Lorenzo was a center for extended trade (Norman, "San Lorenzo as the Jaredite City of Lib," p. 6).

EVIDENCE NO. 751: THE CITY DID NOT SPREAD SOUTHWARD

Evidence: Poisonous serpents prevented southward expansion of Jaredites for five generations prior to Lib. Under the reign of Lib, the serpents were destroyed, but he continued to preserve the land southward for wild game (Ether 9:31; 10:19). The Olmecs of the lowland tropics of Vera Cruz for unknown reasons did not spread southward into the lowland tropics of Peten. (See Norman, "San Lorenzo as the Jaredite City of Lib," pp. 6-7, where other authorities are cited.)

EVIDENCE NO. 752: DESTRUCTION AROUND 900 BC

Evidence: During the takeover by the brother of Shiblom, in about 900 BC, the prophets were killed, and there was great destruction in all the land by war and famine (Ether 11:5-7). Based on Norman's research, there was massive destruction around 900 BC during a takeover by Nacaste-phase invaders (see Norman, "San Lorenzo as the Jaredite City of Lib," pp. 5-6).

EVIDENCE NO. 753: NEW CULTURE INTRODUCED AROUND 500 BC

Evidence: According to Book of Mormon chronology, the civilizations of the Jaredites and the Mulekites overlapped. Eventually, at least one Jaredite is recorded to have made contact with the Mulekites (see Omni 1:20-22). Clearly, there could have been other contacts that were not recorded. Between 600 and 400 BC, San Lorenzo made cultural ties with Chiapa III (Escalera) phase in the Central Depression of Chiapas and Mamom phase in the Maya lowlands.   Norman noted that this cultural interaction created a "catalytic effect that produced the distinctive and rich cultural tradition known as Izapan civilization, that had spread across much of Mesoamerica by the time of Christ (see Norman, "San Lorenzo as the Jaredite City of Lib," p. 8).

Brian F. Fagan, made a summary of what occurred during the decline of Olmec and the rise of post-Olmec civilization:

> We believe that the spread of the Olmec [-influenced] art style [Izapan art] and the beginning of the Late Preclassic period in approximately 500 to 300 BC signals the period during which a common religious system and ideology began to unify large areas of Mesoamerica. A powerful priesthood congregated in spectacular ceremonial centers, commemorating potent and widely recognized deities. Distinctive art and architecture went with the new religion, the practice of which required precise measurements of calendar years and of longer cycles of time. Writing and mathematical calculations were developed to affirm religious practices, a unifying political force in the sense that they welded scattered village communities into larger political units. (Brian F. Fagan, *Peoples of the Earth: An Introduction to World Prehistory* [Little, Brown, and Co.: Boston, 1983, 4th edition], p. 392.)

Robert J. Sharer's summary of the same era is included below:

> It would appear that Olmec interaction had a catalytic effect on the cultural development of the Preclassic societies along the Pacific plain, for the growth of these societies continued at an accelerated pace after the waning of Olmec connections in the region. In the wake of the Olmec, the Pacific coastal plain was host to a rich sculptural tradition in the Late Preclassic, known as the Izapan style,

and the earliest examples of Maya hieroglyphic texts and calendrical notations. These appear to represent the direct ancestors to the dynastic monuments that characterize lowland Maya civilization during the subsequent Classic period. (Robert J. Sharer in *Journal of Field Archaeology*, Vol. 9 [1982], p. 257; Cited in Norman, "San Lorenzo as the Jaredite City of Lib," p. 8.)

EVIDENCE NO. 754: SOUTHERN LANDS ABANDONED

Claim: The Book of Mormon mentions that the great Nephite civilization was abandoned around 326 AD when they retreated to "the north countries" (Mormon 2:3). The abandonment of a Mesoamerican site around 300 AD corresponds with the abandonment of the Land Southward by the Nephites as mentioned in the Book of Mormon.

Evidence: The following is quoted from the "Summary of Report of the BYU-*University Archaeological Society Newsletter* Middle-American Expedition of 1956" (UAS. Newsletter 34.0):

> Work at the Chiapa de Corzo site revealed more than 50 mounds, dating from the first century BC to 300 AD, about 15 burials, over 100,000 potsherds, and what are probably the earliest discovered structures of cut stone in southern Mesoamerica. The site was evidently abandoned around AD 300 and lay unoccupied for several centuries. (This date is of particular interest when compared with the Book of Mormon claim [Mormon 2] that the Nephites abandoned the Land Southward—that is southern Mesoamerica—about AD 327-350.)

> Later the group worked at Puerto, Mexico, across the river from Acala, and there discovered some 15 Late Classic-period mounds with the typical rectangular arrangement and ball court.

> The party also conducted extensive reconnaissance of the Grijalva valley from Chiapa de Corzo nearly to the Guatemalan border, locating over a dozen "Preclassic" (Book of Mormon-period) sites and numerous late ones. (Also cited in Christensen, *Progress in Archeology* [1963], p. 177.)

EVIDENCE NO. 755: POSSIBLE LOCATION OF THE HILL SHIM

Claim: The Book of Mormon states that Mormon received the records from Ammaron on the hill Shim (Mormon 1:3). The hill *Cintepec,* located east of Lake Catemaco in the Tuxtla Mountain Range in the State of Vera Cruz, Mexico, correlates with the Book of Mormon hill Shim.

Evidence: As mentioned above, the last part of Cintepec, "tepec," means hill or mountain in the Nahuatl (Aztec) language. The first part of the word, "Cin" means corn. Hence, the word Cintepec means "corn hill." Shim in the Maya language also means corn. Therefore, when Ammaron told Mormon where to find the records, he may well have meant corn hill when he referred to the hill called Shim (Joseph L. Allen, *Exploring the Lands of the Book of Mormon,* [1989], p. 38).

EVIDENCE NO. 756: THE LOCATION OF THE HILL CUMORAH

Claim: Critics have attempted to prove the Book of Mormon false by arguing that *the Hill Cumorah* (near Manchester, New York, where Joseph Smith unearthed the Golden Plates of the Book of Mormon [see Joseph-Smith—History 1:51-52]), is too far away from Central America where the events of the Book of Mormon are supposed to have occurred. Some Book of Mormon scholars have answered this criticism by suggesting that the location of the Hill Cumorah is actually in Central America or Mexico, and that the plates were later moved to New York in preparation for their translation by Joseph Smith. However, the real Hill Cumorah could indeed have been in the state of New York where Joseph Smith was shown the gold plates from which he translated the Book of Mormon.

Evidence: The following is quoted from an article by Hugh W. Nibley entitled "The Book of Mormon and the Ruins; the Main Issues" (N-BMA, Nibley Archive, *Foundation for Ancient Research and Mormon Studies*, University Station, Provo, Utah, July 13, 1980), pp. 5-6: "Cumorah, a Hill Too Far? What were the people of Zarahemla doing in New York State? Some have made this a major stumbling block to the accepting of the Book of Mormon. The Peruvian archaeologist F. Kauffmann-Diog shows us that this is a premature and naive way of thinking." The following is from his *Manual de Arqueologia Peruana* (Lima: Peisa, 1973), p. 174:

The Fallacy of Distance: A variety of things has contributed to hindering the progress of thinking about the intercommunications between remotely-separated American cultures. A superficial concept of distances ... reinforced by a false perception of present-day boundaries of the Americas is one of those things, perhaps the most popular, not to say vulgar position, which absolutely refuses to admit cultural contacts and derivations. But let us bear in mind that global distances were no impediment to the arrival of man in America, and that upon arrival there no barriers prevented him from occupying every part of the continent. The same fundamental ... comparative archaeology shows that in the Mexican area the Formative period ... is older than in Peru. The adjoining map may appear elemental but we see that it offers interesting information. It is designed to correct the usual geographical perspective. It shows in the first place that the boundaries of the Incan Empire, between Ancasmayo and Maulo or the Bio Bio River embrace a distance equivalent to that between the northern boundary of Incaland (Ancasmayo) and New York. That fact, elementary as it seems, though none has made use of it, raises salutary reflections on how small a world it is.

Dr. Nibley continues: "From the northern limit of the Incan Empire to Mexico City is almost as far as from Mexico City to Cumorah in New York State. Incan armies which marched form end to end of the Empire through the Andes covered more distance and a far more difficult terrain than the stretch between Mexico and New York State covered in the great military withdrawal occupying many years."

Another possibility to consider is that the Nephites could have sailed from Middle America to the eastern coast of North America. Since the Book of Mormon records that the Nephites were ship builders, this is a very logical possibility (Alma 63:5-8).

Figure 15. North and South America.

6. Book of Mormon Culture

Introduction

The Book of Mormon indicates that the peoples of the earlier periods of pre-Columbian history developed an advanced culture and became highly civilized. (For example see 2 Nephi 5:15-16; Helaman 3:9, 11.) This was in stark contrast to the prevailing view of the Native Americans. Victor Wolfgang von Hagen, in his biography of John Lloyd Stephens, gives an excellent idea of the generally held views on the Indians and information available about them in 1830. He writes:

> The acceptance of an "Indian civilization" demanded, to an American living in 1839, an entire reorientation, for to him an Indian was one of those barbaric half-naked teepee-dwellers against whom wars were constantly waged. A rude subhuman people who hunted with the stealth of animals, they were artisans of buffalo robes, arrowheads, and spears, and little else. Nor did one ever think of calling the other indigenous inhabitants of the continent "civilized." In the universally accepted opinion, they were like their North American counterparts—savages. No one dreamed that throughout the tablelands of Mexico, in the tangled scrub-jungles of Yucatan, there stood, covered by jungle verdure, ruins of temples, acropolises, and stone causeways of a civilization as great in extent as Egypt's. (Reprinted from Victor Wolfgang von Hagen, *Maya Explorer: John Lloyd Stephens and the Lost Cities of Central America and Yucatan*, [University of Oklahoma Press, 1947], p. 78; also cited in Harris, *The Book of Mormon Message and Evidences* [1961], p. 60.)

Similarly, A. B. French concluded the following in 1892:

> Joseph Smith revealed to the world, over sixty years ago, historical and scientific truths that every research of the modern archaeologist has tended to confirm...Remember that at the date of Joseph Smith's revelations nothing was known of the extensive ruins in Central America. The explorer had not then penetrated the great tropical forests to learn of this decayed civilization. An unlettered boy tells of a great civilization that had faded away more than 2,000 years ago. How came he to know of the ruins in Central America? ...Joseph Smith was an ignorant boy, and not a learned and cultured man, when he began his revelations, but he anticipated science and led the way. (*Gleanings from the Rostrum* quoted in *Liahona*, vol. 31, pp. 4-5 [1933-1934]; cited in Harris, *Book of Mormon Message and Evidences*, p. 58.)

Lionel Casson concluded that the mounds of the Eastern United States were built by a superior race, or more probably a people of foreign and higher civilization who had occupied America long before the North American Indians. See Lionel Casson et. al., *Mysteries of the Past*, edited by Joseph J. Thorndike Jr., (American Heritage Publishing Company, Inc.: New York, 1977), p. 121.

According to *The Works of Ixtlilxóchitl:* "The Tultecas were the second settlers of this land after the decline of the giants...Tulteca means artisan and wise man because the people of this nation were great artisans, as is seen ... in the ruins of their buildings, in this town of Teotihuacán, Tula and Cholula." (*The Works of Ixtlilxóchitl,* English translation by Hunter and Ferguson, *Ancient America and the Book of Mormon,* [1950], p. 57.)

The study of ancient American culture provides many strong evidences supporting the Book of Mormon claim that ancestors of the American Indians were a highly cultured and industrious people who brought their advanced culture with them when they migrated from the Middle East. A few of the more compelling similarities between ancient American cultures and that of the Old World are presented in this chapter.

EVIDENCE NO. 757: STORING VALUABLES IN STONE BOXES

Claim: When Joseph Smith related his account of uncovering the gold plates, he explained that they had been deposited in a stone box (Joseph Smith—History 1:52).

Evidence: Joseph Smith's description of ancient records deposited in a stone box stood alone for nearly a century. Recently, however, it has been established that the hiding of valuables, and particularly important records in stone boxes, was a common practice in ancient cultures. Nearly 50 stone boxes have been located in different parts of the world. See Cheesman, *The World of the Book of Mormon* (1978), pp. 77-78; and Cheesman, *Ancient Writing on Metal Plates* (1985), p. 77-80.

EVIDENCE NO. 758: EGYPTIAN CULTURE IN THE BOOK OF MORMON

Claim: The influence of Egyptian culture in the Book of Mormon (for example 1 Nephi 1:2, Mormon 9:32-33) is to be expected because Egyptian influence was very strong in Palestine where the Nephites and Mulekites of the Book of Mormon originated. The fact that Egyptian culture can be found throughout the Book of Mormon is another evidence of its truthfulness.

Evidence: Not only does the Book of Mormon contain ample evidence of Egyptian cultural influence, critics have complained that it contains far *too much* Egyptian culture. However, as is often the case, what was once considered a weakness of the Book of Mormon, has turned out to be another evidence of its truthfulness. Modern scholars have found compelling evidence that Egypt had great influence on Palestine, and that countries around Egypt were taught in the language of the Egyptians as was Nephi (1 Nephi 1:2). Often, sons were sent from other countries to be educated in Egypt, such that it was said: "foreigners became Egyptians everywhere." See, D. G. Bogarth, "Egyptian Empire in Asia," *Journal of Egyptian Archeology*, vol. 1, pp. 13-14; A. S. Cook, *Cambridge Ancient History*, vol. 3, p. 257; A. Moret, *Histoire de l'Orient*, [Paris: Presses Universitaires, 1945] vol. 2, p. 787; Edward Meyer, *Geschicthe des Altertums*, 1928, vol. 2, 1, p. 132; H. Frankfort, "Egypt and Syria in the First Intermediate Period," *Journal of Egyptian Archeology*, vol. 12, (1926), p. 96; and D. G. Hogarth, "Egyptian Empire in Asia," *Journal of Egyptian Archeology*, vol. 1, p. 12. All of the above evidences are cited in Nibley, *An Approach to the Book of Mormon,* (1988), chapter 7, pp. 84-92.

EVIDENCE NO. 759: EGYPTIAN INFLUENCE IN ANCIENT AMERICAN ARCHITECTURE

Claim: The Book of Mormon was written by people whose architecture was influenced by Egyptian culture. See 1 Nephi 1:2 and Mormon 9:32-33.

Evidence: Renowned scientist Robert Wauchope writes his thoughts about the origin of the Mesoamericans:

Perhaps the most popular theory about American Indian origins derives the famous ancient civilizations of Mexico, Central America, and the Andes from Egypt. There were pyramids in both America and Egypt, there were mummies in Peru and Egypt, sun worship was practiced in many parts of the New World as well as in Egypt, and both areas produced hieroglyphic writing, royal tombs, bas-relief sculpture, and a number of other similar customs and cultural traits. To most people the word "archaeology" conjures up but one picture: towering pyramids, the brooding Sphinx, King Tut's tomb, and the Valley of the Nile. It is only natural that when they see ancient relics like these somewhere else, even in faraway America, they see a connection with the classic expression of ancient civilizations—Dynastic Egypt. (See Robert Wauchope, *Lost Tribes and Sunken Continents* [Chicago: University of Chicago Press, 1956] p. 7; and Francis C. Kelley, *Blood-Drenched Altars* [Milwaukee: Bruce Publishing Co., 1935] p. 38. Both above sources are cited in Cheesman, *The World of the Book of Mormon*, p. 2.)

EVIDENCE NO. 760: MERCY BALANCED WITH JUSTICE

Claim: While Egyptology was still in its infancy and before any decoded hieroglyphics were made available in English—much less in the American frontier of New England, Joseph Smith dictated the translation of the Book of Mormon. The Book claims to be sacred record from a people who were familiar with Egyptian culture and who wrote in reformed Egyptian (Mormon 9:32).

The Book of Mormon clearly teaches of the balance between justice and mercy: "mercy cannot rob justice" (Alma 42:25) and God's plan of mercy was designed to "appease the demands of justice" (Alma 42:15). It further states that "mercy can satisfy the demands of justice" (Alma 34:16), and that the Lord counsels "in justice and in great mercy, over all his works" (Jacob 14:10-12).

Evidence: The concept of balancing mercy with justice was not invented by Joseph Smith, but is of ancient origin. Discoveries that were made after the Book of Mormon was published clearly show that this belief was prevalent among the ancient Egyptians—who were taught the gospel by Abraham, and tried to imitate the aspects of the true gospel (Abraham 1:26).

Many illustrations of the Pharaoh, as seen in frescoes, bas-reliefs, and on entombed sarcophagi, show him holding the shepherds crook in one hand and the flail in the other. Egyptologists have translated the meanings of the crook as a symbol of *mercy*, while the flail is a symbol of *justice*. The figures of the pharaoh with such symbols in each hand demonstrate his ability and obligation to use godly wisdom in balancing the demands of justice with the gift of mercy. (See Jacquetta Hawkes, *Pharaohs of Egypt*, [New York: American Heritage Publishing Co., Distributed by Harper and Row, 1965], pp. 21, 39, 101, 139.)

Figure 16. Egyptian figure holding the Crook of Mercy and the Flail of Justice.

EVIDENCE NO. 761: THE BOOK OF MORMON CONVERTS AN EGYPTIAN PROFESSOR

Claim: While translating the Book of Mormon into Arabic, Dr. Sami Hanna, a non-LDS professor at the University of Utah, clearly recognized that the Book of Mormon was indeed a true record of ancient origin. He was touched by the Holy Spirit and received a witness from God as to the importance of receiving baptism by those holding the priesthood of God.

Evidence: Dr. Sami Hanna left his native land of Egypt in 1955 to come to the states as a Fulbright Scholar. His first contact with the Church of Jesus Christ of Latter-day Saints was through the weekly radio program of "Music and the Spoken Word." Each Sunday he would listen to the inspiring music offered by the Tabernacle Choir in his apartment in New York. In 1958 he was offered a fellowship at the University of Illinois, and moved to Urbana. After his first year in Urbana his former professor from Egypt, Dr. Assiz Atiya, invited him to join the faculty at the University of Utah.

Upon sharing the offer with his department chairman he was immediately discouraged from accepting the invitation. He was told that it would not be wise to go "*anywhere* in Utah," because of the dreadful Mormon people living there. His salary was increased in an effort to retain him, but finally after another year of negotiations he was transferred on a one-year loan to the University of Utah.

After arriving in Salt Lake City, Dr. Hanna recalls that his impression of the Mormon people was quite different from what he was told to expect:

> I soon found that all of my Mormon colleagues were really not as dreadful as I had been led to believe, but were in reality living examples of a Christianity that teaches brotherly love. Because of the great friendship shown me, I began to make my associations more with the Mormons than with any other group and soon became fast friends with Dr. Faust, the brother of Elder James E. Faust, [of] the Twelve. My work at the University was challenging and rewarding and my association with my Mormon colleagues was so comfortable that the one-year period that I was on loan from the University of Illinois came and went and I was still in Salt Lake City. Another year came and went and I found myself quite contented to remain among the Mormon people and to imitate their way of life.

> Time went by, and my admiration for the Mormon people and their church continued to grow. I was so impressed by the dedication and service of all Church members, of *all* stations. I was rather amazed to find that the members of the Church who were financially well established, and even members of the "hierarchy" of the Church, would give of their precious time free of charge to work on farms picking vegetables, canning food and other menial chores. I was so impressed by this love and dedication to the Church and concern for the well being of their fellowmen that I too wanted to join in and assist in these programs, even though I was not a member. I was told to be patient, that the time would come when I would be called upon to participate in the Welfare Program.

Still wanting to do something for the Church, and hearing that the Church had just started sending missionaries to Arabic-speaking countries, Dr. Hanna asked if he could be of service by translating Church literature into Arabic. After translating *The Joseph Smith Story*, and while preparing to translate the Book of Mormon, he received a divine witness, in the form of a dream, and accepted baptism into the Church.

> Many new horizons and opportunities to serve my fellowmen have opened to me since my baptism. Besides having the choice experience of translating the Book of Mormon into Arabic, I see that more of the Church literature should be translated into Arabic, a task which I feel privileged to undertake.

> The Lord knew that I needed to be baptized to bring about the fulfillment of my fondest dreams, but he also knew that if I were to accomplish this, I needed the prodding and assurance that he provided in his special dream to me, for which I shall be eternally grateful. (*Stories of Insight and Inspiration*, compiled by Margie Jensen, [1976], pp. 58-64.)

EVIDENCE NO. 762: THE EFFICIENCY OF THE NEPHITE MONETARY SYSTEM

Claim: An impostor might have based monetary descriptions on those in existence in their day, for example, the decimal system known by contemporaries of Joseph Smith.

Evidence: It has been shown that the unique monetary system used in the Book of Mormon (1-2-4-7) as described in Alma 11:5-19 is the most effective system requiring the fewest number of coins. See R. P. Smith in *Improvement Era*, vol. 57, (1954), pp. 316-317; cited in Nibley, *Since Cumorah*, (1988), p. 225.

EVIDENCE NO. 763: MONEY VALUED BY WEIGHT

Claim: The practice recorded in the Book of Mormon of relating value of precious metals and commodities to their weight was consistent with ancient Near Eastern practice.

Evidence: The Book of Mormon indicates that certain metal pieces were "equal" or "twice the *value*" of certain other combinations (Alma 11:5-10) or equal to a measure of grain, such as barley (Alma 11:7); however, the account compares certain metal pieces as being "as great" or "greater" than another. The greater or lesser descriptions likely refer to weight. Weighing to assess value was the custom in ancient times. (See Ed. Meyer, *Geschides Altertums* [1909] vol. 1, pp. ii, 517; and E. G. Kraeling, *Brooklyn Aramaic Papyri*, p. 38. Both cited in Nibley, *Since Cumorah*, [1988] p. 225.)

Evidences Concerning the Migrations of Ancient American Settlers

Claim: The Book of Mormon asserts that at least *some* of the ancient American settlers crossed the ocean in ships (1 Nephi 17-18; Omni 1:15-22; Ether 6). Most anthropologists have held to the theory that *all* ancestors of the American aborigines migrated by foot from Asia during the time when the sea level was lower and the Bering Land Bridge connected Alaska to Siberia. Thus for many years critics have mocked the Book of Mormon for making such an unsubstantiated claim concerning the migrations of the ancient Americans. More recently, however, several leading authorities on the subject have accumulated a large body of evidence supporting the possibility that ancient travelers could have migrated to the Americas from across the ocean. The following several evidences are a small sampling of the documentation concerning this Book of Mormon claim.

EVIDENCE NO. 764: NEW EVIDENCE THAT THE FIRST AMERICAN INHABITANTS CAME BY SEA

The Church has never claimed that the *Book of Mormon* peoples were the only ancient inhabitants of the Americas. Nor has it ever denied that some early immigrants may have crossed the Bering Strait. No Latter-day Saint prophet has denied the possibility of mixtures with Asiatic immigrants. In fact, as early as 1929, President Anthony W. Ivins of the Quorum of the Twelve pointed out that, the Book of Mormon "does not tell us that no one was here before them [the Book of Mormon peoples]. It does not tell us that people did not come after." (See *Conference Reports*, April 1929, pp. 15-16, cited in Franklin S. Harris, *The Book of Mormon Message and Evidences,* [Deseret News Press: Salt Lake City, 1961] p. 56.)

Elder Bruce R. McConkie has said:

> It is quite apparent that groups of Orientals found their way over the Bering Strait and gradually moved southward to mix with the Indian peoples. We have records of a colony of Scandinavians attempting to set up a settlement in America some 500 years before Columbus. There are archeological indications that an unspecified number of groups of people probably found their way from the old to the new world in pre-Columbian times...(McConkie, *Mormon Doctrine*, [1958], p. 31).

The Book of Mormon hints that other peoples inhabited ancient America concurrently with the Book of Mormon peoples. The prophet Mormon, states that he was a "pure descendent of Lehi" (3 Nephi 5:20). For Moroni to specifically mention this part of his ancestry, implies that there were others who were not "pure descendants of

Lehi—therefore, Mormon may have been describing his ancestry in contrast to others whose ancestors had inter-married with other peoples not mentioned in the Book of Mormon.

Evidence: Book of Mormon critics often refer to a few scientists who have held to the theory that *all* migrations to America originated from Asia via the Bering Strait. However, these critics are facing increasing difficulty in finding support for their weakening position. Such a position is rapidly losing credibility in the light of mounting evidence to the contrary. (See Rivet, *Paul Maya Cities* [London: Elek Books, 1960] p. 227; L. Sprague, and Catherine de Camp, *Ancient Ruins and Archeology*, Thesis [Garden City, New York: Doubleday, 1964] p. 167; Robert Wauchope, *Lost Tribes and Sunken Continents* [Chicago: University of Chicago Press, 1956] p. 7. All three above sources were cited in Cheesman, *The World of the Book of Mormon*, [1978], p. 1.)

Froelich Rainey has written: "Northwestern America and northeastern Siberia, under present climatic conditions, together form one of the most formidable barriers to human communications one can find anywhere in the world. To refuse Neolithic man the ability to cross the southern Pacific and to accept his ability to penetrate this region is straining at a gnat and swallowing a camel." (See *American Antiquity*, vol. 18, no. 3, part 2, [January 1953] "Asia and Transpacific Contacts." cited in Harris, *Book of Mormon Message and Evidence*, [1961], p. 64.)

The following is from *Foundation for Ancient Research and Mormon Studies*, (February 1996), no. 104, p. 2:

> Traditionally, most anthropologists have accepted the theory that the ancestors of all Native American cultures in the New World migrated by foot from Asia during the Pleistocene era when the sea level was lower and a narrow strip of land called the Bering Land Bridge connected the two continents. But [Dr. E. James Dixon of the University of New Mexico] challenges this traditional model. (Dixon, *Quest for the Origins of the First Americans*, [Albuquerque: University of New Mexico Press, 1993].)

> Dixon is a leading authority on the archaeology of eastern Beringia, the chain of Islands that once formed the ancient land bridge connecting Asia with present-day Alaska. Although no one doubts the existence of this land bridge, or its potential as a conduit for human migration, Dixon demonstrates that this could not have been the sole mechanism for populating the Americas. He presents impressive and compelling evidence that suggests that the first, or at least early, inhabitants of ancient America actually arrived on ocean-worthy vessels.

> The geology and paleoecology of the Beringia region suggest that it was not until about 9,500 BC that the Bering Land Bridge became passable for human overland migration. Consistent with this date, there is no documented evidence of human occupation anywhere in the Beringian corridor until about 9,000 BC. Yet there is ample evidence of early occupations along the west coasts of both North and South America that date at least two or three thousand years and in some cases many thousands of years before that. Since it appears that there was no way of crossing overland at such early dates, Dixon asserts that these settlements must have been founded by seagoing peoples.

> … carefully presented research findings like Dixon's (and those from an increasing number of others) make it clear that humans anciently were capable of long-distance voyages across the oceans to visit or colonize parts of the New World. By extension, it is reasonable to conclude that the small colonies of Jaredites, Lehites, and Mulekites could have made such trips as well.

Many critics of the Book of Mormon make much ado about the Mongolian spot, claiming that such a genetic feature found among Native Americans proves a link between the natives and Asia. Dr. Ariel Crowley noted that during World War 2, Germany assigned one of its best ethnologists to research the trail of the Mongolian spot. They established beyond question its occurrence in German, Irish, Russian, English and other ethnic groups, and concluded that the spot is not peculiar to the Mongolians. (Crowley, *About the Book of Mormon*, [1961], p. 144.)

Franklin S. Harris, Jr. noted the following in, *Book of Mormon Message and Evidence*, (1961), p. 64:

> The usual view then is that the Indians are of Mongoloid origin, which means straight hair, broad high cheek bones, etc. We cannot deny that many American peoples are of Mongoloid type. With the Indians, all Mongoloid racial characteristics are variable except dark brown eyes, dark brown hair and

the skin yellowish or reddish brown. All anthropometric indices are variable. The epicanthic fold which gives the almond-shaped eye is common but not universal. Mongoloid faces are broad, the American Indian variable. The Mongoloid nose is low in the bridge, the American Indian variable, but among high culture peoples high in the bridge. Mongoloids are short, the Indians variable in stature. Some traits do not fit in with the Mongoloid pattern, such as wavy hair. The Maya nose is high bridged with a convex tip and flaring nostrils. The Maya are very broad-headed, and the Mongoloids usually only slightly broad-headed.

Dr. E. A. Hooten in his studies in Southwest anthropometry reports [he] found a race which duplicated one of the Near East (*The Indians of Pecos Pueblo* [1930], p. 363). Said he: "The theory of the originally and perpetually Mongoloid character of the American population is difficult to accept in view of the decidedly non-Mongoloid character of the stratigraphically early types."

...And Dr. Hooten (*The Maya and Their Neighbors*, pp. 277, 280) in the same volume: "It is of considerable interest to ponder the fact that intentional artificial deformation of the skull in a people with hooked, beaky noses is associated with the development of high civilization in two widely separated areas—the Near East and the Western cordillera of the Americas. It intrigues me to note that cranial deformation is conspicuous by its absence in Northeastern Asia, and, in fact, among the peoples of Asia who can be described from a racial point of view as Mongoloid, and that prominent, convex noses, although observable in Asia among mixed Mongoloid peoples, are absolutely incompatible with a full development of Mongoloid physical characters. I should say that neither these flattened heads nor those proboscis-like noses are, nor have been, at home in Mongoloid Asia...I am inclined to think that the ancestors of the classical Mayas were not very different from the White hybridized type which we call Armenoid... Eventually they picked up some Mongoloid features—hair, pigmentation, cheek bones, etc. These may have been recent accretions..."

EVIDENCE NO. 765: NON-MONGOLIAN BLOOD TYPES

Evidence: The following is quoted from an article by Hugh W. Nibley entitled "The Book of Mormon and the Ruins; The Main Issues," N-BMA, Nibley Archive, *Foundation for Ancient Research and Mormon Studies*, University Station, Provo, Utah, July 13, 1980, page 3:

A. A. Anguiano: "There are among the Indians ...Mongoloids ...Negroids ...Southern European types ...giants (Patagonian) ...pigmies (Venezuela and Brazil). Many anthropologists consider it impossible that all these types should be traced to a single Bering route from Asia. South American skulls and dialects both have strong Oceanian resemblances and indicate a Pacific crossing." See, A. A. Anguiano, *Mexico Antes de los Aztecas*, (Mexico: 1967), p. 16.

Edward Seler: "The two main native traditions have the ancestors coming from the East by sea and from the West by sea...All agree that their ancestors came in boats." (Edward G. Seler, *Gesammelte Abhandlungen zur Amerikanischen Sprach und Alterthumskunde*, [Berlin: 1902], vol. 4, p. 3.)

Those favoring single-shot explanations of everything have been significantly silent on the subject of blood types. According to G. A. Matson, a leading authority in the field, the dominant blood type among the American Indians is type "O," though some tribes, for example, the Blackfeet, are almost 100% type "A" as are the Hawaiians. Mongolians on the other hand are almost exclusively type "B" which is exceedingly rare among the Indians. This should pretty well settle the race question but the issue has been carefully avoided. (G. Albin Matson, "Distribution of Hereditary Blood Groups among Indians in South America," *American Journal of Physical Anthropology*, vol. 27 [1967], p. 188.)

See also Lionel Casson, et. al., *Mysteries of the Past*, (American Heritage Pub.: New York, 1977), pp. 221-215, who poses the question: "Why do North American Plains Indians look so 'European' in certain of their facial features and so little like the living Asian descendants of their own Asian forebears?"

EVIDENCE NO. 766: ANCIENT AMERICAN LEGENDS CONCERNING ORIGINS ACROSS THE OCEAN

Evidence: The Mayas believed that their civilization originated across the sea. Brinton noted that: "The Mayas did not pretend to be autochthonous, but claimed that their ancestors came from distant regions in two bands. The largest and most ancient immigration was from the East, across or rather through the ocean—for the gods had opened twelve paths through it—and this was conducted by the mythical Itzamna. The second band, less in number and later in time, came in from the West, and with them was Kukulcan. The former was called the Great Arrival, the latter, the Less Arrival." (Brinton, *American Hero Myths* [1882] pp. 145, 146; quoted in Harris, *Book of Mormon Message and Evidence* [1961], p. 70.)

Another source indicates that: "Some of the old people of Yucatan say that they have heard from their ancestors that this land was occupied by a race of people, who came from the East and whom God had delivered by opening twelve paths through the sea." (Diego de Landa, *Relación de las Cosas de Yucatán*, translated by Alfred M. Tozzer, *Harvard University, Peabody Museum of American Archaeology and Ethnology Papers*, [Cambridge: Peabody Museum, 1941], vol. 18, p. 16, see also p. 214. Both of the above sources are quoted in Harris, *Book of Mormon Message and Evidence* [1961], pp. 70-72.)

The *Popol Vuh: The Sacred Book of the Ancient Quiche Maya*, also confirms that the earliest settlers came from across the sea. "We shall bring it to light because now the *Popol Vuh*, as it is called, cannot be seen any more, in which was clearly seen the coming *from the other side of the sea* and the narration of our obscurity…The original book, written long ago, existed, but its sight is hidden to the searcher and the thinker." (Delia Goetz & Sylvanus Morley, *Popol Vuh*, [Norman: University of Oklahoma Press, 1950], pp. 79-80.)

Similarly, the Aztecs claimed that their ancestors arrived in ships. (See Guy E. Powell, *Latest Aztec Discoveries*, [San Antonio: Naylor Co., 1967], p. 45; Francis C. Kelly, *Blood Drenched Altars*, [Milwaukee: Bruce Pub. Co., 1935], p. 38. See also Karl Sapper, *Forschchungen Und Fortschritte*, [November 1, 1939], p. 81,. p. 45. p. 38; Frank Waters, *Book of the Hopi* [New York: Ballentine Books, 1969], p. 31; Sahagun, *A History of Ancient America*, pp. 190-192. The above sources are also cited in Harris, *Book of Mormon Message and Evidences*, [1961], p. 65; and Cheesman, *The World of the Book of Mormon*, [1978] pp. 2, 3, 15.)

EVIDENCE NO. 767: ORIGINS FROM THE NEAR EAST

Evidence: Some Scholars are changing their opinion that ancient American civilizations developed out of New World hunting cultures without any help from the ancient civilizations of the Old World. The following is quoted from an article by Hugh W. Nibley entitled "The Book of Mormon and the Ruins; the Main Issues" (N-BMA, Nibley Archive, *Foundation for Ancient Research and Mormon Studies*, [University Station, Provo, Utah, July 13, 1980] pp. 3-4):

Related to the question of race is that of migration, a subject on which the experts have recently taken to bold speculation, which has hitherto been crippled by the fallacy that the *first* comers to the land must be the only comers.

…But if the people came from Asia, there is a puzzling lack of cultivated plants and domestic animals of the Old World in the New World as well as the absence in the latter of the plow, potter's wheel, bellows, glass, iron, stringed instruments and the true arch. This is more than out-balanced by more important cultural items such as political patterns, cosmology, art, religion, symbolism, ceremonial, architecture, etc., which are far too much alike in the two hemispheres to be explained by the recent and far-fetched theory of "convergence." How to explain a super abundance of one type of cultural equipment along with a complete deficiency of another kind of stuff? The solution is in the *type* of migration indicated. The people who crossed the sea were not artisans or technicians but cultivated folk of a religious and intellectual—priestly—persuasion. What is indicated according to Heine-Geldern is "carefully planned and prepared undertakings primarily with *missionary* goals." Then, why no trace of South Eastern Asiatic religious teachings in America? Why no Hinduism and Bud-dhism? The answer again is to look to the *Near East* where Spanish priests and Puritan divines instantly detected an abundance of parallels between the rites and teachings of the Old World and the New. (See W. Krickeberg, *Altmexkanische Kulturen*, [Berlin: Safari-Verlag 1966] p. 569.)

The following quotation is based on an article by Dee F. Green entitled "Recent Finds Have Revived the Old Theory of the origin of the Ancient American Civilizations in a Transoceanic Influence from the Old World" (*University Archaeological Society Newsletter* 70.0). Also quoted in Ross T. Christensen, *Progress in Archaeology* [1963], pp. 71-72:

Weaknesses in the independent-origin doctrine [the theory that they developed out of the primitive hunting cultures of the New World without any help from the ancient civilizations of the Old World] began appearing as early as 1896, when British anthropologist E. B. Tylor discussed the Aztec game of *patolli* and its striking similarities to the Hindu game of *parchisi* (*parcheesi*). Though this was an essay in method, the obvious question raised by these similarities could not be overlooked.

...The debate received new impetus in 1947, however, when Harold S. Gladwin published his *Men Out of Asia*, and again in 1950, when Thor Heyerdahl followed with *The Kon-Tiki Expedition*—works arguing anew the possibility of ancient transoceanic migrations. Although the migrations they suggested went in opposite directions, both rammed the bulwark of independent inventionism and the fight was on. Now a new generation of Americanists is taking a second look at the doctrine of independent native origin of the American civilizations, and seriously considering influence from the Old World not only by land *via* Bering Strait but also across the Pacific.

...The more recent studies seem to point to a compromise solution; namely, that both transoceanic influence and independent native development were factors in the origin of the American civilizations.

EVIDENCE NO. 768: NEPHITE VOYAGE SUSTAINED BY THE PACIFIC TRADE WINDS

Evidence: The following is from a *Foundation for Ancient Research and Mormon Studies Update,* April 1986:

Professor Ben Finney, an authority at the University of Hawaii on Pacific Island voyaging, has recently pointed out how early voyagers could have moved from Melanesia out into the broad Pacific to the east. Until recently, he notes, scholars have been puzzled about easterly travel by Polynesians across the Pacific, since the normal trade winds would appear to have posed an almost insurmountable barrier to easterly movement. Finney reports that new meteorological information about the phenomenon known on the west coast of South America as El Niño now changes the picture (Ben Finney, "Anomalous Westerlies, El Niño, and the Colonization of Polynesia," *American Anthropologist,* vol. 87, [1985], pp. 9-26.)

When El Niño conditions prevail, warm surface water from the equatorial zone floods south down the coast of South America, upsetting many normal conditions. It is now known that the trouble begins with a slackening of the normal trade winds. This causes a strong easterly flow of water from the western Pacific all the way to South America. This is accompanied by unusual westerly winds in place of the trades. Under these conditions, travel from Melanesia to South America is quite feasible. Finney proposes that the makers of Lapita pottery sailed out of Melanesia on such westerlies, reaching western Polynesia before 1000 BC. Their descendants would have used the same winds to move, perhaps all the way to the Marquesas Islands from Tonga. Finney further suggests that these spells of westerlies have occurred every seven to sixteen years throughout the past. Other combinations of winds and routes eastward are also possible, as Finney notes. (For coverage of one of the most powerful El Niños on record, that in the winter of 1982-1983, see T. Y. Canby, "El Niño's Ill Wind," *National Geographic,* vol. 165, [February 1984], pp. 144-183.)

The FARMS Update further explains that travel from Arabia to Indonesia by the Book of Mormon voyagers is easily explained along well-known sea routes that have remained "essentially the same from very early times until the development of steamships." See G. Hourani, *Arab Seafaring in the Indian Ocean in Ancient and Early Medieval Times,* (1951), G. R. Tibbetts, *Arab Navigation in the Indian Ocean before the Coming of the Portuguese,* (Royal Asiatic Society, Oriental Translation Fund, new series, London, 1981), vol. 42, pp. xi-50; Pliny the Elder, *Natural History,* 6.26, pp. 101-106; T. Severin, "In the Wake of Sinbad," *National Geographic,* (July 1982), vol. 162, pp. 2-40.

EVIDENCE NO. 769: EARLIEST MIGRATION CAME AFTER THE FLOOD

Evidence: The first migration to the Americas of the Book of Mormon peoples took place after the flood and shortly after the building of the great tower (Ether 1-6). Non-Mormon scholars have concluded America began to receive population "immediately after the flood..." See Pedro Sarmiento de Gamboa, *History of the Incas* (1572), Hakluyt Society, 2nd Series, No. 22, Cambridge, 1907, p. 32; J. W. LeSuer, *Indian Legends*, 1928, pp. 39-40, 61; Victor W. Von Hagen, *Realm of the Incas*, New York, 1957, pp. 29-30 (Peru and Andes); Priest, *American Antiquities*, 1934, p. 219; Lowry, "Reply to Official Inquiries Respecting the Aborigines of America"; Nadillac, *Prehistoric America*, p. 261.

EVIDENCE NO. 770: THE EIGHT BARGES OF THE JAREDITES

Evidence: The Book of Mormon records that the first people to migrate from the Old World were known as Jaredites and crossed the ocean in eight watertight, dark vessels around 2000 BC (Ether 3:1). Critics scoffed at the idea that the "primitive" Mesoamericans could have had the technology to travel to America in boats. Franklin Harris, Jr. writes the following in his book *The Book of Mormon: Messages and Evidences*, (1961) p.64:

Many voyages anciently and in modern times have been made across the Atlantic and Pacific. Columbus on his second voyage saw on the island of Guadeloupe the stern-post of a vessel supposed to have been the fragment of some unknown ship that had drifted across the Atlantic (J. T. Short, *North Americans of Antiquity,* [1880], p. 506).

Two modern books have many stories of long and early voyages such as Japanese junks being blown or drifting across the Pacific to the Coast of Mexico, Elsdon Best, *Polynesian Voyagers,* (1923), and C. Daryll Forde, *Ancient Mariners* (1927). The latter book also gives similarities in boat design in Old and New Worlds.

The most dramatic modern voyage is that of Thor Heyerdahl from Peru to Papeete. (Thor Heyerdahl, *Kon Tiki,* [1950]. The scientific basis for the voyage is given in *American Indians in the Pacific* [1952], this includes discussion of evidence for origins of race and culture relations outside America.)

According to the legends of the Toltec Indians, the giants, or ancient ones who first settled Mesoamerica, crossed the waters in seven wooden barges which were dark and cavern-like. See *Works of Ixtlilxóchitl* and *Sahagun* in Hunter and Ferguson, *Ancient America and the Book of Mormon* (1950), pp. 33-35. The latter records the old Indian legend that the group crossed the ocean through seven dark "caves."

EVIDENCE NO. 771: ORDEAL BY WATER

Claim: The Book of Mormon contains many references to the ancient American *ordeals by water*. This recurring theme is a reflection of Near Eastern culture from where the ancestors of the ancient Americans migrated.

Evidence: A thorough treatment comparing Book of Mormon ordeals by water with those of the Near East and Asia is presented in the following reference: Michelle Mitchell, "Ordeal by Water," *Foundation for Ancient Research and Mormon Studies*, MIT-83, 1983. The following are excerpts from pages 22-25:

God prepared the Jaredites for a Noah-like water ordeal by instructing them to build barges and by explaining that he would save them from their ordeal in the watery depths (see Ether 2:16, 24, 25)... The language is as cosmic as that of the Psalms and the basic elements of the Psalmist's river ordeal are also satisfied: The Jaredites are beset by raging waters, they rely upon God and they are drawn out of the waters and set in a safe place (see Ether 6:5-7).

Before Nephi and his family faced their trial by water, Nephi's brothers wanted to expose Nephi to an impromptu river ordeal: "And now it came to pass that when I had spoken these words, they were angry with me and were desirous to throw me into the depths of the sea." But it was the brothers who felt the effects of an ordeal since Nephi stretched out his hand by the Lord's command to shock his brothers and make them aware of God's judgment. Nephi reminded them of God's power and justice in supporting their worthy ancestors through water ordeals (1 Nephi 17:26, 27, 29, 32).

But in spite of all warnings, Nephi's brothers misbehaved during the voyage and made Nephi fear that they would lose the Lord's protection in their trial by water: "And I, Nephi, began to fear exceedingly lest the Lord should be angry with us, and smite us because of our iniquity, that we should be swallowed up in the depths of the sea" (1 Nephi 18:10). He worried with good cause. His brothers tied him up and did not release him until they were about to be drowned and realized that "...the judgments of God were upon them and that they must perish save that they should repent..." (1 Nephi 18:15). Following the Psalmist's pattern, only after Nephi had cried out to the Lord did the storm cease and the ship come safely to land (1 Nephi 18:21).

...The internal water ordeal is also mentioned in the Book of Mormon: "Therefore they have drunk damnation to their own souls. Therefore, they have drunk out of the cup of the wrath of God..." Here again is the bitter cup which judges the guilty when they submit to the ordeal of drinking it. Similarly, Jacob quotes from Isaiah: "O Jerusalem, which hast drunk at the hand of the Lord the cup of his fury" (2 Nephi 8:17). Christ once more characterizes His ordeal as a test by water: "And I have drunk out of that bitter cup which the Father hath given me..." (3 Nephi 11:11).

We may dismiss ordeals as superstitious indulgence of the credulous, but there is a wealth of symbolism associated with water and its power to save or destroy.

EVIDENCE NO. 772: TEXTILES IN ANCIENT AMERICA

Claim: Textile technology in ancient America was similar in some respects to those in the ancient Near East. These similarities help prove that ancestors of ancient Americans originated in the Near East as recorded in the Book of Mormon.

Evidence: The following is quoted from a paper by John L. Sorenson entitled "The Significance of an Apparent Relationship Between the Ancient Near East and Mesoamerica," SOR-71, *Foundation for Ancient Research and Mormon Studies*, 1971, p. 240:

Documentation

Cultural Features	Mesoamerica	Near East
Purple cloth dye prepared from coastal mollusk by "milking," then replacing it. Elite and hieratic connotation.	Nuttall, 1909; Born, 1937	Jackson, 1916; Born, 1937; Wright, 1943
Use of scarlet cloth dye (cochineal/kermes) prepared from plant louse.	Born, 1938; McBryde, 1945	Born, 1938
Resist dyeing	Kroeber, 1952; Hewes, 1961	Kroeber, 1952; Hewes, 1961
Loom	Kroeber, 1952; Hewes, 1961	Kroeber, 1952; Hewes, 1961
Cotton	Kroeber, 1952; Hewes, 1961	Kroeber, 1952; Hewes, 1961
Head Clothing: Turban or "Nightcap"	Stirling, 1940, p. 317	Albright, 1949;
Pointed-toe shoes	Stirling, 1940, p. 327	Chiera, 1938; Irwin, 1963
Long robes with sash, mantle, sandals & loincloth	Irwin, 1963	Irwin, 1963

Z. Nuttall, "A Curious Survival in Mexico of the Use of the Purpura Shellfish for dyeing," *Putnam Anniversary Volume,* edited by F. Boas, (Cedar Rapids, Iowa, 1909), pp. 368-384.

J. W. Jackson, "The Geographical Distribution of the Shell Purple Industry," *Manchester Literary and Philosophical Society Memoirs and Proceedings,* (1916), vol. 60.

W. Born, "The Use of Purple Among the Indians of Central America," *Ciba Review,* (1937), vol. 4, pp. 124-127.

G. E. Wright, "How Did Early Israel Differ From Her Neighbors?" *Biblical Archaeologist,* (1943), vol. 1, p. 3.

W. Born, "Scarlet," *Ciba Review,* (1938), vol. 7, pp. 206-217.

F. W. MacBride, "Cultural and Historical Geography of Southwestern Guatemala," *Smithsonian Institution Social Anthropology,* (1959), Publication no. 4.

A. L Kroeber, "The Ancient Oikoumene as a Historical Culture Aggregate," *The Nature of Culture,* (Chicago: 1952), pp. 389-390.

G. W. Hewes, "The Ecume as a Civilizational Multiplier System," *Kroeber Anthropological Society Papers,* (1961), no. 25, pp. 73-109.

M. W. Stirling, "Great Stone Faces in the Mexican Jungle," *National Geographic Magazine,* (1940), vol. 77, pp. 317, 327.

William F. Albright, *The Archaeology of Palestine,* (Baltimore, 1949), pp. 211-212.

E. Chiera, *They Wrote on Clay,* (Chicago, 1938), p. 205.

C. Irwin, *Fair Gods and Stone Faces,* (New York: 1963), pp. 146-157.

EVIDENCE NO. 773: ORIENTATION OF SACRED SITES

Claim: One of the many customs that the ancient Americans brought with them from the Near East is the practice of orienting sacred buildings to face East (1 Nephi 21:13). This similarity helps prove that ancestors of ancient Americans originated in the Near East as recorded in the Book of Mormon.

Evidence: Examples from the Near East can be found in: Ezekiel 41:14; 43:2-4; 47:1; Jack Finegan, *Handbook of Biblical Chronology, Principles of Time Reckoning in the Ancient World and Problems of Chronology in the Bible,* (Princeton, New Jersey, 1964), p. 37; and F. J. Hollis, *The Sun Cult and the Temple at Jerusalem, Myth and Ritual,* (London, 1933).

Examples from Mesoamerica are found in: J. W. Dow, "Astronomical Orientations at Teotihuacán: A Case Study in Astroarchaeology," *American Antiquity* (1967), vol. 32, pp. 326-334; and J. E. S. Thompson, *Maya Hieroglyphic Writing: An Introduction,* Revised Edition, (Norman, Oklahoma, 1960), p. 249. The above sources are also cited in a paper by John L. Sorenson entitled "The Significance of an Apparent Relationship Between the Ancient Near East and Mesoamerica," *Foundation for Ancient Research and Mormon Studies,* SOR-71, (1971), p. 228.

In contrast, see the evidence concerning the "EVILS OF THE NORTHERLY DIRECTION" which appears in this same chapter.

EVIDENCE NO. 774: TEMPLE SYMBOLISMS

Claim: Inasmuch as the Book of Mormon claims that the temples of ancient America were fashioned after the Temple of Solomon (2 Nephi 5:16), we should expect to find characteristics of these temples similar to those in the ancient Near East. Evidence of these similarities help prove that ancestors of ancient Americans originated in the Near East as recorded in the Book of Mormon.

Evidence: The following is quoted from a paper by John L. Sorenson entitled "The Significance of an Apparent Relationship Between the Ancient Near East and Mesoamerica," SOR-71, *Foundation for Ancient Research and Mormon Studies*, 1971, p. 227:

Documentation

Cultural Features	Mesoamerica	Near East
Temple atop large platform (see Figure 17)		Parrot, 1949; Wales, 1953
Temple and its platform as an artificial representation or natural elevation of cosmic significance	Wicke, 1965; Holland, 1964	Frankfort, 1949; Hastings, 1951, vol. 6; Wales, 1953
Ascent of temple platform signifies rising to the heavens	Holland, 1964, p. 303; Vaillant, 1950	Psalms 24:3-4; Wales, 1953, p. 8-11
Interior of temple partitioned, "holy of holies" idea, which is contact point with heavenly powers	Wicke, 1965, p. 412; Holland, 1964, pp. 303-305	1 Kings 7:50; Ezekiel 41:4; Wales, 1953, p. 8
Omphalos concept, "navel of the world"	Thompson, 1950; Alexander, 1916	Wensinck, 1916; Wales, 1953; Nibley, 1951; Burrows, 1941, pp. 43-53
Waters confined beneath temple[*]	Prescott, 1877	Hastings, 1951, vols. 2 &4; Ezekiel 47
Cosmic axis, connection of heavens, earth, underworld at the point	Wales, 1953, pp. 8-13	Holland, 1964; Burrows, 1941
Occasional burial beneath this cosmic axis point	Wicke, 1965, pp. 410-412	Hastings, 1951, vol. 1; Edwards, 1961

[*] At the great pyramid at Cholula, when Cortéz was attacking, native priests in their extremity (in accord with a "tradition") expected water to flood out of the structure when they made an opening in its side. The temples at Byblos and Jerusalem were believed to be over the watery abyss, confining the contents from bursting forth. (On this motif in Ezekiel 31, see W. R. Farmer, "The Geography of Ezekiel's River of Life," *Biblical Archaeologist,* [1956], vol. 19, p. 18.)

A. Parrot, *Ziggurats et Tour de Babel,* (Paris: 1949), pp. 33-36.

C. R. Wicke, "Pyramids and Temple Mounds: Mesoamerican Ceremonial Architecture in Eastern North America," *American Antiquity,* vol. 30, pp. 410-412.

W. R. Holland, "Contemporary Txotxil Coxmological Concepts as a Basis for Interpreting Prehistoric Maya Civilization," *American Antiquity,* (1964), vol. 29, p. 301-306.

H. Frankfort, H. A. Frankfort, J. A. Wilson and T. Jacobsen, *Before Philosophy,* (1949), pp. 30-31.

J. Hastings, editor, *Encyclopedia of Religion and Ethics,* (New York, 1951), vol. 1, p. 609, vol. 2, p. 705, vol. 4, pp. 128-129, vol. 6, p. 678.

G. C. Vaillant, *The Aztecs of Mexico,* (Bungay, Suffolk: 1950; Garden City, New York: 1941), pp. 157-158.

J. E. S. Thompson, "Maya Hieroglyphic writing: Introduction," *Carnegie Institution of Washington, DC,* Publication no. 589, (1950), p. 71.

H. Nibley, "The Hierocentric State," *Western Political Quarterly,* (1951), vol. 3, pp. 229.

H. B. Alexander, *The Mythology of All Races, North American,* (New York, 1916), vol. 10, pp. 286-287.

A. J. Wensinck, "The Ideas of the Western Semites Concerning the Navel of the Earth," *Koniklijke Akademie van Wetenschappen. Verhandelingen,* Nieuwe reeks, (1916), vol. 17, no. 1.

M. Burrows, *What Mean These Stones,* (New Haven, 1941), pp. 43-53.

W. H. Prescott, *History of the Conquest of Mexico,* (Philadelphia, 1877), vol. 2, p. 20.

I. E. S. Edwards, *The Pyramids of Egypt,* (London: 1961).

Figure 17. The "Mountain of the House of God" (or Ziggurat) from Ur, Southern Mesopotamia about 2100 BC (left), and the Temple of Kukulcan at Chichtzen Itza, Yucatan, Mexico, dated from the tenth century AD (right). See Bruce W. Warren and Thomas Stuart Ferguson, *The Messiah in Ancient America*, (1987), pp. 164-167, (which also shows a photograph of the Quetzalcoatl pyramid of Cholula, in Puebla, Mexico, in perfect alignment with mount Popocatepetl—the shape of the pyramid was apparently fashioned to exactly match the shape of the nearby mountain.)

EVIDENCE NO. 775:   USE OF WOOD AND ADOBE RATHER THAN STONE

<u>Claim</u>: The general lack of stone construction in early Nephite history (Preclassic period) as indicated in the Book of Mormon has been verified. (For Book of Mormon references see those cited in the evidence below.)

<u>Evidence</u>: The following are quotes from a book review by John L. Sorenson, published in *University Archaeological Society Newsletter* 17.0, and is quoted in Christensen, *Progress In Archaeology*, [1963], pp. 168-170. The book is *Lugares Arqueológicos del Altiplano Meridional Central de Guatemala* by Edwin M. Shook.

> Perhaps the most impressive features of Preclassic Kaminalijuyu architecture is the non-use of building stone, even for the most important religious and civic structures. The Guatemala Valley is a large basin whose floor is composed of layers of decomposed volcanic turf, pumiceous ash, brown clay, and surface soil, and these were the materials almost exclusively utilized in early architecture, as adobe or puddled earth. State the authors: "No stones of any kind were to be had on the surface in the immediate vicinity of Kaminaljuyu…To our knowledge …no masonry of either cut or uncut stone was ever employed at Kaminaljuyu during Preclassic times. The first use of stone at the site for construction purposes occurred in the Esperanza or Early Classic Period." (pp. 45-46).

> The general lack of stone construction seems true of the Preclassic everywhere in southern Mesoamerica, and is in remarkable agreement with the Book of Mormon account! This record makes repeated mention of the use of wood for buildings in the "land southward," beginning in the sixth century BC, but the use of stone for construction is not mentioned until 72 BC (Alma 48:8), and here it is for fortification walls only. (Compare Nephi's stated lack in the building of his temple at Nephi of the *"precious things"* used by Solomon [2 Nephi 5:16] with the repeated reference in 1 Kings 7:9-11 to the sawed and hewed building stones used by Solomon's builders as *"costly stones."* Note also that Helaman 5:44 [circa 29 BC] implies that even prison walls were [flammable] and therefore of wood and not of brick or stone, contrary to some modern illustrations of the Book of Mormon. See also Mosiah 11:8-10.) The evidence from both archaeology and the Book of Mormon, then, requires that we visualize Book of Mormon religious and civic structures (at least in early times in the "land southward") in a different form from that of the Near Eastern homeland of the New World colonizers.

How Joseph Smith, in 1829, could have fitted the Book of Mormon text to the architectural pattern in use in pre-Christian times in America, when such knowledge has been obtained by science only in the last decade or two, is a question which ought to cause some scholarly head- scratching. It is another evidence of the historicity of the record translated by Joseph Smith.

...Construction (of the pyramidal mounds) was almost universally of earth or adobe. Surface mounds were protected by adobe brick or wet-smoothed adobe. Stone was apparently not used in any construction.

EVIDENCE NO. 776: MOTIFS AND AESTHETIC FEATURES

Claim: Motifs and aesthetic features in ancient America were similar to those in the ancient Near East. These similarities help prove that ancestors of ancient Americans originated in the Near East as recorded in the Book of Mormon.

Evidence: The following is quoted from a paper by John L. Sorenson entitled "The Significance of an Apparent Relationship Between the Ancient Near East and Mesoamerica," in *Man Across the Sea—Problems of Pre-Columbian Contacts*, edited by Carroll L. Riley, J. Charles Kelley, Campbell W. Pennington, and Robert L. Rands, (Austin: University of Texas Press, 1971), pp. 219-241:

Documentation

Cultural Features	Mesoamerica	Near East
Double-headed eagle (see Figure 18)	Barlow, 1954	Ward, 1910
Winged sun disc (globe) or sun as body of bird[1] (see Figure 19)	Barlow, 1954; Kroeber, 1948	D'Alviella, 1894; Hinke, 1907
Pennated tail, dependent from a circular feature	Barlow, 1954; Kroeber, 1948	D'Alviella, 1894
Horseshoe-shaped, curled-end device representing hair curls of a female deity[2] associated with: childbirth, vegetational fertility, and with Venus as the morning star (see Figure 20)	Ferguson, 1958; Covarrubias, 1957; Thompson, 1958	Ferguson, 1958; Hinke, 1907; Frankfort, 1944
Star of David—intertwined triangles (see Figure 21)	Smithsonian, 1883, p.57	
Motif, ring transfixed from below by a stick with pentad on ring face (see Figure 22)	Caso, 1947, figs. 1, 4, 21, 62	Ackerman, 1950; Ferguson, 1958, pp. 115-116
Motif, ritual bucket held by figure in hieratic scene (see Figure 23)	Drucker, Heizer, & Squier, p. 198	Frankfort, 1955, p. 83
Motif, floating figure ("Scraph?")	(La Venta Stela 3)	Irwin, 1963, p. 169
Frontality in representations of human figure (head in profile; eye, torso, and shoulders full front—see Figure 24)	Ferguson, 1958, p. 112	Ferguson, 1958
Turquoise and lapis lazuli mosaics	Kidder, 1946, pp. 115-117; Vaillant, 1935, p. 245	Woolley, 1934
Trumpets (several types)	Thompson, 1954	
Cylinder stamps[3] (see Figure 25)	Borhegyi, 1950	Woolley, 1937; Frankfort, 1939
Flat stamps (see Figure 26)	Borhegyi, 1950	
Antiphonal poetic style[4]	Thompson, 1950	Ginsberg, 1945

1. The maximum version shows the disc as the body of a partially stylized bird with outstretched wings and pennated tail below. The Assyrian example is more stylized, lacking the bird's head and feet, although wings and tail are very similar to the Mexican one.

2. This is Ishtar/Hathor in Mesopotamia/Egypt. See fertility figurine complex above.

3. "The cylinder seal is a peculiar type not likely to be invented independently in two different countries...Paper-using people would never invent the cylinder seal" (Woolley, 1937). Frankfort (1939: 311) suggests a link in art styles between the Near East and Mexico.

4. "There are close parallels in Maya transcriptions of the colonial period, and, I am convinced, in the hieroglyphic texts themselves to the verses of the Psalms, and the poetry of Job" (Thompson, 1950, pp. 61-62). Ginsberg (1945) shows that the same style was Ugaritic.

The complete references for the above evidence are listed below in order of appearance:

R. Barlow, *Las Joyas de Martin Oceletl., Yan*, (1954), vol. 3, pp. 57, 59.

W. H. Ward, *Seal Cylinders of Western Asia*, (Washington: 1910), p. 420.

A. L. Kroeber, *Anthropology*, (New York: 1948), pp. 474-514.

E. G. D'Alviella, *The Migration of Symbols*, (London: 1894), p. 207.

J. Hinke, *A New Boundary Stone of Nebuchadnezzar I from Nippur*, The Babylonian Expedition of Pennsylvania University, (Philadelphia: 1907), ser. D, vol. 4, p. 89.

Thomas Stuart Ferguson, *One Fold and One Shepherd*, (San Francisco: 1958), pp. 112-125.

M. Covarrubias, *Indian Art of Mexico and Central America*, (New York: 1957).

J. E. S. Thompson, "Symbols, Glyphs, and Divinatory Almanacs for Diseases in The Maya Dresden and Madrid Codices," *American Antiquity*, (1958), vol. 23, pp. 300-306.

H. Frankfort, H. A. Frankfort, J. A. Wilson, and T. Jacobsen, *The Birth of Civilization in the Near East*, (Bloomington, Indiana: 1954), pp. 198-200.

Smithsonian Institution, *Collections: Indians of North and South America*, (1883), Bureau of American Ethnology Annual Report for 1882-1883, p. 57.

A. Caso, *Calendario y Escritura de Antiguas Culturas de Monte Alban*, (Mexico City: 1947), Figs. 1, 4, 21, 62.

P. Ackerman, "The dawn of religions," In *Ancient Religions: a symposium*, edited by V. Ferm, (New York: 1950), pp. 3-24.

P. Drucker, R. Heizer, and R. Squier, "Excavations at La Venta, Tabasco, 1955" *Smithsonian Institution*, (1959), Bureau of American Ethnology, Bulletin 170, p. 198.

H. A. Frankfort, *The Art and Architecture of The Ancient Orient*, (Baltimore: 1955), p. 83.

C. Irwin, *Fair Gods and Stone Faces*, (New York: 1963), p. 169.

A. V. Kidder, J. D. Jennings and E. M. Shook, "Excavations at Kaminaljuyu, Guatemala," *Carnegie Institution of Washington, D.C.*, Publication no. 561, (1946), pp. 115-117.

G. C. Vaillant, "Excavations at El Arbolillo," *American Museum of Natural History Papers*, (1935), vol. 35, p. 245.

L. Woolley, *Ur excavations, Volume 2, The Royal Cemetery*, (London: 1934).

J. E. S. Thompson, *The Rise and Fall of Maya Civilization*, (Norman, Oklahoma: 1954), p. 185.

S. F. de Borhegyi, "Notas Sobre Sellos de Barro, Existentes en el Museo Nacionál de Arqueológicos y Etnológia de Guatemala," *Rev. Instituto de Antropológico Historia de Guatemala*, vol. 2, (1950), pp. 16-26.

L. Woolley, *Digging Up The Past*, (Baltimore, 1937), p. 76.

H. Frankfort, *Cylinder Seals*, (London, 1939).

J. E. S. Thompson, "Maya Hieroglyphic writing: Introduction," *Carnegie Institution of Washington, DC*, Publication no. 589, (1950), pp. 61-62.

H. L. Ginsberg, "Ugaritic Studies and the Bible," *Biblical Archaeologist*, vol. 8, (1945), pp. 55-56.

Figure 18. Two-headed eagles from Asia Minor (Left) and Mexico (right). See T. S. Ferguson, *One Fold*, (1958), p. 128.

Figure 19. Winged sun discs from Assyria (left) and Mexico (right). See Thomas Stuart Ferguson, *One Fold and One Shepherd*, (1958), p. 127.

Figure 20. Horseshoe-shaped, curled-end device representing childbirth, vegitational fertility and hair curls of a female deity. From Assyria (top left), Mesopotamia (bottom far left), Egypt (bottom center) and Mesoamerica (right). See Thomas Ferguson, *One Fold and One Shepherd*, (1958), pp. 174-177, 182.

Figure 23. Religious person holding a holy bucket from the Old (left) and New (right) Worlds. See Fergusen, *One Fold*, p. 89.

Figure 21. A Star of David symbol from Uxmal, Yucatan, Mexico about 1000 AD. See Warren and Ferguson, *The Messiah*, p. 173.

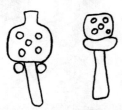

Figure 22. Pentad of Monte Alban, Mexico (Ferguson, *One*, p. 115).

Figure 24. Examples of *frontality* from Egypt (left) and Vera Cruz, Mexico (right). See Ferguson, *One Fold*, (1858), p. 112.

Figure 25. Seals from Chiapa de Corzo, Chaipas, Mexico. Cylinder seal from about 400 BC (left), Seal 5 with a bar-and-dot number 8, from about 500 BC, (right). See Bruce W. Warren and Thomas Stuart Ferguson, *The Messiah in Ancient America*, (1987), p. 206.

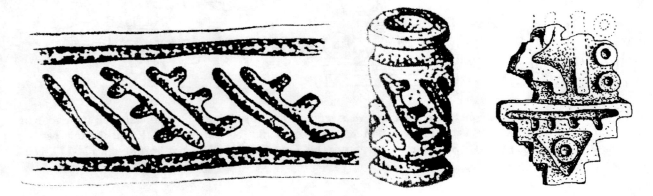

EVIDENCE NO. 777: NEW ARROWS FOR NEPHI'S NEW BOW

Claim: The fact that Nephi made new arrows for his new bow is an evidence of the accuracy of detail in the Book of Mormon.

Evidence: After Nephi broke his steel bow, he made not only a new wooden bow, but he also made a new arrow (1 Nephi 16:18, 23). A false prophet would not have given any thought to the need for new arrows with a new bow. This is yet another evidence that Joseph Smith was a true prophet and that the Book of Mormon is true and authentic.

The arrows that had been used previously with the steel bow were thicker and heavier and would not have been useful with his new wooden bow—hence the need for lighter arrows. A July 1984 *FARMS Update* comments that "One doubts that such information was known to Joseph Smith or to many of his contemporaries. Archery as a means of self-defense or as a serious method of hunting or warfare, went out of vogue among Europeans many years before the time of Joseph Smith. On the other hand, archery as a sport, did not emerge until the later half of the 19th Century." (See Nahum Waldman, "The Breaking of the Bow," *Jewish Quarterly Review,* [October, 1978], vol. 69, pp. 82-88; Cited in *Re-exploring the Book of Mormon,* Edited by John W. Welch and Alan Goff, [1992], pp. 41-43.)

EVIDENCE NO. 778: THE DATE OF CHRIST'S BIRTH

Claim: The date of Jesus Christ's birth as given by revelation (D&C 20:1) is consistent with Mayan calendar dating.

Evidence: M. Wells Jakeman noted the following in his article "The Ancient Middle American Calendar System: Its Origin and Development" (*University Archaeological Society Newsletter,* [BYU.: Provo, Utah] 31.0, Cited in Ross T. Christensen, *Progress in Archaeology* [1963], p. 135-136):

> Still another contribution, which should have great interest to both Book of Mormon and New Testament students, is the identification of the beginning point of one of the ancient time-counts of the Middle American calendar system, which appears to coincide with the beginning point of one of the time-counts in the Book of Mormon and also the beginning point of the Christian era of the Old World! It will be recalled that the Book of Mormon indicates that, between about AD 1 and 10, its ancient Nephite calendricists of Mesoamerica—like the early Christians in the Old World—adopted a new time-count the beginning point of which was the day of the birth of Christ, the life god of the Nephites (3 Nephi 2:5-8). That great event as dated by Book of Mormon statements, when interpreted in light of New Testament and Babylonian calendar evidence, to the early spring of one of the years from 4 BC to AD 5; and was possibly revealed by the Lord himself to the Prophet Joseph Smith as having occurred on the day April 6 (*Doctrine and Covenants,* Sec. 20, preface and v. 1). Now the beginning point of the new time-count discovered in the Middle American calendar system was the day 7.18.0.0.1 of the Maya era or Long Count, the equivalent of which in the European-Christian calendar was the day April 6 of the year AD 2! (That is, if the Maya day 7.18.0.0.1 is translated according to the original Thompson version of the 11-16 correlation. The three other versions of this correlation so far proposed would give as the European-Christian equivalent April 1, AD 2 [Goodman version], April 2, AD 2 [Martinez version], and April 4, AD 2 [revised Thompson version]. This remarkable correspondence presents, of course, important further support for the Book of Mormon, as well as new evidence for solving the long-time problem of the actual date of the birth of the Savior. (Note further—as a consideration rendering this correspondence even more complete and arbitrary— that since there is no special calendrical or astronomical reason for the adoption, by the ancient Mesoamerican calendricists, of the particular day 7.18.0.0.1 or April 6, AD 2, as the epoch of a new chronological count, the reason for this must have been historical. That is, some event of such great

political or religious importance occurred on this day, that the ancient Mesoamericans thereafter considered it the beginning of a new era in their history—quite possibly the mysterious "Dawn" frequently mentioned in the native histories as an early event apparently connected with the religion or history of Quetzalcoatl, the "Fair God" or life god of the ancient Mesoamericans, when, it is stated, "a new world dawned for them" [*Book of Chilam Balam of Chumayel*, edited and translated by Ralph L. Roys, Washington, 1933, p. 102].)

The following reference cites evidence to support the view that the Mayan calendar was actually the invention of a pre-Maya (e.g., Nephite) people: "Cycle 7 Monuments in Middle America: A Reconsideration," by Michael D. Coe, Reviewed by Bruce W. Warren (*University Archaeological Society Newsletter,* vol. 50, p. 2).

EVIDENCE NO. 779: SIMILARITIES OF THE MESOAMERICAN AND ISRAELITE CALENDARS

Claim: Features of the Mesoamerican calendar correlate with that of Israel's calendar. The Book of Mormon speaks of the lunar month (Omni 1:21) and the seven-day week (Mosiah 13:18).

Evidence: The following is quoted from an article by M. Wells Jakeman entitled: "The Ancient Middle American Calendar System: Its Origin and Development" (*University Archaeological Society Newsletter*, 31.0, Cited in Ross T. Christensen, *Progress in Archaeology* [1963], p. 135):

> Early Features of the Mesoamerican Calendar. The principal contribution of this paper is a reconstruction of the successive steps involved in the development of the main "Maya" version of the ancient Middle American calendar system. As shown by hieroglyphic and other evidence, most of the earlier of these steps took place in the latter part of the so-called Preclassic period of ancient Mesoamerican history, dating to the later centuries of the first millennium BC and first four centuries AD (that is, the period of the second or Israelitish Lehite-Mulekite civilization of the Book of Mormon). Several of these earlier steps were discovered to duplicate features of the ancient *Israelite* calendar indicated in the Book of Mormon to have been that of the Lehite-Mulekite peoples of Mesoamerica in this "Preclassic" period—among them a year of 12 months (instead of 18 as in the later Maya calendar), and a cycle of seven days, which is the period in the Israelite-Nephite calendar called the week. The latter especially—since it involves an arbitrary number—constitutes an important addition to the growing list of trait-correspondences between the ancient American and Near Eastern civilizations confirming the claims of the Book of Mormon.

For further evidence that the Mesoamericans and the Near Easterners both measured their time with the lunar month and the seven-day week see *Man Across the Sea, Problems of Pre-Columbian Contacts,* edited by Riley et. al., [Austin & London: University of Texas Press, 1971], p. 228; cited in Sorenson, "The Book of Mormon as a Mesoamerican Codex," (The Society for Early Historic Archaeology, 1976) p. 5.

EVIDENCE NO. 780: NUMBERING OF DAYS AND MONTHS

Claim: The Book of Mormon writers referred to days and months by numbers rather than by names. For example, they would speak of the first day of the week, the second, or third etc. (See Alma 10:6; 14:23; 16:1; 49:1; 52:1; 56:1,42.)

Evidence: Modern scholars have verified that this was the practice in both Mesoamerica and the ancient Near East. (See J. Eric Thompson, *Maya History and Religion,* [Norman: University of Oklahoma Press, 1971]; and Manor S. Edmonton [1971], "The Book of Counsel: The *Popol Vuh* of the Quiche Maya of Guatemala," *Tulane University, Middle American Research Institute,* Publication 35, [New Orleans: Mari, 1971], p. xv; Jack Finegan, *Handbook of Biblical Chronology* [Princeton: Princeton University Press, 1946], cited in John L. Sorenson, "The Book of Mormon as a Mesoamerican Codex," [1976], p. 5.)

Dr. Franklin S. Harris writes: "With the designation of months, G. Schiaparelli points out that at the time Lehi and Mulek left Palestine at 600 BC the Israelites did not give names to the months but called them by numbers in their order, and in a dozen references scattered through the Book of Mormon (Alma 10:6) the months are always referred to by number and not given any special name." (Harris, *Book of Mormon Message and Evidence* [1961], pp. 96; who cites Kenneth MacGowan, *Astronomy in the Old Testament* [1905], p. 104)

EVIDENCE NO. 781: EACH DAY BEGAN AT SUNSET

<u>Claim</u>: The Nephites, having descended from tribes of Israel undoubtedly started each day at sunset as did the ancient Israelites.

<u>Evidence</u>: According to Oliver LaFarge and Douglas Ryers this was also the practice in Mesoamerica. "The Jacaltecs' days begin at sunset as was probably the case with the old Maya." (See LaFarge and Ryers, *Year Bearer's People* [1931], pp. 171-172; cited in Harris, *Book of Mormon Message and Evidence* [1961], pp. 96.)

EVIDENCE NO. 782: SIGNIFICANCE OF THE NEW YEAR CELEBRATION

<u>Claim</u>: The Book of Mormon implies that observance of the New Year was a very significant event to the ancient Americans. Indeed, many important events transpired at the beginning of the New Year, such as the birth of Christ, and thirty-four years later his appearance on the American Continent (3 Nephi 1:4; 2:8; 10:18). There are several other significant events that occurred at the commencement of the New Year. See, for example, Alma 28:6-7; 30:5-6; 44:24; 45:1.

<u>Evidence</u>: According to scholars and historians of the Middle East, the new year was celebrated in ancient times as the birthday of the world. It was the day of coronation of divine and earthly kings, a day of victory over chaos, and a day of renewal of covenants. In the Book of Mormon, a number of significant happenings transpired at the time of the New Year. (See "New Year's Celebrations," *Foundation for Ancient Research and Mormon Studies Update*, January 1985.)

King Amalickiah was murdered on New Year's Eve (Alma 51:34-37; 52:1), perhaps to prevent him from re-enthroning himself in the rites of the New Year. Amalickiah's brother Ammoron was also killed on New Year's Eve (Alma 62:36-39), most likely to prevent him from being crowned in place of his brother. Jesus appeared to the Nephites as the most divine King just after the beginning of the New Year (3 Nephi 10:18).

King Benjamin's address, discussed elsewhere in this work as a series of separate evidences because of its close resemblance to the Feast of Tabernacles, also occurs at the first of the Jewish year (Mosiah 2-5). (See also the related information on "THE GREAT ASSEMBLY OR YEAR-RITE" in the chapter on "Historical Accuracy of the Book of Mormon.")

EVIDENCE NO. 783: HEBREW MARRIAGE CUSTOMS

<u>Claim</u>: Expressions concerning marriage are similar to Hebrew expressions. For example, "his sons should take daughters to wife" (1 Nephi 7:1). Verification of this custom strengthens the claim that the Book of Mormon is Authentic and true, that Joseph Smith was a prophet of God and hence that the Church of Jesus Christ of Latter-day Saints is true.

<u>Evidence</u>: In Hebrew, a man does not marry a woman; he takes "her to wife" or "she is given to him to wife." (See McFadyen, John Key to *Introductory Hebrew Grammar*, 3rd edition [Edinburgh: T&T Clark, 1951], p. 13. Cited in Cheesman, *Ancient Writing on Metal Plates*, p. 19.)

EVIDENCE NO. 784: DANCING MAIDENS

Claim: The Book of Mormon account of dancing maidens is consistent with ancient Near Eastern practice.

Evidence: The Book of Mormon, contains a number of authentic details, including the incident of the dancing maidens at Shemlon (Mosiah 20:1-5). At first glance, the story may seem strange to readers who are unacquainted with the ways of ancient Middle Eastern culture. For example, it appears that the priests knew where and when the maidens would be dancing, for they hid themselves ahead of time, in order to lie in wait. Also, it is strange that after the maidens were abducted, none of them made any attempt to escape. In fact, they actually pled with their brothers and fathers not to kill their captor-husbands (Mosiah 23:33).

Since the publication of the Book of Mormon, information has come to light that verifies the authenticity of the incident of the dancing maidens. It now appears that the maidens went to Shemlon at a customary place and at a designated time for the very purpose of announcing their availability to men who might be "bride-hunting" and to purposely attract their attention.

In ancient Israel, such a day was the Fifteenth of *Av* and was known as a "matrimonial holiday" for all those concerned. In the Old World, the designated location was in the fields just outside Shiloh and later at Jerusalem. As in the Book of Mormon, dancing was an important part of the rituals. (See Abraham Bloch, *The Biblical and Historical Background of the Jewish Holy Days* [New York: KTAV, 1975], pp. 215-219; and the Babylonian Talmud *Baba Batra* 121a, both cited in John W. Welch, Robert F. Smith, Gordon C. Thomasson, "Dancing Maidens and the Fifteenth of Av," *Foundation for Ancient Research and Mormon Studies Update*, February 1985; reprinted in *Re-exploring the Book of Mormon*, edited by John W. Welch, [1992], pp. 139-141.)

EVIDENCE NO. 785: INTERVENTION OF WOMEN

Claim: The Book of Mormon contains authentic customs of the ancient Middle East, such as men yielding to the petitions of women.

Evidence: The Book of Mormon tells of Nephi's life being spared by the intervention of one of the daughters of Ishmael and her mother. Nephi wrote that his brothers "were angry with me again, and sought to lay hands upon me; but behold, one of the daughters of Ishmael, yea, and also her mother...did plead with my brethren, insomuch that they did soften their hearts; and they did cease striving to take away my life" (1 Nephi 7:19).

This account is true to the custom of the ancient Middle East. Indeed, the influence of a woman was great in this ancient culture (William Smith, *A Bible Dictionary,* [McLean, Virginia: MacDonald Publishing Co.], p. 749).

Dr. Hugh Nibley writes the following (*Approach to the Book of Mormon* [1988], pp. 250-251) regarding the Middle Eastern respect for women:

> The women have their own quarters, which no man may invade; and an older woman may talk up boldly to the sheikh when no one else dares to, just as Sariah took Lehi to task when she thought her sons were lost in the desert (1 Nephi 5:2-3). All that saved Nephi's life on one occasion was the intervention of "one of the daughters of Ishmael, yea, and also her mother, and one of the sons of Ishmael" (1 Nephi 7:19), for while "the Arab can only be persuaded by his own relations," he can only yield to the entreaties of women without losing face, and indeed is expected to yield to them, even robbers sparing a victim who appeals to them in the name of his wife, the daughter of his uncle. If a courageous woman demands that a raiding sheikh give back something so that her people will not starve, he is in honor bound to give her a camel. (See Claude R. Conder, *Tent Work in Palestine,* [London: Bentley, 1878], vol. 2, p. 283; John L. Burckhardt, *Notes on the Bedouins and Wahábys,* [London: Colburn & Bentley, 1831], vol. 1, p. 33.)

Women also had great influence in ancient American and Polynesian cultures. For example, members of the Ancient Inroqis tribal council were nominated by women. Women also held the power to remove members who misbehaved. (See article on "Iroquois," in *World Book Encyclopedia,* [Chicago, 1992], vol. 9, p. 455.)

EVIDENCE NO. 786: THE SIGNIFICANCE OF THE NUMBER TWENTY-FOUR

<u>Claim</u>: One of the many authentic details that substantiate the truthfulness of the Book of Mormon is the frequent, and appropriate use of the number "twenty-four." (For Book of Mormon references see those cited in the evidence below.)

<u>Evidence</u>: While it may be general knowledge in our present day of greater availability of information that certain numbers represented specific meanings in Biblical times, it is clear that such bits of information were not as readily available in the days of Joseph Smith. Even so, the Book of Mormon is full of such authentic details. In ancient times, the number 24 symbolized heavenly government—and, as a multiple of 12, symbolized government in general and priestly judgment in particular. For more information, see E. Bullinger, *Number in Scripture* (1894, reprinted Grand Rapids: Kregel Pub. 1969).

Not only does the Book of Mormon make frequent use of the number 24, but it is also used appropriately according to its original meaning. For example, there were apparently 24 judges or priests on King Noah's court, since his priests captured 24 Lamanite daughters (Mosiah 20:5). The 24 plates of Ether appropriately contained the judgments of God upon his people (Mosiah 8:9; Alma 37:21; Ether 1:2).

The prophet Mormon was chosen as the keeper of the sacred records when he was ten years old, but was told to wait until he was 24 before he should assume this great responsibility (Mormon 1:2-4). As part of his addition to the history of his people, Mormon emphasizes that there were only 24 survivors of the great battle between the Lamanites and Nephites—symbolizing their witness to the judgments of God poured out upon them for their disobedience (Mormon 6:11, 15-22).

The Jaredite King Orihah was said to have executed judgment in righteousness most likely with the help of his 23 sons sitting with him as judges (Ether 7:1-2). The Jaredite King Hearthom reigned over his kingdom for 24 years before it was taken away from him (Ether 10:30). For more examples see John W. Welch, *Foundation for Ancient Research and Mormon Studies Update*, "Number 24," December 1985; reprinted in *Re-exploring the Book of Mormon*, edited by John W. Welch, [1992], pp. 248-249.

EVIDENCE NO. 787: INCENSE BURNING

<u>Claim</u>: Several features of the ancient American practice of incense burning have a close parallel with the practices of the Near East—providing further support for the Book of Mormon claim that ancient Americans had roots in the Near East. (For those who assume that incense burning was strictly a pre-Christian practice, see Revelation 5:8; 8:3-4).

<u>Evidence</u>: The following is quoted from a paper by John L. Sorensen entitled "Incense-Burning and 'Seer' Stones in Ancient Mesoamerica; New Evidence of Migration of Biblical Peoples to the New World" *University Archaeological Society Newsletter* 21.00, (cited in Christensen, *Progress in Archaeology* [1963], pp. 118-119):

Among many evidences of early contacts between Mesoamerica and the Near East which are coming to light through current research, some of the more striking concern the use of incense. In the Near East, incense was used ceremonially in ancient times probably to a greater extent than anywhere else in the world except Mesoamerica. The importance of incense burning in Hebrew ritual is clear in the Old Testament. Examination of the uses of incense in these two widely- separated areas, the Near East and Mesoamerica, shows many parallels. Some of these are: use in periodic temple rites, in incensing holy objects and officiants, in divinations, in New Year renewal ceremonies, in accompanying sacrifices, etc. In both areas the ascending smoke symbolized prayer rising to heaven. Other details of concept and practice are equally striking.

Confirming these parallels is a remarkable likeness in the incense-burners themselves. Numerous specific details link those found in early highland Guatemalan sites with a type quite common to the Near East about 3000 years ago. Significant is the fact that the likeness is strongest in the earliest pronged examples yet found in Guatemala, dating to perhaps 500 BC, while the same general pronged type had already had a long history in the Near East by then and passed out of fashion soon after.

The complex parallels in ideas, practices, and paraphernalia involving incense in religious ceremonies of both the Near East and Guatemala seem explainable only on the basis of a movement of people from the former area to the latter.

The following comparison is from another paper by John L. Sorenson entitled "The Significance of an Apparent Relationship Between the Ancient Near East and Mesoamerica," SOR-71, *Foundation for Ancient Research and Mormon Studies*, (1971), p. 230-231:

Documentation

Cultural Features	Mesoamerica	Near East
Strong emphasis on incense accompanying most rituals	Kidder, Jennings & Shook, 1946; Tozzer, 1941	Hastings, 1951
As route for ascent of soul	Bancroft, 1883, vol. 2	Pederson, 1945, p. 488; Hastings, 1951
For purification	Tozzer, 1941	Hastings, 1951
For offering to gods, sweet, attractive	Kidder, Jennings & Shook, 1946	Hastings, 1951
Symbolizing prayer	Bancroft, 1883, vol. 3.	Psalms 14:2; Hastings, 1951
To hide holy object in temple by incense smoke	Satterthwaite, 1946	Pederson, 1945, p. 266
Incense procured from trees after ritual preparation of gatherers	Tozzer, 1941, p. 143	Pederson, 1945, p. 357; Hastings, 1951, p. 201
Gum considered the 'blood' of tree that produced it	Tozzer, 1941, p. 142 (rubber)	Pederson, 1945, p. 357 (frankincense)
Association with fertility and rain	Sahagún, 1946; Brinton, 1885	Hastings, 1951
Serpent association*	Hastings, 1951, p. 203	Schaeffer, 1936,
Tall, cylindrical ceramic burners, with Horizontal rows of inverted triangle "windows," and four horns on the rim.	Borhegyi, 1950, 1951; Ferguson, 1958; García Payón 1959	Cook, 1930; May, 1935; Albright, 1942-1943, 1949; McCown, 1947
Limestone burners	Borhegyi, 1951, p. 110	May, 1935, p. 12

* According to Hastings, incense was said to be favored by Quetzalcoatl, represented as the feathered serpent, as a form of bloodless sacrifice, while frankincense was gathered from trees in Arabia that were supposedly guarded by winged serpents.

A. V. Kidder, J. D. Jennings & E. M. Shook, "Excavations at Kaminaljuyu, Guatemala" *Carnegie Institution of Washington, D.C.*, Publication no. 561, (1946), pp. 93, 260.

A. M. Tozzer, editor, "Landa's Relación de las Cosas de Yucatán, a Translation," *Harvard University, Peabody Museum of American Archaeology and Ethnology Papers*, vol. 18 (Cambridge: Peabody Museum, 1941), pp. 142-143, 153, 155, 158, 163-164.

J. Hastings, editor, *Encyclopedia of Religion and Ethics*, (New York, 1951), vol. 7, pp. 201-205.

H. H. Bancroft, *The Native Races of the Pacific States*, (1883), vol. 2, p. 799; vol. 3, p. 7.

J. Pederson, *Israel, Its Life and Culture*, (Copenhagen: 1945), pp. 266, 357, 484.

Linton Satterthwaite, "Incense Burning at Piedras Negras," *Pennsylvania University Museum Bulletin,* (1946) Bulletin number 11.

B. de Sahagún, *Historia General de las Cosas de Nueva España,* edited by M. Acosta Saignes, (Mexico City, 1946) pp. 482-483.

D. Brinton, *The Annals of the Cakchiquels,* (Philadelphia, 1885), p. 14.

C. F. A. Schaeffer, *La Septième Campagne de Fouilles à Ras-Shamra Ugarit,* (Paris, 1936), fig. 3.

S. F. de Borhegyi, "Notas Sobre Sellos de Barro, Existentes en el Museo Nacional de Arqueología y Etnología de Guatemala," *Rev. Instituto de Antropológico Historia de Guatemala,* vol. 2, (1950), pp. 16-26.

S. F. de Borhegyi, "A Study of Three-pronged Incense Burners from Guatemala and Adjacent Areas, *Carnegie Institute of Washington DC, Notes of the Middle American Archaeological and Ethnological Association,* (1951) no. 101.

S. F. de Borhegyi, "Further Notes on Three-pronged Incense Burners and Rim-head Vessels in Guatemala, *Carnegie Institute of Washington DC, Notes of the Middle American Archaeological and Ethnological Association,* (1951) no. 105, p. 112.

T. S. Ferguson, *One Fold and One Shepherd,* (San Francisco, 1958), p. 87.

J. García Payón, "Prehistória de Mesoamérica," *Excavaciones en Trapiche y Chalahuite, Veracruz México,* (1959) Cuadernos de la Facultad de Filosofía, Letras, y Ciencias, Universidad Veracruzana, Xalapa, Vera Cruz, Mexico, p. 49.

H. G. May, "Material Remains of the Megiddo Cult," *University of Chicago Oriental Institute Publications,* vol. 26, p. 12-13.

S. A. Cook, *The Religion of Ancient Palestine in the Light of Archaeology,* (London, 1930), pp. 29-31.

William F. Albright, "The Excavation of Tell Beit Mirsim, *American Schools of Oriental Research Annual,* (1942) vol. 1, pp. 30-31; vol. 3, pp. 28-30;

William F. Albright, *The Archaeology of Palestine,* (Baltimore, 1949), pl. 19.

C. C. McCown, "Tell En-Nasbeh," *Palestine Institute and American Schools of Oriental Research,* (Berkeley, 1947), vol. 1, pp. 211, 236.

EVIDENCE NO. 788: THE ZORAMITE PRAYER

<u>Claim</u>: The Zoramite prayer, as recorded in Alma 31:15-18, provides some interesting details that are parallel to some of the Jewish forms of worship and strengthens the case for the authenticity of the Book of Mormon.

<u>Evidence</u>: J. Heineman reports that the Jewish *Amida* or "standing prayer" (*Shemone–`Esreh*) was a communal prayer which made use of the plural first person pronouns such as "we" and "us," and utilized eighteen benedictions to the "Holy God" in petitions, praise and thanksgiving. (See J. Heineman, *Prayer in The Talmud,* [Berlin: de Gruyter, 1977], pp. 26-29. See also *Berakot 4:3* in the *Babylonian Talmud*; both cited in "Nephite Daily Prayers," *Foundation for Ancient Research and Mormon Studies Update,* Fall, 1986.)

Similarly, the Zoramites stood in prayer, used "we" and "us" in communal form, and repeatedly referred to the "Holy God" six times in their short prayer. But as the FARMS Update indicates, the Zoramite prayer, though similar to the Jewish *Amida,* was obviously "a shocking corruption of what had been a legitimate expression of Israelite piety."

EVIDENCE NO. 789: CHARACTERISTICS OF SACRIFICES

Claim: The Book of Mormon makes frequent reference to the practice of offering sacrifices unto the Lord. For example, see 1 Nephi 5:9; Mosiah 2:3; and Alma 34:10-15. Characteristics of sacrifice in ancient America were similar to those in the ancient Near East. These similarities help prove that ancestors of ancient Americans originated in the Near East as recorded in the Book of Mormon.

Evidence: The following is quoted from a paper by John L. Sorenson entitled "The Significance of an Apparent Relationship Between the Ancient Near East and Mesoamerica," SOR-71, *Foundation for Ancient Research and Mormon Studies*, 1971, p. 232-233:

Cultural Features	Documentation Mesoamerica	Near East
Offerings burned on altar in ceremonial area	Lothrop, 1926	Leviticus 3:2
Communion sense in consumption	Tozzer, 1941, p. 120; Hastings, 1951: vol. 11, p. 6	Leviticus 3
Accompanied by censing. Incense mixed with cereal, as one type of offering.	Tozzer, 1941, pp. 104, 142	Leviticus 2:1-3
Parched grain or meal as offering	Tozzer, 1941, p. 144	Hastings, 1951, vol. 11, p. 34
Blood offered as sacrifice, scattered over area and participants	Lothrop, 1926; Squier, 1860, p. 71	Hastings, 1951, vol. 11, p. 32; Exodus 30:223; Leviticus 1:11; 3:8;
Scape-goat concept	Tozzer, 1941, p. 226	Leviticus 16
Circumcision sacrificial connotation	Loeb, 1923	Loeb, 1923

The following is quoted from Harris regarding the scapegoat concept in Mesoamerica:

> An interesting rite of the scapegoat is described where boys and girls took from a priest some ground maize and incense and threw them into a brazier, which then was mixed with a little wine and carefully taken out of town, "by this they said that the evil spirit had been driven away." The rite of expiation of sins and placation of the gods by a communal ceremony has a woman bearing the sins of all on her shoulders to represent the community to their gods to appease their anger.

> The smearing of the idols with blood in offering sacrifices was also practiced in Yucatan and on the altar and other places by the Israelites. (Diego de Landa, *Relación de las Cosas de Yucatán*, translated by Alfred M. Tozzer, *Harvard University, Peabody Museum of American Archaeology and Ethnology Papers*, [Cambridge: Peabody Museum, 1941], vol. 18, p. 114; Harris, *Book of Mormon Message and Evidence*, [1961], pp. 73-74.)

S. K. Lothrop, "Pottery of Costa Rica and Nicaragua," *Contrib. Museum of the American Indian, Heye Foundation*, (1926), vol. 1, no. 8, p. 71-73.

A. M. Tozzer, editor, "Landa's Relación de las Cosas de Yucatán, a Translation," *Harvard University, Peabody Museum of American Archaeology and Ethnology Papers*, vol. 18 (Cambridge: Peabody Museum, 1941), pp. 104, 110, 120, 144, 142.

J. Hastings, editor, *Encyclopedia of Religion and Ethics*, (New York, 1951), vol. 11, pp. 6, 32, 34.

E. Squier, *Collection of Rare and Original Documents and Relations*, No. 1, "Carta por ...el Lic. Garcia de Palacio, 1576," (New York, 1860), p. 71.

E. Loeb, "The Blood Sacrifice Complex," *Memos of the American Anthropological Association*, (1923), no. 30.

EVIDENCE NO. 790: SERPENT SYMBOLISM

<u>Claim</u>: Snake symbolism in ancient America was similar to that in the ancient Near East. This similarity helps prove that ancestors of ancient Americans originated in the Near East as recorded in the Book of Mormon.

<u>Evidence</u>: The Book of Mormon adds depth and meaning to the Biblical episode in which the children of Israel were bitten by poisonous serpents while in the wilderness (Numbers 21:6-9). It refers to the incident in which Moses caused the children of Israel to be healed by lifting up a brazen serpent as a symbol of the Savior who would also be lifted up to save us from our iniquities (2 Nephi 25:20; Alma 33:19-22; Helaman 8:14-15).

The following gives further evidence of the link between the Old and New World serpent symbolism. It is quoted from a paper by John L. Sorenson "The Significance of an Apparent Relationship Between the Ancient Near East and Mesoamerica," SOR-71, *Foundation for Ancient Research and Mormon Studies*, 1971, p. 234-235:

Documentation

Snake Symbolism	Mesoamerica	Near East
Signifying wisdom, knowledge	Ixtlilxóchitl, 1952	Burrows, 1941
Signifying healing	Ixtlilxóchitl, 1952	Hastings, 1951, vol. 11
'Flying,' feathered serpent	(Quetzalcoatl)	Hastings, 1951, vol. 11, p. 406; Numbers 21:4-9; 2 Kings 18:4
Associated with water holes	Smith, 1919	Hastings, 1951, vol. 11, p. 403
Motif, undulating serpent (or intertwined serpents—see Figure 26)	Vaillant, 1935; Paddock, 1955	Perrot, 1884
Seven-headed serpent motif (see Figure 27)	García Payón, 1948-1949; Ferguson, 1958	Frankfort, 1955
Rain, fertility association	Ferguson, 1958; Caso, 1958	Budge, 1926
Dragon, water-monster association	Thompson, 1950	Hastings, 1951, vol. 4, pp. 128-129, 154

F. De Alva Ixtlilxóchitl, *Obras Históricas,* (Mexico City, 1952), vol. 1, p. 21.

M. Burrows, *What Mean These Stones,* (New Haven, 1941), pp. 106-107.

J. Hastings, editor, *Encyclopedia of Religion and Ethics,* (New York, 1951), vol. 4, pp. 128-129, 154, vol. 11, pp. 403, 406.

G. E. Smith, "Dragons and Rain-gods," *John Rylands Library Bulletin no. 5,* (Manchester, 1919), pp. 317-380.

G. C. Vaillant, "Excavations at El Arbolillo, *American Museum of Natural History Papers,* (1935), vol. 35, p 53.

J. Paddock, "The First Three Seasons at Yagul," *Mesoamerican Notes,* (1955), no. 4, pp. 25-47, Fig. 8a.

G. Perrot, and C. Chipiez, *History of Art in Chaldea and Assyria,* (London, 1884), vol. 1, pp. 286-294.

J. García Payón, "Una 'Palma' in Situ.," *Revista de Mexicano Estudios Antropológicas,* (1948-1949), vol. 10, pp. 121-124.

T. S. Ferguson, *One Fold and One Shepherd,* (San Francisco 1958).

H. Frankfort, *The Art and Architecture of the Ancient Orient,* (Baltimore, 1955), Fig. 13.

A. Caso, *The Aztecs, People of the Sun,* (Norman, Oklahoma, 1958), p. 45.

E. A. T. Budge, *Babylonian Life and History,* Revised Edition, (New York, 1926), p. 132.

J. E. S. Thompson, "Maya Hieroglyphic Writing: Introduction," *Carnegie Institution of Washington DC Publication no. 589,* (1950), pp. 75, 110.

Figure 26. Intertwined serpent-necked felines from Southern Mesopotamia (left) and stylized serpent-necked design (right) of the Mixtec Codex Vienna from Mesoamerica (1350 AD). See Bruce W. Warren and Thomas Stuart Ferguson, *The Messiah in Ancient America*, (1987), pp. 157-158.

Figure 27. Seven-headed serpent from Southern Mesopotamia (left), seven-serpent headed man from El Tajan, Veracruz, Mexico (right). See Warren and Ferguson, *The Messiah*, pp. 160-162.

EVIDENCE NO. 791: BURIAL CUSTOMS

Claim: Characteristics of burial in ancient America were similar to those in the ancient Near East. These similarities confirm the Book of Mormon claim that ancestors of ancient Americans originated in the Near East.

Evidence: The Book of Mormon mentions several instances of burial in Mesoamerica, such as Alma 3:1; 30:1; 57:28; Helaman 9:10. If Joseph Smith had written the Book of Mormon, as critics claim, he would not have mentioned burial, since most Indian tribes of his day did not bury their dead, but laid them on raised platforms until only their bones remained. See Carl Waldman, *Encyclopedia of Native American Tribes,* (Facts on File: 1988), pp. 62, 115; Benjamin Capps, *The Indians,* (Time-Life Books: Alexandria, Virginia, 1973), pp. 120-121.

The following is quoted from an article by Ross T. Christensen entitled "An Egyptian-like Pyramid Discovered in Mesoamerica" (*University Archaeological Society Newsletter,* [BYU: Provo, Utah] vol. 12, p. 2):

One of the most spectacular archaeological discoveries in the western hemisphere occurred in December of 1952, when the jewel-laden tomb of a seventh century AD personage was found beneath the Pyramid-Temple of the Inscriptions at Palenque, southern Mexico.

The presence of a subterranean construction was suspected in 1949, when archaeologist Alberto Ruz of Mexico's *Instituto Nacionál de Antropológia e História* inspected rows of plugged-in holes along the edges of a flagstone in the floor of the temple. Investigation disclosed the uppermost steps of a series of rubble-choked stairways leading down through the 72-foot-high pyramid on which the temple stands, to a point six feet below the level of the surrounding plaza. Here, the skeletons of six victims of human sacrifice and an offering of jade and pearls were found. Beyond, the excavators came upon a crypt, the walls of which were embellished with a frieze showing a procession of nine larger-than-life-sized personages bedecked in elaborate Maya style. In the center of the chamber was a construction, which was at first taken to be a sacrificial altar. The top consisted of a slab of fine, hard stone measuring twelve feet six inches by seven feet two inches by ten inches, upon which was carved in low relief, with exquisite workmanship, the ancient religious symbol of the Tree of Life.

The discovery that the "altar" was hollow prompted Dr. Ruz to lift off the ponderous carved top-slab with the aid of truck jacks. The slab proved to be a lid, and beneath it lay an inner lid. This also was removed and the secret of Palenque lay bared. The "altar" was a sarcophagus! Within lay the moldering remains of a Maya king or priest laid to his last rest around AD 633 and among the bones lay fabulous quantities of beads, rings, and other jewelry fashioned from that most precious substance known to the ancient Maya, jade.

...Further significance may lie in the fact that we have here a generalized Egyptian-like trait: the burial of an important person within or beneath a pyramid-like construction. This trait is exceedingly rare in the New World. Most American "pyramids" have much more in common with the Mesopotamian stepped towers than with Egyptian pyramids in that, unlike the latter, both served as substructures for temples or sanctuaries, rather than as tombs for the dead. Yet, just how rare is this Egyptian-like trait? Will close examination reveal the presence of similar tombs beneath other New World temple pyramids, so well hidden as to have remained heretofore unnoticed? If so, this would also tend to support the Book of Mormon account, since according to that record the homeland of its later peoples of the New World was Palestine, a land which, according to archaeological findings, had long been familiar with Egyptian customs and influenced by them when the original colonies of these peoples departed for the New World. (Quoted in Christensen, *Progress in Archaeology* [1963], pp. 109-110.)

The following is from a paper by John L. Sorenson entitled "The Significance of an Apparent Relationship Between the Ancient Near East and Mesoamerica," SOR-71, Foundation for Ancient Research and Mormon Studies, 1971, p. 229-230:

Documentation

Cultural Features	Mesoamerica	Near East
Burial tomb in elevated structure	Wicke, 1965	Edwards, 1961, (Egypt)
with or without temple atop	Linné, 1942	Hastings, 1951, (Mesopotamia)
with hidden entry	(Palenque)	Edwards, 1961
Conspicuous display of royal tombs	Adams, 1966	Kroeber, 1952: 389-90
Dedicatory sacrifice	Vaillant, 1950	Bailey, 1943
Sub-foundation burial of children	Vaillant, 1950	Hastings, 1951
Urn burial of children	Meggers & Evans, 1963	Macalister, 1912; Free, 1956
Deep-shaft tombs	Covarrubias, 1957	Franken & Franken-Battershill, 1963
Bench, niche arrangement along walls of tombs	(Monte Alban, Kaminaljuyu)	Franken & Franken-Battershill, 1963
Family re-use of tombs	Sellars, 1945	Franken & Franken-Battershill, 1963
Retainer sacrifice	MacLeod, 1923; Tozzer, 1941	
Stone sarcophagus (see Figure 28)	Stirling, 1943	Irwin, 1963
Rope motif surrounding	Stirling, 1943	Irwin, 1963
Ancestor heads preserved	Morley, 1956	
Fires made at burial site upon death of notable	Bancroft, 1883; Kidder, Jennings & Shook, 1946	Pederson, 1945; Jeremiah 34:5; 2 Chronicles 16:14

The complete references for the above evidence are listed below in order of appearance:

C. R. Wicke, "Pyramids and Temple Mounds: Mesoamerican Ceremonial Architecture in Eastern North America," *American Antiquity,* (1965), vol. 30, pp. 409-420.

I. E. S. Edwards, *The Pyramids of Egypt,* (London: 1961), pp. 199-204.

S. Linné, "Mexican Highland Cultures," *Ethnog. Mus. Sweden Pub.,* (1942), n.s., no. 7.

J. Hastings, editor, *Encyclopedia of Religion and Ethics,* (New York, 1951), vol. 1, pp. 690-691; vol. 6, p. 114; vol. 11, p. 32.

R. M. Adams, *The Evolution of Urban Society: Early Mesopotamia and Pre-Hispanic Mexico,* (Chicago: 1966), p. 145.

A. L Kroeber, "The Ancient Oikoumene as a Historical Culture Aggregate," *The Nature of Culture,* (Chicago: 1952), pp. 389-390.

G. C. Vaillant, *The Aztecs of Mexico,* (Bungay, Suffolk: 1950; Garden City, New York: 1941), p. 76.

A. E. Bailey, *Daily Life in Bible Times,* (New York: 1943), Figure 53.

B. J. Meggers and C. Evans, "The Machalilla Culture: An Early Formative Complex on the Ecuadorian Coast," *American Antiquity,* (1962) vol. 28, pp. 186-192, table 2, appendix 1.

R. Macalister, *The Excavations of Gezer,* (London: 1912).

J. P. Free, "The Excavation of Dothan," *Biblical Archaeologist,* (1956), vol. 19, p. 47.

M. Covarrubias, *Indian Art of Mexico and Central America,* (New York: 1957), p. 89.

H. J. Franken, and C. A. Franken-Battershill, *A Primer of Old Testament Archaeology,* (Leiden: 1963), pp. 70-71, 159-160.

O. R. Sellars, "Israelite Belief in Immortality," *Biblical Archaeologist,* (1945) vol. 8, pp. 1-16.

W. C. MacLeod, "On the Diffusion of Central American Culture to Coastal British Columbia and Alaska," *Anthropos,* (1929), vol. 24, p. 424.

A. M. Tozzer, editor, "Landa's Relación de las Cosas de Yucatán, a Translation," *Harvard University, Peabody Museum of American Archaeology and Ethnology Papers*, vol. 18 (Cambridge: Peabody Museum, 1941), pp. 129-130.

M. W. Stirling, "Stone Monuments of Southern Mexico," *Smithsonian Institute, Bur. American Ethnology.,* bulletin no. 143, (1943), p. 59.

C. Irwin, *Fair Gods and Stone Faces,* (New York: 1963), p. 159.

S. G. Morley, *The Ancient Maya,* Third Edition, (Palo Alto, California: 1956), revised by G. W. Brainerd, p. 206.

H. H. Bancroft, *The Native Races of the Pacific States,* (San Francisco: 1883), vol. 2, p. 799.

J. Pederson, *Israel, Its Life and Culture,* (Copenhagen: 1945), p. 484.

A. V. Kidder, J. D. Jennings, and E. M. Shook, "Excavations at Kaminaljuyu, Guatemala, *Carnegie Institute of Washington Publications,* (1946), no. 561, p. 93.

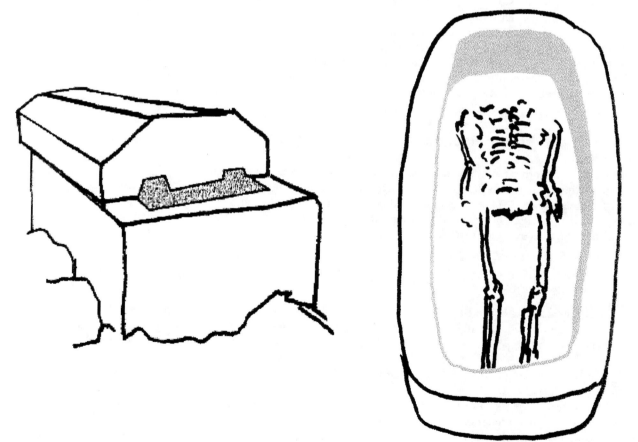

Figure 28. Sarcophagi from Egypt (left) and Mesoamerica (right). See Thomas Stuart Ferguson, *One Fold and One Shepherd,* (San Francisco, 1958), p. 105.

EVIDENCE NO. 792: THE DEATH OF LABAN

Claim: The Book of Mormon relates an incident in which Nephi was told by the Lord to take the life of Laban. Nephi, being a righteous man—with no desire to shed blood, delayed in his obedience to the Lord. Finally, after being commanded by the Lord three different times, Nephi obeyed (1 Nephi 4:6-18).

Evidence: Some have wondered if God could have actually ordained such an event for righteous purposes. However, we find God commanding actions similar to that of Nephi in several Biblical passages. See, for example, Exodus 2:11-16; 1 Kings 18:40; 2 Kings 2:23-4; 10:1,7,11,30; 1 Samuel 15:33; Judges 7:20-22; Psalms 144:1; Jeremiah 48:10; Matthew 15:4; 18:5- 6; Mark 9:42; Luke 17:2; 19:27; Romans 1:28, 32.

According to Israelite law, it was a sin to lie in wait to slay someone—even if the victim deserved to die. It is clear from Nephi's account that he was careful to follow the letter and the spirit of this law. He did not lie in wait to slay Laban, rather he was "led by the spirit, not knowing beforehand the things which [he] should do" (1 Nephi 4:6). The spirit told Nephi that "the Lord hath delivered him into [his] hand" (1 Nephi 4:11). This is the very wording of the law (Exodus 21:12-14). The law further specifies that those who slay a person under such circumstances must flee to an appointed place. This Nephi also did.

Dr. Hugh Nibley tells of an incident in which he was discussing the death of Laban before a class that included a few Arab students. Dr. Nibley was prepared to justify this event against the usual objections typical of Western students. However, from the Arab students came a much different response. They questioned the authenticity of the Book of Mormon for the simple reason that it took Nephi too long to do the deed. They could not understand why it was necessary for God to command Nephi three times before he obeyed. The Nephi-Laban incident, which often invites protests of shock and disgust from Western readers, easily fits into the setting of the Mid-Eastern culture. See Nibley, *An Approach to the Book of Mormon* (1957), Preface, p. viii.

Four Evidences Concerning the Execution of Zemnarihah

The Book of Mormon contains the narration of a strange execution (3 Nephi 4:28-33). By western standards it was strange for four reasons: (1) A man was hanged rather than stoned; (2) after the accused was dead, the tree was chopped down; (3) the execution was done before all the people; and (4) the people shouted "with one voice" as if it were a common recitation. Some have questioned the authenticity of these strange proceedings and ridiculed them as evidence that the Book of Mormon was the product of Joseph Smith's fertile imagination.

EVIDENCE NO. 793: EXECUTION BY HANGING

Claim: The account in the Book of Mormon of the hanging of Zemnarihah (3 Nephi 4:28-33) is consistent with occasional Jewish practice in Old Testament times, even though execution by stoning was much more common. This consistency supports the Book of Mormon claim of transoceanic influence in ancient America.

Evidence: According to the *Foundation for Ancient Research and Mormon Studies Update*, November 1984:

> The text suggests that the Nephites read Deuteronomy 21:22 as allowing execution by hanging—a reading which the rabbis saw as possible. While they viewed hanging as a means only of exposing the dead body after it had been stoned, they were aware of a penalty of "hanging until death occurs." For example, there were rare Jewish instances of hanging: 70 women were "hung" in Ashkelon and 800 Pharisees were crucified by Alexander Jannaeus the High Priest (Josephus, *War*, 1:97) but the rabbis rejected that means of execution, since this was "as the government does." *Babylonian Talmud*, Sanhedrin, VI. 5-6. (See John W. Welch, *Re-exploring the Book of Mormon*, [1992], pp. 250-252.)

EVIDENCE NO. 794: THE TREE WAS FELLED

<u>Claim</u>: The account in the Book of Mormon of cutting down the tree which Zemnarihah was hanged is similar to Jewish practice in Old Testament times.

<u>Evidence</u>: The *FARMS Update* continues:

Was this ever done in antiquity? Apparently it was. For one thing, Israelite practice required that the tree upon which the culprit was hung be buried with the body. Hence the tree had to be chopped down. Since the Rabbis understood that this burial should take place immediately, the *Babylonian Talmud, Sanhedrin* VI. 6, recommends hanging the culprit on a detached tree so that, in the words of Maimonides, "no felling is needed." (*Code of Maimonides, Sanhedrin*, XV .9.)

Second, consider why the tree was chopped down and buried. As Maimonides explains: "In order that it should not serve as a sad reminder, people saying: 'This is the tree on which so-and-so was hanged.'" In this way, the tree became associated with the person being executed. In a similar way, the Nephites identified the tree with Zemnarihah and all those like him, when they cried out: "May [the Lord] cause to be felled to the earth all who shall seek to slay [the Lord's people]...even as this man hath been felled to the earth" (3 Nephi 4:29). See John W. Welch, *Re-exploring the Book of Mormon*, (1992), pp. 250-252.

EVIDENCE NO. 795: THE EXECUTION BEFORE ALL THE PEOPLE

<u>Claim</u>: The account in the Book of Mormon of executing Zemnarihah in front of the people is similar to Jewish practice during Old Testament times.

<u>Evidence</u>: The *FARMS Update* suggests that the reason the execution was done before all the people was that it followed the ancient Mid-Eastern practice that the punishment should be fashioned to fit the crime.

For example, if a thief broke into a house, under Section 21 of the Babylonian Code of Hammurabi, he was to be put to death and "hung in front of the place where he broke in." Punishment was often related symbolically to the offense. Likewise, under Section 2 of those laws (compare Deuteronomy 19:19), the punishment for a false accuser was to m ake him suffer that which would have happened to the person he falsely accused. In Zemnarihah's case, he was hung in front of the very nation he had tried to destroy, and he was "felled to the earth" much as he had tried to bring that nation down. (See John W. Welch, *Re-exploring the Book of Mormon*, [1992], pp. 250-252.)

EVIDENCE NO. 796: THE LOUD CHANT IN UNISON

<u>Claim</u>: The account in the Book of Mormon of the people chanting loudly at the execution of Zemnarihah is similar to ancient Jewish practice during Old Testament times.

<u>Evidence</u>: The *FARMS Update* concludes with the following observations:

The people all chanting loudly, proclaiming the wickedness of Zemnarihah, may be reminiscent of the ancient practice of heralding a notorious execution. Deuteronomy 19:20 says that "those which remain shall hear, and fear, and shall henceforth commit no more any such evil among you." How was this to be accomplished? Rabbi Jehudah explained: "I say that he is executed immediately and messengers are sent out to notify the people." Indeed, public matters, such as the execution of a rebelling judge (3 Nephi 6:23, 28), had to be heralded. An even clearer example of heralding is found in Alma 30:57. In both these cases, it appears, the requirement of publishing the wickedness of the culprit was satisfied, that all who remained would "hear and fear" and the evil would be removed from among God's people. (See *Babylonian Talmud*, Sanhedrin X.6; John W. Welch, *Re-exploring the Book of Mormon*, [1992], pp. 250-252.)

EVIDENCE NO. 797: WORLD DIVIDED INTO FOUR QUARTERS

Claim: Methods of designating world quarters in ancient America were similar to those in the ancient Near East. These similarities help prove that ancestors of ancient Americans originated in the Near East as recorded in the Book of Mormon. The Book of Mormon discusses this concept in such references as 1 Nephi 19:16; 22:25; 2 Nephi 10:8; 21:12; 3 Nephi 5:24-26; 16:5; Ether 13:11.

Evidence: The following is from a paper by John L. Sorenson entitled "The Significance of an Apparent Relationship Between the Ancient Near East and Mesoamerica," SOR-71, Foundation for Ancient Research and Mormon Studies, 1971, p. 228:

Documentation

Cultural Features	Mesoamerica	Near East
World quarters, symbolized by colors	Nuttall, 1901	Nuttall, 1901
Symbolized by patolli-parchisi[1] game		Culin, 1898; Piggott, 1950
Symbolized by swastika	Nuttall, 1901	
Symbolized by cross within a cross (see Figure 29)	Ferguson, 1958	Frankfort, 1939:
Symbolized by pattée cross (see Figure 30)	Covarrubias, 1946	Perrot, 1884

[1] Indian parcheesi was known as far west as Syria. A similar dice game was shared between Sumer and the Inus Valley as early as the Early Bronze Age (Piggott, 1950).

The complete references for the above evidence are listed below in order of appearance:

Z. Nuttall, "The fundamental principles of Old and New World civilization," *Papers of Peabody Museum*, (Harvard University: 1901), vol. 2, pp. 143-146.

S. Culin, "Chess and Playing Cards," *United States Natural Museum Report*, (1896), p. 854.

S. Piggott, *Prehistoric India to 1000 BC*, (Baltimore: 1950), p. 190-191.

M. Covarrubias, *Mexico South, The Isthmus of Tehuantepec*, (New York: 1946) p. 134.

A. Perrot, *Ziggurates et Tour de Babel*, (Paris: 1949) 1, pp. 286-294.

T. S. Ferguson, *One Fold and One Shepherd*, (San Francisco, 1958) pp. 102-103.

H. Frankfort, *Cylinder Seals*, (London: 1939) pl. 30.

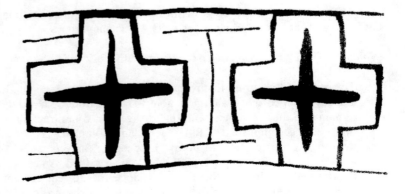

Figure 29. A Cross within a cross from Southern Mesopotamia about 2000 BC (left), and from Monte Alban, Oaxaca, Mexico. See Warren and Ferguson, *The Messiah in Ancient America*, (1987), p. 171.

Figure 30. An Assyrian pattée (Maya Kan) cross on breast, from Nineveh about 800 BC (left). Two renderings of Quetzalcoatl from ancient Mexico with the pattée cross on the shield. See Warren and Ferguson, *The Messiah*, (1987), pp. 104, 169; and Ferguson, *One Fold*, (1958), p. 102.

EVIDENCE NO. 798: TREE SYMBOLISM

Claim: Tree symbolism in ancient America was similar to that in the ancient Near East. This similarity helps prove that ancestors of ancient Americans originated in the Near East as recorded in the Book of Mormon. *The tree of life*, first mentioned in chapters 2 and 3 of Genesis, is given great emphasis in the Book of Mormon. It is mentioned sixteen times throughout the Book of Mormon, starting with 1 Nephi 8:10, where it is a symbol of major focus in Lehi's dream. The recurring references to the tree of life in ancient literature of both the old and new worlds verifies the teachings of the Book of Mormon and provides evidence that the Mesoamericans did indeed migrate from the Middle East as it claims.

Evidence: The tree of life was also a sacred symbol of great importance among the peoples of the ancient Middle East. See Layard, *Monuments of Nineveh,* and Hugo Gressman, *The Tower of Babel* (1928), Fig. 3. and discussion relating thereto. The Cakchikeles of Guatemala (close relatives of the Mayas) call themselves descendants of the tree of life. See Sylvanus Morley, *The Ancient Maya,* [1946], pp. 8, 221; cited in Hunter and Ferguson, *Ancient America and the Book of Mormon,* p. 214.

The ancient Americans called their tree of life *Quiahuiteotlchica-hualizteotl* or *Quiauhtzteotlchicahualizteotl,* which means "the God of rains and of health and *the tree of sustenance or of life.*" The ancient Americans worshipped the tree of life as the first tree in the world. (Andres de Avendano y Loyola, *Relación de las dos Entrades que hize a Peten Ytza,* [1697], English translation by Philip Ainsworth Means cited in *History of the Conquest of Yucatan and of the Itzas,* [1917], p. 135.)

The ancient Maya called themselves descendants of the tree of life. See Paul Henning, Francisco Plancarte, Cecilio A. Robelo and Paul Gonzalez, "Tamoanchan Estudio Arqueológicos e Histórico," in *Añales del Museo Nacionál de Arqueológica,* vol. 4, pp. 433-462. Above sources cited in Hunter and Ferguson, *Ancient America and the Book of Mormon,* (1950), pp. 211-214. See also Alma M. Reed, *The Ancient Past of Mexico* (New York: Crown Publishers, 1966), p. 11 cited in Cheesman, *The World of the Book of Mormon,* (1978), p. 2; and Mackenzie, *Migration of Symbols,* p. 170; Diego de Landa, *Relación de las Cosas de Yucatán,* translated by Alfred M. Tozzer, *Harvard University, Peabody Museum of American Archaeology and Ethnology Papers,* (Cambridge: Peabody Museum, 1941), vol. 18, pp. 131, 194, both cited in Harris, *The Book of Mormon Message and Evidence* (1961), p. 79.

The following is quoted from a paper by John L. Sorenson entitled "The Significance of an Apparent Relationship Between the Ancient Near East and Mesoamerica," SOR-71, *Foundation for Ancient Research and Mormon Studies*, 1971, p. 236-237:

Documentation

Cultural Features	Mesoamerica	Near East
"Tree of Life" scene representations include: tree in center, two (or four) figures facing—one (or two) each side, serpent/monster element beneath, and bird/(winged) motif above (see Figures 31 & 32)	Briggs, 1950	Briggs, 1950
'Tree of God' Cedar[1]	Tozzer, 1941, p. 197	Hastings, 1951, vol. 2; James, 1966, p. 33
Named after deity	Tozzer, 1941, p. 197	James, 1966, p. 33
Sacred tree bears blue/green stone[2]	Henning, 1911	James, 1966, p. 13; Kramer, 1952; Kunz, 1938
Tree representing a people	Henning, 1911	Henning, 1911; Ezekiel 17; Genesis 49:22; Isaiah 61:3
World tree spreading protectively over all[3] rooted at contact with upper and underworld point. Route for upward and downward movement.	Thompson, 1950; Tozzer, 1961, pp. 131-132; Holland, 1964	James, 1966, pp. 13, 143

[1.] Cedar of Yucatan was called kuche, "tree of God"; it was the preferred wood for idol-making. In Babylonia the sacred cedar had the name of Ea written in its core (Hastings, 1951, vol. 12, p. 456); at Susa the cuneiform sign for cedar tree was part of the name of the dominant deity (Hastings, 1951, vol. 2, p. 705).

[2.] Jade is referred to figuratively as the "heart" of the maize plant (which appears as the "tree" of life); a codex apparently represents jade leaves; jade, "the exudation of leaves," was fed to the infant ancestors of some Middle American peoples. In Mesopotamia the sacred kiskana tree was shown with leaves that appear to be lapis lazuli; the Epic of Gilgamesh mentions the tree of life bearing lapis lazuli fruit.

[3.] See E. W. Count, "The Earth-driver and the Rival Twins: A Clue to Time Correlation in North-Eurasiatic and North American Mythology," *Indian Tribes of Aboriginal America,* edited by S. Tax, (Chicago, 1952), pp. 55-62 where this and other folkloric motifs, not all mentioned in this paper, are considered as to significance for inter-hemispheric movement.

A. M. Tozzer, editor, "Landa's Relación de las Cosas de Yucatán, a Translation," *Harvard University, Peabody Museum of American Archaeology and Ethnology Papers,* vol. 18 (Cambridge: Peabody Museum, 1941), pp. 131-132, 197.

J. Hastings, editor, *Encyclopedia of Religion and Ethics,* (New York, 1951), vol. 1, pp. 690-691; vol. 6, p. 114; vol. 2, p. 705.

E. O. James, *The Tree of Life,* (Leiden, 1966), pp. 13, 33, 143.

P. Henning, "Apuntes Sobre la Historia del Chalchiuitl en América," *Mem. Sociedad "Alzate,"* no. 31, pp. 29-46.

S. N. Kramer, *Enmerkar and the Lord of Aratta,* (Philadelphia, 1952), vol. 2, pp. 620-626.

G. Kunz, *The Curious Lore of Precious Stones,* (New York, 1938), pp. 232-238.

J. E. S. Thompson, "Maya Hieroglyphic writing: Introduction," *Carnegie Institution of Washington, D.C.,* (1950), Publication number 589, p. 71.

W. R. Holland, "Contemporary Txotxil Coxmological Concepts as a Basis for Interpreting Prehistoric Maya Civilization," *American Antiquity,* (1964), vol. 29, p. 303.

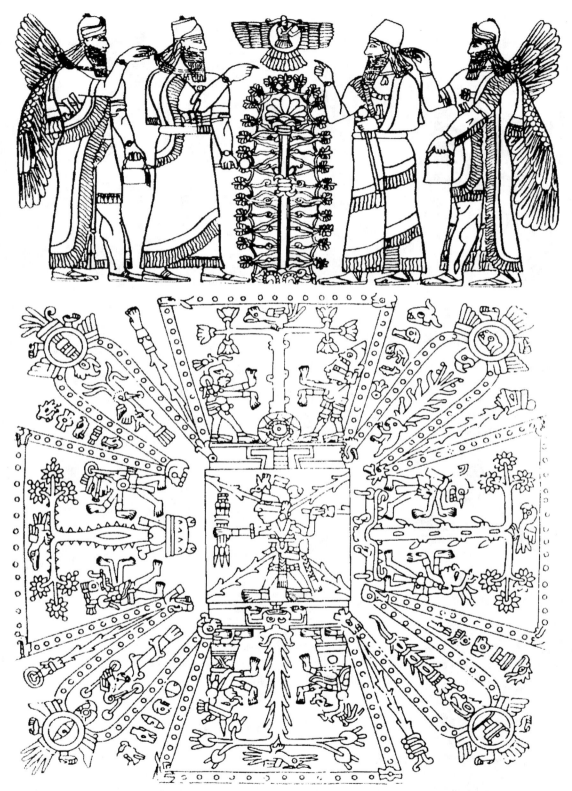

Figure 31. Ancient *Tree of Life* scenes. Assyrian Tree of Life from Nineveh in the eighth century BC (top), and directional Trees of Life from the first page of the Codex Fejervary-Mayer from Central Mexico, fourteenth century AD (bottom). See Warren and Ferguson, *The Messiah*, (1987), p. 78.

Figure 32. Tree of Life scenes from the Maya Codex Dresden, page 3, 1000 AD (left), and from the tomb lid of Pacal in the Temple of the Inscriptions at Palenque, Chiapas, Mexico (right). See Warren and Ferguson, *The Messiah,* **(1987), pp. 79, 148. See also pp. 77-88.**

Legend, Folklore and Superstition

<u>Claim</u>: The following several evidences compare Mesoamerican legends, folklore and superstitions with those of the ancient Near East. They provide further evidence that the ancient Americans borrowed much of their culture from their ancestral home in the near east as claimed by the Book of Mormon (1 Nephi 1:2; 2 Nephi 25:1-6; Alma 16:13).

EVIDENCE NO. 799: RELIGIOUS AND HISTORICAL BELIEFS

<u>Evidence</u>: Features in ancient American beliefs were similar to those in the ancient Near East. These similarities help substantiate that ancestors of ancient Americans originated in the Near East as recorded in the Book of Mormon. Some of the Book of Mormon beliefs regarding heaven and hell can be found in the following citations: 1 Nephi 12:16-17; 14:3-4; 2 Nephi 1:13-15; 9:13; Alma 40:11-14; 4 Nephi 1:14; Moroni 10:34.

The following is from a paper by John L. Sorenson entitled "The Significance of an Apparent Relationship Between the Ancient Near East and Mesoamerica," SOR-71, *Foundation for Ancient Research and Mormon Studies*, 1971, p. 239:

Documentation

Cultural Features	Mesoamerica	Near East
Paradise concept	Tozzer, 1941	James, 1966
Underworld, "hell" concept	Tozzer, 1941	Smith, 1966; Sellars, 1945
Dualism	Thompson, 1950b	Briggs, 1955; Count, 1952
Earth, air, fire, water as basic elements[1]	Nuttall, 1901	Nuttall, 1901
Deluge motif	Moura Pessoa, 1950	Genesis 6-8
A few persons saved in a vessel		
Bird sent forth to check drying		
Tower built for safety against future deluge	Bancroft, 1883	Genesis 11
Destroyed by being blown down by wind[2]	Ixtlilxóchitl, 1952	Parrot, 1949

[1] Nuttall reports the concept(s) present in Greece and perhaps in India as early as the seventh century BC The intervening area likely shared them, too.

[2] Note that this destruction concept is not biblical, hence unlikely to have been transmitted by Spanish missionaries.

A. M. Tozzer, editor, "Landa's Relación de las Cosas de Yucatán, a Translation," *Harvard University, Peabody Museum of American Archaeology and Ethnology Papers*, vol. 18 (Cambridge: Peabody Museum, 1941), vol. 18, pp. 131-132.

E. O. James, *The Tree of Life*, (Leiden, 1966), p. 74.

R. H. Smith, "The household lamps of Palestine in Old Testament times," *Biblical Archaeologist*, (1966) vol. 27, p. 11.

O. R. Sellars, "Israelite belief in immortality," *Biblical Archaeologist*, (1945), vol. 8, pp. 1-16.

J. E. S. Thompson, "Maya hieroglyphic writing: introduction," *Carnegie Institute of Washington, DC*, Publication no. 589, (1950), p. 83.

C. W. Briggs, "Eastern sage to western man," *Rev. Religion*, vol. 19, pp. 115-130.

E. W. Count, "The earth-driver and the rival twins: a clue to time correlation in North-Eurasiatic and North American mythology," *Indian Tribes of Aboriginal America*, edited by S. Tax, (Chicago: 1952), pp. 55-62.

Z. Nuttall, "The fundamental principles of Old and New World civilization," *Papers of Peabody Museum*, (Harvard University: 1901), vol. 2, pp. 143-146.

M. Moura Pessoa, "O Mito do Diluvias nas Americas," *Rev. Mus. Paulista*, (São Paulo, Brazil, 1950), n.s., vol. 4, pp. 7-48.

H. H. Bancroft, *The Native Races of the Pacific States*, (San Francisco: 1883), vol. 5, p. 200.

F. de Alva Ixtlilxóchitl, *Obras Históricas*, (Mexico City: 1952), vol. 1, p. 21.

A. Parrot, *Ziggurats et Tour de Babel*, (Paris: 1949), pp. 33-36.

EVIDENCE NO. 800:   COSMOLOGICAL SYMBOLISM IN MESOAMERICA

Evidence: Astronomy was well developed and stellar symbolism was rich in Mesoamerica and in the Near East. Figure 33 below depicts the "churning of the Milky Way" as viewed in both the Old and New Worlds. The Biblical gospels of Matthew and Luke speak of the wise men that followed the signs in the heavens in order to find the Christ-child. For Mesoamerican sources, see S. G. Morley, *The Ancient Maya,* Third Edition, (Palo Alto, California: 1956), revised by G. W. Brainerd, pp. 304-311; and Diego de Landa, *Relación de las Cosas de Yucatán,* translated by Alfred M. Tozzer, *Harvard University, Peabody Museum of American Archaeology and Ethnology Papers,* [Cambridge: Peabody Museum, 1941], vol. 18, pp. 132-138, both cited in Sorenson, "The Book of Mormon as a Mesoamerican Codex," (*The Society for Early Historic Archaeology*, 1976), p. 5.

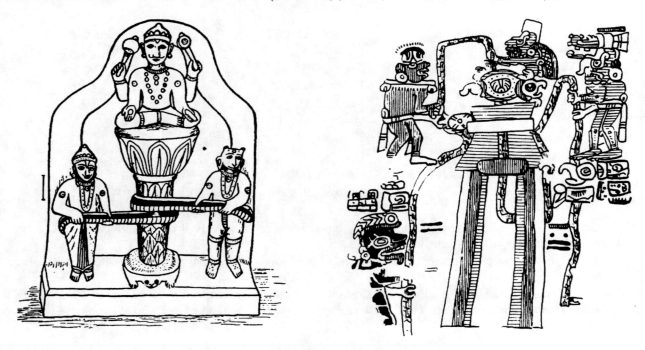

Figure 33. The churning of the Milky Way, a Hindu example (left) and a Mayan Example (right) from the Maya Codex Madrid. See Warren and Ferguson, *The Messiah in Ancient America,* (1987), pp. 192-193.

EVIDENCE NO. 801:   DIVINATION IN ANCIENT TIMES

Evidence: Both the Mesoamerican and the ancient inhabitants of the Near East looked to the stars as a means of divining the future. In the Book of Mormon, the new star along with other "signs and wonders" in the heavens were used to divine the time of Christ's birth in the Old World (3 Nephi 1:21). The Book of Mormon also speaks of other signs and wonders in the heavens (for example, see 2 Nephi 26:8; 23:10; 25:3; Alma 18:30-32; 30:44; Helaman 12:14-15).

Furthermore, both cultures practiced captoptromancy (mirror gazing). See *Encyclopedia of Religion and Ethics,* edited by J. Hastings, (New York, 1951), vol. 4, pp. 780-782, 807; J. E. S. Thompson, *The Rise and Fall of Maya Civilization,* (Norman, Oklahoma, 1954) p. 138; T. Besterman, *Crystal Gazing,* (New Hyde Park: New York, 1965), pp. 73-77; *The Jaguar's Children,* edited by M. Coe, (Museum of Primitive Art: New York, 1965); All sources cited in John L. Sorenson, "The Significance of an Apparent Relationship Between the Ancient Near East and Mesoamerica," SOR-71, *Foundation for Ancient Research and Mormon Studies*, 1971, p. 233.

Critics who dismiss the Book of Mormon as occultic literature simply because it mentions prophets of God looking for signs of divine guidance should consult their own Bible. The following passages demonstrate that men of God believed in such forms of divination in Biblical times. For examples of Biblical aeromancy (seeking for signs in the skies) see Genesis 9:12-17; Numbers 24:7; Judges 4:5; 5:20; Daniel 5:11 and Matthew 2:1-2.

Additionally, the following types of divination are alluded to in the Bible:

1. Aeromancy (seeking for signs in the skies) Genesis 9:12-17.
2. Alectryomancy (seeking for signs from birds and chickens) Genesis 8:7-12; Matthew 26:34; Mark 14:30; Luke 3:22; Luke 22:34.
3. Alphitomancy (signs of guilt by trial of ordeal) Numbers 5:15-22.
4. Anmiomancy (signs observed in entrails) 1 Samuel 16:6-7; Psalms 7:9; 16:7; 26:2.
5. Astrology (seeking for signs in the stars) Judges 5:20; Daniel 5:11-12; Matthew 2:1-2; Revelation 8:10.
6. Austromancy (signs in the wind: direction, sounds, damaged caused, etc.) 2 Samuel 5:22-24; Acts 2:1-4.
7. Axinomancy (signs from hatchets and axes) 2 Kings 6:5-7.
8. Belomancy (signs from arrows) 1 Samuel 20:20-22; 2 Sam.22:15; 2 Kings 13:17; Psalms 7:13; Ezekiel 5:16.
9. Botanomancy (seeking signs in leaves) Genesis 8:11; Matthew 24:32.
10. Capnomancy (seeking signs in smoke or clouds) Exodus 13:21-22; Deuteronomy 29:20; Psalms 74:1; Isaiah 6:4; 44:22; Revelation 8:4; 15:8.
11. Catoptromancy (seeking signs through glass or mirrors) 1 Corinthians 13:12; 2 Corinthians 3:18.
12. Cleromancy (casting lots) Joshua 18:6; Jonah 1:7; Acts 1:26.
13. Geomancy (seeking signs in random lines found in the dirt) Psalms 19:1-4.
14. Hydromancy (signs in water) Exodus 7:19-20; Judges 6:36-40; 1Kings 17:1; Revelation 17:15.
15. Lampadomancy (using fires, lamps and candles) Exodus 3:2; 13:21-22; Leviticus 9:24; Judges 6:21; 1 Kings 18:24,38; Revelation 1:14; 4:5; 8:10.
16. Margaritomancy (seeking signs in pearls) Matthew 13:46; Revelation 21:21.
17. Necromancy (signs from the spirits of the dead) 1 Samuel 28:3-20.
18. Numerology (signs in numbers) Revelation 13:18.
19. Onieromancy (signs from dreams) Genesis 37:9-10; 40:5-19; 41:1-32; 1 Samuel 28:6, 15; Daniel 2:1-45; Joel 2:28; Acts 2:17.
20. Palmistry (palm reading) 1 Samuel 26:18; Job 37:7; Proverbs 3:16; Isaiah 49:16.
21. Rhabdomancy (seeking for signs with the use of divining or dowsing rods, wands, witching forks, arrows, sticks, etc.) Exodus 17:6; Numbers 17:8; Hosea 4:12.
22. Stones and pebbles for divination Exodus 28:13-30; Leviticus 8:8; Numbers 27:21; Deuteronomy 33:8; 1 Samuel 28:6; Ezra 2:63; Nehemiah 7:65; Revelation 2:17.
23. Tasseography (cup divination) Genesis 44:1-5, possibly alluded to in Psalms 116:13.

EVIDENCE NO. 802: THE LAYERED COSMOS

Evidence: Just as the Near Easterners viewed the heavens, Book of Mormon prophets inferred that the cosmos existed in layered fashion, with multiple realms above and below the earth. (See, for example, 1 Nephi 1:3; Alma 1:15; 18:30 which refer to the plural heavens, and 1 Nephi 12:16; 14:3; 2 Nephi 24:9; Moroni 8:14; Mosiah 13:12 which refer to the underworld.)

Dr. Caroll L. Riley has verified that the Mesoamericans as well as the Near Easterners believed in a layered cosmos, with multiple realms above the earth's surface between, and in one or more underworlds. (See *Man Across the Sea, Problems of Pre-Columbian Contacts,* edited by Caroll L. Riley [Austin & London: University of Texas Press, 1971], p. 227; also cited in Sorenson, "The Book of Mormon as a Mesoamerican Codex," [The Society for Early Historic Archaeology, 1976], p. 7.)

EVIDENCE NO. 803: FLOWING VASES OF THE OLD AND NEW WORLDS

<u>Evidence</u>: The Babylonian "lord of the watery deep," *Enki,* is often depicted in ancient artwork as holding a vase, out of which flows two streams that represent the Milky Way. This theme has been found in Mesopotamia, as well as ancient Oaxaca Mexico. Several examples of this theme are shown below.

Figure 34. Flowing vases in the hands and at the feet of a king from Lagash, Iraq (top left). Flowing vase from Ur in ancient Mesopotamia about 2000 BC (top right). Flowing vase in the hands of a goddess about 2400 BC from ancient Mesopotamia (middle right). Sumerian King Gudea, holding the flowing vase about 2100 BC (bottom left). A person holding a flowing vase from a Zapotec urn of ancient Oaxaca, Mexico (bottom middle). Zapotec urn also from Oaxaca, Mexico, with the flowing vase (bottom right). See Warren and Ferguson, *The Messiah in Ancient America,* (1987), pp. 138-145.

EVIDENCE NO. 804: MONSTERS BELIEVED TO INHABIT THE SUBTERRANEAN WATERS

Evidence: The Book of Mormon indicates that some people of that period believed in monsters or dragons of some kind which supposedly inhabited the subterranean waters (2 Nephi 8:9; 9:10, 19, 26; 23:22; Mosiah 20:11; Alma 43:44).

This is also verified by modern research from Mesoamerica: See J. Eric Thompson, "Maya Hieroglyphic Writing: Introduction," in *Man Across the Sea, Problems of Pre-Columbian Contacts,* edited by Caroll L. Riley [Austin & London: University of Texas Press, 1971], p. 227. From the Near East: See William F. Allbright, *Yahweh and The Gods of Canaan, A Historical Analysis of Two Contrasting Faiths,* (Garden City, New York: Doubleday, 1968), pp. 92-93, 97, 184-185, 201, 227, also cited in Sorenson, "The Book of Mormon as a Mesoamerican Codex," (The Society for Early Historic Archaeology, 1976), p. 7.

Some critics have branded the Book of Mormon occultic or paganistic because of its mention of monsters and dragons. However, such are unwittingly condemning the Bible, which contains similar imagery. Indeed the Bible speaks of such mythological creatures as the *Behemoth* which could drink up whole rivers (Job 40:15-24), the *cockatrice* (Isaiah 11:8), *dragons,* (Isaiah 11:8; 13:21-22; 27:1; 43:20; Ezekiel 29:5; Psalms 143:7; the fire breathing *leviathan* (Job 41), the *satyr* (Isaiah 13:21-22), *sea dragons* and *sea serpents* (Psalms 74:13; Isaiah 27:1), and even the *unicorn* (Numbers 23:2; 24:8; Deuteronomy 33:17; Job 39:9-10; Psalms 22:21; 29:6; 92:10; and Isaiah 34:7).

EVIDENCE NO. 805: CAVES AND WATER HOLES CONNECTED WITH THE LOWER WORLD

Evidence: The Book of Mormon compares the depths of certain waters with the depths of hell (see 1 Nephi 12:16; 15:27).

Non-Mormon scholars have found that the ancient mind in the Near East as well as in the early Americas, regarded caves and water holes as being connected with the lower world. (See the same sources cited as evidence for ELEVATIONS AS CONTACT POINTS WITH THE HEAVENS.) The areas below the surface of the earth were thought to be primal water that might flow above ground from certain locations. This subterranean water was usually connoted as evil. (See Caroll L. Riley, "The Significance of an Apparent Relationship between the Ancient Near East and Mesoamerica," in *Man Across the Sea, Problems of Pre-Columbian Contacts,* Edited by Riley et al. [Austin & London: University of Texas Press, 1971], p. 227; J. E. S. Thompson, "Maya Hieroglyphic Writing: Introduction," *Carnegie Institute of Washington, DC,* Publication 589, [1950], p. 72; William F. Allbright, *Yahweh and the Gods of Canaan, A Historical Analysis of Two Contrasting Faiths* [Garden City, New York: Doubleday, 1968], pp. 92-93, 97, 184-185, 201, 227; J. E. S. Thompson, *Maya History and Religion* [Norman: University of Oklahoma Press, 1971], p. 184. All above sources also cited in Sorenson, "The Book of Mormon as a Mesoamerican Codex" [The Society for Early Historic Archaeology, 1976], p. 7.)

EVIDENCE NO. 806: THE CITY OF ENOCH

Evidence: The *Book of Moses* in the *Pearl of Great Price* was revealed to the prophet Joseph Smith as he was working on the inspired translation of the Bible between June of 1830 and February of 1831. It tells of a city "called the City of Holiness, even ZION" which was built by Enoch the father of Methuselah. The residents of Enoch's city "were of one heart and one mind, and dwelt in righteousness; and there was no poor among them." Eventually the entire City of Enoch was taken up into heaven (Moses 7:18-27, 69).

The Book of Mormon claims that the ancient inhabitants of the Americas had with them a record containing the history found in the Old Testament (1 Nephi 5:10-13), which undoubtedly would have contained the account of Enoch's city and its departure into heaven. A strikingly similar legend is found among the Maricopa Indians, which provides further evidence that the Native Americans came from the Middle East, and that they did indeed have knowledge of the history of the Old Testament.

In November 1926, Burns French, a Maricopa Indian boy, told the following to the Chandler—Gilbert Seminary, on the Salt River Indian Reservation. It is quoted from J. W. Lesuerur, *Indian Legends,* (1927), p. 69, also cited in Joshua M. Bennett, *The Gospel of the Great Spirit,* (1990), pp. 71-72.

> Long, long time ago, so the story goes among my people, when our people lived way south of here, some hunters traveled a long ways from home toward the East on a hunting trip. After going on and on they finally reached the great waters (ocean), then hunting there a long time, they decided to return to their home in the West, returning in the same way they had traveled, and following their tracks.

> Something strange had happed while they were away, as the tracks led right into a large body of water and they could not understand it—how there was water now where before was land—but looking upward they saw the land high in the sky and still going farther and farther until it finally went out of sight. All the people on the land went up with it, and have never come back. Many of the people had relatives and friends living on the land that was taken away and they mourned because they were gone.

The fact that the account of Enoch's city has a parallel in Native American tradition is especially significant since the account is not found in the modern versions of the Bible. Therefore, it would not have been possible for the Native Americans to learn of Enoch and his city from the early Christian missionaries. (See also the evidence CITIES OF ENOCH AND ZION in the chapter on the Pearl of Great Price in volume 1 of this work.)

EVIDENCE NO. 807: ELEVATIONS AS CONTACT POINTS WITH THE HEAVENS

Evidence: The Book of Mormon alludes to an apparent belief among the Mesoamericans that elevations, such as mountains, were contact points with the multiple realms above (1 Nephi 11:1).

This has also been verified by modern research from Mesoamerica: See *Man Across the Sea, Problems of Pre-Columbian Contacts,* edited by Caroll L. Riley (Austin & London: University of Texas Press, 1971), p. 227; and "Landa's Relación de las Cosas de Yucatán, a Translation," edited by A. M. Tozzer, *Harvard University, Peabody Museum of American Archaeology and Ethnology Papers*, vol. 18 (Cambridge: Peabody Museum, 1941), index under "Cenote." From the Near East: Roland de Vaux, *Ancient Israel* (London: McGraw-Hill, 1961), pp. 277-278, also cited in Sorenson, "The Book of Mormon as a Mesoamerican Codex," [The Society for Early Historic Archaeology, 1976], p. 7.)

This concept is also Biblical. For example, Abraham offered sacrifice and communed with the Lord on Mount Moriah (Genesis 22), Jacob on Mount Gilead (Genesis 31:54), Moses on Horeb (Exodus 3) and Sinai (Genesis 19-20; 24:9-11), Elijah on Mount Carmel (1 Kings 18:20-39), and Jesus Christ, together with Peter, James and John communed with God the Father and other angelic messengers on a "high mountain" (Matthew 17:1-18; Mark 9:2-8).

EVIDENCE NO. 808: THE EVILS OF THE NORTHERLY DIRECTION

Evidence: The Book of Mormon often refers to the land northward as the land of Desolation. (See, for example, Mosiah 8:8; Alma 16:11; 22:30-1; Helaman 3:5-6; 3 Nephi 3:24; 8:12.)

In both the ancient Near Eastern and Mesoamerican mind, the world was divided into four quarters. Sorenson has noted that the prime orientation was to the east as though an observer faced that direction. South was then termed "on the right" while north was "the left." The north sector was considered cursed, foreboding and unlucky. See Munro S. Edmonson ("The Book of Counsel: The Popol Vuh of the Quiche Maya of Guatemala," *Tulane University, Middle American Research Institute Publications,* no. 35, [New Orleans: 1971], pp. 36, 178; S. H. Weingarten, "Yam Sufddiam Ha'adom," *Beth Mikra,* no. 48 [1971], pp. 200-204. Both cited in Sorenson, "The Book of Mormon as a Mesoamerican Codex," [1976], p. 5.)

Desolation is said to be a descriptive place-name often used by the ancient Semites to designate "any scene of defeat." Their word "Hormah" meant destruction or desolation. See L. Woolley and T. E. Lawrence, *The Wilderness of Zin,* (London: J. Cape, 1936), p. 107. Cited in Nibley, *Since Cumorah* (1988), p. 171.

EVIDENCE NO. 809: MANA AND TAPU IN POLYNESIA

Evidence: The Book of Mormon tells of an incident in which Nephi warned his angry brothers that if they tried to harm him they would be smitten by the power of God. "Touch me not, for I am filled with the power of God, even unto the consuming of my flesh; and whoso shall lay his hands upon me shall wither even as a dried reed; and he shall be as naught before the power of God, for God shall smite him" (1 Nephi 17:48). The discharge of this power to which Nephi had access was apparently similar to a shock of static electricity (1 Nephi 17:53).

This same concept is found among the Polynesian islands, which Latter-day Saints claim was settled (at least in part) by the voyage of Hagoth (Alma 63:5-8). A significant link between Polynesia and the Book of Mormon is the belief that certain people had the power to harm others by a mere touch. In fact the word *taboo* is of Polynesian origin. The Native Polynesians believed *mana* was a supernatural power or spiritual life-force in all living things but some individuals, such as chiefs and priests, had more of it than others. Comparable to static electricity, this power "could build up on these a charge of very high, dangerous potential that was quite capable of blasting ordinary people to death." (See Gene Lisitzky, *Our ways of Being Human, An Introduction to Anthropology,* [New York, Viking Press, 1956], p. 141.)

Those people or objects that were believed to be thus charged with *mana* were said to be *tapu* (taboo), meaning, forbidden, untouchable, holy or sanctified. (See Lisitzky, *Our Ways,* p. 142. See also T. Barrow, *Art and Life in Polynesia,* [Sydney: A.H. & A.W. Reed, 1972], p. 47; and Thor Heyerdahl, *Aku Aku,* [Rand McNally, Chicago, 1958].)

During his five years in the Pacific Islands one of the authors, Allen Richardson found this superstitions still survives in modern times. Some islanders are still afraid to tread even upon the graves of certain dignitaries—not just out of respect, but because they feared that they would be struck dead. The authors believe that this superstition grew out of a tradition that had been handed down from Book of Mormon peoples.

Ancient Americans as well as Polynesians believed that illness was caused by the breach of taboo. Likewise, the cure for illness was the confession of the offender. These superstitions were borrowed from the culture of the Near East. (See Diego de Landa, *Relación de las Cosas de Yucatán,* translated by Alfred M. Tozzer, *Harvard University, Peabody Museum of American Archaeology and Ethnology Papers,* [Cambridge: Peabody Museum, 1941], vol. 18, p. 106; E. S. C. Handy, "Dreaming in Relation to Spirit Kindred and Sickness in Hawaii," in *Essays in Anthropology,* presented to A. L. Kroeber, [Berkeley, 1936], p. 127. See also Job 8:4-6; 11:6, 14-16 and John 9:1-3.)

EVIDENCE NO. 810: EVIDENCE RELATIVE TO CURSINGS

Claim: Some critics have questioned the truthfulness of the Book of Mormon because of its use of curses. (For example see 1 Nephi 2:23.) They claim that the use of curses is a negative, unchristian practice. However, those who make such statements are inadvertently criticizing their own Bible, particularly the New Testament.

Evidence: The Bible makes mention of cursings even more frequently than the Book of Mormon. For example, Jesus cursed a fig tree for not bearing fruit out of season (Mark 11:12, 20). He also instructed his disciples to wipe or shake off the dust of their feet as a curse against any city that would not receive them (Matthew 10:12-14; Mark 6:11; Luke 9:5; 10:10-12; Acts 5:9-10; 13:44-51).

In a similar ritual, Paul shook his clothing as a curse against the Jews (Acts 18:4-6). On a previous occasion Paul cursed a sorcerer with blindness (Acts 13:8-11). Peter struck Ananias and Sapphira dead for holding back money meant for the apostles (Acts 5:1-11). For other cursings and threats see 1 Corinthians 16:22 and Galatians 1:8.

The *simile curse* was part of both the Mesoamerican and ancient Near Eastern cultures. Mark J. Morrise explains that the simile curse consists of two parts. First, an event (for example "just as this is burned by fire…") followed by an application of that event to the subject of the curse ("…so shall Arpad be burned.") From an Aramaic treaty of approximately 750 BC. Quoted in Mark J. Morrise, "Simile Curses in the Ancient Near East, Old Testament, and Book of Mormon," *Journal of Book of Mormon Studies,* vol. 2, no. 1, [spring 1993], pp. 124-125.

For Biblical examples of the simile curse see: Jeremiah 18:1-10; 24:1-10; Ezekiel 4:1-8, 9-17; 5:1-14; 12:3-12.

The *treaty curse* was often ritualistic in nature. But during the treaty negotiations between the Nephites and Lamanites, a spontaneous act of striking off a piece of scalp from the disgruntled Lamanite leader Zerahemnah lead to the uttering of a treaty curse. "Even as this scalp has fallen to the earth … so shall ye fall to the earth except ye will deliver up your weapons of war" (Alma 44:14). See also Helaman 13:18-20, 34-36.

Six examples of the *treaty curse* have been identified in the Old Testament. See, for example Genesis 4:15 where God makes a "treaty" with Cain which includes a curse. See also, Joshua 6:26 where Israel is warned not to rebuild Jericho: "Cursed be the man before the LORD, that riseth up and buildeth this city Jericho: he shall lay the foundation thereof in his firstborn, and in his youngest son shall he set up the gates of it."

Joshua 9:3-23 includes a treaty curse between the Israelites and the Gibeonites, and Psalms 137:1-9 contains a treaty or covenant with the Israelites which carries with it a curse upon them should they forget Jerusalem while held captive in Babylon. (Delbert R. Hillers, *Treaty Curses and the Old Testament Prophets,* [Rome: Pontifical Biblical Institute, 1964], pp. 8-11, 20-21.)

In his masterful discourse, King Benjamin taught that just as a man would not take his neighbor's animal, but would drive it from his own flock to return it to his neighbor, "so shall it be among you if ye know not the name by which ye are called" (Mosiah 5:14). This particular covenant was ratified by voice (Mosiah 5:5) and was enforced by the blotting out of the names of those who violated the covenant (Mosiah 26:36). Hillers cites a similar curse of expulsion in an Ashurnirari treaty "Just as this ram [is taken] away from his fold … so may … the people of this land [be taken away] from this land…" (Hillers, *Treaty Curses,* [1964], p. 34).

The Book of Mormon speaks of the curse of *rending the garment* as follows: "If they should transgress [this covenant] the Lord should rend them even as they had rent their garments (Alma 46:21). Although all curses contained a conditional penalty that was often prophetic in nature, Abinadi's prophecy about the demise of the evil king Noah is an authentic example of an unconditional *prophetic simile curse.* "And it shall come to pass that the life of king Noah shall be valued even as a garment in a hot furnace; for he shall know that I am the Lord …thou shalt be as a stalk, even as a dry stalk of the field, which is run over by the beasts and trodden under foot. And again, he saith thou shalt be as the blossoms of a thistle, which, when it is fully ripe, if the wind bloweth, it is driven forth from upon the face of the land" (Mosiah 12:3, 10-12).

Hillers refers to several examples of prophetic simile curses, some of which were done in ritual (Hillers, p. 132). See also Isaiah 29:7-8 for one of many biblical examples. Also see the several evidences concerning Captain Moroni's *Title of Liberty* in the Chapter on War of this same volume.

EVIDENCE NO. 811: ABINADI AND THE TEACHER OF RIGHTEOUSNESS

Claim: The Book of Mormon tells of a prophet of uncommon courage named Abinadi who preached to the corrupt court of the wicked king Noah. Because of his harsh criticism, the king became wroth but he had no power over Abinadi until after he had delivered his message from God (Mosiah Chapters 11-17). Once Abinadai had delivered his message, the king burned Abinadi at the stake. The teachings and tribulations of this New World prophet have an uncanny resemblance to the "Teacher of Righteousness" that is mentioned in several of the Dead Sea Scrolls which were found many years after Joseph Smith first published the Book of Mormon. The similarities between the two incidents reaffirms that both men were directed by the same God, that two books which record their respective missions were inspired by that same God and that the culture of the Book of Mormon peoples is indeed of Middle Eastern origin as claimed in the Book of Mormon.

Evidence: Dr. Hugh Nibley writes the following in this subject in his book, *The Prophetic Book of Mormon,* (1989), pp. 302-303:

> Of many striking parallels, I would like to speak of one here that goes to the root of things. It is an episode that opens in the Book of Mormon in the middle of the second century BC with "a man whose name was Abinadi," in deep trouble with the establishment. In the Old World we find about the same time a certain "Teacher of Righteousness" in much the same fix: his story is told in the Manual of Discipline, the Damascus or Zadokite Fragment, the commentary on Habakkuk, and the Thanksgiving Hymns from Qumran. He is being given a bad time by certain corrupt priests who are in the saddle. In the Book of Mormon we find them cross-examining the righteous man as they sit at a special tribunal with comfortable seats.

The following table lists the many similarities between the teachings of these two prophets:

Similarities	Abinadi	Teacher of Right.
Both accused the establishment of speaking "lying and vain words."	Mosiah 11:11	1QH 4:7, 9-10, 20
The reaction of the court was an unsuccessful attempt on their lives.	Mosiah 11:26	1QH 2:21-23, 32-35
They respond with an interesting figure of speech by combining two elements of *fire* and *weaving*.* Abinadi: " "The life of King Noah shall be valued even as a *garment in a hot furnace*." Teacher of Righteousness: "For those who stubbornly oppose [God] there shall be violence and overpowering of great terror by the *flame of fire* ...Their *weaving* is a flimsy thing, the weaving of spiders."	Mosiah 12:3; 12:10	CD 2:5; 5:13-14
Those who fight against the prophet shall be like chaff before the wind.	Mosiah 12:12	1QH 7:20-21
The court tries to snare the prophet in cross-examination, but this backfires upon the accusers.	Mosiah 12:19	1QH 2:15-16, 29-33
The prophets accuse the court of pretending to keep the law while being guilty of heinous sins such as adultery and greed.	Mosiah 12:27-29, 33	CD 8:4-8; 19:15-20
The prophets teach that the law is a preparation for the Messiah to come: every aspect of the law must be kept until the Messiah comes.	Mosiah 13:27, 30-32	1QS 9:9-11; CD 12:21-23
Moses prophesied about the coming of the Messiah.	Mosiah 13:33	1QS 1:3; 1QS 9:4-5
Those who believe the Messiah will be his seed and shall inherit the kingdom of God, and become kings.	Mosiah 15:10-11	1QSb 3:2-5; 1QS 5:21-22
"When the glory of God is openly revealed to Israel, then shall all the evil-doers of Judah be cast out."	Mosiah 16:1-3	CD 20:26

As a result of Abinadi's teachings, Alma, one of the priests of King Noah, became converted and pleaded for the life of the prophet. Subsequently, Alma fled into the wilderness to escape the wrath of the king. While in exile, he secretly built up a community of believers in the wilderness (Mosiah 17-18). This pattern of withdrawing from the establishment and going into the wilderness as a preparation for a sacred mission has been followed several times throughout the history of the Hebrews. This is exactly what Ether, Moroni, Lehi, Moses, John the Baptist and Jesus Christ did. Similarly, the Qumran community from whom we have inherited the Dead Sea scrolls withdrew from Judah and gathered in the desert to obtain their freedom to worship in peace.

From the many similarities between the Book of Mormon and the writings of the Qumran community, Dr. Hugh Nibley concludes in *The Prophetic Book of Mormon,* (1989), pp. 325:

> It would be easy to supply many times more such parallels between the Book of Mormon and the other ancient records. If the latter are authentic (and both the Qumran and the Enoch writings were once

challenged as late forgeries), it is hard to see how we can brush aside the Joseph Smith production as nonsense. Even if every parallel were the purest coincidence, we would still have to explain how the prophet contrived to pack such a dense succession of happy accidents into the scriptures he gave us. Where the world has a perfect right to expect a great potpourri of the most outrageous nonsense, and in anticipation has indeed rushed to judgment with all manner of premature accusations, we discover whenever ancient texts turn up to offer the necessary checks and controls, that the man was astonishingly on target in his depiction of general situations, in the almost casual mention of peculiar oddities, in the strange proper names, and countless other unaccountable details. What have Joseph Smith's critics really known about the true nature of those ancient societies into which his apocalyptic writings propose to take us? As the evidence accumulates, it is not the Prophet but his critics who find themselves with a lot of explaining to do.

---

* Dr. Nibley notes: "Here both prophets are borrowing from Isaiah 50:9, 11: 'Who is he that shall condemn me? lo, they all shall wax old as a garment; the moth shall eat them up. Behold, all ye that kindle a fire, that compass yourselves about with sparks; walk in the light of your fire, and in the sparks that ye have kindled.' The idea is that those who have foolishly started such fires will themselves perish by them. In the Zadokite Fragment the precarious position of the persecutors is compared with playing with fire and a flimsy weaving of spiders. Abinadi combines the images with characteristic wit: Noah himself is the flimsy garment in the hot fire, to suffer the very death he is inflicting on Abinadi."

EVIDENCE NO. 812: ABINADI AND PENTECOST

Claim: One of the many authentic details contained in the Book of Mormon is the incident in which the prophet Abinadi returned to King Noah's court apparently during Pentecost (Mosiah Chapters 11-17).

Evidence: Even in our modern times, with more and better libraries than were available in Joseph Smith's day, better schools and easier access to information through computer storage and photocopies, very few people today understand the ramifications of Hebrew Holy Days, such as Pentecost. Some critics assume that Joseph Smith, at the young age of 22 and with no higher education, had the extensive knowledge and understanding of ancient Hebrew culture to be able to work into the Book of Mormon so many little-known authentic elements.

In Mormon's abridgment of the Book of Mosiah, many minor details were obviously omitted from Abinadi's ministry. However, modern scholarship has enabled the reader to understand in greater detail the religious and cultural setting of the incident.

Without directly so stating, Abinadi must have chosen to return to King Noah's court during the festival of Pentecost in order to meet a more receptive audience. His speeches deal with the themes of Pentecost, which particular festival was an agricultural holiday (sometimes called "The Day of the First Fruits") rejoicing in the new bounty. Abinadi cursed the crops when a bounteous grain season was at hand, by prophesying hail, dry winds, and insects (Mosiah 12:6). Just as the Passover marked Israel's deliverance from bondage, Abinadi proclaimed that the wicked shall be brought into bondage; and none shall deliver them (Mosiah 11:21), and "they shall have burdens lashed upon their backs" (Mosiah 12:2, 5).

As the Talmud explains, Pentecost commemorates giving the law to Moses. Likewise, Abinadi repeated the Ten Commandments (Mosiah 12:33). Just as Moses' face seemed to glow as he descended from Mt. Sinai (Exodus 34:29-30), Abinadi's "face shone with exceeding luster" as he taught the Ten Commandments to king Noah and his corrupt priests (Mosiah 13:5).

When Abinadi predicted that King Noah would be like "a garment in a hot furnace" (Mosiah 12:3), no doubt King Noah (who claimed to follow the Law of Moses) recalled that Sinai became like a furnace (Exodus 19:18).

Some may question why Abinadi's trial was postponed for *three* days (Mosiah 17:6). However, it must be understood that this festival may have lasted several days. For more information, see John W. Welch, Gordon C. Thomasson, and Robert F. Smith, "Abinadi and Pentecost," *Foundation for Ancient Research and Mormon Studies Update*, September 1985; reprinted in *Re-exploring the Book of Mormon*, edited by John W. Welch, (1992), pp. 135-138.

EVIDENCE NO. 813: ANCIENT NEAR EASTERN JUDICIAL SYSTEM IN ANCIENT AMERICA

Claim: The description of Nephite law in the Book of Mormon is evidence that those laws were solidly rooted in ancient Near Eastern jurisprudence and legal tradition.

Evidence: The following is quoted from the *Foundation for Ancient Research and Mormon Studies Update*, "The Law of Mosiah," March 1987; reprinted in *Re-exploring the Book of Mormon*, edited by John W. Welch, (1992), pp. 158-161:

> The Law of Mosiah was primarily procedural and administrative in nature, like the legal reform of King Jehoshaphat in 2 Chronicles 19:5-11. It changed the judicial system. It abolished the kingship and instituted judges and officers (Alma 11:1-2; Deuteronomy 16:18), also establishing an innovative procedure whereby a judge could be judged by a "higher judge" if he did not judge according to the law (Mosiah 29:28). It further established a procedure for expelling unjust higher judges. If they did not judge righteously (i.e., according to the law given by the fathers), a small number of the lower judges could be authorized by the people to judge the higher judges and remove them from office. This law departed most significantly from traditional law by providing for the payment of judges (Alma 11:1). The fixing of wages for various other services, however, was one of the main subjects of most ancient Near Eastern law codes.

> In order to set statutory wages of any kind, it was often necessary for ancient laws to recognize a system of legal exchange equivalents. Similarly, the Law of Mosiah gave exchange ratios for gold, silver, barley and all kinds of grain (Alma 11:7). Prior to the Law of Mosiah, Nephite weights and measures had been altered "according to the minds and the circumstances of the people, in every generation" (11:4), but here, they were standardized by decree of the king. Much the same thing can be found in the Mesopotamian Laws of Eshnunna, which begin with a list of thirteen exchange equivalencies, e.g., "1 *kor* barley for 1 shekel silver," and then establish fixed prices for services of harvesters, boatmen, and other workers. (R. Yaron, "The Laws of Eshnunna," *Israel Law Review*, vol. 5, [1970], pp. 327-336.)

See also, John W. Welch, "What was a 'Mosiah'," *Re-exploring the Book of Mormon*, (1992), pp. 105-107.

EVIDENCE NO. 814: TRIAL BY ORDEAL

Claim: The trial of Abinadi (Mosiah 17), which may sound strange to those who are unfamiliar with ancient Near Eastern law, is yet another evidence that the Book of Mormon is true and authentic.

Evidence: Paul Y. Hoskisson, Assistant Professor of Ancient Scriptures at Brigham Young University, noted that King Noah unexpectedly became afraid (verse 11) when Abinadi was convicted of a capital crime by Noah's court. Hoskisson suggests that the reason for Noah's fear was that the court, corrupt as it was:

> ...still operated under the guise of ancient Near Eastern law. One aspect of the law, trial by ordeal, may explain Noah's behavior. If a case came down to one person's word against another's, the case could not be dismissed but had to be resolved through trial by ordeal.

> The accused person, by winning the ordeal, was proven innocent, and the accuser would become guilty of bearing false witness and would suffer the punishment for the crime he falsely charged. (See Deuteronomy 19:16-19.) Abinadi had been accused of a capital crime, so he proposed such a trial: They could put him to death, but he would not take back his words (Mosiah 17:10). By dying without recanting, Abinadi would win the trial by ordeal and thus prove that he was telling the truth.

> At this point, Noah refused the trial by ordeal and would have released Abinadi had it not been for the priests' words "He has reviled the king" (Mosiah 17:12), a treasonable offense which stirred the king's anger. Instead, the king delivered him up to be slain, and Abinadi was tortured with scourging, and was killed by fire, without taking back his words. In the process of winning the trial by ordeal, Abinadi could prophesy that Noah and the other accusers would therefore suffer, as he did, death by fire. (See "New Developments in Book of Mormon Research," *Ensign*, February 1988, pp. 12-13.)

Note that the priests of King Noah's court claimed to follow the law of Moses which included the above-mentioned provision for bearers of false accusations (Mosiah 12:27-28). True to ancient Near Eastern law and according to Abinadi's prophecy, King Noah later suffered death by fire.

EVIDENCE NO. 815: TRIAL PROCEDURE

Claim: The trial at which King Limhi presided (Mosiah 7:9-11) followed the procedures that were common in the Middle East, from where the Nephites migrated.

Evidence: In both the Middle Eastern and Nephite culture the trial procedure was as follows:

1. The King gives his name and titles (Mosiah 7:9)
2. The King asks a question of the prisoners, giving the charge of which they are accused (Mosiah 7:10)
3. The King tells the prisoners the penalties that depend on their answers (Mosiah 7:11)
4. The King pronounces the verdict of the court (Mosiah 7:14-15)

Numerous Middle Eastern sources are given for each step in the trial procedure in John Gee, "Limhi in the Library," *Journal of Book of Mormon Studies*, vol. 1, no. 1, (1992), pp. 54-66.

EVIDENCE NO. 816: SHEREM AND ISRAELITE LAW

Claim: The Book of Mormon contains a detailed narrative that demonstrates a remarkable familiarity with the intricacies of Israelite law. In the relation of Jacob's encounter with Sherem (Jacob 7), the latter accuses Jacob of three offenses, which were punishable by death: 1) causing public apostasy, 2) blasphemy, and 3) false prophecy.

> And ye have led away much of this people that they pervert the right way of God, and keep not the law of Moses which is the right way; and convert the law of Moses into the worship of a being which ye say shall come many hundred years hence. And now behold, I, Sherem, declare unto you that this is blasphemy; for no man knoweth of such things; for he cannot tell of things to come (Jacob 7:7).

These serious charges were of a capital nature punishable by death. But instead of Sherem's accusations bringing about an execution for Jacob, he himself is stricken and dies. This *boomerang judgment* is a little-known feature of Israelite law. Had Joseph Smith been the author of the Book of Mormon, it is highly improbable that he (an uneducated backwoods farm boy) could have known about this in order to put this into the Book of Mormon. Rather, the Book was written by ancient Israelite prophets and translated by Joseph Smith through the gift and power of God.

Evidence: It is extremely unlikely that a non-Jewish, unlettered, frontiersman of the early eighteen hundreds could have devoted the time and resources necessary to enable him to invent a story which so authentically discloses major aspects of ancient Hebraic law as detailed in the Jewish Talmud. Though the Bible was available in Smith's day, and though it makes oblique references to the Mosaic Law, its overwhelming size and convoluted structure would have intimidated any impostor of young Joseph's age. The following references, obscure even to the most astute Bible scholars, warn of the seriousness of all three offenses of which Sherem accused Jacob:

1. Causing Public Apostasy: Israelite law specified the fate of anyone who tells Israel to "go and serve other gods which ye have not known, ...shall not consent unto him, nor hearken unto him, ...but thou shalt surely kill him. ...And thou shalt stone him with stones, that he die; because he hath sought to thrust thee away from the LORD thy God, which brought thee out of the land of Egypt, from the house of bondage" (Deuteronomy 13: 1-18).

2. Blasphemy: Anyone who spoke "a word in my name, which I have not commanded him to speak, or that shall speak in the name of other gods, even that prophet shall die." (Deuteronomy 18:20).

3. False Prophecy: Similarly, if a person made a prophecy, in the name of the Lord, which did not come true, he too was put to death (Deuteronomy 18:20-22).

In the end, Sherem demanded a sign of the Holy Ghost. Accordingly, "the power of the Lord fell upon him, insomuch that he fell to the earth" (Jacob 7:13-15). A few days later he died, suffering that fate which he had obviously sought for Jacob. This is also in accordance with the Mosaic law: "if the witness be a false witness, and hath testified falsely against his brother; Then shall ye do unto him, as he had thought to have done unto his brother" (Deuteronomy 19:16-19). For more information, see John W. Welch, *Foundation for Ancient Research Mormon Studies Update*, No. 74, January 1991.

7.   Names Used in the Book of Mormon

Introduction

<u>Claim</u>: Great writers, such as Shakespeare, are lauded for their ability to introduce new and unique names into their works. Not so with Joseph Smith. Critics who have suspected that he fabricated the Book of Mormon have accused him of "letting his fancy run free." They have said that the strange names in his book are not authentic. However, below are listed a number of names with documentation from non-Mormon scholars who have found that the names are authentic after all, and were common to the various cultures from which the Book of Mormon peoples emigrated. Indeed, many of the newly discovered names carry the same or similar *meaning* as expressed in the Book of Mormon. In each case, the findings were documented many years after the Book of Mormon was first published.

Of these remarkable evidences relating to the use of proper names in the Book of Mormon, Dr. Nibley wrote the following in *The Improvement Era,* January 1966, p. 33, (also found in Nibley, *Since Cumorah,* [1988], p. 464):

> The Book of Mormon is so generous with proper names that no other evidence should be necessary to establish its authenticity. Along with a sprinkling of Arabic, Greek, and possibly Hittite or Hurrian names, more than two hundred proper names are almost equally divided between Hebrew and Egyptian forms. Incidentally, the prevalence in Palestine of Egyptian culture circa 600 BC is one of the claims for which our text was long held up for ridicule, but today a lot is known about the really intimate cultural ties between the two peoples.

Evidences Relative to Names Used in the Nephite Monetary System

The Nephite monetary system is described in detail in Alma chapter 11 of the Book of Mormon. Critics have mocked Joseph Smith for the "silly" names used in the Nephite monetary system mentioned in the Book of Mormon. However, in recent years the critics have been silenced on this topic since it was discovered that most of the names mentioned in the Book of Mormon are indeed words of ancient origin. The following evidences document this fact, and provide additional evidence that the Book of Mormon is indeed a true work of ancient history.

EVIDENCE NO. 817: ANTION

Evidence: The *antion* as mentioned in Alma 11:19 as the name of a monetary unit of gold, is an authentic ancient term—making use of the prefix *anti* which was common in the Americas as well as in the Middle East.

B. H. Roberts noted that according to the *Encyclopedia Britannica*, the term *anti* was an ancient American word that meant copper. Since gold and copper are both soft metals it is logical that they would be called by similar words. A small *antion* of gold could have been equivalent to a larger quantity of copper. (See B. H. Roberts, *New Witness for Christ in America,* vol. 3, p. 520, who cites Varcilasso, *Conquest of Peru*, vol. 1, p. 113. See also Garcilasso de la Vega, *Royal Commentaries*, Book 5, chapter 14.)

Reynolds and Sjodahl, noted the following concerning the prefix *anti*:

> In the Book of Mormon, anti means a "mountain" or a "hill." When it is used to denote a country, it probably means a hilly or mountain country, and when the name is applied to a city, it may indicate its location in a mountain region. In the same way Anti-Nephi-Lehies may mean that they were located in a hilly or mountainous country. As applied to a piece of money, the word would indicate that they were made of an alloy in which copper formed a considerable part." (George Reynolds and Janne. M. Sjodahl, *Commentary on the Book of Mormon*, vol. 2, p.320.)

> ...The old Indian equivalent for anti is *anta,* which means *copper,* and from this we have the name of the *Andes Mountains.* The word appears in the Peruvian *Antisuyu,* the name given to the eastern part of the country which is traversed by the loftiest of the Andes Mountains. (Reynolds and Sjodahl, *Commentary*, vol. 3, p.336.)

See also the related information in the sections on proper names under "Anti" and "Manti."

EVIDENCE NO. 818: EZROM

Evidence: The *ezrom* of silver was a unit in the Nephite monetary system (Alma 11:6). This word is likely related to the similar-sounding word of ancient Jewish origin *Hezron*. See R. A. S. Macalister, "The Craftsmen's Guild of the Tribe of Judah," *Palestine Exploration Fund Quarterly,* 1905, p. 328; cited in Nibley, *Lehi in the Desert and The World of the Jaredites,* (1988), p. 32.

This name is most likely the root for a personal name, mentioned in the Book of Mormon, *Zeezrom*. The name Zeezrom was given to a corrupt lawyer who tried to bribe the prophet with money (Alma 11:22). This name can be read in Hebrew as "the ezrom (money)" or "the one with money." This name was most likely a title rather than a name given at birth. See *Foundation for Ancient Research and Mormon Studies Insights,* June 1984, p. 1.

EVIDENCE NO. 819: LIMNAH

Evidence: *Limnah* is mentioned as a unit of money in Alma 11:5. Money units were counted out in measures or weighed. This word is not only authentic, but it also carries with it the same general meaning as is used in the Book of Mormon. *Limnah* is Hebrew for "to count or weigh." See Francis Brown, S. R. Driver and C. A. Briggs, "A Hebrew and English Lexicon of the Old Testament" (Clarendon Press: Oxford, 1968), p. 584, cited in Paul Richard Jesclard, "A Comparison of the Nephite Monetary System with the Egyptian System of Measuring Grain," a paper read at the *Twenty-first Annual Symposium on the Archaeology of the Scriptures*, B.Y.U., October 16, 1971, which was cited in Wirth, *A Challenge to the Critics,* (1986), p. 47.

EVIDENCE NO. 820: ONTI

Evidence: An *Onti* of silver is mentioned in Alma 11:6, 13 as a unit of ancient American money. Not only is this word authentic, but it also is related to the same word in Egyptian. *Onti* is Egyptian for a "small amount" or "short of an amount." See *Woerterbuch der Aegyptische Sprache*, vol. 1, pp. 206-207, cited in Paul Richard Jesclard, "A Comparison of the Nephite Monetary System with the Egyptian System of Measuring Grain," a paper read at the Twenty-first Annual Symposium on the Archeology of the Scriptures, BYU, October 16, 1971, which was cited in Vestal and Wallace, *The Firm Foundation of Mormonisim*, (1981), p. 177.

EVIDENCE NO. 821: SENUM

Evidence: A unit of money mentioned in Alma 11:3, 6-7 is the *Senum*. This coin is halved or doubled to get the next lower or higher unit. Not only is this word authentic, but its actual meaning is synonymous with the way in which it is used in the Book of Mormon. The root *Sen* is Egyptian for "one half" or "doubling." See Worterbunch, *der Aegyptischen Sprache*, vol. 4, pp. 164-165, cited in Paul Richard Jesclar, "A Comparison of the Nephite Monetary System with the Egyptian System of Measuring Grain," *Newsletter and Proceedings of the Society of Early Historic Archaeology*, No. 134, October 1973, p. 2, which in turn is cited in Wirth, *A Challenge to the Critics* (1986), p. 47.

EVIDENCE NO. 822: SHIBLUM

Evidence: *Shiblum* is a Nephite measurement of value in the Nephite monetary system, mentioned in Alma 11:16. This word is authentic in meaning as well as being a word of ancient origin. *Shiblum* is very close to the Hebrew *Shilum*. Actually, according to the printer's manuscript of the Book of Mormon, the word should have been spelled *Shilum*, not *Shiblum*. The Hebrew word means "payment, reward or retribution." See Sue Bergin, "Volunteers Team up to Study Book of Mormon," *BYU Today*, February 1985, pp. 15-16, cited in Wirth, *A Challenge to the Critics* (1986), p. 48.

EVIDENCE NO. 823: SHUM

Evidence: *Shum* is mentioned in Alma 11:5-9 as a unit of gold. This name could have been derived from several ancient names including *Shem* (the son of Noah), *Sum*, and *Ishim*. See Genesis 5:32; Jose Gabriel, *Idiomas Aborigines*, (Buenos Aires: Dibujos de Carlos J. Abregu Mittelbach, 1941), p. 273; Marcos E. Becerra, *Volcabulario de la Lingua Chol.*, (Mexico City: Talleres Graficos de la Nación, 1937), p. 24; both cited in Vestal and Wallace, *The Firm Foundation of Mormonism*, (1981), p. 121.

EVIDENCE NO. 824: DIFFERENCES BETWEEN NEPHITE AND JAREDITE PROPER NAMES

Evidence: The Book of Mormon is an ancient history of two entirely separate groups of people who migrated to America at different times. The first group mentioned is comprised of the Family of Lehi and the Mulekites. Both of these families migrated separately to America from Jerusalem around 600 BC, but later merged into one group, whose history was preserved by the Nephites (1 Nephi 10:4; Omni 1:15-19; Mosiah 25:2).

The second group mentioned in the Book of Mormon, called the Jaredites, lived at the time of the Tower of Babel, and migrated much earlier than the first groups mentioned. The Jaredite civilization did not interact with the Lehites. Thus their cultures were essentially separate, and the few cultural features that survived from the Jaredites, to be handed down to the Lehites, existed in the historical records, and ruins. (See the Book of Ether in the Book of Mormon.)

A strong evidence which helps prove the authenticity of the Book of Mormon is that the proper names of the Lehites differ significantly from those of the Jaredites. The names of the Lehites are basically Hebrew, Arabic and Egyptian in origin, while the names of the Jaredites are mainly Akkadian and Sumerian.

The following review appeared in newsletter proceedings of the *Society for Early Historic Archaeology* (SEHA), No. 141, December 1977. The editor reviewed an article by John A. Tvedtnes, (M. A. graduate student in Semitic linguistics and archaeology, Hebrew University, Jerusalem) entitled "A Phonemic Analysis of Nephite and Jaredite Proper Names" Presented at the *Twenty-second Annual Symposium on the Archaeology of the Scriptures and Allied Fields*, held at Brigham Young University on October 28, 1973.

> The author of this paper explores the fascinating subject of the names of persons and places found in the Book of Mormon. He accepts the many indications that the principal tongue of the Lehite-Mulekite peoples of the Book of Mormon was essentially Hebrew, and that the names of persons and places recorded therein are therefore mostly in that language. Tvedtnes also proposes that the proper names of the Jaredites as recorded in the Book of Mormon were drawn from the Akkadian and Sumerian languages, confirming the Mesopotamian origin of that earlier people. The reader will notice that Joseph Smith, the professed discoverer and translator of the Nephite record in the 1820s, could not possibly have had knowledge of those extinct Mesopotamian languages (they did not become known to scholars until after the decipherment of the ancient cuneiform writing of Mesopotamia in the mid-nineteenth century).

Tvedtnes examined 63 Jaredite proper names and 186 Lehite names, showing their relationships to the two separate language systems.

EVIDENCE NO. 825: METONYMS IN THE BOOK OF MORMON

Evidence: The Book of Mormon demonstrates its authenticity by the use of *metonymic* naming. This is an ancient practice of bestowing names like titles on people whose deeds or life resemble that of others with the same name. For example, someone who has betrayed a close friend might be called a "Judas." The Roman emperors who followed Julius Caesar used his name in addition to their own so that their people would see in them the same greatness. Carrying on the use of Caesar as a title, the Kaisers of Germany and the Czars of Russia took the names of their predecessors as metonymic titles.

Similarly, the Nephite and Lamanite kings as well as their people were known by the name of their first king. (See Jacob 1:11; Mosiah 7:21-22; Omni 14). This practice transcended bloodlines for those who moved from one group to another (4 Nephi 20).

The Nephite *Coriantumr* of Helaman chapter 1 may well be a metonym of the much earlier Jaredite king Coriantumr—since his revolt led to a scene of carnage, though not as extensive, as did the wars of the earlier Coriantumr (Ether 13-15). Similarly, the Jaredite name Coriantumr is quite certainly a metonym of the two righteous Jaredite kings both named *Coriantum,* the first of whom actually saw Jehovah (Ether 9:21-25; 10:31).

The roots of these names can be found in Strong's *Exhaustive Concordance*. When broken down we find that the first syllable, *kor* means, "measure," the second, *ayin,* means "where," and the third, *tom,* means "prosperity, integrity, perfection." These segments could collectively represent the name-title of a newly-crowned king who, it is hoped, would be an example of perfectly measured judgment, and would bring prosperity to his people." (See James Strong, "A Concise Dictionary of the Hebrew Bible," in *Exhaustive Concordance,* [1973], entries nos. 370, 3734, 8537, pp. 11, 57, 124.)

The following are other possible metonyms in the Book of Mormon. The Hebrew roots are all found in James Strong, *Exhaustive Concordance,* (1973). Beside each root is given the entry and page number in Strong's Concordance.

Name	Hebrew Roots	Meaning	Meaning of Name
Ablom, a Jaredite city by the sea (Ether 9:3)	*ab:* 1&2, p. 12 *lom:* 3816, p. 58	father a community, or people	"City of our fathers"
Amgid, a Jaredite warrior king (Ether 10:32)	*ayam:* 5868, p. 87 *gidown:* 1439, p. 26	strength, mighty warrior	"Strong and mighty warrior"
Amnigaddah, a Jaredite king (Ether 1:14-15)	*am:* 5971, p. 89 *na:* 4994, p. 75 *gadah:* 1415, p. 25	a people, tribe or nation prayer, entreaty a border of a river	"A man whose people will entreaty of him at the river bank."
Amnihu, a hill mentioned in Alma 2:15	*emunah:* 530, p. 14 *huw:* 1931, p. 32	firmness, security, stability	"A place of firmness, security and stability."
Amulon, a land mentioned in Mosiah 23:31; 24:1	*am:* 5971, p. 89 *yalown:* 3210, p. 49 or *luwn:* 3885, p. 59	a people, a tribe, a nation lodging to stay permanently or dwell	"The people's permanent place of dwelling."
Antion, a unit of gold (Alma 11:19)	*antah:* 607, p. 15 *own:* 202, p. 9	thou, thee wealth, goods, substance	"Thy wealth," or "thy treasures."
Antionum the name for an area of land (Alma 31:3)	*antah:* 607, p. 15 *ownam:* 208, p. 9	thou, thee strong	"Thy stronghold" (a place of safety)
Antiparah, a Nephite city (Alma 56:14)	*antah:* 607, p. 15 *para:* 6500, p. 96	thou, thee to bear fruit, to be fruitful	"Thou fruitful, populous, city."
Antum, the hill Shim was located in the land of Antum (Mormon 1:3)	*an:* 575, p. 14 *tom:* 8537, p. 124	where or whither Completeness, prosperity, perfection, uprightness.	"The land where perfection is found."
Archeantus, a Nephite military officer (Moroni 9:2)	*ar:* 6146, p. 91 *kiy:* 3587, p. 55 *ayin:* 370, p. 11 *toos:* 2907, p. 45	enemy brand, scar where pounce, hasten	"One who will hasten or pounce on his enemies, causing great injuries and scars."
Comnor, a hill mentioned in Ether 14:28	*quwm:* 6965, p. 102 *nahar:* 5102, p. 76	to rise, lift up, rear up to sparkle, be lightened	"High place from which light shines."
Corom, a Jaredite king (Ether 1:19)	*kor:* 3734, p. 57 *ruwm:* 7311, p. 107	measure high, raise, exalt, lift up	"Exalted one, who measures out justice and mercy."
Emer, a king (Ether 1:28)	*emer:* 561, p. 14	answer, saying, speech	"Appointed to speak."
Gadiomnah, a city mentioned in 3 Nephi 9:8	*gadiy:* 1424, p. 26 *omnah:* 545, p. 14	fortunate training, brought up	"A city where the fortunate are brought up."
Luram, a Nephite officer (Moroni 9:2)	*lu:* 3863, p. 59 *ram:* 7410, p. 109	a wish, "would that" high	"One who desires to be lifted up."
Sherrizah, a tower from which was taken many prisoners (Moroni 9:7-17)	*sheroshuw:* 8332, p. 121	eradication, exile, banishment	"The tower of exile or banishment"

For more information on metonyms in the Book of Mormon see Gordon C. Thomasson, "What's in a Name? Book of Mormon Language, Names and [Metonymic] Naming," *Journal of Book of Mormon Studies,* vol. 3, no. 1, (Spring 1994), pp. 1-27.

EVIDENCE NO. 826: PATRONYMIC NAMES

Evidence: Personal names such as *Abinadom, Abinadi, Aminadi* and *Aminadab*, mentioned in the Book of Mormon (Omni 1:10; Mosiah 11:20; Omni 1:10; Helaman 5:39), contain Semitic (Near Eastern) elements. John A. Tvedtnes said the following: "Book of Mormon personal names containing such Semitic patronymic elements as Abi- ("father") and Ami- ("paternal kinsman/clan") fit the biblical pattern and are evidence for a strong patrilineal kinship system." (John A. Tvedtnes, "Book of Mormon Tribal Affiliation and Military Caste," TVE-89, *Foundation for Ancient Research and Mormon Studies*, [1989], p. 1, note 3.)

EVIDENCE NO. 827: ABISH

Evidence: *Abish* is the name of a woman mentioned in Alma 19:16 of the Book of Mormon. The Book of Mormon first introduced this name into the Western world, however, it is actually of ancient origin.

For the similar-sounding *Jabish*, see 2 Barnabas 5:5. The ancient Hebrew language had no "J." The letter "J" which we see in modern spellings was pronounced like an "Y" or an "I." Substituting "Y" for "J" makes *Yabish*—which is even closer to the Abish from the Book of Mormon. (See James Strong, *Exhaustive Concordance of the Bible*, [New York: Abingdon Press, 1973].)

Since *ab* is the Hebrew word for "father" and *ish* is Hebrew for "man" the name *Abish* would seem to carry the meaning of "a man who is a father." This being the case, it may seem strange that *Abish* is used as the name of a woman in the Book of Mormon. However, we find that the prefix *Ab* was used consistently in ancient Hebrew names for women. For example, consider the following names. *Abi,* which means "fatherly," is the name of the mother of Hezekiah (2 Kings 18:2). *Abigail,* means "father of joy" is the name for at least two Israelite women in the Bible (1 Samuel 25:3; 2 Samuel 17:25; 1 Chronicles 2:16). *Abihail,* which means "father of might," was used as the name of two Israelite women in (1 Chronicles 2:29; 2 Chronicles 11:18). King David was married to *Abital,* which means "father of dew" (2 Samuel 3:4). *Abishag,* which means "father of error," was the name of David's concubine (1 Kings 1:3-4).

Note that the last syllable *ish* was also used in female names such as *Abishag* (mentioned above) and *Elisheba,* the wife of Aaron (Exodus 6:23), from which the modern name of Elizabeth is formed. See James Strong, "A Concise Dictionary of the Hebrew Bible," in *Exhaustive Concordance,* (1973), entries no. 1, 2, 21, 26, 32, 37, 49, 376 & 472, pp. 7, 12, 13.

EVIDENCE NO. 828: ADAM—IXANOM

Evidence: One of the many links between the Middle East and the Americas is the similarity in pronunciation of the name of the first man, Adam. The Book of Mormon states that Adam and Eve could not eat from the Tree of Life after they had partaken of the Tree of Knowledge (Alma 12:21-26; 42:3, 5). However, they were able to partake of it in a figurative sense—the Tree of Life symbolizing the Love of God (1 Nephi 11:22).

Ancient Americans believed that their first father, who in their language was called *Ixanom*, ate of the fruit of the Tree of Life. See Andres de Avendano y Loyola, *Relación de las dos Entradas que hize a Peten Ytza* (1967), English translation by Philip Ainsworth Means, cited in *History of the Conquest of Yucatan and of the Itzas* (1917), p. 135, cited in Hunter and Ferguson, *Ancient America and the Book of Mormon* (1950), p. 213.

Note that the "Anom" in *Ixanom* is not far from the Hebrew rendering of Adam in the Old Testament. The prefix Ix, with its "sh" sound in the Aztec tongue, resembles the Hebrew *ishi,* meaning *man*—hence "the man Adam" in English, "Ishi, Adam" in Hebrew, and "Ixanom" in Aztec. Note: As stated elsewhere in this work under the Literacy Chapter, *Ishi* is also the word for *man* in several of the ancient American dialects.

EVIDENCE NO. 829: ADONAI—ATANOTI

Evidence: One of the many striking parallels which link the Middle East to the Americas is that the Cherokee Indian name for God "Atanoti," is close to the Hebrew word for *Lord*. Since the Book of Mormon claims to be written by people from a Hebraic culture, one would expect to find traces of the Hebrew language in the language and culture of the ancient American peoples. For example, one of the most sacred words in the Hebrew language is *Adonai*, which means *Lord*.

Atanoti is the name of <u>one of the three</u> supreme gods of the Cherokees (Spence, Lewis, *Myths and Legends*: The North American Indians [Boston: David P. Nickerson, 1932], p. 3; cited in Cheesman, *The World of the Book of Mormon*, [1978], p. 3.)

EVIDENCE NO. 830: ALMA

Evidence: The name *Alma*, is introduced in Mosiah 17:2. Critics have questioned the authenticity of the Book of Mormon assuming that Alma was not an ancient near-Eastern name, rather a Latin word in the feminine gender meaning *soul*. Once again, what critics once used to mock the Book of Mormon has proved to be additional evidence that the Book of Mormon is true.

While Alma is a Latin word, recent findings have led to the conclusion that the word was also used in ancient Palestine and means *young man*, *servant*, or *eternity*. See Jaussen & Savignac, *Mission Archaeologique in Arabie*, (Paris, 1909), No.'s 277, 335, 394, 430, 475, 622, 984, 1292; *Survey of Western Palestine*, "Name Lists," E. H. Palmer, *Comment*, (London, 1881), pp. 40, 17, 66; Nibley, *Lehi in the Desert*, (1980), p. 45.

In 1966, Professor Yadin found the deed to a farm in the floor of the Cave of Manuscripts of the Dead Sea. Written on that deed, as one of the owners of the farm, is the name "Alma, son of Judah." This deed can be found at the *Shrine of the Book of Jerusalem*, a strip of papyrus mounted on glass with a light shining through. (See Nibley, *The Prophetic Book of Mormon*, [1989], p.310.)

Also, a Native American chief in the 1800's was named Alma (*Conference Report*, Oct. 1947, p. 17).

EVIDENCE NO. 831: ANTI

Evidence: The affix *Anti* as used in such names as *Manti*, *antion*, *Ani-Anti*, *Antiomno*, *Anti-Nephi-Lehi*, *Antiparah*, etc., is found throughout the Book of Mormon (Alma 2:22; 11:19; 21:11; 20:4; 24:3; 56:14). This is an authentic affix common among the ancient Americans and in the Middle East. Though used primarily as a prefix or a suffix, the term *anti* is an actual word from Book of Mormon times. For example, see Alma 21:11.

B. H. Roberts noted that according to the Encyclopedia Britannica, *anti* is an ancient American word meaning copper. He also cited Prescott who observed that the *Anta* or *Antis* are names for a tribe in the *Andes* Mountains of Peru. See William H. Prescott, *History of the Conquest of Peru*, [New York, 1898], vol. 1, p. 113, cited in B. H. Roberts, *New Witness for Christ in America*, vol. 3, p. 520.

See also the word *Andi* in A. Gustav, "Die Personnenamen id den Tontafeln von Tell Táannek," *Zeitschrift des Deutsch-Palästina Vereins*, vol. 50, (1927), pp. 1-19 and vol. 51 (1928), pp. 191, 198, 207 cited in Nibley, *An Approach to the Book of Mormon* (1988), p. 286.

EVIDENCE NO. 832: CHEMISH—SHEM-ASH

Evidence: The name *Chemish* is mentioned as a Nephite record keeper in the Book of Omni 1:8-10. Not only is this name found to be of ancient Hebrew origin, but also the meaning of the name is fitting for the calling of the individual who bore that name. The Hebrew equivalent *shem-ash* can be found in Strong's *Exhaustive Concordance*, which means "to serve, minister"—a possible name-title that symbolized the calling to serve as a record keeper for his Nephite brethren. (See James Strong, "A Concise Dictionary of the Hebrew Bible," in *Exhaustive Concordance,* [1973], entries no. 8120, p. 119.)

EVIDENCE NO. 833: CUMORAH

Evidence: *Cumorah*, a hill mentioned in Mormon 6:6, 11-15; and Ether 15:11, is an authentic name and strengthens the claim that the Book of Mormon is an accurate record of the ancient Americans. Not only is the word *Cumorah* authentic but its meaning corresponds with its use in the Book of Mormon. The word *Cumorah* is a combination of *Kamau* or *Qowmah* meaning "height, high, tall" and *rah* meaning "high" in Hebrew. (Strong, *Concordance of the Bible Hebrew & Chaldee Dictionary,* [New York: Abingdon Press, 1890, 1973], Words 6966, 6967 cited in Hunter and Ferguson, *Ancient America and the Book of Mormon* [1950], pp. 363-335.)

See also the evidence concerning the word *Ramah* later on in this same section.

EVIDENCE NO. 834: ETHER

Evidence: *Ether* is the name of an ancient American prophet who wrote the history of his people that migrated to America at the time of the tower of Babel. This history was later abridged by the prophet Moroni and included in the Book of Mormon as the *Book of Ether*. This name has also been found to be of ancient origin. For example see the names *Ether, Epher, Jether* mentioned in R. A. S. Macalister in *Palestine Exploration Fund Quarterly,* 1905, p. 333; cited in Nibley, *Lehi in the Desert, The World of the Jaredites,* (1980) p. 33.

EVIDENCE NO. 835: GAZELEM

Evidence: In his translation of the Book of Mormon, Joseph Smith used the strange name *Gazelem* to describe a servant of the Lord who would use "a stone, which shall shine forth in darkness unto light. ...And now, my son, these interpreters were prepared that the word of God might be fulfilled" (Alma 37:23-24). Here, the word *Gazelem* is used as a metaphor for the prophet who made use of the sacred stone as well as a synonym for the *Urim and Thummim* (Exodus 28:30; Leviticus 8:8; Deuteronomy 33:8; Ezra 2:63; Nehemiah 7:65).

While the name Gazelem is not found in dictionaries of ancient Hebrew, it was recently discovered that the name is actually a compound Hebrew word. It is apparently a combination the Hebrews words *Geh* and *Zelem*. The prefix *geh* is simply a demonstrative pronoun meaning "this," and the suffix *zelem* means "illusion, resemblance, representative figure, or image" as one might see by means of the seer stone or Urim and Thummim. (See James Strong, "Hebrew and Chaldee Dictionary," in *Exhaustive Concordance of the Bible,* [New York: Abingdon Press, 1890], entry nos. 1454, 6754, pp. 26, 99).

EVIDENCE NO. 836: ISABEL

Evidence: The harlot *Isabel* is mentioned in Alma 39:3. While critics have assumed that Joseph Smith simply borrowed this name from modern usage, the name was actually of ancient origin. Though not found in the Bible, it is Hebrew and is more often spelled *Ishabaal*. See *Hasting's Dictionary,* (New York, 1951), vol. 1, p. 209; vol. 2, p.501; *Interpreter's Bible*, Note on 2 Samuel 2:8; 1 Chronicles 9:39. See also Crowley, *About the Book of Mormon* (1961), pp. 109-110.

The similarity of the name Isabel with the Old Testament name Jezebel (2 Kings 9:22) is another example of metonymy, the practice of giving a person a name that reflects a trait associated with another person with the same name. (The "J" in Hebrew was pronounced as a "Y.") Both Isabel and Jezebel were examples of immoral behavior. (See Gordon Thomasson in *FARMS Insights*, June 1984, p. 1.)

Furthermore, this name may very well have provided the root for *Lake Izabal* in Central America, located approximately 89° west longitude, and between 15° and 16° north latitude.

EVIDENCE NO. 837: ISHMAEL—IZAMAL—UXMAL

Evidence: Ishmael, who was the father of Lehi's daughters-in-law (1 Nephi 7), may very well have formed the etymological basis for the name of the Mayan god *Izamal*, as well as the name *Uxmal*, a Mayan city on the Yucatan Peninsula. Since the "x" is pronounced with the "sh" sound, the two words are nearly identical. Such honoring of an ancestor as the father of the Lehite matriarchy would be a significant part of the culture of the ancient Americans. It is well known that their society was often matriarchal in nature.

Among the Hopi Indians of Arizona, matrilineal households took leading roles in public ceremonies. "Women played a profound role in Iroquois political life." The female heirs to the chieftain titles of the league were part of a matrilineal system headed by a "clan mother." The oldest daughter of the head of a clan often succeeded her mother at her death. Also, the Huron Indians traced their ancestry through the female line. Males who became chief were chosen from the female line. (See Joy Miller, in *Encyclopedia of North American Indians,* edited by Frederick E. Hoxie, [New York: Houghton Mifflin Co., 1996], p. 194; and B. E. Johansen, in *Encyclopedia of North American Indians,* edited by D. Birchfiel, [New York: Marshall Cavendish Co. 1997], vol. 4, pp. 503-4.)

EVIDENCE NO. 838: JACOB—ECAB—LLOCAB

Evidence: The name Jacob, mentioned in the Book of Mormon as a Nephite prophet (Jacob 1:1), may well have been the basis for a Mesoamerican site on the northeastern tip of the Yucatan Peninsula called *Ecab*. Anciently, the Hebrew name Jacob was pronounced as *Yakob* or *Iacob*—the similarity to *Ecab* is quite obvious. Furthermore, the Book of Mormon indicates that Lehi and his family were descendants of *Israel* (3 Nephi 10:17; 20:22) who was first known as *Jacob* (Genesis 32:28). See James Strong, *Hebrew and Chaldee Dictionary,* (New York: Abingdon Press, 1890), word #3290, *Yáaqob*, p. 51.

Evidence: The *Popol Vuh*, the sacred book of the ancient Quiché-Maya in the highlands of Guatemala, mentions that the people of *Llocab* came to this land from the "other side of the sea" in the East. The double "L" in Llocab is pronounced "Y." Thus, Llocab would be pronounced exactly like the Hebrews pronounced the name Jacob—Yah·ak·obe'. (See Delia Goetz and Sylvannus G. Morley, *Popol Vuh*, English translation by Adrian Recinos, [University of Oklahoma Press: Norman, 1950], pp. 69-80, 171; cited in Hunter and Ferguson, *Ancient America and the Book of Mormon,* [1950], p. 64).

EVIDENCE NO. 839: JARED AND HIS BROTHER

Evidence: Two righteous brothers referred to as Jared and "the brother of Jared" led the Jaredites to the Promised Land of America. These two prophets petitioned the Lord at the time of the confounding of the languages to allow them and their people to continue to speak their native tongue (Ether 1:33-37). The name of the brother of Jared is not given in the Book of Mormon. The authenticity of the Book of Mormon is verified by the recent discovery of this same story in ancient tradition.

According to a Mandaen tradition, when the human race was broken up into different tongues, after the world had been purged, there were two righteous brothers whose language was not changed: *Ram* and his brother *Rud*. Both names are contractions, *Rud* is short for *Jared,* and *Ram* is from some unknown name. The legend goes on to say that these two men led a migration to the east, founded "a race of mankind" and were never heard of again. Robert Eisler points out that *Ram* means "high" and *Rud* means "wanderer", as does the name *Jared*. See Robert Eisler, *Iesous Basileus ou Basileusas,* vol. 2, p. 109, n. 1, cf. 180; Ethel S. Drower, *The Mandaeans of Iraq and Iran,* pp. 22-23, 132; both cited in Nibley, *An Approach to the Book of Mormon,* (1988), p. 333; and Nibley, *Since Cumorah,* (1988), p. 274.

EVIDENCE NO. 840: JERSHON

Evidence: *Jershon* is mentioned in the Book of Mormon as the land given "for an inheritance" to the converted Lamanites (Alma 27:22). The Hebrew equivalent of *Jershon* is *Yershon,* which also means, "place of inheritance." See John A. Tvedtnes, in *A Sure Foundation* (Deseret Book Co., 1988), p. 24.

EVIDENCE NO. 841: LAMAN

Evidence: The name *Laman* was first introduced is in 1 Nephi 2:5. Laman, the oldest of Lehi's four sons, may have been given his Arabic name during Lehi's travels among Arabic traders. Critics have asked: if an entire civilization was named after *Laman,* why has not the name *Laman* or even a corrupted form of it survived down through the centuries—especially in light of the fact that the *Lamanites* were victorious over their enemies the *Nephites,* and continued to live as a nation? See Mormon 5:6; 6:8; 8:2-8; Moroni 9:7-21.

However, not only is the name *Laman* authentic, but it is actually the name by which several groups of Indians are called—just as the Book of Mormon records. The names *Lamans, Layamon, Laymones, Laimon, Liamone, Laymona, Limon,* and *Limonies* have all been found in early American tribal groups: See Elisee Reclus, *The Earth and Its Inhabitants* (New York: Appleton & Co., 1891), vol. 1, p. 283; Maria Francisco Picolo, *Memoir in Recueil de Voyages au Nord,* vol. 3, p. 279; Miguel Venegas, *Juan Maria Salvatierra,* (Madrid, 1757), translated by Margaret Wilbur (Cleveland, 1920), p. 37; *Historical Memoir of Pimeria Alta,* vol. 2, p. 50, translated by Herbert E. Bolton, (University of California); Jacob Baegert, 1864 *Report Smithsonian Institute,* pp. 378, 393; An account of the aboriginal inhabitants of the California peninsula, by Baegert's *Nachrichten* translated by Charles Rau, parts 1-4, 1863, *Report Smithsonian Institute,* p. 352, parts 5-10; Gerard Decorme, *Da Obra De Los Jesuitas Mexicanos,* translated by Barbara Crowley, (1949); J. Ross Browne, "The Indian Tribes and Languages of the Peninsula," *Resources of the Pacific Slope,* (1869), pp. 53-54; "Lamani," in *Enciclopedia Universal Illustrada;* "Mapa Linguistico de Norte y Centro-America" in *Instituto Nacional de Anthropologie e Historia* of Costa Rica and *Museo Nacional de Mexico* (1936), Grupo Siux-Hokano, Sub-grupo Hokano-Subtiaba, XXIX Familia Yumana 95; *Lenguas Indigenas de Mexico Mendizabal-J. Moreno, Distribucion Prehispanica de las Lenguas Indigenos,* (1939), Map 5. All above sources are also cited in Ariel L. Crowley, *About the Book of Mormon* (Deseret News Press, 1961), pp. 76-85.

The name Laman is also the clear root for a Mesoamerican site called *Lamanai* located about one third of the way up the east coast of the Yucatan peninsula at approximately 18° north and 90° west longitude.

Furthermore, the name *Laman* was also found in the Old World with various spellings as: *Anlaman, Lamon, Leimun,* and even *Laman.* See F. L. Griffith, *Journal of Egyptian Archaeology,* vol. 4, (1917), pp. 169, 161, 216; C. Clenmont-Ganneau, "Moslem Mukams," *Survey of Western Palestine, Special Papers,* p. 325 and C. R. Conder, same volume, p. 272; E. ben Yehuda, "The Edomite Language," *Journal of Palestine Oriental Society,* vol. 1, (1921), pp. 113-115. All cited in Nibley, *Since Cumorah,* (1988), p. 171; and Nibley, *Lehi in the Desert,* (1952), p. 45.

EVIDENCE NO. 842: LEHI

Evidence: *Lehi,* the name of the great prophet and patriarch of the Nephite and Lamanite nations, is introduced in 1 Nephi 1:4. The use of this name in ancient Palestine is documented in *Survey of Western Palestine,* "Name Lists" edited by E. H. Palmer, (London, 1881), p. 358; Ed. Meyer, *Israeliten,* p. 322, No. 336, p. 313;

The similar name *Lahai* or *LHI* is documented in Nelson Glueck, "Ostraca From Elath," *Bulletin of the American Schools of Oriental Research*, No. 80, December 1940, p. 5; *Journal of Biblical Literature*, vol. 33, (1914), pp. 290-295. Also cited in Nibley, *Lehi in the Desert* (1952), p. 44.

EVIDENCE NO. 843: LIAHONA

Evidence: The Book of Mormon describes an instrument that was built by Jehovah, and given to the prophet Lehi as a "director" called the "*Liahona*, which is, being interpreted, a compass; and the Lord prepared it" (Alma 37:38). It was equipped with "two spindles" which directed their course of travels as described in 1 Nephi 16:10.

Not only is this word authentic, but it carries the same meaning in Hebrew. A literal translation of this strange word is: "to Jehovah for light." (See George Reynolds and Janne Sjodahl, *Commentary on the Book of Mormon*, [Deseret Book: 1959], vol. 4, p. 178.)

Furthermore it also fits the description of a similar word in the Hebrew language. For the similar name *lahab-hennah*, see Hebrew for "point" and "whither," in James Strong, *A Concise Dictionary of the Words in the Hebrew Bible*, appendage to his *Exhaustive Concordance of the Bible*, (Abingdon Press, 1890), words 3851-3852 and 2008, cited in Hunter and Ferguson, *Ancient America and the Book of Mormon* (1950), p. 71.

EVIDENCE NO. 844: MATHONI, MATHONIHAH, & MIDDONI

Evidence: *Mathoni* and his brother *Mathonihah* are listed in the Book of Mormon as two of the twelve disciples chosen by Jesus Christ during His visit to ancient America after his resurrection (3 Nephi 19:4). The land of *Middoni* is mentioned several times in the Book of Mormon, starting in Alma 20:2. These are authentic Egyptian and Hebrew names.

Compare these Book of Mormon names with the following Hebrew names: *Mittani, Matianoi, Mitanni* and *Mattanyahu*. See Théodore Reinach, "Un Peuple Oublié: Les Matiènes," *Revue des Études Grecques*, vol. 7, (1894), pp. 313-318; Walter Otto, "Zur Universalgeschichte des Altertums," *Historische Zeitschrift*, vol. 146, (1932), pp. 205-206; Harry Torczyner, *Lachish I (tell ed-Duweir): The Lachish Letters*, (London: Oxford, 1938), p. 24; The above are also cited in three of Dr. Nibley's Books namely: *Since Cumorah*, (1988), p. 171; *Approach to the Book of Mormon*, (1988), p. 19; and *The Prophetic Book of Mormon*, (1989), p. 388, respectively.

The following is quoted from a report by Dr. Hugh Nibley entitled "The Book of Mormon as a Mirror of the East." (This paper was reprinted as F.A.R.M.S. Report, N-BMM from the *Improvement Era* vol. 73, November 1970, pp. 115-120. Elements of this report also appeared in Dr. Nibley's book entitled *Lehi in the Desert*, [1988], p. 22.)

> A reflection of the Egyptian picture may be detected in the coast cities of Palestine, regularly under Egyptian influence, where government was also by priests and judges, who occasionally usurped the office of king. This happened both at Sidon and Tyre; in the latter city two priestly usurpers bore the name of *Maitena* or *Mattena*—a name which has a number of variants and strongly suggests the Book of Mormon *Mathoni*. (See A. Moret, *Histoire de l'Orient*, [Paris: Presses Universitaires, 1941], vol. 2, p. 610.)

Furthermore, the roots of these names can be found in Strong's *Exhaustive Concordance*. Mathonihah: the first syllable, *math*, means "an adult," while the second, *anaya*, means "Jehovah has answered." Combining these two words results in a name which would seem to indicate "a man, whose prayers have been answered by Jehovah." Similarly, Mathoni seems to be a combination of *math*, and *adoni*, which means "Lord." Putting the two together would represent "a man of the Lord." Both names are fitting for apostles or emissaries of the Lord Jehovah. (See James Strong, "A Concise Dictionary of the Hebrew Bible," in *Exhaustive Concordance*, [1973], entries nos. 136, 2123, 7311, pp. 8, 35, 107.)

EVIDENCE NO. 845: MELCHIZEDEK

Evidence: The Book of Mormon Refers to *Melchizedek* as a high priest who had lived many years previously in the Old World (Alma 13:14). It is highly significant that the same name is found in ancient American writings, even though the spelling is slightly different.

In a Mayan account of the creation known as "The Birth of the Uinal," which is found in the *Book of Chilam Balam of Chumayel*, the following is recorded: "Thus it was read by the first sage, *Melchisedek*, and the first prophet, Puc Tun, the priest, and the first sun priest..." (This document is translated in Munro S. Edmonson, *Chilam Balam of Chumayel*, [Austin:University of Texas Press,1986], P. 120-126, Cited in Roberta H. and Peter T. Markman, *The Flayed God—The Mythoology of Mesoamerica*, [NY: Harper San Francisco, 1992], P. 98.)

The Markmans do not comment on the name—possibly because they were not aware that it is Hebraic. Some critics may say that Edmonson could have been influenced by possible knowledge of the Biblical Melchizedek. But this is unlikely because of several reasons: 1) the non-Biblical spelling, 2) most Christians are not familiar with Melchizedek, 3) and most of those who have heard of him do not believe he was an actual person, rather a figurative illusion to the per-mortal Christ. Furthermore, scholars have found that "during the classic period, the Maya wrote in what linguists called a 'mixed' script, composed of both phonetic syllables and logographs (that is, word pictures) that allowed them to replicate most of the nuances of speech." (See Mary Miller and Karl Taube, *The Gods and Symbols of Ancient Mexico and the Maya*, [NY: Thames and Hudson, 1993], P. 187.)

EVIDENCE NO. 846: MINON

Evidence: The land of *Minon* is mentioned in Alma 2:24. The Nephite emigrants who left Palestine most likely borrowed this authentic name from the Philistine civilization and used it in the Western Hemisphere. See D. W. Thomas, *Palestine Exploration Fund Quarterly*, 1950, pp. 5, 8, cited in Nibley, *An Approach to the Book of Mormon* (1957), p. 234.

EVIDENCE NO. 847: MORMON

Evidence: The prophet *Mormon* was one of the last of the Nephite leaders who compiled and abridged the history of his people into what was later named by his son: *the Book of Mormon*. He was named after his father who was also named *Mormon* (Mormon 1:5). *Mormon* was also employed in the Book of Mormon as a geographical name (Mosiah 18:4).

Although some antagonists have attempted to find a parallel between the name *Mormon* and a somewhat similar-sounding word said to be from the Far East, the name *Mormon* itself comes from the Middle East as is—without the deletion of any consonant. The name is typical Hebrew, Egyptian and Arabic. See C. Clermont-Ganneau, "Moslem Mukams," *Survey of Western Palestine, Special Papers*, p. 325.

The Egyptian *Mr-monh* means "good master" according to the *History of Sinuhe*, an ancient Egyptian romance, cited in Webb, *Joseph Smith as Translator,* (1936), pp. 62, 66. This is especially significant in light of the fact that the prophet Joseph Smith explained that part of the word means "good." See Smith, *Teachings of the Prophet Joseph Smith* (1976), pp. 299-300.

EVIDENCE NO. 848: THE NAME-TITLE OF MOSIAH

Evidence: The name-title *Mosiah* as employed in the Book of Mormon and introduced in Omni 1:12 is an ancient Hebrew term which could not have been known to Joseph Smith. This provides additional evidence that Joseph Smith was indeed a prophet of God, and that he translated the Book of Mormon though the gift and power of God. The following is taken from F.A.R.M.S. (*Foundation for Ancient Research and Mormon Studies Update*, April 1989, SAW-65 by John Sawyer).

In 1965, John Sawyer published an article entitled "What was a Mosia?" *Vetus Testamentum*, vol. 15, (1965), pp. 475-486. He argues that the term "mosiah" was an ancient Hebrew term, like *go'el* ("redeemer, avenger of blood"), or *sedek* ("victor, savior"), that originally had meaning in Hebrew daily life and culture but came to be used among their titles for God. The word mosia (pronounced moe-shee-ah) is a word peculiar to Hebrew, a "word invariably implying a champion of justice in a situation of controversy, battle or oppression" (Sawyer, "What was a Mosia," p. 476). Sawyer's analysis may shed interesting light on the word Mosiah in the Book of Mormon.

It appears that the form of the word Mosiah is a Hiphil participle in Hebrew. It occurs in Deuteronomy 22:27; 28:29; Judges 12:3; Psalms 18:42; Isaiah 5:29—texts that in all probability were on the Plates of Brass. This word, however, was not transliterated into the English by the King James translators, and thus it would not have been known to Joseph Smith. It was, however, known and used as a personal name in the Book of Mormon, as well as by people in the Jewish colony at Elephantine in the 5th century BC.

The meaning of the word *mosia* was "savior." People in danger cry out, "but there is no *mosia*" (Deuteronomy 22:27). After examining all occurrences of this term in the Hebrew Bible, Sawyer concludes that the term *mosia* applied to a particular kind of person and was sometimes a title designating "a definite office or position" (Saywer, "What was a Mosia," p. 477). Typical of this office are the following traits:

(a) A *mosia* is a victorious hero appointed by God;
(b) he liberates a chosen people from oppression, controversy and injustice after they cry out for help;
(c) their deliverance is usually accomplished by means of a non-violent escape or negotiation;
(d) the immediate result of the coming of a *mosia* was "escape from injustice, and a return to a state of justice where each man possesses his rightful property." Ibid., 480.
(e) On a larger scale "final victory means the coming of *mosi'im* [pronounced moe-shee-**eem** = mosiahs] to rule like Judges over Israel" (Saywer, "What was a Mosia," p. 482).

Thus the term had judicial or forensic connotations, similar to the word "advocate." A *mosia* gives refuge to those on his "right hand" from their accusers in court (Psalm 17:7; Moroni 7:28).

The exact derivation of the Book of Mormon name Mosiah is unknown, but it appears to be the same as *mosia*, which derives from the Hebrew *hasa* ("to be wide open, free, deliver, rescue, preserve, save"), and so it is quite different from the word *messiah*, derived from the Hebrew word *masiah* ("anointed," Greek *christos*). It might also contain a theophoric element (-iah), thus meaning "the Lord is a *mosia*."

Interestingly, the term *mosia* applies perfectly to the mosiahs in the Book of Mormon. King Mosiah I was a God-appointed hero who delivered the chosen people of Nephi from serious wars and contentions by escaping out of the land of Nephi (Omni 1:12-4). It is unknown whether he was called Mosiah before he functioned as a *mosia* of his people or if he took this well-earned title upon himself afterwards, but either is possible.

Indeed, the book of Mosiah tells of one *mosia* after another. Alma was a God-inspired *mosia* who peaceably saved his people from King Noah and the Lamanites. Zeniff tried to return to the land of Nephi to repossess the rightful property of the Nephites, but his efforts failed and his grandson Limhi eventually functioned as a *mosia* in leading his people in their escape back to Zarahemla. The themes of God's salvation and the deliverance of his people are strong in the book of Mosiah. At the end of the book of Mosiah the reign of Judges was established, a fitting development for a people that had been best served by *mosi'im* for over a century. Thus, the book of Mosiah, like the book of Judges in the Old Testament, appears to have been very meaningfully named.

EVIDENCE NO. 849: THE NAME-TITLE OF MULEK

Evidence: The name *Mulek* is first mentioned in Mosiah 25:2, as the youngest son and the only surviving heir of King Zedekiah of Jerusalem when the massacre took place during the destruction of Jerusalem in 600 BC. (See also Helaman 6:10.) Though 2 Kings 25:4-7 records that the Zedekiah's sons were all slain, some fascinating conclusions have recently been drawn about *Malchiah* (mentioned in Jeremiah 38:6) that link him to the Mulek mentioned in the Book of Mormon.

Dr. Yohanan Aharoni, the late head of the Department of Archaeology at Tel Aviv University concluded that the Biblical Malchiah was actually the Son of Zedekiah. Furthermore, it is now known that many Hebrew names were shortened in the 6th century BC. For example the name BerekYahu became Baruch, and Malchiah (MalkiYahu) would have been shortened to something very much like Mulek as in the Book of Mormon. When a prominent Old Testament scholar visiting Brigham Young University learned that the Book of Mormon names Mulek as a son of Zedekiah, he remarked, "If Joseph Smith came up with that one, he did pretty well!" (See *Foundation for Ancient Research and Mormon Studies Insights,* June, 1984, p. 1.)

Not only is the name *Mulek* an authentic Hebrew word, but it also happens to be a noble title meaning *royal* or *king*, according to James Strong, *A Concise Dictionary of the Words in the Hebrew Bible,* (New York: Abingdon Press, 1890), words 4429-4432. The royal connotations of the name *Mulek* correspond to its use in the Book of Mormon as the name of a prince. See also Robert F. Smith, W. Benjamin Urrutia, *Foundation for Ancient Research and Mormon Studies Update*, February 1984; cited in *Re-exploring the Book of Mormon*, Edited by John W. Welch (1992), pp. 142-144.

EVIDENCE NO. 850: NAHOM

Evidence: *Nahom* is mentioned in the Book of Mormon as the place where the daughters of Ishmael mourned their father's death, and where he was buried (1 Nephi 16:34). Not only is this word authentic, but its meaning corresponds to the way it is used in the Book of Mormon. *Nahom, Nahum* or *NHM* are Arabic for "to sigh or mourn." Just as the daughters of Ishmael mourned their father's death, the obvious conclusion is that the mourners named the place Nahom as a symbol of their grief.

The fact that the Book of Mormon specifically mentions *daughters* mourning but not *sons* is another evidence of the veracity of the Book of Mormon. It is the custom in the Middle East for only the women to mourn. See Nibley, *Lehi in the Desert* (1952), pp. 90-91.

There is related evidence elsewhere in the "Geography" chapter of this same volume suggesting that Nahom may have existed prior to the arrival of the Lehi party. This possibility would indicate that its very location in the hot dry Arabian Desert would be logically named by previous travelers who suffered and mourned, as did Lehi's party. Indeed, in such a harsh, lifeless locale, it would be surprising if any group of travelers did *not* mourn.

EVIDENCE NO. 851: OMNI—LOMNI

Evidence: One of the ancient American prophets who contributed to the writing of the Book of Mormon is named *Omni*, introduced in the first verse of the *Book of Omni*. While this name sounds like a word from a science fiction magazine, it was actually used in the ancient Middle East. For the similar *Lomni*, see R. A. Stewart Macalister, "The Craftsmen's Guild of the Tribe of Judah," in *Palestine Exploration Fund Quarterly*, 1905, p. 333; K. Sethe, *Zeitschrift für Ägyptische Sprache und Altertumskunde*, vol. 43, (1906), pp. 147-149. Both cited in Nibley, *Since Cumorah*, (1988), pp. 171.

EVIDENCE NO. 852: RAMAH, RAMEUMPTOM

Evidence: The names and meaning of *Ramah* and *Rameumptom* are given in the Book of Mormon—that of *Ramah* to a high hill (Ether 15:11), and *Rameumptom* to a high and "holy stand" used by a group of apostates for offering vain prayers (Alma 31:21). These names are not only authentic, but carry the same meanings as similar ancient Near Eastern words.

Rah-mah means "height" or "high place." *Ra'am* is Hebrew for "high," or "to rise:—be lifted up." *Rameem* means "the heights" in the hills near Lebanon. When *raam* is combined with *yowm,* which means "perpetually" it suggests that the people continually ascended to the high holy place to repeat the same prayer each time. The words *tom* and *tam,* which mean "perfect, complete, pious and uprightly," add the element of self-righteousness that the apostate Nephites exhibited in their prayer. (See James Strong, "A Concise Dictionary of the Hebrew Bible," in *Exhaustive Concordance of the Bible,* [New York: Abingdon Press, 1973], words 3117, 7213, 7215, 7216, 7311, 7413, 8537 & 8535, pp. 48, 106-107, 109, 124; *Funk & Wagnall's New Standard Bible Dictionary,* 1936 edition, p. 760; Daniel H. Ludlow, *A Companion to Your Study of the Book of Mormon* [Deseret Book Co., 1976], p. 213.)

Remb, Ramp, and *Rhamph* are Greek words that describe the ancient Christian stylites, which consisted of endless gyrations atop a high pillar. The pillar-sitting monks of Syria carried on an ancient pagan tradition in which the man on the pillar at some important ceremonial center would pray for the people. See Henrico Stephano, *Thesaurus Graecae Linguae,* (Reprint Graz: Akademische Druck–und Verlagsanstalk, 1954), vol. 7, pp. 2337-2338; Johannes Leipoldt, *Religionsgeschichte des Orients in der Weltreligionen,* Edited by B. Spuler (Leiden: Brill, 1961), p. 10; cited in Nibley, *Since Cumorah,* (1988), p. 244.

Though the name *Ramah* is listed throughout the Bible together with its variants of *Raamah* and *Rama,* the meaning of this strange word is not given in the sacred text. It is highly significant, therefore, that the Book of Mormon utilizes these words and gives their meaning which Joseph Smith would not have known—being relatively uneducated.

EVIDENCE NO. 853: RIPLIANCUM

Evidence: The name of a large body of water is mentioned in the Book of Mormon as *Ripliancum* "which, by interpretation, is large, or to exceed all" (Ether 15:8). The authenticity of this name strengthens the claim that the Book of Mormon is an accurate history of ancient Hebrews in America.

In spite of critics who have accused Joseph Smith of fabricating words that make no sense, the word *Ripliancum* fits very well into ancient Middle Eastern linguistics. *Ripliancum* is almost identical to a combination of three words from classical Hebrew and Chaldee: *rab, lahen* and *koom.* The meanings of these ancient words are also consistent with the interpretation given in the Book of Mormon. These words are defined in James Strong, "A Concise Dictionary" in *Exhaustive Concordance,* (1973):

   rab: "abundant, exceedingly, full, great, much" (word no. 7227, p. 106)
   lahen: "to or for ... therefore" (word 3860, p. 59)
   koom: "to rise ... lift up" (word 6965, p. 102) which is closely related to
   komaw: "height, high, stature" (word 6967, p. 102).

EVIDENCE NO. 854: SARIAH

Evidence: *Sariah,* the wife of the Book of Mormon prophet Lehi, is first introduced in 1 Nephi 2:5. The name *Sariah* has its roots in the Middle East just as the Book of Mormon implies. Although Sariah is not found as a *female* name in the Bible, the name *Seraiah* is used nineteen times in the Old Testament, representing eleven different *men* (2 Samuel 8:17; 2 Kings 25:18; 25:23; 1 Chronicles 4:13-14; 4:35; 6:14; Ezra 2:2; 7:1; Nehemiah 10:2; 11:11; 12:1, 12; Jeremiah 36:26; 40:8; 51:59, 61; and 52:24).

However, the name Sariah has more recently been found as the name of a Jewish woman living at Elephantine in Upper Egypt during the fifth century BC. A reference to *"Sariah daughter of Hoshea son of Harman"* is found in the Aramaic Papyrus of Elephantine #22 (also called Cowley #22 or C-22) and appears in *Aramaic Papyri of the Fifth Century BC,* Edited and Translated by Arthur E. Cowley, (Oxford: Clarendon, 1923), p. 67.

This is particularly interesting in light of the fact that Sariah left Jerusalem with her family around 600 BC, and had close ties to Egypt (1 Nephi 1:2; 10:4). Her name is phonetically identical to *Seriah* as mentioned in 2 Barnabas 5:5 (though spelled differently). See Jeffrey R. Chadwick, "Sariah in the Elephantine Papyri," *Journal of Book of Mormon Studies,* vol. 2, no. 2, (Fall 1993), pp. 196-200; and George Reynolds and Janne Sjodahl, *Commentary on the Book of Mormon,* (Deseret Book: 1959), vol. 1, p. 14.

EVIDENCE NO. 855: SHAZER

Evidence: *Shazer* is mentioned in 1 Nephi 16:13-14 as a place where Lehi and his people stopped and camped for a time during their travels through the desert. The fact that this word was properly employed in the Book of Mormon provides further evidence that the Joseph Smith made an accurate translation of this ancient history.

Shajer is a common Palestinian place name for *trees,* which is pronounced *Shazher* by the Arabs. *Shazer* is Arabic for "a weak but reliable water supply—or a clump of trees." *Shisur* is a famous water hole in Southern Arabia. Other variations on this ancient word include *Shisar, Shihor, Sozura, Shaghur* and *Segor.* See Bertram Thomas, *Arabia Felix,* (New York: Scribner, 1932), p. 136-137; Harry S. J. B. Philby, *The Empty Quarter,* (New York: Holt, 1933), p. 231; Claude R. Conder, *Survey of Eastern Palestine,* (London: Palestine Exploration Fund, 1889), vol. 1, pp. 239, 241; Edward H. Palmer, "Arabic and English Name Lists," *Survey of Western Palestine,* (London: Palestine Exploration Fund, 1881), vol. 8, pp. 29, 93, 116, 134; Claude R. Conder, "Notes on the Language of the Native Peasantry in Palestine," *Palestine Exploration Fund Quarterly* (1879), p. 134; Claude R. Conder and H. H. Kitchener, "Memoirs of the Topography, Orography, Hydrography and Archaeology," *Survey of Western Palestine,* (London: Palestine Exploration Fund, 1881), vol. 2, p. 169. All sources for variants of the Book of Mormon *Shazer* are cited in Nibley, *Lehi in the Desert,* (1988), p. 78-79.

Furthermore, Lynn and Hope Hilton have identified a possible location for this oasis. Assuming that Lehi's party traveled approximately twenty miles per day, a four-day journey from the previous camp at the Valley of Lemuel would put *Shazer* at an oasis called *al-Muwaylih*—a natural stopping place for weary travelers. (See Hilton, *Discovering Lehi,* [1996], pp. 33-34, 109.)

EVIDENCE NO. 856: SHELEM, SHILOM

Evidence: *Shelem* is the name of a high mountain mentioned in Ether 3:1. Not only is this an authentic name, its meaning fits the way it is used in the Book of Mormon. *Salam* is a Semitic word for "a high place." A secondary meaning may be the similar-sounding word *Shalom* that means "peace." The high mountain may have been a place of peace and safety. In Arabic *Sullam* means *ladder, stairway,* or *elevation.* See Nibley, *Lehi in the Desert* (1988), p. 242.

The name *Shilom* is introduced in Mosiah 7:5, 21 as both a land and an ancient American city. This name resembles one of the names mentioned in the *Lachish Letters* (military reports written at the very time of the fall of Jerusalem, and discovered in the twentieth century). This remarkable body of documents mentions the name of *Tobshillem.* See Harry Torczyner, *Lachish I (Tell ed-Duwer): The Lachish Letters,* (London: Oxford, 1938); cited in Nibley, *The Prophetic Book of Mormon,* (1989) p. 388.

Both names are most likely a variant of the Hebrew word *shalom,* which means "peaceable, perfect, quiet"—a fitting title for a city and land occupied with those how hope for peace and perfection. (See James Strong, "A Concise Dictionary of the Hebrew Bible," in *Exhaustive Concordance,* [1973], entry no. 8004, p. 117.)

The probability that Joseph Smith could have made up these names together with the many others mentioned in this work **and** to have used them correctly—in accordance with their ancient meanings, is so small as to allow only one conclusion: Joseph Smith was truly a prophet of God, and the Book of Mormon was not his fabrication, but rather was a divinely inspired translation of an ancient document, as he claimed it was.

EVIDENCE NO. 857: SHEUM

Evidence: *Sheum,* a strange word is mentioned as a name for a New World crop in Mosiah 9:9. Very similar words of ancient American origin have recently been documented. Two words found in the language of the ancient Americans are *sum* and *ishim*. *Sum* means corn or maize among the Aymara of Argentina. *Ishim* means corn or maize in the Chol Mayan dialect of Chiapas near Izapa. See the word SUM in Jose Gabriel, *Idiomas Aboriginales* (Buenos Aires, Argentina: Dibujos de Carlos J. Abregu Mittelbach, 1941), p. 273. The word ISHIM can be found in, Marcos E. Becerra, *Vocabulario de la Lengua Chol.* (Mexico City: Talleres Graficos de la Nación, 1937), p. 24. Both cited in Vestal and Wallace, *The Firm Foundation of Mormonism,* (1981), p. 121.

EVIDENCE NO. 858: SHULE

Evidence: *Shule* was a Jaredite king mentioned in Ether 1:30-31. The authenticity of this name makes a significant contribution to the case for the truthfulness of the Book of Mormon. The Maya place name *Xul,* which is also the name of one of the Maya months, is pronounced exactly the same as *Shule,* the "x" being the Spanish spelling for the Maya sound "sh." (See Allen, *Exploring the Lands of the Book of Mormon* [1989], p. 37.)

EVIDENCE NO. 859: ZARAHEMLA

Evidence: The great Nephite city *Zarahemla* is introduced in the Book of Omni verse 14. It is described as being located in the region of the Land of Bountiful—a name that reflected is lush environment. It was in an area that had "many plants and roots," having frequent rains and seasonal fevers—typical of a tropical rain forest (Alma 22:32-33; 46:40). *Bountiful* was also the name of another Nephite city to the north of *Zarahemla* in the same general area (Helaman 1:23). This strange name is not only an authentic word, but also its meaning precisely fits its use in the Book of Mormon. *Zara-hamullah*: compounded from the Hebrew *Zara* meaning "to sow, plant, yield," and *Hamullah* meaning "too fully." Also *Hemla* meaning, "fully, overflowing abundance." See James Strong, *Dictionary of the Words in the Hebrew Bible,* (New York: Abingdon Press, 1890, 1973), words 1890, 1998, 1999, and 2232. See also *Bountiful* in the same volume. Also cited in Hunter and Ferguson, *Ancient America and the Book of Mormon* (1950), p. 152.

The Mesoamerican cite called *Yarumela,* is quite likely another variant of the name Zarahemla. Yarumela is located approximately 15° north latitude and 88° west longitude in Central America.

EVIDENCE NO. 860: ZENOS

Evidence: Jacob chapters 5-6 indicate that *Zenos* was an Israelite prophet who compared apostate Israel to a vineyard with corrupt fruit. Critics have long objected to the Book of Mormon mention of a prophet, not listed in the Bible, who was supposed to have lived in Jerusalem sometime before 600 BC.

However, since the discovery of the Dead Sea Scrolls, the world has learned that such a man did indeed exist by the name of *Zenez.* In 1893 M. R. James published Greek and Latin versions of "The Vision of Zenez, the Father of Gothoniel," from the Dead Sea Scrolls. Not only does the prophet *Zenez* share the same name as the *Zenos* mentioned in the Book of Mormon, but both compared apostate Israel to a vineyard with corrupt fruit. The only logical assumption is that *Zenez* and *Zenos* are one and the same. See M. R. James, *Apocrypha and Anecdota* Texts and Studies, edited by J. A. Robinson (Cambridge University, 1893), vol. 2, part 3, pp. 174-179. Also James' *The Biblical Antiquities of Philo* (London: SPCK, 1917), p. 34, cited in Nibley, *Since Cumorah,* (1988), p. 278.

Again, it was not possible for Joseph Smith to have known about the *Zenez* of the Dead Sea Scrolls, which had not yet been discovered, and it is not statistically possible for him to have invented both the prophet and his message—both which are verified in the Scrolls. So the only logical conclusion is that Joseph Smith made an accurate translation of an authentic record of ancient history when he translated the Book of Mormon, through the "gift and power of God."

EVIDENCE NO. 861: ZORAM

<u>Evidence</u>: *Zoram*, a Hebrew servant in the house of Laban at Jerusalem is introduced in 1 Nephi 4:35. Though this name is of ancient Hebrew origin, it is not found in the Bible. For documentation that *Zoram* is an authentic Hebrew and Arabic name, see Alfred F. L. Beeston, "Old South Arabian Antiquities, *Journal Royal Asiatic Society* (1952), p. 21, cited in Nibley, *Approach to the Book of Mormon*, (1988), p. 286.

EVIDENCE NO. 862: THE FREQUENCY OF "-AN" AND "-ON" NAME ENDINGS

<u>Evidence</u>: Many Book of Mormon names end with the Arabic suffixes -an and -on, such as *Helaman, Laman, Pahoran, Emron, Heshlon, Jashon, Mormon*, etc. Names ending in -an and -on are generally older and more Arabic than Hebraic. This is consistent with the fact that Lehi and his family belonged to the tribe of Manasseh (Alma 10:3) which lived farther out in the desert than any other tribe, and, hence, were in more frequent contact with Arabs than any of the other tribes.

See James L. Montgomery, *Arabia and the Bible*, (Philadelphia: University of Pennsylvania Press, 1934), p. 47; William F. Albright, *The Vocalization of Egyptian Syllabic Orthography*, (New Haven: The American Oriental Society, 1934), vol. 10, p. 12; Abraham Bergman, "The Israelite Tribe of Half-Manasseh," *Journal of the Palestine Oriental Society*, vol. 16, (1936), pp. 225, 228, 249; Moses H. Segal, "The Settlement of Manasseh East of the Jordan," *Palestine Exploration Fund Quarterly*, (1918), p. 124; all cited in Nibley, *Lehi in the Desert* (1988), p. 38.

EVIDENCE NO. 863: THE FREQUENCY OF "I" NAME ENDINGS

<u>Evidence</u>: The Book of Mormon practice of ending names in "i," (such as *Moroni, Lamoni* and *Muloki*) has been found to be an authentic Hebrew practice. The letter "i" at the end of some names is the Hebrew *Nisbeh*, or gentilic suffix, rendered in English as "-ite." Thus, as John A. Tvedtnes noted, *Moroni* could be rendered as *Moronite*—from the land of *Moron* mentioned in the Book of Mormon. Similarly, *Lamoni* (a righteous Lamanite king) could be rendered *Lamanite*, *Muloki* could be written *Mulekite*, and *Amaleki* probably means *Amalekite*. See John A. Tvedtnes, in *A Sure Foundation* (Deseret Book Co., 1988), p. 23.

EVIDENCE NO. 864: THE FREQUENCY OF "-IAH" NAME ENDINGS

<u>Evidence</u>: There is a strong tendency of Book of Mormon names to end in *-iah*, such as *Sariah*, or with the same sound but with slightly variant spelling as in *Ammonihah* and *Zemnarihah*. This is significant, because the vast majority of Hebrew names found in the Lachish Letters end the same way, proving that the -iah suffix, which is quite foreign to the English reader, was very popular in the ancient Hebrew Culture. See Harry Torczyner, *Lachish I (tell ed-Duweir): The Lachish Letters*, (London: Oxford, 1938), vol. 1, p. 198, cited in Nibley, *Lehi in the Desert* (1988), p. 32.

EVIDENCE NO. 865: GREEK NAMES

Evidence: The Book of Mormon contains names of Greek origin. For example, *Lachoneus* in 3 Nephi 6:19, and *Timothy* in 3 Nephi 19:4. Some have ridiculed the idea that Greek names would be found in ancient America. However, what *appeared* as anachronisms in the Book of Mormon, have now become another evidence that it is an accurate history. It has recently been discovered that the Jews were closely connected with the ancient Greeks, and considered each other as "brethren." (See 1 Maccabees 12:21; and A. Powell Davies, *The Meaning of the Dead Sea Scrolls*, [New York: Signet Key Book, The New American Library, 1956] p. 65.)

Dr. Hugh Nibley writes: "It is interesting to note in passing that *Timothy* is an Ionian name, since the Greeks in Palestine were Ionians (hence the Hebrew name for Greeks: "Sons of Javanim") and—since *Lachoneus* means 'a Lachonian,'—that the oldest Greek traders were Laconians, who had colonies in Cyprus (Book of Mormon Akish) and, of course, traded with Palestine" (Nibley, *Lehi in the Desert* [1988], p. 33).

Nibley cites: Robert H. Pfeiffer, "Hebrews and Greeks Before Alexander," *Journal of Biblical Literature*, vol. 56, (1937), pp. 91-95, 101; William F. Albright, "A Colony of Cretan Mercenaries on the Coast of the Negeb," *Journal of the Palestine Oriental Society*, vol. 1, (1921), pp. 187-194; Joseph G. Milne, *A Journal of Egyptian Archaeology*, vol. 25, (1939), p. 178; F. B. Welch, *Palestine Exploration Fund Quarterly*, (1900), pp. 342-350; William M. F. Petrie, *Palestine Exploration Fund Quarterly*, (1890), p. 235; Nelson Glueck, "Ostraca from Elath," *Bulletin of the American Schools of Oriental Research*, vol. 80, (December 1940), p. 3; Edward Meyer, *Geschichte des Altertums*, 2nd Edition (Stuttgart: Cotta, 1928), vol. 2, part 1, p. 553;

Evidences Regarding Egyptian Names in the Book of Mormon

Claim: A large number of proper names listed in the Book of Mormon have been found to be Egyptian in origin. This should not be surprising since the Book of Mormon claims that the ancient inhabitants of America wrote in reformed Egyptian, and were influenced by the Egyptian culture (1 Nephi 1:2; Mormon 9:32-33). It is important to note that at the time of Joseph Smith, very little was known about the ancient Egyptian culture and history. It would not have been possible for Joseph Smith to simply copy these names from Egyptian literature. In fact, it was not until 1822 that Jean Francois Champollion became the first to decipher the Egyptian hieroglyphics on the Rosetta Stone, and published his discovery in French. It is ludicrous to assume that Joseph Smith could have had access to a then little-known publication written in a foreign land and tongue.

The following several evidences were first compiled by Dr. Hugh Nibley, and lists several Book of Mormon names that have Egyptian origin (such as Ammon, Korihor, Nephi and Sam). As an introduction to these evidences, we quote from his article entitled "The Book of Mormon as a Mirror of the East." (*The Improvement Era*, vol. 73, [November 1970], pp. 115-120. This paper was reprinted as *Foundation for Ancient Research and Mormon Studies Report*, N-BMM; and also appeared in Dr. Nibley's book entitled *Lehi in the Desert*, [1988], pp. 25-34, 131-132.):

> It requires no great effort of the imagination to detect a sort of parallelism between the two short listings. But aren't we using unjustified violence when we simply take the names at random and place them side by side? That is just what is most remarkable; we *did* pick names at random, and we had the whole Near East to draw on, with Egyptian names by no means predominating numerically in the lists before us. Yet the *only* Old World names that match those in our Book of Mormon episode all come from Egypt, nay, from one particular section of Egypt, in the far south, where from an indefinite date, but at least as early as the mid-seventh century, a Jewish colony flourished. What is more, all these names belong to the later dynasties, after the decline.

The Book of Mormon tells us that Lehi was a rich merchant, who, though he "dwelt in Jerusalem all his days," enjoyed an Egyptian education and culture, which he endeavored to transmit to his children. The book continually refers to the double culture of the people of Lehi: Hebrew to the core, but proud of their Egyptian heritage. "Egyptian civilization was one to be admired and aped," writes H. R. Hall, speaking of Lehi's own land and time. The only non-Hebraic names to enjoy prominence among the Nephites *should*, by the Book of Mormon's own account, be Egyptian, and such is found to be the case. (See Harry R. Hall, *Cambridge Ancient History,* [New York: Macmillan, 1925], vol. 3, p. 268.)

It will be noted that the names compared are never *exactly* alike, except in the case of the monosyllables *Sam* and *Hem*. This, strangely enough, is strong confirmation of their common origin, since names are bound to undergo some change with time and distance, whereas if the resemblance were perfect we should be forced to attribute it, however fantastic it might seem, to mere coincidence. There *must* be differences; and what is more, those differences should not be haphazard but display definite tendencies. This brings us to a most impressive aspect of Book of Mormon names.

Let us take for example the case of *Ammon*. Being so very popular a name, one would expect it to occur in compounds as well as alone, and sure enough, it is the commonest element in compound names, in the West as in Egypt. But in compound names *Amon* or *Amun* changes form following a general rule. Gardiner, in his *Egyptian Grammar* (page 431), states: "A very important class of personal names is that containing names known as theophorous, that is, compound names in which one element is the name of a deity. Now in Graeco-Roman transcriptions it is the rule that when such a divine name is stated at the *beginning* of a compound [the italics are Gardiner's] it is less heavily vocalized than when it stands independently or at the end of a compound."

The author then goes on to show that in such cases *Amon* or *Amun* regularly becomes *Amen*, while in some cases, the vowel may disappear entirely. One need only consider the Book of Mormon *Aminadab, Aminadi, Amnihu, Amnor*, etc., to see how neatly the rule applies in the West.

EVIDENCE NO. 866: ISRAELITES WITH PAGAN NAMES

Evidence: Critics have ridiculed Joseph Smith when they find names such as Sam, Nephi and Ammon (which are Egyptian) and Timothy and Lachoneus (Greek), in the Book of Mormon, assuming that Israelites would not name any of their children with names from pagan nations. However, this practice is supported by evidence. Scholars have found that the Israelites had no aversion to giving non-Jewish names to their children—even some of pagan origin. (See A. Reifenberg, "A Hebrew Shekel of the Fifth Century BC," *Palestine Exploration Fund Quarterly*, [1943], p. 102; William Foxwell Albright, *Archaeology and the Religion of Israel*, [Baltimore: John Hopkins Press, 1946], p. 113; Samuel A. Cook, "The Jews of Seyene in the Fifth Century BC," *Palestine Exploration Fund Quarterly*, [1907], pp. 68-73.)

The Above are cited in Nibley, (*Lehi in the Desert,* [1988], p. 42) who also writes (on page 31):

> The Egyptian Empire at all times during the later period (after 930 BC) pretends to embrace Palestine and regard Jerusalem as a dependent. Egypt (in the seventh century), "never ceased to claim the west lands as an ancient dominion," regarding Hittites and Assyrians as mere interlopers. (A. Moret, *Histoire de l'Orient*, [Paris: Presses Universitaires, 1945] vol. 2, p. 658; Harry R. H. Hall, *Cambridge Ancient History,* [New York: Macmillan, 1925], vol. 3, p. 280.)

Furthermore, the Egyptian names used in the Book of Mormon follow the same pattern of predominance as is found in the Old World statistical pattern. Ammon with its many variations are used most often in both patterns, then Manti, with strong emphasis on names beginning with "Pa" and high frequency of the elements "mor" and "hor." See: W. M. Flinders Petrie, "The Historical Value of Egyptian Names," *Ancient Egypt* (1924), p. 79. P. Langlois, "Essai por Remonter à L'original Égyptien du Terme Sémitique Désignant L'égypte," *Revue Egyptologique*, vol. 1, (1919), pp. 148-162. Theodore Hopfner, "Graezisiert, Grechisch-Ágyptische, bzw., Ágyptisch Griechische und Hybride Theophore Personennamen," *Archiv Orientálni,* (1946) vol. 15, pp. 22-27. All cited in Nibley, *Since Cumorah* (1988), p. 170.

EVIDENCE NO. 867: NAMES AND CULTURAL RELATIONSHIPS

Claim: As a result of translating the Book of Mormon, Joseph Smith knew typically Egyptian names, meanings, and events associated with those names, and the cultural relationship between Egypt and Israel.

Evidence: The following is quoted from page 5 of a report by Dr. Hugh Nibley entitled "The Book of Mormon as a Mirror of the East." (This paper was reprinted as *Foundation for Ancient Research and Mormon Studies Report*, N-BMM from the *Improvement Era* 73, November 1970, pp. 115-120. Elements of this report also appeared in Dr. Nibley's book entitled *Lehi in the Desert*, [1988], pp. 25-34.)

What did Joseph Smith, translator of the Book of Mormon, know about the Old World? So much seems certain, that he knew:

1. A number of typically Egyptian names, queer-sounding words in no way resembling Hebrew or any other language known to the world of Joseph Smith's time.

2. He knew the sort of plot and setting in which those names would figure in the Old World and seems quite at home on the Egyptian scene.

3. He gives a clear and correct picture of cultural relationships between Egypt and Israel, with due emphasis on its essentially commercial nature, in the remarkably convincing picture of Lehi—a typical merchant prince of the seventh century BC. The picture of life in the ancient East which the Book of Mormon allows us to reconstruct is more wonderful in the light of those fantastic conceptions of the gorgeous East which bedizened the heads of even the best scholars at the time the book came forth.

EVIDENCE NO. 868: AHA, AHAH

Evidence: *Aha* is a Nephite name mentioned in Alma 16:5. *Ahah* is mentioned as a Jaredite king in Ether 1:10; 11:10 whose father was named Seth. Though these names may sound a little silly in English, they have been shown to be of ancient origin. Since the LDS claim that the Book of Mormon is an authentic record of an ancient civilization that emigrated from the Middle East to the Americas, correlations between the two geographic regions would substantiate that claim. In the Book of Mormon, a Nephite general bestowed the name *Aha*, which means *warrior*, upon his son.

Aha was also the name of the first hero-king of Egypt, and like King *Ahah* in Ether, his father was also named Seth. (See Philip K. Hitti, *History of Syria*, [New York: Macmillan, 1951], p. 149; Hermann Ranke, *Die Ägyptischen Personennamen*, [Hamburg, 1934]; J. Lieblein, *Dictionnaire de Noms Hieroglyghiques*, [Christiana, 1971]; Jörgen A. Knudtzon, *Die El-Amarna-Tafeln* [Leipzig: Hinrich, 1915; reprinted Aalen: Zeller, 1964], vol. 2, pp. 1555-1583; cited in Nibley, *Lehi in the Desert, The World of the Jaredites*, [1988], pp. 27-30, 261).

The name *Aha* is also mention in Egyptian literature as the successor of *Narmer*. (See Paul Johnson, *The Civilization of Ancient Egypt*, [Atheneum: NY, 1978], p. 25.)

EVIDENCE NO. 869: AKISH

Evidence: The name *Akish*, introduced in Ether 8:10 is also a name of ancient Egyptian origin. *Akish* was also an authentic name that the Egyptians and Hittites used for Cyprus. See *Journal of Egyptian Archaeology* XVII, vol. 4, p. 304, line 10; cited in Nibley, *Lehi in the Desert and the World of the Jaredites*, [1988], p. 32).

EVIDENCE NO. 870: AMMON, AMINADI, AMINADAB, AMMONIHAH, CAMENIHAH & HELAMAN

Evidence: The most common name in the Book of Mormon is *Ammon*. It appears in various forms with the names *Helaman, Ammonihah, Aminadi, Aminadab and Camenihah* (Mosiah 1:2; 7:3; Alma 8:6-8; 10:2-3; Helaman 5:35-37; Mormon 6:14). Note, in current editions of the Book of Mormon *Camenihah* is spelled *Cumenihah,* this change was made in 1981 based on a study of the original manuscript of the Book of Mormon. However, prior to 1981 *Camenihah* was spelled with an "a" as shown above.

The chief governor of Egypt was "the high priest of Amon" (or Ammon). See A. H. Gardiner, *Egyptian Grammar,* (oxford, 1927), p. 429. The name *Amon* is also the most common and most revered name in the later Egyptian Empire, and originated from southern Egypt. Dr. Nibley writes:

> Though the name of *Nephi* occurs oftener, *Ammon* in various forms seems to turn up as an element in proper name compounds far oftener than any other in the Book of Mormon. This is entirely in keeping with the behavior of the name of *Amon* in the East. Compare the *Amarna* names (*Amandi, Amanappa, Amanathabi,* etc.), with Book of Mormon *Aminadi, Aminadab*; also *Ammuni-ra* has the same relationship to Book of Mormon *Ammoni-hah* as the derived *Amarna* name *Khamuni-ra* has to Book of Mormon *Cameni-hah*. For *Amarna* names, see Jörgen A. Knudtzon, *Die El-Amarna-Tafeln* (Leipzig: Hinrich, 1915; reprinted Aalen: Zeller, 1964), vol. 2, p. 1557. For the various vocalizations of *Amon,* as *Amen-, Amun-,* etc., see Gardiner, *Egyptian Grammar,* p. 431.

> Compare also Book of Mormon *Helaman* with Egyptian *Heramon* (Egyptian always writes "r" for Semitic "l"). Nibley, "The Book of Mormon as a Mirror of the East." *The Improvement Era* vol. 73, November 1970, pp. 115-120.

Similarly, compare the Hebrew name *Amminaadbi* with the Book of Mormon *Aminadab*. See M. Noth, "Gemeinsemitische Erscheinungen in der Israelitischen Namengebung," *Zeitschrift der Deutschen Morgenländischen Gesellschaft,* vol. 81, (1927), p. 27. Cited in Nibley, *Since Cumorah,* (1988), p. 171.

EVIDENCE NO. 871: CUMENI, CUMENIHAH, KUMEN & KUMENONHI

Evidence: *Cumeni* is the name of a city mentioned in Alma 56:14; 57:7. The names *Kumen* and *Kumenonhi* are both mentioned in 3 Nephi 19:4. *Cumenihah* is mentioned as a Nephite military commander in Mormon 6:14.

Compare the names *Cumeni, Kumen, Cumenihah* and *Kumenonhi* with the Egypto-Hittite names *Kumani* (also an important city) *Khamuni-ra* and *Kumendi*. See Sidney Smith, "Kizzuwandna," *Journal of Egyptian Archaeology,* vol. 10, (1924), p. 108; Anton L. Mayer and John Garstang, "Kizzuwanda and Other Hittite States," *Journal of Egyptian Archaeology,* vol. 11, (1925), p. 26; Jörgen A. Knudtzon, *Die El-Amarna-Tafeln* (Leipzig: Hinrich, 1915; reprinted Aalen: Zeller, 1964), vol. 1, 528-529, tablet 122; vol. 1, p. 562-563, tablet 132; notes in vol. 2, p. 1222; vol. 2, p. 1561; and vol. 2, p. 1566 index; cited in Nibley, *Lehi in the Desert* (1988), p. 22, note 64; p. 26, note 2, p. 32, note 14.

EVIDENCE NO. 872: DESERET

Evidence: *Deseret* is mentioned in the Book of Mormon as an ancient Jaredite word for "honeybee" in Ether 2:3. Not only has this word been found to be authentic, but also its meaning corresponds with its use in the Book of Mormon.

The symbol for the *bee* in ancient Egypt was the *Red Crown*. The name of the *Red Crown* was "dsrt" probably because "dsrt" also means red. See A. H. Gardiner, *Egyptian Grammar,* (Oxford, 1927), p. 491; cited in Nibley, *Lehi in the Desert* (1952), pp. 184-189.

EVIDENCE NO. 873: GID, KIB

Evidence: The city of *Gid* is mentioned in Alma 51:26. *Gid*, the Nephite Commander is mentioned in Alma 57:28-36.

The name *Kib* is found in a list of genealogical names in Ether 1:32. These strange names are very close to the similar-sounding Egyptian names of: *Kib, Keb* and *Kibkib* see K. Sethe, *Zeitschrift für Ägyptische Sprache und Altertumskunde*, vol. 43, (1906), pp. 147, 149; Harry R. H. Hall, *Cambridge Ancient History*, (New York: Macmillan, 1925), vol. 3, p. 273; cited in Nibley, *Since Cumorah*, (1976), p. 194; and Nibley, *Lehi in the Desert, The World of the Jaredites*, (1980), p. 25.

EVIDENCE NO. 874: GIDDONAH, GIDGIDDONI, GIDGIDDONAH, GADIANDI & GIDDIANHI

Evidence: The name *Giddon* appears in the Book of Mormon under several different forms such as: *Giddonah, Gidgiddoni, Gidgiddonah, Gadiandi & Giddianhi* (Alma 10:2; 3 Nephi 3:9, 18; 9:8; Mormon 6:13). They refer to a high priest, two Nephite generals and a notorious robber. Dr. Nibley has shown that these too have parallels in ancient Egyptian—they are *Dji-dw-na, Djed-djhwt-iw-f, Djed-djhwti-iw-s, Cadyanda,* and *Djhwti-ankhi.* While the Egyptians spellings are different from the Book of Mormon spellings, their pronunciations are very similar. (*Journal of Egyptian Archaeology*, vol. 11, pp. 20-24 cited in Nibley, *Lehi in the Desert*, [1988], p. 26.)

Furthermore, the meaning of name of the notorious gangster Giddianhi (3 Nephi 3:9-12; 4:5-14) has been shown to correspond with his violent character—implying that his name may have been a title rather than his birth name. When the name is broken down we find that the its segments can be found in Strong's *Exhaustive Concordance, Gidoniy,* which means "warlike." The center syllable of this name is also found in Strong's Concordance, *Iyown,* which means, "ruin." Combining these two words results in a name-title that means "a warlike robber who brings people or cities to ruin." Similarly, the name of the Nephite military commander *Gidgiddoni* (mentioned in 3 Nephi 3:18-21, 26; 4:13-14, 24-26; 6:6) could also be a name-title for the same reasons. (See James Strong, "A Concise Dictionary of the Hebrew Bible," in *Exhaustive Concordance*, [1973], entries nos. 1441, 5859, pp. 26, 86.)

EVIDENCE NO. 875: HELAMAN—HERAMON

Evidence: *Helaman*, the name of three great Nephite prophets mentioned in the Book of Mormon, (Mosiah 1:2; Alma 31:7; 63:11) is also found in ancient Egyptian. The Semitic "l" is always written "r" in Egyptian, which has no "l," thus the Egyptian equivalent of *Helaman* is *Heramon*—which means "in the presence of Amon." Also, note the similar Egyptian proper name *Heri-i-her-imn."* See Ranke, *Die Ägyptischen Personennamen*, p. 252, line 15; cited in Nibley, *Lehi in the Desert*, (1988), p. 26.

EVIDENCE NO. 876: HEM

Evidence: Hem is mentioned in the Book of Mormon as the brother of Ammon (Mosiah 7:6). The title of the Egyptian *Amon* is *neter hem tep*—"chief servant (*Hem*) of the God. See A. Moret, *Histoire de l'Orient*, [Paris: Presses Universitaires, 1945] vol. 2, p. 518; Harry R. H. Hall, *Cambridge Ancient History*, (New York: Macmillan, 1925), vol. 3, p. 268. Both cited in Nibley, *Lehi in the Desert*, (1988), pp. 30, who writes:

Hem is an element in Egyptian proper names and means the same as the extremely common *Abdi* element in western Asiatic names of the time (compare to the modern Arabic *Abdullah*, "servant of God"). It is most interesting that the brother of *Ammon* in the Book of Mormon actually bears the name of *Hem* (Mosiah 7:6). See Harry R. H. Hall, *Cambridge Ancient History*, (New York: Macmillan, 1925), vol. 3, p. 266.

EVIDENCE NO. 877: HIMNI—HMN

Evidence: One of the sons of King Mosiah mentioned in the Book of Mormon is *Himni.* He was asked to succeed his father as King, but refused so that he could serve as a missionary to the Lamanites (Mosiah 28:1-10).

Himni, spelled anciently (without the vowels) in the Egyptian language would be *Hmn. Hmn,* is the name of the Egyptian hawk-god, and is also the symbol of the Pharaoh. (See Hermann Ranke, *Die Ägyptischen Personennamen,* [Hamburg, 1934]; J. Lieblein, *Dictionnaire de Noms Hieroglyghiques,* [Christiana, 1971]; Jörgen A. Knudtzon, *Die El-Amarna-Tafeln* [Leipzig: Hinrich, 1915; reprinted Aalen: Zeller, 1964], vol. 2, pp. 1555-1582; cited in Nibley, *Lehi in the Desert and the World of the Jaredites,* [1988], pp. 26-27.)

EVIDENCE NO. 878: HERMOUNTS

Evidence: *Hermounts* is mentioned in Alma 2:37 as a name for a wilderness infested by wild beasts. Not only is this word authentic, but it is also associated with an Egyptian word with an identical meaning. The name *Hermonthis* is Egyptian for "Land of Month." *Month* was the Egyptian god of wild places and wild things. See Grapow, "Hermonthis" in Pauly-Wissowa, *Paulys Realencyclopadie,* vol. 8, p. 901; C. F. Herodatus, *History,* vol. 2, p. 46. Both cited in Nibley, *Since Cumorah,* (1988), p. 169.

See also the related information on Hermounts in the Geography chapter of this same volume.

EVIDENCE NO. 879: KORIHOR—KERIHOR

Evidence: *Korihor* was a political agitator who was seized by the people of Ammon and brought before the king under charges of "perverting the ways of the Lord" (Alma 30). *Kerihor* (also *Khurhor*) was the great high priest of Ammon who seized the throne of Egypt at Thebes around 1085 BC. A. Moret, renders the name *Herihor,* the "h" being hard "kh" (the vowels are largely guesswork). See A. Moret, *Histoire de l'Orient,* (Paris: Presses Universitaires, 1941), vol. 2, p. 591; E. A. W. Budge, *The Mummy* (Cambridge, 1925), p. 103;

Other renditions of this name include *Heriher, Hurhor, Her-Heru. Her-Hor* and *Hrihor.* In this study we have chosen to follow Moret, whose recent and thorough study largely supersedes the others. (See *Zeitschrift für Ägyptische Sprache und Altertumskunde,* vol. 20, [1882], Suppl. pl. ii; E. A. W. Budge, *The Nile,* [1912], p. 50; A. Wiedermann, "Beitrage zur aegyptischen Geschichte," *Zeitschrift für Ägyptische Sprache und Altertumskunde,* vol. 23 (1885), p. 83; all cited in Nibley, *Lehi in the Desert,* [1988], p. 27.)

EVIDENCE NO. 880: KISHKUMEN

Evidence: *Kishkumen,* the name of a notorious leader of a band of robbers, is introduced in the Book of Mormon in Helaman 1:9. This name is also ancient, being a possible combination of the Hebrew *Cush* and the Egypto-Hittite name of an important city, *Kumani.* The "reformed" Egyptian names, *Kumen, Khamuni-ra* and *Kumani* are mentioned in Anton L. Mayer and John Garstang, "Kizzuwanda and Other Hittite States," *Journal of Egyptian Archaeology,* vol. 11, (1925), p. 26; Jörgen A. Knudtzon, *Die El-Amarna-Tafeln* (Leipzig: Hinrich, 1915; reprinted Aalen: Zeller, 1964), vol. 1, 528-529, tablet 122; vol. 1, p. 562-563, tablet 132; notes in vol. 2, p. 1222; vol. 2, p. 1561; and vol. 2, p. 1566; Both cited in Nibley, *Lehi in the Desert* (1988), p. 26, note 2, p. 32, note 14.

EVIDENCE NO. 881: MANTI AND MATHONI

Evidence: *Manti* was the name of a Nephite soldier, a land, a city, and a hill (Alma 2:22; 16:6-7; 56:13-14). *Manti* was also the Semitic form of an Egyptian proper name, such as *Manti-mankhi,* who was a prince in Upper Egypt around 650 BC. It is also a form of the name *Month,* the god of *Hermonthis.*

Similarly, *Mathoni* was one of the twelve Nephite disciples chosen by Jesus as apostles to minister unto the Nephites (3 Nephi 19:4). This name is closely related to Egyptian names such as *Maitena*, and *Mattenos*—"two judges of Tyre, who at different times made themselves king, possibly under the Egyptian auspices" (Nibley, *Lehi in the Desert*, [1988], p. 27).

EVIDENCE NO. 882: MORIANTON, MORIANTUM AND MORIANCUMER

Evidence: *Morianton* is mentioned as the name of a man, a Nephite city, a land, a people, and a Jaredite King (Alma 50:25-28; Ether 1:22-23). *Moriantum* is mentioned as an apostate Nephite land (Moroni 9:9-10), and *Moriancumer* is mentioned as a Jaredite camp (Ether 2:13).

These names clearly have their parallels in ancient names of Egyptian princes: *Meriaton* and *Meriamon*, "Beloved of Aton" and "Beloved of Amon" respectively. Variations on the name of the Egyptian King *Meriamon* include *Meryamon* and *Moriamon*. (See Hermann Ranke, *Die Ägyptischen Personennamen*, [Hamburg, 1934]; J. Lieblein, *Dictionnaire de Noms Hieroglyghiques*, [Christiana, 1971]; Jörgen A. Knudtzon, *Die El-Amarna-Tafeln* [Leipzig: Hinrich, 1915; reprinted Aalen: Zeller, 1964], vol. 2, pp. 1555-1582; *Zeitschrift für Ägyptische Sprache und Altertumskunde*, XX, [1882], Taf. ii, V [7a]. Also cited in Nibley, *Lehi in the Desert*, [1988], p. 27, and Nibley, *Approach to the Book of Mormon*, [1988], p. 287.)

Furthermore, the meaning of the name chosen for the *land of Moriantum* (mentioned in Moroni 9:9-10), correlates with its apostate attitude of self-righteousness. The prefix of the name can be found in Strong's *Exhaustive Concordance, Maw-ray*, which means "domineering; a master or Lord." The last syllable of this name is also found in Strong's Concordance, *tom*, which means "completeness, prosperity, perfection, uprightness." (See James Strong, "A Concise Dictionary of the Hebrew Bible," in *Exhaustive Concordance*, [1973], entries nos. 608, 4756, 8537, pp. 15, 72, 124.)

EVIDENCE NO. 883: NEAS

Evidence: The Book of Mormon uses the word *neas* as a crop cultivated by the Nephites in Mosiah 9:9. The word *neas* has been found to be of Egyptian origin. (See F. L. Griffith in *Journal of Egyptian Archaeology*, [1917], vol. 4, pp. 161, 169, 216.) The Mayan Chol morpheme *niche* (pronounced "neesh,") meaning flowers, is close to the word neas and is connected with the fruit chinquapin. (See Schumann G. Otto, *La Lengue Chol, de Tila* [Chiapas], [Mexico City: Unam, 1973], p. 88; Also see Alfa Hurley Vda. de Delgaty and Agustin Ruiz Sanchez, *Diccionaria Tzotzil*, [Mexico City: Instituto Linguistico de Verano, 1978], see entry under *nich*. Also cited in Vestal and Wallace, *The Firm Foundation of Mormonism*, [1981] pp. 121, 135.)

EVIDENCE NO. 884: NEPHI—NEHI, NEHRI, NFY AND NIHPI

Evidence: The name *Nephi* is the first to be mentioned in the Book of Mormon. It is the name that occurs most often in the Book of Mormon. It refers to: 1) the son of Lehi, a great prophet and founder of the *Nephite* nation, 2) a nation or people, 3) a land, 4) the title assumed by the kings of the *Nephite* nation, 5) a city, 6) the great missionary son of Helaman, 7) the grandson of Helaman, son of *Nephi*, and one of the twelve apostles called by Jesus to minister to the *Nephites*, 8) and four historical records engraven on plates of gold (1 Nephi 1:1; 9:2; 12:20; 2 Nephi 5:8; Jacob 1:9-14; Mosiah 9:15; Helaman 3:21; 3 Nephi 1:2; Mormon 1:4). Additionally, there is the name *Nephihah*, which refers to: 1) the second chief judge of the *Nephites*, 2) another city, 3) a land, 4) a people, 5) and some plains near the city of *Nephihah* (Alma 4:17-18; 50:14; 59:5; 62:18).

Almost fifty years ago, Dr. Hugh Nibley raised the question of whether the personal names contained in the Book of Mormon are "satisfactory for that period and region". After over forty years of investigations on the names in the Book of Mormon, the name Nephi is perhaps the most thoroughly documented name from the ancient Middle East. John Gee has summarized the extensive evidence regarding the name of Nephi in his article entitled "A Note on the Name of Nephi," *Journal of Book of Mormon Studies*, vol. 1, no. 1, (Fall 1992), pp. 189-191.

In his article, John Gee lists eleven variants of the name Nephi that are of Phoenician, Egyptian, Semitic and Coptic origin. In Summary he concludes: "Nephi is an attested Syro-Palestinian Semitic form of an attested Egyptian man's name dating from the Late Period in Egypt. It is appropriate that Nephi notes early the connections between Egypt and Israel at his time (1 Nephi 1:3), for his own name is Egyptian. It is the proper form of a proper name of the proper gender from the proper place and proper time."

For example, consider the following Egyptian names: 1) *Nehi*, great administrator who "united all the south under his direction," 2) *Nehri*, Count of Thebes who claimed independent dominion in the south of Egypt, 3) *Nfy*, the name of an Egyptian captain, 4) and *Nihpi*, the original name of the god *Pa-nepi*. See Wilhelm Spiegelberg, "The God Panepi," *A Journal of Egyptian Archaeology*, vol. 12, (1926), p. 35; cited in Nibley, *Lehi in the Desert*, (1988), p. 27.

EVIDENCE NO. 885: PAHORAN

Evidence: The Book of Mormon speaks of a chief judge named *Pahoran*, and his son who was also named *Pahoran* (Helaman 1:1-13). This name closely resembles an Egyptian name *Pa-her-an*, who was an ambassador of Egypt in Palestine. Other forms of his name include *Pahura*, *Pakhoras*, *Bakharas*, *Horan* and *Pa-her-y*. (See F. L. Griffin, "Pakhoras–Bakharas–Faras in Geography and History," *Journal of Egyptian Archaeology*, [1925] vol. 2, p. 259; J. Gray, "The Canaanite God Horon," *Journal of Near-Eastern Studies*, vol. 8, pp. 29, 32, 34, p. 194; Hermann Ranke, *Die Ägyptischen Personennamen*, [Hamburg, 1934]; J. Lieblein, *Dictionnaire de Noms Hieroglyghiques*, [Christiana, 1971]; Jörgen A. Knudtzon, *Die El-Amarna-Tafeln* [Leipzig: Hinrich, 1915; reprinted Aalen: Zeller, 1964], vol. 2, pp. 1555-1582; all cited in Nibley, *Lehi in the Desert* [1988], p. 22 and Nibley, *Since Cumorah,* [1988], p. 170.)

When the name Pahoran is broken down we find that the first syllable *peh*, means "the mouth, speech, appoint or command." The suffix of this name is also found in Strong's Concordance, *Haran*, which means "mountain or mountaineer." Combining these two segments results in a name-title could represent "a ruler [chief judge] who gives commands from high places." (See James Strong, "A Concise Dictionary of the Hebrew Bible," in *Exhaustive Concordance,* [1973], entries nos. 2039, 6310, pp. 34, 93.)

EVIDENCE NO. 886: PAANCHI, PACUMENI AND PACHUS

Evidence: The Book of Mormon chief judge Pahoran, had two other sons besides Pahoran, namely: *Paanchi* and *Pacumeni*. When Pahoran (the father) passed away there was contention between the people regarding which of his three sons should succeed him as chief judge. Eventually Pahoran (the son) was elected "by the voice of the people," and *Paanchi* led a rebellion against the government in which Pahoran was assassinated, and his brother *Pacumeni* was elected in his stead (Helaman 1:1-13).

The Book of Mormon also mentions a man named *Pachus* who also led a rebellion against the Nephite government and tried to usurp the throne (Alma 62:6-10).

All three of the above mentioned names have been identified in ancient Egyptian literature:

1. *Paanchi:* Paanchi was the son of *Kherihor* (mentioned above), the chief high priest of *Amon* and ruler of the south who conquered all of Egypt and was high priest of *Amon* at Thebes."

2. *Pacumeni:* Pakamen, is an Egyptian proper name meaning "blind man." Other forms of his name include: *Pa-menech*, *Pa-mnkh*, *Pakhaamnata*, *Pamenches* and *Pachomios* (Greek) who was the "commander of the south and high priest of *Horus*."

3. *Pachus:* Finally there are the Egyptian proper names: *Pa-ks*, *Pach-qs* and *Pa-ches-i*, which means, "he is praised."

See Wilhelm Spiegelberg, "Der Stratege Pamenches," *Zeitschrift für Ägyptische Sprache und Altertumskunde,* (1922) vol. 57, pp. 88-92; Jörgen A. Knudtzon, *Die El-Amarna-Tafeln* (Leipzig: Hinrich, 1915; reprinted Aalen: Zeller, 1964), vol. 2, p. 1566; Both cited in Nibley, *Lehi in the Desert,* (1988), pp. 23, 27-28.

EVIDENCE NO. 887: SAM

Evidence: The Book of Mormon mentions *Sam*, the elder brother, and humble follower of the prophet Nephi (1 Nephi 2:5, 17). Though many have assumed that this name was borrowed from English, it is also of ancient Egyptian origin. *Sam Tawi*, is the title taken by the brother of *Nehri* (mention above) when he became king of Southern Egypt. His name means "uniter of the lands." (See Nibley, *Lehi in the Desert,* (1988), p. 28.)

Also, the name Sam is Arabic for the Biblical Shem. See *The Qur'an,* translated by Abdullah Yusufali, edited by Sayed A. A. Razwy, (Elmhurst, New York: Tahrike Tarsile Qur'an Inc., 1995), list of names, p. vi.

EVIDENCE NO. 888: ZENOCK, ZENIFF AND ZEMNARIHAH

Evidence: The Book of Mormon mentions an ancient Hebrew prophet named *Zenock* who prophesied about the future mission of Jesus Christ (1 Nephi 19:20; Alma 33:15; 34:7; Helaman 8:20; 3 Nephi 10:16). Though he was contemporary with the Bible, he is not mentioned in it. *Zenekh* is also a proper Egyptian name that was once identified with a serpent god. Note that it may seem strange to some that a prophet of God should share a name with that of a serpent. However, this is consistent with an episode in the Bible where a serpent fastened to a pole was used to represent Jesus Christ being lifted up on the cross (Numbers 21:8; 2 Kings 18:4; John 3:14-16; Helaman 8:14).

Also mentioned in the Book of Mormon is *Zeniff*, the ruler of a relatively small Nephite colony (Mosiah 7:9). *Znb* and *Snb* are very common elements in Egyptian proper names, such as *Senep-ta* for example.

Finally, there is the notorious robber chief *Zemnarihah* mentioned in 3 Nephi 4:17. A common Egyptian practice was to create new names by rearranging the segments of another name. Thus in Egyptian we find the name *Zmn-ha-re* as a form of the *Zemnarihah* mentioned in the Book of Mormon. See Hermann Ranke, *Die Ägyptischen Personennamen*, [Hamburg, 1934]; J. Lieblein, *Dictionnaire de Noms Hieroglyghiques*, (Christiana, 1971); Jörgen A. Knudtzon, *Die El-Amarna-Tafeln* (Leipzig: Hinrich, 1915; reprinted Aalen: Zeller, 1964), vol. 2, pp. 1555-1583; cited in Nibley, *Lehi in the Desert,* (1988), pp. 28.

Furthermore, the meaning of the notorious gangster's name *Zemnarihah* (3 Nephi 4:16-28) has been shown to correspond with his evil nature—implying that his name may have been a title. When the name is broken down we find that the root *zammah*, means "an evil plan, heinous crime, mischief or wickedness." The suffix of this name is also found in Strong's Concordance, *neriyah*, which means, "light of Jehovah." Combining these two words suggests a name-title that means "one whose plan is to sin against the light of the Lord." (See James Strong, "A Concise Dictionary of the Hebrew Bible," in *Exhaustive Concordance,* [1973], entries nos. 2154, 5374, pp. 35, 80.)

EVIDENCE NO. 889: ZEEZROM, CEZORAM AND SEEZORAM

Evidence: The Book of Mormon mentions the name *Zeezrom* which refers to both a wicked lawyer who repents and becomes a righteous missionary, and a city (Alma 10-15; 56:14). It later mentions a depraved judge named *Seezoram* who was murdered by his brother *Seantum* (Helaman 9:19-38). The Egyptian forms of these names are *Zoser* or *Zeser* who was one of the greatest Pharaohs to rule during the Third Dynasty. See Hermann Ranke, *Die Ägyptischen Personennamen*, [Hamburg, 1934]; J. Lieblein, *Dictionnaire de Noms Hieroglyghiques*, (Christiana, 1971); Jörgen A. Knudtzon, *Die El-Amarna-Tafeln* (Leipzig: Hinrich, 1915; reprinted Aalen: Zeller, 1964), vol. 2, pp. 1555-1583; cited in Nibley, *Lehi in the Desert*, (1988), pp. 28.

Cezoram is mentioned in the Book of Mormon as a Nephite chief judge (Helaman 5:1). *Chiziri*, was the Egyptian governor of a Syrian city. (See Jörgen A. Knudtzon, *Die El-Amarna-Tafeln* [Leipzig: Hinrich, 1915; reprinted Aalen: Zeller, 1964], vol. 1, p. 951, tablets 336 and 337 and index in vol. 2, p. 1562; cited in Nibley, *Lehi in the Desert,* [1988], pp. 23, 26.)

The roots of these names can be found in Strong's *Exhaustive Concordance*. When broken down we find that the first syllable, *zeez*, means "fulness or abundance," while the second, *ruwm*, means "high, to raise, exalt or lift up." Combining these two words results in a name which may reflect the hopeful anticipations of parents who desired their children to be "abundantly qualified to serve in high leadership positions." (See James Strong, *Exhaustive Concordance*, [1973], entries nos. 2123, 7311, pp. 35, 107.)

Similarly, the name of Seezoram's murderous brother Seantum, may also be a title. The root word *sow-an* means "a soldier, or warrior," while the suffix *tom* means "prosperity"—suggesting a "warrior who would fight to secure prosperity" (Strong's *Concordance*, entries nos. 5431, 8537, pp. 81, 124).

EVIDENCE NO. 890: THE PREFIX "PA-" FOR PROPER NAMES

Evidence: Nephite practice of naming members of the ruling class with prefix "Pa-" is strikingly similar to the same practice found in the ancient Egyptian culture.

The following is quoted from page 3 of a report by Dr. Hugh Nibley entitled "The Book of Mormon as a Mirror of the East." (This paper was reprinted as FARMS Report, N-BMM from the *Improvement Era*, vol. 73, November 1970, pp. 115-120. Elements of this report also appeared in Dr. Nibley's book entitled *Lehi in the Desert*, (1988), pp. 22-23.):

The experiment with government by priestly judges collapsed, largely due to a rivalry for the chief judgeship among three candidates, all sons of the great chief judge, *Pahoran*. Their names are *Pahoran, Paanchi and Pacumeni* (Helaman 1:1-13).

Such family rivalry for the office of high priest is characteristic of the Egyptian system, in which the office seems to have been hereditary not by law but by usage.[1]

The name of *Pahoran* reflects the eastern *Pahura*, which is "reformed" Egyptian, that is, a true Egyptian title, but altered in such a way as to adapt it to the Hebrew-Canaanite speech.[2] *Pahuia* (also written *Puhuru*) was in Amarna times an Egyptian governor (*rabu*) of Syria.[3] The same man, or another man with the same name, was placed by Pharaoh as governor of the Ube district, with his headquarters at Kumedi.

Paanchi is simply the well-known Egyptian *Paiankh* (also rendered *Pianchi, Paankh*, etc.)[4] The first important man to bear the name was none other than the son of the above-mentioned Kherihor. He did not succeed his father on the throne, being content with the all-powerful office of chief high priest of Amon, but his son, *Panezem*, did become king.[5] In the middle of the eighth century another *Pianhki*, a king of Nubia, conquered virtually all of Egypt, and claimed for himself the office of high priest of Amon at Thebes as well as the title of Pharaoh.[6] His successor, when the Assyrians invaded Egypt, in the days of Lehi, fled to a fortified city, as yet unlocated, which bore the name of Kipkip or Kibkib,[7] a name that strongly suggests the Book of Mormon city-name Gidgiddoni (3 Nephi 9:8). (See also Gimgim-no.)

Pacumeni, the name of the third son, resembles that borne by some of the last priest governors of Egypt, whose names are rendered *Pa-menech, Pa-mnkh, Pamenches*, etc.[8] The Greeks (who often furnish the key to the correct reading of Egyptian names) put the guttural before the nasal, as in the Book of Mormon form, *Pachomios*.[9] The most famous man of the name commanded all the forces of the south, and was also high priest of Horus. At least one other governor-general of Egypt bore the name.[10]

A striking coincidence is the predominance among both Egyptian and Nephite judge names of the prefix *Pa-*. In late Egyptian this is extremely common, and has simply the force of the definite article. For the Egyptian chief priests *Panezem, Pakebis,* and *Panas*[11] we have no Book of Mormon parallel, but from the Nephite list we must not omit the name of *Pachus,* since, though I have not found it in the limited documents at my disposal, it is perfectly good Egyptian (meaning "he–Amon–is praised"), both elements occurring frequently in Egyptian proper names.[12] Another Book of Mormon judge, *Cezoram,* has a name that suggests that of an Egyptian governor of a Syrian city: *Chi-zi-ri.*[13] It should be noted that the above Panezem, upon becoming king, took the name of *Meriamon,* which has a Book of Mormon ring, even if we don't read it *Moriamon*—a perfectly possible variant.

1. A striking parallel to the Book of Mormon account is that given by Harry R. H. Hall, *Cambridge Ancient History,* (New York: Macmillan, 1925), vol. 3, p. 254.

2. W. F. Albright, *The Vocalization of Egyptian Syllabic Orthography,* (New Haven, American Orthographic Society, 1934), deals with the problem of "reformed" Egyptian. The author suggests, pp. 10ff, that a "new orthography was devised in the 'foreign office' of the Egyptian chancellery during the twentieth century" specifically for dealing with Palestine and Syria, since the scribes "found it necessary to devise an orthography which would enable them to read their own records." From this time on the new idiom underwent progressive and constant deterioration until, by the seventh century BC among other things "an almost complete shift in the quality of Egyptian vowels" had taken place.

3. Jörgen A. Knudtzon, *Die El-Amarna-Tafeln* [Leipzig: Hinrich, 1915; reprinted Aalen: Zeller, 1964], vol. 1, pp. 117,123,132, vol. 2, p. 1366.

4. See accompanying cut, which may be found in E. A. Wallis Budge, *The Mummy,* (Cambridge: Cambridge University Press, 1925), pp. 103, 108, and in W. M. F. Petrie, *A History of Egypt* (London, 1905), vol. 3, pp. 202, 290, the latter giving phonetic values, 'Piankh' and 'Pankhy' respectively. *Paanchi* is settled as the correct reading, however, by the principle stated in Alan H. Gardiner, *Egyptian Grammar,* (London: Oxford University Press, 1950), p. 521: the "i" as here occurring "is always final consonant."

5. Lists of priest-kings in the original form may be found in *Zeitschrift für Ägyptische Sprache und Altertumskunde,* Vol. 20 (1882), Taf. ii., V (7a); E. A. Wallis Budge, *The Mummy,* (Cambridge: Cambridge University Press, 1925), p. 103.

6. Harry R. H. Hall, *Cambridge Ancient History,* (New York: Macmillan, 1925), vol. 3, p. 273.

7. The Assyrian Text (British Museum Cyl. No. 12168) is given in L. W. King, *First Steps in Assyrian,* pp. 78ff.

8. The name in its various form is discussed in W. Spiegelberg, "Der Stratege Pamenches," *Zeitschrift für Ägyptische Sprache und Altertumskunde,* vol. 57 (1922), pp. 88-92. An even closer parallel is provided by Amarna *Pa-kha-am-na-ta,* given with variants in Knudtson, Jörgen A. Knudtzon, *Die El-Amarna-Tafeln* [Leipzig: Hinrich, 1915; reprinted Aalen: Zeller, 1964], vol. 2, 1366, he was governor of Amurru under Egypt.

9. W. Spiegelberg, "Der Stratege Pamenches," p. 89, note 2.

10. W. Spiegelberg, "Der Stratege Pamenches," p. 91, Numbers 7 and 9 in Spiegelberg's list.

11. W. Spiegelberg, "Der Stratege Pamenches," p. 91.

12. Herbert E. Winlock, "The Eleventh Egyptian Dynasty," *Journal of Near Eastern Studies,* p. 275, finds Egyptian commoners at Thebes with names *Hesem, Hesi.*

13. Jörgen A. Knudtzon, *Die El-Amarna-Tafeln* [Leipzig: Hinrich, 1915; reprinted: Zeller, 1964], pp. 41, 42.

Supplementary Information Relative to Names

Because of the Book of Mormon practice of naming children after great ancestors it is apparent that both names and ancestry were considered sacred to the Book of Mormon peoples. Indeed the Book of Mormon gives lengthy lists of ancestry such as in Ether 1:6-33. Similarly, scholars have found that names were regarded as a sacred possession in ancient America and Polynesia as well as in the ancient Middle East. (See Ralph W. Andrews, *Indians as the Westerners Saw Them,* [New York: Bonanza Books, 1963], pp. 43-44; and A. Bocher, *Christus Exoreista,* [Stuttgard, 1972], p. 88.)

Names of ancestors were especially held in sacred remembrance. Indeed, the ancient Americans and Polynesians kept oral histories that were recited in lengthy chants and carved the family histories in wood and stone, or otherwise recorded them in pictographs, lengths of knotted twine, etc. This has led some to wrongly accuse these cultures of ancestor worship. More astute scholars realize that these customs were merely a means of remembering and honoring ones ancestors. (See T. Barrow, *Art and Life in Polynesia,* Sydney: A. H. and A. W. Reed, 1972] pp. 34, 43.)

The Polynesians would recite their genealogies in the Kava' ceremony in order to establish seniority with royal lines. Furthermore, when the first explorers and European settlers were invited to participate in the ceremony, the natives were alarmed that their guests had not memorized the names of their ancestry. This may have led to the Hawiian practice of referring to the Europeans as *Hauli*—a word which means "who have no knowledge of their parentage." (See John Martin, *An Account of the Natives of the Tonga Islands,* [Boston: Charles Ewer, 1820], pp. 369-379.)

8. Book of Mormon Literacy

EVIDENCE NO. 891: MANY BOOKS WRITTEN BY ANCIENT AMERICANS

Claim: The Book of Mormon claims that "books of every kind" were written by ancient American prophets (Helaman 3:15).

Evidence: The following is quoted from the abstract of a paper by M. Wells Jakeman entitled "Ancient Maya Hieroglyphic Writings, and their Decipherment and Study" (*University Archaeological Society Newsletter* 44.01), and cited in Christensen, *Progress in Archaeology* (1963), p. 128:

> Ancient Maya hieroglyphic writings are found on stelae (stone monuments) and in codices (paper screen-books), as well as on the walls and steps of temples, on vases, etc. Although more than a hundred Aztec and Mixtec codices and other documents are known to scholars, there exist only three known codices written in Maya hieroglyphs: the Dresden Codex, the Peresianus Codex, and the Tro-Cortesianus Codex.
>
> The most beautiful of these is the Dresden Codex. It contains chapters dealing mainly with the great god of life and light, Itzamna (the counterpart in Maya religion of the famed "Fair God," Quetzalcoatl, of Toltec-Aztec religion), and a page apparently recording the ancient Flood of Maya tradition. A copy printed in color is in the possession of the BYU Department of Archaeology.
>
> There is historical and archaeological evidence that many such codices or paper books were in existence in the Mesoamerican or Book of Mormon area from early times.

Unfortunately, in the sixteenth century when the Spaniards attempted to convert the natives to Christianity, countless volumes of ancient Mayan manuscripts were systematically destroyed. The Spanish monks apparently believed that they could more easily introduce the natives to the Christian faith if they first eradicated what they perceived to be pagan writings. (Diego de Landa, *Yucatan before and after the Conquest,* translated by William Gates [New York: Dover, 1978], p. 29; cited in Allen J. Christensen, "Chiasmus in Mayan Texts," *Ensign,* October 1988, p. 29.)

EVIDENCE NO. 892: WRITING ABILITY OF ANCIENT AMERICANS

Claim: According to the Book of Mormon (1 Nephi 1:1), ancient Americans were capable of recording information in written form. It is highly unlikely that Joseph Smith would have fabricated this claim, since the Indians of his day and locale did not have a written language.

Evidence: Dr. Barry Fell, president of the Epigraphic Society, believes the earliest writing in America was approximately 1450 BC. See Bernard Pottier, "The Indian Languages of America" *Research* (N.Y.: 1977), pp. 15-19; cited in Paul R. Cheesman, *The World of the Book of Mormon,* (1985), p. 16, who also notes that:

> Cortez recorded how the Indians kept a form of writing "which was inscribed in written characters and pictures of a kind of paper they have by which they make themselves understood." Several Mexican books were written in hieroglyphics on paper, which was about the consistency of light pasteboard. Peter Martyr described them as folding tablets. (Francisco Augustus MacNutt, *Hernando Cortez: His Five Letters, Relations to the Emperor Charles V,* [Glendale, CA: Arthur Clark, 1908], pp. 170-171.)

> The Italian humanist Pietro Martire D'Anghiera could not say enough about "the two books such as the Indians use." He remained "wrapped in astonishment," for to him the books were a greater index to the quality of this new civilization than the gold. "The Indians of the golden land write in books," he said in his letters to other humanists as he analyzed the technique of the book and the hieroglyphics, "which almost resemble those of the Egyptians... Among the figures of men and animals are those of kings and great lords..." (Victor Wolfgang Von Hagen, *The Ancient Sun Kingdoms of the Americas* [New York: The World Pub. Co., 1961]; cited in Cheesman, *The World of the Book of Mormon,* [1985], p. 69.)

EVIDENCE NO. 893: ANCIENT STONE TABLETS DISCOVERED IN PERU

Claim: The recent discovery of three ancient stone tablets in Peru's highland jungle may provide further proof of the authenticity of the Book of Mormon.

Evidence: The following is an article from the Associated Press that appeared in the *Deseret News*, December 10, 1989. (Emphasis added.)

> An American explorer [Gene Savoy] says that he has found three ancient *stone tablets* in Peru's highland jungle that ... contain the first writing found from the ancient civilizations of the Andes and that the inscriptions are similar to Phoenician and Semitic hieroglyphs ... [Savoy], said the find could be extremely valuable. "We have found something that is going to revolutionize the archaeological interpretation of Peru's ancient civilizations," he said.

> Peru's pre-Columbian cultures, which culminated with the Incas, were not known to have written languages, said Savoy, 62, a member of the New York Explorers Club. Savoy said he found three tablets, each weighing several tons and measuring about 5 by 10 feet, in August in a cave near Gran Vilaya, the immense ruins of the Chachapoyas Indian civilization he discovered in 1985.

> The Gran Vilaya ruins are 400 miles north of Lima and 9,000 feet above sea level in a fog shrouded region of the Andes that Peruvians call the 'jungle's eyebrow.' Savoy displayed photos of the tablets, which he said remain in the cave, and sketches of rubbings taken from the stones. He pointed out the similarities between the stylized inscriptions and samples of *Phoenician hieroglyphs.*

> The hieroglyphs on the tablets are similar to those used in King Solomon's time and include one identical to the symbol that always appeared on the ships he sent to the legendary land of Ophir, which the Bible described as the source of his gold, Savoy said. "When I first heard about the possible contact between Egypt and Israel and the Americas, nobody was more skeptical than I was," he said.

"I thought it was absolutely ridiculous. They've been talking about this crazy stuff for years. "But now we've got stone tablets and this cannot be denied." Savoy, who has written books on his explorations in Peru, said he has studied his findings since early September and is preparing to publish them.

"The tablets were not brought here from another country like Egypt. This is a Chachapoyas form of hieroglyphic writing," he said, referring to the Indian Empire that once dominated the jungle region. "We're talking about something very old. It's possible the Andean cultures ... are much older than we realize, perhaps older than what we know as the Old World," Savoy said.

EVIDENCE NO. 894: ENGRAVING VS. BRUSHING WITH INK

Claim: The ancient American prophet writers of the Book of Mormon could not have engraved Hebraic character forms onto metal plates. Thus they would have been forced to use another language such as Egyptian.

Evidence: The Book of Mormon was written in the "language of [Nephi's] father, which consists of the learning of the Jews [Hebrew], and the language of the Egyptians" (1 Nephi 1:2). The Hebrew was altered and written "in the characters which are called among us the reformed Egyptian" (Mormon 9:32-33).

The sacred record was "engraved" on gold plates in reformed Egyptian rather than Hebrew because Hebrew characters are not suitable for engraving, but are painted by brush strokes—each part of a given character having thicker or thinner brush strokes to convey a precise meaning. Dr. Hugh Nibley's points out that the Nephites could not have engraved in Hebrew, and that they saved much space by using Egyptian characters. See H. Torczyner, *The Lachish Letters,* (Oxford, 1938), p. 15, cited in Nibley, *Lehi in the Desert and the World of the Jaredites*, (1980), pp. 15-16.

EVIDENCE NO. 895: THE TITLE PAGE OF THE BOOK OF MORMON TAKEN FROM THE LAST PLATE

Claim: Joseph Smith wrote that "the title-page of the Book of Mormon is a literal translation, taken from the *very last leaf*, on the left hand side of the collection or book of plates, which contained the record which has been translated." (See Joseph Smith, *History of the Church of Jesus Christ of Latter-day Saints,* vol. 1, p. 71.)

This small detail, mentioned only in passing, is yet another evidence that the Book of Mormon is true, and that it was indeed translated from an ancient document written by peoples who migrated from the Middle East.

Evidence: Non-Mormon scholar Walter Burkert recently completed a study of the cultural dependence of Greek civilization on the ancient Near East. In his study he points out that "the practice of the *Subscriptio* in particular ... connects the layout of later Greek books with cuneiform practice, the indication of the *name of the writer/ author and the title of the book right at the end, after the last line of the text*; this is a detailed and exclusive correspondence which proves that Greek literary practice is ultimately dependent upon Mesopotamia. It is necessary to postulate that Aramaic leather scrolls formed the connecting link." Walter Burkert, *The Orientalizing Revolution: Near Eastern Influence on Greek Culture in the Early Archaic Age,* p. 32, emphasis added. Also cited in *Foundation for Ancient Research and Mormon Studies Update,* (July 1994), no. 95, p. 2.

EVIDENCE NO. 896: UNIQUE WORDPRINTS OF VARIOUS BOOK OF MORMON PROPHETS

Claim: The unique vocabularies of the different prophets who wrote the Book of Mormon are reflected in the words and phrases of each book, rather that one style as if it had all been written by Joseph Smith.

Evidence: Computer analysis shows that each Book of Mormon writer has his own "wordprint" which is as individual and distinctive as his fingerprints. The following is quoted from an article on "Book of Mormon Authorship" in *Encyclopedia of Mormonism*, (New York: Macmillan Publishing Company, 1992), vol. 1:

Wordprinting has been used to ascertain the authorship of such works as twelve disputed Federalist Papers and a posthumously published novel by Jane Austen. When applied to the Book of Mormon, wordprinting reveals that the word patterns of the Book of Mormon differ significantly from the personal writings of Joseph Smith, Solomon Spaulding, Sidney Rigdon, and Oliver Cowdery, who served as Joseph Smith's scribe. Furthermore, patterns of Nephi are consistent among themselves but different from those of Alma. The results of objectively measuring these phenomena indicate an extremely low statistical probability that the Book of Mormon could have been written by one author. The introduction of new vocabulary into the text is at a low rate, which is consistent with the uniform role of Joseph Smith as translator.

Studies have been conducted in which computers analyzed the "wordprints" of Joseph Smith and some of his associates as well as the various books within the Book of Mormon. One study found that the Book of Mormon is the product of at least 24 different authors. The same study also indicated that the odds against the Book of Mormon having a single author are more than a billion to one. See Alvin C. Rencher and Wayne Larsen, *Brigham Young University Studies*, Spring 1980, cited in Vestal and Wallace, *The Firm Foundation of Mormonism*, (1981), pp. 178-181.

In her book, Diane Wirth referred to the research of Dr. Robert Thomas who (in his "A Literary Critic Looks at the Book of Mormon," in Charles D. Tate; and Truman G. Madsen, *To the Glory of God* [Salt Lake City: Deseret Book Co., 1972], pp. 149-161) commented on these variations in writing styles:

… He found that there is a marked difference in writing styles between the small books written by Enos, Jarom, and Omni.

Enos was impetuous—his sentences indistinct and fragmentary. "His words roll forth in an irresistible flood." In Jarom, the next book in line, we see a drastic shift in style from that of Enos. Jarom is crisp, to the point, and yet there is a sereneness in his writing. He also takes the time to reflect on genealogies and Hebraic law. We see a literal, psychological contrast in the makeup of these two men.

Next is Omni. Again we find an author distinct and separate from both Jarom and Enos. Omni is a soldier: proud, dutiful, and perhaps a bit self-centered. In his first two verses he uses "I" seven times. His writings deal with war and peace, conquests and losses. He is not impulsive like Enos—he is not humble, yet forceful, as is Jarom.

… A personal study of the various writers of the Book of Mormon gives strong evidence of the book's individuality and, of course, its historic and authentic nature. (See Wirth [1986], p. 94.)

The following examples presented by the *Foundation for Ancient Research and Mormon Studies*, clearly demonstrate that one man did not create the Book of Mormon, but that it was the product of many different writers, each having his own style and vocabulary.

… the phrases "Lord God Omnipotent" or "Lord Omnipotent" appear six times in the Book of Mormon, and all six of them are in King Benjamin's Speech. Apparently this name for God, spoken four times by the angel in Mosiah 3, and once by the people and once by Benjamin in Mosiah 5, was distinctive to Benjamin, and perhaps was considered too sacred to have been used by other Nephites outside of Benjamin's text.

And again, as David Fox has pointed out, the phrase "The Holy One of Israel" never appears in the Book of Mormon except in the Small Plates of Nephi and in Isaiah. This name for God appears some 30 times in the Old Testament, and almost all of them are in Isaiah or around the time of Lehi. Perhaps this name reflects a theological understanding of a God who is particularly concerned with the scattering and gathering of Israel.

Many phrases may shed light on the prevailing ideas or particular experiences of Book of Mormon personalities. The word "island" and the phrase "isles of the sea" appear exclusively in the books of 1 Nephi and 2 Nephi. Why should the important prophecies of Isaiah about the Lord remembering "those who are upon the isles of the sea" (2 Nephi 10:21; Isaiah 11:11; 49:1; 51:5) be so prominent here but unmentioned later? Perhaps it took a few years for the Nephites to realize what a large land-mass their territory was a part of.

It is also remarkable that the phrase "great and abominable church" likewise appears only in the early Nephite writings—12 times. Nephi uses the phrase 11 times, and his brother Jacob (in 2 Nephi 6:12) uses it once. This phrase appears to have remained distinctively associated with Nephi's vision. Similarly, Wade Brown has pointed out a number of phrases that are unique to Zenos. Roger Keller is working on the characteristics of the autographic writings of Mormon and Moroni. Paul Hoskisson and Deloy Pack have recently examined words and phrases relating to the "heart." (See "Words and Phrases," *Foundation for Ancient Research and Mormon Studies Update,* April 1987; see also Philip A. Allred, "Alma's Use of *State* in the Book of Mormon: Evidence of Multiple Authorship," *Journal of Book of Mormon Studies,* [Spring 1996], vol. 5, no. 1, pp. 140-149.)

See also "Who Wrote the Book of Mormon?—An Analysis of Wordprints by Wayne A. Larsen and Alvin C. Rencher in *Book of Mormon Authorship,*" Edited by Noel B. Reynolds, (Religious studies Center, Brigham Young University, 1982).

EVIDENCE NO. 897: SYMBOLISM IN THE BOOK OF MORMON

Claim: One of the more common characteristics of ancient writings is the use of symbolism. Since the Book of Mormon claims to be a companion to the Bible, it should be expected to contain similar types of symbolism. Indeed, the Bible teaches that "God is no respecter of persons" or nations (Acts 10:34-35). It also teaches that the Lord is "same yesterday, and to day, and for ever" (Hebrews 13:8). It follows, therefore, that revelations from God to two different nations would be given with similar types of symbolism, especially if those two nations shared a common culture and history.

The fact that the Book of Mormon contains many types of ancient Biblical symbolisms is evidence that it is both authentic and of the same God who revealed the Bible. However, while Book of Mormon symbolism resembles those of the Bible, they are often employed in unique ways not found in the Bible. A few examples of ancient Biblical symbolisms from both books are presented below.

Evidence: For example, both the Bible and the Book of Mormon use the word *white* as a symbol of *purity* (Isaiah 1:18; Daniel 12:10; Alma 5:24). Critics of the Book of Mormon who have insisted that the word *white* can only be used in a literal sense and cannot be synonymous for *pure* are actually criticizing their own Bible.

The Bible uses *light* as a symbol of *knowledge* (Daniel 5:14), as does the Book of Mormon, but in the latter it is further symbolized as a thing that can be "held" (3 Nephi 18:24), such as food that can be "tasted" (Alma 32:35). Similarly, the Bible uses the sun as a symbol for the Savior (Malachi 4:2) as does the Book of Mormon, which further personifies the sun as a male (Helaman 14:20). Both books imply that the sun can *stand* (Joshua 10:13; Habakkuk 3:11; Helaman 12:15), and can *smite* (Psalms 121:6; Isaiah 49:10; 1 Nephi 21:10) as a man would do.

One verse in the Bible alludes to the *olive tree* as a symbol of the *house of Israel* (Romans 11:17). But in the Book of Mormon this concept is fully developed and taught in a detailed allegory of some seventy-seven verses in the fifth chapter of Jacob. In the Bible, a *field* is personified as being able to experience *joy* (Psalms 96:12), and is employed as a symbol for the world (Matthew 13:38). The Book of Mormon uses the symbol of a *ripe field* to represent potential converts who must be *reaped* by the missionaries who thrust in the *sickle* and gather the *sheaves* (Alma 26:5).

The Bible uses *rivers* as symbols of the *spirit,* of *peace* and the *King's heart* (John 7:37-39; Isaiah 48:18; Proverbs 21:1). The Book of Mormon uses the *river* to symbolize the path to "*the fountain of all righteousness,*" as well as a symbol of *wickedness* (1 Nephi 2:9; 15:2). In the scriptures *water, rain* and *dew* are used to symbolize "*counsel in the heart of man,*" the *words of God, affliction* and as a symbol for both *good* and *evil works* (Deuteronomy 32:2; Proverbs 20:5; Isaiah 30:20; James 3:10-12; Moroni 7:10-12). The Book of Mormon makes an interesting extension on these themes by using the imagery of the "*dew before the sun*" as a symbol of the Nephite civilization as they were being *wiped off the face of the land* (Mormon 4:18).

In the Bible, *valleys* are used as a symbol of *death* as well as *revelation* (Psalms 23:4; Isaiah 22:1-5). In the Book of Mormon the word *valley* was used as a symbol of *firmness, steadfastness, sorrow* and *the strait and narrow path* (1 Nephi 2:10; 2 Nephi 4:26, 32).

Both the Bible and the Book of Mormon often symbolize the passage of *time* as *space* by proceeding a measurement of time with the phrase "for the space of..." (such as in Genesis 29:14; and Omni 1:21). The authors find twenty such occurrences in the Bible and eighty-seven in the Book of Mormon.

The Bible uses the *lion* to represent *God, the king's wrath,* and *boldness* (Job 10:16; Proverbs 19:12; 20:2), while the Book of Mormon uses the same symbol to represent the *"remnant of the house of Jacob"* (3 Nephi 20:16; 21:12; Mormon 5:24).

Both books use the *sword* as symbol for the *word of the Lord* (Revelation 1:16; 2:26; 19:15; and 1 Nephi 21:2), but they also use the *sword* to represent other things. For example, the Psalmist used the *sword* to represent both the *tongue* and the *reproach of ones enemies* (Psalms 42:10; 57:4). The Book of Mormon used the *sword* to represent the *power to enforce,* the *wrath of God,* the *justice of God, pestilence* and *vengeance* (Alma 1:12; 54:6; Helaman 11:14; 13:5; 3 Nephi 20:20; Ether 8:23; Mormon 8:41).

The Bible compares the *coming of a chief prince* to a *storm* (Ezekiel 38:9). The Book of Mormon uses the imagery of *storms* and *winds* to represent the *destructions of the last days* as well as the *temptations of the devil* (Alma 26:6; Heleman 5:12).

Both books of scripture make extensive use of the word *visit* in various ways not used in our western culture. For example, the scriptures speak of the Lord *visiting* with *thunderings, lightnings, tempests, fires, smoke* and *vapors of darkness* (Isaiah 29:6: 1 Nephi 19:11). However, they also mention the Lord *visiting* with *Salvation, assurances, the fire of the Holy Ghost* and *"his voice...unto their great joy and salvation"* (Psalms 106:4; 1 Nephi 19:11; Alma 58:11; 3 Nephi 12:2; Moroni 8:26). They further speak of *visiting* with *anger, judgement, evil, famine, hatred, sore curses, great destructions, death* and *the sword* (Job 35:15; Proverbs 19:23; Isaiah 29:6; Jeremiah 23:2; 1 Nephi 13:33; 2 Nephi 1:18; Jacob 2:33; Mosiah 29:29:27; Alma 9:18; 54:10; Helaman 13:9; 3 Nephi 3:4, 6).

In the above references the scriptures speak of *visiting with*...however, the following speak of the Lord *visiting* directly the *iniquity, transgression, sin* and *destruction,* not *upon* or *with,* but *of* his wayward children (Exodus 20:5; 32:34; Leviticus 18:25; Psalms 89:32; Jeremiah 14:10; Mosiah 11:20; 13:13; Helaman 13:10).

Hebrew and Egyptian Influence in the Book of Mormon

Claim: The Book of Mormon, originally written in a language which, consisted of "the learning of the Jews (Hebrew) and the language of the Egyptians," (1 Nephi 1:2) often contains wordings that are foreign and awkward to the English tongue, but which are precisely correct in their original setting. The following several evidences provide specific examples of the influence of Hebrew and Egyptian on the ancient American writers of the Book of Mormon.

Egyptian Influence on the Book of Mormon

EVIDENCE NO. 898: REFORMED EGYPTIAN

Evidence: The Book of Mormon proclaimed that it was written in *reformed Egyptian* because it was more efficient (taking up less space) than Hebrew (1 Nephi 1:2; Mosiah 1:4; Mormon 9:31-33; Ether 12:23-28, 35). When the Book of Mormon was first published, the idea of Hebrews writing in Egyptian must have sounded quite ludicrous. However, one hundred years after the Book of Mormon was first published, scholars found evidence of hieratic (shortened) Egyptian and demotic (a shorthand, even more brief than hieratic). Thus, the Book of

Mormon is substantiated again. Hubert Grimme, Professor of Semitic Language at Munster University has published his findings of ancient engravings on the Sinai Peninsula from 1500 BC *in pure Hebrew language but the script was hieratic Egyptian* "somewhat changed." In the same source, Grimme proves that the Incas and Mayas used Egyptian hieratic script by slightly altering it. (See A. Churchward, "Althebraische Inschriften vom Sinai" *The Origin and Evolution of Religion*, [1924]. See also E. A. W. Budge, *Papyrus of Ani*, [New York: Putnam, 1913], vol. 1, p. 50; Theodore Noeldeke, *Die Semitischen Sprachen*, [Leipzig 1899], p. 34; Edward Meyer, *Geschichte des Altertums*, [1927], vol. 1. p. 297; and William F. Albright, *The Vocalization of Egyptian Syllabic Orthography*, [New Haven: American Orthographic Society, 1934]; S. Sauneron and J. Yoyotte in *Bulletin de l'Institut Francais de'Archaelogie Oriental*, [1952], vol. 50, pp. 107-117; and Wilhelm Spiegelberg, "Zur Definition des 'Demotischen'," *Zeitschrift für Ägyptische Sprache und Altertumskunde*, vol. 37 [1899], p. 19, cited in Nibley, *Since Cumorah* [1988], p. 149. See also Dr. Barry Fell, President of the Epigraphic Society in Paul R. Cheesman, *Ancient Writing on Metal Plates* [Horizon Publishers: Bountiful, 1985], p. 16.)

The following is quoted from a paper by John L. Sorenson entitled "The Book of Mormon as a Mesoamerican Codex," SOR-76, *Foundation for Ancient Research and Mormon Studies*, 1976, p. 3:

> The Book of Mormon text reports it to have been written, in the words of its final custodian in the 4th century AD, in "characters which are called among us the reformed Egyptian, being handed down and altered by us, according to our manner of speech." Furthermore, the Nephite writers in the Book of Mormon complain of their frustration at the ambiguity which the character system forced upon them.[1] Clearly enough they were not using Egyptian glyphs as such, but a variant system which operated on similar principles with the addition of unique symbols. Durbin's classification of the world's writing systems puts the Mesoamerican systems in the same general category as *Egyptian*.[2] The operational principles being essentially the same in the two systems, addition or substitution of new characters could result in a series of transitions to a symbol system "reformed" in comparison with the old because the characters would be unreadable to persons not specifically instructed in their meaning. If the original Book of Mormon text was written in codex form using a glyph system on Mesoamerican principles, as Anthon [Professor Anthon visited by Martin Harris] hints, it could reasonably have been termed a reformed or modified Egyptian system if any significant portion of it had had Egyptian derivation. (Emphasis added.)

[1] Ether 12:24-25; Mosiah 1:3-6, and also J. Eric Thompson's characterization of the Maya system which sounds very similar: "Both space considerations and ritualistic associations militated against precision in writing; and, in addition, the great use of rebus writing … influenced the texts so that the reader had to have a good background of mythology and folklore to comprehend the texts." (J. Eric Thompson, "Maya Hieroglyphic Writing," in *Handbook of Middle American Indians, Volume 3, Archaeology of Southern Mesoamerica*, Part 2, edited by Gordon R. Willey [Austin: University of Texas Press, 1965], p. 646.)

[2] Marshall Durbin, "Linguistics and Writing Systems," *Estudios de Cultura Maya*, vol. 7 (1968), p. 54; and C. F. & E. M. Voegelin, "typological Classification of Systems with Included, Excluded and Self-sufficient Alphabets," *Anthropological Linguistics,* vol. 3 (1961), p. 78. Compare with Ether 12:24-25 on possible bases for Jaredite-Nephite differences in writing capability.

EVIDENCE NO. 899: REFORMED EGYPTIAN CHARACTER FORMS

<u>Evidence</u>: In the late 1820's, Martin Harris persuaded Joseph Smith to copy a few lines of the reformed Egyptian characters as proof that the plates were genuine. These were the characters Harris showed to Professor Charles Anthon of Columbia College. When the anti-Mormons saw the transcript, some claimed that Smith's characters were not reformed Egyptian but "deformed English." However, modern studies have demonstrated that the characters copied from the plates by Joseph Smith are indeed authentic.

Studies have been conducted to determine if the characters are authentic. The conclusion is that each character is authentic—each one has at least one counterpart with ancient writing samples from the Middle East. For example, one character form showing a horizontal line with eight perpendicular strokes above it (shown in Figure 35 below) has been singled out as being a ridiculous attempt at authenticity. However, this glyph is authentic and is called the "sign of the chessboard." See E. A. W. Budge, "Lithographs," *Book of the Dead* (British Museum, 1899).

Another character form that has drawn much criticism is the one resembling a cursive capital "H." This, too, is authentic—representing the meaning "to write" or "writing." Joseph Smith could not have gained access to a demotic (reformed) Egyptian alphabet or a dictionary of this ancient language during the translation of the Book of Mormon. Such resources would not be available for another century until the works of Brugsch, Spiegelberg, Erman, Grapow, Budge, Petrie, Young, Tatam, Lepsius, Birch, Gardiner, etc., were all published years after the first publication of the Book of Mormon. See Ariel Crowley, *About the Book of Mormon* (Deseret News Press, 1961), pp. 20-38.

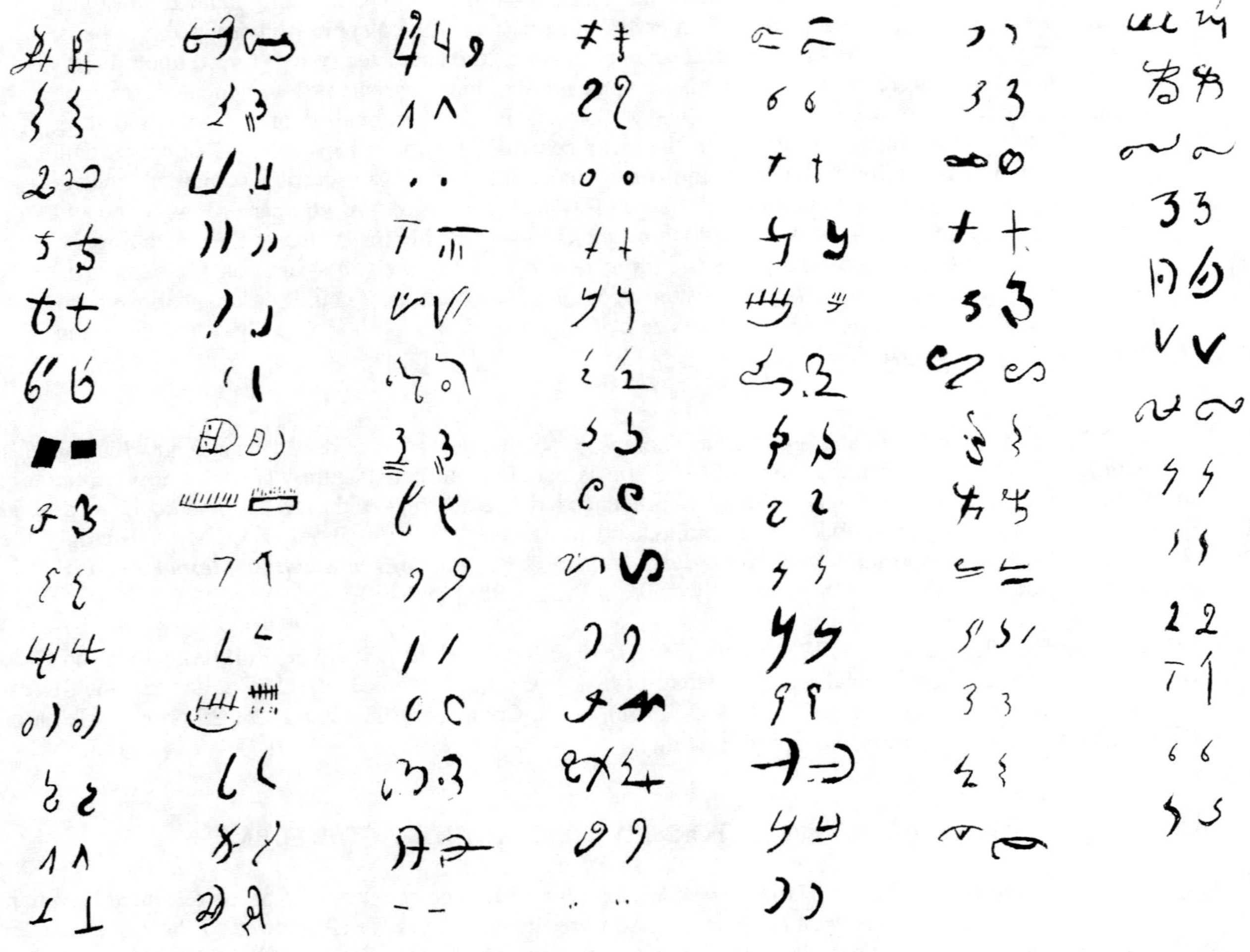

Figure 35. Reformed Egyptian characters from the Book of Mormon (left side of each column) and the Middle East (right side of each column).

EVIDENCE NO. 900: BOOK OF MORMON CHARACTER FORMS RE-AUTHENTICATED

Evidence: In addition to the assurance from Professor Charles Anthon of Columbia College that the Book of Mormon characters were authentic (Joseph Smith—History 1:64-65), a modern professor—more qualified than Dr. Anthon, has reaffirmed the authenticity of the character forms copied from the golden plates of the Book of Mormon.

Dr. William C. Hayes, Curator of the Egyptian Department of the Metropolitan Museum of Art in New York City, recognized the Harris character forms as resembling hieratic Egyptian characters and indicated their possible meaning. (See Stanley H. B. Kimball, "I Can Not Read a Sealed Book," *Improvement Era*, [1957] vol. 60, p. 80; cited in Sydney B. Sperry, *The Problems of the Book of Mormon* [Bookcraft, 1964], p. 60.)

EVIDENCE NO. 901: A MODERN TRANSLATION OF THE ANTHON TRANSCRIPT

Evidence: A careful examination of the Anthon transcript has shown that the sequence of characters correlates with a portion of the Book of Mormon that tells of the Jaredite voyage to ancient America. Stanley and Polly Johnson have produced a translation of the Anthony transcript by comparing each character to similar hieroglyphics in Egyptian, Polynesian and Native American cultures. A truly astonishing result of this tedious work was the discovery that the Anthon transcript correlates with Ether 6:3-13. (See Stanley Quenton and Polly Ivory Johnson, *Translating the Anthon Transcript*, [Parawan, Utah: Ivory Books, 1999].)

To effect this translation the authors drew upon such authorities as E. A. Wallis Budge, La Van Martineau, Ettie Rout, and Polly Sschaafsma. (See Budge, *An Egyptian Hieroglyphic Dictionary*, [New York: Dover Publications Inc., 1978]; Martineau, *The Rocks Begin to Speak*, [Las Vegas: K. C. Publications, 1976]; Rout, *Maori Symbolism*, [London: Harcourt, Brace and Co., 1926]; and Sschaafsma, *Indian Rock of the Southwest*, [Santa Fe: University of New Mexico Press, 1980].)

The fact that the Anthon characters provide a logical and meaningful flow of thought, from right to left (as Hebrew words are written), it remarkable, but the fact that they also match the actual wording in Ether 6:3-13 is truly astounding.

EVIDENCE NO. 902: MESOAMERICAN CHARACTER FORMS

Evidence: Not only have many of the Anthon characters been identified as actual reformed Egyptian characters, but many have also turned up on a roller stamp found at *Tlatilco, Valley of Mexico*. Some of the clearest similarities between the Book of Mormon characters and their Mesoamerican forms are shown below in Figure 36. (See Carl Hugh Jones, "The 'Anthon Transcript' and Two Mesoamerican Cylinder Seals," *Society for Early Historic Archaeology Newsletter and Proceedings*, [Provo, Utah], no. 122, fig. 8; and no. 145, [August 1980].)

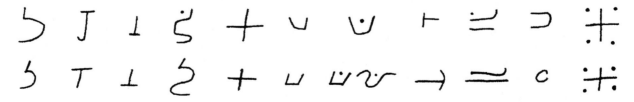

Figure 36. Markings found at Tlatilco Valley of Mexico (top), Anthon Transcript equivalents (bottom)

EVIDENCE NO. 903: MAYAN WRITTEN LANGUAGE SIMILAR TO EGYPTIAN

Evidence: The Mayan written language was strikingly similar to Egyptian. Below is a table comparing the Maya alphabet with that of the Egyptians. The table below is found in Peter Tompkins, *The Mysteries of the Mexican Pyramids*, (Harper & Rowe, 1976), p. 116.

The following is a quotation from the abstract of a paper by M. Wells Jakeman entitled "Ancient Maya Hieroglyphic Writings and Their Decipherment and Study" (*University Archaeological Society Newsletter* 44.01):

> About 1930, a Harvard scholar named Benjamin Whorf came out in support of a phonetic theory of Maya decipherment; that is, he believed the elements of the glyphs to be primarily phonetic, rather than ideographic. ... William Gates (whose famous collection of Middle American linguistic documents has been in the posses-sion of Brigham Young University since 1946, and who compiled a dictionary of Maya glyphs) believed, with Whorf, in the phonetic principle.

> Late last year, the announcement was made that a young Russian linguist, Yuri Knorozov, had succeeded in a preliminary decipherment of the non-calendrical hiero-glyphs, proposing phonetic as well as ideographic values for about 300 glyphs. ... His work in general is in harmony with that of Whorf, Gates, and the other phone-ticians, and is favored by the prominent Mexican archae-ologist Alberto Ruz.

> According to Knorozov, the Maya system (quite like the Egyptian) is composed of four varieties of elements: ideo-graphic signs, phonetic signs, determinatives (affixes tacked on to clarify meaning), and particles. Latter-day Saints will find this view intriguing, since according to the Book of Mormon one of the writing systems of its ancient peoples of America was a "reformed Egyptian" (probably an adaptation of Demotic Egyptian script). Christensen, *Progress in Archaeology,* (1963), p. 130.

Mayan	Egyptian

EVIDENCE NO. 904: THE COLOPHON

Evidence: The Book of Mormon's extensive use of the ancient Egyptian composition device called *colophon* provides additional evidence of its authenticity. The Book of Mormon opens with a perfect example of the ancient *colophon*, a literary form of composition characteristic of Egyptian writing in which the author writes:

1) His name,
2) The merits of his parents, and the learning of his father,
3) A solemn avowal that the record is true,
4) An assertion that he writes it himself, and
5) Ends various sections with a phrase such as "And thus it is." See 1 Nephi 1:1-3.

For other *colophons*, see 1 Nephi 9:6; 14:30; 22:30-31; Jacob 1:2; 7:27; Jarom 1-2; Omni 1:1, 3-4; Words of Mormon 9; and Mosiah 1:4; 9:1.

For documentation of this unique form of writing on the Old World, see E. J. Bickerman, "Colophon of the Greek Esther," *Journal of Biblical Literature*, (1944), vol. 63, p. 339; R. O. Faulkner, "The Bremer-Rind Papyrus-II," *Journal of Egyptian Archaeology*, (1937), vol. 23, p. 10; F. L. Griffith, "The Teaching of Amenophis, the Son of Kanakht," *Journal of Egyptian Archaeology*, (1926), vol. 12, p. 195; and K. Sethe, *Aegyptische Lesestuecke* (Leipzig, 1924), pp. 17, 42-43. Above sources are cited in Nibley, *Lehi in the Desert and the World of the Jaredites,* (1988), pp. 17-18. See also John A. Tvedtnes, "Colophons in the Book of Mormon," *Re-exploring the Book of Mormon*, edited by John W. Welch, (1992), pp. 13-16.

EVIDENCE NO. 905: "LANGUAGE" FOR "SPEECH"

Evidence: The Book of Mormon was written by people who were influenced by Egyptian culture. The use of the word "language" as a substitute for the word "speech" in the Book of Mormon is borrowed from the Egyptian tongue. (See 1 Nephi 1:2, 15 and Mormon 9:32-3). Among the Egyptians, the word "language" was commonly substituted for "speech." See A. S. Yahuda, *The Language of the Pentateuch in its Relation to Egyptian,* (London: Oxford University Press, 1933), p. 51, cited in Nibley, *Lehi in the Desert*, (1988) p. 14.

EVIDENCE NO. 906: ONE'S SEED

Evidence: The numerous references to "seed" in the Book of Mormon to symbolize one's descendants (1 Nephi 2:23; 8:3; 4:14; Mosiah 17:15; Mormon 5:10) was typical wording for writers influenced by the Egyptian language as were the Nephites (1 Nephi 1:2; Mosiah 1:4; Mormon 9:32).

The word "seed" has been found to be a common idiomatic expression in the ancient Egyptian language which is used to designate "son" or "descendant." See H. Crapow, *Die Bildlichen Ausdrucke des Aegyptischen*, (Leipzig: Hinrich, 1924), p. 126. Cited in Nibley, *Since Cumorah* (1988), p. 166.

EVIDENCE NO. 907: THE PHRASE "AND IT CAME TO PASS" USED IN ANCIENT LANGUAGES

Evidence: The Book of Mormon states that it was written "in the language of the Egyptians" (1 Nephi 1:2). This explains why it uses the phrase "it came to pass" so much more than the Bible—which was written in Hebrew and Greek.

Though this wording may seem awkward to the western reader, the phrase "and it came to pass" used so frequently in the Book of Mormon, was common in the Hebrew, Egyptian and Mayan languages. Since the Hebrew language uses no punctuation, the phrase "and it came to pass" functions much like a period to signal the end of one thought and the beginning of another. Angela Crowell noted that:

"And it came to pass" is probably the most frequently used phrase in the Book of Mormon. This phrase in the idiom of King James English is a rendering of the Hebrew word "vayehee." Its frequent use in the Book of Mormon is consistent with the frequent use of "vayehee" in the Old Testament Hebrew text. In J. Weingreen's *A Practical Grammar for Classical Hebrew* (2nd edition [Oxford: The Clarendon Press, 1959], p. 92), the author comments concerning the meaning of this phrase: "This, rather than implying a continuation with what has preceded, has little more force (when translated) than 'now it happened.' This phrase, 'and it came to pass' and the frequent use of 'and' are two of the most important proofs of Hebrew language structure found in the Book of Mormon." (Angela Crowell, "Hebraisms in the Book of Mormon," *The Zarahemla Record* [1982], p. 2.)

The monotonous repetition of "it came to pass" as a replacement for punctuation, was also standard Egyptian practice. Egyptian historical texts, Crapow noted, "begin in monotonous fashion" always with the same stock words; at some periods even every speech was introduced with the unnecessary "I opened my mouth." Also dramatic texts are held together by the constant repetition of *Khpr-n*, "It happened that..." or "It came to pass..." See H. Crapow, *Das Hieroglyphensystem*, pp. 23-25, 31; and P. Humbert, in *Archiv fur Orient forschung*, 10 (1935), pp. 77-80, cited in Nibley, *Since Cumorah*, (1988), p. 150.

The following is quoted from Bruce W. Warren and Thomas Stuart Ferguson, *The Messiah in Ancient America*, (Provo, Utah: 1987), pp. 62-64.

> The phrase "and it came to pass" occurs frequently throughout the Book of Mormon. It has a fascinating parallel in Mayan hieroglyphs. J. Eric Thompson, probably the leading Mayan scholar until his death in the early 1970s, discussed what he called posterior and anterior date indicators in Classic Maya Hieroglyphs. He discovered that the posterior date indicators meant, "to count forward to;" the anterior date indicators meant "to count backward to." When he wrote this in 1950, he did not know of an equivalent phrase in contemporary Yucatec or other Mayan dialects (J. Eric Thompson, "Maya Hieroglyphic Writing," *Carnegie Institution of Washington,* [1950] vol. 589, 162-164).
>
> Proto-Cholan is now considered to be the main Mayan dialect used in the Classic period hieroglyphs. In 1984 David Stuart gave a Proto-Cholan reading of *uht* as "to finish, come to pass," or Chontal *ut* with the same meaning. Schele, a professor of anthropology at the University of Texas, considered one of the leading scholars of ancient Maya hieroglyphs, also translated this Maya hieroglyph as "then it came to pass" (Linda Schele, *Maya Glyphs: The Verbs,* [Austin: University of Texas Press, 1982] pp. 21-25).
>
> ... A couple of hieroglyphic examples of this usage can be found on the Palace Tablets at Palenque, Chiapas, Mexico and are shown below in Figure 37.

Figure 37. "And then it came to pass" and "it had come to pass" Mayan glyphs from 600 AD.

In 1982 Schele illustrated with Maya glyphs and verbal descriptions four types of directional count indicators, posterior date indicators, posterior event indicators, anterior date indicators, and anterior event indicators (Linda Schele, *Maya Glyphs: The Verbs,* pp. 22, 68-69).

Many examples of several types of these directional count indicators can be found in the Book of Mormon:

Posterior Date Indicator: "And it came to pass that thus passed away the ninety and fifth years also" (3 Nephi 2:1).

Posterior Event Indicator: "And it came to pass that the people began to wax strong in wickedness and abominations" (3 Nephi 2:3).

Posterior Date and Event Indicators: "And it came to pass in the thirteenth year there began to be wars and contentions throughout the land" (3 Nephi 2:11).

Anterior Date Indicator: "And thus did pass away the ninety and sixth year" (3 Nephi 2:4).

Anterior Event Indicator: "And it had come to pass, yea, all things, every whit, according to the words of the prophets" (3 Nephi 1:20).

Combined Anterior Date and Event Indicator: "And six hundred and nine years had passed away since Lehi left Jerusalem" (3 Nephi 2:6).

Hebrew Influence in the Book of Mormon

<u>Claim</u>: The Book of Mormon claims to have been written "in the language of [Lehi], which consists of the learning of the Jews and the language of the Egyptians" (1 Nephi 1:2). The similarities between the Hebrew language and that of the various Indian nations caused Dr. Fray Diego Duran to conclude that they are "so like that of the Hebrews." See Fray Diego Duran, *The Aztecs—The History of the Indies of New Spain.* Translated with notes by Doris Heyden and Fernando Horcastes (New York: Onion Press, 1964) p. 3. See also Cheesman, *World of the Book of Mormon,* (Salt Lake City: Deseret Book Co. 1978).

The following several evidences document the striking similarity between the Hebrew Language and those of the ancient Americans. They further demonstrate the profound influence of the Hebrew language on the literary styles of the Book of Mormon. Hebrew scholars have noted that the language of the Book of Mormon "is not English freely composed but is rather that type of English that would be produced by a translator who frequently follows the original too closely, the syntax of which is thus made plain in the English dress. In other words … the English of the Book of Mormon often betrays a too-literal adherence to an apparent Hebrew original. Let us call it Hebrew-English" (*Journal of Book of Mormon Studies,* [FARMS, Spring 1995], vol. 4, no. 2, p. 214).

EVIDENCE NO. 908: ANAPHORA

<u>Evidence</u>: The Book of Mormon was written by prophets who were conversant with Hebrew customs and language (1 Nephi 1:2). This is made evident by the frequent use of an ancient Hebrew literary device known as *anaphora*. Anaphora is defined as "the repetitions of the same word at the beginning of successive sentences." (See E. W. Bullinger, *Figures of Speech Used in the Bible,* [Grand Rapids, Michigan: Baker Book House, 1968], pp. 199, cited in Hugh Pinnock, *Ancient Literary Forms,* [Provo, Utah: FARMS, 1999], p. 18.)

An excellent example of this *anaphora* is found in 2 Nephi 9:31-38 where the word "wo" is used eight times:

> And *wo* unto the deaf that will not hear; for they shall perish. *Wo* unto the blind that will not see; for they shall perish also. *Wo* unto the uncircumcised of heart, for a knowledge of their iniquities shall smite them at the last day. *Wo* unto the liar, for he shall be thrust down to hell. *Wo* unto the murderer who deliberately killeth, for he shall die. *Wo* unto them who commit whoredoms, for they shall be thrust down to hell. Yea, *wo* unto those that worship idols, for the devil of all devils delighteth in them. And, in fine, *wo* unto all those who die in their sins; for they shall return to God, and behold his face, and remain in their sins.

See also 2 Nephi 15:20-22; Heleman 13:11-16 for other examples of using "wo" in this literary technique.

This ancient Hebrew form is found in about one forth of the verses in the Book of Mormon, but only one out of every 24 verses in the Bible. Other words and clauses that are used in this fashion include: "How is it" (1 Nephi 7:9-12), "Believe" (Mosiah 4:9-10), "I say unto you" (Alma 5:3-60), "Yea" (Alma 5:32-35; 5:48-55), "Verily" (3 Nephi 11:29-39; 15:19-21), "Then" (3 Nephi 20:32-36), "For" (3 Nephi 22:3-10) and "Behold" (Mormon 5:16-20).

Biblical examples of anaphora include "Cursed" (Deuteronomy 28:16-19), "Praise" (Psalms 13:1-3; 148:1-4), "Blessed are" (Matthew 5:3-11) and "Faith" (Hebrews 11:13-31).

EVIDENCE NO. 909: EPISTROPHE AND AMOEBAEON

Evidence: Other Hebrew literary forms found in the Book of Mormon are *epistrophe* and *amoebaeon*. *Epistrophe* is defined as "the repetition of an identical word and/or expression at the end of successive sentences." While epistrophe is used in the poetic writing of sentence endings, *amoebaeon* is used in narrative writings for paragraph endings. While these literary techniques seem awkward and redundant to the modern reader, they were quite fashionable in ancient times. (See E. W. Bullinger, *Figures of Speech Used in the Bible*, [Grand Rapids, Michigan: Baker Book House, 1968], pp. 18, 241, 343; Donald W. Parry, *The Book of Mormon Text Reformatted according to Parallelistic Patterns,* [Provo, Utah: FARMS, 1992], p. xliii.)

An example of *epistrophe* is found in Ether 2:17 which uses the phrase "tight like unto a dish":

And they were built after a manner that they were exceedingly *tight*, even that they would hold water *like unto a dish*; and the bottom thereof was *tight like unto a dish*; and the sides thereof were *tight like unto a dish*; and the ends thereof were peaked; and the top thereof was *tight like unto a dish*; and the length thereof was the length of a tree; and the door thereof, when it was shut, was *tight like unto a dish*.

Other Book of Mormon examples of epistrophe and amoebaeon can be found in 1 Nephi 10:12-13; Mosiah 1:6; Alma 9:2-3, 32-33; 14:4-5, 8-14, 18-19; 26:31-32; 29:11-12; 31:7-8; 33:11-18; 35:1-2; 37:9-10; 39:16 through 40:2, 40:18-20; 43:62:18; Helaman 7:23-24; 10:8-10.

Biblical examples of epistrophe and amoebaeon include Deuteronomy 27:16-26; Job 1:15-19; Psalms 115:9-11; 118:10-12; 136:1-26; Isaiah 9:12, 17, 21; Joel 2:26-27; Amos 4:6-11. See also Hugh Pinnock, *Ancient Literary Forms,* (Provo, Utah: FARMS, 1999), pp. 36, 38.

EVIDENCE NO. 910: POLYSYNDETON (THE EXCESSIVE USE OF THE CONJUNCTION "AND")

Evidence: The excessive use of the monotonous conjunction "and" in the Book of Mormon seems awkward and somewhat annoying to the western reader, however, it follows perfect Hebrew syntax. The word "and" often stands before each word (or phrase) in a series; possibly because there was no punctuation in the Hebrew language.

Notice the structure of Enos 1:21 from the Book of Mormon: "*And* it came to pass that the people of Nephi did till the land, *and* raise all manner of grain, *and* of fruit, *and* flocks of herds, *and* flocks of all manner of cattle of every kind, *and* goats, *and* wild goats, *and* also many horses." See also 1 Nephi 2:4; 4:9; 2 Nephi 33:9; Alma 1:29; 7:27; 8:21-23; 9:21; Helaman 3:14; 3 Nephi 4:7; 11:19-20; 17:13-25; 4 Nephi 1:5-7; Mormon 8:37 and Ether 9:17-27 for other examples.

William Gesenius explained that "Contrary to English usage, which in lengthy enumerations uses the *and* to connect only the last member of the series, in Hebrew *polysyndeton* is customary." (See William Gesenius, *Hebrew Grammar* [Oxford: The Clarendon Press, 1956], p. 484; cited in Angela Crowell, "Hebraisms in the Book of Mormon," *The Zarahemla Record* [1982], p. 2. See also Hugh W. Pinnock, *Ancient Literary Forms,* [Provo, Utah: FARMS, 1999], pp. 21-27.)

This same literary usage can also be found in Genesis 8:22; 20:14; 22:9-13 and 1 Samuel 13:20. See Cheesman, *Ancient Writing on Metal Plates*, (Horizon Publishers: Bountiful, Utah 1985), p. 19.

EVIDENCE NO. 911: PRONOMINAL OBJECTS

<u>Evidence</u>: Some have scoffed at the awkward passages in the Book of Mormon as poor grammar when in fact, such passages provide additional evidence that the Book of Mormon is true. For example, Jacob awkwardly says "hear the words of me" instead of "hear my words" (Jacob 5:2). John A. Tvedtnes pointed out that "in Hebrew, pronouns used for direct objects are ordinarily attached as suffixes to the verb in case of direct objects. (See Tvedtnes, "Hebraisms in the Book of Mormon: A Preliminary Survey," *BYU Studies,* [1970], p. 54.)

At the end of the first decade of this century, Thomas W. Brookbank, published a groundbreaking series of articles in the *Improvement Era* entitled "Hebrew Idioms and Analogies in the Book of Mormon." This was the beginning for what has become an entire literature devoted to examining Hebraisms in the Book of Mormon. Brookbank cites several examples of what appears to be bad grammar known as *number switching*—when the texts switches between singular and plural pronouns in the same verse. For instance: "And it came to pass that the Lord spake unto me saying, Blessed art *thou*, Nephi, because of *thy* faith, for *thou* hast sought me diligently, with lowliness of heart. And inasmuch as *ye* shall keep my commandments, *ye* shall prosper and shall be led to a land of promise, yea, a land which is choice above all lands" (1 Nephi 2:19-20).

Brookbank pointed out that the Lord began by speaking to Nephi using singular pronouns. However, the promised blessings which the Lord gives to Nephi on account of his righteousness pertained not only to Nephi but also to his companions as well, so the Lord switched to plural pronouns in order to broaden the scope of his blessing. Thus, Brookbank concludes, "the characteristic switches in pronominal usage in the Book of Mormon are not to be ridiculed as grammatical errors, but rather understood as reflecting a peculiar Hebrew idiom evidenced in the Bible." (Kevin L. Barney, "Enallage in the Book of Mormon," *Journal of Book of Mormon Studies*, vol. 3, [FARMS, Spring and Fall 1994], pp. 113-147; who cites Thomas W. Brookbank, "Hebrew Idioms and Analogies in the Book of Mormon," *Improvement Era*, vol. 13 [1909-1910] pp. 117-121, 234-239, 336-342, 418-420, 538-543; vol. 17 [1914], pp. 189-192.)

For other examples of pronominal objects see Sidney B. Sperry, "The Book of Mormon as Translation English," *Improvement Era,* vol. 38 (March 1935), pp. 140-141, 187-188, and "Hebrew Idioms in the Book of Mormon," *Improvement Era,* vol. 57 (October 1954), pp. 703, 728-729; E. Craig Bramwell, "Hebrew Idioms in the Small Plates of Nephi," Master's thesis, Brigham Young University, 1960; John A. Tvedtnes, "Hebraisms in the Book of Mormon," *BYU Studies,* vol. 11 (Autumn 1970), pp. 50-60; Melvin Deloy Pack, "Possible Lexical Hebraisms in the Book of Mormon," Master's thesis, Brigham Young University, 1973; and Angela Crowell, "Hebraisms in the Book of Mormon," *Zarahemla Record,* vol. 17-18 (Summer and Fall 1982), pp. 1-7, 16.

EVIDENCE NO. 912: "TO THE CONVINCING OF THE JEW"

<u>Evidence</u>: The Book of Mormon uses a grammatically strange expression on its title page: "... to the convincing of the Jew and Gentile that Jesus is the Christ..." Critics have questioned the claim of an inspired translation that included improper English. They say that the expression *For the convincing of the Jew...*" would be more grammatically correct.

While the Church does not teach that Joseph Smith translated the Book of Mormon through a word-for-word dictation from God, there is evidence that it was, indeed, originally written in a language consisting of elements of Hebrew and Egyptian. The evidence for this conclusion is that idioms and characteristics peculiar to the Hebrew language filters through the language barrier even after translation. Though the words "to the convincing of the Jew..." may be imperfect English, it is proper Hebrew, based on the Hebrew particle ל (*lamedh*) which is "an inseparable preposition, prefixed to nouns, pronouns, and verbs." (See Tvedtnes, *Hebraisms in the Book of Mormon: A Preliminary Survey* [1970], p. 58.)

EVIDENCE NO. 913: HIDING COUNSEL

Evidence: People have wondered what was meant by Nephi's statement about the wicked who "seek...to hide their counsel from the Lord" (2 Nephi 27:27; 28:9). Tvedtnes explains that the "Hebrew word for conversing, consulting, or counseling, *sod*, also means "*secret*." One can more readily imagine the wicked attempting to hide their "secrets" from the Lord. (With this meaning, another rendition of Amos 3:7 would be: "Surely the Lord God will do nothing, but he revealeth his **counsel** [instead of "secret"] unto his servants the prophets." In many ways, this is preferable. (See Tvedtnes, "Hebraisms in the Book of Mormon, A Preliminary Survey," *Brigham Young University Studies* [1970], p. 59.)

EVIDENCE NO. 914: "I SAID IN MY HEART"

Evidence: The expression "He said in his heart" or "I said in my heart..." as is found in 1 Nephi 4:10, is authentic ancient wording. This phrase is typical of Hebrew speech (see Tvedtnes, "Hebraisms in the Book of Mormon, A Preliminary Survey," *BYU Studies* [1970], p. 58). Had Joseph Smith authored the Book of Mormon himself, as critics claim, he would undoubtedly have used the English expression, such as "He thought," or "I thought."

EVIDENCE NO. 915: "LAY HOLD"

Evidence: The Book of Mormon use of the expression "lay hold upon the word of God" (see, for example, Helaman 3:29 and Mormon 7:8) is authentic. Had Joseph Smith or any of his contemporaries written the Book of Mormon rather than ancient prophets, he might have written that people were exhorted to "accept" the word of God or to "receive" it. Yet "lay hold" upon the "word of God" or "upon every good thing" was a common expression among ancient peoples of the Middle East. For example, a Jewish document urges the people to "take hold of the way of God." See Chaim Rabin, *The Zadokite Documents*, (Oxford: Claredon, 1954) pp. 22, 40; cited in Nibley, *Since Cumorah*, (1988), pp. 166-167.

EVIDENCE NO. 916: MORONI WAVED THE "RENT" OF HIS GARMENT

Evidence: The Book of Mormon often uses wording which is awkward in English, but denotes good Hebrew. Some of this awkward wording which appeared in the first edition of the Book of Mormon has since been changed to make it easier for English-speaking readers to understand the content.

One example from the 1830 edition of the Book of Mormon is that "when Moroni had said these words, he went forth among the people, waving the *rent* of his garment in the air" (Alma 46:19). Specialist in linguistics and Semitic languages, John A. Tvednes observed that:

> When the word "rent" is used as a noun in English, it may refer to a hole caused by rending, but not, to my knowledge, to a portion of rent cloth; the unlikely usage of "rent" in English as a noun no doubt contributed to the fact that, in subsequent editions of the Book of Mormon, it was changed to read "rent part" (Alma 46:19). But the Hebrew would, in this instance, use but one word, *qera'*, "rent (part)," coming from *qara'*, "he rent, tore," for nouns, in Hebrew, are derived from roots—as are Hebrew verbs—by the addition of certain vowel patterns that distinguish them from other parts of speech. (See John A. Tvedtnes, "Hebraisms in the Book of Mormon: A Preliminary Survey," *Brigham Young University Studies,* vol. 2, [1970], p. 51.)

EVIDENCE NO. 917: "SPAKE, SAYING"

Evidence: Joseph Smith translated Nephi's description of a revelation from the Lord in the following authentic manner of Hebrew speech: "And it came to pass that the Lord *spake unto me saying*" (1 Nephi 2:19). If Joseph Smith had tried to fabricate the Book of Mormon, he would most probably have used the more common and less awkward English wording: "The Lord said to me," or "The Lord told me." (See Tvedtnes, "Hebraisms in the Book of Mormon: A Preliminary Survey," *Brigham Young University Studies,* vol. 2, [1970], p. 52.)

EVIDENCE NO. 918: "THAT" OR "WHICH" INSTEAD OF "WHO" OR "WHOM"

Evidence: The 1830 edition of the Book of Mormon frequently used "that" or "which" where in English, "who" or "whom" properly belongs. Most of these instances were later changed to be grammatically correct, however, some examples remain in the current edition of the Book of Mormon. For example: "...after they had tasted of the fruit they were ashamed, because of those *that* [instead of who] were scoffing at them..." (1 Nephi 8:28) and "the mixture of thy seed, *which* [instead of who] are among thy brethren" (1 Nephi 13:30).

John A. Tvedtnes, of the University of Utah, notes that "The change to the latter is, of course, warranted in the English language, but unfortunately a Hebraism is lost by such a transformation. For, in Hebrew, the relative pronoun *aser* is used for both human and non-human, as well as for place relativization." (Tvedtnes, "Hebraisms in the Book of Mormon: A Preliminary Survey," *Brigham Young University Studies,* [1970], vol. 2, p. 51.)

EVIDENCE NO. 919: THROWING ARROWS

Evidence: Alma 49:22 in the Book of Mormon strangely speaks of "throwing" arrows rather than shooting them. Rather than being an awkward weakness in the Book of Mormon, this is an authentic detail that lends further credibility to the work.

The *Foundation of Ancient Research and Mormon Studies* has reported that "William Hamblin examined all descriptions of the bow and arrow in the Book of Mormon, relating them to a wide variety of archaeological and art evidence from the Near East and Mesoamerica." He found that "the Hebrew idiom for 'shooting' an arrow literally means 'throwing'..." See *FARMS Update*, Sept. 1987, "Conference on Warfare in the Book of Mormon" reporting on an August 21-22, FARMS-sponsored conference in Provo, Utah.

EVIDENCE NO. 920: "WOMAN" FOR WIFE

Evidence: Nephi wrote in characteristic Hebrew when he spoke of "our women" (1 Nephi 17:20 instead of "our wives." The substitution of "women" for "wives" was not disrespectful, but correct, common Hebrew. The Hebrew word for "wife" is the same word for "woman." (See Tvedtnes, "Hebraisms in the Book of Mormon: A Preliminary Survey," *Brigham Young University Studies,* vol. 2, [1970], p. 59.)

EVIDENCE NO. 921: CONSTRUCT FORM OF ADJECTIVE PHRASES

Evidence: There are approximately 2,700 word roots throughout the pages of the Book of Mormon—adjectives are rarely used. This is one of the characteristics of the Hebrew language.

Instead of adjectives, the Book of Mormon uses the construct form of adjectival phrases, which is also typical Hebrew. The correct English expression "an iron rod," for example, is incorrect Hebrew. The correct Hebrew form "rod of iron" is used in the Book of Mormon (Nephi 8:19-30). "House of Laban" is used in the Book of Mormon (1 Nephi 3:4-7) rather than "Laban's house." "Daughters of Ishmael" (1 Nephi 7:6, 19) is the Hebrew form for "Ishmael's daughters." (See Andrew B. Davidson, *Hebrew Syntax* [New York: Charles Schribner's and Sons, 1950], p. 61; cited in Angela Crowell, "Hebraisms in the Book of Mormon," *The Zarahemla Record* [1982], p. 3; Paul R. Cheesman, *Ancient Writing on Metal Plates* (Horizon Publishers: Bountiful, Utah 1985), pp. 18-19. Also, Thomas W. Brookbank, *Improvement Era*, XVII, 1914, p. 1061.)

EVIDENCE NO. 922: PLURAL NOUNS

Evidence: A common characteristic of the Hebrew language is to use some words only in their plural form. For example, the Hebrew word *shamayim* (heavens) is always rendered in the plural number. In the Book of Mormon, the word *heavens* is always used rather than the singular *heaven*. Also *waters* (from the Hebrew *mayim*) is found much more often in the Book of Mormon than is *water*. (See Tvedtnes, "Hebraisms," [1970], pp. 51-52.)

Nephi describes their bows as "having lost their *springs*" (1 Nephi 16:21). This is the Semitic use of a plural for a noun of quality. See E. Craig Bramwell, *Hebrew Idioms in the Small Plates of Nephi* [thesis], BYU, 1960 cited in Cheesman, *Ancient Writing,* p. 20.

The Book of Mormon also speaks of "great *slaughters* with the sword" (1 Nephi 3:99); and "I did exhort them with all the *energies* of my soul" (1 Nephi 4:42); "and by *bloodsheds*, and by pestilence" (2 Nephi 5:39); "and did reap with your *mights*" (Alma 14:84).

William Gesenius indicates that these plural forms are used to intensify or heighten the idea of the singular, while in English we would use the singular form. (William Gesenius, *Hebrew Grammar*, edited by E. Kautzsch, second edition [Oxford: The Clarendon Press, 1956], p. 397; cited in Crowell, "Hebraisms" [1982], p. 5.)

EVIDENCE NO. 923: PLURAL NOUNS IN THE SINGULAR FORM

Evidence: Just as the Hebrew language uses plural nouns where the English language would call for singular nouns, the Hebrew uses singular nouns where English would prefer the plural. The Book of Mormon demonstrates its authenticity by employing such reversals in number. In it, for example, we see singular-for-plural nouns as: "by the *voice* of his *angels*" (Alma 8:29), "by the *mouth* of his holy *prophets*" (2 Nephi 6:2), and "with the *tongue* of *angels*" (2 Nephi 13:17).

Andrew B. Davidson stated that: "Words such as *hand, head, mouth, tongue* and *voice* are generally used in Hebrew in the singular form when the word is common to a number of persons. In English we would use the plural form." (Andrew B. Davidson, *Hebrew Syntax*, 3rd edition [New York: Charles Scribner's Sons, 1950], p. 20. Cited in Crowell, "Hebraisms..." [1982] p. 5.)

EVIDENCE NO. 924: THE COGNATE ACCUSATIVE

Evidence: A verb accompanied by a direct object derived from the same root is a common Hebrew idiom. Some examples from the Book of Mormon are: "I *dreamed* a *dream*" (1 Nephi 3:2; 8:2), they were "*cursed* with a sore *cursing*" (2 Nephi 1:22; Jacob 3:3), he did "*work* all manner of fine *work*" (Mosiah 11:10; Ether 10:23-24, 27), and even "*work* a *work,* which shall be a great and a marvelous *work*..." (3 Nephi 21:9). See also 2 Nephi 5:15, 23; Mosiah 9:8; 11:13; 23:5.

For documentation that this was, indeed, an ancient characteristic of the Hebrew language, see William Gesenius, *Hebrew Grammar*, edited by E. Kautzsch, translated by A. E. Cowley, 2nd Edition (Oxford: The Clarendon Press, 1956), pp. 366-367, cited in Crowell, "Hebraisms..." (1982), p. 4. See also Tvedtnes, "Hebraisms in the Book of Mormon: A Preliminary Survey," *Brigham Young University Studies,* vol. 2, (1970), pp. 50-60.

EVIDENCE NO. 925: REPEATED PREPOSITIONS

Evidence: The Book of Mormon demonstrates a common characteristic of Hebrew expression in the form of repeating the same preposition several times in the same sentence. It involves repeating the (same) preposition, rather than using compound objects to one preposition. For example, the Book of Mormon speaks of the Lord manifesting Himself unto the people, "*in* word... *in* power, ...*in* very deed" (1 Nephi 14:1). Likewise, Nephi wrote that he armed himself "*with* a bow and an arrow... *with* a sling, and *with* stones" (1 Nephi 16:23). Nephi also wrote that the Lord shall visit the people "*by* tempest, *by* fire and *by* smoke...and *by* the opening of the earth, and *by* mountains which shall be carried up" (1 Nephi 19:11).

While this style is quite awkward in English, it is perfect Hebrew. See A. B. Davidson, *Hebrew Syntax* [3rd Edition, Edinburgh: T. & T. Clark, reprinted 1950], p. 159 cited in E. Craig Bramwell, "Hebrew Idioms in the Small Plates of Nephi," *The Improvement Era*, vol. 64, July 1961, p. 517.

EVIDENCE NO. 926: COMPOUND PREPOSITIONS

Evidence: In addition to the repeated prepositions, the Book of Mormon makes use of the authentic Hebrew usage of two prepositions that introduce a single prepositional phrase. For example, 1 Nephi 4:28 tells of some that "fled *from before* my presence." Jacob 5:30 indicates that "the servant went *down into* the vineyard." Also, in Mosiah 5:7, "They went *down into* the land of Nephi." Moroni 1:52 speaks of those who "did not flee *from before* the Lamanites." See also 1 Nephi 3:51; 11:12; 2 Nephi 6:20; Alma 20:83; Mormon 2:22.

Angela Crowell observed the following in her article entitled "Hebraisms in the Book of Mormon," *The Zarahemla Record*, (1982), p. 4:

Hebrew syntax calls for compound prepositions rather than the single preposition common in English. This usage is traced back to the literal translation of the Hebrew text. Compound prepositions are used to indicate the locale and direction of the action as well as the action itself. (Crowell cites William Gesenius, *Hebrew Grammar*, edited by E. Kautzsch [Oxford: The Clarendon Press, 1956], p. 377.)

Sometimes two prepositions are expressed, and at other times only one is expressed and a second implied in the verb.

The example "from before" is a literal translation of the Hebrew words *mippene* and *milliphene*. The writer found that it was used twenty-three times in the Old Testament Hebrew text, but that it was translated into English (KJV & IV) only four times (for example, Genesis 23:4, Exodus 4:3, 1 Chronicles 11:13, Judges 11:23). The other verses all translate it "from," giving us a more precisely worded English sentence, even though in the Hebrew text it reads, "from before." It would have been quite difficult for Joseph Smith to have copied this Hebraism from the King James Version of the Bible when the construct only appears four times in the entire English text. Yet there are at least ten instances where the combination "from before" is found in the Book of Mormon. In this instance, the Book of Mormon contains a Hebraism "more literally" translated than its counterpart form the King James Version of the Bible.

How can we account for this? It is remote that Joseph Smith on his own would have been able to identify this construct as a Hebraism. Rather, we see original Hebraic authorship and a correct translation through divine aid.

EVIDENCE NO. 927: REPEATED POSSESSIVE PRONOUN

Evidence: While this style is very awkward in English, the repeated possessive pronoun as used in the Book of Mormon is yet another evidence that the latter-day scripture was influenced by the Hebrew language as it claims (1 Nephi 1:2). An example of this practice is the description of Lehi's departure into the wilderness: "And he left *his* house, and the land of *his* inheritance, and *his* gold, and *his* silver, and *his* precious things" (1 Nephi 2:4). A modern writer would more likely have written that Lehi left his house, land, gold, silver and precious things. (See A. B. Davidson, *Hebrew Syntax* [3rd edition Edinburgh: T. & T. Clark, reprinted 1950], p. 2, cited in E. Craig Bramwell, "Hebrew Idioms in the Small Plates of Nephi," *Improvement Era*, July 1961, p. 517.)

For other examples of the repeated pronoun see 1 Nephi 2:11; Alma 4:6; 3 Nephi 3:22.

EVIDENCE NO. 928: THE PROPHETIC PERFECT

Evidence: In the prophetic perfect style of writing, the prophet who speaks of the future describes the event as if it had already occurred. For example, "But behold I have obtained a land of promise" (spoken while in the wilderness before they left on their journey, 1 Nephi 1:150); "After [Christ] was baptized with water, the Holy Ghost descended upon him in the form of a dove" (spoken 559-545 BC, 2 Nephi 13:10); "These are they whose sins [Christ] has borne; these are they for whom he has died, to redeem them from their transgressions" (spoken 148 BC, Mosiah 8:44).

Angela Crowell noted the following in her article entitled "Hebraisms in the Book of Mormon," *The Zarahemla Record,* (1982), p. 4:

> In Hebrew thinking, an action is regarded as being either 'completed' or 'incompleted.' Hebrew, therefore, knows no past, present, or future tenses, but has instead a Perfect and an Imperfect (which in context lend themselves to a variety of shades of meaning). The Hebrew Perfect may be taken to represent action in the past. The equivalent of the English present tense is supplied by the participle, and the English future tense (with other varieties) by the imperfect.

> The Prophetic Perfect is a common usage in the language of the prophets. The prophet so transports his mind ahead that he describes a future event as if it had been already seen or heard by him. This happens in making promises or threats, and also in the language of contracts. (Crowell cites William Gesenius, *Hebrew Grammar*, edited by E. Kautzsch, 2nd edition [Oxford: The Clarendon Press, 1956], pp. 312-313.)

For Biblical examples of the prophetic perfect see Isaiah 53:4-9 and Revelation 14:6-7.

EVIDENCE NO. 929: COMPOUND SUBJECTS

Evidence: The Book of Mormon use of the compound subject "I and my brethren" (1 Nephi 3:9-10; 5:30; 7:2; 3:2; 22:31) may be poor English grammatical construction but is good Hebrew.

Angela Crowell also reported that: "In biblical Hebrew, when the compound subject consists of different persons, the first person—i.e., the person speaking—precedes any others. In proper English usage, the order is reversed: the speaker always comes last. We say, 'My father and I' instead of 'I and my father,' as in Hebrew. This phenomenon in Hebrew is a literal translation, i.e., 'I' is written in Hebrew before 'and my father.'" (See Crowell, "Hebraisms" [1982], p. 3 who cites Andrew B. Davidson, *Hebrew Syntax* [New York: Charles Schriber's Sons, 1950], p. 159.)

EVIDENCE NO. 930: ADIEU

Claim: The closing word in the book of Jacob has been the subject of harsh criticism by faultfinders. However, the fact that Jacob ends his book with the French word *adieu* (Jacob 7:27), has actually become another evidence for the truthfulness of the Book of Mormon.

Evidence: The word *adieu* that Joseph Smith employed in the translation of the Book of Mormon, is in fact the best word to convey the original meaning that Jacob had written and therefore strengthens the case for the accuracy of the *translation*. There are several factors that one should consider in this matter:

1) Those who have for many years asked: "How did a French word get into the writings of a *supposedly* Hebrew prophet?" might just as well have asked how so many *English* words got into the Book of Mormon. The obvious fact is that the prophet writers of the Book of Mormon wrote neither French nor English, but Joseph Smith used these words as he *translated* the meanings of their ancient Hebrew thoughts into words that we could understand. As a translator, Joseph Smith naturally used words that were common to him in his time and locale. It is a matter of history that the New England area where Joseph Smith was born and raised was populated by many French who had migrated down from over the French-Canadian border.

2) Being a composite of several older languages, the English language borrows from many countries especially France. Indeed, many of the words in our English language are actually French. Such English words as *faith, repent,* and *prison* originated in the French Language. These and many others appear in the King James Bible.

3) Some uniquely French words also appear in the King James Bible such as *tache* (Exodus 26:6, 11), *laver* (Exodus 30:18, 28) and *brute* (Jeremiah 10:22; Nahum 3:19). Those who criticize the Book of Mormon for using a French word are inadvertently criticizing the Bible, which is *guilty* of the same charge.

4) The last written word of the prophet Jacob is most likely a translation of the Hebrew word *Lehitra'ot* which carries virtually the same meaning as the French word *adieu.* Both words convey much more than a simple farewell—each includes the invocation of a blessing. (See Daniel H. Ludlow, *A Companion to Your Study of the Book of Mormon,* [1977], p. 163.)

EVIDENCE NO. 931: HISSING

<u>Claim</u>: The Bible makes several references to the words *hiss* and *hissing* (1 Kings 9:8, 2 Chronicles 29:8; Jeremiah 19:8; 25:9, 18; 29:18; 50:13; 51:37; Lamentations 2:16). Many readers of the Bible have probably wondered about the meaning of the word. James Strong defines its Hebrew equivalents *Sharaq* and *Sheriqah,* as having to do with "a call or scorn," or "a derision." (See "Hebrew and Chaldee Dictionary" in, *Strong's Exhaustive Concordance of the Bible,* entry nos. 8319 and 8322.)

<u>Evidence</u>: The Book of Mormon strengthens its authenticity by making use of the word *hiss* some eight times. Consistent with the Hebrew meaning, it is used as "a call" when the Lord hisses (2 Nephi 17:8; 29:2; and Moroni 10:28), and it is used "in scorn" where it mentions that Israel will become a "hiss and a by-word" (1 Nephi 19:14; 3 Nephi 16:9).

A related evidence that the Pacific Islanders are descendants of Israel through the Book of Mormon peoples, is the Polynesian custom—specifically in Tonga—of hissing when hearing or speaking of a disagreeable subject. Their hissing is not done with their teeth but with their throat as if clearing it. It is not vocalized, but sound is created by air passing through a tightened throat, as if gargling.

EVIDENCE NO. 932: ANTENANTIOSIS IN ANCIENT WRITINGS

<u>Claim</u>: Another evidence that the Book of Mormon is an authentic record of ancient history is its use of antiquated writing styles such as *antenantiosis.* Antenantiosis is defined as the use of a proposition in terms of its opposite. For example see Jacob 5:48:

> And it came to pass that the servant said unto his master: Is it *not* the loftiness of thy vineyard—have *not* the branches thereof overcome the roots which are good? And because the branches have overcome the roots thereof, behold they grew faster than the strength of the roots, taking strength unto themselves. Behold, I say, is *not* this the cause that the trees of thy vineyard have become corrupted?

Other examples of antenantiosis can be found in Mosiah 4:19; 29:24; and Mormon 9:29.

Evidence: While this writing style seems awkward in our modern culture, it was a common form of speech in Biblical times. For Biblical examples of antenantiosis see Deuteronomy 4:15-19; 1 Samuel 1:8; Isaiah 43:10-12; 45:18-21; Matthew 13:55; Mark 6:3; Corinthians 13:1-4, 8-13. This is further discussed in Gail Call, "Antenantiosis in the Book of Mormon," *Foundation for Ancient Research and Mormon Studies Insights,* (1991), no. 4; reprinted in *Re-exploring the Book of Mormon,* edited by John W. Welch, (1992), pp. 96-97.

EVIDENCE NO. 933: EPANALEPSIS IN ANCIENT WRITINGS

Claim: Another antiquated writing style used in the Book of Mormon is *epanalepsis.* Epanalepsis is the practice of repeating a phrase in a long sentence to pick up a previous train of thought after a parenthetical aside to remind the reader of the original idea of the sentence. For example see Alma 3:1:

> And it came to pass that the Nephites who were not slain by the weapons of war, *after having buried those who had been slain*—now the number of the slain were not numbered, because of the greatness of their number—*after they had finished burying their dead* they all returned to their lands, and to their houses, and their wives, and their children.

Larry Childs has identified 84 occurrences of epanalepsis in the Book of Mormon. "Epanalepsis in the Book of Mormon;" printed in *Re-exploring the Book of Mormon,* edited by John W. Welch, (1992), pp. 96-97; 165-166.

Evidence: Biblical examples of this writing style are found in E. W. Bullinger, *Figures of Speech used in the Bible,* (Baker Book House: Grand Rapids, Michigan, 1989), pp. 159-164.

EVIDENCE NO. 934: IRONY AND SARCASM

Claim: Book of Mormon prophets used irony and sarcasm similar to that used by Hebrew prophets.

Evidence: Irony and sarcasm were commonly used by Hebrew prophets as noted by W. L. Holladay in "Style, Irony, and Authenticity in Jeremiah," *Journal of Biblical Literature,* (1962), vol. 81, pp. 44-54. Cited in Nibley, *Since Cumorah,* (1988), p. 153.

The Book of Mormon tells of the prophet Abinadi quoting extensively from Hebrew prophets. For example, Abinadi quotes Isaiah 52:7-10 in Mosiah 12:21-24, and Isaiah 53 in Mosiah 14, the revelation of the Lord, to Moses as recorded in Exodus 20:2-4 in Mosiah 12:34-36, and Exodus 20:5-17 in Mosiah 13:13-24, etc. Since Abinadi was a student of Hebrew prophets, it is expected that he would indulge in irony and sarcasm as was customary among the Hebrew prophets.

Abinadi's irony and sarcasm is observed in such verses as Mosiah 12:25. In this verse, Abinadi sarcastically asks why men (who "pretend" to be priests) ask him the meaning of his quotations. In Mosiah 17:18, he prophesies that his enemies would ironically suffer "death by fire" just as they were burning him at the stake.

For other Book of Mormon examples see 2 Nephi 28:7-8 and 29:4-5.

EVIDENCE NO. 935: THE IMPORTANCE OF REMEMBERING

Claim: The Book of Mormon prophet writers frequently emphasize the importance of remembering. For example 1 Nephi 10:20: "Therefore *remember*, O man, for all thy doings thou shalt be brought into judgment." Other classic examples are found in Mosiah 2:41: "O *remember, remember* that these things are true; for the Lord God hath spoken it," and Mosiah 4:30: "And now, O man, *remember*, and perish not."

The charge to "remember" is repeated seven times in Helaman 5:5-6. Note that seven is a number that was used in ancient Hebrew culture to signify perfection or completion. (See also, 1 Nephi 15:25; 19:15-16; Jacob 3:9-11; Alma 37:35; 3 Nephi 18:7, 11; and Moroni 4-5.)

All in all, the Book of Mormon prophets stress the importance of remembering the Lord's dealings with their fathers some seventy-nine times! The frequent emphasis on *remembering* throughout the Book of Mormon is consistent with the Hebrew literature. (See Wallace E. Hunt Jr., "Moses' Brazen Serpent as It Relates to Serpent Worship in Mesoamerica," *Journal of Book of Mormon Studies*, [1993], p. 126.)

Evidence: The following is quoted from John W. Welch, *Re-exploring the Book of Mormon*, (1992) pp. 127-129:

> From numerous statements [in the Book of Mormon], it is evident that "remembering" is a saving principle of the gospel. Just as faith looks forward in Christ to actualize the present power of his redemption, so remembrance looks back on covenants and gifts from God and keeps the past alive... By placing emphasis on the concept of "remembering," the Book of Mormon significantly captures one of the most distinctive aspects of Israelite mentality.

> Brevard S. Childs has shown that various forms of the Hebrew verb *zakhor* (to remember) occur in the Old Testament well over two hundred times. He shows that what the Old Testament understands by "memory" goes well beyond the mere mental recall of information, though of course that is part of its meaning. To remember often means to be active, to consider, to keep divine commandments, or to act. The word in Hebrew thus carries a wider range of meaning than is common with the verb *remember* in English. Indeed, to remember involves turning to God, or repenting, or acting in accordance with divine injunctions. (See Brevard S. Childs, *Memory and Tradition in Israel*, [London: SCM, 1962], pp. 9-10, 50-55; Hayim Yerushalmi, *Zakhor: Jewish History and the Jewish Memory*, [Seattle: University of Washington Press, 1982].)

> Not only man, but also God "remembers." He remembers covenants he has made with Noah (see Genesis 9:15-16), with Abraham, Isaac and Jacob (see Exodus 2:24; Leviticus 26:42), and with all of Israel (see Ezekiel 16:60; Luke 1:72).

> Conversely, the antonym of the verb *to remember* in Hebrew—*to forget* does not merely describe the passing of a thought from the mind, but involves a failure to act, or a failure to do or keep something. Hence, failing to remember God and His commandments is the equivalent of apostasy.

> Interestingly, words for memory and remembrance also occur well over two hundred times in the Book of Mormon. This high density is not noticed by causal readers, but it vividly reflects a religious sensitivity on the part of Book of Mormon prophets that is similar to that of other Israelite prophets. Though the range of uses of remembering in the Book of Mormon is perhaps not quite as extensive as that identifiable in the Old Testament, the idiom of remembrance in both books includes warnings, promises, threats, pleas, and complaints, and the same deep connection between memory and action can be found in both. To remember is to hearken, to awaken, to see, to hear, to believe, to trust. (See Jacob 3:9-11; Mosiah 2:41; 4:30; 13:29-30; Alma 7:16; 9:13-14; 18:10; 36:1-2; 37:35; 46:23; 58:40 and compare with Numbers 15:39-40; Psalms 103:18.)

> ...In such ways the Book of Mormon shows a clear link between the ways of remembrance or forgetfulness and the blessings or cursings associated with the covenant people of God. Since one of the main purposes of the Book of Mormon, as stated on its title page, is to show that God remembers the covenants he has made with his people (see also 1 Nephi 19:15-16; 2 Nephi 29:1-2; 3 Nephi 16:11), it is especially appropriate that the renewal of covenants includes a commitment to "always remember him, and keep his commandments," as the faithful affirm their willingness to take upon them the name of Jesus Christ (Moroni 4:3).

Similarly, Psalms 137:1-9 contains a covenant with the Israelites which carries with it a curse upon them should they forget Jerusalem while held captive in Babylon. A More complete treatment of this topic of remembering is found in Louis C. Midgley, "The Ways of Remembrance," in *Rediscovering the Book of Mormon,* edited by John Sorenson and Melvin Thorne, (Salt Lake City: Desert Book and FARMS, 1991), pp. 168-176.

EVIDENCE NO. 936: MERISMUS IN THE BOOK OF MORMON

Claim: An ancient Hebrew poetic form, known as *merismus,* (the comparing and contrasting of adjectives and nouns) has been found in the Book of Mormon—further substantiating the claim that the Book of Mormon was written by descendants of the Hebrews.

Evidence: The Foundation for Ancient Research and Mormon Studies reported on an article by Angela Crowell in the *Zarahemla Record*, No. 32-33, pp. 2-9, in which she described merismus as one of twenty three poetic devices found in the Book of Mormon. This poetic form, according to *FARMS Update*, December 1986, allowed Hebrew poets to express an:

> Inclusive concept by a pair of adjectives: young and aged = everybody (Job 29:8); sea and dry land = the universe (Psalms 95:5); flesh and blood = sacrificed animals (Psalms 50:13). Crowell notes in Alma 37:37 the use of "night" and "morning" to convey the concept "all the time." In Mesoamerica the same device is known as difrasismo or kenning. Among the Aztecs, for example, skirt and blouse signified woman in her sexual aspect, flower and song meant poetry and art, and face and heart signified personality (M. Leon-Portilla, *Pre-Columbian Literatures of Mexico,* [1969], p. 77).

> "My hand, my foot" meant my body, while "in the clouds, in the mist" conveyed the idea mystery. Thus, Edmonson comments on "the extraordinary difficulty" in reading such texts. The "obvious" meaning of an expression frequently must be modified to extract its "synthetic or esoteric meaning," and a translator is faced with "complex puns, metaphors, and traditional religious symbolisms." Furthermore, "these [religious] texts are purposely obscure. They are not intended to make sense to outsiders—and they don't." They were meant to be "read and pondered rather than skimmed over or recited." (See C. McGowan, *Katunob,* [December 1977], vol. 10, p. 45; *The Ancient Future of the Itza: The Book of Chilam Balam of Tizimin,* [1982], pp. xiii-xiv; cited in John L. Sorensen, Angela Crowell, & Allen J. Christensen, "View of the Hebrews an Unparallel," *Re-exploring the Book of Mormon*, Edited by John W. Welch, [1992], pp. 83-87.)

EVIDENCE NO. 937: MANNER OF SPEECH

Claim: Moroni claimed that the written characters he engraved on the plates represented the "manner of speech" used by the Nephites (Mormon 9:32).

Evidence: The Soviet scholar, Yuri Knorosov led the way in correcting the assumption that the Mayan glyphs represented no real phonetic features. Dr. John L. Sorenson of Brigham Young University noted that "Today, it is generally acknowledged that 'the Maya system had a strong phonetic-syllabic component,' much like Moroni's description of the Nephite system." (See Sorenson, "Digging into the Book of Mormon," *Ensign*, October 1984, p. 13; who cites Michael D. Coe, "Ancient Maya Writing and Calligraphy," *Visible Language,* [1971], vol. 5, p. 301; and David H. Kelley, *Deciphering the Maya Script* [Austin: University of Texas Press, 1976], M. D. Coe, *The Maya Scribe and His World* [New York: Grolier Club, 1973], p. 11.)

EVIDENCE NO. 938: "BEYOND THE MARK"

<u>Claim</u>: The expression "beyond the mark" used in Jacob 4:14 is a characteristic of the languages of the ancient cultures of the Middle East, the area from which the peoples of the Book of Mormon emigrated.

<u>Evidence</u>: This was, indeed, a common expression in ancient times. In the *Gospel of Truth* it is written that Israel turns to error when the people look for that which is *beyond the mark* (*Gospel of Truth*, folio xi, line 24, [1967 edition] 42:33-43:6). See also *The Damascus Document* (Zadokite Fragment), 1:16; 20B:25f. Both are cited in Nibley, *Since Cumorah* (1988), p. 167.

EVIDENCE NO. 939: A FIRM, STEADFAST, AND IMMOVABLE VALLEY

<u>Claim</u>: The Book of Mormon makes the following simile: "firm, steadfast, and immovable" as a *valley* (1 Nephi 2:9-10). This is consistent with Middle Eastern literature, while writers of Western literature would not have used the word *valley* in such a phrase but would typically refer to *mountains* as being firm, steadfast, and immovable.

<u>Evidence</u>: The peoples of the Middle East, particularly the Arabs, with whom Lehi and his family associated, attributed firmness, steadfastness and immovableness to valleys rather than mountains. See Al-Hariri of Basra, *Makamat of Kufa* (Preston, p. 216), and *Al-Mu^c allaqot*, translated by Frank E. Johnson, (Bombay: Education Society's Steam Press, 1893; reprinted at New York: AMS Press, 1973), p. 71, line 13. Both cited in Nibley, *An Approach to the Book of Mormon*, (1988), p. 271.

EVIDENCE NO. 940: THE "FOUNTAIN OF THE RED SEA"

<u>Claim</u>: While camped near a river that "emptied into the Red Sea" (1 Nephi 2:8), Lehi "saw that the waters of the river emptied *into the fountain* of the Red Sea (1 Nephi 2:9). People of western cultures would expect a river to flow *from* its fountain rather than *into* it.

<u>Evidence</u>: There are two explanations for this statement—one literal and another figurative: First of all, the Gulf of Aqaba, serving as the northeast extension of the Red Sea, could be called the fountain of that larger body of water. Dr. Hugh Nibley has shown that in ancient times the Gulf of Aqaba was known in Hebrew as *Yam*—a "source" or "fountain"—to distinguish it from a large sea or ocean. See Hugh Nibley, *Lehi in the Desert and the World of the Jaredites* (Salt Lake City: Bookcraft, 1952), pp. 88-89; cited in Lynn M. and Hope Hilton, *In Search of Lehi's Trail*, p. 64.

Secondly, though strange to most others, this manner of speaking and thinking is authentic to Near Eastern cultures. In their minds, the river somehow "drinks" from the larger body of water even as it flows into it. See Samuel Noah Kramer in *Bulletin of The American Schools of Oriental Research*, (1944) no. 96, p. 28, notes 27, 41; and W. G. Lambert, "The Cosmology of Sumer and Babylon," *American Cosmologies*, pp. 55-60. Both cited in Paul Y. Hoskisson, "Textual Evidences for the Book of Mormon," an article in Nyman and Tate, *The Book of Mormon: First Nephi, the Doctrinal Foundation* (Provo: BYU, 1988), pp. 289-290.

EVIDENCE NO. 941: "THEIR SOULS DID EXPAND"

<u>Claim</u>: The phrase "Their souls did expand," used in Alma 5:9, is an authentic idiom of the language and time of the Book of Mormon culture. See also Alma 32:28,34.

<u>Evidence</u>: Joseph Smith could not have borrowed this phrase from any source because it had not been uncovered and printed in any scientific publication prior to 1830. It is not found in the Bible, nor any phrase similar to it, even though it is an authentic phrase among Middle Eastern cultures. Additionally, the phrase "expand the soul"

has been found in Europe, which strongly suggests its origin in nearby Near Eastern cultures. See Jacob Grimm and Wilhelm Grimm, *Deutsches Worterbuch*, 9. Band: Schiefeln-Seele (Leipzig: Hirzel, 1899), columns 2867-2868 cited in Paul Y. Hoskisson "Textual Evidences for the Book of Mormon," *The Book of Mormon: First Nephi, The Doctrinal Foundation* (Provo: Religious Studies Center, BYU, 1988), pp. 284-287.

EVIDENCE NO. 942: "THOU SHALT HAVE PLACE WITH US"

Claim: The expression "thou shalt have place with us" (1 Nephi 4:34) is a typical Bedouin expression that carries with it a profound meaning. Nephi used this phrase to persuade Zoram to leave his home in Jerusalem and flee with his family into the wilderness.

Evidence: Dr. Hugh Nibley writes the following in regards to this ancient Bedouin phrase:

> Nephi's invitation to Zoram was: "If thou wilt go down into the wilderness to my father thou shalt have *place* with us (1 Nephi 4:34). Accordingly, after an exchange of oaths, "We ... departed into the wilderness, and journeyed unto the tent of our father" (1 Nephi 4:38). The first thing a suppliant does seeking "place" with a tribe is to "put up his tent near that of his protector, take a woolen string from his head and lay it around the neck of his new patron, saying, 'I seek protection with thee, O So -and-so.'" To this the answer is: "Be welcome to my authority! We receive all of you but what is bad. Our *place* is now your *place*." From that moment the newcomer is under the full protection of the sheikh and "has place" with the tribe. The immemorial greeting of welcome to those accepted as guests in any tent is *Ahlan wa-Sahlan wa-Marhaban:* in which *ahlan* means either a family or (as in Hebrew) a tent, *sahlan* a smooth place to sit down, and *marhaban* the courteous moving aside of the people in the tent so as to make room for one more. The emphasis is all on "having place with us." (See Frederic D. Thornton, *Elementary Arabic* [Cambridge: Cambridge University Press, 1943], p. 156; cited in Nibley, *An Approach to the Book of Mormon* [1988], p. 243-244.)

EVIDENCE NO. 943: "ALPHA AND OMEGA"

Claim: Some critics have charged that the Book of Mormon use of the Greek words "Alpha and Omega" is an anachronism (3 Nephi 9:18). However, this is one of several supposed problems in the Book of Mormon that has actually become another evidence.

Evidence: Of course the English words found in the copies of the Book of Mormon were not engraved as English on the plates. The ancient engravings were translated *into* English. Yet, the English language is actually a combination of several languages and thus contains words from Latin, German, French, and, significantly, Greek. For example, many English words, such as "critical", "music", and "poetry" may be thought to be purely English words, but were actually borrowed from the Greek language. So when the word "critical" is used in Alma 51:9 and 57:16, it must be remembered that the word was not originally engraved upon the plates, but was employed by the English translator (Joseph Smith). Likewise, *Alpha and Omega* has become an accepted English expression, though it was once purely Greek. To use a literal English translation by saying, "I am the A and the O," or the more ancient "I am the A and the T" would be meaningless to English-speaking readers.

Furthermore, in the ancient ritual alphabet of the Mandaeans, a Semitic alphabet, "the first and last letters, the "alpha and omega," are the same and represent "perfection of light and life." Both letters, as E. S. Drower explained, "have as their sign a circle, possibly representing the sun-disk as *a symbol of light*." Hence, as Nibley contemplated, there may be more behind 3 Nephi 9:18 than a mere literary convention: "I am the light and the life...I am Alpha and Omega." See E. S. Drower, *The Mandaeans of Iraq and Iran* (Oxford, 1937), p. 241. Quoted in Nibley, *Since Cumorah,* (1988), pp. 165-166.

EVIDENCE NO. 944: NEPHI'S PSALM

Claim: Nephi's Psalm, as recorded in 2 Nephi 4:16-35, provides an example of a Hebrew literary pattern called the *individual lament* and thus provides evidence of the Hebrew roots of the Book of Mormon Prophets.

Evidence: The individual lament consists of five parts, all of which are contained in Nephi's Psalm as shown below along with a Biblical example from the book of Psalms:

	Feature	2 Nephi	Psalms
1.	Invocation	4:16-17	54:1-2
2.	Complaint	4:17-19	54:3
3.	Confession of Trust	4:20-30	54:4
4.	Petition	4:31-33	54:5
5.	Vow of Praise	4:34-35	54:6-7

See Herman Gunkel, *The Psalms: A Form-Critical Introduction,* translated by Thomas M. Horner (Philadelphia: Fortress, 1967), pp. 10, 30-39; cited in Matthew Nickerson, "Nephi's Psalm: 2 Nephi 4:16-35 in the light of Form-Critical Analysis," *Journal of Book of Mormon Studies,* (Provo, Utah: FARMS 1997), vol. 6, no. 2, pp. 26-42.

Evidences in Hebrew Parallelism

Claim: The authenticity of the Book of Mormon is further substantiated by the fact that it contains the type of Hebrew poetry called "parallelism." The following is from an article by Donald W. Parry entitled "Hebrew Literary Patterns in the Book of Mormon," *The Ensign*, October 1989, pp. 58-61:

"The poetry contained in the inspired books, the most ancient and the most simple, is superior to all others, and deserves exclusively to be denominated sublime. As it had no model, so it will find no successful imitators." (Philip Sarchi, *An Essay on Hebrew Poetry,* [London: 1824], p. vi.)

These words, published six years before the Book of Mormon was printed, proved to be prophetic. Biblical scholars of the early nineteenth century had not the slightest hint that a companion volume to the Bible would soon come forth, with poetic forms equal in value and style to biblical poetic verse. In fact, 159 years later, few are yet aware of the prevalence and nature of scriptural poetry in the Book of Mormon.

One of the most impressive types of Hebrew poetry is called parallelism. Robert Lowth is usually credited with drawing attention to the importance of this form. Though others before him had mentioned parallelism in passing, his two-volume work, *Lectures on the Sacred Poetry of the Hebrews* (Hildescheim: George Olms Verlag, 1787), developed the idea of poetic structures in Holy Writ. He defined poetic parallelisms as words, phrases, or sentences that correspond, compare, contrast, or repeat. More recent scholars, like Adele Berlin, extend the definition to include both equivalent phrases scattered throughout a text as well as parallel words and sounds in dissimilar phrases.

Words or phrases can be parallel by appearing as synonyms or near-synonyms (heart/soul, statutes/commandments, preacher/teacher); repetitions of identical phrases (cry unto him/cry unto him); antonyms (holy/unholy, poor/rich); complementaries (bow/arrows, river/sea); inflections of the same root (to judge/a judge/judgment/judgment seat); gradations (holy/most holy, thousands/tens of thousands); superordinates (wine/drink, gold/metal); or reciprocals (to retire/to sleep, to eat/to be full, sin/pain of conscience).

The Book of Mormon is replete with parallelisms. The poetic patterns serve, as they do in the Bible, to emphasize messages, define and expand them, make them more memorable, and structure them. One form of parallelism, chiasmus, has been extensively studied, but surprisingly, almost nothing has been written on the abundance of other parallelisms in the Book of Mormon.

The parallel nature of biblical writing is apparent to most readers. However, the study of Hebrew poetics—the classification and analysis of many different kinds of parallel structures—began in the first half of the nineteenth century. Not until the turn of the twentieth century did scholars introduce specific definitions of the various parallelisms. A critic might say that the prophet Joseph Smith could have been able to imitate the parallel nature of biblical writing; but it is extremely unlikely that he could have produced such a huge number of parallelisms—sometimes several per verse—of more than twenty-five types. Only the Book of Mormon prophets, who used the structural forms of ancient Hebrew poetry and who were inspired from on high, could have written such beautiful poetic structures.

The following several evidences demonstrate the various Hebrew forms of poetic parallelism that are found in the Book of Mormon.

EVIDENCE NO. 945: CONTRASTING IDEAS PARALLELISM

Evidence: One kind of parallelism compares a subject or idea with another to create a contrast between the two. By this form, prophets could more easily compare sin and righteousness, life and death, deliverance and captivity. Paul, for example, underscores what the Resurrection does for us by pairing two phrases that echo each other (1 Corinthians 15:53-54):

> For this corruptible must put on incorruption,
> and this mortal must put on immortality.

> So when this corruptible shall have put on incorruption,
> and this mortal shall have put on immortality,
> then shall be brought to pass the saying that is written, Death is swallowed up in victory.

Anther examples are found in Hosea 2:23:
> And I will *have mercy* upon her that had *not obtained mercy*;
> and I will say to them which were *not my people*,
> Thou *art my people*; and they shall say, *Thou art my God*.

and Proverbs 21:9:
> It is better to dwell in *a corner of the housetop*,
> than with a brawling woman in *a wide house*.

Other Biblical examples can be found in Joshua 25:15; Isaiah 5:20; Micah 6:7; Malachi 4:6 and Matthew 23:23.

An example from the Book of Mormon is found in 2 Nephi 9:39:
> Remember, to be carnally-minded is *death*,
> and to be spiritually-minded is *life eternal*.

This kind of parallelism also allows for specific contrasts within a broad category. Moroni, for instance, compares the love of riches with the absence of charity (Mormon 8:37):

"For behold, ye do love money, and your substance, and your fine apparel, and the adorning of your churches, more than ye love the poor and the needy, the sick and the afflicted."

More examples of *contrasting ideas parallelism* are found in 2 Nephi 26:25; Alma 5:40-41; 9:28; 36:21; Helaman 10:6; and 3 Nephi 27:33.

A similar parallelism in which contrasting ideas appear as opposites is called *antithetical*. Biblical and Book of Mormon prophets often noted the sharp divergence of good and evil by pointing out that the two were opposites. Alma employed a double antithetical parallelism to point out what is truly the source of divine knowledge and what is not (Alma 36:4):

> I would not that ye think that I know of myself—
> not of the *temporal*
> but of the *spiritual*,
> not of the *carnal mind*
> but *of God*.

More examples of *antithetical parallelism* are found in 1 Nephi 17:45; Jacob 4:10; Mosiah 4:24; Ether 12:26; and Moroni 10:6. (See Parry, *Ensign*, October 1989, pp. 59-61.)

EVIDENCE NO. 946: SYNONYMIA (SIMPLE SYNONYMOUS PARALLELISM)

<u>Evidence</u>: Perhaps the most basic parallelism found in the scriptures is *simple synonymous parallelism* or *synonymia*, in which the second phrase repeats or echoes the idea of the first. When the prophets introduced an idea, then repeated it in different words, their hearers could more easily grasp their meaning. The idea thus received a double emphasis (the fundamental effect of most parallelisms). One example of simple parallelism can be found in Hosea 2:19-22:

> And I will *betroth* thee unto me for ever; yea,
> I will *betroth* thee unto me in *righteousness*,
> and in *judgment*, and in *lovingkindness*, and in *mercies*.
> I will even *betroth* thee unto me in *faithfulness*: and thou shalt know the LORD.
>
> And it shall come to pass in that day, I will *hear*, saith the LORD,
> I will *hear the heavens*,
> and they *shall hear the earth*;
> And the earth *shall hear the corn*, and the wine, and the oil;
> and they *shall hear Jezreel*.

Other Biblical examples can be found in Genesis 4:23; Isaiah 2:31; Joel 2:28-29; Ruth 1:16-17; Psalms 19:1; and Proverbs 1:8.

A simple example can from the Book of Mormon be found in 1 Nephi 17:47:

> my soul is rent with anguish ...,
> and my heart is pained;

More Book of Mormon examples of *simple synonymous parallelism* are found in 1 Nephi 1:15; 2 Nephi 9:52; 25:2; 30:11; Mosiah 16:10; Alma 34:32; 3; 41:13; Nephi 5:21; 20:42; 29:5; and Ether 6:10.

Simple synthetic parallelism consists of two phrases in which the second explains or adds something new or instructive to the first. The following example shows how the second element defines the first (Moroni 8:17):

I am filled with *charity*,
which is *everlasting love*.

The structure also can establish relationships between actions, as in the next example (2 Nephi 4:23), where the situation in the second phrase is the result of the situation in the first phrase:

Behold, he hath *heard my cry by day*,
and he hath *given me knowledge by visions in the nighttime*.

More examples of *simple synthetic parallelism* are found in 2 Nephi 4:35; Mosiah 23:21; Alma 37:35; and 3 Nephi 10:15.   (See Donald W. Parry, "Hebrew Literary Patterns in the Book of Mormon," *Ensign*, October 1989, pp. 59-61; James L. Kugel, *The Idea of Biblical Poetry,* [New Haven: Yale Univerisy Press, 1981], p. 8; Robert Alter, *The Art of Biblical Poetry,* [New York: Basic Books, 1985], p. 11; cited in Hugh W. Pinnock, *Ancient Literary Forms,* [Provo, Utah: FARMS, 1999], p. 56.)

EVIDENCE NO. 947: SIMPLE ALTERNATE PARALLELISM

Evidence: One of the most common longer forms of parallelism is *simple alternate*, in which four phrases contain two repetitions alternating with each other (A-B/A-B pattern). In this formation, the 'A' phrases are identical, synonymous, or closely related, as are the 'B' phrases. Such a pattern emphatically reinforces a teaching. By reading a pair of thoughts repeated twice, the reader is more apt to remember the two facets of the message. The sentence comes through with greater intensity. One example is found in 1 Corinthians 14:1-5:

A   Follow after charity, and desire spiritual gifts, but rather that ye may *prophesy*.
B   For he that *speaketh in an unknown tongue* speaketh not unto men, but unto God: for no man understandeth him; howbeit in the spirit he speaketh mysteries.
A   But he that *prophesieth* speaketh unto men to edification, and exhortation, and comfort.
B   He that speaketh in an *unknown tongue* edifieth himself;
A   but he that *prophesieth* edifieth the church.
B   I would that ye all spake with *tongues*,
A   but rather that ye *prophesied*: for greater is he that *prophesieth*
B   than he that *speaketh with tongues*, except he interpret, that the church may receive edifying.

Following is a Book of Mormon example in Alma's analogy of the compass (Alma 37:44):

A   It is as easy to give heed to the word of Christ,
B   which will point to you a straight course to eternal bliss,
A   as it was for our fathers to give heed to this compass,
B   which would point unto them a straight course to the promised land.

A reader can easily identify a simple alternate parallelism by recognizing the word pairs in the four phrases. The prophets of the Book of Mormon were inspired in their choices, employing word combinations that greatly expand our understanding of what they had to say. Even in the lengthy parallel phrases above, the heed to/heed to and straight course to/straight course to combinations tag what is being compared—the word of Christ/this compass and eternal bliss/ promised land.

More examples of *alternate parallelism* are found in Isaiah 1:18; Ezekiel 37:16; Zechariah 1:3; Job 1:6; 2:1; 1 Nephi 5:1; 11:25; 17:19, 36, 39; 20:18-9; 2 Nephi 4:17, 28; 6:6; 10:25; 26: 12; 27:4; 30:17; Mosiah 4:8; Alma 1:26; 2:29; 28:11; 63:2; and Helaman 3:21.

Sometimes the two alternating lines will repeat more than once: such a structure is called a repeated *alternate parallelism*. In the following example, the pattern strongly links the message—the Savior's sacrifice—to those who delivered the good tidings—the prophets (1 Nephi 19:10):

A ...the God of Jacob, yieldeth himself,
B according to the words of the angel,
A as a man, into the hands of wicked men, to be lifted up,
B according to the words of Zenock,
A and to be crucified,
B according to the words of Neum,
A and to be buried in a sepulcher,
B according to the words of Zenos...

More examples of *repeated alternate parallelism* are found in 1 Nephi 19:9 Alma 30:24-6; and Alma 30:10. (See Parry, *Ensign*, October 1989, pp. 59-61.)

EVIDENCE NO. 948: EXTENDED ALTERNATE PARALLELISM

<u>Evidence</u>: Another variation in the same family as simple and repeated alternates is the *extended alternate*. This pattern adds additional alternating lines, such as A-B-C/A-B-C or A-B-C-D/A-B-C-D. This parallelism typically delivers more complex messages than the other two, as in this example found in Matthew 7:7-8:

A Ask, and it shall be given you;
B seek, and ye shall find;
C knock, and it shall be opened unto you:
A For every one that asketh receiveth;
B and he that seeketh findeth;
C and to him that knocketh it shall be opened.

The Book of Mormon also uses this form of parallelism such as is found in (Mosiah 7:30-31):

A And again, he saith:
B If my people shall sow filthiness
C they shall reap the chaff thereof in the whirlwind;
D and the effect thereof is poison.
A And again he saith:
B If my people shall sow filthiness
C they shall reap the east wind,
D which bringeth immediate destruction.

More examples of *extended alternate parallelism* are found in Deuteronomy 18:20-22; Ecclesiastes 1:6-7; Isaiah 3:16-24; 1 Nephi 8:24; 9:3-4, 11-12; and Alma 5:19. (See Parry, *Ensign*, October 1989, pp. 59-61.)

EVIDENCE NO. 949: CLIMAX PARALLELISM

<u>Evidence</u>: When the same word or words are found at the end of one phrase and at the beginning of the next, they form a type of parallelism called *climax*. The continuation of thought from phrase to phrase adds power to the discourse, while also connecting lines into an inseparable body. A Biblical example of this can be found in Romans 10:13-15:

For whosoever shall **call upon the name of the Lord** shall be saved. How then shall they **call on him** in whom they have not **believed**? And how shall they **believe** in him of whom they have not **heard**? And how shall they **hear** without a **preacher**? And how shall they **preach**, except they be **sent**? As it is written, How beautiful are the feet of **them that preach** the gospel of peace, and **bring glad tidings of good things**!

Moroni 8:25-26 shows this easily recognized pattern:

> And the first fruits of repentance is **baptism**;
> and **baptism** cometh by faith unto the **fulfilling the commandments**;
> and the **fulfilling the commandments** bringeth **remission of sins**;
> And the **remission of sins** bringeth **meekness, and lowliness of heart**;
> and because of **meekness and lowliness of heart** cometh the visitation of the **Holy Ghost**,
> which **Comforter** filleth with hope and perfect **love**,
> which **love** endureth by diligence unto prayer,
> until the end shall come, when all the saints shall **dwell with God**.

The idea of ascension accompanies climax, where the discourse moves from a beginning point to a climactic situation. Note in the above verses that the series begins with repentance, which is an essential step onto the path of eternal life. Repentance is followed by baptism, then obedience, and the process finally culminates with the righteous receiving an eternal station with God.

More examples of *climactic parallelism* are found in 2 Nephi 2:25; Alma 42:22-23; and Mormon 9:12-13. (See Parry, *Ensign*, October 1989, p. 61.)

EVIDENCE NO. 950: REGULAR OR CIRCULAR REPETITION PARALLELISM

Evidence: This kind of parallelism is found when a phrase is repeated at intervals in a longer passage, as if the message keeps coming back in a circular motion to the key phrase. This is one of the most striking forms of parallelism, as the following example from James 2:14-26 indicates:

> What doth it profit, my brethren, though a man say he hath **faith, and have not works**? can faith save him?

> If a brother or sister be naked, and destitute of daily food, And one of you say unto them, Depart in peace, be ye warmed and filled; notwithstanding ye give them not those things which are needful to the body; what doth it profit? Even so **faith, if it hath not works**, is dead, being alone.

> Yea, a man may say, Thou hast **faith, and I have works**: shew me thy **faith without thy works**, and I will shew thee my **faith by my works**.

> Thou believest that there is one God; thou doest well: the devils also believe, and tremble. But wilt thou know, O vain man, that **faith without works** is dead?

> Was not Abraham our father justified by **works**, when he had offered Isaac his son upon the altar? Seest thou how faith wrought with his works, and by works was **faith** made perfect? And the scripture was fulfilled which saith, Abraham believed God, and it was imputed unto him for righteousness: and he was called the Friend of God. Ye see then how that by **works** a man is justified, and not by **faith** only.

> Likewise also was not Rahab the harlot justified by **works**, when she had received the messengers, and had sent them out another way? For as the body without the spirit is dead, so **faith without works** is dead also.

Other Biblical examples of *circular repetition parallelism* can be found in 1 Corinthians 13:1-13; Hebrews 5:6, 10; 7:17, 21; and Hebrews chapter 11. The following is an example from the Book of Mormon (Alma 5:6):

> I say unto you, my brethren,
> you that belong to this church,
> **have you sufficiently retained in remembrance**
> the captivity of your fathers? Yea, and
> **have you sufficiently retained in remembrance**
> his mercy and long-suffering towards them?
> And moreover, **have ye sufficiently retained in remembrance**
> that he has delivered their souls from hell?

By this repetition (in a sermon full of many kinds of parallelisms), Alma arouses his hearers' conscience and brings to their remembrance the divine interventions of God.

More examples of *circular repetitive parallelism* are found in Mosiah 3:25-26; 11:21; Alma 3:15-16; 14:29; 24:7-10; 60:20; 62:41; Helaman 11:10-16; and Mormon 7:2-5. (See Parry, *Ensign*, October 1989, p. 61.)

EVIDENCE NO. 951: CHIASMUS

<u>Evidence</u>: Chiasmus (pronounced ki-az-mus) is an ancient poetic form, which was used by many Hebrew prophets for about 3,000 years. The existence of this literary style was not discovered by the western world until after the publication of the Book of Mormon. The Book of Mormon contains many examples of this ancient literary device—providing additional evidence that the ancient Americans were Hebrew as the Book of Mormon claims (1 Nephi 1:2).

Chiasmus consists of a progression of ideas or elements written in such a way as to lead to a central point, and then the same ideas or elements are written in reverse order moving away from the central point. For example, a simple chiasmus is found in Psalms 3:7-8:

A. "<u>Save</u> me
B.   O my <u>God</u>,
C.   For thou has <u>smitten</u>
D.   All my <u>enemies</u>
E.   On the <u>cheek-bone</u>.
E.   The <u>teeth</u>
D.   Of the <u>wicked</u>
C.   Thou hast <u>broken</u>,
B.   To <u>Yahweh</u>
A. The <u>salvation</u>" (emphasis and indentation added).

There are many examples of chiasmus throughout the Book of Mormon especially in the first half. After being separated from their Hebrew ancestors for many centuries the use of chiasmus becomes less frequent in the second half of the Book of Mormon. Chiasmus can be found in verses, or an entire chapter can be written in that form. The example below illustrates chiasmus in verse.

A. "Men will drink damnation to their souls unless they <u>humble</u> themselves
B.   and become as little <u>children</u>
C.   believing that salvation is in the <u>atoning blood of Christ</u>;
D.   for the <u>natural man</u>
E.   is an enemy to <u>God</u>
F.   and <u>has been</u> from the fall of Adam
F.   and <u>will be</u> forever and ever
E.   unless he yieldeth to the <u>Holy Spirit</u>
D.   and putteth off the <u>natural man</u>
C.   and becometh a saint through the <u>atonement of Christ</u>
B.   and becometh as a <u>child</u>
A. submissive, meek and <u>humble</u>. (See Mosiah 3:18-19.)

More Book of Mormon chiasma can be found in 1 Nephi 15:9-20; 17:35-40; 19:6-24; 2 Nephi 1:13-23; 9:5-13; 9:18-21; 29:12-14; Mosiah 5:10-12; 12:25-27; 23:7; Alma 36 (whole chapter); 41:13-15; 3 Nephi 20:10-46; 21:1-29; 28:30-36. For more information, see *New Era*, February 1972, pp. 6-11; John W. Welch, "Chiasmus in the Book of Mormon," *BYU Studies*, Autumn 1969, pp. 69-84; Avraham Gileadi, *The Last Days,* (Covenant 1991), pp. 86, 89, 97, 198.

Dave McFarland pointed out that the entire book of 1 Nephi is a chiasmus which centers around the appearance of the Savior both in Jerusalem, and then the American continent and the destruction of the wicked due to pride:

A. Beginning of life "I Nephi having been born of goodly parents" (1:1).
  B. "I make a record in the language of my father" (1:2).
    C. Record consists of the learning of Jews and language of Egyptians (1:2).
      D. Nephi testifies it is true (1:3).
        E. Jerusalem must be destroyed (1:4).
          F. Many prophets testified (1:4).
            G. Coming of Jesus Christ prophesied (1:9-10).
              H. Inhabitants of Jerusalem about to be dispersed (1:13).
                I. Rebellion and repentance of Laman and Lemuel (2:11-14).
                J. Nephi is commanded to obtain the brass plates (3:1-8).
                  K. Laman and Lemuel are confounded by an angel (3:28-30).
                    L. Death of Laban (4:6-18).
                      M. Sariah complains against Lehi (5:1-3).
                        N. Lehi obtains the brass plates which contain the word of God (5:21).
                          O. Ishmael agrees to join the house of Lehi (chapter 7).
                            P. Lehi's vision of the tree of life (chapter 8).
                              Q. Lehi prophesies the Babylonian captivity (10:1-3).
                                R. Nephi's vision opens (11:1).
                                  S. The twelve apostles carried away by the Spirit (11:29).
                                    T. Jesus Christ ministers to the Jews (11:30-33)
                                      U. Multitudes of Earth fall because of pride (11:34-36).
                                      U. Multitudes of Lehites fall in war (12:1-5).
                                    T. Jesus Christ ministers to the Nephites (12:6).
                                  S. The Holy Ghost falls upon the twelve apostles (12:7).
                                R. Nephi's vision closes (14:30).
                              Q. Captivity of the devil (14:3-4).
                            P. Nephi interprets Lehi's vision of the tree of life (15:21-36).
                          O. Daughters of Ishmael marry sons of Lehi (16:7-8).
                        N. Lehi obtains the Liahona which contains messages from the Lord (16:10-29).
                      M. Lehi complains, and daughters of Ishmael complain against Lehi (16:20, 35).
                    L. Death of Ishmael (16:34-35).
                  K. Laman and Lemuel are confounded by power of God (17:52-55).
                J. Nephi is commanded to build a ship (17:8).
                I. Rebellion and repentance of Laman and Lemuel (18:10-11, 17-20).
              H. Scattered Israel to be gathered together (22:4-8, 12, 25, 28).
            G. Coming of the "Holy One of Israel" prophesied (22:20-21).
          F. "I and my father are [not] the only ones that have testified" (22:31).
        E. All who fight against God shall be destroyed (22:23).
      D. Nephi testifies his record is true (22:30).
    C. Gospel preached to all nations, kindreds, tongues and people (22:28).
  B. "I and my father" (22:31).
A. End of life "if ye shall be obedient ... and endure to the end, ye shall be saved at the last day" (22:31).

There is no conceivable way that Joseph Smith could have learned this literary style through academic channels, since it was not discussed in depth until 1854. Therefore, the only logical explanation for the extensive use of the Chiastic structure in the Book of Mormon is that Joseph Smith was indeed inspired by God in the translation of an authentic record of ancient Hebrew Scripture. (See John Forbes, *The Symmetrical Structure of Scripture*, [Clark: Edinburgh, 1854]; *Chiasmus in Antiquity: Structures, Analyses, Exegesis*, edited by John W. Welch, [Hildesheim, West Germany: Gerstenberg, 1981]; Victor L. Ludlow, *Isaiah: Prophet, Seer, and Poet*, [1982], pp. 36-38; John W. Welch, "Chiasmus in the Book of Mormon," *BYU Studies*, [Fall 1969], vol. 10, no. 1, p. 73.)

See also the evidence regarding Chiasmus in the Doctrine and Covenants in the chapter on Joseph Smith in volume I of this same work.

EVIDENCE NO. 952: MAYAN CHIASMUS

Claim: Not only is chiasmus found extensively in the Book of Mormon, but the ancient Mayas—whose ancestors wrote the Book of Mormon, also employed it.

Evidence: Considering the frequency of chiasmus in the Book of Mormon, it would be reasonable to expect to find this literary tool also employed in other ancient American writings. The following are quotations from an article by Allen J. Christenson entitled "Chiasmus in Mayan Texts," *Ensign*, October 1988, pp. 28, 31:

> One firm indication that the Book of Mormon is an ancient work is its extensive use of chiasmus... Chiasmus also appears in the Book of Mormon. Many of these chiasmus have been identified and discussed,[3] but very little research has been done on the use of chiasmus in other ancient American writings. It is entirely possible that descendants of the Book of Mormon peoples knew of the device and used it in their own records. As a translator of ancient Indian languages from Guatemala, I was intrigued with the possibility. Although I knew of no one who had documented the presence of chiasmus in these languages, I knew that Mayan writings, particularly, contain extensive selections of poetry and might contain this rhetorical pattern used so liberally in the Book of Mormon. Such a pattern could exist even though Maya and Hebrew are such dissimilar languages. (See Munro S. Edmonson, *The Book of Counsel: The Popol Vuh of the Quiche Maya of Guatemala*, Middle American Research Institute, publication no. 35, [New Orleans: Tulane University, 1971], pp. xi-xii.)

> I began by reviewing thirty-seven ancient Mayan texts written shortly after the Spanish conquest in the sixteenth century. To my surprise, I found that chiasmus was relatively common in many of the documents, though not in all of them.

> ... Of the thirty-seven Mayan documents I examined, chiastic patterns abound in sixteen. I discovered that the texts with chiasmus had several traits in common: They had early sixteenth-century dates of composition, authorship by royal family members, internal evidence of reliance on pre-Columbian hieroglyphic books, significant references to Mayan history and religion, and relative freedom from European words and cultural influences.

> None of the highland Mayan documents composed after 1580 include passages of chiasmus. By that time, the people familiar with ancient hieroglyphic books were, for the most part, gone.

See also John W. Welch, "Chiasmus in the Book of Mormon," *BYU Studies*, Autumn 1969, pp. 69-84; John W. Welch, "Chiasmus in the Book of Mormon," in *Book of Mormon Authorship*, edited by Noel B. Reynolds, (Provo: Brigham Young University, 1982), pp. 33-52; Noel B. Reynolds, "Nephi's Outline," in *Book of Mormon Authorship*, pp. 53-74; Paul Cracroft, "A Clear Poetic Voice," *Ensign*, January 1984, p. 28.

EVIDENCE NO. 953: GOD CURSES THE LAND

Claim: Enos 1:10 and Alma 37:28 in the Book of Mormon speak of a curse upon the land. Some have wondered why the wording depicts the land rather than the people themselves being cursed.

Evidence: This was an authentic idiomatic expression in ancient times. It meant that those who dwell in certain lands would be cursed if they refuse to obey the commandments of the Lord, and will be blessed if they obey. (See W. Richter, "Urgeschichte und Hofftheologie," *Biblische Zeitschrift* 10 [1966]: 99; and L. I. Newman, *Hasidic Anthology* [New York: C. Scribner's, 1934], p. 297, both cited in Nibley, *Abraham in Egypt,* [1981], pp. 189 and 214 respectively.)

EVIDENCE NO. 954: THE SYMBOLIC PROPHETIC CURSE

Claim: The Book of Mormon makes extensive use of the Biblical symbolic prophetic curse on the more wicked inhabitants of ancient America, thus providing additional evidence that the Book of Mormon was inspired by the very same God who revealed the Bible.

Evidence: The following is quoted from a *Foundation for Ancient Research and Mormon Studies Update,* entitled "Symbolic Action as Prophetic Curse," (FARMS, July 1991), no. 77, p. 2:

At one point in his ministry, Isaiah was instructed by the Lord to remove his garment and shoes and walk "naked [like a slave, without an upper garment] and barefoot" among the people. Isaiah's action was to be a sign, for as Isaiah walked like a slave, even so would the Egyptians become slaves to the Assyrians (Isaiah 20:2-4). This prophetic symbolic action by Isaiah represented a prophetic curse that destruction and ruin would come upon the Egyptians.

Ezekiel conducted a symbolic act which had anathematical tones. He cut off the hair of his beard and his head, and divided it into three portions. One third Ezekiel burned, one third he scattered into the wind, and the third he smote with a knife. This was a prophetic curse, demonstrating the three ways in which Israel would perish—by fire, by scattering, and by the sword of war (Ezekiel 5:1-17).

Such prophetic symbolic curses are well attested in the Bible. G. Fohrer and David Aune, take a broad approach to prophetic symbolic actions, listing several examples (see for instance, Numbers 21:6-9; 1 Kings 22:11; 2 Kings 13:14-19; Isaiah 2:9-10; 3:1-4; 8:1-4; 7:10-17; Jeremiah 19:1-15; 27-28; 32:6-44; Ezekiel 4:1-3; 4:4-8; 4:9-17). See G. Fohrer, *Die Symbolischen Handlungen der Propheten,* (Zürich: Zwingli Verlag, 1953), pp. 17-19; and David E. Aune, *Prophecy in Early Christianity and the Ancient Mediterranean World,* (Grand Rapids: Erdmans, 1983), pp. 100-101.

Several *FARMS* publications have noted various types of symbolic actions that are present in the Book of Mormon. M. Morrise and T. Szink, present examples of simile curses. John W. Welch discusses parabolic acts performed by prophetic oracles. (See Morrise, "Simile Curses in the Ancient Near East, Old Testament, and Book of Mormon" [FARMS, 1982]; Szink, "An Oath of Allegiance in the Book of Mormon" in *Warfare in the Book of Mormon,* edited by Steven D. Ricks and William Hamblin, [1990], pp. 36-38; and Welch, "Law and War in the Book of Mormon," in *Warfare in the Book of Mormon,* p. 62; "Was Helaman 7-8 an Allegorical Sermon?" *FARMS Update,* May 1986.)

Book of Mormon prophets carried on the Old World tradition of performing symbolic actions which revealed a prophetic curse. The incident of the *title of liberty* was much more than a rally behind a standard. Moroni rent his coat, wrote upon it the title of liberty, placed it upon a pole, and "went forth among the people, waving the rent part of his garment in the air, that all might see" (Alma 46:19). After this dramatic act, Moroni likened his rent coat to the garment of Joseph which had been rent by Joseph's brothers, and proclaimed, "let us remember to keep the commandments of God, or our garments shall be rent by our brethren, and we be cast into prison, or be sold, or be slain."

Those who witnessed Moroni's symbolic activity responded in turn with another symbolic action by casting their garments at Moroni's feet and then promising not to fall into transgression, lest God "cast us at the feet of our enemies, even as we have cast our garments at thy feet to be trodden under foot" (Alma 46:22).

A Prophetic symbolic action accompanied by a curse is found in the hanging of Zemnarihah on the top of a tree. After his death the Nephites felled the tree and called, "may the Lord preserve his people in righteousness and in holiness of heart, that they may cause to be felled to earth all who shall seek to slay them … even as this man hath been felled to the earth" (3 Nephi 4:28-29). This act predicted the way the wicked would be slain if they continued their attempts to murder the righteous.

A final example of symbolic action as a prophetic curse is found in the episode of the scalping of Zerahemnah. After Moroni's soldiers scalped Zerahemnah, the war-mongering chief of the Lamanites, he displayed the scalp on the point of his sword and stated with a loud voice, "even as this scalp has fallen to the earth … so shall ye fall to the earth except ye will deliver up your weapons of war and depart with a covenant of peace" (Alma 44:12-14).

The symbolic actions in these examples were so effective that in each instance the audience reacted immediately and positively. Those who viewed Moroni gathered around the title of liberty. Those who witnessed the felling of the tree had a great emotional and spiritual experience; and the followers of Zerahemnah who were present when he was scalped "were stuck with fear" and "threw down their weapons of war" and promised to live in peace. (See Alma 44:15; 46:28-29; 3 Nephi 4:30-33.)

EVIDENCE NO. 955: SIMILARITIES BETWEEN HEBREW AND NATIVE AMERICAN LANGUAGES

Claim: According to the Book of Mormon, the language of the ancient Americans had been influenced by the learning of the Hebrews (1 Nephi 1:2) with their written language a blend of Hebrew and Egyptian.

Evidence: Scholars have found hundreds of striking similarities between early American Indian words and Hebrew as well as other Mideastern dialects. This provides strong evidence that the ancient Americans came from the Middle East, as the Book of Mormon claims. These discoveries were published many years after the Book of Mormon was printed in 1830.

The following examples demonstrate that the language of the ancient Americans has many parallels in the Middle East. One scholar said, "Several early Spanish writers claim that the natives of some portions of the land still spoke a corrupt Hebrew; Las Casas so affirms with regard to the inhabitants of the island of Haiti. Lafitu wrote a history wherein he maintained that the Caribbee language was radically Hebrew." (Claverigo, *Memories de l'Amerique*; *Millennial Star*, vol. 59, p. 374; cited in Widtsoe, *Seven Claims of the Book of Mormon*, [Zion's Printing and Publishing: Independence, Missouri, 1939], p. 98.)

Dr. Starr writing in the *Proceedings of the Davenport Academy of Sciences* (vol. 9, appendix 3) found a number of Hebrew words which appear to have provided the roots for similar words in native American languages. Also, J. Fitzgerald Lee in *The Great Migration*, pp. 60-64, 223-229 (both cited in Josiah E. Hickman, *The Romance of the Book of Mormon* [1937], pp. 173-174). The following comparisons are from the above sources together with: James Strong, *The Exhaustive Concordance of the Bible* (1973), Hebrew word entry nos. 376, 2128, 4277; and Theodora Kroeber, *Ishi* (1964), p. 212. See also Brian Stubbs, "Looking Over vs. Overlooking Native American Languages: Let's Void the Void," in *Journal of Book of Mormon Studies*, (Spring 1996), vol. 5, no. 1, pp. 1-49.

Meaning	Hebrew	Native American
pronoun I	*ano, ani*	The same in ancient Mexico. It is *anoki* in Peru.
a planet, a sign in the heavens	*oth*	*to* or *oth*, in Maya.
night or a dark period	*laila, leila*	*lailo*, in Mexico.
food	*zaid*	*zeeta*, in Mexico.
fire, burning	*attun*	*tunni, etunni*, in Peru and northern South America.

Meaning	Hebrew	Native American
chief, leader	*Khazek* or *Khezek*	*Kazique*, in Central America and West Indies.
whiteness, brightness	*zach*	*zach*, in Central America, especially in Yucatan.
hold water, to drink in hand	*kaph*	*kab, kabh*, in Maya.
morning, brightness of dawn	*boker*	*bokarina*, in northern parts of South America.
bouquet, wreath of flowers	*zizah*	*zizza*, or *zissah*, in Maya.
a tree	*yaar*	*yaor*, Peru and Central America. In Haiti, *yaarooma* is a forest.
a brother	*aach*	*aak* or *aaki*, in Alaska.
to double, to repeat	*kaphal*	*kappal*, in Yucatan.
poison, terror causing death	*puggul*	*pugguly*, to North American Indians, was the name of a poisonous tree .
firewood	*kamar*	*kaamery*, in Venezuela.
hair of the head	*zizith*	*zoz*, in Yucatan.
a ruler, or king	*gabach*	*capach*, in Mexico.
a son	*ben*	*pen*, in Guatemala.
"it passed away"	*makak*	*maqui*, in Maya and Mexican.
to light, to shine	*nagah*	*nagah*, in Maya.
a plague	*nega*	*nega*, in Haitian language is applied to a sand louse that burrows into the flesh of the feet.
flowing, a large river, or over-flowing of a small river	*zuph*	In American Indian dialects the word for river is *ziph, zeph*, or *zipi*. Their great river was called "the fish river": *na messi zippi*; hence the word *Mississippi*.
the chief musician of the king	*Asaph*	*asaphi* is a North American word for "to sing" or "a song."
to strike, to kill by striking	*makhak* or *machaq*	The North American Indian word for "the weapon for killing" is *ta-mahakan*, hence the word *tomahawk*.
"the mighty one"	*Yahova*	*Yehowa* ,Was once used by several North American tribes and those of Central America.
man	*ish*	In some American Indian dialects, the word "man" is *Ishi*.
Sit, dwell	*yasov*	*yasiva*, in Hopi
lightning	*baraq*	*berok*, in Tepiman of Arizona and Mexico
shoulder	*sikm*	*sikum*, (Panamint)
man, person	*adam*	*otam*, (Pima, Southern Tepehuan)
water/ocean	*mayim/mem*	*memet*, (Cupeño)
smooth/plane off, shave or scrape	*sippah*	*sipa*, in Mono (of California, Oregon and Nevada)
squirrel	*siggob*	*sikku*, in Southern Paiute
low/below	*daniy*	*tani*, in Uto-Aztecan
siege-wall	*dayeq*	*tiyiqa*, in Hopi
believe	*ya'amin*	*yawamin*, in Serrano of Southern California
wing	*kanap*	*'anap*, in Tubatulabal of Southern California
grinding stone	*maktes*	*ma'ta*, in Uto-Aztecan
want	*neki*	*onek*, in Uto-Aztecan
chew, chewed	*pawia*	*opawi*, in Uto-Aztecan
boil, boiled	*posoni*	*oposon*, in Uto-Aztecan
lion	*'ari*	*wori*, in Uto-Aztecan
Deity, supernatural judge	*massiah*	*masawi*, in Hopi

EVIDENCE NO. 956: THE TEN COMMANDMENTS IN ANCIENT AMERICA

<u>Claim</u>: Along with discoveries of ancient Hebrew writing is a discovery of Paleo-Hebrew writing near Albuquerque New Mexico which contains the ten commandments that were given to Moses on Sinai—written by the finger of Jehovah. While the origin of these inscriptions is still somewhat controversial, unless they are proven to be a modern hoax, they suggest clear evidence of pre-Columbian contact between the Old and New Worlds.

<u>Evidence</u>: The following is quoted from David Allen Deal, *Discovery of Ancient America,* (Kherem La Yah Press: Irvine, California, 1984), p. 1:

> On the Right Bank of the Rio Puercos, some thirty miles southwest of Albuquerque, in the brown, barren waste of Valencia County, New Mexico, stands a volcanic mesa. The people in the general area call it "Hidden Mountain" or "Mystery Mountain" but the Indians retain its more ancient title, "Cerro Los Moqujino" ("Cliff of the Strange Writings"). These names aptly apply, for upon its slopes a secret is revealed that, if accepted, would change the basic concepts upon which ancient American history is built. Few even dare its challenge. Nevertheless, the emerging evidence compels us to conclude that this wilderness region was in ancient times visited by adventurers from the Middle East.

> Atop these natural volcanic ramparts is found the ancient ruins of a camp laid out in military fashion … At first one might casually dismiss these ruins as some relic of a band of ancient Indians that roamed the area. But closer examination of the details makes such a conclusion patently amiss. Comparison of the building formations with other Indian sites proves them unique in the Americas, but surprisingly similar to finds in the Middle East. Yet the greatest shock, causing much disbelief and offhanded accusations of fraud, comes from the accompanying inscriptions found at the site. … The words chiseled on these rocks are without a doubt ancient Hebrew. The greater inscription recites the Ten Commandments; the smaller reads "Yahweh [Jehovah] is our Mighty One." The ramifications of these words, if authentically composed by an ancient scribe, are enormous, giving direct proof that a connection anciently existed between the Americas, through explorations or mariners, with the Middle East. The evidence would tend to indicate naval power for some countries as early as 3500 years ago. It is within this framework that we must examine the Ten Commandments of New Mexico.

Also found at this site is a zodiac map chiseled into the basalt rock at the top of the mountain. This map, discovered by Bill McGlone and published in *Western Epigraphy,* (vol. 1, no. 2, December 1983), proved to be "a most important key for dating the inscriptions in New Mexico" to 107 BC. After a thorough scrutiny of the evidence, David Deal concludes on page 32 of his work:

> The more we ponder the evidence, the more difficult it is to believe that someone, with the intent to perpetuate a hoax, conceived of a plan whereby he would find a mountain at some remote spot, build pit-houses and a chieftain's complex, and then provide inscriptions and a zodiac to complete the illusion. For what purpose? Indeed, never has so much detail gone into any known hoax. How would anyone have known to combine such evidence, relating to a Shemetic zodiac, Hebrew writing, and a building plan from the mind-set of men living in the Middle East, especially composing the project in the 1800's long before much of such knowledge was known.

The following line drawing of the ten-commandment inscription was copied from a photograph taken by David Nuckols of Edgewood, New Mexico—one of the reviewers of this work. Along side each line of text is shown the English translation found in David Deal's work. Note that the parenthetical text of the first line has been brought up from the third line of the inscription (which is preceded by a "caret" ^ symbol). Also note that Hebrew is read from right to left—thus the English lines are "mirror images" of each Hebrew line.

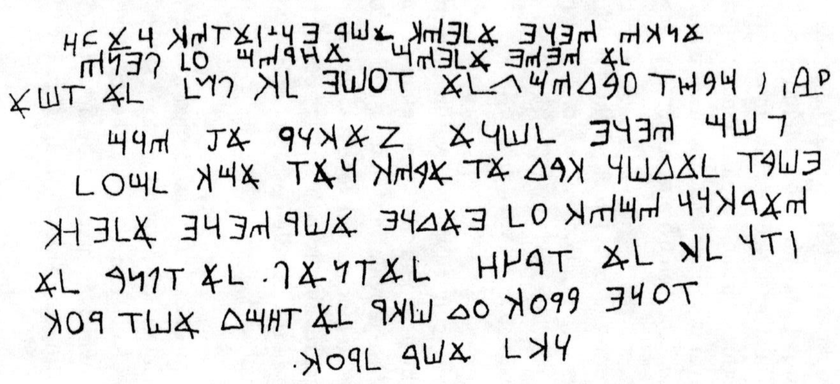

I Yahweh your Mighty One who has brought you out land of (Egypt from the house of bondage.)* not shall there be ones mighty any other besides Me.

^Not you shall make for yourselves a graven image. Not shall take

You the name of Yahweh in vain. Remember Thee day

the Sabbath holy to keep it. Honor Thou your father and your mother so that

may be long your days on the land which Yahweh your mighty one

is giving to you. Not you shall murder. Not you shall commit adultery. Not you shall steal. Not

You shall testify against your neighbor a witness false. Not you shall covet wife your neighbor's

Or anything which (belongs) to your neighbor.

Figure 38. The Ten Commandments written in Paleo-Hebrew found in New Mexico.

*"Note: the caret ^ symbol in the third line was placed there by the inscription's creator as the result of an error on his part. He had left a line out by mistake and corrected his error by writing the missing sentence between line 1 and line 2. *Codex Sinaticus* provides evidence for the use of the caret as early as 2nd century AD. Barry Fell gave demonstration of this point at the Epigraphical Society meeting in Albuquerque, New Mexico, October 23, 1984." (See David Allen Deal, *Discovery of Ancient America*, [Kherem La Yah Press: Irvine, California, 1984], p. 5.)

9. Ancient American Science

EVIDENCE NO. 957: IMPLEMENTS OF IRON IN ANCIENT AMERICA

Claim: The Book of Mormon records that the ancient inhabitants of the American continent made implements of iron (2 Nephi 5:15). Book of Mormon critics have frequently pointed to this as an error in the Book of Mormon, assuming that iron metallurgy was absent from the American continents until it was brought by the Europeans. Once again, what was originally assumed to be a fallacy in the Book of Mormon, has now become an indication of its truthfulness, as evidence has been unearthed that the Mesoamericans did indeed work iron.

Evidence: The capability of ancient Americans to make implements of iron is consistent with the Bible lands where the Book of Mormon peoples originated. Biblical references to the use of iron include: Genesis 4:22; Numbers 31:22; 35:16; Deuteronomy 3:11; Joshua 17:16-18; and Judges 1:19; 4:3; There are over 80 verses in the Bible which refer to the ancient use of iron. Hence, those who criticize the Book of Mormon for its mention of iron as an anachronism are unwittingly criticizing the Bible.

Early Peruvian Spanish writer Cristobal de Molina says the Incas had traditions about the use of iron in Previous ages and that they had names for it in their languages. In Peruvian, iron is *quilly* and in old Chilean it is *panilic*. (See J. D. Baldwin's *Ancient America* [Morriston, New Jersey: Silver Burdett Co., 1871] pp. 225, 248, 1871; also Bancroft's *Native Races,* vol. 4, p. 794.)

The following is excerpted from an abstract of a paper by Franklin S. Harris, Jr. entitled: "Iron in Ancient America" (*University Archaeological Society Newsletter* 4.5):

> The importance of metals in our civilization may exaggerate our view of the importance of iron in ancient times. But the apparent absence of iron metallurgy in the New World before the coming of the Europeans has been a point frequently made by Book of Mormon critics, since the Book of Mormon speaks of iron-working among its people in ancient America (working in iron, as well as gold, silver, and "brass" or bronze, by true metallurgical processes). Although a number of writers have reported finds of worked iron at pre-Columbian sites, these have always been objects cold-hammered from meteoric iron, not cast from smelted terrestrial iron. However, the occurrence of words in two South American languages possibly referring to terrestrial iron, plus claimed discoveries of ancient mines and refining sites in a few places, is suggestive. A recent book by Arlington H. Mallery also claims the discovery of prehistoric iron smelting furnaces in the Ohio valley, which show resemblances to European smelting sites of the Middle Ages. (See Mallery, *Lost America; the Story of the Pre-Columbian Iron Age in America*, [Washington, 1951]; cited in Christensen, *Progress in Archaeology*, [1963], pp. 113-114).

The Aztecs used war clubs studded with iron instead of the usual obsidian. (H. H. Bancroft, *The Native Races* [of the Pacific States], vol. 2, [San Francisco: A. L. Bancroft and Co., 1882], pp. 407-408, quoted by William Hamblin in "Hand-held Weapons in the Book of Mormon," *Foundation for Ancient Research and Mormon Studies*, HAM-85, 1985.)

The following are quotations from Harris, *The Book of Mormon Message and Evidences*, pp. 83-35:

In North America, W. K. Moorehead reports: "Much that both the historic and the prehistoric Indian made use of was composed of cloth, iron, wood, brass, leather, etc." And H. C. Shetrone in *The Mound Builders* (1930) lists many iron objects that have been found from pre-Columbian times. (See Moorehead, *The Stone Age in North America* [1910], pp. 2, 344. See also John L. Myers, "Useful Metals: Copper and Iron" in *Early Man, His Origin and Culture*, edited by G. Elliot Smith [1931].)

An example is the finding near Havana, Illinois, of 22 rounded beads, less than one inch in diameter, composed of strongly oxidized iron. From the structure of the iron and its nickel content the iron is of meteoric origin. This should not be confused with the use of iron minerals such as hematite in the natural form to make hatchets and other objects. (See R. M. Grogan, *American Antiquity*, [1948] vol. 13, pp. 302; Andre Clement, "L'Emplois des Minerals ferreux dans l'Amérique précolombienne," ["The Pre-Columbian use of Ferrous Minerals in America"] *Revista del Museo Nacionál*, [Lima, Peru 1938], vol. 7, p. 131.)

In Central America iron was used, too, because forty-three grams of iron oxide were found in a jar at Uaxactun, as reported by Oliver G. Ricketson Jr. and E. B. Ricketson. Several pieces of iron oxide were found in excavations at Kaminaljuyu, Guatemala. (Ricketson, "Uaxactun, Guatemala," *Carnegie Institution of Washington, DC,* Publication 477, [1937], pp. 71-72; A. L. Smith, "Uaxactun, Guatemala: Excavations of 1931–1937," *Carnegie Institution of Washington, Publication 588*, [1950], p. 90, Table 6, Fig. 133a; Edwin M. Shook and Alfred V. Kidder, "Mound E-III-3, Kami-naljuhu, Guatemala," *Carnegie Institution of Washington, Contributions,* XI, 53, Publication 596 [1952], pp. 63, 118.)

In his article on "The Origin and Early Spread of Iron working," Harold Peake summarizes: "Meteoric iron has attracted the attention of men at different times and in widely separated regions. In the New World, for instance, it was used not only by the Incas of Peru, but also by the Mayas of Yucatan and the Aztecs of Mexico. Amerigo Vespucci found the Indians of the La Plata region of South America making arrowheads and small tools of this metal; the Indians of North America considered it so precious a material that they used it to overlay their beads of gold. Ornaments and tools of meteoric iron have been discovered in the mounds of the Mississippi and Ohio valleys." (See Peake, *The Geographical Review*, [1933], vol. 23, p. 639.)

Here is another interesting statement from H. Hensoldt: "When Cortez had completed the conquest of Mexico, the Spaniards, ... were particularly struck and puzzled by one fact. They noticed that the Aztecs possessed certain implements, such as knives, daggers, etc., made of iron, but it seemed that only the most distinguished of the natives possessed such, that iron was a great rarity and was prized higher than gold.... Their iron was, in fact of meteoritic origin, like that of the Mayas of Yucatan and the Incas of Peru of which many weapons are still preserved in the collections." (See Hensoldt, *The American Geologist*, [1889], vol. 4, pp. 37-38.)

There have recently been some remarkable developments in the knowledge of early iron working in America. Most of the details are given in a book by Captain Arlington H. Mallery, *Lost America, The Story of Pre-Columbian Iron in America*, (1951). Captain Mallery has found large quantities of iron in iron-smelting furnaces of two types, one he calls Celtic and the other Nordic. More interesting still is the beehive type found in the Allyn mound in Ohio. The beehive type was in common use in Asia and Africa (p. iv). There is some evidence of iron associated with Folsom type points (pp. 175, 214). James V. Howe has also found considerable hand-forged pre-Columbian wrought iron and inscriptions with eastern Mediterranean signs in Virginia. (*Gus of Gisholt*, nos. 36-37, May and June 1952, Published by Gisholt Machine Co., Madison, Wisconsin.)

Other evidences of ancient American iron-working include Foster, *Prehistoric Races*, p. 333; *Kansas City Post*, October 19, 1915; Bradford, *American Antiquities*, p. 431, 1841; W. H. Holmes, *Smithsonian Institution Annual Report*, 1903 (1904), "Traces of Aboriginal Operations in an Iron Mine Near Leslie, Missouri", p. 723; Samuel F. Haven, "Archeology of the United States," *Smithsonian Contributions to Knowledge*, vol. 8 (1956), p. 34; All above sources were also cited in Harris, *The Book of Mormon Message and Evidences* (1961), pp. 85-87.

EVIDENCE NO. 958: METALLURGY IN MESOAMERICA

Claim: The Book of Mormon, first published in 1830, recorded that men living on the American continent in ancient times worked metals such as *iron, copper, brass, steel*, etc. (2 Nephi 5:15; Ether 7:9). Although critics have claimed this was evidence that the Book of Mormon is false, it actually provides additional evidence that the book is true.

Evidence: We now know that the ancient Americans were expert in casting copper, tin, lead, iron and Steel. For example see, Sahagun, *A History of Ancient America*, pp. 190-192; Victor W. Von Hagen, *Realm of the Incas*, (New York, 1957), pp. 29-30, 34; Nadaillac, *Pre-Historic America*, pp. 275-277; Helps, *The Life of Pizarro*, p. 123; Miles Poindexter, *The Ayar Incas*, (New York, 1930), vol. 1, pp. 232, 236-239.

Furthermore, archaeologists have found that ancient American metallurgy utilized such advanced techniques as lost-wax casting, smelting, alloying, forging and gilding similar to those used in the ancient Near East. These similarities provide additional evidence that ancestors of ancient Americans originated in the Near East as recorded in the Book of Mormon. See B. J. Meggers & C. Evans, "The Machalilla Culture: An Early Formative Complex on the Equadorian Coast," *American Antiquity,* (1962) vol. 28, appendix, table 2; S. Linné, "Zapotecan Antiquities," *Ethnog. Mus. Sweden Pub.*, no. 4, (1938), p. 74. Both references are also cited in John L. Sorenson, "The Significance of an Apparent Relationship Between the Ancient Near East and Mesoamerica," SOR-71, *Foundation for Ancient Research and Mormon Studies*, 1971, p. 241.

See also H. Lechtman, "Pre-Columbian Surface Metallurgy," *Scientific American,* vol. 250 (June 1984), p. 56-63, cited in the *F.A.R.M.S. Update* for October 1984, "The 'Golden' Plates"; John L. Sorenson, "A Reconsideration of Early Metal in Mesoamerica," *Katunob*, vol. 9 (March 1976), pp. 1-18, reprinted by F.A.R.M.S. as SOR-82a, and Sorenson, *An Ancient American Setting*, pp. 278-288. Consult also Reed Putnam, "Were the Golden Plates Made of Tumbaga?" *Papers, 15th Annual Symposium on the Archaeology of the Scriptures* (Provo: BYU Extension Publications, 1964): 101-9, available from F.A.R.M.S. as PUT-64.

EVIDENCE NO. 959: IMPLEMENTS OF STEEL IN THE BOOK OF MORMON

Claim: The Book of Mormon mentions that the ancient Americans used implements made of steel (2 Nephi 5:15; Ether 7:9). It further states that steel bows and steel swords were common in Palestine in 600 BC (1 Nephi 4:9; 16:18).

Evidence: Critics have contended that instruments of steel would have been extremely unlikely at that early period of history. However, evidence of the use of steel in ancient America includes: A. Hyatt Verrill, "The Pompeii of Ancient America," in *World's Work*, vol. LIII, #3, p. 286, January 1927. Also Radomir Pleiner "Rediscovering the Techniques of Early Blacksmiths," *Archaeology*, (1963), vol. 16, p. 242, cited in Nibley, *Since Cumorah*, (1988), p. 221-223.

Not only was steel used in Mesoamerica, but it was also used concurrently in the ancient Middle East. Swords of beautifully worked gold and steel have been found in the Mideastern area and have been dated to the Book of Mormon period (around 600 BC).   See G. A. Wainwright, "The Coming of Iron," *Antiquity* (1936), vol. 10, pp. 7-9, 14, 17-18; G. A. Wainwright, "Iron in Egypt," *Journal of Egyptian Archaeology*, p. 3; both cited in Nibley, *Lehi in the Desert and the World of the Jaredites* [1980], p. 107-108).

Those who criticize the Book of Mormon for mentioning the use of steel in ancient times are also criticizing the Bible. Evidence of the use of steel in Biblical times includes, 2 Samuel 22:35; Psalms 18:34; and Job 20:24.

EVIDENCE NO. 960: ZIFF

Claim: The word *Ziff* is mentioned in the Book of Mormon to describe a type of metal used in ancient America (Mosiah 11:3, 8).

Evidence: Remarkably, *Ziff* is a Hebrew word which means *bright*, *shining*, or *plated*, likening it to the metal mentioned in the Book of Mormon. See Sorenson, *An Ancient American Setting for the Book of Mormon* (1985), p. 284. See also R. A. S. Macalister, "The Craftsmen's Guild of the Tribe of Judah," *Palestine Exploration Fund Quarterly* (1905), pp. 333, 328; and K. Sethe in *Zeitschrift für Ägyptische Sprache und Altertumskunde*, vol. 43, (1906), pp. 147, 149; cited in Nibley, *Lehi in the Desert* (1988), p. 32; and *Since Cumorah*, (1988), p. 171.

EVIDENCE NO. 961: THE CUBIT IN ANCIENT AMERICA

Claim: The unit of measure called the cubit in the ancient Near East was also used by the ancient Americans.

Evidence: The following is a quotation from Harris, *Book of Mormon Message and Evidences* (1961), p. 74: "Thomas W. Brookbank has shown that of one hundred twenty-five measurements from Stephen's Incidents of Travel in Central America, Chiapas and Yucatan (1843), 41.5 percent of the definite measurements of buildings given can be expressed in whole cubits, halves or thirds, within an average variation of about a half inch, when the Jewish cubit of 21.888 inches is used, and of these measurements, ninety per cent can be expressed in multiples of five or ten cubits. This is remarkable since the unit of measurement of any people is arbitrary."

Others have come to this same conclusion. For example Joseph E. and David Vincent points out that the basic unit of measure used by the ancient Zapotec architects of Yagul, Oaxaca was about 17 inches long. He notes that all dimensions at the site seemed to be a multiple of 17 inches—usually five.   Knowing the basis for the Near Eastern unit of measure, the cubit, he checked the physical characteristics of the Zapotec descendants, and found that 17 inches is a fairly good average of distance from the tip of the fingers to the elbow of the present-day Zapotec inhabitants. See Joseph E. Vincent, "The Cubit in Ancient America?" *University Archaeological Society Newsletter* 47.2; cited in Christensen, *Progress in Archaeology,* (1963), pp. 112-113.

EVIDENCE NO. 962: TRUE ARCH IN ANCIENT AMERICA

Claim: The use of the true arch by ancient Americans is further evidence of Old and New World contacts in pre-Columbian times.

Evidence: The following is quoted from a *Foundation for Ancient Research and Mormon Studies Update*, entitled "Lost Arts," (July 1985), p. 1:

The true arch is often cited to support the idea that there was no contact between the pre-Columbian Eastern and Western Hemispheres. Professor Linton Satterthwaite had accepted that view, but then found himself having to change: "It has been usual to suppose that the principle of the true arch was unknown to the American Indian, though here and there in some particular structure it has been argued that the principle, though not obvious, was really present." Yet finally, on the basis of field reconnaissance, he was left with "no doubt that the Maya at La Muñeca roofed a long room with the true arch, *and that they knew exactly what they were doing.*" (Linton Satterthwaite's review of Karl Ruppert and John H. Denison, Jr., "Archaeological Reconnaissance in Campeche, Quintana Roo, and Peten," *Carnegie Institution of Washington, DC*, Publication no. 543, [1943]; printed in *American Antiquity* [1944], vol. 10, no. 2, pp. 216-218, Emphasis added. See also H. Befu and G. F. Ekholm, "The True Arch in Pre-Columbian America?" *Current Anthropology,* vol. 5, no. 4, [1964], pp. 328-9.)

Earlier, Alfred Tozzer had reported that at Nakum, Guatemala, "two lateral doorways have what may be truthfully called concrete arches ... the only examples of the true arch which I have met with in Maya buildings." G. Squire had [also] reported an arch of adobe bricks from Pachacamac, Peru, in 1878. There are other examples that are either not complete arches or for which a pre-Columbian date remains in question. But a single good example proves the point without necessarily multiplying cases. (See Alfred Tozzer, *Memoirs, Peabody Museum, Harvard,* [1913], vol. 5, no. 3, p. 167; G. Squier, *Peru: Incidents of Travel,* 2nd edition, p. 70.)

See also Bruce W. Warren, "The True Arch in Ancient America" *University Archaeological Society Newsletter,* vol. 17, p. 2; Quoted in Ross T. Christensen, *Progress in Archaeology* (1963), p. 112.

EVIDENCE NO. 963: CEMENT IN ANCIENT AMERICA

Claim: The Book of Mormon claims that around 46 BC Nephite settlers began migrating from the land of Zarahemla to the north, where they began building cities with cement. "The people who went forth became exceedingly expert in the working of cement; therefore they did build houses of cement, ... both of wood and of cement." See Helaman 3:7-11.

Evidence: This claim has been the object of ridicule by critics of the Book of Mormon. They claim that any mention of cement in ancient American History is an anachronism—allegedly proving the Book of Mormon a hoax. Recent discoveries, however, have vindicated this claim and have provided solid evidence that the Book of Mormon is true. A few references which prove that the ancient Americans did indeed use cement include: Thompson, *People of the Serpent,* pp. 173-174; Gann, *Ancient Cities, Modern Tribes,* p. 114, cited in Nibley, *Since Cumorah* (1988), p. 254.

The following is quoted from a *Foundation for Ancient Research and Mormon Studies Update,* (May 1991), no. 76, p. 2:

Recent research shows that cement was in fact used in Mesoamerica beginning at this time. One of the most notable uses of cement is in the temple complex at Teotihuacán, north of present-day Mexico City. According to David S. Hyman, the use of cement appears suddenly in the archaeological record. Its earliest sample "is a fully developed product." Where it came from remains obscure. The cement floor slabs at this site "were remarkably high in structural quality"; although exposed to the elements for nearly 2000 years, they still "exceed many present-day building code requirements" (David S. Hyman, *A Study of the Calcareous Cements in Prehispanic Mesoamerican Building Construction* [Baltimore: Johns Hopkins University, 1970], pp. ii, 6-7).

After its discovery, cement was used at many sites in the Valley of Mexico and in the Maya regions of southern Mexico, Guatemala, and Honduras. It was used in the construction of buildings at such sites as Cerro de Texcotzingo, Tula, Palenque, Tikal, Copan, Uxmal, and Chichen Itza. Further, the use of cement "is a Maya habit, *absent* from non-Maya examples of corbelled vaulting from the south-eastern United States to southern South America" (George Kubler, *The Art and Architecture of Ancient America,* [Baltimore: Penguin, 1975], p. 201).

Mesoamerican cement was almost exclusively lime cement. The limestone was purified on a "cylindrical pile of timber, which requires a vast amount of labor to cut and considerable skill to construct in such a way that combustion of the stone and wood is complete and a minimum of impurities remain in the product." The fact that very little carbon is found in this cement "attests to the ability of these ancient peoples." (See Tatiana Proskouriakoff, *An Album of Maya Architecture,* [Norman: University of Oklahoma Press, 1963], p. xv; Hyman, *Calcareous Cement,* [1970], pp. 6-5.)

John Sorenson further noted the expert sophistication in the use of cement at El Tajin, east of Mexico City, after Book of Mormon times. Cement roofs covered areas of 75 square meters! "Sometimes the builders filled a room with stones and mud, smoothed the surface on top to receive the concrete, then removed the interior fill when the [slab] on top had dried" (John Sorenson, "Digging Into the Book of Mormon," *Ensign*, [October 1984], p. 18).

The presence of expert cement technology in prehispanic Mesoamerica is a remarkable archaeological fact. Cement first appears in Mesoamerican architecture very close to the time when the Book of Mormon says this development occurred. It is also a significant factor in locating the Book of Mormon lands of Zarahemla and Desolation, for Zarahemla must be south of areas where cement was used as early as the middle of the first century BC. Until samples of cement are found outside of the southwest areas of North America, one may reasonably assume that the Book of Mormon lands were not far to the south of these sites where early cement is found.

See also Matthew G. Wells and John W. Welch, "Concrete Evidence for the Book of Mormon," *Re-exploring the Book of Mormon*, edited by John W. Welch, [1992], pp. 212-213.

EVIDENCE NO. 964: GREAT HIGHWAYS

Claim: The Book of Mormon records that the ancient Americans had great *highways* (Helaman 7:10; 14:24; 3 Nephi 6:7-8; 8:13). The stone highways found in Central and South America equaled or surpassed the ancient Roman highways.

Evidence: Before the publication of the Book of Mormon no paved highways had been discovered in any of the native American lands—only dirt trails. Furthermore, it was considered fantastic to suggest that the ancient Americans even had the technology to build elaborate highways. Once again, the critics ridiculed and dismissed the Book of Mormon as false. Yet in recent times, overwhelming evidence has been uncovered that the ancient Americans did indeed build great highways—vindicating the Book of Mormon, and Joseph Smith as a true prophet of God. See Thompson, *People of the Serpent*, pp. 173-174; Gann, *Ancient Cities and Modern Tribes*, p. 114; Nadaillac, *Pre-Historic America*, pp. 275-277; William Prescott, in *History of the Conquest of Peru* (New York: A. L. Burt Publishers, 1928), pp. 478-479, cites a Spanish explorer whose descriptions were originally published in *Relación de Sarmiento*. Cortez is quoted in Constance Irwin's *Fair Gods and Stone Faces* (New York: St. Martin's Press, 1963), p. 7. Victor Wolfgang Von Hagen quotes Pedro Cieza de Leon in *Highway of the Sun* (New York: Duell, Sloan, Pierce, 1955), pp. 3-7.

EVIDENCE NO. 965: THE WHEEL IN ANCIENT AMERICA

Claim: The Book of Mormon mentions the use of chariots in ancient America (see Alma 18:9-12; 3 Nephi 3:22). This claim implies the use of wheels, yet there was no indication in Joseph Smith's day that the Mesoamericans had any knowledge of the wheel prior to making contact with the Western World.

Evidence: Until recent years, critics have insisted that the ancient Americans did not use the wheel. However, once again, what was once considered by a few skeptics to be a flaw in the Book of Mormon became another proof of its authenticity, when conclusive evidence was found that the wheel was indeed used throughout Mesoamerica. Franklin S. Harris, Jr. writes the following about the discoveries of the wheel in ancient America in his work, *The Book of Mormon Messages and Evidences*, (1961), pp. 93-94:

The knowledge of the wheel in Ancient America has been almost uniformly doubted until very recently. Désiré Charney[1] found some wheeled toys, but this discovery was almost ignored by scholars. There have been several sets of these wheeled toys, usually animals, found by different archaeologists in the last few years at various places in Mexico. [See Figure 39 below.] One of them had hollow tubes for the axles to run through with the tops of the holes worn smooth from the axles rubbing against the sides. Gordon E. Elkholm[2] concludes in his article, "Wheeled Toys In Mexico," "The evidence reviewed so far seems to me to indicate fairly conclusively that miniature wheeled vehicles were made, and there was therefore some knowledge of the principle of the wheel, in pre-Conquest Mexico."

In 1946 a group of six outstanding American scholars contributed a discussion with many pictures[3] under the heading, "Did the Middle-American Natives Know the Wheel?" Alfonso Caso concluded: "In summary, at the present it appears that there is sufficient evidence to confirm that at least the Indians of Mexico and perhaps also of Central America knew and used the wheel for small animals which may have had a special significance, or simply may have been used as toys."

Time Magazine (October 7, 1946, p. 68) tells of the work of the Smithsonian Institution in the state of Vera Cruz, Mexico: "Other clay figures showed animals mounted on wheels. This discovery thrilled archaeologists. They had thought the wheel, basic device of mechanical civilization, was unknown in the New World. But the La Ventas had wheels some two thousand years ago, or had seen representations of them. How they learned about wheels, and why their knowledge died with them, remains a mystery."

Figure 39. Wheeled Toys from Ancient Mexico. See Thomas Stuart Ferguson, *One Fold and One Shepherd,* (San Francisco, California: Books of California, 1958), pp. 103, 104.

For more information see Paul R. Cheesman, "The Wheel in Ancient America," *BYU Studies*, (Winter 1969), vol. 9, no. 2, pp. 185-197; Professor Clyde Kluckholm, *Saturday Review*, (September 22, 1956); Andre Vigneau, *Encyclopedia Photographic de l'Art*, (Paris), vol. 11.

[1.] Désiré Charney, *Ancient Civilizations of the New World* (1887) p. 175.

[2.] Gordon E. Elkholm, "Wheeled Toys In Mexico," *American Antiquity*, (1946), vol. 11, p. 222. See also pictures in Matthew Stirling, *National Geographic Magazine*, (September 1940), vol. 78, p. 314.

[3.] Alfonso Caso, "Did the Middle-American Natives Know the Wheel?" *Cuadernos Americanos*, (Mexico City: Imprenta Mundial, January-February 1946), vol. 25, p. 193; see also the illustrated article by Thomas S. Ferguson, "The Wheel in Ancient America," *Improvement Era*, (1946), vol. 49, p. 785 and *Science News Letter,* (January 3, 1948), vol. 53, p. 71. These wheeled toys are also found in the Middle East: *Science News Letter*, (December 17, 1949), p. 394; E. A. Speiser, *Excavations at Tope Gawra*, vol. 1, pp. 68–69, plate XXXV, a.1.

EVIDENCE NO. 966: THE POTTER'S WHEEL USED IN ANCIENT AMERICA

Claim: Though not specifically mentioned in the Book of Mormon, the discovery that ancient Americans used the potter's wheel is evidence that the Mesoamericans migrated from the Old World. (Potter's *clay* is mentioned in 2 Nephi 27:27, but does not presuppose the use of the wheel in working the clay.)

Evidence: The following is quoted from a *Foundation for Ancient Research and Mormon Studies Update*, entitled "Lost Arts," (July 1985), p. 1:

> The potter's wheel is another feature long supposed to have been entirely absent from the New World. That notion too has now had to change. Samuel Lothrop reported decades ago seeing in an archaeological context in Peru what "seemed to be" just such a device. In the early seventies, Terence Grieder settled the matter. In the grave of a high status woman near the Peruvian site of Pashash, he found scores of wheel-turned hemispherical ceramic cups. These offerings accompanied the burial of an aristocratic woman (although cups of the same shape in commoner's graves showed no evidence of being done on the wheel). Furthermore, the grave offerings showed 15 stone cups evidently turned on a "lathe," perhaps consisting of a wooden shaft to which a flywheel was attached to be set in motion by pulling a cord wrapped around it. Evidence of these wheeled devices for clay and stone processing lasted a maximum of 200 years, then totally disappeared. (Samuel Lothrop, "¿Conocieron la Rueda los Indigenas Mesoamericanos?" ["Did Indigenous Mesoamericans Know About the Wheel?"] *Cuadernos Americanos*, [1946], vol. 25, no. 1, p. 201; Terence Grieder, *Archaeology*, [1975], vol. 28, pp. 178-185; "Lost Wheels," *Scientific American*, [October 1975], p. 54).

EVIDENCE NO. 967: THE CONCEPT OF ZERO

Claim: Development of the mathematical concept of *zero* is historically attributed to the Arabs. However, recent discoveries have shown that the concept was also known in ancient America—giving evidence to the Book of Mormon claim of ancient American roots in Palestine.

Evidence: A paper by John L. Sorenson compares the ancient American *zero* concepts, with those of the Old World. In both worlds the zero was not only a representation of the lack of quantity but also as a placeholder for large numbers. (See A. L. Kroeber, *Anthropology*, [New York, 1948], pp. 468-472; and O. Neugebauer, *The Exact Sciences In Antiquity*, [Copenhagen, 1951] pp. 18, 20, 26, 140-146. Both sources are cited in John L. Sorenson, "The Significance of an Apparent Relationship Between the Ancient Near East and Mesoamerica," SOR-71, *Foundation for Ancient Research and Mormon Studies*, 1971, p. 228-229.)

While the *zero* concept may seem trivial to the casual reader, it is actually one of the most significant developments in the history of mathematics—making possible calculations which had previously been impossible, and leading to the development of all the higher branches of mathematics. (See Article entitled "Zero" in *The World Book Encyclopedia*, [Chicago: Field Enterprises, 1992] vol. 21, p. 606.)

EVIDENCE NO. 968: ASTRONOMY IN ANCIENT AMERICA

Claim: The Book of Mormon infers that the ancient Americans were skilled in astronomy (2 Nephi 23:10; Alma 30:44; Helaman 12:14-15).

Evidence: Many critics of the Book of Mormon have assumed that the American Indians were ignorant savages who had no knowledge of astronomy and navigation. Some of them have used this assumption to assert that Joseph Smith was a false prophet. However, it has now been confirmed that the ancient Americans were familiar with the fixed positions and movements of heavenly bodies. (See Bradford, "Conclusions," *American Antiquities*, p. 431, 1841. See also Sahagun, *Libro Noveno Capitulo*, 29, Sec. 1, Vol. 2, pp. 276, 268-269, 280-281; cited in Hunter and Ferguson, *Ancient America and the Book of Mormon*, [1950], p. 291.)

Astronomy was actually well developed and stellar symbolism was rich in Mesoamerica. Lionel Casson writes that the Maya's "great genius was astronomy. As astronomers ... the Maya understood the movements of the moon, the sun, Venus, and possible other planets ... they accurately calculated the length of the solar year... Their calendar reached millions of years into the past encompassing more than one creation." (See Lionel Casson, et. al., *Mysteries of the Past,* edited by Joseph J. Thorndike, Jr., [American Heritage Publishing Co., 1977], p. 295. See also Sylvanus G. Morley, *The Ancient Maya,* [Stanford: Stanford University Press, 1947], pp. 304-311; and A. M. Tozzer, editor, "Landa's Relación de las Cosas de Yucatan. A Translation," *Harvard University, Peabody Museum of American Archaeology and Ethnology,* papers, vol. 18, [Cambridge: Peabody Museum, 1941], pp. 132-138. Both cited in Sorenson, "The Book of Mormon as a Mesoamerican Codex," *Foundation for Ancient Research and Mormon Studies* [1976], p. 5.)

Once again, the critic who condemned Joseph Smith from his pulpit and/or his writings on this particular issue has turned out to be the charlatan—not Joseph Smith. One by one their cries fade out as they become aware of the mounting evidences in favor of the Book of Mormon.

EVIDENCE NO. 969: ASTRONOMICAL CALENDAR OF 365 DAYS

Claim: The Book of Mormon describes the ancient Americans as having a profound and accurate knowledge of astronomy and being a highly cultured people (2 Nephi 23:10; Alma 30:44; Helaman 12:14-15). Since the Book of Mormon was first published, solid evidence has been discovered (such as the ancient American calendar of 365 days) that proves these otherwise improbable claims.

Furthermore, certain aspects of astronomical calendars in ancient America were similar to those in the ancient Near East. This similarity helps prove that ancestors of ancient Americans migrated from Jerusalem as recorded in the Book of Mormon.

Evidence: The following is from J. M. Sjodahl, *An Introduction to the Study of the Book of Mormon*, p. 345:

> They had also a solar year. This was called *Haab.* This year consisted of 365 days, divided into 18 *uinals,* or months, of 20 days each, with the addition of an extra 5 days at the end of the year...By an ingenious combination of the *tonalamatl* and the *haab* the Mayas obtained a cycle of 18,980 days, or 52 solar years, which have been called the "calendar round" for want of a better name. By calculation it was found that the precise order of the 260 days of the *tonalamatl,* with reference to the 365 positions each could occupy in the *haab,* repeated itself in 52 years, as the order of our weekdays does in seven years. By fixing an "initial date" which they called *4 ahau 8 cumhu,* and by dividing time into *kins, uinals, tuns, katuns, cycles, great cycles,*[1] etc., they could fix any date within a period of 374,000 years. (See Dr. Sylvanus Grisvold Morley, "Introduction to the Study of the Maya Hieroglyphics," *Smithsonian Institution, Bulletin 57,* p. 58.)

Lord Kingsborough noted that the Mesoamericans reckoned 365 days to the year, but did not add what is termed the intercalary day every four years, to make what we call leap year. Instead they added thirteen days once every fifty-two years, which exactly made one day for every four years. This shows that they had a very good idea of the length of the year. (See Lord Kingsborough, *Antiquities of Mexico,* [London: Henry G. Bohn 1848]; cited in *Journal of Discourses,* vol. 15, pp. 260-261, Orson Pratt, December 29, 1872.) See also *Man Across the Sea, Problems of Pre-Columbian Contacts,* edited by Riley et al, (Austin & London: University of Texas Press, 1971), p. 228; S. G. Morley, *The Ancient Maya* (Stanford: Stanford University Press, 1947), pp. 265-295, cited in Sorenson, "The Book of Mormon as a Mesoamerican Codex," *Newsletter and Proceedings of the S.E.H.A.* (Provo, UT: Brigham Young University, The Society for Early Historic Archaeology), December 1976, No. 139, p. 5. Reprinted by *the Foundation for Ancient Research and Mormon Studies,* Reprint SOR-76.

Sorenson also points out that the Maya calendar used a very accurate method for calculating very long periods of time by *tuns*, the 360, rather than 365-day unit. Similarly in the Near East, the Egyptian "year" consisted of 360 days plus 5 epagomenal days. (See James Breasted, *A History of Egypt*, [New York, 1909], pp. 32-33; Margret Bunson, *Encyclopedia of Ancient Egypt*, [New York, 1991], p. 50.)

John L. Sorenson has shown that both Mesoamerica and the Near East had highly developed astronomically "articulated lunar, solar and stellar calendars" that were quite similar in their various features. His findings are summarized in the table below, and are quoted from his paper entitled "The Significance of an Apparent Relationship Between the Ancient Near East and Mesoamerica," SOR-71, *Foundation for Ancient Research and Mormon Studies*, (1971), p. 228-229:

Documentation

Features	Mesoamerica	Near East
360-day calendar plus 5 extra	Morley, 1947	Breasted, 1909;
Cycle of 7 days	Thompson, 1954, p. 144	
Day measured from sunset to sunset	Dow, 1967	Finegan, 1964; Gen. 1:5
Observatories, eclipse records non-permutating eras and year counts	Kroeber, 1952; Hews, 1961	Kroeber, 1952; Hews, 1961
Day names with associations like Eurasian constellations,[2] ordered like alphabet order, and lunar houses; similar names and associations in sequence.[3]	Kelley, 1960	Kelley, 1960

---

[1] The day was called *kin*. 20 kins was a *uinal*; 18 uinals, a *tun*; 20 tuns, a *katun*; 20 katuns, a *cycle*; 20 cycles, a *great cycle*. The cycle, then, was equal to 144,000 days, and the great cycle to 2,880,000 days.

[2] Kelley shows that half the names and animals of Aztec days recur in Eurasia in correct sequence as the same or related animals in the constellation list.

[3] Kelley also shows that the Maya day name *manik*, represented by a hand glyph, probably pronounced *ka*, corresponding in sequence in Hebrew letter *k*, probably representing the hand, pronounced *kaph*. (Compare Hebrew *kaph* "hand," with Yucatec *kab* "hand," or Mam *kop* "hand.") Following letter of the alphabet is Hebrew *lamed*; compare with next Yucatec Maya day name *lamat* (or Greek *lambda*; compare with Tzental-Zotzil *lambat*). Next is day-name *mulu(c)*, which is ruled by shark and has the Aztec equivalent "water." Greek *mu* (from Assyrian *mu*, "water?"), or Hebrew *mem*, is next in alphabet sequence. "I suggest the possibility that the Hebrew second month, *Ziv*, may relate to the third of the Yucatec Maya list, *Zip*."

S. G. Morley, *The Ancient Maya* (Stanford: Stanford University Press, 1947), pp. 265-295.

J. Breasted, *A History of Egypt*, (New York, 1909) pp. 32-33.

J. E. S. Thompson, The Rise and Fall of Maya Civilization, (Norman, Oklahoma, 1954), p. 144.

J. W. Dow, "Astronomical Orientations at Teotihuacán: A Case Study in Astroarchaeology," American Antiquity, (1967) vol. 32, pp. 326-334.

J. Finegan, *Handbook of Biblical Chronology, Principles of Time Reckoning in the Ancient World and Problems of chronology in the Bible*, (Princeton, New Jersey, 1964).

A. L Kroeber, "The Ancient Oikoumene as a Historical Culture Aggregate," *The Nature of Culture,* (Chicago: 1952), pp. 389-390.

G. W. Hewes, "The Ecume as a Civilizational Multiplier System," *Kroeber Anthropological Society Papers,* (1961), no. 25, pp. 73-109.

D. Kelley, "Calendar Animals and Deities," *Southwest Journal of Anthropology*, vol. 16, pp. 317-337.

EVIDENCE NO. 970: SHIPBUILDING IN ANCIENT AMERICA

<u>Claim</u>: The Book of Mormon records that ancient Americans were capable of constructing and sailing large ships, and were accomplished maritime traders (Alma 63:5-8).

<u>Evidence</u>: Again, critics are quick to mock the idea that Mesoamericans could have been so advanced. However, Columbus reported seeing a ship of considerable size, capable of carrying scores of people for days at a time, off the coast of the Yucatan Peninsula. (See Albert Collier, *The American Mediterranean, Handbook of Middle American Indians,* edited by Robert Wauchope, [Austin: University of Texas Press, 1964] pp. 128-129, cited in Sorenson, *An Ancient American Setting for the Book of Mormon,* [1985] p. 268.

EVIDENCE NO. 971: JAREDITE "SUBMARINES"

<u>Claim</u>: The Book of Mormon describes the strange ships that were used by the Jaredites as "tight like unto the ark of Noah" so that if they were submerged at times, they would not sink. The record says, "they were many times buried in the depths of the sea, because of the mountain waves which broke upon them..." (Ether 6:6-7).

<u>Evidence</u>: Critics have always ridiculed the idea that ancient people could have constructed such advanced sea vessels. However, the oldest Sumerian accounts of Noah's ark, describe it as a "magur boat," which was completely covered by the waters from time to time. (See H. V. Hilprecht, *The Earliest Version of the Babylonian Deluge Story and the Temple Library of Nippur; The Babylonian Expedition of the University of Pennsylvania*, [Philadelphia: University of Philadelphia, 1910] vol. 5, Fasc. i, pp. 51-56.)

Dr. Nibley makes the following comparison between the Jaredite vessels and the Sumerian account of Noah's ark in his Book *Approach to the Book of Mormon,* (1988) pp. 343-348:

What we wish to point out here is that there are various versions of the Flood story floating about, all of which tell some of the story, none of which tell all of it. The most ancient of these versions substantiates the Bible account to a remarkable degree. Let us place these side by side with Ether's description of the Jaredite ships, matching some twelve peculiarities of the latter with the same peculiarities of the magur-boat which was the ark of *Utnapishtim,* that being the Babylonian name for Noah:

Jaredite Vessels	**Noah's *Magur* Boat**
1. They were built "after the manner of barges which ye have hitherto built" (Ether 2:16). That is, except in some particulars, these boats were not a new design but followed an established and familiar pattern—there really were such boats.	"This class of boats [writes Hilprecht], according to the Nippur version [the oldest], [were] in use before the Deluge." In historic times the type still survived but only in archaic vessels used in ritual, the gods "in their boats ... visiting each other in their temples during certain festivals ... the Babylonian canals, serving as means of communication for the magur-boats. ... [Billerbeck and Delitzsch] show that a certain class of boats really had such a shape." All the main features of the prehistoric ritual divine magur-boat seem to have survived even to the present time in some of the huge river craft still found on the streams of southeast Asia—veritable arks built in the shape of Jared's barges.
2. They were built "according to the instructions of the Lord" (Ether 2:16).	"In all three versions of the Deluge story Utnapishtim receives special instructions concerning the construction of the roof or deck of the boat." Oddly enough he received instructions by conversing with *Anu,* the Lord of Heaven, through a screen or partition of matting, a *kikkisu,* such as was ritually used in the temple. In the Sumerian version God announces the Flood thus: "By the wall at my left side stand, by the wall a word will I speak to thee. ... My pure one, my wise one, by our hand a deluge [shall be caused], the seed of mankind to destroy."

Jaredite Vessels

3. "They were exceedingly tight, even that they would hold water like unto a dish; and the bottom thereof was tight like unto a dish; and the sides thereof were tight like unto a dish" (Ether 2:17)

4. "And the ends thereof were peaked" (Ether 2:17).

5. "And the top thereof was tight like unto a dish" (Ether 2:17).

6. "And the length thereof was the length of a tree" (Ether 2:17). "And they were small, and they were light upon the water, even like unto the lightness of fowl upon the water" (Ether 2:16).

7. "And the door thereof, when it was shut, was tight like unto a dish" (Ether 2:17)

8. "And the Lord said ... thou shalt make a hole in the top, and also in the bottom; and when thou shalt suffer for air thou shalt unstop the hole and receive air. And if it be so that the water come in upon thee, behold, ye shall stop the hole, that ye may not perish in the flood" (Ether 2:20).

9. "Ye shall be as a whale in the midst of the sea; for the mountain waves shall dash upon you" (Ether 2:24).

Noah's *Magur* Boat

There was in the ship "of course a solid lower part, strong enough to carry a heavy freight and to resist the force of the waves and the storm."

"Jensen explains MA-TU as a 'deluge boat,' ... adding, that when seen from the side it probably resembled the crescent moon. ... Moreover, the representations of the sea-going vessels of the *Tyrians* and the *Sidonians* ... show that a certain class of boats really had such a shape."

"The principal distinguishing feature of a magur-boat [was] ... the roof or deck of the boat. ... We notice that in the Biblical as in the Babylonian Version great stress is laid on the preparation of a proper 'roof' or 'cover.' ... 'Cover it with a strong deck' [Nippur Version, line 9] ' ... with a deck as strong as the earth,' or 'let its deck be strong like the vault of heaven above.' " (Second Nineveh Version, lines 2-3) It is quite plain from the emphasis on tightness in Ether that the ordinary vessel was not nearly so closely or firmly constructed.

The lines containing "a brief statement concerning the measures of the ark" have been effaced in the Nippur version. The first Nineveh text says simply: "Its measures be in proportion, its width and length shall correspond." Since only one ark was built, as against eight Jaredite vessels, one would hardly expect the dimensions to be the same.

"Furthermore in the First Nineveh Version the boat ... has a door to be shut during the storm flood." The various names for the boat "designate 'a boat which can be closed by a door,' that is, practically a 'house boat,' expressed in the Hebrew story by an Egyptian loanword, *Tevah*, 'ark' originally meaning 'box, chest, coffin,' an essential part of which is its 'cover' or 'lid.' "

"The boat has ... a door to be shut during the storm flood and at least one 'air-hole' or 'window' (Nappashu, line 136)." The word *nappashu*, meaning "breather" or "ventilator," designates no ordinary window.

"The vessel built by Utnapishtim being such a 'house boat' or magur, this word could subsequently also be rendered ideographically by MA-TU, a 'deluge boat.' ... A magur-boat, then is a 'house boat' in which gods, men and beasts can live comfortably, fully protected against the waves washing overboard, the drenching rain from above and against the inclemencies of wind and weather." The fact that the magur-boat was built to be completely submerged gives strong support to our preceding point.

Jaredite Vessels	Noah's *Magur* Boat
10. "Their flocks and herds, and whatsoever beast or animal or fowl that they should carry with them ... got aboard of their vessels or barges" (Ether 6:4).	In a magur-boat "men and beasts live comfortably." In the second Nineveh version Utnapishtim is to take "domestic animals of the field, with wild beasts of the field, as many as eat grass." The Nippur version mentions "the beasts of the field, the birds of heaven." C. S. Coon, writing of the earliest water transportation known, says, "Dogs howled, pigs grunted, and cocks crowed on these sea-going barn-yards." The idea that the oldest sailing vessels might have been built for the specific purpose of transporting men and animals together, often for vast distances, may strike the reader as strange at first, yet there is ample evidence to show that such was the case. The Asiatic river boats mentioned in point no. 1 above keep whole households afloat for months with their animals and poultry—an idea which, like the riding of buffaloes, seems utterly incomprehensible to the Western mind.
11. "The Lord ... caused that there should be a furious wind blow upon the face of the waters, ... they were tossed upon the waves of the sea before the wind" (Ether 6:5). "The wind did never cease to blow ... and thus they were driven ... before the wind" (Ether 6:8).	"The Storm-winds with exceeding terror, all of them together raced along the deluge, the mighty tempest (?) raged with them ... and the mighty ship over the great waters the storm-wind had tossed." Thus the Sumerian version. "Jensen explains MA-TU as a 'deluge-boat,' seeing in it 'a boat driven by the wind,' 'A sailing vessel' ... [But] a magur-boat was written ideographically MA-TU, literally 'a deluge boat,' not because it was a sailing boat driven by the wind or rather hurricane (*abubu, shubtu*), but because it possessed certain qualities which rendered its use especially effective during the deluge, when its exclusive purpose was to carry the remains of life and to protect men and beasts against the waters from below and the pouring rain from above." Though driven by the storm it had "nothing in common with a boat in full sail, (and) nowhere ... is a sail mentioned, nor would it have been of much use in such a hurricane as described. ... Besides, we observe that the pictures of the *Tyrian* boats referred to have no sails." A magur-boat was driven by the wind, but not with sails.
12. "They were many times buried in the depths of the sea" (Ether 6:6). "When they were buried in the deep there was no water that could hurt them, their vessels being tight like unto a dish, and also they were tight like unto the ark of Noah" (Ether 6:7). "And no monster of the sea could break them, neither whale that could mar them" (Ether 6:10).	"It shall be a house-boat carrying what is saved of life," says the Nippur version, its purpose being to preserve life and offer full protection "against the waves washing overboard."

10.   Warfare in the Book of Mormon

EVIDENCE NO. 972: THE GARRISON OF FIFTY

Claim: The Book of Mormon speaks of a military leader from Jerusalem who had an army of 50 as well as tens of thousands (1 Nephi 3:31; 4:1). Critics have often declared this to be a contradiction, when in fact it is another evidence that the Book of Mormon is an authentic history of ancient peoples who originated in the Near East.

Evidence: It was typical of the Mid-Eastern generals to conquer or defend with tens of thousands and to leave a small permanent garrison of around 50 men in each city. Dr. Hugh Nibley writes the following in his work, *Lehi in the Desert* (1988), pp. 97-98:

> As to the garrison of fifty, it seems pitifully small for a great city. It would have been just as easy for the author of 1 Nephi to have said "fifty thousand," and made it really impressive. Yet even the older brothers, though they wish to emphasize Laban's great power, mention only fifty (1 Nephi 3:31), and it is Nephi in answering them who says that the Lord is "mightier than Laban and his fifty," and adds, "or even than his tens of thousands" (1 Nephi 4:1). As a high military commander Laban would have his tens of thousands in the field, but such an array is of no concern to Laman and Lemuel: it is the "fifty" they must look out for, the regular, permanent garrison of Jerusalem. The number fifty suits perfectly with the Amarna picture where the military forces are always so surprisingly small and a garrison of thirty to eighty men is thought adequate even for big cities. It is strikingly vindicated in a letter of Nebuchadnezzar, Lehi's contemporary, wherein the great king orders: "As to the fifties who were under your orders, those gone to the rear, or fugitives return them to the ranks." Commenting on this, Offord says, "In these days it is interesting to note the indication here, that in the Babylonian army a platoon contained fifty men;" (Joseph Offord, "Archaeological Notes on Jewish Antiquities," *Palestinian Exploration Fund Quarterly*, [1916], p. 148).

EVIDENCE NO. 973: ARMIES OF TEN THOUSAND

Claim: The Book of Mormon records that the Nephite armies were divided into detachments of ten thousand with a captain over each detachment. (See Alma 56:28; Mormon 6:10-15.)

Evidence: It has been found that this type of military structuring was the standard among the people of ancient America. This is precisely the arrangement that Cortez described in Mexico. He found himself opposed by an army with each section of *ten thousand under a chief*. The Tlaxcalans, "were deployed in the battle field by *ten thousand*, each such unit headed by its *captain with his ten thousand*." And in ancient Mexico, "The chief of the warrior class was the Hunpictok; he was the *chief of ten thousand* lances." (See Landa, *Relación de las Cosas de Yucatan*, pp. 32, 35, 121; Bernal Diaz del Castillo, *True History of the Conquest of Mexico* [1927], p. 426. Both above sources cited in Harris, *Book of Mormon Message and Evidence* [1961], pp. 95-96; *Bernal Diaz Chronicles*, [1956],, pp. 105-106 and *México a Traves de los Siglos*, [Mexico City: Editorial Cumbre, 1979], vol. 1, p. 201; cited in Jerry L. Ainsworth, *The Lives and Travels of Mormon and Moroni*, [2000], p. 181.)

EVIDENCE NO. 974: THE OLD TESTAMENT PERSPECTIVE ON WAR

<u>Claim</u>: Critics have often questioned why the Book of Mormon, which purports to be the word of God, would contain so many details on the warfare of the ancient inhabitants of America. "Does not the *God of Love* abhor war," they ask? While it is true that war is always tragic and hideous, nevertheless, there are times when God has used wars to accomplish His purposes, and the fact that warfare is so prevalent in the Book of Mormon is yet another evidence of its authenticity as a book of sacred scripture.

<u>Evidence</u>: The fact that the modern prophet Joseph Smith wrote of warfare in the perspective of the Biblical culture helps to ensure his role as a translator, not the author, of the Book of Mormon. To the ancient Middle Eastern mind, war was a part of the whole religious philosophy. Indeed, those who criticize this perspective are unwittingly criticizing the Biblical concept of God and his chosen people.

For example, the God of the Bible is sometimes portrayed as a war god who taught his people to fight (Exodus 15:3; 17:16; Numbers 21:14; Deuteronomy 32:26; Joshua 10:13-14; 1 Samuel 17:45; Psalms 18:34). He was known by military titles (Joshua 5:14; 2 Chronicles 13:12). As a sky god he would shoot down lightning like arrows from heaven (Psalms 18:13-14), or cast down stones upon the enemies of Israel (Joshua 10:11). He is portrayed as a tribal god (Exodus 23:22; Joshua 11:20), or a territorial god, who could be approached only by those who worshipped from within the boundaries of his conquered lands (2 Kings 5:17; Jeremiah 16:13; Psalms 137:4).

The Bible prophets refer to God as the "Most High God" (Genesis 14:19) or "the Highest" (Luke 1:32, 35, 76; 6:35) implying the existence of other competing gods (Daniel 11:36). This naturally led to a belief in a literal *war in heaven* (Revelation 12:7). Indeed, *Israel,* the name of God's chosen people, denotes combat, conflict and conquest: *One who prevails with God,* a name-title which originated at Peniel, where Jacob fought with the Lord (Genesis 32:28-30).

The Children of Israel were part of a culture that worshipped a warrior-God, whose chosen people were given a divine mandate to wage war on the peoples occupying the lands promised to them by the Lord. Such were often wars of extermination where women, children and the aged were slaughtered along with the enemy warriors. See Genesis 7:4, 23; 18:13; 19:24-25; Exodus 17:16; 22:20; 32:27-29; Deuteronomy 2:24-36; 3:1-6; 7:2-16; 20:10-7; Numbers 6:2, 21; 8:18-26; 10:8-41; 25:6-15; 31:7-18; Joshua 15:1 -9, 33; 19:15-17; Judges 11:32; 2 Kings 2:23-41; 10:1-30; Psalms 144:1; Isaiah 13:18 and Ezekiel 9:4-7.

Though war occupies a substantial portion of the Book of Mormon, as well as the Bible, there are significant differences between the two. While the Bible seemingly glorifies the slaughter of innocent children (Psalms 137:9), the Book of Mormon justifies the tragedy of war **only** as a means of defense (Alma 43:45-47; 46:12-21).

EVIDENCE NO. 975: POLITICAL & RELIGIOUS LEADERS IN BATTLE

<u>Claim</u>: Some skeptics, in their attempts to disprove the Book of Mormon, have criticized the irony of prophets of God participating and even leading their people into battle (Alma 2:29; 46:12-21; Mormon 2:1-2). These critics demonstrate their lack of understanding the Bible, and unknowingly condemn it, since both books of sacred scripture were written in part by prophet-generals. Such criticisms lead the serious investigator to the conclusion that each book supports the other.

<u>Evidence</u>: Just as the Book of Mormon tells of such prophets as Alma, Mormon and Moroni leading their people into battle, so does the Bible tell of the military campaigns of such prophets as Abraham, Moses, Joshua and David (Genesis 14:14-16; Exodus 17:9-16; 1 Samuel 23:4-5).[1]

The Book of Mormon accounts of political and religious leaders fighting battles and leading armies are also consistent with Mayan tradition. The following is quoted from John A. Tvedtnes, "Book of Mormon Tribal Affiliation and Military Caste," TVE-89, *Foundation for Ancient Research and Mormon Studies*, 1989, p. 121:

Typically, Mesoamerican peoples had six basic classes or occupations: peasants, merchants, warriors, priests, judges, and government officials. Among the Aztecs, all of these were directly involved in war. For example, the merchants formed, when necessary, their own military units. Warriors and priests replenished the ranks of the judges and other government officials and most priests began their service for a time in special military units. (Victor W. Von Hagen, *The Aztec: Man and Tribe* [New York: Mentor, 1962], pp. 48, 170, and *World of the Maya* [New York: Mentor, 1963], p. 117.)

… There was also a war captain (*nacom*) who was elected for three years, but during all-out war, the *batab* was expected to lead the army (Von Hagen, *World of the Maya*, p. 117).

It was Nephi who had taken the rather special sword from Laban in Jerusalem (1 Nephi 4:9). Using it as a pattern, he made other swords (2 Nephi 5:14) and personally wielded the sword of Laban in the defense of his people (Jacob 1:10). In this, he appears to have been following the ancient Near Eastern practice of the king being commander of the army.[2] Jarom noted that the Nephite kings led their people in battle (Jarom 1:7, 14).

[1.] To those who would say that Nathan was the prophet in David's time—not David, it should be remembered that Peter refers to David as a prophet in Acts 2:29-30. Indeed, he wrote many of the scriptures in Psalms.

[2.] Saul, Israel's first universally-acknowledged king, is called, in the earlier parts of Samuel, by the term *nagid*, "commander" (KJV "captain"), indicating his role as leader of the army (1 Samuel 10:1; 1 Samuel 11). David's troubles began when he neglected to personally lead the army of Israel in battle (2 Samuel 1:1). From Egyptian, Assyrian and Babylonian records, we learn that it was typical for kings to accompany their armies into the field.

EVIDENCE NO. 976: MILITARY LEADERS IN RITUAL COMBAT

Claim: One of many authentic details in the Book of Mormon is the face-to-face combat between Alma and Amlici (Alma 2:29).

Evidence: In ancient times a military leader was expected to directly confront the enemy's leader in battle. The reasons for this custom frequently resulted from the animosity between leaders of differing territories. See Hans Van Wees, "Kings in Combat: Battles and Heroes in the Iliad," *Classical Quarterly*, (1988), vol. 38, pp. 1-24; and Robert O'connell, *Of Arms and Men: A History of War Weapons and Aggression*, (Oxford University Press, 1989), pp. 25, 46-50; both cited in David B. Honey, "Paradigms and Pitfalls of Approach to Warfare in the Book of Mormon," *Review of Books on the Book of Mormon*, (1991), vol. 3, pp. 118-140, which is a review *Warfare in the Book of Mormon*, edited by Stephen D. Ricks and William J. Hamblin (1990).

EVIDENCE NO. 977: TRIBAL AND MILITARY STRUCTURE

Claim: Similarities in tribal structure and customs between the Near East and ancient America, as recorded in the Book of Mormon, are further evidence of the authenticity of that sacred record.

Evidence: The following is quoted from John A. Tvedtnes, "Book of Mormon Tribal Affiliation and Military Caste," TVE-89, *Foundation for Ancient Research and Mormon Studies*, (1989), pp. 1-15:

In ancient Israel, tribal affiliation generally determined one's political loyalties to one or another of the two kingdoms, which dominated the land of Israel during much of its history as known from the Bible. Thus, for example, the tribes of Judah, Benjamin, Simeon and, to a large extent, Levi, comprised the

Kingdom of Judah. The other tribes comprised the Kingdom of Israel. In the Book of Mormon, we have a similar situation with two nations (Nephites and Lamanites), each of which was really a confederation of tribes.

As early as the second generation in the New World, descendants of Lehi's colony were calling themselves Nephites, Jacobites, Josephites, Zoramites, Lamanites, Lemuelites, and Ishmaelites, after the founders of their lineage groups. Jacob, however, preferred to call them by the collective terms Nephites and Lamanites, according to their political allegiance (Jacob 1:13-14).[1]

Despite the paucity of genealogical details in the Book of Mormon, it is clear that the people were very concerned about their tribal affiliation.[2] One of the evidences for this is that the ancestry of certain individuals is specified, indicating that they either kept genealogical records or that they had family traditions. For example, we learn that Ammon was a descendant of the Mulekite leader Zarahemla (Mosiah 7:3), that Alma was a descendant of Nephi (Mosiah 17:2), and that Amulek of the "Nephite" city of Ammonihah had to take pains to specify that "I am a Nephite" (Alma 8:20). He subsequently spoke of his descent from Nephi and even from Joseph who was sold into Egypt (Alma 10:2-3). Lamoni, king of the land of Ishmael (Alma 17:19) is said to be a descendant of Ishmael (Alma 17:21), though his father, who lived in the land of Nephi (Alma 22), was king over all the Lamanite lands (Alma 20:8). Even Mormon, who lived centuries after the coming of Christ, made a point of his descent from Nephi (Mormon 1:5) and specified that he was a "pure descendant of Lehi" (3 Nephi 5:20)—an idea repeated by his son Moroni (Mormon 8:13). As late as circa 20 BC, Nephi spoke of "the seed of Zedekiah [who] are with us" (Helaman 8:21).

... In Alma 43:13, we read that the Lamanites were "a compound" of descendants of Laman and Lemuel, the sons of Ishmael, and Nephite dissenters such as the Amalekites, Zoramites, and descendants of the priests of Noah. Despite this, there are indications of a clear separation between some of these elements. For example, we read of the Lamanites, Amalekites, and Amulonites who built the city of Jerusalem, with the notation that many of the Amalekites and Amulonites were after the order of Nehors (Alma 21:1-4; 24:28-29). This group seems to have remained separate from the main Lamanite body, at least in their tribal identification. Despite their political unity, these groups appear to have comprised separate "tribal" groups within the Lamanite kingdom. There was a sort of "high king" in the land of Nephi, to whom other kings were subservient.

... We read in 4 Nephi 1:17 that there were no more "-ites" after the coming of Christ, but that all of the people were united in the kingdom of God. However, this evidently has reference to political factionalism, rather than the abandonment of lineage ties. As noted above, not long before the coming of Christ, the people had dissolved their political ties and retained tribal allegiances (3 Nephi 7:2-4). There is reason to believe that these tribal units continued to exist after the time of Christ.

---

[1] We should note the wording of Jacob 1:14: "those who are friendly to Nephi I shall call Nephites, or the people of Nephi, *according to the reigns of the kings*." It has been noted that descendants of Lehi's party are consistently divided into the same seven tribes, always listed in the Book of Mormon in the same order. Dividing the polity into seven groups may correspond to the seven "churches" set up by Alma in the land of Zarahemla (Mosiah 25:23) and are perhaps the "large bodies" into which the people assembled at the time these ecclesiastical units were organized (Mosiah 25:15). See Ross T. Christensen, "The Seven Lineages of Lehi," *New Era* (May 1975): pp. 50-51; John L. Sorenson, *An Ancient American Setting for the Book of Mormon* (Salt Lake City: Deseret Book and F.A.R.M.S., 1985), 310-13; and the F.A.R.M.S. Update "Seven Tribes: An Aspect of Lehi's Legacy," November 1987.

[2] Book of Mormon personal names containing such Semitic patronymic elements as *Abi-* ("father") and *Ami-* ("paternal kinsman/clan") fit the biblical pattern and are evidence for a strong patrilineal kinship system. Note the names Abinadi, Abinadom, Aminadab, and Aminadi.

EVIDENCE NO. 978: THE LOGISTICS OF WARFARE

<u>Claim</u>: The authenticity of the Book of Mormon is enhanced by its many realistic details relative to war.

<u>Evidence</u>: It is highly unlikely that an uneducated farm boy (who had never experienced war) could understand and accurately describe the many necessary details that are part of organized warfare. Yet the Book of Mormon contains a wealth of information on such military logistics as strategy, tactics, weaponry, propaganda, handling of prisoners, and burying of the dead (Alma 16:11; 44:22; 46:12; 49:25; 52:19, 28; 54:1-24; 55:1-35; 62:31). It also makes reference to the difficulties in supplying food to the soldiers, the support (or lack thereof) of the people, and the difficulties of the weather (Alma 58-61). The logistics of four major movements are chronicled in the Zoramite battle recorded in (Alma 49:39-42).

Armor is described in detail with head plates, breastplates, arm shields, bucklers, etc., but no leg armor is mentioned—most likely because the latter would have restricted movement in battle. Hence their wounds were more often on their exposed legs (Alma 43:38; 49:24; Helaman 1:14; 3 Nephi 3:26; Ether 15:15).

The following is quoted from William J. Hamblin, "Warfare in the Book of Mormon," *Rediscovering the Book of Mormon,* edited by John L. Sorenson and Melvin J. Thorne, (1991), pp. 241, 248:

> The wars and battles described in the Book of Mormon include some of the most detailed narratives of the book. Those accounts provided us with an excellent chance to examine how consistent and complex the text is. Joseph Smith lived in an age of warfare with guns, yet the Book of Mormon displays patterns of warfare that made sense only before gunpowder was used. This can be seen in both the general patterns and in the tiny details of the text. Descriptions of weapons and tactics in the Book of Mormon are definitely ancient. Furthermore, the warfare in the Book of Mormon differs from what we read about in the Bible. It differs in the same way that war in ancient Mesoamerica (Mexico and northern Central America) differed from Biblical warfare.

> … The Book of Mormon manifests parallels to ancient patterns of military behavior… There were also the martial implications of shifting populations, the exchange of written or oral challenges between leaders, and the centrality of war to the elite class of society, to name a few more areas. In so many ways, the Book of Mormon uniquely reflects its dual heritage of the ancient Near East and Mesoamerica.

For more details, see the book, *Warfare in the Book of Mormon,* edited by Stephen D. Ricks and William J. Hamblin, [1990].)

EVIDENCE NO. 979: THE CIMETER

<u>Claim</u>: The Book of Mormon makes mention of a strange weapon called the *cimeter* (Enos 1:20; Mosiah 9:16; 10:8; Alma 2:12; 27:29; 43:18, 20, 37; 44:8; 60:2; Helaman 1:14). Less-informed critics brand this as a "fanciful" weapon that was one of many products of Joseph Smith's "active imagination." Other skeptics, aware that the cimeter is an earlier spelling for the more recently standardized *scimitar,* label the mention of this weapon in the Book of Mormon as an anachronism. However, the cimeter mentioned in the Book of Mormon, is neither a product of Joseph's imagination, nor an anachronism, but an actual instrument of war that was used in ancient times.

<u>Evidence</u>: The curved scimitar, with its single-edged blade, was thought to have originated in sixteenth century Persia (George Smith, "Is There Any Way to Escape These Difficulties?': The Book of Mormon Studies of B. H. Roberts," *Dialogue,* [Summer 1984], vol. 17, p. 2).

However, according to recent documentation, the scimitar could easily have been in existence in the time of Nephi (600 BC). See Yigael Yadin, *The Art of Warfare in Biblical Lands in the Light of Archaeological Study*, [New York: McGraw-Hill Book Co., 1963], vol. 2, pp. 253, 349, 359; cited in William Hamblin, "Handheld Weapons in the Book of Mormon," *Foundation for Ancient Research and Mormon Studies Preliminary Report*, HAM-85, pp. 30-31, 36.)

Hamblin also presents evidence of scimitar-like weapons that have been found in Mesoamerica. (See Earl Morris, et. Al. *The Temple of the Warriors at Chichen Itza, Yucatan*, [Washington DC Carnegie Institution, Publication number 406, 1931], vol. 2, plate 77, and column 11 N, plate 79, Izapa Stelae 3 and 4; and George C. Stone, *A Glossary of the Construction, Decoration and Use of Arms and Armor*, [New York: Jack Brussel, 1961], p. 275, fig. 342; and many other sources cited by Hamblin, p. 37.)

EVIDENCE NO. 980: NEPHITES ESCAPE WHILE CAPTORS ARE DRUNK

<u>Claim</u>: The Book of Mormon records that a group of Nephite slaves obtained their freedom by getting their captors drunk prior to their escape (Mosiah 22:3-14).

<u>Evidence</u>: *The Works of Ixtlilxóchitl* tells of a similar incident in which a group of Ulmecas was enslaved by a race of powerful "giants." The Ulmecas prepared a great feast for their oppressors, and after the giants were "replete and drunk," the Ulmecas attacked and were victorious. (*The Works of Ixtlilxóchitl*, English translation by Hunter and Ferguson, *Ancient America and the Book of Mormon*, [1950], p. 140.)

EVIDENCE NO. 981: KILLING THE OLD KING

<u>Claim</u>: Certain sensational aspects of royal succession recorded in the Book of Mormon are similar to Old World practices.

<u>Evidence</u>: The Book of Mormon tells of an evil Jaredite princess who persuaded her father to assume the kingdom by killing the king. To do this she reminded her father of the earlier practice of beheading the old king and suggested he use such an unholy means to usurp the throne (Ether 8:7-18; 9:6).

Dr. Hugh Nibley discovered that one of the more sensational aspects of ancient royalty was "that sinister mode of succession that prevailed in the earliest days, when the old king would be beheaded by the new king who would then proceed to marry the queen." (Examples are given in Robert Graves, *The Greek Myths*, 2 vols. [New York: Penguin, 1960]; and Marie Renault, *The King Must Die* [New York: Pantheon, 1958] cited in Nibley, "Howlers in the Book of Mormon" reprinted by *Foundation for Ancient Research and Mormon Studies* from the *Millennial Star*, [February 1963] vol. 125, pp. 28-34.)

EVIDENCE NO. 982: THE BOW—A SYMBOL OF POLITICAL POWER

<u>Claim</u>: At the time when Nephi was told that he was to be a ruler over his brethren (1 Nephi 2:22; 3:29) there is a deeper significance in the account of Nephi's broken bow (1 Nephi 16:23).

<u>Evidence</u>: The fact that Nephi makes a new bow to replace his steel bow (while everyone else, including the patriarch were murmuring) is symbolic of his calling as a leader over his brethren. It has been well established that the bow was a symbol of political power in the ancient Near East. For example, see Hahum M. Waldman, "The Breaking of the Bow," *Jewish Quarterly Review*, (October 1978) vol. 69, pp. 82-88; cited in "The Political Dimension in Nephi's Small Plates," *Brigham Young University Studies*, (Fall 1987) vol. 27, No. 4, pp. 28, 37.

EVIDENCE NO. 983: THE SWORD OF LABAN AS A SYMBOL OF AUTHORITY

<u>Claim</u>: The authenticity of the Book of Mormon is further demonstrated by its allusions to the *sword of Laban* as a symbol of authority and power. For example, in Mosiah's coronation ceremony King Benjamin passed the sword on to his heir to symbolize the transfer of power (Mosiah 1:15-16).

<u>Evidence</u>: Down through the centuries in Middle Eastern cultures, the sword was seen as more than just a weapon. It helped to establish the possessor as the ruler. The following is quoted from Brett L. Holbrook, "The Sword of Laban as a Symbol of Divine Authority," *Journal of Book of Mormon Studies,* vol. 2, no. 1, (Spring 1993), pp. 39-72:

> Swords have often been seen as symbols of divine authority and kingship. Numerous examples from the mythology, literature, and history of the world attest to distinct patterns. The sword of Laban from the Book of Mormon fits these patterns and can be compared to the sword of Goliath. The sword of Laban can also be traced as part of the royal regalia that gives authority throughout Nephite history, and later as it appears in the Restoration.

> … The swords of kingship originated in association with historic figures or deities and ratified one's office. Anciently, and even in some cultures today, military, religious, and civil offices were often combined in the person of the king. This tripartite responsibility defined "the king's role in the protection of society as warrior, the guarantor of justice as judge and the right ordering of worship as priest." (Keith W. Whitelam, "Israelite Kingship: The Royal Ideology and Its Opponents," *The World of Ancient Israel,* edited by in R. E. Clements, [Cambridge University Press, 1989], p. 130. See also Daniel J. Elazar, "Dealing with Fundamental Regime Change," in *From Ancient Israel to Modern Judaism: Essays in Honor of Marvin Fox,* edited by Jacob Neusner, [Atlanta, Georgia: Scholars, 1989], pp. 105-106.) …

> Yahweh himself is known to have a sword that he used in the cosmogonic battle before creation (Deuteronomy 32:41; Judges 7:18-20; Isaiah 27:1; 66:16), and his word was frequently equated with a sword (Ephesians 6:17; Hebrews 4:12; Revelations 1:16). As the Messiah of Christianity, Jesus Christ was to come a second time wielding a sword in the last days of judgment (Revelations 14:14-16).

(See also Frank Moore Cross, Jr., "The Divine Warrior in Israel's Early Cult," in *Biblical Motifs,* edited by Alexander Altmann, [Cambridge: Harvard University Press, 1966], pp. 11-30; G. G. D. Kilpatrick, *This Book of Isaiah,* vol. 6 in The Interpreter's Bible, 12 vols. [New York: Abingdon, 1956], p. 356; George Elliot, "Does God Have and Use a Sword?" *Methodist Review,* [December 1924] vol. 40, pp. 934-940; Hoyle, "The Weapons of God in Samuel," *This World,* vol. 7 (Winter 1984), pp. 120, 126, 130-134; Gordon C. Thomasson, "Mosiah: The Complex Symbolism and the Symbolic Complex of Kingship in the Book of Mormon," *Journal of Book of Mormon Studies,* [Spring 1993] vol. 2, no. 1, pp. 21-38; MacCulloch, *The Mythology of All Races,* vol. 6, p. 109; Compare to Ezekiel 21:15; Ronald S. Hendel, "The Flame of the Whirling Sword: A Note on Genesis 3:24," *Journal of Biblical Literature,* [December 1985] vol. 104, pp. 671-674; all cited in Holbrook, "The Sword of Laban," *Journal of Book of Mormon Studies,* [Spring 1993] vol. 2, no. 1, pp. 39-72.)

EVIDENCE NO. 984: CITIES FORTIFIED BY DEFENSIVE EARTHWORKS

<u>Claim</u>: The Book of Mormon records that a number of cities located in the east wilderness, such as Ammonihah and Bountiful, were each fortified by a high bank of earth surrounded by a deep trench (see Alma 49:2, 4, 18-22; 50:1-4; 53:4-5).

<u>Evidence</u>: Some ruins in Belize and Peten, Guatemala, which have been suggested by scholars as Nephite cities in the "east wilderness," were surrounded by defensive trenches and high banks of earth—just as the Book of Mormon described them.

Archaeologists Puleston and Callender describe one such site near the ruins of Tikal. They describe a man-made trench with a continuous raised embankment along the south side, following a straight line. They concluded that its potential as a barrier to human movement was obvious. They added that there were causeways (just as the Book of Mormon describes 'passes' or 'entrances' to the cities) where people could cross over. They also added that it was impossible to say that defensive earthworks of this nature were unique to Tikal. (See Dennis E. Puleston and Donald W. Callender, Jr., "Defensive Earthworks at Tikal," *Expedition*, [Spring, 1967] vol. 9, no. 3, pp. 40-48.)

The Book of Mormon mentions walled cities twenty-seven times. For example: "And thus they did cause the Lamanites to labor, until they had encircled the city of Bountiful round about with a strong wall of timbers and earth to an exceeding height" (Alma 53:4). In many cases, ditches or moats were dug outside the walls. "The walled city of Mayapan (Yucatan) contained 60,000 dwellings within the walls." (See M. Wells Jakeman, *The Origins and History of the Mayas*, p. 96.)

The eastern states were once "dotted" with earth mounds that were created by the Natives. Many of these earth mounds were built as fortifications according to Lionel Casson, et. al., *Mysteries of the Past*, edited by Joseph J. Thorndike, Jr. (American Heritage Publishing Co.: New York, 1977), pp. 120, 122.

These words were written in an appeal to save some of these great mounds in Ohio: "There are numbers of structures of earth and stone scattered throughout our state... All such earthworks are, of course, placed on the summits of high hills, or on plateaus overlooking river valleys." At Fort Miami, "it seems as if blockhouses or bastions of wood had been burned down when once protecting the gateway." (See Warren K. Moorhead, *Fort Ancient* [Cincinnati: Clark, 1890], pp. 102-103.)

Of this description, Dr. Nibley wrote: "This is not only an excellent description of Book of Mormon strong places, but it also suits exactly the picture of the standard fortified places of the Old World. Hundreds of such hill forts have been located all over Europe and the British Isles, where they seem to represent the normal life of the people over long periods of time." (Hugh Nibley, *An Approach to the Book of Mormon*, [1988], p. 440.)

EVIDENCE NO. 985: BODY ARMOR

Claim: The Book of Mormon mentions that the ancient Americans used thick clothing for armor (Alma 43:19; 49:6), and large breastplates made of brass and copper (Mosiah 8:10).

Evidence: At the time of the Spanish Conquest, the natives of the Yucatán wore body armor made of quilted cotton. The Spaniards themselves eventually adopted this wartime protection. (See Landa, *Relación de las Cosas de Yucatán*, pp. 32, 35, 121; Bernal Diaz del Castillo, *True History of the Conquest of Mexico* [1927], p. 426; cited in Harris, *Book of Mormon Message and Evidence*, [1961] p. 93.)

For other evidence for the use of thickened textile armor in both ancient America and the Near East see: G. C. Vaillant, *The Aztecs of Mexico*, (Bungay, Suffolk: 1950; Garden City, New York: 1941), p. 210; P. H. F. Follett, "War and Weapons of the Maya," *Tulane University, Middle America Resurvey Institute*, (1932), no. 4; G. E. Smith, "Arms, Armor," in *The Popular and Critical Bible Encyclopedia and Scriptural Dictionary*, edited by S. Fallows, vol. 1, pp. 158; and M. S. Miller, *Encyclopedia of Bible Life*, (New York, 1944), p. 187; all cited in John L. Sorenson entitled "The Significance of an Apparent Relationship Between the Ancient Near East and Mesoamerica," SOR-71, *Foundation for Ancient Research and Mormon Studies*, (1971), p. 240.

Von McLaughlin said: "At the Ohio State University Museum in Columbus is a copper tempered ax weighing thirty eight pounds. Who but a man large in stature builds himself a tool weighing thirty eight pounds to wield as he clears the land of timber?" Mr. McLaughlin says there are also in the museum at least twenty large breastplates of copper and also large spear points including one, "twenty inches in length." (Von McLaughlin, *The Serpent and the Cross*, p. 6.)

Similarly, evidence for the use of the "kettle-shaped helmet" in both the old and the new worlds can be found in C. Irwin, *Fair Gods and Stone Faces,* (New York, 1963), pp. 145-157; also cited in Sorenson "The Significance of an Apparent Relationship... ," SOR-71, *Foundation for Ancient Research and Mormon Studies*, 1971, p. 240.

EVIDENCE NO. 986: THE USE OF THE DART IN ANCIENT AMERICA

<u>Claim</u>: The Book of Mormon mentions that the dart was used as a weapon in ancient America (Jarom 1:8).

<u>Evidence</u>: When the Book of Mormon was first published in 1830, it was not likely that Joseph Smith nor his contemporaries could have known that the dart was a common weapon in ancient America. Even though it was still in use by the Indians of such regions as the Amazon jungles, that information was not available to Joseph Smith. See Sahagun, Fray Bernardino de, *Historia General de los Casas de Nueva España: Florentine Codex*, Translated and edited by Charles E. Dibble and Arthur J. O. Anderson, (Santa Fe: The School of American Research 1950), vol. 2, p. 109; cited in Cheesman, *The World of the Book of Mormon*, (1978) p. 14.

EVIDENCE NO. 987: SLINGS IN ANCIENT AMERICA

<u>Claim</u>: The use of the stone and sling as a weapon of war is mentioned several times in the Book of Mormon. For example, see Alma 2:12. Critics have sneered at this claim, but recent evidence has now turned up to establish the fact that slings were actually used in Mesoamerica.

<u>Evidence</u>: Had Joseph Smith fabricated the Book of Mormon, he would have safely limited his story to bows and arrows, spears, etc. However, this "stumbling block" has become a "stepping stone" with the discovery that ancient Americans did, indeed, use slings. See *Scientific American*, (October 1973), vol. 229, no. 4, pp. 34-42; and G. C. Vaillant, *The Aztecs of Mexico,* (Bungay, Suffolk: 1950; Garden City, New York: 1941), p. 210.

EVIDENCE NO. 988: THE LAW OF APOSTATE CITIES

<u>Claim</u>: One of the many authentic details in the Book of Mormon is its descriptions of apostate cities and the fate of such cities. An example is Ammonihah and its subsequent destruction (see Alma 16:9-11). The law that called for the destruction of apostate cites is found in Deuteronomy 13:12-16.

<u>Evidence</u>: The *Foundation of Ancient Research and Mormon* Studies has noted that:

Alma lacked either the desire or the power to destroy the city of Ammonihah by military force and certainly no legal decree was ever issued calling for the extermination of the city. Nevertheless, Alma carefully recorded and documented the fact that the inhabitants of Ammonihah had satisfied every element of the crime of being an apostate city, so that when the justice of God destroyed that city, it was clear that this fate was in accordance with divine law. Consider the following elements:

1. This law pertains to "certain men [who] are gone out from among you." Alma clearly states that the leaders in Ammonihah were apostates: "If this people, who have received so many blessings from the hand of the Lord, should transgress contrary to this light and knowledge which they do have ... it would be far more tolerable for the Lamanites than for them" (Alma 9:23).

2. The law applies when men have led the city to withdraw from God to serve other gods. Alma accordingly explains that certain men in Ammonihah, the followers of Nehor, had undertaken to study ways to pervert the nation, to turn it away from the statutes, and judgments, and commandments of the Lord (Alma 8:17).

3. Deuteronomy describes the offenders as "the children of Belial." Likewise, Alma made it a matter of record that "Satan had gotten great hold upon the hearts of the people of the city of Ammonihah" (Alma 8:9).

4. The law required officers to investigate the situation thoroughly, to inquire, search and ask, to be sure that the offensive condition in fact existed. Alma did this too. After being rejected, Alma was instructed to return to preach in the city, to give them the necessary warning that they would be destroyed if they did not repent (Alma 8:16). Then, acting as the two required eyewitnesses (Deuteronomy 17:6), Alma and Amulek stood and witnessed an awful scene of utter abomination (Alma 14:9). This was a revolting experience for them, but it completed the case against the city and sealed its eternal fate (Alma 14:11).

5. The prescribed mode of execution was by "the sword, destroying it utterly." This is the only place in the Law of Moses where slaying by the sword is called for. When the day of judgment came upon Ammonihah, the Lamanites did "slay the people and destroy the city" (Alma 16:2), presumably by the sword, their primary weapon of hand-to-hand combat.

6. The law demanded that the city should be destroyed completely by fire, "and it shall be a heap for ever." Alma records, "Every living soul of the Ammonihahites was destroyed, and also their great city … and their dead bodies were heaped up upon the face of the earth" (Alma 16:9-11). Alma does not say how Ammonihah was destroyed, but that fire was involved would have been normal.

7. Finally, the law stated that the ruins "shall not be built again." A similar fate befell Ammonihah: "And people did not go in to possess the land of Ammonihah for many years … and their lands remained desolate" (Alma 16:11). These lands were deemed untouchable for just over seven years, a ritual cleansing period (there are eight years, nine months and five days between Alma 16:1 and Alma 49:1). In a similar fashion, an early Christian synod removed the ban requiring that the island of Cyprus remain unoccupied seven years after its inhabitants had been annihilated. (See Constantinus Prophyrogenitus, *De Administrando Imperio* p. 47, in *Patrologiae Cursus Completus … Series Graeca*, J. P. Migne editor, [Paris: 1857-1866] vol. 113, p. 366.)

Thus, the destruction of Ammonihah conforms quite thoroughly to the legal provisions of Deuteronomy 13, making this a remarkable case of the falling of the vengeful sword of God's justice (Alma 54:6). See John W. Welch, "The Destruction of Ammonihah and the Law of Apostate Cities," *Foundation of Ancient Research and Mormon Studies Update*, (July 1987); reprinted in *Re-exploring the Book of Mormon*, edited by John W. Welch, (1992), pp. 176-179.

EVIDENCE NO. 989: THE OATH OF ALLEGIANCE

<u>Claim</u>: The Book of Mormon records a strange incident in which Captain Moroni rallies his people to defend their country by rending his coat, writing on it, and fastening it to the end of a pole. He then uses this banner, which he calls "the title of liberty," as a symbol for an oath of allegiance which he requires to be taken by his soldiers (Alma 46). This incident has been found to fit the pattern of similar oaths in the ancient Near East.

<u>Evidence</u>: The following are quotations from an article by Terrence L. Szink entitled, "An Oath of Allegiance in the Book of Mormon," *Foundation for Ancient Research and Mormon Studies*, SZI-89, (1989), pp. 1-6:

An important element in any military endeavor is the loyalty of the soldiers. Obviously even the most brilliant military tactics will fail if the troops are unfaithful in fulfilling their duty. Often, to instill this loyalty an oath of allegiance is administered to the recruits. The well-known title of liberty episode of the Book of Mormon (Alma 46) includes an interesting example of just such an oath.

... Amalickiah, "the man who would be king," had drawn a considerable portion of the Nephite population after him. Moroni, chief captain of the Nephite army, perceived the danger and realized that he needed the support of the people. He rent his coat and used it as a banner to rally the people. After a fervent prayer and a speech,

> Behold, the people came running together with their armor girded about their loins, rending their garments in token, or as a covenant, that they would not forsake the Lord their God; or, in other words, if they should transgress the commandments of God, or fall into transgression, and be ashamed to take upon them the name of Christ, the Lord should rend them even as they had rent their garments. Now this was the covenant which they made, and they cast their garments at the feet of Moroni, saying: We covenant with our God, that we shall be destroyed, even as our brethren in the land northward, if we shall fall into transgression; yea, he may cast us at the feet of our enemies, even as we have cast our garments at thy feet to be trodden under foot, if we shall fall into transgression (Alma 46:21-22).

This oath is similar to a number of Near Eastern oaths, which have two characteristics. First, they are self execrative in nature; the party making the covenant or treaty takes upon himself a conditional curse, swearing that if he fails to fulfill his part of the agreement he is willing to endure a specified punishment. Second, they are accompanied by various rites that in some way symbolized the punishment to be inflicted. I have employed the term 'simile oath' to refer to oaths of this type.

Simile oaths occur throughout the ancient Near East. They are most generally used to strengthen the validity of treaties between states, the weaker of the two states being forced to swear the oath by the stronger one.

... The interested reader can find information on these types of oaths in the following: J. M. Munn-Rankin, "Diplomacy in Western Asia in the Early Second Millennium BC," *Iraq* vol. 18 (1956): pp. 68-110; Robert Polzin, "HWQY and Covenantal Institutions in Early Israel," *Harvard Theological Review* vol. 62 (1969): pp. 227-40; Angel Gonzalez-Nunez, "El Rito de la Alianza," *Estudios Biblicos* vol. 24 (1965): pp. 217-38; P. J. Henninger, "Was bedeutet die rituelle Teilung eines Tieres in zwei Halften?" *Biblica,* vol. 34 (1953): pp. 344-53; Gerhard Wallis, "Eine Parallele zu Richter 19:29 ff. und 1 Samuel 11:5 ff.," *Zeitschrift fur alttestamentliche Wissenschaft* vol. 64 (1952): pp. 57-61; see also Mark Morrise, "Simile Curses in the Ancient Near East, Old Testament, and Book of Mormon," FARMS Preliminary Report MOR-82.

See also Terrence L. Szink's article "Oaths," in *Encyclopedia of Mormonism,* (New York: Macmillan Publishing Co., 1992), vol. 3,

EVIDENCE NO. 990: TREADING ON THE GARMENTS

<u>Claim</u>: As part of the covenant taken by the people in the "title of liberty" incident mentioned above, the people "cast their garments at the feet of Moroni" for him to trample upon. This symbolized the casting away of the old life with old sins, and that God "may cast us at the feet of our enemies, even as we have cast our garments at thy feet to be trodden under foot, if we shall fall into transgression" (Alma 46:22). This strange custom was unknown to the western world in Joseph Smith's day, but has been recently shown to originate in the Near East.

<u>Evidence</u>: The ancient Hittites took an oath of allegiance in an identical fashion. "Before their eyes [the priest throws the garment] on the ground; they trample it under foot and he speaks as follows: 'Whoever breaks these oaths, even so let the Hatti people come and trample that man's town under foot.'" (See Yigael Yadin, *The Scroll of the War of the Sons of Light Against the Sons of Darkness,* [Oxford: Oxford University Press, 1962], pp. 311, 323; Terrence L. Szink entitled, "An Oath of Allegiance in the Book of Mormon," *Foundation for Ancient Research and Mormon Studies,* SZI-89, [1989], pp. 1-6; J. Z. Smith, "The Garments of Shame" in *History of Religions,* vol. 5, [1966], pp. 224-233, cited in Nibley, *Since Cumorah,* [1988], p. 243.)

Captain Moroni followed the ancient Mideastern custom of naming the chosen land for his armies during a blessing and pronouncing a curse on their enemies before battle. The curse was to consign the enemies to a desolate region (Alma 46:17). See L. Wooley and T. E. Lawrence, *The Wilderness of Zin,* [London: J. Cape, 1936], p. 107).

Dr. Hugh Nibley writes the following in his work, *Since Cumorah,* (1988), pp. 242-243:

> … In confronting the enemy, Moroni reminds his people that they are the poor and the outcasts of the world, fittingly following a banner which was his own rent coat, representing the torn garment of their ancestor Joseph, the outcast and suffering servant (Alma 46:18-23). Again, the Battle Scroll described the hosts of the Children of Light as the poor and outcast of the earth, despised and now threatened with extermination by the haughty gentiles.

> Following the example of Moroni, all the people who were willing to enter his army and take the covenant rent their garments as he had his, only they went further and proceeded to tread upon their garments, saying as they did so, "We covenant with God, that … he may cast us at the feet of our enemies, even as we have cast our garments at thy feet to be trodden under foot, if we shall fall into transgression" (Alma 46:22).

> In a very recent study J. Z. Smith considers under the title of "Treading upon the Garments" an ancient ritual practice attested in the newly discovered early Christian Coptic texts in which a person upon becoming a member of the church would take off his garment and trample on it "in token" of having cast away an old way of life and as a symbol of trampling his old sins underfoot, with "curses placed on the inciter" to sin.[1] Heretofore the custom has been traced to Hellenistic sources, but it now appears from the newly found documents that it is an original and very old Jewish rite "probably to be traced back to Jewish exegesis of Genesis 3:21."[2] It has all the marks of being archaic and shows that peculiar blend of ritual and real-life behavior which at first made the understanding of the Battle Scroll so difficult and which puts such a distinctive stamp upon some of the historical events in the Book of Mormon.[3]

> Before the battle "when he had poured out his soul to God," Moroni "named all the land which was south of the land Desolation, … and … all the land, both on the north and on the south—a chosen land" (Alma 46:17). Whether we punctuate this to mean that he named the enemy land Desolation and the rest "Chosen," or that he named the "chosen land" and let the rest keep its ill-omened title, the point is that we have here the practice, now attested by the Battle Scroll, of formally blessing the hosts of Israel and cursing the land of their enemy before the battle.[4]

See also the evidences on cursings in the Book of Mormon in the Culture and Literacy chapters, included in this same volume.

---

[1] Jonathan Z. Smith, "The Garments of Shame," *History of Religions,* vol. 5 (1965-1966): pp. 224-233; quotation is from p. 229.

[2] Jonathan Z. Smith, "The Garments of Shame," pp. 230-233. It has special reference to the skin garment of Adam. The quote is from, p. 231.

[3] See our discussion in Hugh W. Nibley, "Old World Ritual in the New World," *An Approach to the Book of Mormon,* (1988), chapter 23; pp. 295-310.

[4] Yigel Yadin, *The Scroll of the War of the Sons of Light Against the Sons of Darkness,* (Oxford University Press, 1962), pp. 15, 215, 223-225; and *Battle Scroll* (1QM—Cave 1, Qumran, *Milhamah*), section 17-19.

EVIDENCE NO. 991: THE REMNANT OF JOSEPH'S COAT

<u>Claim</u>: During his speech to rally the people, Captain Moroni mentioned that a remnant of Joseph's coat of many colors had been preserved as a symbol of a remnant of his (Joseph's) seed which would also be preserved. The other decayed fragment had symbolized the apostate corruption of Israel (see Alma 46:23-6). These symbolisms were unknown to the Western world in Joseph Smith's day but have since been well documented—providing additional evidence that Joseph Smith indeed translated the Book of Mormon by "the gift and power of God."

<u>Evidence</u>: The modern discovery of the Dead Sea scrolls restored an ancient tradition that speaks of two fragments of the garment of Joseph. One was bloodstained and decayed and represented the corruption of Israel. The other fragment was freshly preserved through the centuries and represented the blessed remnant of Israel. (See Marc Philonenko, *Les Interpolations Chretiennes des Testaments des Douze Patriarches et les Manuscrits de Qumran* [Paris: Presses Universitaires de France, 1960], pp. 51-52.)

Other traces of the *remnant of Joseph's coat* were found in the Tha°labi legend:

> And when Joseph had made himself known unto them [his brethren] he asked them about his father, saying, "What did my father after [I left]?" They answered, "He lost his eyesight [from weeping]." Then he gave them his garment [qamis, long outer shirt]. According to ad-Dahak that garment was of the weave [pattern, design] of Paradise, and the breath [spirit, odor] of Paradise was in it, so that it never decayed or in any way deteriorated [and that was] a sign [omen]. And Joseph gave them that garment, and it was the very one that had belonged to Abraham, having already had a long history. (Kitab Qisas al-Anbiyá Tha°labi, [Cairo: Mustafa al-Babli al-Halabi wa-Awladuhu, 1314 A. H.], pp. 80-81, 96; cited in Nibley, *Approach to the Book of Mormon,* [1988], pp. 211-221.)

Tha°labi also mentions that Joseph's torn garment had "three marks or tokens" in it. See also Marc Philonenko in *Revue d'Histoire et de Philosophie Religieuses*, vol. 39, (1959), p. 33.

EVIDENCE NO. 992: FIGHTING IN SMALL GROUPS

<u>Claim</u>: The Book of Mormon states that one of the most efficient and successful military campaigns of the Nephites involved Helaman's "two thousand stripling soldiers." This small group of warriors "who were true at all times in whatsoever thing they were entrusted. Yea, they were men of truth and soberness, for they had been taught to keep the commandments of God and to walk uprightly before him" (Alma 53:17-22). Because of their faith and personal righteousness, these young soldiers were not only victorious but not one of them were slain in battle (Alma 56:45-56; 57:25).

<u>Evidence</u>: According to scholars of Middle Eastern military history, the preference of the people in and around ancient Israel was to choose small groups of carefully selected men, in a state of ritual purity, to defend their country. These people believed that God would march at the head of such a vanguard. (See Roland de Vaux, *Ancient Israel,* [New York: McGraw Hill, 1965], pp. 217, 258-259; cited in John Welch, "Finding Answers to B. H. Roberts' Questions," *Study Aid,* [Provo, Utah: Foundation Ancient Research Mormon Studies, n.d.], p. 16.)

EVIDENCE NO. 993: CIVIL WAR FOLLOWED BY PROSPERITY, THEN NATURAL DISASTERS

<u>Claim</u>: The Book of Mormon records that the Jaredite civil war was followed by a period of reconstruction and prosperity (Ether 9:16). The Book of Mormon further states that 150 to 200 years after the Jaredite civil war (calculated by the reign of kings), famine and poisonous serpents caused the death of many of the inhabitants of Ancient America (Ether 9:28-35). These are both verified by Ancient American history.

Evidence: The *Works of Ixtlilxóchitl* states that after the second great calamity, "they began to rebuild anew and to multiply." Then, 158 years after the second great calamity was a "third great calamity" in the form of natural disasters [primarily a great earthquake] which caused the death of all but a few living inland. Cited in Hunter and Ferguson, *Ancient America and the Book of Mormon* (1950), pp. 42, 46.

EVIDENCE NO. 994: WARS OF ANNIHILATION

Claim: The Book of Mormon describes a war of annihilation: "... a cry went forth throughout the land—who can stand before the army of Shiz? Behold, he sweepeth the earth before him!" (Ether 14:18). Some critics have doubted that such a war could ever occur—why conquer a kingdom leaving no subjects to pay taxes? However, newly recovered ancient documents suggest that wars of extermination were common in antiquity.

Evidence: The Book of Mormon records, "And so terrible was the destruction among the armies of Shiz that the people began to be frightened, and began to flee before the armies of Coriantumr; and they fled to the land of Corihor, and swept off the inhabitants before them, all them that would not join them" (Ether 14:27). Of this account Dr. Hugh Nibley writes the following in his work, *Lehi in the Desert and the World of the Jaredites,* (1988), pp. 231-237:

> This is the classic Asiatic method of forced recruiting: "If the neighboring province to that which they invade will not aid them," says an eyewitness of the Tartar technique, "they waste it, and with the inhabitants, whom they take with them, they proceed to fight against the other province. They place their captives in the front of the battle, and if they fight not courageously put them to the sword."[1] In such a way the Asiatic war-lords from the beginning "[swept] the earth before [them]" like Shiz (Ether 14:18), and like the Communist hordes of our day, forcing all that lay in their path to become part of them. "I counted them among my people," says the Assyrian conqueror of one nation after another, and this ancient formula would seem to go back to our old friend Nimrod, whom popular superstition saw reincarnated in Jenghiz Khan as he "became a mighty hunter," according to Carpini. "He learned to steal men, and to take them for prey. He ranged into other countries taking as many captives as he could, and joining them to himself," as Nimrod had done by awful oaths.[2] This system of "sweeping the earth" explains how it was possible for small and obscure Asiatic tribes to rise very quickly to be conquerors of all Asia and most of Europe: The tribe that gave its name to the conquering hordes was merely the nucleus of an army which snowballed into a world-army by forced recruiting of all it met.
>
> A great deal has been written about the calculated Schrecklichkeit of the great conquerors, especially Jenghiz Khan, whose practices have been condoned by recent biographers on the grounds that there is no better weapon than terror to soften up opposition, provoke early surrender, and thus save lives. Certainly terror is the keynote of Asiatic warfare in which its "contempt for human life,"[3] and the boast of an Assyrian king might be echoed by many an ancient and modern successor: "I marched victoriously, like a mad dog, spreading terror, and I met no conqueror."[4] Being a mad dog seems to us a poor thing to boast of, but the terror was carefully calculated. Shiz would have understood, as in his pursuit of Coriantumr "he did slay both women and children, and he did burn the cities. And there went a fear of Shiz throughout all the land; yea, a cry went forth throughout the land—Who can stand before the army of Shiz? Behold, he sweepeth the earth before him!" (Ether 14:17-18). When Coriantumr gained a victory, it was his turn to be the terror of the earth, and "the people began to be frightened, and began to flee before the armies of Coriantumr" (Ether 14:27).[5]

---

[1]. John de Pian de Carpini, *Contemporaries of Marco Polo,* edited by Manuel Komroff, (New York: Liveright, 1928), chapter 16, p. 26.

[2]. Carpini, *Contemporaries of Marco Polo,* chapter 6, p. 12, 22, 37

[3]. R. Grousset, *L'asie orientale des origines au XVe siècle* (Paris: Presses Universitaires, 1941), pp. 291, 304-305, 307; quote on p. 305.

4. David D. Luckenbill, *Ancient Records of Assyria and Babylonia*, (Chicago: University of Chicago Press, 1927), vol. 2, pp. 99, 152, 310-311.

5. See also, E. A. Wallis Budge, *The Chronography of Bar Hebraeus*, (Oxford: Oxford University Press, 1932), vol. 1, pp. 103, 111, 124, 465; Herodotus, *Histories* vol. 4, pp. 64, 66, 70; Pliny, *Natural History,* vol. 7, pp. 2, 10; Ammianus Marcellinus, *Rerum Gestarum,* vol. 31, pp. 2, 14; Luckenbill, *Ancient Records of Assyria and Babylonia*, vol. 2, p. 396 (No. 1050); McGovern, *The Early Empires of Central Asia*, p. 54; M. E. Moghadam, "A Note on the Etymology of the Word Checkmate," *Journal of the American Oriental Society,* (1938), vol. 58, p. 662; L. Thorndike, "All the World's a Chessboard," *Speculum* (1931), vol. 6, pp. 461-465; F. E. A. Krause, *Cingis Han*, (Heidelberg: Winter, 1922), pp. 17, 26; Michael Prawdin, *The Mongol Empire*, (London, 1940), pp. 191-193, 221, 329, 469, 472; Constantine Porphyrogenitus, *De Administrando Imperio 47*, in *Patrologiae Cursus Completus ... Series Graeca*, J. P. Migne editor (Paris: 1857-66), vol. 113, p. 365; Jordanes, in Mierow, *The Gothic History of Jordanes*, 131; chapter 53; Eunapius, *De Legationibus Gentium ad Romanos 6*, in *Patrologiae Graeca*, vol. 113, pp. 656-657; William M. McGovern, *The Early Empires of Central Asia*, (Chapel Hill: University of North Carolina Press, 1939), pp. 189-191, 335-336, 366; Henning Haslund, *Men and Gods in Mongolia*, (New York: Dutton, 1935), pp. 206-207; and Lord John of Joinville, *Memoirs of Louis IX. King of France*, in Lord John of Joinville, *Chronicles of the Crusades* (London: Bohn, 1848), p. 476.

EVIDENCE NO. 995: EXTERMINATION OF THE JAREDITES

Claim: The Book of Mormon records that the great Jaredite civilization ultimately destroyed itself in a series of civil wars. The demise of this great nation was the direct result of a curse on the land brought on by their wickedness (Ether 13:15-22, 25-26; 14:1-2, 21-25; 15:2, 13-17, 20-22, 33).

Evidence: According to the *Works of Ixtlilxóchitl,* 1,715 years after the great deluge, there was a second great calamity in the form of a hurricane which destroyed all but a few of all the people. In the ancient American account, the hurricane could have been symbolic of the terrible fury with which the army of Shiz "sweepeth the earth before him" (Ether 14:18).

Ixtlilxóchitl also states that the "giants" or "ancient ones" suffered total destruction by war, dissensions and calamities as punishments from heaven for sins. "They were destroyed and e xterminated by great calamities and punishments from heaven for some grave sins that they had committed." See *Works of Ixtlilxóchitl*, English translation by Hunter and Ferguson, *Ancient America and the Book of Mormon* (1950), pp. 41-42, 49-54.

EVIDENCE NO. 996: THE DEATH OF SHIZ

Claim: The Book of Mormon describes the terrifying end to the murderous king Shiz as follows: "... and they fought again with the sword. And it came to pass that when they had all fallen by the sword, save it were Coriantumr and Shiz, behold Shiz had fainted with the loss of blood. And it came to pass that when Coriantumr had leaned upon his sword, that he rested a little, he smote off the head of Shiz. And it came to pass that after he had smitten off the head of Shiz, that Shiz raised upon his hands and fell; and after that he had struggled for breath, he died" (Ether 15:30-31).

Evidence: The following is quoted from a *Foundation for Ancient Research and Mormon Studies Update,* [November 1994] no. 97, p. 2:

> People have long wondered how Shiz could raise himself up, fall, and gasp for breath if his head had been cut off. Dr. Gary M Hadfield, M. D., professor of pathology (neuropathology) at the Medical College of Virginia Commonwealth University, in Richmond, Virginia, has recently published in *BYU Studies,* vol. 33, (1993), pp. 324-325, the following diagnosis:

Shiz's death struggle illustrates the classic reflex posture that occurs in both humans and animals when the upper brain stem (mid-brain/mesencephalon) is disconnected from the brain. The extensor muscles of the arms and legs contract, and this reflex action could cause Shiz to raise up on his hands.[1] ... In many patients, it is the sparing of vital respiratory and blood pressure centers in the central (pons) and lower (medulla) brain stem that permits survival.[2] ...

The brain stem is located inside the base of the skull and is relatively small. It connects the brain proper, or cerebrum, with the spinal cord in the neck. Coriantumr was obviously too exhausted to do a clean job. His stroke evidently strayed a little too high. He must have cut off Shiz's head through the base of the skull, at the level of the mid-brain, instead of lower through the cervical spine in the curvature of the neck.... Significantly, this nervous system phenomenon (decerebrate rigidity) was first reported in 1898, long after the Book of Mormon was published.[3]

Thus, the account of the staggering death of Shiz is not a figment of dramatic imagination, but the Book of Mormon account is plausibly consistent with medical science.

Moreover, linguistic analysis sustains the foregoing clinical analysis by confirming the words *smote off* need not mean that Shiz's head was completely severed by Coriantumr. In Judges 5, and equally gruesome account is given of Sisera's death at the hands of Jael, the wife of Heber. The English translation of the relevant verses reads:

She put her hand to the nail and her right hand to the workmen's hammer; and with the hammer she smote Sisera, she *smote off* his head, when she had pierced and stricken through his temples. At her feet he bowed, he fell, he lay down: at her feet he bowed, he fell: where he bowed, there he fell down dead (Judges 5:26-27).

This text shows that the English words *smote off* need not refer to a total decapitation, for surely Jael did not cleanly chop off Sisera's head using a hammer. Instead, the English words *smote off* here simply mean that Jael struck Sisera extremely hard. Indeed, both the Hebrew and Greek words translated as *smote off* mean "to hammer" or "to strike down with a hammer or stamp," but not generally to smite *off*, and accordingly the New English Bible reads, "with the hammer she struck Sisera, she crushed his head." No more necessarily does Joseph Smith's translation in Ether 15:30 need to mean that Shiz's head was completely cut off. Fifty or sixty percent off would easily have been enough to get the job done, leaving Shiz to reflex and die.

Other deaths, similar to that of Shiz, are a matter of history. B. H. Roberts, wrote the following in his work *New Witness for God*, (1951), vol. 3, pp. 556-557:

It is claimed that this represents an impossible thing—a man with his head stricken off rising upon his hands! And yet equally marvelous things of this nature have occurred, and are matters of record.

Mr. G. W. Wightman, of the Seventeenth Lancers of the British Light Brigade, and a survivor of the wild charge at Balaclava, relates, in the "*Electric* Magazine*" for June 1892, the incident of Captain Nolan's death during that charge. Captain Nolan was of the Fifteenth Hussars, and he met his fate, according to Wightman, as follows:

We had ridden barely two hundred yards and were still at the "trot," when poor Nolan's fate came to him. I did not see him cross Cardigan's front, but I did see the shell explode, of which a fragment struck him. From his raised sword-hand dropped the sword, but the arm remained erect. Kinglake writes that "what had once been Nolan' maintained the strong military seat until the 'erect form dropped out of the saddle;' but this was not so. The sword-hand indeed remained upraised and rigid, but all other limbs so curled in on the contorted trunk as by a spasm, that we wondered how for the moment the huddled form kept the saddle."

It is quite as remarkable that a man stricken unto death by the fragment of a shell should continue erect in the saddle, with sword-arm upraised and rigid, while the other limbs so curled in on the contorted trunk that those who saw him "wondered how the huddled form kept the saddle," as that a man as his head is stricken off should momentarily rise on his hands.

Mr. Wightman, in the same article, relates the still more remarkable case of Sergeant Talbot's death:

> It was about this time that Sergeant Talbot had his head clean carried off by a round shot, yet for about thirty yards farther the headless body kept the saddle, the lance at the charge firmly gripped under the right arm.

After this well attested fact, and many others of a similar nature that might be cited, it is not worth while being skeptical about Shiz convulsively rising on his hands for a moment after his head was stricken off.

---

[1] A. B. Baker and L. H. Baker, *Clinical Neurology,* (New York: Harper and Row, 1975), vol. 1, pp. 40, 65.

[2] J. Adams and L. W. Duchen, *Greenfield's Neuropathology* (Oxford University Press, 1992), pp. 195-200.

[3] C. S. Sherrington, "Decerebrate Rigidity, and Reflex Coordination of Movements," *Journal of Psychology,* (1898), vol. 22, p. 319.

* Note: This may be a typographical error; the magazine is most likely the *Eclectic Magazine* of New York.

EVIDENCE NO. 997: THE TIME PERIOD OF THE JAREDITE EXTERMINATION

Claim: The Book of Mormon tells of a large stone in the ancient city of Zarahemla with engravings on it which told of the destruction of the Jaredites and of Coriantumr, the last king of the Jaredite people (Omni 1:20-22). From the chronology given in the Book of Mormon, this period is estimated as being between 279 and 130 BC, (as indicated on the bottom of the page). When a party of Nephite explorers found the Jaredite battleground, they noted that the Jaredite weapons and armor were still in good condition (Mosiah 8:10-11). This would indicate that the Jaredite battle could not have occurred more than about 20 years prior to the 279 BC date, making the earliest possible date for this fatal battle to be around 300 BC.

Evidence: Ixtlilxóchitl recorded that "The greatest destruction that these Quinametzin had was in the year and figure (picture) that the natives called *ce Toxtli,* which means *rabbit number first,* 299 years before the incarnation of Jesus Christ." Quoted in Hunter and Ferguson, *Ancient America and the Book of Mormon* (1950), p. 50.

EVIDENCE NO. 998: THE FALL OF THE NEPHITE CIVILIZATION

Claim: Specific reasons given in the Book of Mormon for the destruction of the Nephite civilization closely parallel reasons proposed by scholars for the collapse of the Mayan civilization.

Evidence: The following is quoted from an article by Hugh W. Nibley entitled "The Book of Mormon and the Ruins; the Main Issues" (N-BMA, *Nibley Archive, Foundation for Ancient Research and Mormon Studies,* University Station, Provo, Utah, July 13, 1980), pp. 7-9:

> At the center of Ancient American studies today lies the sovereign question, Why did everything collapse so suddenly, so completely, and so mysteriously? To this question "no solution acceptable to the majority of students has yet appeared." J. Eric Thompson's theory is that people "in an increasingly complex society had largely lost the ability to act for themselves." But the valuable collection of studies edited by T. P. Culbert, *The Classic Maya Collapse* reaches an overall consensus, which is

worth setting forth in the words of the various contributors. It may help to put the Book of Mormon statement in a roughly parallel column. (See T. P. Culbert, *The Classic Maya Collapse* [University of New Mexico, 1973], p. 263.)

The Book of Mormon

Jacob 2:13-21: "… you have obtained many riches …ye are lifted up in the pride of your hearts…God …condemneth you, and if ye persist…his judgments must speedily come upon you."

3 Nephi 6:5, 10-12: "… many merchants…and also many lawyers, and many officers…and people began to be distinguished by ranks…And thus there began to be great inequality…insomuch that the church began to be broken up."

Moroni 1:7-8, 12: "The whole face of the land had become covered with buildings, and the people were as numerous almost…as the sand of the sea… And…there began to be a war between the Nephites…and the Lamanites and the Lemuelites and the Ishmaelites (until)…the Lamanites withdrew their design (conquest)."

Alma 28:10-13: "… the destruction of many thousand lives…an awful scene of bloodshed…And thus we see how great the inequality of man is because of sin and transgression."

Alma 5:54: "… will ye persist in supposing that ye are better one than another…in the persecution of your brethren who humble themselves…?"

Alma 46:23, 27: "… we who are despised…shall not be trodden down…let us preserve our liberty…I shall stir up insurrection…I do not fear your power nor your authority."

Helaman 6:5, 8-9, 17-20: "… whether it were among the Lamanites or…the Nephites…they did have frequent intercourse one with another, to buy and sell, and to get gain, according to their desire…and they became exceeding rich. (Within a few years)…to get gain…they began to commit secret murders, and to rob and to plunder…(leading to a series of wars)."

3 Nephi 6:12: "And the people began to be distinguished by ranks, according to their riches and their chances for learning, yea, some were ignorant because of their poverty, and others did receive great learning because of their riches."

The Classic Maya Collapse

Culbert, p. 91: "Over successful, overstrained, and probably overbearing, Tikal would have been at the mercy of…ecological, social and political catastrophes…"

E. W. Andrews, p. 263: "As civilization becomes more complex, it becomes more vulnerable—as we are discovering to our increasing horror in recent years…the problems of maintenance and unity increase geometrically."

W. T. Sanders, p. 359: "… rise of population density, decline of per capita income, increasing local specialization in crops, heavier reliance upon…the periphery for basic materials and more highly organized trade…closely correlated with militarism (and)…a shift from egalitarian to ranked and stratified society."

p. 363: "Recent studies favor political and economic causes…military incursions… disrupted the trade network…farmland gobbled up the forests…"

p. 364: "… an increasing distance between peasant and noble, an economic deterioration in the average peasant's lifestyle, and an increase of nutritionally based diseases… The only reasonable explanation (for sudden and catastrophic population decline) for the loss (of population) is migration, stimulated by peasant dissatisfaction and permitted by the breakdown of the political system."

M. C. Webb, pp. 402-403: "… rivalry over trade was a major cause of war…Probably in many cases allegiance was simply transferred to the intruders…. the proximate cause (of the great collapse) was the spread of the Post-classic pattern of secular trade and commercial war into the Maya area."

General Summary (G. R. Willey and D. B. Shimkin), p. 458: "… Late Classic society was more sharply differentiated into elite and commoner strata than…Early Classic times. As this process of an elite consolidation went on (there was)…a related development of a class of bureaucrats and craft specialists…"

The Book of Mormon

Helaman 13:22, 31: "… ye do always remember your riches…unto great swelling, envyings, strifes, malice, persecutions and murders…the time cometh that he curseth your riches, that they become slippery, that ye cannot hold them…"

Helaman 11:1: "… contentions did increase…that there were wars throughout all the land among all the people of Nephi."

3 Nephi 6:15, 17: "… Satan had great power…stirring up of the people…tempting them to seek for power, and authority, and riches, and the vain things of the world… And thus…they were in a state of awful wickedness."

Alma 45:21, 24: "… many little dissensions and disturbances among the people…they grew proud…because of their exceeding riches."

Alma 51:8: "… those of high birth…were supported by those who sought power and authority over the people."

Helaman 6:31 "… the Nephites…turned out of the way of righteousness…did build up unto themselves idols of their gold and silver."

3 Nephi 30:2: "Turn…from…your idolatries, and your murders, and your priestcrafts, and your envyings and your strifes…"

Alma 26:25: "… Let us take up arms against them, that we may destroy them…out of the land, lest they overrun and destroy us."

Helaman 11:1-2: "… there were wars throughout all the land among all the people of Nephi. And it was this secret band of robbers who did carry on this work of destruction."

3 Nephi 2:17-19: "(It was economic warfare) between the robbers and the people of Nephi…the Gadianton robbers did gain many advantages over them…inasmuch that they were about to be smitten down, and this because of their iniquity.

Helaman 6:38: "… the Nephites (instead of reform) did build up and support them (the robber societies)…they had come down to believe in their works and partake of their spoils…"

Alma 10:27: "… the foundation of the destruction of this people is beginning to be laid by…your lawyers and your judges."

The Classic Maya Collapse

p. 461: In the 7th and 8th Centuries "Maya civilization…was integrated at the elite level in a more impressive fashion than ever before," as "signs of regionalism" appear.

P. 470: "Intensified fighting among cities, inter-city fighting, crop loss and destruction, malnutrition, and disease…reduced the population" (e.g., 90% at Tikal—Culbert).

p. 480: "… the Maya elite…shared like training…prestige, beliefs, inter-regional cooperation…which acted to control warfare and promote geographical expansion," while it "increasingly separated them from the commoners."

p. 484: "The most vital aspects" of the collapse are: "(1) the role of the elite class, (2) the widening social gulf between the elite and the commoners, (3) the competition between centers, (4) agricultural problems, (5) demographic pressures and disease burdens, and (6) the changing effects on…external trade…. The expansion of the hereditary elite population was clearly a major force in the geographic expansion of the Late Classical…"

p. 486: "Add to this the competition for trade…and we can see the situation brought to a fighting pitch." All leading to a "rapid down-spiraling to extinction."

"Population growth increased demand for resources…growing manpower allows economic expansion…differential growth and longevity divided social classes (the poor were short-lived)…efforts to compensate for manpower shortage…were increasingly important causes of war." The economy forced everything in the direction of war.

p. 491: The elite "made no technological or social adaptive innovations which might have mitigated these difficulties. In fact, the Maya managerial elite persisted in traditional directions up to the point of collapse." With religion and law on their side, the elite needed to make no concessions.

The Book of Mormon

3 Nephi 7:2-3, 6-7, 11: "The people…did separate one from another into tribes, every man according to his family and his kindred and his friends; and thus they did destroy the government of the land. And every tribe did appoint a chief…And the regulation of the government were destroyed (by the king-men)…the more righteous part of the people had nearly all become wicked…the tribes of the people…were united (only) in the hatred of those who had entered into a covenant to destroy the government."

The Classic Maya Collapse

Sejourne, p. 183: "The spiritual anemia was followed by a state of permanent struggles for power…the whole country (Central Mexico) broke up into little communities, each claiming its own history and origin." The battle scenes of the fulfillment of the message of the American Prophet…"Mesoamerica fell little by little into a ruinous materialism…It is as if the message of Quetzalcoatl, the American Prophet, had been consumed by the organic inertia which it was his mission to denounce."

EVIDENCE NO. 999: THE WITNESS OF THE SURVIVOR

Claim: Another authentic detail of the Book of Mormon is the accurate portrayal of Ether, Mormon and Moroni's burning desire to testify to the wickedness of their people and the tragic destruction of their society as a result of sin (Words Of Mormon 1:1-2; Mormon 2:14-15; 4:11-23; 8:1-4; Ether 15:33-34; Moroni 9:22).

Evidence: The research of Terrence Des Pres shows that throughout the several holocausts recorded in history, aside from all the bitterness, anger and despair caused by such annihilations, the most basic reaction to the man-made genocide is to survive. Even when death would clearly be a more merciful termination of the pain and suffering, they choose to survive—if for no other reason, than to witness the unspeakable atrocities they endured. (See Terrence Des Pres, "Survivors and the Will to Bear Witness," Social Research, [1973], vol. 40, pp. 668-690; and The Survivor: An Anatomy of Life in the Death Camps, [New York: Pocket Books, 1977].)

In a Foundation for Ancient Research and Mormon Studies Update, (April 1984), several parallels between the conclusions of Des Pres and the Book of Mormon are presented, such as the following:

1. The survivors feel an overwhelming obligation to remember and to record the savagery they have witnessed. In doing this, they are able to overcome their fears. (See Mormon 2:15; 4:11-21.)

2. They see this task as a sacred duty (Mormon 4:23).

3. They usually work in secret and often hide their record of these events (Mormon 8:3-5).

4. The survivor sees himself as a necessary link between the past and the future—speaking on behalf of those who did not survive (2 Nephi 26:15-18; 27:6; Mormon 3:16-18; 5:8-10; 6: 17-22; 8:26).

5. The survivor sees good and evil much clearer in retrospect. Their mission is to record the evil they have witnessed (Alma 14:9; Helaman 12:3; Mormon 8:36-41).

EVIDENCE NO. 1000: FINAL DESTRUCTION OF THE NEPHITE CIVILIZATION

Claim: The Book of Mormon records that due to the wickedness of the Nephite civilization they were destroyed by their brothers the Lamanites. The final battles of this unholy war took place near a hill that was called Cumorah. At Cumorah, hundreds of thousands of Nephites were slain, and the prophet/historian Moroni buried the history of his people in that hill (Mormon 6:2-15; 8:1-5). Hundreds of years later, that same history was unearthed in upstate New York, by the boy prophet Joseph Smith and translated to become the Book of Mormon (Joseph Smith—History 1:51-52).

Evidence: When Joseph Smith made his "fantastic" claims and published the Book of Mormon as an ancient history of the American Indians, some scoffed at the idea that a major battle had anciently taken place in the local vicinity. However, evidence was soon produced that documented that this region of the country did indeed once possess a heavy Indian population, and that a terrible battle had taken place in that locality.

Writing in 1851, E. G. Squier says that in the region: "Human bones of men, women, and children of both sexes were thrown together promiscuously by the thousands." He notes large quantities of pottery, pipes, flint arrowheads, stone hatchets and other implements were also found there. He further states that the ancient relics unearthed in the vicinity (which he estimates to be several hundred years old) showed considerable evidence of Hebrew origin. See E. G. Squier, *Antiquities of New York,* (1851), pp. 137-138.

Josiah Priest states that "We are far from believing the Indian of the present time to be the aborigines of America: but quite contrary, are usurpers who have by force of bloody warfare, exterminated the original inhabitants, taking possession of their country and property." See Josiah Priest, *American Antiquities,* (Albany: Hoffman & White, 1834), p. 396; see also the preface.

In *New York State Bulletin #2,* it is documented that several miles south of "Mormon Hill," as it was then called, a site was found where flint arrowheads and spear points and many unfinished weapons were found in great abundance. All of the above sources are cited in Brenton G. Yorgason, *Little Known Evidences of the Book of Mormon,* (1989), p. 10.

Conclusion

The purpose of the presentation of evidence in a court of law is to assist jurors in arriving at a fair and logical verdict. Similarly, the purpose of the 1,000 evidences presented in this two-volume work is to assist those who seek the truth to arrive at a rational conclusion relative to the truthfulness of the Church of Jesus Christ of Latter-day Saints.

When these 1,000 evidences are weighed in the balance with the criticisms against the church, it should be clear that these evidences, when taken as a whole, far outweigh the claims of the opposition.

In light of such evidence, coupled with earnest prayer, the authors add their testimonies that the most logical verdict is that the Church of Jesus Christ of Latter-day Saints is all that it claims to be. That it offers to the entire world the pathway that leads to eternal life with God our Father and His Son Jesus Christ, and that it has the authority to act in the name of God in ministering the ordinances of salvation.

It is the hope and prayer of the authors that all who seek for confirmation of their faith may find it in the prayerful study of this two-volume work.

Partial Bibliography for Volumes 1 and 2

Ainsworth, Jerry L. *The Lives and Travels of Mormon and Moroni,* (Peacemakers Publishing, 2000)

Allen, James B. and Richard Cowan, *Mormonism in the Twentieth Century* (Provo, Utah: Brigham Young University, 1964)

Allen, Joseph L., *Exploring the Lands of the Book of Mormon* (Orem, Utah: S. A. Publishers, Inc., 1989)

Anderson, Richard Lloyd, *Investigating the Book of Mormon Witnesses,* (Salt Lake City: Deseret Book, 1981)

Ballard, M. Russell, Counseling with our Councils, (Salt Lake City: Deseret Book, 1997).

Barker, James L., *The Divine Church, Course of Study for Melchizedek Priesthood Quorums for 1952* (Salt Lake City, Utah: The Council of the Twelve, The Church of Jesus Christ of Latter-day Saints, 1951). Later republished as *Apostasy from the Divine Church,* (Salt Lake City: Bookcraft, 1984)

Barrett, Ivan J., *Joseph Smith and the Restoration,* (Provo, Utah: Brigham Young University Press, 1973)

Bennett, edited by Joshua Moses, *The Writings of the Rabbis and Other Important Discoveries,* (Washington, DC: Morning Star Publishing Co. 1990 by the Bennett Foundation)

Benson, Alvin K. "Joseph Smith on Modern Science," *Joseph Smith, The Prophet, The Man,* edited by Susan Easton Black and Charles D. Tate, Jr., (Brigham Young University, 1993).

Benson, Ezra Taft, *This Nation Shall Endure,* (Salt Lake City, Utah: Deseret Book Company, 1977)

Berrett, William E. *The Restored Church,* (Salt Lake City, Deseret Book Co., 1953)

Berrett, William E. and Alma P. Burton, eds., *Readings in LDS Church History*, 3 volumes (Salt Lake City: Deseret Book Co., 1967)

Burton, Alma P. and Clea M. Burton, *Stories From Mormon History* (Salt Lake City: Deseret Book Co., 1960)

Burton, Alma P. *Doctrines From The Prophets* (Salt Lake City: Publishers Press, 1970)

Britsch, R. Lanier, *Unto the Islands of the Sea* (Salt Lake City: Deseret Book Co., 1986)

Cheesman, Paul R., *Ancient Writing on Metal Plates* (Bountiful, Utah: Horizon Publishing Co., 1985)

Cheesman, Paul R., *These Early Americans* (Salt Lake City: Deseret Book, 1974)

Cheesman, Paul R., *The World of the Book of Mormon,* (Salt Lake City, Utah: Deseret Book Co., 1978)

Christensen, Ross T., *Progress in Archaeology* (Provo, Utah: Brigham Young University, 1963)

Clark, David L., editor, *Of Heaven and Earth,* (Salt Lake City: Deseret Book Co., 1998)

Clark, James R., *The Story of the Pearl of Great Price* (Salt Lake City: Bookcraft, 1955)

Clark, James R., *The World of the Book of Mormon* (Salt Lake City: Deseret Book Co., 1978)

Cole, William A. and Edwin Jensen, *Israel in the Pacific* (Salt Lake City: Genealogical Society, 1961)

Cook, Melvin A., *Science and Mormonism* (Salt Lake City: Deseret Book Co., 1967)

Cowan, Richard O., *The Church in the Twentieth Century* (Salt Lake City: Bookcraft, 1985)

Crowell, Angela, "Hebraisms in The Book of Mormon," *The Zarahemla Record* (Independence, Missouri: Zarahemla Research Foundation), Issue Nos. 17 and 18, Summer and Fall, 1982

Crowley, Ariel L., *About the Book of Mormon* (Salt Lake City: Deseret News Press, 1961)

Crowley, Ariel L., *Statement of Beliefs of The Church of Jesus Christ of Latter-day Saints* (Salt Lake City: Deseret Book Co., 1963)

Crowther, Duane S., *Prophecies of Joseph Smith* (Salt Lake City: Bookcraft, 1963)

Crowther, Duane S., *Prophecy—Key to the Future* (Salt Lake City: Bookcraft, 1962)

Dyer, Alvin R., *The Refiner's Fire* (Salt Lake City: Deseret Book Co., 1980)

Evenson, Darrick T., *The Gainsayers* (Bountiful, UT: Horizon, 1989)

Ferguson, Thomas Stewart, *One Fold and One Shepherd,* (San Francisco, 1958)

Gibson, Stephen W., *From Clergy to Convert* (Salt Lake City: Bookcraft, 1983)

Gileadi, Avraham, *The Book of Isaiah, A New Translation with Interpretive Keys from the Book of Mormon,* (Salt Lake City, Deseret Book, 1988).

Godfrey, Kenneth and Jill Derr, *Women's Voices, An Untold History of LDS Women from 1830 to 1900* (Salt Lake City, Utah: Deseret Book, 1982).

Gorton, H. Clay, *The Language of the Lord, New Discoveries of Chiasma in the Doctrine and Covenants,* (Bountiful, Utah: Horizon Publishing Co., 1993).

Gunn, Roger S., *Mormonism: Challenge and Defense* (Salt Lake City: Hawkes Pub. Co., 1973)

Harris, Franklin S., *The Book of Mormon Message and Evidences* (Deseret News Press: Salt Lake City, 1961)

Hickman, Josiah E., *The Romance of the Book of Mormon* (Salt Lake City: Deseret News Press, 1937)

Hilton, Lynn M. and Hope, *In Search of Lehi's Trail,* (Salt Lake City: Deseret Book Co. 1976)

Hilton, Lynn M. and Hope, *Discovering Lehi,* (Springville, Utah, 1996)

Hunter, Milton R. and Thomas Stuart Ferguson, *Ancient America and the Book of Mormon* (Oakland, California: Kolob Book Co., 1950)

Hunter, Milton R., *Great Civilizations and the Book of Mormon,* (Salt Lake City: Bookcraft, 1970)

Hunter, Milton R., *Utah in Her Western Setting* (Salt Lake City, Utah: Sun Lithographing Co., 1956)

Jensen, Margie Calhoun, *Stories of Insight and Inspiration,* (Salt Lake City: Bookcraft, 1976)

Johnson, Stan and Polly, *Translating the Anthon Transcript,* (Parawan, Utah: Ivory Books, 1999)

Journal of Discourses, (Liverpool: Franklin D. Richards, 1855-1886), 26 vols.

Lindquist, John M., and Stephen D. Ricks, *By Study and Also by Faith,* (Deseret Book 1990), 2 vols.

Lerchen, Frank H., *A Study Guide for Investigators of The Church of Jesus Christ of Latter-day Saints* (Fairfax, Virginia: Classic Printing Center, 1972)

Ludlow, Daniel H., *A Companion to Your Study of the Book of Mormon,* (Salt Lake City: Deseret Book, 1977)

Ludlow, Victor L. *Isaiah: Prophet, Seer, and Poet,* (Salt Lake City: Deseret Book, Co., 1982)

Madsen, Truman G., "Are Christians Mormon?" *Brigham Young University Studies,* Vol. 15 (Autumn, 1974)

Madsen, Truman G., *Joseph Smith the Prophet* (Salt Lake City: Bookcraft, 1989)

McConkie, Bruce R., *Mormon Doctrine* (Salt Lake City, Utah: Bookcraft, 1958)

McConkie, Bruce R., *The Promised Messiah,* (Salt Lake City, Utah: Deseret Book, 1978)

Melville, J. Keith, "Joseph Smith, the Constitution and Individual Liberties," *BYU Studies* (Provo, UT: 1988)

Millet, Robert, editor, *To Be Learned is Good, If ...* (Salt Lake City: Bookcraft, 1987)

Nibley, Hugh, *Abraham in Egypt* (Salt Lake City: Deseret Book Co., 1981)

Nibley, Hugh, *An Approach to the Book of Mormon* (Salt Lake City: Deseret Book Co., 1957)

Nibley, Hugh, *Enoch the Prophet* (Salt Lake City: Deseret Book Co., 1986)

Nibley, Hugh, *Old Testament and Related Studies,* (Salt Lake City: Deseret Book Co. and Provo: Foundation for Ancient Research and Mormon Studies [F.A.R.M.S.], 1986).

Nibley, Hugh, *Lehi in the Desert and the World of the Jaredites* (Salt Lake City: Bookcraft, 1952)

Nibley, Hugh, *The Message of the Joseph Smith Papyri* (Salt Lake City: Deseret Book Co., 1975)

Nibley, Hugh, *Mormonism and Early Christianity* (Salt Lake City: Deseret Book Co., 1987)

Nibley, Hugh, *Nibley on the Timely and the Timeless* (Provo, UT: BYU, Religious Studies Center, 1978)

Nibley, Hugh, *The Prophetic Book of Mormon,* Volume 8 of the Collected Works of Hugh Nibley (Salt Lake City and Provo: Deseret Book and F.A.R.M.S., 1989)

Nibley, Hugh, *Since Cumorah* (Salt Lake City: Deseret Book Co., 1988)

Nibley, Hugh, *The World and the Prophets* (Salt Lake City: Deseret Book, 1962)

Nibley, Hugh, "Sacred Vestments," *Temple and the Cosmos,* (Salt Lake City: Deseret Book Co., 1992)

McGavin, E. Cecil, *The Family of Joseph Smith* (Salt Lake City, Utah: Bookcraft, 1963)

Nyman, Monte S., editor, *Isaiah and the Prophets,* (Provo, Utah: Religious Studies Center, B.Y.U., 1984).

Nyman, Monte S. and Charles D. Tate, Jr., editors, *The Book of Mormon: First Nephi, The Doctrinal Foundation* (Religious Studies Center, Provo, Utah: Brigham Young University, 1988)

Ostler, Blake, "Clothed Upon: A Unique Aspect of Christian Antiquity," *Brigham Young University Studies* (Provo, Utah: BYU, Winter, 1982), vol. 22, pp. 31-45

Palmer, Spencer J., *Mormons and Muslims* (Provo, Utah: Religious Studies Center, Bookcraft, 1983)

Palmer, Spencer J., *The Expanding Church*, (Salt Lake City: Deseret Book, 1978)

Palmer, Spencer J., *Deity and Death* (Provo, Utah: Religious Studies Center, Brigham Young University, 1978)

Parry, Jay A. and Larry E. Morris, *The Mormon Book of Lists* (Salt Lake City: Bookcraft, 1987)

Rector, Hartman and Connie, *No More Strangers* (Salt Lake City: Bookcraft, 1971-1976), 3 Volumes

Richards, LeGrand, *A Marvelous Work and a Wonder* (Salt Lake City: Deseret Book Co.: 1950)

Ricks, Stephan D., editor, *Journal of Book of Mormon Studies,* , 2 vols. (Foundation for Ancient Research and Mormon Studies, 1992-1993).

Ricks, Stephen D. and William J. Hamblin, editors, *Warfare in The Book of Mormon,* (Salt Lake City: Deseret Book and Foundation for Ancient Research and Mormon Studies, 1990)

Roberts, B. H., *New Witnesses for God*, 3 Vols. (Salt Lake City: Deseret News Press, 1951)

Robinson, O. Preston and Christine H. Robinson, *Christ's Eternal Gospel* (Salt Lake City: Deseret Book, 1976)

Robinson, O. Preston and Christine H. Robinson, *Dead Sea Scrolls and Original Christianity* (Deseret, 1958)

Sampson, Joe, *Written By the Finger of God,* (Sandy, Utah: Wellspring Publishing and Distributing, 1993).

Seaich, Eugene, *Ancient Texts and Mormonism,* (Sandy, Utah: Mormon Miscellaneous, 1983)

Scharffs, Gilbert W., *The **Truth** about "The God Makers"*, (Salt Lake City, Utah: Publishers Press, 1986)

Shumway, Eric B., *Tongan Saints—Legacy of Faith*, (Laie, Hawaii: The institute for Polynesian Studies. Funded by the Polynesian Cultural Center, Brigham Young University, Hawaii, 1991)

Skousen, W. Cleon, *Fantastic Victory* (Salt Lake City: Bookcraft, 1967), Second printing

Skousen, W. Cleon, *Treasures from the Book of Mormon*, 4 Vols (Salt Lake City: W. Cleon Skousen, 1974)

Skousen, W. Cleon, *The Third Thousand Years,* (Salt Lake City: Bookcraft, 1987), 25th printing

Smith, Joseph, *History of the Church,* 7 volumes, plus index (Salt Lake City: Deseret Book Co., 1951)

Smith, Joseph, *Lectures on Faith,* (Salt Lake City: Deseret Sunday School Union, 1913)

Smith, Joseph Fielding, editor, *Teachings of the Prophet Joseph Smith* (Salt Lake City: Deseret Book Co., 1967)

Sorenson, John L., *An Ancient American Setting for the Book of Mormon* (Deseret Book Co., 1985)

Sorenson, John L., "The Book of Mormon as a Mesoamerican Codex," *Newsletter and Proceedings of the SEHA* (Provo, UT: BYU, The Society for Early Historic Archaeology), December 1976, No. 139, reprinted by the *Foundation for Ancient Research and Mormon Studies* in F.A.R.M.S. Reprint SOR-76

Sorenson, John and Melvin Thorne editors, *Rediscovering the Book of Mormon,* (Desert Book, 1991)

Sperry, Sydney B., *Book of Mormon Testifies,* (Salt Lake City: Bookcraft, 1952)

Sperry, Sydney B., *The Voice of Israel's Prophets* (Salt Lake City: Deseret Book Co., 1952)

Talmage, James, E., *The House of the Lord,* (Salt Lake City: Deseret Book Co., 1976)

Tvedtnes, John A., "Hebraisms in the Book of Mormon: A Preliminary Survey," *BYU Studies* 1970, Vol. 2

Vestal, Kirk Holland and Arthur Wallace, *The Firm Foundation of Mormonism* (Los Angeles: L. L. Co., 1981)

Wallace, Arthur, *Can Mormonism Be Proved?* (Los Angeles, 1973)

Warner, Ross, *Book of Mormon Prophecies* (Salt Lake City: Hawks Publishing Co., 1975)

Warren, Bruce W., and Thomas Stewart Ferguson, *The Messiah in Ancient America,* (Provo, Utah: Book of Mormon Research Foundation, 1987).

Homans, J. C. (writing under the pen name of R. C. Webb), *Joseph Smith as a Translator* (Salt Lake City: Deseret News Press, 1936)

Webb, R. C., *The Real Mormonism* (New York: Sturgis and Walton Co., 1916)

Welch, John W., Editor, *Re-exploring the Book of Mormon,* (Salt Lake City: Deseret Book Co., 1992)

Widtsoe, John A., *Seven Claims of the Book of Mormon*, (Independence, Missouri: Zion's Printing, 1936)

Wirth, Diane E., *A Challenge to the Critics* (Bountiful, Utah: Horizon Publishing, 1986)

Yorgason, Brenton, *Little Known Evidences of the Book of Mormon,* (Covenant Communications 1989)

Index to Evidences Volume II

Abandonment of the Nephite empire, 166.

Abinadi and Pentecost, 216.

Abinadi and the Teacher of Righteousness, 214.

Abish, 224.

Adam—Ixanom, 224.

Adam and Eve, are expelled from the garden, 72.

Adam, fall of led to moral agency, 40.

Adam, fall of, anticipated, 40.

Adieu, 268.

Adjectives rarely used, 265

Adobe and wood used rather than stone, 182.

Adonai—Atanoti, 225.

Agency, moral, was result of the fall of Adam, 40.

Agriculture in ancient America, 131.

Aha—Ahah, 239.

Akish, 239.

Alma, 225.

America,

    A chosen land, 97.

    A land of promise, 129.

    Polynesians came from, 33.

    Reserved for the righteous, 96.

    To be a land of liberty, 97.

    To be fortified against all other nations, 98.

American Indians, see Native Americans

Ammon, Aminadi, Aminadab, Ammonihah, 240.

Amnihu and Gideon east of Sidon River, 161.

Amoebaeon and Epistrophe, 262.

Anaphora, 261.

Ancient America, see Mesoamerica

And, used extensively, 262.

Another testament of Jesus Christ, 13.

Antenantiosis in ancient writings, 269.

Anthon transcript, 255-257.

Anthon transcript, A modern translation of, 257.

Anti, 225.

Arabia, Lehi's travels through, 152-158.

    Bountiful, 157.

    Coastal climate, 157.

    Interior climate, 157.

    Lehi's converts in, 153.

    Lihyanite temple in, 154.

    Nephi's name found, 155.

    The Valley of Lemuel and the River of Laman, 155.

Archaeologist, converted by the Book of Mormon, 152.

Arches used in ancient America, 292.

Armies of ten thousand, 303.

Arrows, made new for Nephi's new bow, 187.

Ascension of Christ, 63.

Assembly, great, or year-rite, Benjamin's address, 135.

Astronomical calendar of 365 days, 297.

Astronomy in ancient America, 296.

Astronomy/stellar symbolism of Mesoamerica, 208.

Aztec and Mayan names for Lehi on Stela, 117.

Aztec hieroglyphs of the Codex Borgia, 70-77, 123.

Aztec prayer circle in the Codex Borgia, 77.

Aztec temple and holy city, 70.

Aztec tree of life in Codex Borgia, 123.

Baptism in ancient America, 78.

Baptism of infants condemned, 79.

Barges, the eight Jaredite, 177.

Beards in ancient America, 104.

Benjamin's kingly address, 134-139.

    A farewell, 138.

    Coronation ceremony, 137.

    Guardian of covenant, 136.

    Great assembly, 135.

    Held 130 BC, 135.

    Renounces absolute power, 139.

Bible,

    A testament to the truth of, 13.

    Book of Mormon restores original text from, 20.

    Deletions from, 16.

    Many will declare it sufficient, 91.

    Missing instructions for officers, 20.

    Missing instructions on ordinances, 20.

    Missing prophets of, 19.

    Prayers missing from, 19.

    Scholars condemn infant baptism, 80.

    Scholars on missing scriptures, 18.

    Scriptures missing from, 17-18.

Biblical evidence that Quetzalcoatl is Jesus Christ, 49.

Blood of Christ restores life, 64.

Blood types of native Americans, 175.

Body armor in ancient America, 310.

Book of Mormon,

    A latter-day miracle, 13.

    A Testament to the Bible, 15.

    Character forms, 254-257.

    Converts an Archaeologist, 152.

    Converts an Egyptian professor, 172.

    Crimes in the, 140.

    Described by Isaiah, 83.

    Environmental description, 158.

    Internal consistency of, 99.

    Jews to gather after printed, 98.

    New Testament references in, 67.

    Ranked sixth in nation, 12.

    Restored original text from Bible, 20.

    Symbolism in, 253.

Time period of, 100.
Title page from the last leaf, 251.
To be rejected by many, 90.
To go to all nations, 90.
Book, sacred, buried by ancient Americans, 108.
Books, many written by ancient Americans, 249.
Bountiful,
    Ancient American city, 162.
    Jesus' Appearance at, 62.
    Mineral deposits there, 158.
    Of the Arabian Peninsula, 157.
Bow, a symbol of political power, 308.
Box, Hawaiian prophesy of the square, 90.
Boxes of stone, 170.
Broken bow incident, 156.
Brothers, four, 103.
Building, great and spacious on Stela, 115.
Burial customs, 197.
Calendar changed with Quetzalcoatl's birth, 53.
Calendars, Mesoamerican and Israelite, 188.
Calendars, the numbering of days and months, 189.
Camenihah, 240.
Cannibalism, self-mutilation in Mesoamerica, 142.
Cave of Lehi, refugees of, 111-113.
    Fled to avoid Babylonian invaders, 112.
    Lived in tents, 113.
    Looked forward to redemption of Jerusalem, 113.
    Occupied around 600 BC, 112.
    Sailed by ship, 113.
Caves and water holes, and the lower world, 211.
Cement in ancient America, 293.
Cezoram—Chiziri, 245.
Chemish, 226.
Chiasmus, 281-283.
Children of God, 81.
Chosen land, America, 97.
Christ, see Jesus Christ
Christianity in the New World before Columbus, 46.
Cimeter, 307.
Cities of Mesoamerica,
    Designed with spaces for gardens, 129.
    Fortified by defensive earthworks, 309.
    Large buildings in Mesoamerica, 126.
    Submerged during destruction, 60.
    The law of apostate, 311.
City of Enoch, 211.
Civil war followed by prosperity, then disasters 315.
Civilizations to be swept off the land, 86.
Codex Borgia, Aztec hieroglyphs of, 70-77, 123.
    Aztec initiatory ordinances, 76.
    Depicts an Aztec Prayer Circle, 77.
    Review of the creation, 71.
    Review of the fall of Adam, 72.
    Reviews the crucifixion, 73.
    Savior's wounds provide life, 74.
    Tree of life depicted in, 123.
Cognate accusative, 266.
Colophon, 258.
Columbus to be led by the Spirit, 86.
Commandments, the ten found in New Mexico, 287.
Compass or Director, 121.
Consecration, law of in ancient America, 139.
Consecration, law of in Polynesia, 140.
Construct form of Adjective phrases, 265.
Contents of the Book of Mormon are inspired, 22.
Coronation ceremony, Benjamin's kingly address, 137.
Cosmological and historical beliefs, 207.
Cosmos, the layered, 209.
Covenant, King Benjamin as guardian of, 136.
Cowdery, Oliver, testimony of, 6.
Creation, ancient American account of, 35.
Creation, Aztec review of, 71.
Creation, Polynesian account of, 35.
Crime in the Book of Mormon, 140.
Crucifixion reenacted in ancient America, 45.
Crucifixion, caused great destruction in America, 58.
Crucifixion, depicted in the Codex Borgia, 73.
Cubit used in ancient America, 292.
Cumeni—Cumenihah, 240.
Cumorah, 226.
Cumorah, the hill location, 166.
Cuna Indians, evidences from, 66-67.
Cureloms and cummoms in ancient America, 149.
Curse, symbolic prophetic, 284.
Cursings in ancient America, 213, 284.
Dancing maidens, 190.
Darkness followed wickedness, 66.
Darkness, thick vapor of, 61.
Dart used in ancient America, 311.
Death, Latter-day Saints to suffer, 93.
Death, three Nephites not to taste of, 94.
Deceits, lyings and hypocrisy of the Gentiles, 91.
Deletions from the Bible, 16.
Descendants referred to as seed, 259.
Destruction in the first days of the year, 59.
Deseret, 240.
Destruction at the time of the crucifixion, 58.
Destruction caused new mountains to appear, 60.
Director or Compass, 121.
Divination in ancient America, 208.
Duties of officers, Bible missing instructions for, 20.
Early Christians knew of saints beyond the ocean, 28.
Earth, the spirit of, 38.
Earth, to be cleansed by fire, 38.
Earth, truth to come out of, 89.
Earthquake triggered lightning, 60.
Earthworks, built to defend cities, 309.

Egyptian professor converted by Book of Mormon, 171.

Egyptian culture in the Book of Mormon, 170.

Egyptian influence in the Book of Mormon, 254-259.

Egyptian influence on Mesoamerican architecture, 170.

Egyptian language similar to Mayan, 258.

Egyptian names in the Book of Mormon, 237-246.

Egyptian, reformed, 254.

Eight witnesses, testimony of , 11.

El Niño and reversal of the pacific trade winds, 177.

Elephants in ancient America, 146.

Elevations as contact points with the heavens, 212.

Engraving vs. brushing with ink, 251.

Enoch, City of, 211.

Environment of the Book of Mormon lands, 158.

Epanelepsis in ancient writings, 270.

Epistrophe and amoebaeon, 262.

Ether, 226.

Eve, the first to partake of forbidden fruit, 41.

Expulsion from the garden in Codex Borgia, 72.

Ezekiel and John on the Remnants of Israel, 88.

Fall of Man anticipated, 40.

Fall of Man let to moral agency, 40.

Fame of the Book of Mormon, 12.

Famous scholars on the Book of Mormon, 11

Farewell address of King Benjamin, 138.

Fasting, and Israelite custom in ancient America, 42.

Fasting, the purpose of , 42.

Father, worship of the, 24.

Fighting in small groups, 315.

Figures of speech in the Book of Mormon

"Alpha and Omega," 274.

"Beyond the mark," 273.

"Firm, steadfast and immovable valley," 273.

"Fountain of the Red Sea," 273.

"I said in my heart," 264.

"It came to pass," 259.

"Lay hold," 264.

"Manner of speech," 272.

"Rent" of Moroni's garment, 264.

"Spake, saying," 265.

"That" or "which" for "who" or "whom," 265.

"Their souls did expand," 273.

"Thou shalt have place with us," 274.

"Throwing arrows," 265.

"To the convincing of the Jew," 263.

"Woman" for wife, 265.

Fire, curtain of represented on Stela, 118.

Fire, earth to be cleansed by, 38.

Fires, not permitted in the Arabian desert, 122.

Flood, ancient American migration came after, 178.

Flood, the tower, confusion and scattering, 41.

Flowing vases of the Old and New Worlds, 210.

Folklore and superstition of Mesoamerica, 206-213.

Forbidden fruit, Eve was first to partake, 41.

Fountain of living water on Stela, 116.

Gadianton Robbers in ancient America, 141.

Gardens, cities designed with spaces for, 129.

Garments, sacred and protective, 78.

Garrison of fifty, 303.

Gathering held approximately 130 BC, 135.

Gazelem, 226.

Gentiles to assist the Lamanites, 88.

Gentiles, lyings, deceits and hypocrisy of , 91.

Gentiles, murders of the, 92.

Gentiles, whoredoms of the, 92.

Giants in ancient America, 149.

Gid—Kib, 241.

Giddonah, Gidgiddoni, Gidgiddonah, 241.

Gideon and Amnihu east of Sidon River, 161.

God curses the land, 284.

God, America reserved for those who worship, 96.

God, children of, 81.

Godhead of three deities in ancient America, 31.

Gospel preached before Christian era, 30.

Grace, salvation by, 24.

Grains in ancient America, 131.

Great White God of the Pacific Islanders, 56.

Greek names, 236.

Hagoth, Migratory expeditions of, 132.

Hair as a symbol of strength, 42.

Harris, Martin, testimony of, 8.

Hawaiian prophesy of the square box, 90.

Heaven, pre-mortal council in, 39.

Heavenly Mother, 38.

Heavens, a voice from, 66.

Hebrew influence on the Book of Mormon, 261-290.

Hebrew marriage customs, 189.

Hebrew parallelism, 275-284.

Chiasmus, 281-283.

Circular repetition, 280.

Climax, 279.

Contrasting ideas, 276.

Extended alternate, 279.

Simple alternate, 278.

Simple (synonymia), 277.

Hebrew similarities with Native American, 285.

Hebrew writing in ancient America, 285-288.

Helaman—Heramon, 241.

Hem, 241.

Hermounts, 242.

Hermounts, wilderness of, 159.

Heuman linked with Mormon, 143.

Hiding counsel, 264.

Highways in ancient America, 294.

Himni—Hmn, 242.

Hissing, 269.

Historical and cosmological beliefs, 207.

History, the recurrence of, 101.

Holy Ghost, witness of, 1.
Horses in ancient America, 147.
Horticulture of olives, 132.
Hud as Lehi, 124.
Hypocrisy, lyings and deceits of the Gentiles, 91.
Iah, 236.
Illness, causes and cures of, 213.
Incense burning in ancient America, 191.
Infants, baptism of, condemned, 79.
Initiatory ordinances in the Codex Borgia, 76.
Inspired contents of the Book of Mormon, 22.
Instructions for officers missing from Bible, 20.
Instructions on ordinances, missing from Bible, 20.
Interpreters or Urim and Thummim, 27.
Iron metallurgy in ancient America, 289.
Irony and sarcasm, 270.
Irreantum, 157.
Isabel, 226.
Isaiah describes the Book of Mormon, 83.
Ishmael—Izamal—Uxmal, 227.
Israel, Mesoamericans are descendants of, 227.
Israel, Polynesians are descendants of, 34.
Israel, the remnants of, 88.
Israelite law and Sherem, 218.
Israelite marriage customs, 189.
Israelites with pagan names, 238.
Israelite calendar, similar to Mesoamerican, 188.
Jacob—Ecab—Llocab, 227.
Jacob prophesied of his descendants in America, 84.
Jacob, Mesoamericans are descendants of, 227.
Jaredite language not confounded, 145.
Jared and his brother, 227.
Jaredites,
    Barges of, 177, 299.
    Calamity of the serpents, 150.
    Extermination of, 317.
    Extermination time period, 319.
    Giants, 149.
    Luminous stones, 145.
    Nephite vs. Jaredite proper names, 221.
    "Submarines" of, 177, 299.
Jehovah—Yehowa, 32.
Jehovah, and the Maori God Io, 33.
Jershon, 228.
Jerusalem,
    Refugees anticipated the redemption of, 113.
    Temples outside of, 130.
    To be destroyed, 86.
    Under rule of corrupt leaders 600 BC, 102.
Jesus Christ,
    Another testament of, 13.
    Appearance of at Bountiful, 62.
    Appeared as a man of light in America, 66.

    Ascension of, 63.
    Birth brought many signs and wonders, 53.
    Birth date revealed, 187.
    Birth place of, 53.
    Elder Brother, 32.
    Crucifixion caused great destruction, 58.
    Embraced the children in America, 67.
    Fed a great multitude in America, 62.
    Healed the sick in America, 62.
    His wounds provide life, 74.
    Ministered in ancient America, 46-67.
    Name known before Christian era, 31.
    New insights on his teachings, 68.
    Promised to return to America, 63.
    Quetzalcoatl, Biblical evidence for, 49.
    Sacrifice of, commemorated in the Pacific, 44.
    Took each person by the hand in America, 67.
    Visited ancient America, 48.
    Was hung on a pole, 56.
Jews to gather after Book of Mormon comes forth, 98.
John and Ezekiel on the remnants of Israel, 88.
Joseph's coat, a remnant of, 315.
Joseph's descendants in America prophesied, 84.
Justice balanced with mercy, 171.
Justice, mercy cannot rob, 27.
Justice, robbers as instruments of divine, 142.
Killing the old king, 308.
King's renunciation of absolute power, 139.
King as guardian of covenant, 136.
Kishkumen, 242.
Korihor—Kerihor, 242.
Kumen—Kumenonhi, 241.
Laban, the beheading of, 120.
Laban, the death of, 200.
Laban, the sword of, as a symbol of authority, 309.
Lachoneus gathers his people, 164.
Laman and Lemuel rebelled against Nephi, 104.
Laman represented on Stela, 118.
Laman, 228.
Laman, the river of in Arabian Peninsula, 155.
Lamanites, see Native Americans
Lamoni, possible location for his kingdom, 160.
Land of promise, America, 129.
Land to be taken from the Lamanites, 87.
Language for speech, 259.
Languages, confusion of, 41.
Latter-day priestcrafts, 91.
Latter-day Saints to suffer death, 93.
Law of apostate cities, 311.
Law of Consecration in ancient America, 139.
Law of Consecration in Polynesia, 140.
Law, ancient Near Eastern, in ancient America, 217.
Legends and folklore of Mesoamerica, 206-213.

Lehi,
> As Hud, 124.
> **Cave of,** see **Cave of Lehi**, 111-113.
> His converts in the Arabian Peninsula, 153.
> His name found on Stela, 116.
> **His travels through Arabia**, 152-158.
> The name of, 228.
Lemuel represented on Stela, 118.
Lemuel, the valley of in Arabian Peninsula, 155.
Leprosy in ancient America, 143.
Levi tribe of, Priests not of, 129.
Liahona, 121, 229.
Lib's city linked with San Lorenzo, 164-165.
Liberty, America to be a land of, 97.
Life, Jesus Christ is the source of, 64.
Lightning during the earthquake, 60.
Lihyanite temple in the Arabian Peninsula, 154.
Linen and silk in ancient America, 128.
Luminous stones, 145.
Lyings, deceits and hypocrisy of the Gentiles, 91.
Man of light appeared in America, 66.
Mana and Tapu (Taboo) in Polynesia, 213.
Manti—Mathoni, 242.
Manti located on the west bank of Sidon, 161.
Marriage customs of the Hebrews, 189.
Materialism, naturalism and relativism, 94.
Mathoni—Mathonihah—Middoni, 229.
Mayan and Aztec names for Lehi on Stela, 117.
Mayan Chiasmus, 283.
Mayan language similar to Egyptian, 258.
Meat, to be eaten raw in the Arabian desert, 122.
Melchizedek, 230.
Mercy balanced with justice, 171.
Mercy cannot rob justice, 27.
Merismus in the Book of Mormon, 272.
Mesoamerica,
> Agriculture of, 131.
> Architecture, influenced by Egypt, 170.
> Cannibalism and self-mutilation in, 142.
> Character forms, 258-259.
> Cement used in, 293.
> Cureloms and cummoms in, 149.
> Cursings of, 213.
> Elephants in, 146.
> Giants in, 149.
> Grains in, 131.
> Great cities, large buildings in, 126.
> Horses in, 147.
> Incense burning in, 191.
> Knowledge of the resurrection, 61.
> Law of consecration in, 139.
> Legends of origins across the sea, 175
> Leprosy in, 143.

> Linen and silk in, 128.
> Metal plates found in, 109.
> Migration came after flood, 177.
> Migrations, three separate, 144.
> Oracle stones of, 133.
> Population of, 126.
> **Religious beliefs of, 28-60.**
> Sacred book buried in, 108.
> Secret criminal societies of, 141.
> Silk and linen in, 128.
> textiles of, 179.
> Transoceanic influence on, 176.
> Two different societies in, 104.
> Urim and Thummim in, 133.
Mesoamericans,
> Are descendants of Israel, 227.
> First came by sea, 145.
> Hidden record of, 108.
> **Migrations of, 173-199.**
> With fair skin and beards, 104.
> Writing ability of, 250.
> Wrote many books, 249.
Metallurgy in ancient America, 291.
Metonyms in the Book of Mormon, 222.
Mexico, the period of migration to, 144.
Middle East, metal plates found in, 110.
Migration to Mexico and North America, 144.
Migrations from both the Middle and Far East, 173
Migrations of the Mesoamerican settlers, 173-199.
Migrations to America, three separate, 144.
Migratory expeditions of Hagoth, 132.
Military leaders in ritual combat, 305.
Mineral deposits in Old World Bountiful, 158.
Minon, 230.
Miracle of the Book of Mormon, 13.
Mists of darkness on Stela, 119.
Monetary system of the Nephites, 173, 219-221.
> Antion, 220.
> Ezrom, 220.
> Limnah, 220.
> Money valued by weight, 173.
> Onti, 221.
> Senum, 221.
> Shiblum, 221.
> Shum, 221.
Monsters believed to inhabit subterranean waters, 211.
Months, the numbering of days and, 189.
Morianton, Moriantum, Moriancumer, 243.
Mormon linked with Heuman, 143.
Mormon, 230.
Moroni waved the "rent" of his garment, 264.
Moses ascends to heaven, 81.
Moses, Joseph Smith to become great like, 96.
Mosiah, 230.

Mother in heaven, 38.
Motifs and aesthetic features in ancient America, 183.
Mulek, 232.
Mulekites unite with Nephites, 134.
Murders of the Gentiles, 92.
Nahom, 156, 232.
Names and cultural relationships, 238.
National survey ranks Book of Mormon sixth, 12.
Native Americans,
    Among the Polynesians, 107.
    Blood types, 175.
    Land to be taken from, 87.
    Peaceful Lamanites, 108.
    To be assisted by the gentiles, 88.
    To be converted to the Gospel, 89.
    To be preserved from destruction, 87.
    To know they are of Israel, 89.
    With dark skin, 106.
Native American similarities with Hebrew, 285.
Naturalism, materialism and relativism, 94.
Neas, 243.
Nephi,
    As ruler over his brothers on Stela, 117.
    His name glyph on Stela, 117.
    His name in Southern Arabia, 155.
    His Psalm, 275.
    Laman and Lemuel rebelled against, 104.
    Nehi, Nehri, Nfy, Nihpi, 243.
Nephites,
    Built great cities with large buildings, 126.
    Civilization falls, 319.
    Civilization final destruction, 324.
    Escape while captors are drunk, 308.
    History began in 600 BC, 101.
    Industrious and cultured, 169.
    Jaredite vs. Nephite proper names, 221.
    Monetary system efficiency, 173.
    Three not to taste of death, 95.
    Unite with the Mulekites, 134.
    Voyage sustained by pacific trade winds, 177.
    With fair skin, 104.
New mountains appeared during destruction, 60.
New Testament references in the Book of Mormon, 67
New World Christianity before Columbus, 46.
New year celebration, the significance of, 189.
North America, the period of migration to, 144.
Northerly direction, the evils of, 212.
Nouns, plural, 266.
Oath of allegiance, 312.
Oaths, the practice of swearing, 121.
Ocean, Early Christians knew of saints beyond the, 28.
Olive Horticulture, 132.
Olive tree vineyards, 132.
Omni—Lomni, 232.

Opposition in all things, 17, 22, 40.
Oracle stones in ancient America, 133.
Ordeal by water, 178.
Ordeal, trial by, 217.
Ordinances, instructions on, missing from Bible, 20.
Orientation of sacred sites, 180.
Pa-prefix, 246.
Paanchi, Pacumeni, Pachus, 244.
Pacific Islanders believed in a Great White God, 56.
Pacific Islanders commemorated Christ's Sacrifice, 44.
Pacific trade winds sustained Lehi's voyage, 177.
Pahoran, 244.
Parallelism, se Hebrew Parallelism
Passover feast in ancient America, 44.
Peaceful Lamanites, 108.
Patronymic names in the Book of Mormon, 224.
Pentecost and Abinadi, 216.
Plates of metal in ancient America, 109.
Plates of metal in the Middle East, 110.
Plates uncovered, significance of the day, 109.
Pole, ancient American Savior was hung on a, 56.
Political and religious leaders in battle, 304.
Pollutions of modern times prophesied, 93.
Polynesia, law of consecration in, 140.
Polynesia, Mana and Tapu (Taboo) in Polynesia, 213.
Polynesian account of the creation, 35.
Polynesians came from America, 32
Polynesians are descendants of Israel, 34.
Polynesians with dark skin, 107.
Polysyndeton, 262.
Popol Vuh's account of the creation, 35.
Population in Mesoamerica, 126.
Potter's wheel used in ancient America, 296.
Prayer to the Father, 24.
Prayer, of the Zoromites, 193.
Prayers missing from the Bible, 19.
Pre-mortal council in heaven, 39.
Pre-mortal existence, 39.
Prepositions repeated, 266.
Prepositions compound, 267.
Priestcrafts in the latter-days, 91.
Priests not of the tribe of Levi, 129.
Pronominal objects, 263.
Pronoun, repeated possessive, 267.
Prophetic perfect, 268.
Prophets, missing from the Bible, 19.
Psalm of Nephi, 275.
Purifications ceremonies of the ancient Americans, 69.
Quetzalcoatl, 49-65.
    As giver of rain, 63.
    As the source of life, 50, 63.
    Bible connects him to Jesus Christ, 49.
    Born of a fair virgin, 54.
    Calendar changed to coincide with his birth, 53.

His blood restores life, 64.
    Ordained priests in ancient America, 62.
    Worship suddenly declined 196 AD, 65.
Ramah—Rameumptom, 233.
Read Sea, travel route along the borders, 156.
Record, hidden, of the ancient Americans, 108.
Reformed Egyptian, 254.
Relativism, naturalism and materialism, 94.
Religious and political leaders in battle, 304.
Religious beliefs of the ancient Americans, 28-60.
Remembering, the importance of, 270.
Remnant of Joseph's coat, 315.
Resurrection, ancient American knowledge of, 61.
Righteous, America reserved for, 96.
Rio Grijalva linked with River Sidon, 160-161.
Ripliancum, 233.
River of filthy water on Stela, 116.
Robbers and thieves, 141.
Robbers as instruments of divine justice, 142.
Rod of Iron on Stela, 116.
Sabbath in ancient America, 78.
Sacrament in ancient America, 43.
Sacrament in Polynesia, 44.
Sacrifice of Christ, commemorated in the Pacific, 44.
Sacrifices, characteristics of, 194.
Saints, Early Christians knew of, beyond the ocean, 28.
Salvation by grace, 24.
Salvation by works, 25.
Sam represented on Stela, 118.
Sam, 245.
Samuel the Lamanite in native American legend, 102.
San Lorenzo linked with Lib's city, 164-165.
    A center of government and trade, 165.
    Built on an Isthmus, 164.
    Destroyed around 900 BC, 165.
    Did not spread southward, 165.
    New culture introduced 500 BC, 165.
    Settled around 2360 BC, 164.
Santa Rosa linked with Zarahemla, 162-164.
Sarcasm and irony, 270.
Sariah's name glyph on Stela, 117.
Sariah, 233.
Satan in ancient American Beliefs, 82.
Scattering of Noah's children, 41.
Scholars and statesmen on the Book of Mormon, 11.
Scholars of the Bible, on missing scriptures, 18.
Scriptures missing from the Bible, 17-18.
Sea, ancient Americans first came by, 145.
Secret Combinations, 93.
Secret criminal societies in ancient America, 141.
Seed, descendants referred to as, 259.
Seezroam—Zeezrom, 245.
Self-mutilation and cannibalism in Mesoamerica, 142.

Serpent Symbolism, 195.
Serpents, the calamity of, 150.
Seven tribes, 133.
Shazer, 234.
Sheep, others of the house of Israel, 67.
Shelem—Shilom, 234.
Sherem and Israelite law, 218.
Sheum, 235.
Shim, the hill possibly located, 166.
Shipbuilding in ancient America, 299.
Shiz, the death of, 317.
Shule, 235.
Sidon head waters flow westward, 160.
Sidon River carried bodies out to sea, 161.
Sidon River flowed on the east side of Manti, 161.
Sidon River linked with Rio Grijalva, 160-161.
Sidon River to the west of Amnihu and Gideon, 161.
Sidon River turns northward near a hill, 160.
Sidon River was crossed on foot, 161.
Silk and linen in ancient America, 128.
Symbolism in the Book of Mormon, 253.
Sin, unintentional, 81.
Skin, fair in ancient America, 104.
Skin, Lamanites with dark, 106.
Skin, Polynesians with dark, 107.
Slings in ancient America, 311.
Smith, Joseph, to be made strong, 95.
Smith, Joseph, to become great like Moses, 96.
Steel, implements of in ancient America, 291.
Stela 5, evidences relative to, 114-120.
    Aztec and Mayan names for Lehi on, 117.
    Curtain of fire represented on, 118.
    Fountain of living water on, 116.
    Great and spacious building on, 115.
    Iron rod on, 116.
    Laman represented on, 118.
    Lehi on, 116.
    Lemuel represented on, 118.
    Mists of darkness on, 119.
    Nephi's name glyph on, 117.
    Nephi as ruler over his brothers, 117.
    Partakers of the fruit of the tree on, 119.
    River of filthy water on, 116.
    Robed man represented on, 119-120.
    Sam represented on, 118.
    Sariah's name glyph on, 117.
    Spirit of the Lord on, 119-120.
    Tree of life on, 115.
Stellar symbolism of Mesoamerica, 208.
Stone boxes, used for storing valuables, 170.
Stones, luminous, 145.
Stones, oracle in ancient America, 133.
Strength symbolized in hair, 42.

Subjects, compound, 268.
Submergence of cities, 60.
Superstitions and legends of Mesoamerica, 206-213.
Survivor, the witness of, 320.
Swearing Oaths, 121.
Synagogues before the destruction of the temple, 130.
Tablets of stone discovered in Peru, 250.
Tapu (Taboo) and Mana in Polynesia, 213.
Teacher of Righteousness and Abinadi, 214.
Temples of Mesoamerica,
    At Teotihuacan, 159.
    Orientation of, 180.
    Outside of Jerusalem, 130.
    Rites of the ancient Americans, 69.
    Symbolisms in ancient America, 180.
Ten Commandments found in New Mexico, 287.
Tents, Cave of Lehi refugees lived in, 113.
Teotihuacan, the temples at, 159.
Testament to the Bible, 15.
Testament, another of Jesus Christ, 13.
Textiles in ancient America, 179.
Thieves and robbers, 141.
Three witnesses, testimony of, 2.
Thummim, and Urim, 27.
Thummim, and Urim, in Mesoamerica, 133.
Time period of the Book of Mormon, 100.
Title page of Book of Mormon from last leaf, 251.
Tongues, confusion of, 41.
Tower of Babel, 41.
Treading on the Garments, 313.
Tree of Life,
    Depicted in Aztec Codex Borgia, 123.
    Depicted on Stela, 115.
    Partakers of the fruit of the, 119.
    White fruit of, 41.
Tree symbolism, 203.
Trial by ordeal, 217.
Trial procedure, 218.
Tribal and military structure, 305.
Tribes, seven, 133.
Truth to come out of the Earth, 89.
Twenty-four, the significance of , 191.
Unintentional sin, 81.
Urim and Thummim, 27.
Urim and Thummim in ancient American, 133.
Vapor of Darkness, 61.
Vases, flowing of the Old and New Worlds, 210.
Vineyards of olive trees, 132.
Voice from the heavens, 66.
War, Old Testament perspective on, 304.
Warfare, the logistics of, 307.
Wars of annihilation, 316.
Water holes and caves, and the lower world, 211.
Water, ordeal by, 178.

Waters, subterranean, believed to house monsters, 211.
Wheel, used in ancient America, 294.
White fruit of the Tree of Life, 41.
Whitmer, David, testimony of, 2.
Whoredoms of the Gentiles, 92.
Wickedness followed by darkness, 66.
Wilderness of Hermounts, 159.
Wilderness, extended time in, 122.
Witness of the survivor, 320.
Women, the intervention of, 190.
Wood and adobe used rather than stone, 182.
Wordprints of the Book of Mormon, 251.
Works, salvation by, 25.
World divided into four quarters, 202.
Worship God, America reserved for those who, 96.
Worshipping the Father, 24.
Writing ability of ancient Americans, 250.
Year-rite or great assembly, 135.
Zarahemla,
    Linked with Santa Rosa, 162-164.
    Reached it's peak around 50 BC, 163.
    Rebuilt, 163.
    Sudden growth of, 163.
    Temple the central structure, 163.
    The name of, 235.
    Turning point at 196 AD, 164.
    Two groups of people, 163.
Zeezrom—Seezoram, 245.
Zemnarihah, concerning the execution of, 200-201.
    Executed before all the people, 201.
    Executed by hanging, 200.
    His tree was felled, 201.
    Loud chant after his execution, 201.
Zenock, Zeniff, Zemnarihah, 245.
Zenos, 235.
Zero, concept of in ancient America, 296.
Ziff, a type of metal used in the Book of Mormon, 292.
Zoram, 236.
Zoramite prayer, 193.
Zosimus, Narrative close parallel to First Nephi, 125.